Psycho

ONE WEEK LOAN

WITNESS TESTIMONY

Psychological, Investigative and Evidential Perspectives

Edited by

ANTHONY HEATON-ARMSTRONG
ERIC SHEPHERD
GISLI H. GUDJONSSON
DAVID WOLCHOVER

OXFORD
UNIVERSITY PRESS

OXFORD

UNIVERSITY PRESS

Great Clarendon Street, Oxford OX2 6DP

Oxford University Press is a department of the University of Oxford.
It furthers the University's objective of excellence in research, scholarship,
and education by publishing worldwide in

Oxford New York

Auckland Cape Town Dar es Salaam Hong Kong Karachi
Kuala Lumpur Madrid Melbourne Mexico City Nairobi
New Delhi Shanghai Taipei Toronto

With offices in

Argentina Austria Brazil Chile Czech Republic France Greece
Guatemala Hungary Italy Japan Poland Portugal Singapore
South Korea Switzerland Thailand Turkey Ukraine Vietnam

Oxford is a registered trade mark of Oxford University Press
in the UK and in certain other countries

Published in the United States
by Oxford University Press Inc., New York

British Library Cataloguing in Publication Data
Data available

Library of Congress Cataloging in Publication Data
Data available

Typeset by RefineCatch Limited, Bungay, Suffolk
Printed in Great Britain
on acid-free paper by
Biddles Ltd., King's Lynn, Norfolk

ISBN 978–0–19–927809–1 (Pbk.)

3 5 7 9 10 8 6 4 2

This book is dedicated to victims—whether of crime or miscarriage of justice.

FOREWORD

This is not a book about the law of evidence, or more accurately, it is not a book which confines itself to an analysis of the legal principles which enable relevant evidence to be brought before or apparently relevant evidence to be excluded from consideration by the Court. These processes are addressed in a number of respected and familiar works. The focus here is different. It concerns itself with the much deeper and more complex and subtle problem of the search for the truth in the forensic process. Like our knowledge of the world itself, our understanding of these issues is constantly changing.

It was once believed that a confession produced by or as a result of torture would be likely to be true. We now appreciate that to bring torture to an end its victim is at least as likely to tell the torturer whatever the victim believes the torturer wants to hear as to tell the actual truth. Quite apart from our moral repugnance against the use of torture, nowadays confessions produced by torture are regarded as unreliable. Until recently the competency requirements relating to the evidence of children who described sexual abuse were extremely convoluted. The trial process was based on the proposition that a child would be more likely to tell the truth if he or she believed that the consequence of lying would be the condemnation to the eternal fires of hell. A belief in God, or hell, is no longer treated as a prerequisite to a truthful complaint of abuse.

Research and analysis, and the accumulation of greater knowledge and wisdom calling accepted beliefs into question are inevitable. New fields of expertise are constantly identified. It does not follow that the latest fashionable belief is right. We must evaluate whether new areas of expertise are anything like as valuable as the claims made for them. Sometimes they are, sometimes not.

This book addresses these issues. The list of contents is self-explanatory. They are wide-ranging. Very few of us (whether legal practitioners and judges, or individuals with an interest in these topics) have a complete command of the results of recent research into each of these fields. This book provides them. These studies will impact on, and may assist, the forensic process of ascertaining the truth. Moreover, assuming that the evidence is admissible, before being overwhelmed by increasingly detailed and bulky reports from expert witnesses who are likely to appear in court just because some other equally distinguished expert has reached a different conclusion, the book provides readily assimilated, up-to-date information, which enables the broad picture to be assessed and specific points raised in the individual litigation to be put in an overall context.

We have cause to be grateful to the authors and editors for making the latest understanding of and insight into these areas available to us in such a clear and readable form. The book's predecessor was described by Lord Bingham of Cornhill as 'challenging'. Indeed it was, and so, for precisely the reasons identified by Lord Bingham, this successor remains. It is very welcome.

Lord Justice Judge
President of the Queen's Bench Division

ACKNOWLEDGEMENTS

First and foremost, we express heartfelt thanks to our publishers, Oxford University Press, and to those members of its staff who over four years have seen this project through with imagination, fortitude and patience. We are especially grateful to Annabel Moss, the Assistant Commissioning Editor, without whose encouragement and forbearance the production of such a mammoth task, involving thirty-four contributors based at all four corners of the globe, would have been significantly harder to bear. In our more pressing moments, welcome inspiration has been readily and wholeheartedly offered by Tom Bingham, whose foreword to the book's forerunner, *Analysing Witness Testimony*, and chapter in this volume have made our efforts seem very much more worthwhile. We gratefully recognise the generosity of our hard-pressed authors in contributing their chapters without reward and in responding to our requests so diligently and stoically. We pay tribute to the long suffering efforts of our sub-editor Douglas Page, press-ganged into his role when he might, being Anthony Heaton-Armstrong's pupil, have felt that he had little option but to comply. His humble and uncomplaining performance of such a time-consuming and nerve-shattering task has been exemplary. Anthony's long suffering daughter Celestine has been a great help in enabling him, with much stoicism, to understand the complexities of his computer.

PREFACE

When Blackstone Press published *Analysing Witness Testimony* in 1999 this was a ground-breaking attempt for Commonwealth jurisdictions to break the mould of the traditional approach to assessing witness testimony. The project's aim was to change the mindset of key decision makers concerning the reliability and accuracy of witness evidence: decisions traditionally made without reference to psychological considerations. We never anticipated that the book would bring about a rapid sea-change in thinking. However, there seems little doubt that in the intervening years those involved in the conduct of criminal litigation have become increasingly open-minded and many now seem to appreciate the need for critical analysis of witness testimony whilst taking into account the lines of thought and expertise contained in *Analysing Witness Testimony*.

In his Foreword to *Analysing Witness Testimony*, Lord Bingham, then Lord Chief Justice, commented: '. . . we should be grateful to the editors and authors of this book for making available much learning not readily available to lawyers; and we can be confident that these contributions, appropriately tested, properly understood and wisely used, will serve to deepen our understanding and advance the ends of justice'. The worth of the original project has been proven. The text has been the subject of widespread complimentary review, reference in academic texts, and cited in argument in court cases. It has assisted practitioners to advance lines of defence or argument relating to the reliability of witness testimony: lines which might not, otherwise, have been pursued.

The contents of *Analysing Witness Testimony* remain applicable. However, we never intended it to offer the last words on the topics it covered. Several important areas were not touched upon. Others deserve further consideration. We decided that a complementary, sister, volume would enable coverage of new territory and different perspectives on already visited scenes. Our thoughts on content have been usefully assisted by published reviews of *Analysing Witness Testimony*, by commentary from colleagues and, when this text was in gestation, by constructive observations of peer reviewers commissioned by Oxford University Press. We believe that together the two texts will assist readers to reach what Tom Bingham, in his Foreword to the first, described as the 'elusive but crucial evidential goal of distinguishing the truth from the false'.

An extract from our Preface to *Analysing Witness Testimony* is as apt now as it was in 1999:

> There has been considerable resistance amongst lawyers to the acceptance of wisdom from scientists as to mental processes. This may have been caused by and is undoubtedly reflected in the absence of reference to learning from other disciplines in professional training courses. Legal education has, understandably, been apt to focus on legal concepts but the drawback of such a narrow approach is that the importance of significant areas of knowledge which might assist lawyers in forensic practice whether as practitioners or

members of the judiciary tends to be minimized and even sneered at. And until quite recently judicial education, at least, has concentrated almost exclusively on the mechanics of trial procedures and sentencing policy. Habits collected during professional practice which involve the acceptance of bad practice amongst evidence gatherers are thus perpetuated on the first instance bench and, ultimately, in the Appeal Courts. We are not afraid to acknowledge that we have been influenced by the American approach to the use of psychological and psychiatric expertise in the unravelling of issues created by contentious witness testimony. The work of Elizabeth Loftus, [one of the] forerunner[s] in her field, has been well known to US jurisdictions for over 20 years but we doubt whether, in spite of the undoubted value of her writings, she is perceived as anything other than an obscure, unimportant and American psychologist, with all that this reputation implies, amongst those few legal practitioners here who have even heard of her.

We do not seek to revolutionize the law on the admissibility of expert evidence concerning the reliability of witness testimony and recognize that change must, if [it is] to be valuable, come slowly and on mature consideration. We have set out, however, to provide some insight into the workings of the human mind to those involved in making decisions and helping others to do so, as to whether testimony is accurate or historically correct and can, thus, be relied upon when decisions as to fact need to be made in the forensic setting.

During the last seven years there has been a notable increase in focus on the needs and interests of witnesses. A raft of legislative initiatives, protocols and guidelines indicate how these should be met and also the proper treatment of witnesses in investigative and forensic settings. The 'hearsay' provisions of the Criminal Justice Act 2003 have revolutionized the law relating to the admissibility and status of out-of-court statements made by witnesses. Anything said by a witness prior to oral testimony now has the potential to be adduced in evidence to establish the factual truth of what was said earlier or, even, to act as an effective substitute for statements made in the witness box. In the watershed case of *R v. Momodou and Limani* ([2005] EWCA Crim 177; [2005] 1 WLR 3442) the Court of Appeal set an essential benchmark for the proper avoidance of 'coaching' of witnesses in criminal cases. On 23 January 2006 in a number of Crown Prosecution Service areas a pilot project commenced, of a scheme originally authorized by the Attorney-General, allowing prosecutors to interview potential prosecution witnesses concerning the content of their prospective evidence, i.e. after the witness's statement to the police and prior to trial. These developments justify the need for a considered, detailed understanding of the way investigators obtain statements from witnesses. Hence the major focus of this text is upon the inter-relation between witnesses and those to whom they disclose their experiences. In combination with *Analysing Witness Testimony* it seeks to increase understanding and to provoke thought concerning the realms of testimonial anthropology and archaeology.

We three editors of *Analysing Witness Testimony* are fortunate to be joined by Gisli H. Gudjonsson. His expertise and worldwide reputation in the field of the vulnerability of suspects and witnesses to investigative suggestion, and his proposals for the addition of chapters covering new fields, have proved invaluable. Furthermore Chapter One is notable in allowing those unfamiliar with the work of Elizabeth Loftus to appreciate her inestimable contribution to knowledge of the psychology of witnesses.

Our principal target readerships are the judiciary, criminal court advocates, prosecuting and defence lawyers, police investigators, forensic psychologists, and teachers and students of the law of evidence and psychology.

Anthony Heaton-Armstrong
Eric Shepherd
Gisli H. Gudjonsson
David Wolchover
London/Abingdon/Purley
2006

CONTENTS—SUMMARY

SECTION 3 EVIDENTIAL PERSPECTIVES

DETAILED TABLE OF CONTENTS

SECTION 1 PSYCHOLOGICAL PERSPECTIVES

SECTION 2 INVESTIGATIVE PERSPECTIVES

SECTION 3 EVIDENTIAL PERSPECTIVES

LIST OF EDITORS AND CONTRIBUTORS

EDITORS

Anthony Heaton-Armstrong
barrister in independent practice

Eric Shepherd
psychologist in private practice

Gisli H. Gudjonsson
Professor of Forensic Psychology, Institute of Psychiatry, King's College London

David Wolchover
barrister in independent practice

CONTRIBUTORS

Tom Bingham
The Right Honourable Lord Bingham
of Cornhill
Senior Law Lord

Chris R. Brewin
*Professor of Clinical Psychology,
University College London*

Sven Å. Christianson
*Professor of Psychology,
Stockholm University*

Dr Isabel C.H. Clare
*Consultant Clinical and Forensic
Psychologist, Department of Psychiatry,
University of Cambridge*

Amanda Clement
*Deputy Head, Linguistic and Forensic
Medical Services Branch,
Metropolitan Police Service*

David Corker
Partner, Corker Binning, Solicitors

Ann Corsellis OBE
Chartered Institute of Linguists

H. Valerie Curran
*Professor of Psychopharmacology,
University College London*

Graham Davies
*Professor of Psychology,
University of Leicester*

Peter Dunn
*Head of Research & Development,
Victim Support National Office*

Peter French
*forensic consultant,
JP French Associates*

Dr Tim Grant
*Lecturer in Forensic Psychology,
University of Leicester*

Philip Harrison
*forensic consultant,
JP French Associates*

Saul Kassin
Professor of Psychology,
Williams College, Massachusetts

Sam Katkhuda
Circuit Judge

Michael Kopelman
Professor of Neuro-Psychiatry,
King's College London

Jim Kyle
Professor of Deaf Studies,
University of Bristol

Elizabeth F. Loftus
Distinguished Professor,
Psychology and Social Behaviour,
Criminology, Law and Society,
University of California

Annabel Maxwell-Scott
barrister in independent practice

Harald Merckelbach
Professor of Experimental Psychology,
Maastricht University

Dr Rebecca Milne
Principal Lecturer,
Institute of Criminal Justice Studies,
University of Portsmouth

Glynis H. Murphy
Professor of Clinical Psychology,
University of Lancaster

David Ormerod
Professor of Criminal Law,
University of Leeds

Douglas Page
barrister in independent practice

Andrew Roberts
Lecturer in Law,
University of Warwick

Tim Valentine
Professor and Head of
Psychology Department,
University of London

Aldert Vrij
Professor of Applied Social Psychology,
University of Portsmouth

Helen Westcott
Senior Lecturer in Psychology,
The Open University

William Young
President of the New Zealand
Court of Appeal

EDITORS' CURRICULUM VITAE

Anthony Heaton-Armstrong has been a barrister in independent practice since 1974, specialising in criminal cases. His numerous published articles, many written jointly with David Wolchover, have focussed on evidence-gathering methods used by police investigators, criminal evidence and the disclosure provisions of the Criminal Procedure and Investigations Act 1996. He was the Criminal Bar Association's representative on the Attorney-General's Working Group responsible for drafting his Guidelines on Disclosure of 2000, The Home Office Steering Committee, which oversaw the work of the independent researchers Joyce Plotnikoff and Richard Woolfson which led to the publication of their Report 'A Fair Balance? Evaluation of The Operation of Disclosure Law' in 2001 and various other Criminal Bar Association committees tasked to consider the operation of disclosure law. He was one of the General Council of the Bar's representatives on the Crown Prosecution Working Group which initiated The Attorney-General's scheme for pre-trial interviews by prosecutors with witnesses. He is the joint author, with David Wolchover, of *Confession Evidence* (1996, Sweet and Maxwell) and lead editor of *Analysing Witness Testimony* (1999, Blackstone Press).

Eric Shepherd, a former intelligence officer, qualified as a psychologist and as a psychotherapist. Having held academic and clinical appointments he decided to go into private practice. During the past 25 years he has worked continuously with the police service, the defence, the CPS, the SFO, the PCA, the CCRC, and other agencies. He has authored *Police Station Skills for Legal Advisers*, with Roger Ede *Active Defence*, and *SE3R: A resource book*. He advised the NSPCC in the production of *A Case for Balance*. His latest book *Investigative Interviewing: the Conversation Management Approach* is due to be published this year by OUP.

Gisli H. Gudjonsson is Professor of Forensic Psychology at the Institute of Psychiatry, King's College London, and Head of Forensic Psychology Services for Southwark at the Maudsley and South London NHS Trust. He is a Fellow of the British Psychological Society and an Honorary Fellow of the Icelandic Psychological Society. In 2001 he was awarded an Honorary Doctorate in Medicine from the University of Iceland in recognition for his research in the field of forensic psychiatry and psychology. Professor Gudjonsson has published extensively in the areas of forensic psychology, including violence, psychological vulnerability, false confession, police interviewing, and recovered memories. He pioneered the empirical measurement of suggestibility and provided expert evaluation in a number of high profile cases, including those of the Guildford Four, the Birmingham Six, the Tottenham Three, the Cardiff Three, Judith Ward, Peter Fell, Donald Pendleton, the Jill Dando murder case, Kenneth Erskine (the 'Stockwell strangler'), Derek Bentley, the UDR Four and the 'IRA funeral murders' cases (both in Northern Ireland), Henry Lee Lucas and John Wille (USA), and the Birgitte Tengs and Orderud cases (Norway). He acts as a consultant on cases both for prosecution and defence.

Professor Gudjonsson is the author of *The psychology of interrogations, confessions and testimony* (John Wiley & Sons, 1992), *The Gudjonsson Suggestibility Scales Manual* (Psychology Press, 1997), *Forensic Psychology. A Guide to Practice* (Routledge, 1998, jointly written with Lionel Haward), *The Causes and Cures of Criminality* (Plenum Press 1989, jointly written with Hans Eysenck), and the *Psychology of interrogations and confessions. A handbook* (John Wiley & Sons, 2003).

David Wolchover was called to the Bar by Gray's Inn in 1971 and has for many years practised exclusively in the criminal law field. His works include *The Exclusion of Improperly Obtained Evidence*, dating from 1986, *Confession Evidence* (1996) for the Sweet and Maxwell Criminal Law Library series, co-authored with Anthony Heaton-Armstrong, the second and third editions of *Bail in Criminal Proceedings* (co-written with Neil Corre), *Silence and Guilt* (dealing with inferences from silence under the Criminal Justice and Public Order Act 1994) and, of course, he co-edited *Analysing Witness Testimony*. Over many years he has published numerous articles and papers dealing with criminal evidence and procedure and maintains a website (*www.DavidWolchover.co.uk*) hosting supplements to some of the above works as well as a treatise on gaol cell confessions and a book-length monograph entitled *Visual Identification Procedures under PACE Code D*. He is Head of Chambers at 7 Bell Yard.

TABLE OF CASES

TABLE OF CODES OF PRACTICE

TABLE OF PRIMARY LEGISLATION

Legislation is listed alphabetically by country

TABLE OF SECONDARY LEGISLATION

TABLE OF TREATIES AND CONVENTIONS

INTRODUCTION

This text supplements the contents of *Analysing Witness Testimony* and adds entirely new material. Its sections enable the reader to marry up and navigate the contents of both texts.

The three sections of each text are not mutually exclusive, with themes connecting the contributions in different parts. Some chapters can be viewed as 'stand alone' treatments. Others need to be considered in the context of those that precede and follow them.

The *psychological section* covers the psychological significance of a range of mental processes and factors peculiar to individual witnesses, and the assessment of the impact of these processes and factors upon witnesses' perception of events or their subsequent ability to recount their experiences. Loftus's chapter in this volume supplements Cohen's in *Analysing Witness Testimony*; Curran's is linked to Lader's, and Brewin's, to a narrow extent, to Boakes's. Reading the paired chapters gives the reader a comprehensive oversight of the issues involved. Adopting this strategy with chapters in the other two sections will provide similar benefits. The remaining chapters cover essentially new ground.

A reading of the contents of the psychological section provides a sound foundation for the *investigative section*. This second section describes those factors during the investigative process that have a bearing on methods used to obtain prospective evidential accounts, how investigators and witnesses communicate, the collation of prospective evidential accounts, and methods used for the analysis of the reliability and integrity of the spoken and written word. The pairings between this text and *Analysing Witness Testimony* are: Shepherd and Milne's in both texts; Heaton-Armstrong's, Wolchover's and Maxwell-Scott's chapters are supplemental to Heaton-Armstrong and Wolchover's in '*Recording witness statements*'; Davies and Westcott's contribution is cognate to that of Shepherd and Mortimer; French and Harrison's links with Bull and Clifford's; and Grant's aligns with Shepherd and Mortimer's '*Identifying anomaly in evidential text*'. Again, the outstanding chapters involve consideration of material not previously covered.

The final *evidential section* is best appreciated having read the psychological and, additionally, the investigative sections. Broadly it involves the forensic consequences of these and focuses more on what happens during the preparatory stages of a prosecution and the conduct of the case in court. The contributors consider evidence of identification, best practice for fact-finding, the demeanour of witnesses, the protection of witnesses' interests and consideration of their needs, disclosure, the admissibility of expert evidence and judicial training. In terms of pairing Valentine and Wolchover's and Heaton-Armstrong's chapters supplement McKenzie and Dunk's in *Analysing Witness Testimony*; Bingham's, in limited part, strikes connections with Fife-Schaw's; and

Ormerod and Young's with Mackay, Colman and Thornton's; disclosure and judicial training were briefly touched on in Heaton-Armstrong, Wolchover and Shepherd's '*Problematic testimony*'. Others cover new topics.

Each section is preceded by a summary of each of its chapters' contents.

Chapters in *Analysing Witness Testimony* which have not, generally, been the subject of further specific discussion in this book concern '*Testimony from persons with mental disorder*' (Gudjonsson), '*Witness testimony in sleep and dream-related contexts*' (Fenwick), '*Physical illnesses and their potential influence*' (Norfolk), '*Complaints of sexual misconduct*' (Boakes), '*Hypnotically induced testimony*' (Wagstaff) and '*Police collaborative testimony*' (Clark and Stephenson). Of course the content of these contributions remain as valid as ever.

This is not a text for selected dipping into. As with *Analysing Witness Testimony* its format may be strange at first to those used to legal academic text books or practitioners' guides. We have sought to present the material in a chronological sequence: thus the reader can develop progressive familiarity with core themes. The editors' notes at the end of each chapter point to strategies which might help to achieve 'the elusive goal of distinguishing the true from the false' and to explain some of the practical and political problems which present obstacles to this.

SECTION 1

PSYCHOLOGICAL PERSPECTIVES

Summary

Chapter 1. General Review of the Psychology of Witness Testimony.
Elizabeth F. Loftus, David Wolchover and Douglas Page

A witness's testimony concerning an event said to have been perceived by them through one or more of the senses, will depend for its integrity and reliability on the extent to which things that happened were actually seen, or heard, by the witness and on the workings of their memory at the time and subsequently. Later events, notably when things are said to the witness or overheard by them, may have the potential for corrupting memory in a way which leads to inaccurate evidence being given by the witness subsequently.

Mental or physical characteristics peculiar to the witness may have a bearing on these factors. Fact finders, who are apt to be prone to common misconceptions concerning witness testimony, need to be informed about psychological processes to enable them to reach sound decisions.

Chapter 2. Detecting Deception in Legal Contexts.
Aldert Vrij

When witnesses lie by providing an account—whether to investigators or in court—which they know to be untrue the detection of their deceit, especially if they appear plausible or where there is no supportive or contradictory evidence, is elusive and prone to error. Through psychologically based techniques, however, it may be possible to facilitate the identification of lies through observation of the witness's verbal and non-verbal behaviour, although such techniques are often unreliable. Interviewing methods can assist, but these too are subject to error. Strategies for the making of sound truth/lie judgements are discussed.

Chapter 3. The Effect of Learning Disabilities on Witness Testimony.
Glynis H. Murphy and Isabel C.H. Clare

People with learning disabilities are especially vulnerable to criminal victimization and, later, suggestions that their evidence is unreliable owing to these disabilities. Learning disabilities and their prevalence are defined; the incidence of crimes against people with such disabilities and arrangements for them to participate in the investigative and forensic processes are discussed. Strategies for the best assessment of their evidence are advanced. Subject to effective training of participants in the process, the collation, adduction and consideration of evidence from people with learning disabilities might be improved.

Chapter 4. The Psychological Vulnerabilities of Witnesses and the Risk of False Accusations and False Confessions.
Gisli H. Gudjonsson

A suspect or witness may be vulnerable to false confession or accusation owing to a range of psychological factors, including their suggestibility, compliance or mental disorder. Equally, witnesses in this category may under certain circumstances, if the disorder is severe, be considered unlikely to be able to give reliable evidence by fact-finders. Factors influential of false or unreliable evidence are considered. Particular difficulties may arise where an adult witness describes childhood physical or sexual abuse. Those categories of psychological vulnerabilities which may have a bearing on the reliability of a witness's evidence are listed and discussed. The importance of the use of sound and appropriately informed interview techniques and the desirability of employing psychologists as experts in certain instances are stressed.

Chapter 5. Effects of Drugs on Witness Memory.
H. Valerie Curran

The ingestion and consequent effects of drugs on mentation may have a bearing on the reliability of a witness's memory and, later, their evidence. Drugs may inhibit accurate memory, impair concentration or have disinhibitory effects on behaviour. Such drugs are categorized and their potential for affecting memory and risking reliable evidence are described. The inter-relationship between the effects of drugs and the workings of memory are discussed.

Chapter 6. Recovered Memory and False Memory.
Chris R. Brewin

This controversy has been marked by the advancement of polarized views. By reference to relevant literature and respected psychological and psychiatric learning, the author posits a balanced view which takes account of the realities of witness memory capacity. The history of the debate is detailed in relation to the evidential base for the various views involved. If adequately informed concerning relevant psychological factors, there is little reason why, thus empowered, the courts—fact finders—should not be able to reach sound decisions when a witness has claimed to have been able to remember, subsequently, an event which they believe they had previously 'forgotten'.

Chapter 7. Crime-related Amnesia.
Sven Å. Christianson, Harald Merckelbach and Michael Kopelman

People accused of criminal offences, typically those involving homicide or grave violence, may claim amnesia for the relevant events, thus thwarting attempts to discover the true facts or their state of mind at the relevant time. Claimed amnesia may be genuine or feigned. Different types of amnesia are considered along with methods used to enable experts and courts to discovery the reality.

1

GENERAL REVIEW OF THE PSYCHOLOGY OF WITNESS TESTIMONY

Elizabeth F. Loftus, David Wolchover and Douglas Page

To have a qualified psychologist on the team was a bonus: every jury should have one.

Michael Grove, *The Juryman's Tale*
(London: Bloomsbury, 1998, 49)

A. Introduction

It is often remarked that memory does not work like a video recorder. The process is **1.01** much more complex than that and can be divided into three stages: acquisition, in which perception of the original event is encoded in a person's memory; retention, the interval before the event or information is recollected; and retrieval, when it is recalled. This analysis, central to the whole concept of human memory, has been accepted by almost all psychologists.[1] During each stage there are a host of factors and procedures which can impair its efficiency.

1.02 Our surroundings consist of myriad visual features, only a very small part of which will ever actually be noticed. Following the absorption of these perceptions, the experiences of a witness during the memory retention period—talking or hearing or reading a news story about it—can occasion dramatic changes in the original encoded memory. The witness's replies to subsequent questions may be based both on the actual memory of the event and on information acquired since. One of the greatest challenges facing human memory research has been to explain inaccurate retrieval. It may be the result of a failure of perception in the first instance; of a perception being forgotten or distorted during the retention phase; or of inaccessibility during questioning, i.e. at the retrieval stage. Establishing when the failure occurs will usually be extremely difficult.

B. Perceiving Events

1.03 Self-evidently, an event can hardly be perceived accurately unless it is within the observer's perceptual range. However, errors are still commonplace even though an incident is sufficiently visible or audible and attention is being paid, as is evidenced by two or more witnesses differing widely in their accounts of an event. Ability to perceive is influenced by what are known as 'event factors' and 'witness factors'. It is important to note that intuitive assumptions we make about how these work do not always match actuality.

(1) Event factors

1.04 A number of factors in the interaction between the witness and the observed event will determine the efficiency with which it is observed.

(i) Exposure time

1.05 The longer an observer is exposed to an event the better will it be remembered,[2] a phenomenon which it might be thought hardly warrants strenuous efforts in seeking empirical validation, but which nonetheless has been confirmed by the application of research.[3]

(ii) Frequency

1.06 It also seems obvious that frequency of exposure to particular events will enhance accuracy of memory and indeed this is well established.

---

[1] See, for example, Haberlandt, K., *Human Memory: Exploration and Application*, Needham Heights, Mass: Allyn and Bacon, 1999; Thompson, R. F. and Madigan, S. A., *Memory*, Washington, D.C.: Joseph Henry Press, 2005.

[2] Whipple, G.M., 'The observer as reporter: a survey of the "psychology of testimony" ', (1909) 6 *Psychological Bulletin* 153–170.

[3] E.g. Laughery, K.R., Alexander, J.E. and Lane A.B., 'Recognition of human faces: effects of target exposure time, target position, pose position and type of photograph' (1971) 55 *Journal of Applied Psychology* 477–483.

(iii) Detail salience

Some aspects of an incident will be more salient, or memorable, than others, will attract our attention more readily, are more likely to be mentioned spontaneously and will be recalled more completely and accurately, although the factors governing salience are not always easy to determine. To quote Gardner, 'extraordinary, colourful, novel, unusual, and interesting scenes attract our attention and hold our interest, both attention and interest being important aids to memory'.[4] One feature may simply occlude or distract attention from others: thus, a simple disguise—even the wearing of a hat—may significantly undermine recognition ability.[5]

1.07

(iv) Type of fact

In addition to the salience of some particular detail another event factor, the *type* of detail or fact to be recalled, must be considered: for example the perpetrator's height or build, the duration of an incident, a car's speed, the details of a conversation, or the colour of the traffic signal, details which are not equally easy to perceive or recall. The judgement of speed is especially difficult, and practically every automobile accident results in huge variations from one witness to another.[6]

1.08

(v) Violence of an event

In one well-known study on possible differences in ability to perceive violent and non-violent events, subjects were shown two video sequences, identical except for a middle section, one version of which depicted the mild use of restraining force by police, the other, a gratuitous assault.[7] Recall ability was significantly worse for the violent version than for the details of the non-violent one, suggesting that testimony about an emotionally loaded incident may be more unreliable than testimony about a less dramatic one.

1.09

(2) Witness factors

Certain characteristics of, or conditions in, the witness may diminish perceptiveness, for example stress, fear and preconceptions or expectations. The witness's behaviour may be important. Some may be determined to absorb all the details they can remember while others will be preoccupied with escaping from the situation.

1.10

(i) Stress

The impact of stress on perception was first noted by Yerkes and Dodson as long ago as 1908.[8] They maintained that stress and other emotionally arousing states enhance

1.11

[4] Gardner, D.S., 'The perception and memory of witnesses' (1933) 8 *Cornell Law Quarterly* 324.

[5] Patterson, K.E. and Baddeley, A.D., 'When face recognition fails' (1977) 3 *Journal of Experimental Psychology: Human Learning and Memory* 406–417; Shapiro, P.N. and Penrod, S.D., 'Meta-analysis of facial identification studies' (1986) 100 *Psychological Bulletin* 139–156; Cutler, B.L., Penrod, S.D. and Martins, T.K., 'Improving the reliability of eyewitness identification: putting context into context' (1987) 72 *Journal of Applied Psychology* 629–637; Cutler, B.L., Penrod, S.D. and Martins, T.K., 'The reliability of eyewitness identifications: the role of system and estimator variables' (1987) *Law and Human Behavior* 223–258.

[6] Ibid.

[7] Clifford, B.R. and Scott, J., 'Individual and situational factors in eyewitness testimony' (1978) 63 *Journal of Applied Psychology* 352–359.

[8] Yerkes, R.M. and Dodson, J.D., 'The relation of strength of stimulus to rapidity of habit-formation' (1908) 18 *Journal of Comparative and Neurological Psychology* 459–482.

learning and performance up to a critical point after which it declines, the turning point being determined by the difficulty of the exercise. According to Hilgard *et al*:

> A mild level of emotional arousal tends to produce alertness and interest in the task at hand. When emotions become intense, however, whether they are pleasant or unpleasant, they usually result in some decrement in performance.[9]

When arousal is low, for example upon waking, sensory messages might not register. Performance is best with moderate arousal but declines when arousal is high. The optimal point will obviously vary according to the task. Simple habits which are virtually automatic will be less prone to disturbance by arousal than more complex activity requiring integrated thinking. In a moment of intense fear a person could still spell his name but lose his chess-playing virtuosity.

1.12 Few people are regularly exposed to dangerous situations and so for the majority the experience of danger will tend to have a disabling effect on their perceptions. It is possible that stress will cause a narrowing of attention leading to concentration on a relatively few elements of their surroundings.[10] Thus, '*weapon focus*'—concentrating on a gun or knife being brandished by the robber—often results in, among other consequences, a reduced ability to recall other details such as the assailant's appearance.[11]

(ii) Expectations

1.13 It has long been known that a witness's expectations—or 'expectancies'—and attitudes can undermine testimonial performance by exerting a powerful influence on attention and subsequent recall. According to Whipple, 'observation is peculiarly influenced by expectation, so that errors amounting to distinct illusions or hallucinations may arise from this source . . . We tend to see and hear what we expect to see and hear'.[12]

1.14 Four different sorts of expectations can distort perceptions and the form in which they are stored in the memory: cultural expectations or stereotypes, expectations from past experience, personal prejudices, and temporary biases.

(a) Stereotypical assumptions   Cultural expectations—or stereotypes, as they are often termed—are assumptions characteristically facile and indiscriminately held by large numbers of people in a given culture: fat people are jolly and women make bad drivers.

(b) Expectations from past experience   Prior experience may play a significant part in determining what is perceived and recalled. On the basis of experimental research

---

[9] Hilgard, E.R., Atkinson, R.C. and Atkinson R.L., *Introduction to psychology*, 6th ed, New York: Harcourt, Brace Jovanovich, 1975, at 357.

[10] Easterbrook, J.A., 'The effect of emotion on the utilization and organisation of behaviour' (1959) 66 *Psychological Review* 183–201.

[11] See Loftus, E.F., Loftus, G.R. and Messo, J., 'Some Facts about "Weapon Focus" ', (1987) 11 *Law and Human Behavior* 55–62; Steblay, N.M., 'A Meta-Analytic Review of the Weapon Focus Effect', (1992) 16 *Law and Human Behavior* 413–24.

[12] Whipple, G.M., 'The obtaining of information: psychology of observation and report' (1918) 15 *Psychological Bulletin* 217–248. See also Sommer, R. 'The new look on the witness stand' (1959) 8 *Canadian Psychologist* 94–99; Hirt, E.R., Lynn, S.J., Payne, D.G., Krackow, E. and McCrea, S.M., 'Expectancies and Memory: Inferring the Past from What must Have Been' in Kirsch, I. (ed.), *How Expectancies Shape Experience*, USA: American Psychological Association, 1999.

conducted as long ago as the late-1940s Bruner and Postman demonstrated the important role that experience can play in what we perceive and remember and they concluded that 'the perceiver's behaviour can be described as resistance to the recognition of the unexpected or incongruous'.[13]

(c) Personal prejudices The counterpart of group-held stereotypical beliefs affecting perception is personal prejudice, similarly simplistic, applied indiscriminately to groups and often absurd.

(d) Temporary biases What may be termed a 'temporary bias' can wield a powerful influence on perception and memory. So, for example, a person who is out hunting, and expects to see a deer, may shoot a moving object that looks like a deer. Some tragic hunting accidents have occurred, because of the strong expectation that influences perception. Human beings have been shot because they 'looked' like the animal that the hunter expected to see.

(3) Perceptual activity

Focusing on one aspect of an episode may act to the detriment of the perception **1.15** of another aspect. It has been found, for example, that the memory for minor or peripheral details about a crime is inversely related to the accuracy of a witness's identification of the perpetrator, because attention to such details will reduce the mental resources available to process the perpetrator's face.[14] Again, while on the one hand a witness might be examining a rapist's facial features in an effort to commit them to memory, equally she might be staring in the direction of the face but actually concentrating on how best to escape or survive her predicament. Clearly, the witness's mental processes will determine how well various aspects of a crime are remembered. For example, it has been found that expectations can often impact on perceptions. What we might believe, or assume, in advance about an incident may colour the way we experience it: the details we absorb; the elements we notice; how much we concentrate on particular details; how we react. It is known that the perceived gravity of a crime can strongly influence the accuracy for example of eyewitness identification. It seems likely that a concurrent appreciation of the serious nature of a crime will provide motivation for a witness to pay closer attention to the miscreant's facial features than might otherwise be the case in a commonplace encounter (although, equally, timidity may inhibit the witness from looking directly at or into the criminal's face). A perception may then stay embedded in the memory until the witness attempts to retrieve it, a process governed by a further set of factors.

---

[13] Bruner, J.S. and Postman, L., 'On the perception of incongruity: a paradigm' (1949) 18 *Journal of Personality* 206–223, at 222.

[14] Well, G.L and Leippe, M., 'How do triers of fact infer the accuracy of eyewitness identifications? Using memory for peripheral detail can be misleading' (1981) 66 *Journal of Applied Psychology* 682–687; Cutler, B.L. and Penrod, S., *Mistaken Identifications: The Eyewitness, Psychology and the Law*, Cambridge: Cambridge University Press, 1995.

C. Retaining Information in Memory

1.16 Compounding the problem of the distortion of perception, changes can occur in memories during the period of their storage. The duration of the interval before the episode is retrieved may be a crucial factor. It is probably self-evident, and certainly well established, that recall accuracy often deteriorates with time,[15] although it is perhaps not so well known that the rate of detailed memory loss is often greatest after an event and then levels off over time.[16]

(1) Post-event information

1.17 However, the passage of time itself is a neutral factor in governing the survival of memory intact. It is what happens to the memory during that time which counts. Subsequently absorbing new information about the incident can radically alter a witness's original memory. This has been particularly noticed in relation to the process of identification, in which the showing of a photograph of the suspect will elevate the likelihood of selection from a lineup.[17] The new input might be a coloured or slanted news release, overheard conversation about the episode, or an erroneous assumption embodied in questions asked by a police investigator when taking a statement. 'Post-event information' can sometimes enhance recall (as when witnesses compare notes as to their recollections and serve as mutual triggers in reviving genuine memories) but it can also embellish, distort or result in the incorporation of non-existent detail into a previously encoded memory.[18]

(2) Enhancing memory

1.18 It is human nature for witnesses to a dramatic incident to discuss it together afterwards. As already mentioned this can lead to benign memory enhancement, as where the memory by one witness of some point of detail can trigger a memory of that fact on the part of a second witness. However, whether the purported memory has been genuinely revived or is really no more than a new belief implanted by the force of suggestion will usually be extremely difficult if not impossible to determine.

(3) Compromise memories

1.19 The later acquisition of new information which conflicts with what a witness has seen or heard can lead to the formation of a compromise memory, as demonstrated in one

---

[15] See Ebbinghaus, H.E., *Memory: a contribution to experimental psychology*, New York: Dover, 1964, originally published 1885 (author tested the duration of his own memory of a list of nonsense syllables). See also Einstein, G.O. and McDaniel, M.A., *Memory Fitness*, New Haven, Conn: Yale University Press, 2004.

[16] Deffenbacher, K.A., 'A Maturing of Research on the Behaviour of Eyewitnesses' (1991) 5 *Applied Cognitive Psychology* 377–402.

[17] See e.g. Brown, E., Deffenbacher, K. and Sturgill, W., 'Memory for faces and circumstances of encounter' (1977) 53 *Journal of Applied Psychology* 311–318; Hinz, T. and Pezdek, K., 'The effect of exposure to multiple lineups on face identification accuracy' (2001) 25 *Law and Human Behavior*, 185–198.

[18] See, e.g., Loftus, E.F., 'A 30-year investigation of the malleability of memory' (2005) 12 *Learning and Memory*, 361–366.

version of a well-known type of experiment—the staged disruption of a lecture—in which the subjects tended to compromise between what they had seen and what they were told later. A compromise might be conscious and deliberate, or unconscious.

(4) Ousting of the true by the false

When an investigator taking a statement from a witness happens to mention some **1.20** incorrect fact or description this may not merely induce some people to adopt a compromise memory between what they actually noticed and the new material but may even cause complete assimilation of the novel fact or description at the expense of the original memory.

(5) Central matters compared with peripheral details

In general it is easier to induce the modification of memory on peripheral details than on **1.21** salient matters central to the incident or episode in question and therefore harder to mislead witnesses on important aspects than in respect of unimportant ones.[19]

(6) Timing of new information

As a rule of thumb it can be said that new information supporting the original memory **1.22** improves recall performance; contradictory information impairs it. The furnishing of misleading information immediately after an event influences the memory of it less than when it is imparted just before the witness is required to recall the event. In short, as the memory of detail fades so false facts can more readily take their place.

(7) Non-verbal input

It is not only the conveying of information in the form of words or language which can **1.23** cause post-event memory change. A still picture or film footage can do it, as can intonation and inflexion, a certain look, bodily gestures, posture and bearing and a myriad of other subtle influences. People vary almost infinitely in their ability to communicate non-verbally, as with speech, but up to a point everyone is susceptible to non-verbal influences.

There are a number of potential post-event non-verbal influences which are commonly **1.24** encountered in the arena of criminal justice. For example, the mere fact that a witness is being invited to attend an identification procedure can induce an assumption that the perpetrator is going to appear somewhere on the line-up. Again, communication between witnesses at the scene of a crime or an accident can cause a corruption of their memories well before the arrival of official investigators and the possibility of preventative intervention. Many of the exchanges will be in verbal and non-linguistic form combined. Indications of confidence imparted in this way may enhance the confidence of initially-less-sure witnesses in the validity of a particular scenario. The problem will be exacerbated where the witnesses are members of the same family, friends or workmates.

---

[19] See e.g. Brainerd, C.J. and Reyna, V.F., *The science of false memory*, Oxford: Oxford University Press, 2005.

(8) Post-event influence explained

1.25 Psychologists have endeavoured to explain the process by which external influences can lead witnesses to come to believe the contrary of some fact, which they actually perceived themselves or at least a different version of it. An understanding of the process may help the courts of trial to expose hidden weaknesses in evidence which can result in miscarriage. In theoretical terms it has been postulated that the original perceptions entering the memory at the time of the witnessing become integrated with information supplied subsequently to form a homogenous pseudo-memory. Later, when that memory is explored with the witness in court, most notably by reference to other objectively validated evidence in the case, the separation out of its constituent elements may be difficult if not impossible.

(9) Intrusion of the witness's own thoughts on the memory

1.26 Aside from external input the memory of witnesses may of course be disrupted by their own thoughts, anxieties, emotions, desires, self-image, belief system and other internal processes and structures, propelling them towards a recollection which accords with those elements of their mind. This process is sometimes called autosuggestion.[20]

(10) Labelling

1.27 Labelling is a mental process by which people who experience difficulty in reproducing objects and situations may overcome it. However, the very application of a label to a memory is a form of 'post-event information,' which is itself liable to cause distortion of the reproduced account[21] although it must be noted that no significant difference has been found in performance between those who provided their own label and those to whom the label was furnished by the researchers.[22]

(11) Guessing

1.28 Facts deduced by guesswork can become part of the memory of an incident and, while an initial guess may be attempted with diffidence, once seated in the memory it may be elevated to the point that the witness misreads the guess as a real memory. The process may be reinforced by social pressures in favour of projecting an image of comprehensiveness, accuracy assertiveness and confidence, in contrast with diffidence, which the witness may regard as reflecting intellectual weakness.

(12) Freezing

1.29 It has been noticed that peremptory assertions by witnesses made very soon after an incident may reappear in later accounts, irrespective of their truth or accuracy, a

---

[20] Ibid.

[21] See Carmichael, L.C., Hogan, H.P. and Walter, A.A., 'An experimental study of the effect of language on the reproduction of visually perceived form' (1932) 15 *Journal of Experimental Psychology* 73–86.

[22] See Thomas, D.R. and DeCapito, A.L. 'Role of stimulus labelling in stimulus generalisation' (1966) 71 *Journal of Experimental Psychology* 913–915; Thomas, D.R., Caronite, A.D., LaMonica, G.L. and Hoving, K.L. 'Mediated generalisation via stimulus labelling: a replication and extension' (1968) 78 *Journal of Experimental Psychology* 531–533.

persistence which is known as 'freezing' from the fact that the comment is frozen in the memory and recurs whenever the witness is called upon to relate the incident. It can be seen how the process is similar to guessing. The impact which thoughts, comments and accounts can have on the course of a person's subsequent evidence in court later has long been known. According to Whipple,

> When a given reporter is called upon to make his report several times, the effect of this repetition is complex, for (1) it tends in part to establish in mind the items reported, whether they be true or false, and (2) it tends also to induce some departure in later reports, because these are based more upon the memory of the verbal statements of the earlier reports than upon the original experience itself.[23]

The antidote, Whipple argued, was to reduce occasions upon which witnesses were called upon to testify.

An appreciation of how easily inaccurate facts can be implanted in the memory and why **1.30** this happens may permit the development of preventive strategies and measures.

D. Retrieving Information from Memory

(1) Retrieval environment

Extrapolating from the results of experiments conducted with college students many **1.31** years ago it may be reasonable to conjecture that the narrative performance of eye-witnesses will be poorer for proceeding in an environment (for example a police interview room) different from that where the original incident being described occurred.[24]

(2) Type of retrieval

It may be a truism that the form a question takes will determine the quality of the answer **1.32** but this conventional wisdom was methodically validated by experimental psychologists many decades ago.[25] A thorough understanding of the principle has been enlisted to regulate the questioning of witnesses and suspects alike: for accuracy, narrative is best (in the form of the 'cognitive interview'); for completeness of the topic, the interrogative technique will be preferable. It may be suggested that there remains much of value in an old study indicating that a witness should first be allowed to describe an incident freely or in a controlled narrative which can then be followed by a series of more specific questions to broaden the scope of the witness's account.[26]

Asking specific questions before the narrative is recorded can lead to the information contained in the questions becoming part of the narrative, even when it is incorrect.[27]

---

[23] Cited above, at n.2, at 166–167.
[24] See Abernathy, E.M., 'The effect of changed environmental conditions upon the results of college examinations' (1940) 10 *Journal of Psychology* 293–301; Feingold, G.A., 'The influence of environment on identification of persons and things' (1914) 5 *Journal of Criminal Law and Criminology* 39–51.
[25] Cady, H.M., 'On the psychology of testimony' (1924) 35 *American Journal of Psychology* 110–112.
[26] See Snee, T.J. and Lush, D.E., 'Interaction of the narrative and interrogatory methods of obtaining testimony' (1941) 11 *The Journal of Psychology* 229–336.
[27] See Loftus, E.F., 'Leading questions and the eyewitness report' (1975) 7 *Cognitive Psychology* 560–572.

(3) Question wording

1.33 Slight variation in the wording of a question can produce dramatic variation in the substance of the answer. So asking 'how fast were the cars going when they smashed into each other?' can lead to higher estimates of speed than 'how fast were the cars going when they hit each other?'[28]

(4) The questioner's status

1.34 High-status interrogators can have a significant impact on the recollection of witnesses: they can be very persuasive and can change attitudes and behaviour in untold ways.[29]

(5) Confidence in recollection

1.35 The confidence with which people recollect facts tends intuitively to be taken to reflect their accuracy. In fact the relation between confidence and accuracy is much weaker than people think.[30] Post-event questioning, witness preparation and rehearsal, and confirming feedback can greatly increase a witness's confidence without any corresponding change in accuracy.[31]

(6) The 'knew it all along' effect

1.36 Research has revealed that when people are informed of some fact which *could* have been within their knowledge they tend to imagine—or, at least, to claim—that they 'knew it all along'.[32] This finding may be important in relation to court testimony. Witnesses of a particular incident who learn of some relevant detail, such as a certain feature of the culprit's appearance, may come to believe that they noticed it at the time but forgot to mention it. While the theory is that honest witnesses may 'innocently' integrate the new information into their memory of the incident and truly believe what they claim they

---

[28] Loftus, E.F. and Palmer, J.C., 'Reconstruction of automobile destruction: an example of the inter-action between language and memory' (1974) 13 *Journal of Verbal Learning and Verbal* Behaviour 585–589. See also Harris, R.J. 'Answering questions containing marked and unmarked adjectives and adverbs' (1973) 97 *Journal of Experimental Psychology* 399–401.

[29] See, e.g., Marshall, J., *Law and Psychology in Conflict*, New York: Bobbs-Merrill, 1966; New York: Anchor Books, Doubleday, 1969.

[30] Kassin, S.M., Tubb, V.A., Hosch, H.M. and Memon, A., 'On the general acceptance of eyewitness testimony research' (2001) 56 *American Psychologist*, 405–416.

[31] See e.g. Luus, C.A.E. and Wells, G.L., 'The Malleability of Eyewitness Confidence: Co-witness and Perseverance Effects' (1994) 79 *Journal of Applied Psychology*, 714–23; Shaw, J.S. 'Increases in Eyewitness Confidence Resulting from Postevent Questioning' (1996) 2 *Journal of Experimental Psychology: Applied*, 126–46; Shaw, J.S. and McClure, K.A., 'Repeated postevent questioning can lead to elevated levels of eyewitness confidence' (1996) 20 *Law and Human Behavior*, 629–653; Wells, G.L., Small, M., Penrod, S., Malpass, R.M., Fulero, S.M. and Brimacombe, C.A.E., 'Eyewitness identification procedures: recommendations for lineups and photospreads' (1998) 22 *Law and Human Behavior*, 603–647; Wells G.L. and Bradfield, A.L., 'Distortions in eyewitnesses' recollections: can the postidentification-feedback effect be moderated?' (1999) 10 *Psychological Sciences*, 138–144; Semmler, C., Brewer, N. and Wells, G.L., 'Effects of postidentification feedback on eyewitness identification and nonidentification confidence' (2004) *Journal of Applied Psychology*, 334–346.

[32] Fischhoff, B., 'Hindsight ≠ foresight: the effect of outcome knowledge on judgment under uncertainty' (1975) 1 *Journal of Experimental Psychology: Human Perception and Performance*, 288–299; 'Perceived informativeness of facts' (1977) 3 *Journal of Experimental Psychology: Human Perception and Performance*, 349–358.

previously knew, such avowals should plainly be treated with circumspection. A witness may be anxious to see that justice is done or may want no more than to avoid looking ineffectual or even foolish but there is not always a discernible line between a real memory and the unconscious adoption of a fact not originally noticed.

E. Theoretical Issues

(1) Theories on representation in memory

There is no definitive account as to how knowledge is represented in the memory but several ideas, or models, have been put forward, essentially falling into two categories, the propositional and the non-propositional. According to the first, the information we gain from our environment is represented in the memory as a complex network or series of propositions: the car was red; it was a Nissan; it was stationary at a traffic sign; the sign was a stop sign; there were trees all around. The information will be stored in the memory in some very abstract way but would then be transformed into propositions before retrieval. The non-propositional argument is that there are types of memory representation which are specific to vision, hearing and the other senses and are stored in a format which depends on the particular sense. **1.37**

Aside from the issue of information represented in memory, comprehension of an event will depend upon an interpretation of its various aspects and this may be based on three elements: our actual perception of the event (e.g. a car accident); our previous memory and existing knowledge or preconceptions (about accidents, intersections and pedestrians); and inference (e.g. that some damage must have been caused). It has been suggested that memory storage is probably fragmented.[33] Retrieval would involve reconstruction of whatever fragments are stored and have survived memory decay. **1.38**

(2) Coexistence versus alteration

Following a particular incident a witness might be supplied with further, possibly misleading, information, for example in the form of a question asked by an investigator. It is a matter of debate whether impressions initially stored in memory remain there permanently regardless of whether they are subsequently reinterpreted in the light of misleading information ('coexistence') or whether they are permanently altered by it ('alteration'). A number of research techniques have been developed in an effort to establish which of these two possible explanations is correct. **1.39**

For example, it has been found that witnesses will reject blatantly false information supplied within a short time after the incident but that where the misinformation is delayed the ability of the witness to withstand it will be diminished, suggesting alteration. In fact, without providing conclusive proof, all of the techniques deployed suggest that the original material perceived by the witness is not permanent but rather that

---

[33] Rumelhart, D.E. and Ortony, A. 'The representation of knowledge in memory' in Anderson, R.C., Spiro, R.J. and Montague, W.E. (eds), *Schooling and the acquisition of knowledge*, Hillsdale, N.J.: Erlbaum Press, 1976.

the memory has been altered. However, whether new information alters a previously acquired representation or coexists with it, the fact remains that the totality of the person's memory has changed, no matter what theory of memory is subscribed to, and this may affect the potential response.

F. Additional Factors Influencing the Eyewitness: Individual Differences

1.40 If they are honest about not having conferred beforehand two witnesses are unlikely to give separate but identical accounts of an incident, though close similarities there may be. To begin with every witness will be observing from a slightly different vantage point. Not all witnesses to an incident will be paying the same degree of attention and each is likely to be focusing on a slightly different aspect of the incident as it unfolds. Witnesses will all come loaded with different expectations and pre-conceptions and they will each have internal characteristics which to a greater or lesser extent impair their perceptive and retentive efficiency. While it is virtually impossible to gauge the impact of these hidden factors idiosyncratic to each witness, there are certain more general differentiating factors which research has revealed can affect witness performance—for example, gender, age, general anxiety or unhappiness and training.

(1) General anxiety

1.41 Nearly all victims and witnesses of a serious crime will suffer some degree of stress but certain people are abnormally anxious and this may impair their perceptual and retentive faculties, possibly because being preoccupied they tend to pay less attention than others to events going on around them.[34]

(2) Gender

1.42 Although research into the impact of gender distinction on witness performance has produced conflicting results[35] it may be that cultural factors do operate to encourage the development of different sorts of interest as between the sexes and these in turn may establish a predisposition to notice different aspects of an incident, including physical descriptions of relevant persons.[36] Put another way, men and women are interested in different things, pay attention to different things, and their memory may be better for the things that they paid attention to.

---

[34] Siegel, J.M. and Loftus, E.F., 'Impact of anxiety and life stress upon eyewitness testimony' (1978) 12 *Bulletin of the Psychonomic Society*, 479–480.

[35] E.g. Cady, 1924, above n.25; Bird, C., 'The influence of the press upon the accuracy of report' (1927) 22 *Journal of Abnormal and Social Psychology*, 123–129; Witryol, S. and Kaess, W. 'Sex differences in social memory tasks' (1957) 54 *Journal of Abnormal and Social Psychology*, 343–346; Trankell, A., *Reliability of evidence*, Stockholm, Bechmans, 1972; Ellis, H., Shepherd, J. and Bruce, A., 'The effect of age and sex upon adolescents' recognition of faces' (1973) 123 *The Journal of Genetic Psychology*, 173–174; McKelvie, S., 'The effects of verbal labelling on recognition memory for schematic faces' (1976) 28 *Quarterly Journal of Experimental Psychology*, 459–474; Lipton, J.P., 'On the psychology of eyewitness testimony' (1977) 62 *Journal of Applied Psychology*, 90–93; Clifford and Scott, 1978, above n.7.

[36] See Maccoby, E.E. and Jacklin, C.N., *The psychology of sex differences*, Stanford, Cal: Stanford University Press, 1974.

(3) Age

Studies comparing the eyewitness ability of children in different age groups typically **1.43** demonstrate the perhaps unsurprising fact that older children tend to outperform younger ones.[37] It may be that as children mature they become less prone to guessing but it may also reflect an authentic development in their faculty of perception. Children are not only relatively inaccurate but characteristically they are of course highly suggestible. In later life performance in some areas may decline with age but in other areas, such as memory for logical relationships and the ability to draw complex inferences, it does not. It may tentatively be suggested that memory and recognition ability develops up to the teenage years and then begins to decline after about 60 years of age.

(4) Training

It is widely supposed that police officers are trained to observe and to give more reliable **1.44** eyewitness accounts than civilian witnesses but research has demonstrated no significant differences in performance, although in one study in which the subjects were shown a film of a street scene officers mistakenly identified more thefts than the lay subjects[38] (perhaps because they were culturally predisposed to be suspicious). Training programmes on facial recognition have been shown to have little or no impact.[39] This may be because they have focused on the selection of individual facial features rather than the whole face, there being some evidence that in general facial recognition is more successful when based on a holistic, *gestalt*, approach than when the trainees are asked to concentrate on specific facial features.

(5) Other factors

There are other factors which may have an impact on witness performance, for example, **1.45** education, intellect and the state of a person's physical or mental health.

G. Judicial Knowledge of Psychological Factors Involved in Witness Testimony

In the United States of America some research has been conducted into the state of **1.46** knowledge among the public at large about various psychological factors which may undermine the reliability of eyewitness testimony.[40] This may have some use in formulating appropriate instructions and warnings which ought to be given to juries as a matter of generality but jurors are the shifting sands of criminal justice. One jury may be rich in awareness of the dangers of accepting certain types of evidence; the members of another

---

[37] See e.g. Ceci, S.J. and Bruck, M., *Jeopardy in the courtroom: A scientific analysis of children's testimony*, Washington, DC: American Psychological Association, 1995; Bruck, M. and Ceci, S., 'Forensic developmental psychology: Unveiling four common misconceptions' (2004) 13 *Current Directions in Psychological Science*, 229–232.

[38] Tickner, A.H. and Poulton, E.C., 'Watching for people and actions' (1975) 18 *Ergonomics*, 35–51.

[39] Woodhead, M.M., Baddely, A.D. and Simmonds, D.C.V., 'On training people to recognise faces,' cited in Loftus, E.F., *Eyewitness Testimony*, Camb, Mass: Harvard University Press, 1996.

[40] E.g. that conducted by Loftus *et al* as described in ibid, pp.171–177.

may be blissfully ignorant of even the most basic deficiencies. To be effective instructions need to cater for very nearly the presumed lowest common denominator and this does not really require polling of the public. However, there is a more specific purpose behind the sampling of public perceptions. By demonstrating the extent of public knowledge or ignorance about the psychological factors at work in eyewitness testimony, an assessment can be conducted of the validity of the judicial assumption, where it is made, that such factors are within the 'common knowledge' of the jury. This is important because if such factors are genuinely a matter of common knowledge juries will not require the assistance of experts. In the United States expert evidence on eyewitness testimony is often permitted at trial although the most common reason judges give for *excluding* it is that the expert's testimony is within the knowledge of the jury and would not therefore assist the jury.[41] In the jurisdiction of England and Wales this of course has been the unvarying rule.[42] However, research has suggested that expert evidence is a promising safeguard which is effective in sensitizing jurors to psychological factors involved at least in respect of eyewitness identification.[43] A survey among judges has been conducted in the United States to discover what judges themselves know and believe about eyewitness testimony and how accurately they perceive jurors' knowledge of it to be.[44] It is suggested that this may give some indication of the extent to which they may be persuaded to permit safeguards, notably expert testimony. It may also incidentally throw light on what additional training judges may need in instructing juries on the potential pitfalls of eyewitness evidence.

H. Conclusion

1.47 The traditional approach to assessing the reliability of witnesses was for fact-finders to focus exclusively on the content of their narrative testimony in court, their reactions under cross-examination and their demeanour when giving that evidence. Times have moved on. Through the development of the theory and practice of the discipline of psychology from the end of the 19th century we now know much more about the hidden influences which can interfere with the mental processes of witnesses and hence undermine their testimonial reliability. Our accumulating body of scientifically-based knowledge of these influences has scotched the old-time assumption that all would be revealed in the witness box. We now know how incredibly complicated are the dynamics of testimony; how impoverished are the conventional instruments of the common law—examination and cross-examination; how essential it will often be to apply the findings of psychology in assessing a witness's evidence, whether in general terms or through the

---

[41] O'Hagen, C.J., 'When seeing is not believing: the case for eyewitness expert testimony' (1993) 81 *Georgia Law Review*, 741, at 758.

[42] See Chapter 22, below, 'The admissibility of expert evidence', by Ormerod and Roberts.

[43] Penrod, S.D. and Cutler, B.L., 'Preventing mistaken convictions in eyewitness identification trials' in Roesch, R., Hart, S.D. and Ogloff, J.R.P. (eds), *Psychology and Law: The State of the Discipline*, New York: Kluwer Academic/Plenum Publishers, 1999.

[44] Wise, R.A. and Safer, M.A., 'A survey of judges' knowledge and beliefs about eyewitness testimony' (2003) 40 *American Judges Association Court Review*, 6; same authors, 'What U.S. judges know and believe about eyewitness testimony' (2004) 18 *Applied Cognitive Psychology*, 427–443.

expert evidence of professional psychologists; how important it is for judges to recognize the fact that the totality of knowledge of human behaviour extends beyond their narrow legal horizons. Without expert attention to the detailed chronology between the episode under litigation and its narration on tape, before a camera, or in court, a process which may be complicated and require much digging, fact-finders will be presented with an incomplete, not to say misleading, picture of the facts on which they must make a decision affecting the liberty of the subject.

Further Reading

Loftus, E.F., *Eyewitness Testimony*, Camb, Mass: Harvard University Press, 1996.

Loftus, E.F. and Doyle, J.M., *Eyewitness testimony: Civil & Criminal*, 3rd edn, Charlottesville, Va: Lexis Law Publishing, 1997.

Technical Working Group for Eyewitness Evidence, *Eyewitness evidence: A guide for law enforcement*, Washington, DC: United States Department of Justice, Office of Justice Programs, 1999.

Wells, G.L. and Loftus, E.F. (eds), *Eyewitness Testimony: Psychological Perspectives*, Cambridge: Cambridge University Press, 1984.

Brainerd, C.J. and Reyna, V.F., *The science of false memory*, Oxford: Oxford University Press, 2005

Elizabeth F. Loftus is Distinguished Professor at the University of California, Irvine, holding positions in the Departments of Psychology & Social Behaviour, and Criminology, Law & Society; holds an appointment in the Department of Cognitive Sciences; and is a Fellow of the Centre for the Neurobiology of Learning and Memory. She was formerly Professor of Psychology and Adjunct Professor of Law at the University of Washington, Seattle, where she taught for 29 years. She received her Ph.D. in Psychology from Stanford University, since when she has published 20 books and over 400 scientific articles. Her fourth book, *Eyewitness Testimony*, won a National Media Award (Distinguished Contribution) from the American Psychological Foundation. One of her most widely read works, *The Myth of Repressed Memory* (co-authored with Katherine Ketcham) has gone into a number of translations.

Professor Loftus has been an expert witness or consultant in hundreds of cases, including those of Oliver North, the officers accused in the Rodney King beating case, the Menendez brothers, Michael Jackson, Martha Stewart, Bosnian war crimes defendants, the Oklahoma bombing case defendants, and she has been involved in numerous prominent trials concerning allegations of repressed memory.

Her research over the last 20 years has focused on human memory, eyewitness testimony and also on courtroom procedure. Her work has been funded by the National Institute of Mental Health and the National Science Foundation. In 1983, she was invited to present this work to the Royal Society of London.

She has received five honorary doctorates from world universities and numerous awards and other honours for her research, including the American Academy of Forensic Psychology Distinguished Contributions to Forensic Psychology Award. Citations include tributes to her 'career of significant intellectual contributions to the science of psychology in the area of applied psychological research' and 'ingeniously and rigorously designed research studies . . . that yielded clear objective evidence on difficult and controversial questions'.

Among a number of distinguished honorary positions she held the Presidency of the American Psychological Society in 1998–1999.

Douglas Page was called to the Bar following a career in the music industry as a performer and composer of classical music. He completed his pupillage in the chambers of Lord Carlile of Berriew. His postgraduate law thesis focused on the (then) proposed changes to the rule against double jeopardy and after graduating from the Inns of Court School of Law he worked in the criminal law for a firm of solicitors specialising in criminal defence. He remains in criminal practice at the Bar.

Editors' Note

Elizabeth Loftus's expertise is acknowledged, at least in some American jurisdictions, to be such that her evidence has frequently been adduced to assist jurors there to understand and analyse contentious eyewitness testimony. Owing to the approach by the Higher Courts in England and Wales to the admissibility of expert evidence concerning issues of reliability and credibility, and their very broad interpretation of what is meant by 'common knowledge', it seems doubtful that she or others propounding her intensively research-based theories would be welcome as expert witnesses here. Her contribution therefore provides essential knowledge for judges and advocates, enabling them to impart to fact-finders under the rubric of 'common knowledge' material from her work that is relevant to the factual issues in a case. Furthermore, common sense argues that all professionals within the criminal justice system should become familiar with her work.

2

DETECTING DECEPTION
IN LEGAL CONTEXTS

Aldert Vrij[1]

A. Introduction

In criminal investigations the question often arises whether a suspect, victim or witness's **2.01** account of what has happened is accurate or not. Although inaccurate accounts may occur for various reasons (for example, because the person misremembered certain things), this chapter deals with a specific form of inaccuracy: when the person deliberately reports something that he or she believes to be untrue, or in other words, when the person is lying.

Lies can be detected by comparing a person's statement with physical evidence or with **2.02** information from reliable third parties. There is evidence that this is the way that most

---

[1] Correspondence concerning this chapter should be addressed to: Aldert Vrij, University of Portsmouth, Psychology Department, King Henry Building, King Henry 1 Street, Portsmouth, PO1 2DY, United Kingdom or via email: aldert.vrij@port.ac.uk.

people detect lies in daily life.[2] It is also the most efficient way to detect lies. However, often physical evidence or third-party information is not available. In these situations, lie detectors could observe the communicator's non-verbal behaviour, analyse their speech content, or measure their physiological responses. In this chapter these three ways of detecting lies will be discussed. First, in the psychological perspectives section, I will discuss theories explaining why differences could occur between liars' and truth tellers' non-verbal behaviour, speech content or physiological responses, and whether they in fact do occur. This section shows that no theory predicts the existence of cues uniquely related to deception, like Pinocchio's growing nose, and, indeed, no such cue has been found to date. Then, in the investigative perspectives section, I will describe interview protocols that are developed to detect deception, and will discuss how accurate these tools are. This section reveals that no tool is highly accurate and that errors are frequently made. I will also explain why such errors occur. Finally, in the evidential perspectives section I will discuss how truth/lie judgements could be used in criminal investigations.

B. The Psychological Perspective: Theories About Cues to Deception

(1) Zuckerman, DePaulo, and Rosenthal's multi-factor model

2.03 According to Zuckerman, DePaulo, and Rosenthal[3] liars show signs of deceit as a result of processes triggered by emotion, content complexity and attempted control processes.

2.04 When people lie they may experience certain emotions. For example, they may be worried that they won't be believed. Three polygraph tests described below, the Relevant–Irrelevant test, Control Question test and the Directed Lie test, are based upon this principle.

2.05 Lying might also be cognitively demanding, as liars need to come up with plausible and convincing answers; avoid contradicting themselves; avoid making slips of the tongue; and remember what they have said so that they can say the same things again when asked to repeat their story. Statement validity assessment, a verbal detection tool described below, is based upon this principle.

2.06 Liars might realise that others will observe their demeanour in order to find out whether they are lying. They therefore may feel an urge to control their demeanour so that they will appear honest. While doing so they may try to avoid showing behaviours (e.g. gaze aversion or making fidgety movements) or saying certain things (e.g. self-deprecated comments) that might appear suspicious. Statement validity assessment is also based upon this principle.

2.07 Whether liars actually experience any of the three processes depends on the circumstances and the liar's personality. For example, experiencing fear of not being believed is

---

[2] Park, H. S., Levine, T. R., McCornack, S. A., Morrisson, K. and Ferrara, M., 'How people really detect lies' (2002) 69 *Communication Monographs*, 144–157.

[3] Zuckerman, M., DePaulo, B. M. and Rosenthal, R., 'Verbal and nonverbal communication of deception' in Berkowitz, L. (ed.), *Advances in experimental social psychology*, Volume 14, New York, NY: Academic Press, 1981, 1–57.

more likely when getting away with the lie matters to the liar, in other words, when the stakes (negative consequences of not being believed or positive consequences of being believed) are high. In the majority of lies that people tell in daily life the stakes are low,[4] but the stakes may be higher when people lie in criminal investigations. Fear might also depend on the authority of the lie detector. When liars respect the lie detector's ability, they may become more afraid of not getting away with their lies. Experiencing fear might also depend on the personality of the liar. For example, those who know from experience that they are good liars might experience less fear than those who are less certain of their ability. The extent to which lying is demanding probably depends on the type of lie. Telling an outright lie (i.e. total falsehood) might be more cognitively demanding than concealing information, and telling an elaborate lie might well be more demanding than providing short 'yes' or 'no' answers. Lying is perhaps also more demanding when the lies are not well prepared or rehearsed. There are probably also individual differences. Verbally skilled people might find lying cognitively easier than people who are less verbally skilled. Liars' motivation and efforts to deliberately control their demeanour will probably increase as the stakes arise.

(2) Buller and Burgoon's Interpersonal Deception Theory (IDT)

The second perspective is Interpersonal Deception Theory.[5] IDT embraces Zuckerman[6] **2.08** *et al*'s factors (emotion, content complexity, and attempted control) as underlying reasons for cues to deceit.[7] In addition, it emphasizes that when deception occurs in interactive contexts it is not a unidirectional activity: rather, both liar and interviewer actively participate in constructing the deceptive conversation.[8] According to IDT, interviewers may influence liars' behavioural displays both directly and indirectly.

Regarding the direct effects, it is known that when people communicate with each other, **2.09** matching and synchrony take place.[9] People may mirror each other's posture or they may converge quickly in how loudly they speak. They may also reciprocate each other's gazing, nodding and smiling behaviour, and even accents can converge.[10] This 'chameleon effect'[11] emerges even when total strangers interact with each other and it happens within

---

[4] DePaulo, B.M., Kashy, D.A., Kirkendol, S.E., Wyer, M.M. and Epstein, J.A., 'Lying in everyday life' (1996) 70 *Journal of Personality and Social Psychology*, 979–995.

[5] Buller, D.B. and Burgoon, J.K., 'Interpersonal deception theory' (1996) 6 *Communication Theory*, 203–242; Burgoon, J.K., Buller, D.B. and Guerrero, L.K., 'Interpersonal deception IX: Effects of social skill and nonverbal communication on deception success and detection accuracy' (1995) 14 *Journal of Language and Social Psychology*, 289–311.

[6] Cited above at n.3.

[7] Burgoon, J.K., Buller, D.B., White, C.H., Afifi, W. and Buslig, A.L.S., 'The role of conversation involvement in deceptive interpersonal interactions' (1999) 25 *Personality and Social Psychology Bulletin*, 669–685.

[8] Burgoon, J.K., Buller, D.B., Floyd, K. and Grandpre, J., 'Deceptive realities: Sender, receiver, and observer perspectives in deceptive conversations' (1996) 23 *Communication Research*, 724–748.

[9] Chartrand, T.L. and Bargh, J.A., 'The chameleon effect: The perception–behaviour link and social interaction' (1999) 76 *Journal of Personality and Social Psychology*, 893–910.

[10] DePaulo, B.M. and Friedman, H.S., 'Nonverbal communication' in Gilbert D.T., Fiske S.T. and Lindzey G. (eds.), *The handbook of social psychology*, Boston, Mass: McGraw-Hill, 1998, 3–40.

[11] Chartrand and Bargh, 1999, cited above at n.9.

a few minutes.[12] In other words, the behaviour of the criminal investigator may well influence the behaviour of the suspect, witness or victim, and vice versa.

2.10 The indirect effects are related to feedback from the investigator. When a liar is exposed to negative feedback from the investigator, expressed either through verbal comments or through a lack of conversational involvement such as avoiding eye contact, leaning back in the chair, and turning the body away, he or she might realise that his or her performance is lacking credibility and could therefore attempt to make behavioural adjustments over time to diminish suspicions.

(3) DePaulo's self-presentational perspective

2.11 A key element in DePaulo's self-presentational perspective[13] is emphasising the similarities between liars and truth tellers. She has argued that not only liars but also truth tellers might experience emotions or cognitive demand or might wish to control themselves. Thus, truth tellers also might wish to make behavioural adjustments to diminish suspicions or be afraid of being disbelieved in criminal investigations, etc. Therefore, fundamental to this perspective is that if non-verbal cues to deception occur, they are ordinarily quite subtle. DePaulo argues that a central element in all lies is the claim of honesty, yet this is not what differentiates lies from truths. The difference is that the liar's claim to honesty is illegitimate, and this has two implications. First, deceptive self-presentations might be less convincingly embraced as truthful self-presentations, for example, because liars have moral scruples, lack the emotional investment in their false claims, or lack the knowledge and experience to convincingly back up their deceptive statements. Second, liars typically experience a greater sense of awareness and deliberateness in their performances than truth tellers, because they typically take their credibility less for granted than truth tellers.[14]

(4) Summary

2.12 The three perspectives make clear that the relationship between lying and deceptive behaviour is complex. The assumptions of Zuckerman *et al*[15] that liars might show signs of emotions and cognitive load seem straightforward. However, liars often do not experience emotions and cognitive load,[16] and, to complicate matters further, DePaulo's self-presentation perspective stresses that such experiences are not the exclusive domain of liars and that truth tellers may experience them as well. The attempted control prediction is not straightforward because the behaviours shown by liars as a result of this deliberate control will depend upon their perceptions of what constitutes a credible non-verbal display and their acting skills to perform this display. Finally, IDT's interactive approach

---

[12] Akehurst, L. and Vrij, A., 'Creating suspects in police interviews', (1999) 29 *Journal of Applied Social Psychology*, 192–210; Chartrand and Bargh, 1999, cited above at n.9.

[13] DePaulo, B.M., 'Nonverbal behaviour and self-presentation' (1992) 111 *Psychological Bulletin*, 203–243; DePaulo, B.M., Lindsay, J.L., Malone, B.E., Muhlenbruck, L., Charlton, K. and Cooper, H., 'Cues to deception' (2003) 129 *Psychological Bulletin*, 74–118.

[14] Kassin, S.M. and Norwick, R.J., 'Why people waive their Miranda rights: The power of innocence' (2004) 28 *Law and Human Behavior*, 211–221.

[15] Cited above at n.3.   [16] Cited above at n.4.

implies that deceptive behaviour might be directly influenced by the behaviour of the investigator (a result of the chameleon effect) or indirectly influenced by the suspicions raised by the investigator.

Two more theories might be relevant to explain deceptive behaviour. They differ from **2.13** the previous three theories because they are not specifically developed to explain deceptive responses. As such they are not deception theories, but their implications may explain liars' responses.

(5) Reality Monitoring [17]

Reality Monitoring focuses on how people remember (i) events they have actually experi- **2.14** enced and (ii) events they imagine they have experienced but which in fact they did not experience. The core of Reality Monitoring is the claim that memories of experienced events differ in quality from memories of imagined events. Memories of real experiences are obtained through perceptual processes and are therefore likely to contain, amongst other things, *perceptual information* (details of sound, smell, taste, touch, or visual details) and *contextual information*: spatial details (details about where the event took place, and details about how objects and people were situated in relation to each other, e.g. 'he stood behind me'), and temporal details (details about time order of the events, e.g. 'First he switched on the video-recorder and then the TV', and details about duration of events). These memories are usually clear, sharp and vivid.

Accounts of imagined events are derived from an internal source and are therefore likely **2.15** to contain *cognitive operations*, such as thoughts and reasonings ('I must have had my coat on, as it was very cold that night').[18] They are usually more vague and less concrete. One might argue that 'experienced events' reflect truth telling whereas 'imagined events' reflect deception. Therefore, perhaps the described differences also occur between liars and truth tellers.

(6) Orienting theory [19]

The core of this approach is that an orienting response occurs in response to personally **2.16** significant stimuli, such as in a cocktail party, where people can be unaware of the conversations around them, yet notice when their name is mentioned in one of these conversations. Such an orienting response also has a physiological profile which can be measured. The Guilty Knowledge test, a polygraph test, is based upon this principle.

---

[17] Johnson, M. K., and Raye, C. L., 'Reality Monitoring', (1981) 88 *Psychological Review*, 67–85.

[18] Johnson, M. K., Hashtroudi, S., and Lindsay, D. S., 'Source monitoring', (1993) 114 *Psychological Bulletin*, 3–29; Johnson and Raye, 1981, cited above at n. 17; Johnson, M. K., and Raye, C. L., 'False memories and confabulation', (1998) 2 *Trends in Cognitive Sciences*, 137–145.

[19] Lykken, D. T., *A tremor in the blood: Use and abuses of lie detection*, New York: Plenum Trade, 1998; Pavlov, I. P., *Condition reflex*, Oxford: Clarendon Press, 1927.

C. Cues to Deceit

2.17 Various reviews of deception research have recently been completed or published.[20] Two findings emerged from these reviews. First, as was already predicted, no single cue is uniquely related to deception; in other words, a cue like Pinocchio's growing nose does not exist. Second, in support of DePaulo's self-presentational perspective, in those cases where relationships between cues and deception did occur, those relationships were always weak. The relationships provided support for many of the above-mentioned theories. For example, in support of the emotions approach, liars tend to have more dilated pupils, have a more tense voice, and speak with a higher pitched voice. However, differences in pitch between liars and truth tellers are usually very small and therefore only detectable with sophisticated equipment.

2.18 In support of the cognitive demand approach, liars tend to make more word and phrase repetitions, tell stories which sound less plausible, and include fewer details in their stories. Liars also make fewer illustrators (gestures that accompany the speech) and fewer hand and finger movements (subtle movements of hands and fingers without the arms being moved). This, again, could support the cognitive complexity approach (people tend to move less when they think hard); it could also be the result of deliberate attempts to appear convincing (see attempted control, IDT and DePaulo's self-perspective). That is, perhaps in order to appear honest, liars attempt to avoid all sorts of movements which they think appear suspicious, resulting in atypically stiff behaviour.

2.19 There is also evidence that lies are less convincingly embraced. For example, compared to truth tellers, liars show less vocal and verbal involvement, speak with more vocal and verbal uncertainty, make more negative statements, and show less facial pleasantness. In support of the Reality Monitoring theory, statements of liars include fewer perceptual (visual and auditory) details, fewer spatial details and fewer temporal details (but there is no support that they include more cognitive operations into their speech).

2.20 Cues such as gaze aversion[21] and fidgeting do not seem to be related to deception. This is interesting because these are the cues that many people, including many criminal

---

[20] DePaulo *et al*, 2003 cited above at n.13; Masip, J., Sporer, S.L., Garrido, E., and Herrero, C., 'The detection of deception with the Reality Monitoring approach: A review of the empirical evidence' (2005) 11 *Psychology, Crime, and Law*, 99–122; Vrij, A., *Detecting lies and deceit: The psychology of lying and the implications for professional practice*, Chichester: John Wiley, 2000; Vrij, A., 'Criteria-Based Content Analysis: A qualitative review of the first 37 studies', (2005) 11 *Psychology, Public Policy, and Law*, 3–41.

[21] Sometimes professional lie catchers tell me that they believe that eye movements are associated with deception. They then typically refer to the neuro-linguistic programming (NLP) model. However, not a single scientific study has demonstrated that eye movements are related to deception in the way described in the NLP model (Vrij, A. and Lochun, S.K., 'Neuro-linguistic programming and the police: worthwhile or not?' (1997) 12 *Journal of Police and Criminal Psychology*, 25–31).

investigators, associate with deception.[22] See DePaulo *et al* (2003),[23] Masip *et al* (2005) and Vrij (2000, 2005)[24] for a more comprehensive list of cues to deceit.

(1) Raising the stakes

The deception studies on which these findings were based have one limitation in com- **2.21** mon. They have overwhelmingly been carried out in low-stakes situations. That is, in those studies, liars and truth tellers were typically college students who lied or told the truth in laboratory settings for the sake of the experiment. In such situations, whether or not the students appeared convincing did not result in any serious consequences for them. This is perhaps unavoidable. In laboratory settings serious negative consequences for failing to appear credible can never be introduced for ethical reasons. Yet, in real life, and perhaps in many criminal investigations, truth tellers and liars may face serious negative consequences if they are not believed. Studies of how people respond in criminal investigations are rare, and most of these studies have been carried out in polygraph examinations which will be discussed below.

In only two studies has the behaviour of people in criminal investigations been exam- **2.22** ined.[25] Both studies examined the responses of suspects in police interviews, and the study of Mann *et al* was the more comprehensive of the two. They examined the behavioural responses of 16 suspects while they lied and told the truth during their police interviews. The police interviews were videotaped and the tapes were made available for detailed scoring of the suspects' behavioural responses. The suspects were interviewed in connection with serious crimes such as murder, rape and arson, and were facing long custodial sentences if found guilty.

Results revealed that compared to when they told the truth, the suspects exhibited more **2.23** pauses, fewer eye blinks, and (male suspects) fewer hand and arm movements when they lied. Again popular indicators such as fidgeting and gaze aversion did not emerge. The results suggest that the suspects' cues to deception were more likely to be the result of increased cognitive demand than nervousness. The strongest evidence for this was the reduction in eye blinks during deception. Research has shown that nervousness results in an increase in eye blinking, whereas increased cognitive load results in a decrease in eye blinking. This is an interesting finding because the majority of criminal investigators expect suspects to show signs of nervousness when they lie.[26]

Further support for the suggestion that, while lying rather than being tense the suspects **2.24**

---

[22] Strömwall. L. A., Granhag, P. A., and Hartwig, M., 'Practitioners' beliefs about deception', in Granhag, P. A. and Strömwall, L. A. (eds.), *Deception detection in forensic contexts*, Cambridge: Cambridge University Press, 2004, 229–250; Vrij, A., 'Guidelines to catch a liar', in Granhag, P. A. and Strömwall, L. A. (eds.), *Deception detection in forensic contexts*, Cambridge: Cambridge University Press, 2004, 287–314; Vrij, A., 'Invited Article: Why professionals fail to catch liars and how they can improve', (2004) 9 *Legal and Criminological Psychology*, 159–181.

[23] Cited above at n. 13   [24] Cited above at n. 20

[25] Mann, S., Vrij, A., and Bull, R., 'Suspects, lies and videotape: An analysis of authentic high-stakes liars', (2002) 26 *Law and Human Behavior*, 365–376; Vrij, A., and Mann, S., 'Telling and detecting lies in a high-stake situation: The case of a convicted murderer', (2001) 15 *Applied Cognitive Psychology*, 187–203.

[26] Strömwall *et al*, 2004, cited above at n. 22

appeared to have to think hard, was found in a follow-up study.[27] In this study police officers were shown a selection of the truthful and deceptive clips of Mann *et al*'s study discussed above. After each fragment the officers were asked to indicate, amongst other factors, to what extent the suspect appeared tense and gave the impression that he or she had to think hard. Results revealed that the suspects appeared to be thinking harder when they lied than when they told the truth (supporting the cognitive demand approach); however, in contrast with the emotional approach, they appeared more tense when they told the truth than when they lied.

2.25 The apparent predominance of cognitive load processes compared to emotional processes in those suspects during deception can be explained in several ways. Many of the suspects included in Mann *et al*'s study had regular contact with the police. Therefore, they were probably familiar with the police interview situation which might somewhat limit their nervousness while lying. However, suspects in police interviews are typically of below average intelligence.[28] It has been suggested that less intelligent people will have particular difficulty in inventing plausible and convincing stories.[29] Alternatively, it might well be that the suspects were more tense when they lied but that this was momentarily suppressed when they had to think hard. Leal, van Hooff and Vrij[30] found that when participants were asked to solve complex tasks their skin conductance levels (indicator of tenseness) momentarily decreased when they were engaged in solving the problem, and that a sharp increase in skin conductance levels took place (the compensatory effect) the moment this thinking process was terminated. In a deception setting, this could mean that liars do not appear tense when they actually tell a cognitively demanding lie, but that tenseness becomes apparent directly after the lie has been told. In Mann *et al*'s 2002 study, only the response during the actual lie was investigated, not the response directly after the lie.

D. The Investigative Perspective: Interview Protocols

2.26 Most explicit interview protocols to detect deception exist for polygraph tests. A polygraph is a machine that measures physiological responses. The responses most often measured are skin conductance, blood pressure and respiration. The polygraph accurately records even very small changes by amplifying signals picked up from sensors attached to different parts of the body. A polygraph measures arousal and not deception. Polygraph examiners have no other option but to measure deception in such an indirect way, as a pattern of physiological activity directly related to lying does not exist.[31]

---

[27] Mann, S., Vrij, A. and Bull, R. (in press), 'Police officers' judgements of veracity, tense, cognitive load and impression management in real-life police interviews', *Psychology, Crime and Law*.

[28] Gudjonsson, G.H., *The psychology of interrogations and confessions: A handbook*, Chichester: John Wiley, 2003.

[29] Ekman, P. and Frank, M.G., 'Lies that fail', in Lewis, M. and C. Saarni, C. (eds.), *Lying and deception in everyday life*, New York: Guildford Press, 1993, 184–201.

[30] Leal, S., 'Central and peripheral physiology of attention and cognitive demand: understanding how brain and body work together' *PhD thesis, University of Portsmouth* (2005).

[31] Saxe, L., 'Detection of deception: Polygraph and integrity tests' (1994) 3 *Current Directions in Psychological Science*, 69–73.

Three of the four most popular polygraph tests[32] are built upon the premise that, while **2.27** answering so-called 'relevant' questions, liars will be more aroused than while answering so-called 'control' questions, due to a fear of detection (fear of not being believed: see the emotional approach discussed above). This premise is theoretically unsound. There is no theoretical reason why liars would necessarily be more aroused when answering the relevant questions. In addition, truth tellers might well be more aroused when answering the relevant questions. First, they too might be afraid of not being believed. Polygraph tests are only carried out if other evidence is not available (already discussed above). For an innocent examinee it means that s/he cannot prove his or her innocence, and failing the test may well prolong the negative effects associated with being falsely suspected, such as loss of respect, continuing to be interviewed, continuing to be kept in custody, fear of being falsely convicted, etc. A second occasion why truth tellers also might be more aroused when answering the relevant questions is when the relevant and control questions are not directly comparable, for example, when these relevant questions are by their nature already emotion-evoking questions (e.g. when athletes are asked the question 'did you ever use enhance performing drugs?').

The other popular test[33] is built upon the premise that guilty examinees will be more **2.28** aroused while answering some questions compared to other questions due to different orienting reactions, that is, they will show enhanced orienting responses when recognising crucial details of a crime. This premise has stronger support in psychophysiological research than the first mentioned 'arousal' premise.[34]

(1) Relevant–Irrelevant test

In the Relevant–Irrelevant test ('RIT'),[35] the physiological responses to relevant ques- **2.29** tions ('Did you murder Alan Smith'?) are compared to the responses to irrelevant questions such as 'is today Tuesday?' The examinees are instructed to answer the irrelevant questions truthfully and these truthful responses are then compared to the responses to the relevant questions. In cases where the examinee is more aroused when answering the relevant questions he is thought to be lying. As just mentioned, this assumption is theoretically flawed. Liars do not necessarily show heightened arousal. Also, a strong physiological response could also occur in truthful examinees, for example, when they are afraid of not being believed, and because of the fact that 'did you murder Alan Smith?' is a more arousal-provoking question than 'is today Tuesday?' There is agreement amongst polygraph researchers, including Larson, that the RIT should not be used.[36]

---

[32] Relevant–Irrelevant test, Control Question test and Directed Lie test, all discussed below.

[33] Guilty Knowledge test, discussed below.

[34] Fiedler, K., Schmid, J. and Stahl, T., 'What is the current truth about polygraph lie detection?' (2002) 24 *Basic and Applied Social Psychology*, 313–324; Iacono, W.G. and Lykken, D.T., 'The validity of the lie detector: two surveys of scientific opinion' (1997) 82 *Journal of Applied Psychology*, 426–433.

[35] Larson, J.A., *Lying and its detection: A study of deception and deception tests*, Chicago, Ill: University of Chicago Press, 1932.

[36] Lykken, 1998 cited above at n.19; Raskin, D.C. and Honts, C.R., 'The comparison question test' in M. Kleiner (ed.), *Handbook of polygraph testing*, London: Academic Press, 2002, 1–48.

(2) Control Question test

2.30 In the Control Question test ('CQT') an effort is made to make the relevant and irrelevant questions more comparable (the latter are called 'control questions' in this test). For example, in a murder inquiry, the control question 'have you ever tried to hurt someone to get revenge?' might be used in case the examiner believes that the examinee did indeed hurt someone at some point in his life. The examiner will tell the examinee that admitting this would cause the examiner to conclude that the examinee is the type of person who would commit the crime in question and would therefore be considered guilty. Thus, the examinee has no choice other than to deny this earlier wrongdoing and thus to lie in answering this control question. The CQT is based on the assumption that in the *innocent suspect* control questions ('have you ever tried to hurt someone to get revenge?') will generate more arousal than the relevant questions ('Did you murder Alan Smith?'). This pattern will emerge because the innocent examinee will become more concerned over his or her answers to the control questions, because (i) the examiner puts so much emphasis on the control questions, and (ii) the examinee knows he or she is lying to the control questions but is answering the relevant questions truthfully. However, the same control questions are expected to elicit less arousal in *guilty suspects* than the relevant questions. A guilty suspect gives deceptive responses to both types of question, which in principle should lead to similar physiological responses to both types of question. However, relevant questions represent the most immediate and serious threat to the examinee, and are expected to lead to a stronger physiological response than the control questions.

2.31 Although this method may be an improvement compared to the RIT, it still does not rule out that heightened arousal could occur in truth tellers when answering relevant questions. It still could be that (i) the relevant question evokes more arousal by its nature, and (ii) that innocent suspects are afraid of not being believed when answering the relevant questions. Neither is it guaranteed that liars would always show most arousal when answering the relevant questions.

2.32 Several reviews have been published to date regarding the accuracy of CQT in real-life criminal investigations. These reviews, discussed in Granhag and Vrij,[37] showed that there is reasonable agreement amongst the reviews regarding guilty suspects. Correct classifications were made in 83 to 89 per cent of the cases.[38] There is less agreement

---

[37] Granhag, P. A. and Vrij, A., 'Deception detection' in Brewer, N. and Williams, K. (eds.), *Psychology and law: An empirical perspective*, New York: Guildford Press, 2005, 43–92.

[38] The classification of guilty examinees appears high but these accuracy scores might well be inflated. A problem for researchers in determining the accuracy of polygraph examinations in real-life investigations is to evaluate the accuracy of polygraph examiners' decisions. As mentioned earlier, polygraph examinations are typically carried out when other, conclusive, evidence is not available. Therefore, researchers rely on confessions as evidence. An examinee is judged truly guilty when s/he confesses to the crime, and truly innocent when somebody else confesses to the crime. The problem with confessions is that they are not independent evidence, as the decision to confess may depend on the polygraph outcome. Consider the case of a guilty examinee who passes a polygraph test. This examinee is now unlikely to confess because there is no evidence against him. Since he committed the crime, it is unlikely that somebody else will falsely confess to having committed the crime. The result is that there will be no confession in this case, and that the researcher will not include this case in his/her study, as they only consider cases where confessions did occur. In other words, the incorrect decision made by the polygraph examiner will not appear in the accuracy figures.

regarding innocent suspects, but in all reviews the findings for innocent suspects were less positive than for guilty suspects. Depending on the review, between 53 and 78 per cent of innocent suspects were correctly classified. These relatively low accuracy rates for innocent suspects imply that innocent suspects are frequently more aroused when answering relevant questions than when answering control questions.

An additional problem with the CQT is that the control questions cannot be standard-   **2.33**
ized. For example, control questions such as 'have you ever tried to hurt someone to get revenge?' can only be asked to examinees who are known to have hurt someone in the past. The lack of standardization means that much depends on the skills of the individual polygraph examiner who formulates the questions.

(3) The Directed Lie test

This standardization issue is addressed in the Directed Lie test ('DLT'). In a DLT, the   **2.34**
control questions used could be asked in all situations. Typical examples of such control questions are 'during the first 27 years of your life, did you ever tell even one lie?' and 'Before age 27, did you ever break even one rule or regulation?'.[39] Examinees will be instructed to answer 'No' to these questions. They will also be instructed to think about particular situations in which they did tell a lie or did break a rule during these (control) denials. As was the case with the CQT, guilty suspects are thought to be mostly concerned with the relevant questions and are expected to show the strongest responses to these questions. Innocent suspects, however, are thought to be more concerned with the (control) directed lie questions since they will be concerned that their responses while lying (i.e. to directed lie questions) differ from their responses when telling the truth (i.e. to relevant questions). Although the standardization problem of the CQT might be reduced with the DLT, the problem that innocent suspects could score higher on relevant questions (because the relevant questions are arousal-evoking and because the suspect is afraid of not being believed while replying to relevant questions) remains. Also, the issue that liars do not necessarily show more arousal when answering the relevant questions remains. To date, not enough studies have been carried out to assess the accuracy of DLT.[40]

(4) Guilty Knowledge test

The aim of the Guilty Knowledge test ('GKT') is to probe whether examinees possess   **2.35**
knowledge about a particular crime that they do not want to reveal. For example, suppose that a person is found murdered and that the police know how that person was killed. In a GKT the examiner will describe several possibilities: 'was he drowned?', 'was he stabbed?', 'was he shot?', etc. A guilty examinee will recognise the correct possibility. It is assumed that this so-called *guilty knowledge* will produce a heightened physiological response which will be detected by the polygraph (see the orientation approach discussed above). The GKT, when properly carried out, does not suffer as much from the problems (mentioned above) of arousal-evoking relevant questions and fear of not being believed.

---

[39] Raskin and Honts, 2002, cited above at n. 36.   [40] Ibid.

However, these two problems can also occur in a GKT, for example, when the correct multiple-choice alternative is a more arousal-evoking option than the other alternatives, or when the innocent suspect can guess what the correct alternative is. This problem can be minimized by pre-testing the set of alternatives on mock suspects. That is, on known innocent people. They should give similar responses to all alternatives. Another set of alternatives needs to be chosen if this is not the case.[41]

2.36 There are additional problems. Suppose that the murderer used a revolver and suppose that the innocent examinee owns an unregistered pistol. That examinee might show enhanced responses to questions that mention handguns among the alternatives, even when he has no concealed knowledge about the murder weapon.[42] This problem can probably be avoided by asking more questions.

2.37 Also, innocent suspects might have guilty knowledge because the salient details of the crime are made available to them by the investigators.[43] It is common practice to disclose details of crimes to suspects in police interviews as this is seen as a possible way to make suspects confess.[44] Many suspects, including those who are innocent, therefore might have guilty knowledge after being interviewed. Ben-Shakhar *et al*[45] point out that this might not be problematic as long as innocent suspects are aware of having acquired the guilty knowledge in this way and can account for it. However, if guilty knowledge is leaked without the innocent suspect's awareness, they might incriminate themselves. Leaking relevant crime details to suspects in police interviews might rescue guilty suspects as they then can point out that they obtained this guilty knowledge in the interview rather than through being involved in the crime. Finally, guilty suspects might not possess guilty knowledge because they do not remember what the correct answer is. This might happen when, for example, the question is asked about a minor detail (i.e. 'what was the colour of the shirt the victim was wearing at the time of the attack?').

2.38 Only two field studies regarding the accuracy of the Guilty Knowledge test have been published.[46] Both tests revealed very good results regarding the classification of innocent suspects (94 and 98 per cent of innocent suspects were correctly classified) but rather poor results regarding the classification of guilty suspects (76 and 42 per cent of guilty suspects were correctly classified). This could mean that the last-mentioned problem, that guilty suspects cannot remember the correct answer, is a serious problem in GKT testing.

---

[41] Lykken, 1998, cited above at n. 19.

[42] National Research Council (2003), *The polygraph and lie detection*, Committee to Review the Scientific Evidence on the Polygraph (2003), Washington, DC: The National Academic Press.

[43] Ben-Shakhar, G., Bar-Hillel, M. and Kremnitzer, M., 'Trial by polygraph: reconsidering the use of the guilty knowledge technique in court' (2002) 26 *Law and Human Behavior*, 527–541.

[44] Inbau, F. E., Reid, J. E., Buckley, J. P. and Jayne, B. C., *Criminal interrogation and confessions*, 4th edition, Gaithersburg, Maryland: Aspen Publishers, 2001.

[45] Cited above at n. 43.

[46] Elaad, E., 'Detection of guilty knowledge in real-life criminal investigations' (1990) 75 *Journal of Applied Psychology*, 521–529; Elaad, E., Ginton, A. and Jungman, N., 'Detection measures in real-life criminal guilty knowledge tests' (1992) 77 *Journal of Applied Psychology*, 757–767.

(5) Statement Validity Assessment

The verbal lie detection method probably most widely used in criminal investigations is **2.39**
Statement Validity Assessment ('SVA'). It was developed in Germany for the veracity
assessment of statements made by children in alleged sexual abuse cases, and SVA
decisions are accepted in Germany as evidence in court. There is evidence that SVA could
also be used with adults talking about other events.[47] However, SVA is not used in this
way in criminal investigations. The interview protocol is rather minimal. The method
requires a *semi-structured interview* where the interviewee provides his or her own
account, with as little influence from the interviewer as possible. Psychologists have
designed special interview techniques based on psychological principles to obtain as
much information as possible from interviewees in a free narrative style without
inappropriate prompts or suggestions.[48] The statements are then transcribed and trained
observers look for the presence of 19 specific criteria which are thought to be more often
present in truthful statements. The hypothesis is thus that truthful statements contain
more of these criteria than fabricated statements. This part of the SVA procedure is called
Criterion-Based Content Analysis ('CBCA'). Examples of these CBCA criteria are:
unstructured production (whether the information is not provided in a chronological time
sequence); *contextual embeddings* (references to time and space: 'he approached me
for the first time in the garden during the summer holidays'); *descriptions of interactions*
('the moment my mother came into the room, he stopped smiling'); and *reproduction of
speech* (speech in its original form: 'and then he asked: "Is that your coat?" '). These
elements are more likely to occur in truthful statements because it is thought to be
cognitively too difficult for liars to incorporate them. (See content complexity approach
described above). Other criteria are more likely to occur in truthful statements for
motivational reasons. Truthful persons will not be as concerned with impression management as deceivers. Compared to truth tellers, deceivers will be keener to try to
construct a report which they believe will make a credible impression on others, and will
leave out information which, in their view, will damage their image of being a sincere
person.[49] As a result, a truthful statement is more likely to contain information that is
inconsistent with the stereotypes of truthfulness. Examples of these so-called 'contrary-
to-truthfulness-stereotype' criteria[50] are: *spontaneous corrections* (corrections made without prompting from the interviewer: ('he wore a black jacket, no sorry, it was blue') and
raising doubts about one's own testimony (anticipated objections against the veracity of
one's own testimony: 'I know this all sounds really odd').

A complication in using this method is that the presence of CBCA criteria might be **2.40**
influenced by factors other than veracity. For example, verbally skilled interviewees

---

[47] See Vrij (2005), cited above at n. 20

[48] See Milne, R. and Bull, R., *Investigative interviewing: psychology and practice*, Chichester: John Wiley
and Sons, 1999 for an overview of such techniques.

[49] Köhnken, G., *Statement Validity Assessment*, paper presented at the pre-conference programme of
applied courses 'Assessing credibility' organised by the European Association of Psychology and Law,
Dublin, July 1999.

[50] Ruby, C. L. and Brigham, J. C., 'Can Criteria-Based Content Analysis distinguish between true and
false statements of African-American speakers?' (1998) 22 *Law and Human Behavior*, 369–388.

produce statements which typically contain more CBCA criteria.[51] Moreover, when people talk about familiar events their statements include more CBCA criteria then when they talk about events they are not familiar with.[52] The second phase of the SVA method is to examine whether any of these alternative explanations might have affected the presence of the CBCA criteria. However, the procedure on how to do this is not well defined and often difficult to apply.[53] The risks are that such alternative explanations are disregarded, and there is some evidence that this happens in real-life cases.[54]

2.41 SVA is a truth detection tool rather than a lie detection tool. That is, the presence of each CBCA criterion increases the chance that a statement is truthful, and no criteria are included that indicate fabrication. Statements that are largely truthful but include an incorrectness about an important detail (e.g. the child describes a real abuse but accuses the wrong person of being the perpetrator) might include many CBCA criteria as most of the account is true. It is therefore possible that this false accusation will be judged as truthful by SVA experts.

2.42 Despite the fact that SVA assessments are used as evidence in court in several countries, it is unclear how accurate these assessments are because no reliable data regarding the accuracy of CBCA assessments in real-life cases are currently available.[55] Research has been carried out in laboratory studies. In these studies sometimes children, but more often undergraduate students, told the truth or lied for the sake of the experiment. Such studies showed similar accuracy rates for adults and children. Overall, 73 per cent of the truths and 72 per cent of the lies were correctly classified by using CBCA assessments. Obviously, students or children who tell lies and truths in an experiment are different from children who tell truths and lies in criminal investigations, and the accuracy scores therefore do not necessarily reflect the accuracy scores in criminal investigations.

(6) Reality Monitoring

2.43 There does not exist a standard interview protocol for the use of Reality Monitoring. Furthermore, to my knowledge, Reality Monitoring assessments are not used in criminal investigations. In the Reality Monitoring research published to date[56] a protocol similar to the SVA protocol was used: interviewees were invited to give their account with as little influence from the interviewer as possible. In the five laboratory studies published to date, the average truth accuracy rate was somewhat higher (75 per cent) than the average lie accuracy rate (67 per cent). Reality Monitoring cannot always be used. Not all

---

[51] Vrij, A., Akehurst, L., Soukara, S. and Bull, R., 'Will the truth come out? The effect of deception, age, status, coaching, and social skills on CBCA scores' (2002) 26 *Law and Human Behavior*, 261–283.

[52] Pezdek, K., Morrow, A., Blandon-Gitlin, I., Goodman, G. S., Quas, J. A., Saywitz, K. J., Bidrose, S., Pipe, M. E., Rogers, M. and Brodie, L., 'Detecting deception in children: event familiarity affects criterion-based content analysis ratings' (2004) 89 *Journal of Applied Psychology*, 119–126.

[53] See Vrij (2005), cited above at n. 20.

[54] Gumpert, C. H. and Lindblad, F., 'Expert testimony on child sexual abuse: a qualitative study of the Swedish approach to statement analysis' (1999) 7 *Expert Evidence*, 279–314.

[55] See Vrij (2005), cited above at n. 20.

[56] See Granhag and Vrij, cited above at n. 37, at 43–92 and Masip *et al* (2005), cited above at n. 20 for reviews.

truths are about experienced events. For example, people also lie about abstract issues, such as their attitudes or opinions. Reality Monitoring cannot be used in such instances. Also, not all lies are imagined events. For example, people may recall an event they really experienced but lie about a crucial detail of the event such as on what day or at what time the event took place. Reality Monitoring is not likely to detect such lies.

(7) Non-verbal assessments

The current state of non-verbal assessments in criminal investigations probably resembles **2.44** that of Reality Monitoring. No standard interview protocols are used, and such assessments do not form part of standard criminal investigative procedures. If professional lie catchers, such as police officers, are asked to detect truths and lies just by looking at videotaped statements of truth tellers and liars, their accuracy is typically low. A review of ten of these studies found a truth and lie accuracy of 55 per cent in both cases.[57] However, those studies were laboratory studies where the truthful and deceptive statements were produced by college students for the sake of the experiment. Mann, Vrij and Bull[58] conducted a more ecologically valid study and showed 99 police officers videotapes consisting of 54 truths and lies told by suspects during their videotaped police interviews. A total accuracy rate of 65 per cent was obtained in this study with similar accuracy rates for detecting truths and lies.

Perhaps even higher hit rates can be obtained if systematic and objective analyses of **2.45** non-verbal behaviour take place. That is, when behaviours known to be 'reliable' cues to deception according to deception research are scored in detail by frequency of occurrence, and when truth/lie decisions are then made utilizing multiple cue models which are based upon these reliable cues. In an experiment where participants reported having experienced pleasant feelings when they were telling the truth and unpleasant feelings when they were lying, up to 86 per cent of liars and truth tellers could be correctly justified by observing cues to emotions.[59] In two experiments where liars faced a more cognitively difficult task than truth tellers, 71 and 78 per cent of the truths and lies respectively could be correctly classified by examining cues associated with cognitive load.[60] However, unlike for example polygraph and SVA examinations, where examiners observe a standardized list of cues (skin conductance, blood pressure, respiration, and a list of 19 verbal criteria), the cues researchers examined in these non-verbal studies varied per experiment. This implies that non-verbal assessments are not standardized.

---

[57] See Granhag and Vrij (2005), cited above at n. 37.

[58] Mann, S., Vrij, A. and Bull, R., 'Detecting true lies: police officers' ability to detect deceit' (2004) 89 *Journal of Applied Psychology*, 137–149.

[59] Ekman, P., O'Sullivan, M., Friesen, W. V. and Scherer, K., 'Face, voice, and body in detecting deceit' (1991) 15 *Journal of Nonverbal Behaviour*, 125–135.

[60] Vrij, A., Akehurst, L., Soukara, S. and Bull, R., 'Detecting deceit via analyses of verbal and nonverbal behaviour in children and adults' (2004) 30 *Human Communication Research*, 8–41; Vrij, A., Edwards, K., Roberts, K. P. and Bull, R., 'Detecting deceit via analysis of verbal and nonverbal behaviour' (2000) 24 *Journal of Nonverbal Behaviour*, 239–263.

(8) Interviewing to detect deception by looking at non-verbal cues

2.46 Perhaps interview protocols which would facilitate lie detection via observing someone's behaviour could be developed, and elsewhere I give suggestions of how to do this.[61] One possible way is by utilizing the comparable truth method. There are large individual differences in people's behaviour. Some people typically make many movements, whilst others do not; some people look away often when they speak, whereas others do not, etc. In order to control for these individual differences, the lie detector could establish a baseline of the person's truthful behaviour, and could use this for lie detection purposes. However, an important aspect of this method is that the baseline behaviour must be truly comparable with the behaviour under investigation. That is, comparing the behaviour shown by suspects during the small talk part of the interview with their behaviour during the actual interview, a technique advised by Inbau *et al*[62] in their popular police manual, is *not* a proper method. In fact, Inbau *et al*'s recommendation resembles the RIT polygraph technique, already discussed above. Small talk and the actual investigation are fundamentally different situations. Small talk conversations are low-stakes situations where the suspect's responses are unlikely to have any negative consequences. The investigative part of the interview, on the other hand, is a high-stakes situation where the suspect's responses are intensely scrutinized and where the suspect's reactions may easily heighten suspicion. Suspects are probably aware of this and therefore, not surprisingly, both guilty and innocent people tend to show different behaviours during small-talk compared to the actual interview.[63]

2.47 Lie detectors could be taught how to establish comparable truths and how to compare the response under investigation with the response during this comparable truth. To give an example, during a videotaped real-life police interview a man suspected (and later convicted) of murder was asked to describe his activities on a particular day.[64] The murder suspect described his activities during the morning, afternoon and evening. Detailed analyses of the videotape revealed a sudden change in behaviour as soon as he started to describe his activities during the afternoon and evening. One possible reason for this may have been that he was lying. Evidence supported this view. Police investigations could confirm his story with regard to his morning activities, but revealed that his statement about the afternoon and evening was fabricated. In reality, he met the victim in the afternoon and killed her later on that day. In this case, we were able to make a good comparison. There are no good reasons why different behaviours would emerge while describing different parts of the day, especially when describing such a seemingly normal day as the suspect did. When such differences do emerge, they are remarkable and worth investigating. Interestingly, the question on which we based the baseline method 'what did you do that particular day?' could be asked in many interviews. This method has limitations as well. A serious constraint is that the set of cues on which people might

---

[61] See Vrij (2004) 9 *Legal and Criminal Psychology*, 159–181, cited above at n. 22.
[62] Cited above at n. 44.
[63] Vrij, A., 'Behavioral correlates of deception in a simulated police interview' (1995) 129 *Journal of Psychology*, 15–28.
[64] See Vrij and Mann (2001), cited above at n. 25.

differ when they lie compared to when they tell the truth will probably vary per individual and also per situation. This means that such a test cannot be standardized.

(9) Countermeasures

When people are aware which lie detection methods lie detectors use, they may actively **2.48** attempt to show the responses which will improve their chances of passing such lie detection tests. Methods to achieve this are called 'countermeasures'. Polygraph studies have revealed that people can beat polygraph tests by pressing their toes or biting their tongue at appropriate times during the examination.[65] Instructing participants to include several CBCA criteria into their statements revealed mixed results.[66] Coached adults and 10–11-year-old children included more CBCA criteria in their statements than their untrained counterparts, whereas coaching had no effect in 5–6-year-olds.

(10) Non-intrusive, quick measures

A problem with all the lie detection methods is that they cannot be employed instantly. **2.49** Examinees need to be attached to polygraph machines for their polygraph tests; statements need to be transcribed before CBCA and Reality Monitoring analyses can be carried out, and conducting such analyses is time-consuming; behaviours need to be videotaped and these videotapes often need to be played in slow motion to enable detailed scoring of non-verbal behaviours.

Non-intrusive equipment that produces instant results does already exist, such as voice **2.50** stress analysers. The accuracy of these machines is unknown but I expect the application to be problematic.[67] The underlying assumption that 'arousal means deception' is naive. Moreover, as with polygraph tests, the way the questions are phrased is crucial for its success, and probably requires more training than the average voice stress analyser user receives. Computer software that instantly analyses written statements for cues to deception is currently available.[68] I expect such measures to be less accurate than CBCA or Reality Monitoring analyses, because text interpretation is a necessary requirement for an accurate speech analysis. However, the speed with which computer analyses can be carried out might in some circumstances compensate for its lack of accuracy. A recent study that revealed that CBCA-trained judges were, to some extent, able to assess the frequency of occurrence of several CBCA criteria in statements just by listening to these statements is promising in that respect.[69]

---

[65] See Honts, C. R. and Amato, S. L., 'Countermeasures' in Kleiner, M. (ed.), *Handbook of polygraph testing*, London: Academic Press, 2002, 251–264 for a review.

[66] Vrij, A., Akehurst, L., Soukara, S. and Bull, R., 'Let me inform you how to tell a convincing story: CBCA and Reality Monitoring scores as a function of age, coaching and deception' (2004) 36 *Canadian Journal of Behavioral Science*, 113–126; Vrij, Akehurst, Soukara, and Bull, cited at n. 51 above.

[67] An internet search supports this pessimistic view. See *http://www.polygraph.org/voicestress.htm* for a useful website.

[68] Pennebaker, J. W., Francis, M. E. and Booth, R. J., *Linguistic Inquiry and Word Count: LIWC 2001*, Mahwah, NJ: Lawrence Erlbaum, 2001.

[69] Vrij, A., Evans, H., Akehurst, L. and Mann, S., 'Rapid judgements in assessing verbal and nonverbal cues: their potential for deception researchers and lie detection' (2004) 18 *Applied Cognitive Psychology*, 283–296.

2.51 Progress has been made in developing equipment which can non-intrusively observe and instantly code the non-verbal behaviour displayed by target persons.[70] Such a system has the potential to become more accurate in coding behaviours than humans depending on its ability to pick up subtle behaviours and behavioural patterns which are easily missed by human coders. However, due to the lack of standardization in non-verbal assessments the problem remains of how to interpret the non-verbal differences which arise.

E. The Evidential Perspective: The use of Veracity Assessments in Legal Contexts

2.52 Whether to use lie detection methods in criminal cases can be addressed in two different ways. First, can they help practitioners in making veracity judgements? Second, what importance should be given to such judgements? To answer the first question, as this chapter reveals, several methods appear to discriminate between truth tellers and liars above the level of chance and therefore might help investigators. They could provide a tool to evaluate the veracity of statements given by victims, witnesses, informants and suspects, and such judgements could have consequences for the direction which is given to these investigations (e.g. 'is it worth following that lead?', 'is it worth further considering this man as our main suspect?', etc.). Which lie detection method to use is difficult to tell, as several could be used. It probably depends on individual preferences and circumstances. However, since lie detection methods are prone to error then investigators should always keep in mind the possibility that they might make the wrong decisions by relying upon their outcomes. This should be an especial concern in situations with severe consequences. Therefore, convicting suspects on the basis of veracity judgements, or allowing sex offenders to walk free on the basis of such decisions[71] is undesirable.

Further Reading

For a general overview of all methods discussed:

Granhag, P.A. and Strömwall, L.A. (eds.), *Deception detection in forensic contexts*, Cambridge: Cambridge University Press, 2004.

Vrij, A., *Detecting lies and deceit: The psychology of lying and the implications for professional practice*, Chichester: John Wiley, 2000.

For an overview of polygraph research:

Kleiner, M. (ed.), *Handbook of polygraph testing*, London: Academic Press, 2002.

National Research Council, *The polygraph and lie detection*, Committee to Review the Scientific Evidence on the Polygraph (2003), Washington, DC: The National Academic Press, 2003.

---

[70] See Vrij (2004) 9 *Legal and Criminal Psychology*, 159–181, cited above at n.22.

[71] The latter is currently being tested in the UK, *The Independent*, 29 May 2004.

For an overview of Statement Validity Assessment:

Raskin, D.C. and Esplin, P.W., 'Statement Validity Assessment: Interview procedures and content analysis of children's statements of sexual abuse', (1991) 13 *Behavioral Assessment*, 265–291.

Steller, M. and Köhnken, G., 'Criteria-Based Content Analysis', in Raskin, D.C. (ed.), *Psychological methods in criminal investigation and evidence*, New York: Springer–Verlag, 1989, 217–245.

Vrij, A., 'Criteria-Based Content Analysis: A qualitative review of the first 37 studies', (2005) 11 *Psychology, Public Policy, and Law*, 3–41.

For an overview of Reality Monitoring:

Masip, J., Sporer, S.L., Garrido, E. and Herrero, C., 'The detection of deception with the Reality Monitoring approach: A review of the empirical evidence', (2005) 11 *Psychology, Crime, and Law*, 99–122.

Vrij, A., *Detecting lies and deceit: The psychology of lying and the implications for professional practice*, Chichester: John Wiley, 2000.

For an overview of non-verbal behaviour and deception:

DePaulo, B.M., Lindsay, J.L., Malone, B.E., Muhlenbruck, L., Charlton, K. and Cooper, H., 'Cues to deception', (2003) 129 *Psychological Bulletin*, 74–118.

Ekman, P., *Telling lies: Clues to deceit in the marketplace, politics and marriage*, New York: W.W. Norton and Company, 1985/2001.

Aldert Vrij (1960) is a Professor of Applied Social Psychology at the University of Portsmouth. His main research interest is deception, particularly non-verbal aspects of deception (e.g. how liars behave), verbal aspects of deception (e.g. what they say), people's ability to detect deceit, and ways to improve this ability. He has published almost 300 articles and book chapters and six books to date, the majority of which are related to deception. His book *Detecting lies and deceit* published by Wiley in 2000 (ISBN 0-471-85316-X) provides a comprehensive overview of non-verbal, verbal and physiological correlates of deception.

Professor Vrij currently holds research grants from the Economic and Social Research Council (ESRC), the British Academy and the Nuffield Foundation, and in the past he has held grants from the ESRC, the Nuffield Foundation, the Leverhulme Trust, and the Dutch Ministry of Justice. All of these research grants were related to deception.

Professor Vrij is Editor of *Legal and Criminological Psychology* and sits on the editorial boards of *Law and Human Behavior*, *Human Communication Research* and *Journal of Nonverbal Behaviour*.

Editors' Note

The search for the true or the false in trials involving contentious witness testimony, as Lord Bingham made clear in his foreword to *Analysing Witness Testimony*, should never be considered to be one which ought not to be facilitated through relevant and useful scientific research, for 'the common law is nothing if not pragmatic. It lives and it learns'. If the common law is to continue to live and learn in its pursuit of the elusive goal, those who direct fact-finders should harness psychological expertise that points the way towards more reliable and sound decisions.

3

THE EFFECT OF LEARNING DISABILITIES ON WITNESS TESTIMONY

Glynis H. Murphy and Isabel C.H. Clare

A. Introduction: Witnesses with Learning Disabilities

People with learning disabilities are increasingly living in the community and, like **3.01** other members of the community, they may sometimes be victims of and/or witnesses to crimes. This chapter will consider what is known about people with learning disabilities as witnesses.

(1) Defining learning disabilities

3.02 In the UK, 'learning disabilities' refers to significant deficits in intellectual ability and in adaptive behaviours (normally defined as an intellectual quotient, or IQ, below 70 and adaptive behaviours that are more than two standard deviations below the mean,[1] evident from early childhood).[2]

(2) Learning disabilities and similar terminology

3.03 The term 'learning disabilities' was officially adopted following its use in 1991 in a speech by Stephen Dorrell, then Secretary of State for Health, replacing previous terms such as 'mental handicap', 'mental retardation' and the even more outdated term 'sub-normality'. At times, however, the term 'learning disabilities' causes confusion, even in English-speaking countries. Occasionally it is mistakenly taken to mean *specific* learning disabilities, such as dyslexia, and this is particularly the case in the USA. The table below shows the terms currently in use in a number of English-speaking countries. All refer to significant deficits in intellectual capacity and adaptive behaviours, evident from early childhood.

Table 3.1 Terms for learning disabilities in different countries

Country	Preferred term
UK	Learning disabilities
USA	Mental retardation or developmental disabilities
Ireland	Learning disabilities
Australia	Intellectual disabilities
New Zealand	Intellectual disabilities

3.04 People with learning disabilities themselves have strong views on the terms used to describe their difficulties. Self-advocacy organizations in the UK and USA, such as People First, prefer the term 'learning difficulties' and particularly dislike the phrase 'mental retardation', which they refer to as the 'R' word.[3]

(3) Learning disabilities as a continuum

3.05 People with learning disabilities have varying degrees of disability. The World Health Organisation has proposed a sub-division of learning disabilities according to IQ, as follows[4]:

---

[1] See British Psychological Society, *Learning Disability: Definitions and Contexts*, Leicester: Professional Affairs Board of the British Psychological Society, 2001.

[2] See Emerson, E., Hatton, C., Felce, D. and Murphy, G.H., *Learning Disabilities: The Fundamental Facts*, London: The Foundation for People with Learning Disabilities, 2001.

[3] Bersani, H., 'From social clubs to social movement: landmarks in the development of the international self-advocacy movement' in Ward L. (ed.), *Innovations in Advocacy and Empowerment for People with Intellectual Disabilities*, Chorley, Lancs: Lisieux Hall Publications, 1998.

[4] World Health Organization, *International Classification of Diseases—10th Ed. (ICD–10)*, Geneva: World Health Organization, 1992.

- mild learning disabilities: IQ 50–69;
- moderate learning disabilities: IQ 35–49;
- severe learning disabilities: IQ 20–34 and
- profound learning disabilities: IQ below 20.

In practice, these sub-divisions are infrequently used. Few people with learning disabilities have had recent formal IQ tests and, in any case, exact measurement of IQ is not feasible for those with severe and profound disabilities.

Nevertheless, it is important to note that learning disabilities form a continuum, with a **3.06** small number of people, for example, those with profound disabilities, needing support from carers for almost all their activities, including self care, and having no easily understood expressive language skills. In contrast, others, who have mild disabilities, may be well able to have a conversation and be able to live independently, with support provided only for a few hours each day, to assist with difficult tasks (such as looking after children, budgeting, and meal planning and preparation). Since the term 'learning disabilities' is perceived as stigmatizing, many people with mild learning disabilities will deny that they have been given this diagnosis (although they will often accept that they have some difficulties, such as problems in budgeting or telling the days of the week). Sometimes, this can be problematic in the criminal justice system, which offers some special help for those with learning disabilities (see below).

(4) The causes of learning disabilities

The causes of learning disabilities are sometimes biological and sometimes environ- **3.07** mental; often, they are a mixture of both. Biological causes are more common in people with severe learning disabilities and include genetic conditions (such as Down's syndrome and Fragile-X syndrome), congenital factors (such as foetal alcohol syndrome, cytomegalovirus), and post-natal factors, such as extreme prematurity and infections (such as meningitis). Environmental causes (highly correlated with extreme social deprivation) are more common in people with mild disabilities. However, studies of aetiology have reported that the causes of learning disabilities are 'unknown' in between 20 and 60 per cent of cases.[5] Assumptions about people's disabilities should not be made from knowledge of the cause of their disabilities, however, because, for any condition, the extent of the disability may be very variable.

(5) The prevalence of learning disabilities

The true prevalence of learning disabilities has been established from total population **3.08** studies, like those in Aberdeen[6] and in the Isle of Wight,[7] and it is thought to be about 2–3 per cent for mild learning disabilities and about 3 per 1000 for more severe

---

[5] Emerson *et al*, cited above at n. 2.
[6] Birch, H., Richardson, S.A., Baird, D., Horobin, G. and Illsley, R., *Mental Subnormality in the Community: A Clinical and Epidemiological Study*, Cambridge, Mass: Harvard University Press, 1970.
[7] Rutter, M., Tizard, J., Yule, M., Graham, P.J. and Whitmore, K., 'Research report: Isle of Wight studies, 1964–1974' (1976) 6 *Psychological Medicine*, 313–332.

disabilities.[8] It is thought that, during the school years, the numbers of children known to have learning disabilities approaches the true figure (i.e. that administrative prevalence approaches true prevalence), because the academic demands of the school environment make disabilities obvious. When children leave school, however, it seems that between a half and two-thirds disappear from services (i.e. do not access any specialist learning disabilities services), so that the administrative prevalence falls away from the true prevalence.[9]

3.09　In the UK, each health and social services area provides support to people with learning disabilities and most areas now have adult learning disability registers. Frequently, however, the numbers on these registers fall far short of the likely true prevalence for the area. In Plymouth, for example, which has a total population of about 220,000, a recent study found that 1,326 adults were on the register (i.e. were known to adult learning disability services), even though the true prevalence would probably be more like 4,000 people.[10] The implication of this is that people with learning disabilities who become involved with the criminal justice system may well not be known to adult learning disability services.

B. People with Learning Disabilities as Victims of Crime

3.10　It has been argued that people with learning disabilities are especially vulnerable to crimes and abuse of various kinds, including robbery, theft, verbal abuse, physical assaults, sexual abuse, financial abuse, false imprisonment and even abduction and unlawful killing.[11]

(1) Physical and sexual abuse

3.11　During the 1980s and 1990s, research in numerous Western countries demonstrated that physical and sexual abuse against children and adults with disabilities was common.[12]

---

[8] Emerson *et al*, cited above at n. 2.

[9] Richardson, S.A. and Koller, H., 'Epidemiology' in Clarke, A.M., Clarke, A.B.D. and Berg J.M. (eds.), *Mental Deficiency: The Changing Outlook*, 4th ed, London: Methuen, 1985.

[10] McBrien, J., Hodgetts, A. and Gregory, J., 'Offending and risky behaviour in community services for people with intellectual disabilities in one Local Authority' (2003) 14 *Journal of Forensic Psychiatry*, 280–297.

[11] Williams, C., *Invisible Victims: Crime and Abuse against People with Learning Difficulties*, London: Jessica Kingsley, 1995; Westcott, H. and Jones, D.P.H., 'Annotation: The abuse of disabled children' (1999) 40 *Journal of Child Psychology and Psychiatry*, 497–506.

[12] Sobsey, D. and Varnhagen, C., 'Sexual abuse, assault and exploitation of Canadians with disabilities' in Bagley, C. and Thomlinson, R.J. (eds.), *Child Sexual Abuse: Critical Perspectives on Prevention, Intervention and Treatment*, Toronto: Wall and Emerson, 1991; Sobsey, D. and Doe T., 'Patterns of sexual abuse and assault' (1991) 9 *Sexuality and Disability*, 243–259; Westcott, H., 'The abuse of disabled children: A review of the literature' (1991) 17 *Child: Care, Health and Development*, 243–258; Wilson, C. and Brewer, N., 'The incidence of criminal victimisation of individuals with an intellectual disability' (1992) 27 *Australian Psychologist*, 114–117; Westcott and Jones (1999) cited above at n. 11; Crosse, S.B., Kaye, E. and Ratnofsky, A.C., *A Report on the Maltreatment of Children with Disabilities*, Washington DC: National Center on Child Abuse and Neglect, 1993; Turk, V. and Brown, H., 'The sexual abuse of adults with learning disabilities: results of a two-year incidence survey' (1993) 6 *Mental Handicap Research*, 193–216; Brown, H., Stein, J. and Turk, V., 'The sexual abuse of adults with learning disabilities: a second incidence study' (1995) 8 *Mental Handicap Research*, 3–24; McCarthy, M. and Thompson, D., 'A prevalence study of sexual abuse of adults with intellectual disabilities referred for sex education' (1997) 10 *Journal of Applied Research in Intellectual Disabilities*, 105–124; Mencap, *Living in Fear*, London: Mencap, 1999.

Research by Brown and Stein[13] in two county social service departments in south-east **3.12** England examined adult abuse alerts across all vulnerable care groups (older people, people with physical disability, people with learning disabilities and people with mental health needs). They found that 397 incidents of alleged abuse against vulnerable adults were reported to social services in a single year—an incidence of 14 alerts per 100,000 of the general population in one county and 26 alerts per 100,000 in the other. The majority of these concerned older people, aged 65 or over (about 36 per cent of alerts) and those with learning disabilities (about 34 per cent of alerts), with 16 per cent of alerts for people with mental health needs and 14 per cent of alerts for people with physical impairments. The types of abuse reported across the different groups varied: about 26 per cent appeared to be multiple forms of abuse, while about 33 per cent of the alerts concerned physical abuse alone, about 15 per cent sexual abuse alone, 12 per cent financial abuse alone, and fewer than 5 per cent each for psychological abuse alone and neglect.

People with learning disabilities, though they were fewer in total number than older **3.13** people, were *proportionately* far more likely than any other group to be the victims of abuse, especially physical abuse (36 per cent of abuse alerts) and sexual abuse (33 per cent of abuse alerts). Relatively few were thought to have been financially abused (4 per cent of abuse alerts in intellectual disabilities).

Similar findings have been reported for children with disabilities in the USA, both by **3.14** Crosse *et al*,[14] who reviewed case files for 1,834 American children in a nationally representative sample of substantiated cases of abuse, and by Sullivan and colleagues,[15] in their retrospective analysis of the merged hospital, police and social services records of abused and non-abused children in one area.

(2) The vulnerability of people with learning disabilities

A number of reasons have been suggested for why people with learning disabilities are so **3.15** vulnerable to abuse, including sexual abuse:[16]

- they are in a very powerless position in society;
- they may be very dependent on others for physical and other types of care;
- they may live in settings that make abuse more likely (large institutional settings are particularly problematic);

---

[13] Brown, H. and Stein, J., 'Implementing Adult Protection policies in Kent and East Sussex' (1998) 27 *Journal of Social Policy*, 371–396.

[14] Crosse, S.B., Kaye, E. and Ratnofsky, A.C., *A Report on the Maltreatment of Children with Disabilities*, Washington DC: National Center on Child Abuse and Neglect, 1993.

[15] Sullivan, P.M., Knutson, J.F., Scanlan, J.M. and Cork, P.M. (1997) 'Maltreatment of children with disabilities: Family risk factors and prevention implications' (1997) 4 *Journal of Child-Centred Practice*, 33–46; Sullivan, P.M. and Knutson, J.F., 'The association between child maltreatment and disabilities in a hospital-based epidemiological study' (1998) 22 *Child Abuse and Neglect*, 271–288.

[16] Brown, Stein and Turk, (1995) cited above at n. 12 Brown, H., 'Abuse of people with learning disabilities: layers of concern and analysis', in Stanley, N., Manthorpe J. and Penhale B. (eds.), *Institutional Abuse: Perspectives Across the Life Course*, London: Routledge, 1999; McCarthy, M., *Sexuality and Women with Learning Disabilities*, London: Jessica Kingsley, 1999.

- they are often kept in ignorance of what situations are risky or unacceptable (for example, by a lack of sex education);
- they may have major communication difficulties, so that they may be unable to tell anyone that they have been abused;
- their care staff often have little training in what to do if abuse is suspected;
- they are unlikely to be as able as other people to contact the police themselves to report alleged crimes, and
- they may not be believed, even when they do tell the police or other people what has happened to them.

Some of these characteristics mean that people with learning disabilities may be specifically targeted by some perpetrators.

3.16 In addition, it is known that, even when people with learning disabilities do tell carers about abuse or crimes against them, the carers do not always tell the police, especially if the alleged perpetrator is another person with a learning disability. For example, a study in Cambridge showed that, when asked, staff in 60 per cent of the city's residential and day services said they would not necessarily report a major assault against a person with learning disabilities and 10 per cent said they would not necessarily report a rape, when another person using the service was the alleged perpetrator.[17]

3.17 A more recent study, by McBrien and Murphy,[18] has confirmed the reluctance of staff to report to the police incidents perpetrated by people with learning disabilities. They found that carers tended to think that the alleged perpetrators needed help rather than the intervention of the law. Where non-disabled people were allegedly the perpetrators of crimes against people with learning disabilities, it seems that staff are not so reluctant to report them to the police.[19]

C. People with Learning Disabilities as Witnesses in the Criminal Justice System

(1) The limited involvement of people with learning disabilities

3.18 It appears that relatively few of the alleged crimes against people with learning disabilities are ever investigated by the police, let alone prosecuted, and this seems to be the case in many Western countries.[20]

3.19 For example, in their surveys of sexual abuse of people with learning disabilities in the

---

[17] Lyall, I., Holland, A.J. and Collins, S., 'Offending by adults with learning disabilities and the attitudes of staff to offending behaviour: Implications for service development' (1995) 39 *Journal of Intellectual Disability Research*, 501–508.

[18] McBrien, J. and Murphy, G., 'Police and carers' beliefs about intellectually disabled offenders' (2006), 12 *Psychology, Crime and Law*, 127–144.

[19] McCarthy and Thompson, (1997), cited above at n. 12; McBrien and Murphy, cited above at n. 18.

[20] Luckasson, R., 'People with mental retardation as victims of crime' in Conley, R.W., Luckasson, R. and Bouthilet, G.N. (eds.), *The Criminal Justice System and Mental Retardation*, London: Paul Brookes Publishing Co., 1992.

UK, Brown and her colleagues reported that only 28 per cent of the cases of sexual abuse detected (i.e. known to services) in their 1989/1990 survey and only 14 per cent of cases detected in their 1991/1992 survey led to prosecution/disciplinary actions or to warnings/cautions.[21] Similarly, in McCarthy and Thompson's 1997 study of sexual abuse against people with learning disabilities,[22] only 25 per cent of the cases of sexual abuse that came to light were investigated by police and only 5 per cent of the perpetrators were convicted.

Where other types of crime have been included as well, a similarly small proportion **3.20** has been notified to the police: in a survey of crimes against people with learning disabilities,[23] for example, 90 per cent of those interviewed reported that they had been bullied or been victims of crimes over the previous year, some of the incidents being of an extremely serious nature (such as physical attacks requiring hospitalization). The majority of incidents (73 per cent) had taken place in public and yet only a small minority (17 per cent) had even been reported to the police. Where studies have reported higher reporting and prosecution rates, usually this has been the result of a biased sample, such as a sample of very high profile or serious cases. For example, Sanders *et al* in their study of crimes against people with learning disabilities found that, of 76 high profile cases, charges were brought in 33 (i.e. still less than 50 per cent of cases, despite the seriousness), prosecutions resulting in 32 cases. Only 13 of the alleged perpetrators were convicted.[24]

(2) Why do people with learning disabilities so rarely go to court?

Sharp[25] has reported that the police do not always take crimes against people with **3.21** learning disabilities seriously, partly because it is often believed that they will be unsafe witnesses in Court. Indeed, the Codes of Practice that accompany the Police and Criminal Evidence Act 1984, governing the investigation of alleged offences in England and Wales, still warn the police that:

> although ... people who are mentally disordered or otherwise mentally vulnerable are often capable of providing reliable evidence, they may, without knowing or wishing to do so, be particularly prone in certain circumstances to provide information that may be unreliable, misleading or self-incriminating.[26]

In the face of such warnings, the police may believe that there is no point in talking with **3.22** victims and other witnesses with learning disabilities. They may also think, along with many health and social carers, that the trauma of going to Court may be so severe that it would do the vulnerable person more harm than good and is best avoided; something with which the witnesses themselves do not necessarily agree.[27]

---

[21] Turk and Brown (1993), cited above at n. 12; Brown, Stein and Turk, (1995), cited above at n. 12.
[22] Cited above at n. 12.   [23] Mencap, (1999), cited above at n. 12.
[24] Sanders, A., Creaton, J., Bird, S. and Weber, L., *Victims with Learning Disabilities: Negotiating the Criminal Justice System* (Occasional Paper No. 17), Oxford: University of Oxford Centre for Criminological Research, 1997.
[25] Sharp, H., 'Steps towards justice for people with learning disabilities as victims of crime: the important role of the police' (2001) 29 *British Journal of Learning Disabilities*, 88–92.
[26] Note E2, Code C, *PACE Codes of Practice*, London: The Stationery Office, 2005.
[27] Green, G., 'Vulnerability of witnesses with learning disabilities: preparing to give evidence against a perpetrator of sexual abuse' (2001) 29 *British Journal of Learning Disabilities*, 103–109.

3.23 McCarthy and Thompson[28] have suggested that a number of obstacles commonly prevent cases being prosecuted, including:

- a lack of corroborating evidence (cited in 50 per cent of their cases as the reason for not proceeding);
- the victim being considered an unreliable witness (40 per cent of their cases);
- the victim not wanting action taken (33 per cent of their cases);
- the victim giving an inconsistent account (23 per cent of their cases).

The alleged perpetrator having intellectual disabilities was also cited as an obstacle in 26 per cent of cases.[29]

3.24 It seems therefore that there are a number of barriers to people with learning disabilities becoming witnesses in court. What does research evidence say about what the crucial difficulties are for witnesses with learning disabilities? The evidence suggests that there are four main difficulties that seem to act as obstacles to victims and other potential witnesses with learning disabilities: difficulties coping with interviews; difficulties in providing eyewitness evidence; difficulties in following Court proceedings; and, more generally, difficulties in making decisions. These will be discussed in turn.

(i) Difficulties coping with interviews: acquiescence, confabulation, compliance and suggestibility

3.25 People with learning disabilities are vulnerable to being poor witnesses under certain circumstances.[30] As a group, they tend to show higher degrees of acquiescence (i.e. saying 'yes' to questions requiring a yes/no answer, regardless of their content) and a greater tendency to confabulation (that is, to distorting or fabricating information) than people without disabilities.[31]

3.26 People with learning disabilities are also more likely to be compliant (that is, to say or do what they believe is wanted, regardless of their own views). In addition, it seems that, overall, both children and adults with learning disabilities are more suggestible than people without disabilities.[32] Some studies, such as that of Everington and

---

[28] Cited above at n.12.   [29] More than one obstacle was identified in many cases.

[30] Kebbell, M.R. and Hatton, C., 'People with mental retardation as witnesses in court: a review' (1999) 37 *Mental Retardation*, 179–187.

[31] Clare, I.C.H. and Gudjonsson, G.H., 'Interrogative suggestibility, confabulation, and acquiescence in people with mild learning disabilities (mental handicap): Implications for reliability during police interrogations' (1993) 32 *British Journal of Clinical Psychology*, 295–301; Heal, L.W. and Sigelman, C.K., 'Response biases in interviews of individuals with limited mental ability' (1995) 39 *Journal of Intellectual Disability Research*, 331–340; Finlay, W.M.L. and Lyons, E., 'Acquiescence in interviews with people who have mental retardation' (2002) 40 *Mental Retardation*, 14–29.

[32] Clare and Gudjonsson, (1993), cited above at n.31; Cardone, D. and Dent, H., 'Memory and interrogative suggestibility. The effects of modality of information presentation and retrieval conditions upon the suggestibility scores of people with learning disabilities' (1996) 1 *Legal and Criminological Psychology*, 165–177; Henry, L. and Gudjonsson, G.H., 'Eyewitness memory and suggestibility in children with learning disabilities' (1999) 104 *American Journal on Mental Retardation*, 491–508; Milne, R., Clare, I.C.H. and Bull, R., 'Interrogative suggestibility among witnesses with mild intellectual disabilities: the use of an adaptation of the GSS' (2002) 15 *Journal of Applied Research in Intellectual Disabilities*, 8–17; Everington, C. and Fulero, S., 'Competence to confess: measuring understanding and suggestibility of

Fulero,[33] have found that people with learning disabilities are more vulnerable both to 'yield', that is to being misled by leading questions and 'shift', that is, to changing their responses following interrogative pressure; others, however, have found differences in yield but not in shift, at least among adults.[34]

There have been some claims that this increase in suggestibility amongst people with **3.27** learning disabilities is simply an artefact of the way in which suggestibility is measured: Beail[35] has argued that the Gudjonsson Suggestibility Scale[36] ('GSS'), which is the most widely used measure of suggestibility, relies on semantic memory for a story and that the relatively poor memory of people with learning disabilities automatically means that they will obtain poor scores (i.e. higher suggestibility). However, it seems that, while taking account of the poorer recall for the story in the GSS reduces the differences between groups of people with and without disabilities, it does not eliminate them entirely.[37] Beail[38] also argued that, in real life, witness testimony reflects episodic and autobiographical memory, which may be better than semantic memory in people with learning disabilities. However, when a videotaped incident is used, rather than a story, people with learning disabilities are still more suggestible than their general population counterparts.[39] Moreover, the GSS is a good predictor of suggestibility in responding to questions about real-life events.[40]

Nonetheless, *some* people with learning disabilities are neither acquiescent nor suggest-**3.28** ible; nor do they necessarily confabulate (that is, fabricate or distort) information. In any case, their problems seem to be no greater than those of many children who are accepted as witnesses. Often, the style of questioning can be adjusted to minimize the problems. For example, free recall can be encouraged because when just asked to 'tell what happened', people with learning disabilities make no more errors than others.[41] Moreover, provided questions are phrased simply, are open rather than closed, are not leading, and it is stated clearly that it is acceptable to say 'I don't know' as a response, as witnesses many vulnerable people can be as reliable as other witnesses.[42] Milne, Clare, and Bull[43] have suggested that a cognitive interview approach, in which the questioning becomes increasingly focused, produces the best evidence from people with learning disabilities.

---

defendants with mental retardation' (1999) 37 *Mental Retardation*, 212–220; Gudjonsson, G.H. and Henry, L., 'Child and adult witnesses with intellectual disability: the importance of suggestibility' (2003) 8 *Legal and Criminological Psychology*, 241–252.

[33] Cited above at n. 32.

[34] See Clare and Gudjonsson, (1993), cited above at n. 30; Henry and Gudjonsson, (1999), cited above at n. 32; Milne, R., Clare, I.C.H. and Bull, R., 'Using the cognitive interview with adults with mild learning disabilities' (1999) 5 *Psychology, Crime and Law*, 81–101.

[35] Beail, N., 'Interrogative suggestibility, memory and intellectual disability' (2002) 15 *Journal of Applied Research in Intellectual Disabilities*, 129–137.

[36] Gudjonsson, G.H., *The Gudjonsson Suggestibility Scales*, Hove: Psychology Press, 1997.

[37] Gudjonsson and Henry, (2003), cited above at n. 32.   [38] Cited above at n. 35.

[39] See Milne, Clare and Bull, (2002), cited above at n. 34.

[40] Gudjonsson (1997), cited above at n. 36.

[41] Perlman, N.B., Ericson, K.I., Esses, V.M., and Isaacs, B.J., 'The developmentally handicapped witness' (1994) 18 *Law and Human Behavior*, 171–187. See also Henry and Gudjonsson, (1999), cited above at n. 32.

[42] See Perlman *et al*, cited above at n. 41.   [43] Cited above at n. 34.

(ii) Difficulties in providing eyewitness evidence

3.29 Eyewitness identification may sometimes be the main evidence, or even the only evidence, that suggests that a particular suspect was the perpetrator of a crime and so, in the prosecution of crimes against people with learning disabilities, the ability to act as eyewitnesses following crimes is an important issue. Research on the ability of non-disabled children and adults to act as eyewitnesses has shown that children can make as many correct identifications as adults but they may make more incorrect identifications and fewer 'no selection' responses than adults. Ericson and Isaacs[44] investigated eyewitness identification by people with learning disabilities by showing a film clip of the theft of a purse at a garden shop. Afterwards, they tested examinees' ability to identify the suspect in three conditions (clear film, less distinct film and ambiguous film) and compared it to that of non-disabled adults. They found that people with learning disabilities made as many correct identifications as the non-disabled adults but, whatever the clarity of the film, they made more false identifications.

3.30 According to Malpass and Devine,[45] there are two major factors that affect eyewitness identification:

- information about the appearance of the alleged offender (which may depend on physical factors like lighting or period of time in sight, as well as psychological factors such as the focus of attention at the time and memory), and

- the social value of choosing (which may be heavily influenced by the desire for social approval).

3.31 Ericson and Isaacs concluded from their study that participants with learning disabilities had just as good a memory for the suspect's appearance as other participants but, like children, were more influenced than others by the social value of making an identification. The implication of such compliant responding is that it is extremely important to ensure that eyewitnesses with learning disabilities know that it is acceptable for them to be unable to remember.

(iii) Difficulties in following court proceedings

3.32 Being a witness in court involves not just being able to give an account of events when questioned, but also being able to understand proceedings and survive cross-examination, which is sometimes aggressive in tone.

3.33 People with learning disabilities often find legal terminology and court proceedings very difficult to follow. Ericson and Perlman,[46] in Canada, compared 40 people with learning disabilities with an equal number of men and women without disabilities on their understanding of 34 common legal words that they were likely to come across if they

---

[44] Ericson, K.I. and Isaacs, B., 'Eyewitness identification accuracy: A comparison of adults with and those without intellectual disabilities' (2003) 41 *Mental Retardation*, 161–173.

[45] Malpass, R. and Devine, P., 'Research on suggestion in lineups and photospreads' in Wells G. and Loftus E. (eds.), *Eyewitness Testimony*, Cambridge: Cambridge University Press, 1984.

[46] Ericson, K.I. and Perlman, N.B., 'Knowledge of legal terminology and court proceedings in adults with developmental disabilities' (2001) 25 *Law and Human Behavior*, 529–545.

were to become witnesses in court (including judge, lawyer, crown attorney, defendant, arrest, allegation, charge, prosecute, suspect, testimony, innocent, guilty, jail). With the exception of 'police officer', which was understood equally well by both groups, the people with learning disabilities had a poorer understanding of all the words. 'Allegation' and 'prosecute' were among the most difficult for them, but they also had problems with 'accused', 'guilty', 'trial', 'adjourn', 'charges', 'defendant', 'suspect', 'victim', and 'evidence' (see Ericson and Perlman for the full list). There was considerable variability in the group with disabilities, however, with one person only being able to define one term ('jail') while another could define 32 out of the 34. Like others, Ericson and Perlman have pointed out that asking people if they understand the meaning of a word is not a good basis for judging comprehension. Instead, it is much better to ask them to explain it in their own words.

Once people with learning disabilities are giving evidence in court, especially if they **3.34** happen to be amongst those who find court terminology confusing, it is easy for lawyers to make them appear unreliable as witnesses, particularly when it comes to cross-examination. Kebbell *et al*[47] compared the transcripts of 16 trials in England and Wales involving witnesses with learning disabilities and the same number involving witnesses from the general population. For both groups, they found that lawyers asked significantly more open questions, closed questions and either/or questions in direct examination than in cross-examination. In contrast, significantly more yes/no, leading, negative, and multiple questions were asked in cross-examination. There appeared to be extremely few differences between the kinds of questions asked of witnesses with and without disabilities (slightly fewer leading questions, slightly more repeated questions), indicating that lawyers did not really adjust their questioning style to take account of the needs of witnesses. Not surprisingly, witnesses with learning disabilities were significantly more likely to be affected by leading questions, especially in cross-examination, than were those without disabilities.

In England and Wales, judges are allowed to interrupt court proceedings if they feel **3.35** the court is being misled, or to ensure a fair trial.[48] O'Kelly *et al*[49] compared the number of times in which judges intervened in 32 trials, 16 of which involved witnesses with learning disabilities and in 16 of which the witnesses were not disabled. The transcripts were used to categorize these interventions broadly as interactions with witnesses, inter-actions with lawyers, and interactions with juries and, then, within these three classes, into 18 subcategories (see O'Kelly *et al* for details). No significant differences were found in either the broad classes or the sub-categories. These findings suggest that judges are probably not sensitive to the vulnerabilities of witnesses with learning disabilities.

---

[47] Kebbell, M.R., Hatton, C. and Johnson, S.D., 'Witnesses with intellectual disabilities in court: What questions are asked and what influence do they have?' (2004) 9 *Legal and Criminological Psychology*, 23–25.

[48] Pattenden, R., *Judicial Discretion and Criminal Litigation*, Oxford: Clarendon Press, 1990.

[49] O'Kelly, C.M.E., Kebbell, M.R., Hatton, C. and Johnson, S.D., 'Judicial intervention in court cases involving witnesses with and without learning disabilities' (2003) 8 *Legal and Criminological Psychology*, 229–240.

(iv) Difficulties in making decisions

3.36 The final difficulty facing people with learning disabilities is that of decision making. It has been established that, when they are being interviewed by the police as suspects, people with learning disabilities sometimes confess to crimes of which they are innocent.[50] Clare and Gudjonsson[51] have demonstrated that this may, in part, be due to naivety about the seriousness of making this kind of false confession. There are some reported cases in which people with learning disabilities who are initially interviewed by the police as witnesses have ended up confessing to crimes they did not commit.[52]

D. Supporting Witnesses with Learning Disabilities

(1) The stringent rules for witnesses

3.37 In England and Wales, there was, until recently, no special provision to help people with learning disabilities give evidence in court. Instead, as in many other countries,[53] they had to survive the court proceedings as would any member of the public. The relevant case law in England and Wales was provided by *R* v *Hill*,[54] in which the judge examined the witness in a *voire dire* (a separate hearing before the case itself), in order to determine whether she or he was able to:

- understand the nature and the special responsibility of the oath (and the obligation to tell the truth in Court), and
- give a rational verbal account of what happened (or what had been seen).[55]

Similar abilities are required in the USA.[56]

3.38 It seems, however, that such stringent rules prevented some people with learning disabilities from acting as witnesses. Gudjonsson *et al*[57] assessed 49 men and women with learning disabilities for the police in a case where staff in two large residential services were accused of physical and sexual abuse and ill-treatment of residents. The potential witnesses were assessed for their understanding of the oath, for acquiescence and suggestibility, and for their ability to be interviewed by police (a clinical judgement), as well as for their degree of intellectual disability.

---

[50] Gudjonsson, G.H., *The Psychology of Interrogations and Confessions: A Handbook*, Chichester: John Wiley and Sons, 2003.

[51] Clare, I.C.H. and Gudjonsson, G.H., 'The vulnerability of suspects with intellectual disabilities during police interviews: a review and experimental study of decision-making' (1995) 8 *Mental Handicap Research*, 110–128.

[52] See, for example, the case of Mr Z in Gudjonsson, (2003), cited above at n.50.

[53] See Dinerstein, R.D. and Buescher, M., 'Capacity and the courts' in Dinerstein, R.D., Herr, S.S. and O'Sullivan, J.L. (eds.), *A Guide to Consent*, Washington, DC: American Association on Mental Retardation, 1999; Gudjonsson, G.H., Murphy, G.H. and Clare, I.C.H., 'Assessing the capacity of people with intellectual disabilities to be witnesses in court' (2000) 30 *Psychological Medicine*, 307–314.

[54] (1851) 2 Dennison 254.

[55] The judge was not obliged to decide whether the witness was *reliable*, however. In England and Wales this has always been for the jury to decide.

[56] Herr, S.S., 'Capacity for consent to legal representation' in Dinerstein, Herr and O'Sullivan, (1999), cited above at n.53.

[57] Cited above at n.53.

Understanding of the oath was assessed by asking people to repeat the standard oath and **3.39** then to explain what it meant, including the words 'truth' and 'lie'.[58] In addition, people were asked what would happen to someone who told a lie in Court (to test that the person understood that they had a special responsibility to tell the truth there and knew that they could be prosecuted for telling a lie). Of the 49 men and women, 12 were too severely disabled to be tested. Of the remaining participants, no-one could demonstrate understanding of all four aspects of the oath, but many were able to explain at least some of the concepts:

- the meaning of 'lie' and 'truth';
- the meaning of 'the whole truth';
- the meaning of swearing on a religious book, and
- the special responsibility to tell the truth in court.

Of the 49 participants, 10 (20 per cent) could explain the difference between the 'truth' **3.40** and a 'lie' and a further 9 (18 per cent) could recognize the difference when concrete examples were given. In all, 17 of the 37 were judged to be able to give sufficiently coherent accounts to be interviewed by the police.[59] Excluding those who were unable to explain the oath well would prevent many people who might be able to give accurate and reliable accounts from having access to justice.

(2) The demand for change

In England and Wales during the late-1990s, in the face of mounting evidence of this **3.41** kind, there was a growing feeling that the law needed to change.[60] An increasing number of pressure groups[61] asked for better training for the police[62] and others involved in the criminal justice system, and called for new legislation so that the likelihood of trial and conviction for those guilty of crimes against this group of vulnerable people could be improved. Following the recommendations of an interdepartmental working group,[63] the Youth Justice and Criminal Evidence Act 1999 was enacted, and came into force in 2001. The Act made provision, under Part II, for new rules of evidence for 'vulnerable witnesses', defined as young people, adults with a mental disorder or learning disability or physical disability, or people of any kind suffering from fear or distress (intimidated witnesses).

---

[58] For examples of scoring see Gudjonsson *et al*, (2000), cited above at n. 53.

[59] As Gudjonsson *et al*, (2000), point out, while there is a clear requirement in case law for competence to be a witness in court, there is no such legal requirement for being interviewed by the police and the police will be concerned not just to interview people who could be witnesses in court but also to gather any evidence that will further the investigation of the case. Cited above at n. 53.

[60] See Williams, (1995), cited above at n. 11 and Sanders, A., Creaton, J., Bird, S. and Weber, L., cited above at n. 24.

[61] Mencap, *Barriers to Justice*, London: Mencap, 1997; VOICE UK, *Competent to Tell the Truth*, Derby: Voice UK, 1998.

[62] See also Bailey, A. and Barr, O., 'Police policies on the investigation of sexual crimes committed against adults who have a learning disability' (2000) 4 *Journal of Learning Disabilities*, 129–139.

[63] Home Office, *Speaking Up for Justice. Report of the Interdepartmental Working Group on the Treatment of Vulnerable or Intimidated Witnesses in the Criminal Justice System*, London: HMSO, 1998.

(3) The introduction of the 'special measures'

3.42 Under the new Act, vulnerable witnesses are allowed 'special measures' according to their needs.[64] These can include:

- the removal of wigs and gowns by the judge and barristers;
- the use of screens to protect the victim from seeing the perpetrator;
- exclusion of the public from court;
- giving unsworn evidence rather than the oath;
- giving videotaped evidence-in-chief;
- cross-examination by video;
- the use of an intermediary, to assist the witness to understand the court (and vice versa), and
- communication aids, such as signs, symbol boards and electronic aids.

3.43 The Home Office published guidance on the implementation of these special measures, including material to help in identifying and, in particular, interviewing, vulnerable witnesses.[65] Access to the 'special measures' has to be determined in a Pre-Trial Hearing (Magistrates' Courts) or Plea and Directions Hearing (Crown Courts) and it is recommended that all vulnerable witnesses be assessed prior to these hearings, to determine their needs. Clearly such assessments need to be completed as early as possible after an alleged crime, in order to influence the way the police conduct their interview of the witness.

3.44 Whether the new law improves access to justice for vulnerable witnesses remains to be seen but an early evaluation, carried out by Hamlyn *et al*[66] has suggested that vulnerable witnesses (by no means all of these were people with learning disabilities) felt somewhat less intimidated, more satisfied with the criminal justice system and less anxious in court, than before. However, the number of people who use such special measures as communication aids and intermediaries remains unclear. These, and some other special measures, have been available to witnesses in Australia for some time but the experience there is that they are not often used.[67]

---

[64] Cooke, P. and Davies, G., 'Achieving best evidence from witnesses with learning disabilities: new guidance' (2001) 29 *British Journal of Learning Disabilities*, 84–87.

[65] Home Office, *Achieving Best Evidence in Criminal Proceedings: Guidance for Vulnerable or Intimidated Witnesses, including Children* (Report of the Memorandum Project Steering Group), London: Home Office Communication Directorate, 2002 (see also *http://www.homeoffice.gov.uk*).

[66] Hamlyn, B., Phelps, A., Turtle, J. and Sattar, G., *Are Special Measures Working? Evidence from Surveys of Vulnerable and Intimated Witnesses* (Study 283), London: Home Office Research, Development and Statistics Directorate, 2004.

[67] Balandin, S., 'Witnessing without words' in Shaddock, T., Bond, M., Bowen I. and Hales K. (eds.), *Intellectual Disability and the Law: Contemporary Australian Issues*, Callaghan, NSW: Australian Society for the Study of Intellectual Disability, 2000; Davis, C., 'Systemic abuse: Intellectual disability and the criminal justice system' in Shaddock *et al, Intellectual Disability and the Law*, cited above.

E. Witnesses with Learning Disabilities: Assessment and Support

(1) Carrying out a comprehensive assessment

Many people with learning disabilities will have problems such as memory difficulties, cognitive impairments, executive functioning deficits, language difficulties and social disadvantages[68] that put them at risk of giving poor evidence as witnesses to the police or in court. It is therefore likely that psychologists assessing a vulnerable witness for the police will need to use standardized psychometric assessments to evaluate the person's:

3.45

- cognitive skills;
- language skills, and
- memory functioning.

They will also wish to conduct some more specific assessments relevant to appearance in court. These may include:

3.46

- understanding of the oath or affirmation;
- suggestibility;
- acquiescence;
- confabulation;
- compliance, and
- understanding of the court process and legal terminology.

Any witnesses referred will also need to be assessed for their suitability for special measures, according to the jurisdiction. In England and Wales, this will require the psychologist to consider issues such as:

3.47

- How anxious the person would be in a 'normal' courtroom: (does he/she need the courtroom cleared? What about wigs and gowns? Should he/she give evidence by video?)
- The possible effects of seeing the alleged perpetrator: (does he/she need screens?)
- The communication skills of the witness: (will he or she need to take communication aids into the courtroom? Will he or she need an intermediary? How should lawyers best communicate with the witness?)

(2) The need for pre-trial support

In addition, psychologists might need to interview the vulnerable witness in order to determine what kind of pre-trial support may be appropriate, for example, the witness might wish to go to court prior to the case, to see the courtroom and meet court personnel. Most courts now have witness support schemes that will assist with these matters. There are also a number of books, including 'books without words', which explain the court process and show it in pictures[69] to assist vulnerable witnesses'

3.48

---

[68] Murphy, G.H. and Clare, I.C.H., 'Adults' capacity to make legal decisions' in Carson, D. and Bull R. (eds.), *Handbook of Psychology in Legal Contexts*, 2nd ed, Chichester: John Wiley and Sons, 2003.

[69] Hollins, S., Sinason, V., Boniface, J. and Webb, B., *Going to Court*, London: Gaskell Publications/ Royal College of Psychiatrists, 1994.

understanding of what going to court may be like. It is important to note that during interviews and assessments of this kind, the psychologist should not ask the witness anything about the actual circumstances of the alleged crime he/she witnessed. This can be difficult, since vulnerable witnesses with learning disabilities are very often also the alleged victims and they may wish to talk about their experiences. However, if the alleged offence itself is discussed, it might be alleged that the psychologist 'coached' the witness and the case may not proceed. Nevertheless, it is perfectly acceptable for the witness to be assisted to understand the court process in general, to visit the court and to be taught how to deal with intimidating lawyers by role play, so that they feel confident about saying 'I don't know' or 'please explain'.

(3) Good practice in providing support for witnesses: an example

3.49 Over the last 10 years, some excellent examples of good practice in witness support have arisen. In Merseyside, for example, a multi-agency project involving the local authority, police, the Crown Prosecution Service (CPS) and the courts, which began in 1997, is now sited in an Investigation Support Unit in Liverpool Social Services.[70] The project provides support and preparation for witnesses with learning disabilities, from the investigation stage onwards.[71] A detailed witness profile is drawn up, which is served on the court and provides information on how to ensure the witness will best be enabled to give his/her evidence. Witnesses also have numerous trips to court to familiarize them with the court layout and court procedure, and the success rates (trials resulting in convictions) for the 30 witnesses supported so far are about 90 per cent.

3.50 Staff at the unit argue that their success is due to the preparation of both the witness and the court (lawyers and judge) to support the social interactions that form the real basis of giving evidence; they feel that the 'special measures', which they argue are largely ways to alter the physical environment are less important.[72] This witness support service has received much praise from lawyers, judges, the CPS Inspectorate and the Inspectorate of Constabularies. The CPS Policy Directorate is supporting the spread of similar units around the 42 CPS areas, using the Liverpool initiative as an example of good practice.

F. Conclusion

3.51 People with learning disabilities are vulnerable to abuse and exploitation, but often crimes against them are not reported to the police. Even when reported, the police may not interview them, frequently because of a belief that they will be 'unsafe witnesses'. People with learning disabilities tend to be more acquiescent, compliant, and suggestible than others; in addition, in some circumstances, they can be at greater risk of

---

[70] Monaghan, G. and Pathak, M., 'Silenced witnesses' (2000) *Community Care*, April 27.

[71] *The Times*, 25 January 2005; *Law in Action*, BBC Radio 4, 28 January 2005.

[72] We are very grateful to Mark Pathak, Social Worker for Liverpool Social Services Department for this information.

confabulating information. However, many of these difficulties reflect the use of overly complex language on the part of those involved in the criminal justice system, with leading questions, embedded phrases and repeated questions, and insufficient reminders that it is acceptable for people to say that they 'don't know' or 'can't remember'. In the police station, people with learning disabilities can provide adequate evidence during interviews and eyewitness procedures, if care is taken in the style of interview questions and the manner of witness identification. In court, however, they are likely to feel intimidated, and can be at risk both of being confused by the language and procedures used, and of succumbing to pressurized questioning from lawyers, especially under cross-examination. So far, it seems that lawyers find difficulty in amending their style of questioning to meet the needs of people with disabilities and nor, for the most part, do judges insist on this. In some jurisdictions, such as in England and Wales, new legislation has been introduced to assist people with learning disabilities to give evidence and psychologists or social workers may well be asked to assess people's needs for 'special measures' in court. The aim of such changes, which have been supported by some excellent schemes, has been to improve access to justice for people with learning disabilities and enable them to give 'best evidence'.

Further Reading

Gudjonsson, G.H., *The Psychology of Interrogations and Confessions: A Handbook*, Chichester: John Wiley and Sons, 2003.

Home Office, *Achieving Best Evidence in Criminal Proceedings: Guidance for Vulnerable or Intimidated Witnesses, including Children*, (Report of the Memorandum Project Steering Group), London: Home Office Communication Directorate 2002 (see also http://www.homeoffice.gov.uk).

Glynis H. Murphy is Professor of Clinical Psychology at the University of Lancaster. She is a chartered Clinical & Forensic Psychologist, Fellow of the British Psychological Society and President-Elect of the International Association for the Scientific Study of Intellectual Disabilities. Professor Murphy has had a long term research interest in intellectual disabilities and has published widely on challenging behaviour, forensic issues, abuse and capacity to make decisions.

Isabel C.H. Clare is a Consultant Clinical and Forensic Psychologist, working with men and women with learning disabilities in Cambridgeshire and Peterborough Mental Health NHS Trust. Dr. Clare is also a researcher in the Department of Psychiatry (Section of Developmental Psychiatry), University of Cambridge, and has published widely, particularly on issues relating to offending and abuse, and decision-making capacity.

Editors' Note

There will always be prejudice directed towards those who are 'different' in their communicative styles. This is experienced especially by those with learning disabilities of the 'does s/he take sugar?' variety. They are particularly vulnerable to victimization by abusers confident that their targets' accounts would be unlikely to be believed by investigators or in court. Knowledge of the real effects of learning disabilities and their effects on testimony will enable fact-finders and those who address or direct them to reach dependable and accurate conclusions concerning what they say, free of prejudice.

4

THE PSYCHOLOGICAL VULNERABILITIES OF WITNESSES AND THE RISK OF FALSE ACCUSATIONS AND FALSE CONFESSIONS

Gisli H. Gudjonsson

A. Introduction

'Investigative interviewing' is an important form of evidence gathering. The principal **4.01** objective is to obtain information that is detailed, complete, comprehensible, valid (in legal settings the words 'safe' and 'reliable' are commonly used to describe validity), and relevant to the legal issues in the case that need to be established and proved. A number of governmental and local agencies are involved in conducting investigative interviews, including the police, Customs and Excise, the military and the security services.[1] Interviewing also occurs in other settings, such as mental health and organisational.[2] However, the focus in this chapter is on investigative (police) interviews in relation to 'vulnerable' people. Obtaining a clear and reliable account of events from witnesses, victims and suspects is important in order to achieve a sound conviction and avoid a miscarriage of justice. Witnesses do sometimes give false or misleading evidence, even when motivated to tell the truth.[3] Similarly, self-incriminating statements from suspects, even when false, do on occasions result in a wrongful conviction.[4]

---

[1] Gudjonsson, G. H., 'The psychology of interrogations and confessions' in Williamson, T. (ed.), *Investigative Interviewing. Rights, research, regulations*, Devon: Willan Publishing, 2005, 123–146.

[2] Memon, A. and Bull, R., (eds), *Handbook of Psychology of Interviewing*, Chichester: John Wiley & Sons, 1999.

[3] Kebbell, M. R. and Wagstaff, G. F., 'Face Value? Evaluating the Accuracy of Eyewitness Information,' Police Research Series, Paper 102, Policing and Reducing Crime Unit, London: Home Office, 1999.

[4] Kassin, S.M. and Gudjonsson, G. H., 'The Psychology of Confessions. A Review of the Literature and Issues' (2004) 5 *Psychological Science in the Public Interest*, 33–67; Williamson, T., 'Towards greater

4.02 It is often assumed that persons who suffer from mental disorder lack the capacity and motivation to give an accurate, complete and reliable account of events. This unfounded view was well highlighted during the Ashworth Inquiry,[5] where the evidence of psychiatric patients about alleged ill-treatment and improper care was challenged by the defendants on the basis of the patients' mental status and their inherent lack of credibility as witnesses.

4.03 In this chapter the potential psychological vulnerabilities of persons with mental disorder are set out and it is argued that mental disorder on its own does not usually undermine the credibility of witnesses when interviewed by the police or when giving evidence in court. What is needed is a proper identification of mental problems and other psychological vulnerabilities and an explanation of how these factors may influence the reliability of the witness's account to the police and evidence in court. This is what the present chapter aims to do.

B. Components of Credibility

4.04 The *credibility* of witnesses refers to the extent to which they are capable of being believed and it is determined by the trier of fact, typically the jury. The related concept of *reliability*, in terms of its legal use, focuses specifically on the trustworthiness of the witness's account (i.e. is it safe to rely on it as being an accurate and genuine recollection?). It has to do with the weight that the trier of fact can attribute to the testimony of the witness, having not only considered the credibility of the witness, but also considering all the surrounding circumstances, including the interview tactics used by the police to elicit the witness statement (e.g. the conduct of the police, the nature and circumstances of the disclosure). In contrast to *credibility* and *reliability*, the term *competence* is a legal issue for the court and refers to the personal qualities of the witness to testify in court (e.g. cognitive abilities, understanding of the nature of the oath).[6]

4.05 Psychologists use the term 'reliability' more technically to indicate the *consistency* of a test or measure. They use the term 'validity' to describe the extent to which a test measures what it is intended to measure. In this chapter the term 'reliability' is used with its legal meaning.

4.06 Credibility can be separated into two components.[7] The first component involves the *ability* of people to give reliable evidence at any one given point in time. This aspect of credibility is related to the witness's memory of the event in question, cognitive

---

professionalism: minimizing miscarriages of justice' in Williamson, (ed.), *Investigative Interviewing*, Devon: Willan Publishing, 2005, 147–166.

[5] Blom-Cooper, Sir Louis, Brown, M., Dolan, R. and Murphy, E., *Report of the Committee of Inquiry into Complaints about Ashworth Hospital*, Cmnd 2028 (2 vols), London: HMSO, 1992.

[6] Gudjonsson, G. H., Murphy, G. H. and Clare, I. C. H., 'Assessing the capacity of people with intellectual disabilities to be witnesses in court' (2000) 30 *Psychological Medicine*, 307–314.

[7] Undeutsch, U., 'Statement reality analysis' in Trankell, A. (ed.), *Reconstructing the Past: The Role of Psychologists in Criminal Trials*, Deventer: Kluwer, 1982, 25–56.

functioning (intelligence, memory capacity, tendency to confabulate), personality (suggestibility, compliance, acquiescence), and mental state (anxiety, depression, feelings of guilt, a state of shock, post-traumatic stress disorder, drug or alcohol intoxication or withdrawal symptoms).

Secondly, there is the *willingness* of witnesses to tell the truth. This is the motivational **4.07** aspect of credibility and it is influenced by both 'other-deception' (i.e. lying to others) and 'self-deception' (i.e. lying to oneself). Other-deception occurs when people deliberately lie to others in order either to *conceal* or to *falsify* information. Concealing takes place when they intentionally withhold information which may be important and relevant in establishing facts. Falsifying means that people intentionally give false information which they claim is true. Self-deception involves people lying to themselves (usually in order to stabilize mood and self-esteem) and they accordingly give an account of their feelings and behaviour which is incomplete or distorted but which they themselves believe to be true. Both other-deception and self-deception are important in a forensic assessment, but the former is more readily influenced by the context in which the person is being assessed.[8] That is, the way in which the person deceives others is typically under more conscious control and more deliberate than deceiving oneself. Self-deception indicates a lack of insight into one's problems and psychopathology and it is associated with the denial of painful emotional experiences. The consequence is that underlying psychopathology, such as depression and severe emotional problems, may not be readily apparent during the psychological and psychiatric assessment.

There are two kinds of punishment at stake when people lie to others. First, there **4.08** may be punishment if the lie fails (i.e. punishment associated with people learning about the truth of a matter which is being concealed or falsified). Second, the embarrassment and perceived punishment for being caught deceiving is often worse than the punishment that the lie was designed to avoid in the first place. Thus, once people have lied they are often persistent in maintaining the lie, even when confronted with evidence demonstrating the lying. Commonly this serves to protect their pride and self-esteem.[9]

C. Suspects, Witnesses and Victims

A 'witness' can be defined as any person who is potentially able to provide the police or **4.09** the court with information about an alleged offence or an offender. 'Suspects' and 'victims' are often important 'witnesses' in that they may provide the police and the court with information which is pertinent to the case.

Kebbell and Wagstaff[10] have identified three types of factors that influence the reliability **4.10** of eyewitnesses. These are:

---

[8] Gudjonsson, G.H., 'Self-deception and other-deception in forensic assessment' (1990) 11 *Personality and Individual Differences*, 219–225.
[9] Gudjonsson, G.H., *The Psychology of Interrogations, Confessions and Testimony*, Chichester: John Wiley and Sons, 1992.
[10] Cited above at n.3.

1. The nature of the offence and the situation in which the material event took place if observed, (e.g. factors relating to the offence, such as visibility, the amount of time under observation, distance from which the offence is observed, physical obstructions, and familiarity with the offender or the crime scene).
2. The characteristics of the witness (e.g. their strengths and weaknesses, age).
3. The way in which the information is retrieved (i.e. the nature and type of questioning, time lapsed since the offence).

4.11 As far as police interviewing is concerned, there are important differences between victims, witnesses and suspects. First, witnesses and victims are required to recall events they apparently observed. Suspects, when involved in the offence, would be expected to report their actions and intentions. Innocent suspects would not be in a position to give details of the offence unless they had observed it or been told about it.

4.12 Another important difference between suspects and other witnesses relates to the circumstances and nature of their interview with the police. The former, unlike other witnesses, are suspected of a criminal offence and the likelihood of self-incrimination is high. It is for this reason that they are cautioned against self-incrimination, and if mentally disordered or young persons they are entitled to the presence of an 'appropriate adult' to assist them at the police station. The person acting in this capacity has to be at least 18 years of age and he or she cannot be a police officer or the suspect's solicitor. In the case of a youth, a parent is most commonly called to act as an appropriate adult. In the case of an adult who is suffering from mental disorder, the social services are most commonly approached by the custody officer.

4.13 The use of appropriate adults at police stations is intended as a safeguard that protects 'vulnerable' suspects. These include children and adolescents and those suffering from mental disorder or those who are in a disturbed mental state while at the police station.

4.14 The role of the appropriate adult is threefold: to give advice, to further communication, and to ensure that the interview is conducted properly and fairly. The nature of the advice given is not specified in the Codes of Practice issued under the Police and Criminal Evidence Act 1984 (PACE), but it should not involve legal advice. If the vulnerable suspect is not legally represented, the appropriate adult would be well advised to encourage the suspect to seek legal advice.[11] This is particularly important since the implementation in April 1995 of the Criminal Justice and Public Order Act 1994, under which adverse inferences may be drawn by the court if a suspect chooses to remain silent when questioned by the police, or he or she chooses not to give evidence in court when the case goes to trial. There is no doubt that modifying the right to silence increases the complexity of the decision making required of suspects during questioning. This may cause suspects to feel under pressure to make admissions when they do not wish to do so, admissions which may subsequently turn out to be unreliable. In addition, many suspects may not understand the adverse inferences that can be drawn in court from their

---

[11] Pearse, J. and Gudjonsson, G. H., 'How appropriate are Appropriate Adults?' (1996) 7 *Journal of Forensic Psychiatry*, 570–580.

refusal to answer questions or from their failure to give proper answers. There is evidence that the current caution is very complicated to understand and it is understood fully only by a minority of persons in the general population,[12] and therefore of persons detained for questioning by the police.[13] Persons of low intellectual abilities are particularly disadvantaged in understanding the new caution,[14] which is very important to recognize in view of the fact that the majority of suspects detained at police stations for interviewing are of below average intellectual ability. In their study for the Royal Commission on Criminal Justice, Gudjonsson, Clare, Rutter and Pearse found an average IQ score of 82 for suspects detained for interviewing at two police stations within the Metropolitan Police District.[15] A third of the sample obtained an IQ score of 75 or below, which represents a significant intellectual impairment. This indicates that a substantial proportion of suspects detained at police stations are intellectually disadvantaged.

There are currently many problems with the use of appropriate adults, and the extent to which they provide a safeguard that protects vulnerable suspects has been seriously questioned.[16] The problems identified include the vagueness of their role, the lack of availability of some of the persons used, and the absence of national guidelines and standards for training. If appropriate adult schemes were shown to provide a good safeguard for vulnerable suspects, then such a facility might also be important for use when mentally disordered witnesses are interviewed by the police. For example, there have been instances when persons with learning disability were first interviewed as witnesses and because of their apparently unsatisfactory or misleading answers during questioning they became suspects and made unreliable confessions.[17] Medford, Gudjonsson and Pearse have made an empirical study of the efficacy of appropriate adults.[18] They found that although the presence of an appropriate adult did not influence the confession rate and appropriate adults contributed little to the police interview in terms of verbal interactions, their safeguard is such that their mere presence in the police interview has **4.15**

---

[12] Shepherd, E.W., Mortimer, A.K. and Mobasheri, R., 'The police caution: comprehension and perceptions in the general population' (1995) 4 *Expert Evidence*, 60–67.

[13] Fenner, S., Gudjonsson, G.H. and Clare, I.C.H., 'Understanding of the current police caution (England & Wales) among suspects in police detention' (2002) 12 *Journal of Community and Applied Social Psychology*, 83–93.

[14] Clare, I.C.H., Gudjonsson, G.H. and Harari, P.M., 'The current police caution in England and Wales: How easy is it to understand?' (1998) 8 *Journal of Community and Applied Social Psychology*, 323–329.

[15] Gudjonsson, G.H., Clare, I., Rutter, S. and Pearse, J., *Persons at risk during interviews in police custody: The identification of vulnerabilities*, Royal Commission on Criminal Justice, London: HMSO, 1993.

[16] Pearse and Gudjonsson, (1996), cited above at n.11.

[17] Gudjonsson, G.H. and MacKeith, J., 'Learning disability and the Police and Criminal Evidence Act 1984. Protection during investigative interviewing: a video-recorded false confession to double murder' (1994) 5 *Journal of Forensic Psychiatry*, 35–49; Gudjonsson, G.H., ' "I'll help you boys as much as I can"—how eagerness to please can result in a false confession' (1995) 6 *Journal of Forensic Psychiatry*, 333–342.

[18] Medford, S., Gudjonsson, G. and Pearse, J., *The identification of persons at risk in police custody. The use of appropriate adults by the Metropolitan Police*, London: Institute of Psychiatry and New Scotland Yard (jointly published), 2000; Medford, S., Gudjonsson, G.H. and Pearse, J., 'The efficacy of the appropriate adult safeguard during police interviewing' (2003) 8 *Legal and Criminological Psychology*, 253–266.

three important effects. First, it increases the likelihood that a solicitor is also present. Second, it reduces the interrogative pressure that suspects are placed under by the police in interview. Third, in the presence of an appropriate adult the legal advisor takes on a more active and appropriate role.

4.16 Another important difference between suspects, victims and witnesses is that the statements of suspects are often more self-serving than those of other witnesses and their motive for being deceptive is therefore stronger. This does not mean that witnesses and victims do not on occasions lie to the police. There are numerous instances where this has occurred due to various motives, including obtaining money under false pretences from insurance companies, revenge, in order to protect the offender, to avoid possible feelings of embarrassment or shame resulting from being untruthful, and fear of retaliation or intimidation by the offender, which is not uncommon and may make witnesses reluctant to be forthcoming during police interviewing and testifying in court.

4.17 Problems sometimes arise when witnesses are trying to be over-helpful to the police. For example, extreme eagerness to assist the police with their enquiries can result in false accounts being given of events and during identification parades.[19]

Special problems may arise when the police are interviewing victims of sexual and violent crimes. Such victims are sometimes so traumatized by the experience that they are unable to recount what happened and fear any discussion about it.[20]

4.18 There are many reasons which may prevent suspects from being open, honest and forthcoming during a police interview or when giving evidence in court. The three main reasons are fear of legal sanctions (e.g. being convicted, sentenced), feeling ashamed and embarrassed about the crime, and fear of retaliation for implicating others. Whereas feelings of *shame* inhibit suspects from confessing, feelings of *guilt* facilitate the confession process.[21] Feelings of shame are particularly likely to occur when suspects are interviewed in relation to sexual offending, such as child molestation, which carries strong social stigma. Here the police interview will need to focus on ways of overcoming the feelings of shame associated with such offences.[22] This kind of offender needs to be interviewed particularly sensitively if a reliable confession is to be obtained.

4.19 A neglected group of people are those who confess falsely to the police in order to protect a significant person in their life from being prosecuted (e.g. a relative, a friend, a peer). These types of false confession are probably quite common and do not come to the notice of the judiciary because they are typically not retracted.[23]

4.20 Undoubtedly, one of the most problematic types of case that the police and the courts

---

[19] Gudjonsson, (1992), cited above at n. 9.   [20] Kebbell and Wagstaff, (1999), cited above at n. 3.

[21] Gudjonsson, G. H., *The Psychology of Interrogations and Confessions. A Handbook*, Chichester: John Wiley and Sons, 2003.

[22] Gudjonsson, G. H., 'Sex offenders and confessions: How to overcome their resistance during questioning' (2006), 13 *Journal of Clinical Forensic Medicine*, 203–207.

[23] Sigurdsson, J. F. and Gudjonsson, G. H., 'Alcohol and drug intoxication during police interrogation and the reasons why suspects confess to the police' (1994) 89 *Addiction*, 985–997.

have to deal with is an allegation of childhood sexual abuse. In the United States of America there is currently a large number of cases of alleged childhood sexual abuse which result from so-called 'recovered memories during therapy'.[24] Such accusations also occur in the UK and are typically made against a father by a grown-up daughter, who alleges he sexually abused her in childhood, with the memory of the abuse having been 'repressed' until adulthood when the accuser entered therapy for such problems as depression and eating disorders.[25] It is often assumed that 'recovered memories' are roused by heightened susceptibility to suggestions during therapy.[26] Interestingly, this kind of accuser has not been found to be unduly suggestible on psychometric testing,[27] which suggests that the beliefs or recovered memories of the alleged childhood abuse are internally generated (i.e. they are not primarily the product of leading questions and interrogative pressure). In one case a low score obtained by a female accuser on the Gudjonsson Suggestibility Scale was used by the Crown as an indication that the 'recovered memories' of childhood sexual abuse were genuine and true. The present author does not believe that a low score on the Gudjonsson Suggestibility Scale can be used as evidence that the allegations are necessarily true, because such beliefs and memories can be due to an internal process of influence rather than as a direct result of suggestions from persons, such as siblings, therapists or social workers. However low susceptibility to suggestions during questioning, as measured by the Gudjonsson Suggestibility Scale, does not rule out the possibility that recovered memories of childhood sexual abuse could not be true. Each case must be considered on its own merit.

Recovered memories are held by the accuser with very firm conviction, although retrac- **4.21** tions sometimes do occur.[28] Research among members of the British False Memory Society (BFMS) indicates that only a small minority (7 per cent) of their cases proceed to the Crown Court and when the accusation involved alleged recovered memories obtaining a conviction is extremely rare.[29] It seems that the police, lawyers, judges and jurors are very reluctant to accept the testimony of accusers who claim recovered memories of sexual abuse and as a result such cases are unlikely to succeed in court. A major problem with these cases is the absence of independent corroborative evidence and typically the only evidence presented involves the testimony of the accuser, which is easy to undermine due to its nature.

---

[24] Ofshe, R. and Watters, E., *Making Monsters. False Memories, Psychotherapy and Sexual Hysteria*, New York: Charles Scribner's Sons, 1994.
[25] Gudjonsson, G. H., 'Accusations by adults of childhood sexual abuse: A survey of the members of the British False Memory Society (BFMS)' (1997) 11 *Applied Cognitive Psychology*, 3–18.
[26] Ofshe and Watters, (1994), cited above at n. 24.
[27] Gudjonsson, G. H., 'False memory syndrome and the retractors: Methodological and theoretical issues' (1997) 8 *Psychological Inquiry*, 296–299; Leavitt, F., 'False attribution of suggestibility to explain recovered memory of childhood sexual abuse following extended amnesia' (1997) 21 *Child Abuse and Neglect*, 265–272.
[28] Ofshe and Watters, (1994), cited above at n. 24.
[29] Gudjonsson, G., 'Members of the British False Memory Society: the legal consequences of the accusations for the families' (1997) 8 *Journal of Forensic Psychiatry*, 348–356.

D. Psychological Vulnerabilities

4.22 In the context of a police interview and testifying in court, the term 'psychological vulner-abilities' refers to psychological characteristics or mental states which render a witness prone, in certain circumstances, to providing information which is inaccurate, unreliable or misleading. On occasions misleading information can result in witnesses deliberately or unwittingly implicating an innocent person, and in the case of a suspect a false confession may result in a wrongful conviction. No research has been conducted specifically into differences between suspects, witnesses and victims. However, one recent study investigated differences in the mental state and personality of suspects and witnesses.[30] The suspects and witnesses were assessed psychologically immediately after the interview with the police was completed. Significant differences emerged between the two groups with the suspects being more depressed, hopeless, compliant and personality-disordered than the witnesses. The implication is that suspects interviewed at police stations are in a disturbed mental state, which is not readily identified without a formal clinical assessment. The witnesses, none of whom were victims in the case, in contrast, were relatively symptom free, although some were in a disturbed mental state. Secondly, the nature of those clinical symptoms, which were most marked in relation to depression and hopelessness, raises concern about the suspects' ability to cope effectively with the police interview and to make rational decisions. Research into psychological vulnerabilities of suspects detained at two English (metropolitan) police stations have reported similar findings.[31]

4.23 The forms of psychological vulnerability shown by suspects, witnesses and victims can be categorized into four distinct groups. The first group can be labelled 'mental disorder,' the second, 'abnormal mental state,' the third, 'intellectual functioning,' and the fourth 'personality characteristics'. The table below lists the kind of psychological vulnerabilities sometimes found in cases of mental disorder.

Table 4.1 The psychological vulnerabilities of persons with mental illness, learning disability, and personality disorder

Mental illness	Learning disability	Personality disorder
Faulty reality monitoring	Impaired intellectual capacity	Manipulative
Distorted perceptions and beliefs	Poor memory capacity	Lies readily
Proneness to feelings of guilt	Poor understanding of legal rights	Need for notoriety
Suspicion and paranoia	Heightened suggestibility	Lack of concern about consequences
	Heightened acquiescence	Tendency towards confabulation
	Distorted perception of consequences	

---

[30] Sigurdsson, J. F., Gudjonsson, G. H., Einarsson, E. and Gudmundsson, G., 'Differences in personality and mental state between suspects and witnesses immediately after being interviewed by the police' (in press) *Psychology, Crime and Law.*

[31] Gudjonsson, Clare, Rutter, and Pearse, (1993), cited above at n. 15.

(1) Mental disorder

The term 'mental disorder' implies that the person suffers from diagnosable psychiatric **4.24** problems, such as mental illness (e.g. schizophrenia, depressive illness), learning disability (also known as 'mental handicap'), and personality disorder.

In cases of mental illness, perceptions, emotions, judgement and self-control may be adversely affected. These factors can result in misleading information being provided to the police or when giving evidence in court. Those suffering from paranoid schizophrenia are sometimes difficult to interview because of their suspicion and lack of trust. Breakdown in 'reality monitoring' is an important feature of mental illness. This means that the ability of people to differentiate facts from fantasy is impaired. In extreme cases this may result in people believing that they have committed crimes of which they are totally innocent. Breakdown in reality monitoring also commonly occurs in everyday life in relation to the memory of thoughts, feelings and events and does not require the presence of mental illness. The presence of mental illness makes the breakdown in reality monitoring more pronounced, extensive and frequent.

Severe depressive illness, in extreme cases, can cause people to ruminate and implicate **4.25** themselves falsely in criminal activity as a way of relieving strong feelings of free-floating guilt.

Persons with learning disability, whether witnesses, victims or suspects, may experience **4.26** problems when being interviewed by the police and when giving evidence in court. This is due to the fact that their condition may cause inherent problems with regard to their capacity to give clear and detailed accounts of events during police interviewing and when testifying in court. Difficulties often arise because they may find it difficult to remember clearly the material event; they may become easily led and confused when questioned; they may have problems understanding the questions and articulating their answers; they may not fully appreciate the implications and consequences of their answers; and they may feel easily intimidated when questioned and cross-examined by people in authority.

A useful practical paper on identifying witnesses with learning disability and on how to **4.27** maximize their performance during police interviewing has been produced by Bull and Cullen for the Scottish Crown Office.[32] However, there has been little research carried out into the psychological vulnerabilities of witnesses who suffer from learning disability. Clare and Gudjonsson[33] provide a detailed review of the area and conclude that persons with learning disability are disadvantaged in several respects, including the fact that they are less likely to understand their legal rights, they tend to be acquiescent and suggestible, and fail to appreciate fully the consequences of making a misleading statement.

Three studies provide useful guidance about the type of question format that is required **4.28**

---

[32] Bull, R. and Cullen, C., *Witnesses Who Have Mental Handicaps*, Edinburgh: Crown Office, 1992.

[33] Clare, I.C.H. and Gudjonsson, G.H., 'The vulnerability of suspects with intellectual disabilities during police interviews: A review and experimental study of decision-making' (1995) 8 *Mental Handicap Research*, 110–128.

when interviewing witnesses with learning disability in order to maximize the completeness of the account whilst minimizing the amount of inaccurate recall.[34] This includes avoiding the use of leading questions, allowing the witness to give his or her uninterrupted account, and asking open-ended questions. Milne has provided a helpful guide to investigators who have to interview children with learning disabilities.[35]

4.29 Gudjonsson and Gunn, in a case at the Central Criminal Court, showed how the jury could distinguish between the reliable and unreliable aspects of the evidence of a woman with learning disability who had been a victim of serious sexual assault.[36] The case indicates that persons with severe learning disability may well be capable of providing reliable evidence about factual matters that they clearly remember.

4.30 The concept of personality disorder proved to be an important psychiatric diagnosis in connection with disputed confessions in the case of Judith Ward, who was wrongfully convicted of terrorist crimes in 1974 and had her conviction overturned by the Court of Appeal in 1992.[37] She suffered from a personality disorder with histrionic features. A review of medical records concerning her period on remand prior to the trial revealed evidence of severe mental disorder which had not been disclosed by doctors to the trial court. Psychological assessment indicated a person of average intellectual abilities who scored highly on a test of suggestibility and exhibited a strong tendency to confabulate. (Confabulation refers to the tendency to fill gaps in one's memory by producing imagined material.) Gudjonsson has discussed the importance of confabulatory tendency in relation to personality disorder.[38] Personality disorder may represent an important psychological vulnerability among some witnesses and suspects in that they appear to have a heightened tendency to confabulate in their memory recall[39] and more readily make false confessions as a part of their criminal lifestyle.[40] Recently Gudjonsson, Sigurdsson, Bragason, Einarsson and Valdimarsdottir[41] have shown how antisocial personality traits are significantly correlated with both false confessions and false denials.

---

[34] Dent, H., 'An experimental study of the effectiveness of different techniques of questioning mentally handicapped child witnesses' (1986) 25 *British Journal of Clinical Psychology*, 13–17; Bull and Cullen, (1992), cited above at n.32; Perlman, N.B., Ericson, K.I., Esses, V.M. and Isaacs, B.J., 'The developmentally handicapped witnesses. Competency as a function of question format' (1994) 18 *Law and Human Behavior*, 171–187.

[35] Milne, R., 'Interviewing children with mild learning disabilities' in Memon and Bull, (1999), cited above at n.2, 165–180.

[36] Gudjonsson, G.H. and Gunn, J., 'The Competence and reliability of a Witness in a Criminal Court' (1982) 141 *British Journal of Psychiatry*, 624–627.

[37] Gudjonsson, (2003), cited above at n.21.   [38] Ibid.

[39] Smith, P. and Gudjonsson, G.H., 'The relationship of mental disorder to suggestibility and confabulation among forensic inpatients' (1995) 6 *Journal of Forensic Psychiatry*, 499–515.

[40] Sigurdsson, J. and Gudjonsson, G., 'The criminal history of "false confessors" and other prison inmates' (1997) 8 *Journal of Forensic Psychiatry*, 447–455; Gudjonsson, G.H., Sigurdsson, J.F., Asgeirsdottir, B.B. and Sigfusdottir, I.D., 'Custodial interrogation, false confession and individual differences. A national study among Icelandic youth' (2006), 41 *Personality and Individual Differences*, 49–59.

[41] Gudjonsson, G.H., Sigurdsson, J.F., Bragason, O.O., Einarsson, E. and Valdimarsdottir, E.B., 'Confessions and Denials and the relationship with personality' (2004) 9 *Legal and Criminological Psychology*, 121–133.

(2) Abnormal mental state

Witnesses who are interviewed by the police or give evidence in court can suffer from an **4.31**
abnormal mental state, which may adversely influence the reliability of their testimony,
without their having had a history of mental disorder. For example, in their recent
study for the Royal Commission on Criminal Justice, Gudjonsson *et al* found that about
20 per cent of the suspects were reporting an abnormally high level of anxiety, whilst only
about 7 per cent were suffering from mental illness, such as schizophrenia or depressive
illness.[42]

In addition to a high level of anxiety witnesses may experience specific phobic symptoms, **4.32**
such as claustrophobia (e.g. irrational fear of being locked up in a confined space such as
a police cell) or panic attacks (e.g. victims of crime experiencing a severe panic attack
when attempting to describe what happened to them). Head injury or other organic
conditions may also adversely affect the person's ability to give a reliable account of
events. In the Royal Commission study extreme fear of being locked up in a police cell
was very rare (i.e. only one case out of 171), although many detainees complained that
they were distressed about being locked up at the police station. The most commonly
expressed anxiety was in relation to uncertainties over their predicament. Many of the
detainees expressed concern over what was going to happen to them: they kept asking the
researchers for information about their detention, and wanted to know when they were
going to be interviewed by the police.

Some witnesses are in a state of bereavement when interviewed by the police, because of a **4.33**
loss of a loved one. This may sometimes render them vulnerable to giving unreliable
statements because of feelings of guilt and subjective distress that typically accompany
the condition. For example, self-blame associated with a state of bereavement can make
suspects unwittingly exaggerate their involvement in an offence.

Since provisions of the Police and Criminal Evidence Act 1984 came into force in 1986, **4.34**
it is not rare that suspects are interviewed by the police when visibly under the influence
of alcohol, although on occasions some alcoholics may be experiencing withdrawal
symptoms while in detention. More commonly, suspects who are high on drugs when
arrested may be withdrawing from drugs while in custody and at the time they are
interviewed by the police. Some drug addicts may be vulnerable to giving misleading
accounts of events when being asked leading questions and placed under interrogative
pressure, in addition to saying things in order to expedite their early release from
custody.

Sigurdsson and Gudjonsson[43] found that being interviewed by the police when suspects **4.35**
are under the influence of drugs or withdrawing from drugs causes them to feel confused.
This does not mean that they are unfit to be interviewed, only that special care should be
taken when interviewing them. Two studies have specifically investigated the effects of
drug use and drug withdrawal on interrogative suggestibility, which suggests that opiate
users undergoing opiate withdrawal are significantly more suggestible than opiate users

---

[42] Gudjonsson, Clare, Rutter and Pearse, (1993), cited above at n. 15.   [43] Cited above at n. 23.

who are no longer showing acute withdrawal symptoms,[44] and that there is a subgroup of vulnerable drug addicts who may be more suggestible when under the influence of opiates.[45]

4.36 In a follow-up study to the Gudjonsson *et al* study for the Royal Commission on Criminal Justice, Pearse, Gudjonsson, Clare and Rutter[46] found that the only variable that was significantly associated with making a confession was whether or not detainees reported taking illicit drugs in the 24 hours before the police interview. One possible interpretation of this finding is that withdrawing from drugs encouraged them to make a confession as a way to facilitate their early release.

4.37 Some medical conditions (e.g. cardiovascular problems, diabetes, epilepsy) may result in a disturbed or abnormal mental state whilst the person is being interviewed by the police or giving evidence in court. This may adversely influence the accuracy and reliability of the person's account and his or her ability to function in a stressful situation.

(3) Intellectual abilities

4.38 Impaired intellectual functioning, even when not amounting to mental handicap, can influence the ability of witnesses to understand questions, articulate their answers, and appreciate the implications of their answers.

4.39 There is evidence from the study by Gudjonsson *et al* for the Royal Commission on Criminal Justice that many suspects interviewed at police stations are of low intelligence.[47] The mean IQ for 160 suspects detained at two police stations was only 82, with the range 61–131. Almost 9 per cent of the sample had a pro-rated IQ score below 70, compared with about 2 per cent of the general population, and one-third (34 per cent) had a pro-rated IQ score of 75 or below (i.e. bottom 5 per cent of the general population).

4.40 It is probable that, to a certain extent, the IQ scores obtained represent an underestimate of the suspects' intellectual abilities due to the circumstances and context of testing (i.e. many of the suspects were anxiously waiting to be interviewed by the police at the time of testing). However, the findings highlight the fact that the police are commonly interviewing persons of low intellectual abilities. The average intellectual capacity of witnesses and victims who are being interviewed by the police is not known. Therefore, it is not known how their intellectual functioning compares with that of suspects who are detained for an interview.

---

[44] Murakami, A.T., Edelman, R.J. and Davis, P.E., 'Interrogative suggestibility in opiates users' (1996) 91 *Addiction*, 1365–1373.

[45] Davison, S.E. and Gossop, M., 'The problem of interviewing drug addicts in custody: a study of interrogative suggestibility and compliance' (1996) 2 *Psychology, Crime and Law*, 185–195.

[46] Pearse, J., Gudjonsson, G.H., Clare, I.C.H. and Rutter, S., 'Police interviewing and psychological vulnerabilities: Predicting the likelihood of a confession' (1997) 8 *Journal of Community and Applied Social Psychology*, 1–21.

[47] Cited above at n.15.

(4) Personality characteristics

A number of personality characteristics may be important when evaluating the reliability **4.41** of witnesses' accounts. The three most extensively researched variables are suggestibility, acquiescence, and compliance.[48]

Confabulation has been investigated in relation to the reliability of verbal accounts given **4.42** by witnesses.[49] Extreme confabulation has been found in some cases of personality disorder, as it was in the cases of Joe Giarratano[50] and Judith Ward.[51] However, the study of Clare and Gudjonsson[52] with subjects of low intelligence, and the study of Sigurdsson, Gudjonsson, Kolbeinsson and Petursson[53] with severely depressed mental patients, indicate that persons with mental disorder, such as learning disability and severe depression, have impaired memory recall for events, but the accuracy of their accounts is not undermined by a heightened tendency to confabulate.

'Interrogative suggestibility' refers to the tendency of people to yield to leading questions **4.43** and submit to interrogative pressure. It can be measured by the use of a behavioural test, such as the Gudjonsson Suggestibility Scale. Here subjects are subtly misled in an experimental way and their responses are carefully monitored and compared with those of relative normative groups for the purpose of comparison. If the scores are statistically infrequent, that is, they occur in fewer than 5 per cent of the general population then the person can be described as being abnormally suggestible on the test.[54]

The concept of 'compliance' overlaps, to a certain extent, with suggestibility, but it is **4.44** more strongly associated with eagerness to please and the tendency to avoid conflict and confrontation. It is more difficult to measure compliance than suggestibility by behavioural observation and it is therefore typically measured by a self-report questionnaire. As a result, it is a measure that is easier to falsify than measures of interrogative suggestibility.

'Acquiescence' refers to the tendency of people, when in doubt, to answer questions in **4.45** the affirmative irrespective of content. The reason for this tendency appears to be that they answer questions in the affirmative without properly listening to them or fully understanding them. Acquiescence is more strongly correlated with low intelligence than either suggestibility or compliance.[55]

---

[48] Gudjonsson, (2003), cited above at, n. 21; Clare, I. C. H. and Gudjonsson, G. H. 'Interrogative suggestibility, confabulation, and acquiescence in people with mild learning difficulties (Mental handicap): Implications for reliability during police interrogation' (1993) 32 *British Journal of Clinical Psychology*, 295–301.

[49] Ibid; Sigurdsson, E., Gudjonsson, G. H., Kolbeinsson, H. and Petursson, H., 'The effects of electro-convulsive therapy and depression on confabulation, memory processing, and suggestibility' (1994) 48 *Nordic Journal of Psychiatry*, 443–451.

[50] Gudjonsson, (1992), cited above at n. 9.

[51] Gudjonsson, G.H. and MacKeith, J., *Disputed Confessions and the Criminal Justice System* (Maudsley Discussion Paper No. 2), London: Institute of Psychiatry, 1997.

[52] Cited above at n. 48.   [53] Cited above at n. 49.

[54] Gudjonsson, (1992), cited above at n. 9.   [55] Gudjonsson, (2003), cited above at n. 21.

E. Conclusion

4.46 This chapter has reviewed the literature on the potential psychological vulnerabilities of persons interviewed by the police. A number of factors can influence the reliability and credibility of the accounts given by witnesses, victims and suspects when they are interviewed by the police and when they give evidence in court. These include contextual and environmental factors, which may include the stress of appearing in court, feelings of intimidation, and fear or threat of retaliation. This chapter has focused on the psychological factors that can, under certain circumstances, make witnesses vulnerable to giving unreliable accounts of events. Differences exist between witnesses, victims, and suspects, in terms of the nature and circumstances of their evidence, which have a bearing on their *motivation* to be open and truthful. As far as the *ability* to give reliable evidence is concerned, it is not known how these three groups may differ in their mental, intellectual and personality functioning, although recent research in Iceland has revealed important differences between suspects and witnesses (victims were not included in the study). Within each group there are large individual differences which must not be ignored.

4.47 In many cases the courts rely heavily on the accounts of witnesses and victims. Therefore, careful interviewing of these persons is very important as well as the proper recording of the content of the interviews. It is likely that in the future audio or video recordings will be made of interviews of witnesses in major criminal cases, which will make it easier to evaluate properly the reliability and credibility of the accounts given to the police.

4.48 Problems sometimes arise when mentally disordered people are interviewed and required to give evidence. Their mental problems are not always easily recognized at the time they are interviewed by the police, and even when they are, police officers and the courts may not be familiar with the kind of factors that may undermine the reliability of their reporting of events.

4.49 Psychologists have an important contribution to make in assisting with the identification of factors that influence the reliability of witnesses' information and to develop interviewing techniques and procedures that maximize the reliability of witnesses' reports generally.

Recommended Reading

Gudjonsson, G. H., *The Psychology of Interrogations and Confessions. A Handbook*. Chichester: John Wiley & Sons, 2003.

Gudjonsson, G. H., Clare, I., Rutter, S. and Pearse, J., *Persons at risk during interviews in police custody: The identification of vulnerabilities*. Royal Commission on Criminal Justice. London: HMSO, 1993.

Sigurdsson, J. F., Gudjonsson, G. H., Einarsson, E., and Gudmundsson, G., 'Differences in personality and mental state between suspects and witnesses immediately after being interviewed by the police' (in press) *Psychology, Crime and Law*.

Editors' Note

Until now the author's reputation in this field has mainly rested on his work on false confessions by suspects and defendants vulnerable owing to being compliant or suggestible. But a similarly vulnerable witness to a crime—or one who claims to be a victim—if interviewed by investigators or spoken to by others may equally be prone to provide inaccurate accounts in consequence of their condition and inappropriate investigative techniques. Investigators, fact-finders and those who address or direct fact-finders need to be alert to these sources of vulnerability and the potential for the emergence of false or misleading allegations and of unreliable evidence—particularly when investigators have failed either to make allowance for or to monitor for indicators of compliance and suggestibility.

5

EFFECTS OF DRUGS ON WITNESS MEMORY

H. Valerie Curran

A. Introduction

There are many factors that affect a witness's ability to remember accurately. An important **5.01** one of these is the influence of 'psychoactive' drugs—drugs that have an action on the brain. There are hundreds of them, including alcohol, street drugs and a wide range of prescribed medications. Drugs are frequently a factor in criminal activity and in crime reporting. A victim, suspect and/or eyewitness may have been under the influence of a drug around the time the relevant events of the case occurred. When a judge and jury hear testimony from such a witness, they must take into account the effects the drug(s) may have had upon their memory and all the myriad factors influencing memory, in evaluating the weight to give their testimony.

Some drugs have powerful amnesic effects. This can be medically advantageous. For **5.02** example, anaesthetists value drugs that ensure a patient has a sufficient period and depth of amnesia so that even if s/he regained consciousness during an operation, s/he would not remember doing so afterwards. In this respect, benzodiazepines like diazepam (*Valium*) prove ideal drugs. Indeed, an anaesthetist could be accused of failing in care if a patient could remember events during surgery. Drug-induced amnesia is less advantageous in other situations in which drugs are taken.

Memory does not occur in a vacuum and psychoactive drugs do not only affect memory. **5.03** Most psychoactive drugs alter mood. Some drugs can alter perception and some affect arousal levels, having either stimulant or sedative effects. Some drugs impair concentration so that certain details of events are ignored, often at the expense of other details.

Some drugs may 'disinhibit', interfering with our control processes so that we may say or do things which are uncharacteristic of our normal behaviour.

B. Types of Psychoactive Drug

(1) Prescribed drugs

5.04 A wide range of psychoactive substances are medically prescribed and some others can be bought over the counter in a pharmacy. Many of these are drugs prescribed for psychiatric disorders including tranquillizers (e.g. alprazolam, diazepam), sleeping pills (e.g. temazepam, zopiclone), antidepressants (e.g. fluoxetine, amitryptyline), neuroleptics (e.g. clozapine, haloperidol) and drugs used in treating addiction (e.g. methadone). There are also drugs prescribed for neurological disorders such as epilepsy or Parkinson's disease; and a range of drugs is used in the treatment of other medical disorders or symptoms. These include pain killers (analgesics) which vary from mild, over-the-counter preparations like paracetamol through to powerful opiates like morphine.

(2) Self-administered drugs

5.05 These include the widely used legal drugs—alcohol, nicotine and caffeine—as well as an increasingly large array of illicit substances—such as heroin, cocaine, cannabis, ecstasy (MDMA), amphetamine and ketamine. People's use of such drugs can vary from occasional or 'recreational' through to compulsive, dependent use. Drug dependency is especially associated with opiates, crack cocaine, nicotine and alcohol.

5.06 The brain of course cannot distinguish between a legal and an illegal substance and there is overlap between prescribed and self-administered drugs. Many heroin and crack users will also take benzodiazepine tranquillizers; steroids may be used non-medically by body builders; ketamine is both a medical anaesthetic and a Class C drug of abuse. Although the term drug is used here, there are other substances which act on the brain and change mood (e.g. inhalants like glue or petrol that abusers sniff; psychoactive plants like certain mushrooms and cacti).

5.07 Psychoactive drug use is increasingly common. More than 10 per cent of senior citizens in most Western countries take a sleeping pill every night. In England alone, there were about 9 million prescriptions for antidepressants written in 1992; in 2002 this rose to over 26 million. Recreational use of illicit drugs like cannabis and ecstasy has become so widespread in some parts of the world as to be almost the norm among 16–24-year-olds. And there is that ubiquitous recreational drug, alcohol.

5.08 Sometimes the drug in question is not deliberately taken by a witness. Drugs may be used to aid and abet crimes when given covertly as in so-called drug-assisted rape or in cases where victims are drugged to facilitate theft of their property. A range of drugs has been implicated in such crimes, most often alcohol (a 'Micky Finn') but also benzodiazepines, gammahydroxybutyrate (GHB) and related compounds.

5.09 All psychoactive drugs exert their effects by interfering with how brain cells communicate with each other. This communication depends on many natural chemicals in the brain that are called 'neurotransmitters'. Drugs interfere with the processes of neurotransmission.

C. What Types of Drug Influence Memory?

It is impossible to cover the effects of the many hundreds of psychoactive drugs on memory and related functions in this chapter. However, drugs most often associated with memory impairment include: **5.10**

- sleeping pills and tranquillizers: there are more than thirty different benzodiazepines as well as other drugs (e.g. zopiclone, GHB) which act on the brain's major inhibitory neurotransmitter (gamma aminobutyric acid; GABA);
- drugs with anticholinergic properties such as tricylic antidepressants and several types of neuroleptics that affect the neurotransmitter acetylcholine;
- drugs like ketamine and phencyclidine (PCP) that interfere with the transmission of glutamate (a major excitatory neurotransmitter);
- alcohol acts on several different neurotransmitters and its memory-impairing properties are thought to stem mainly from its actions on GABA and glutamate.

Most research has concentrated on the types of drug listed above and so we know most about how these influence different aspects of memory. However, there are many other drugs that can impair memory and these include opiates (e.g. morphine, methadone), cannabis (marijuana) and ecstasy (i.e. ± 3,4 methylenedioxymethamphetamine, MDMA). **5.11**

D. What Influences a Drug's Effects on Memory?

The degree and duration of memory loss depends on several factors besides the particular drug that has been taken. *Dose* is critical and impairment generally increases with dose. The dose of drug people take is difficult to judge by milligrams. It's a bit like guessing how much alcohol is in a glass without knowing whether the liquid is white wine, vodka or lemonade. Some drugs are more potent than others so a small amount in milligrams can have a large effect on memory. Memory loss after alcohol generally varies with the level of the drug in the blood (blood alcohol concentration or BAC). Severe memory loss as seen in partial or complete blackouts is especially associated with rapidly rising BACs that occur often when someone consumes several drinks in a short space of time, especially if this is on a relatively empty stomach. **5.12**

Each drug has its own *time curve* of absorption, distribution, metabolism and elimination over which effects on memory will vary. For example, following one oral dose of the benzodiazepine lorazepam, peak memory impairments occur from 1.5 to 5 hours later, after which they slowly subside. If the same drug was given intravenously, it would have a more rapid onset of effect and so the *route of administration* is very important. Snorting or smoking a drug will also lead to its rapid absorption in the brain. **5.13**

The effects of a single dose differ in people who have taken the drug before compared **5.14** with those who are drug naive. The brain adapts to repeated administration of a drug so, for example, 1 mg of alprazolam (*Xanax*) can produce marked amnesia in someone who has never taken it before but less impairment in a patient who takes the drug daily for an anxiety disorder. This phenomenon is called '*tolerance*' and is seen when the same dose of a drug has less effect over repeated use or when a person increases the dose over time to maintain the same effect. Tolerance to the various effects of a drug can develop at different rates. For example, a person may no longer experience the sedative effects of a benzodiazepine after taking it every day for a week but still show memory impairment for a time after a daily dose. Or again, a person prescribed a neuroleptic drug to lessen psychotic symptoms can tolerate doses which could render a healthy person semi-conscious.

5.15 Chronic, heavy use of a drug (e.g. heroin, alcohol, cocaine) may sometimes result in impairments to intellectual abilities and memory that persist even after the person stops taking the drug. When a drug used regularly is then abruptly stopped, the person may experience a withdrawal state that is usually characteristic of that particular drug.

5.16 The degree of amnesia also depends on *characteristics of the person* who has taken the drug. Physical changes during ageing affect how a drug is metabolized so that people over 65 can show memory impairments after low doses which have little effect on younger adults. Weight and gender are also factors, and a heavy male will show rather less of an effect than a slim female. Children have a heightened sensitivity to psychoactive drugs not just because of lower body weight but also because of developmental factors. Genetic factors also contribute to individual differences in response to drugs.

5.17 A drug's effects also depend on any *other drugs* that a person took around the same time. For example, if someone took a *valium* and then drank several whiskies, the memory-impairing effects of each drug would combine to be approximately the sum of each.

E. Drugs and Memories

5.18 It is helpful to think of 'memories' rather than 'memory' because people have several interacting but distinct types of memory. Drugs have differential effects on these different types of memory.

5.19 Short-term or *working memory* allows us to hold information 'on line' while we do something with it, like remember a telephone number long enough to dial it. Working memory is relatively unaffected by most drugs. For instance, when we have a conversation, we use working memory because we need to remember the beginning phrases or sentences until the end so we can understand the meaning of what someone said. A person who has drunk several units of alcohol or taken 20 mg of diazepam can often appear to engage in sensible conversation. However, several minutes later they can remember little if anything of what was said. In effect, the information was held in short-term storage but was not transferred into longer-term storage.

5.20 A while ago a television company was making a programme about 'drug-assisted rape'. They filmed an experiment where I tested the memory of the presenter who had volunteered. One of the tests was to recall a news article about the pop group Bon Jovi. Her memory for this was excellent immediately after hearing it and very good when I asked her to recall it again 10 minutes later. She then took 1 mg of the benzodiazepine flunitrazepam (*Rohypnol*), waited until the drug had been absorbed and then did a parallel set of tests, this time hearing a news article about the Rolling Stones. When asked to recall this immediately, she remembered about half. However, when asked to recall it again 10 minutes later, she recounted the Bon Jovi story almost perfectly. I pointed out that this was the first story she had heard over an hour ago and asked again for the one she had just heard 10 minutes before. She was furious, insisting that she had only heard one story and I was trying to trick her. The next day when we looked at the video recording she was dumbfounded that she had no memory of either the Rolling Stones story or her accusation of trickery.

5.21 As this illustrates, though a drug may leave working memory intact, it often prevents the information being transferred to long-term memory. Long-term memory has four subsystems.[1] Two of these store things that you are not consciously aware of. *Procedural memory* stores skills like how to drive your car. You just get in, turn the key and drive without conscious thought. Another subsystem stores *perceptual representations* of words and objects that help you read this text, but again in ways you are not consciously aware of. It is generally the case that drugs have little if any effect on either of these memory subsystems, although there are rare exceptions (e.g. lorazepam may sometimes influence the perceptual representation system).

5.22 Two other subsystems store things that you consciously know and are called semantic and episodic memory. *Semantic memory* is memory for facts, knowledge and language. For example, you know that Madrid is the capital of Spain and that $e=mc^2$ but probably do not remember the exact circumstances of learning those facts—who your teacher was, when it was, who you sat next to in school at the time you learnt the information. In contrast, *episodic memory* lets us recollect episodes or events in our lives. You remember what you ate for dinner last night, who you ate with and what you talked about. You probably also remember the title of the last film you saw, who you went with and whether you had popcorn or a drink afterwards. In this way, episodic memory is unique in that it allows us to travel back in time and mentally relive events in our lives.

5.23 Most drugs have no effect on our ability to remember information that has been stored in semantic memory. People can recall stored facts and knowledge fairly well despite being under the influence of a drug. One notable exception to this is ketamine which recent research has shown to impact negatively on semantic memory. It is also worth noting that most drugs will block the acquisition of new semantic memories (new facts and knowledge) because this relies on the integrity of the episodic memory system.

5.24 In most situations, witnesses are asked to report information that is stored in episodic memory. And most drugs that impair memory exert their major effects upon episodic memory.

[1] Tulving, E. and Schacter, D.L., 'Priming and human memory systems' (1990) 247 *Science*, 301–306.

F. Drugs and Episodic Memory

5.25 Memory-impairing drugs generally interfere with the formation of *new* episodic memories. They do not affect the ability to recall old episodic memories, those that were stored before the drug was taken. Going back to the example of the female television presenter, *after* taking the benzodiazepine, she recalled almost perfectly the news article she had heard *before* taking the drug whilst having total amnesia for the story heard after the drug. Alcohol, benzodiazepines, anticholinergics, ketamine and several other types of drugs all impede acquiring new information into episodic memory. Depending on dose and other factors (section D above), the impairment can be negligible to severe, with the severest effect being total amnesia for events occurring whilst under the influence of the drug.

5.26 Retrieval of previously stored memories is largely unaffected by being intoxicated. People often think that retrieval is 'state-dependent' so that the man who hid the gin bottle when he was drunk should get drunk again to help him find it. However, there is scant scientific evidence that such drug-state dependency actually occurs and when such effects have been shown, they have been remarkably small in magnitude.

5.27 Clearly, our accuracy in remembering depends on how well (or deeply) we processed and encoded details of the relevant events at the time they occurred. This is generally the case whether or not a person is under the influence of a drug. So after a few alcoholic drinks, a person may remember some details of events they found particularly interesting and processed deeply whilst forgetting a host of other details. Our memory accuracy also depends on the circumstances in which we retrieve details of events. For example, trying to freely recall a list of words a person has just been shown is generally more difficult than being asked to decide which of a bigger bunch of words were shown to them before (i.e. recognize the words). And being given clues to the words (e.g. the first few letters of each) is of medial difficulty between free recall and recognition. The same difficulty gradient operates regardless of whether a person was intoxicated or not when they were shown the words, although if intoxicated, there will be impairments across all types of retrieval conditions.

5.28 As we have seen, episodic memory allows us to mentally travel back in subjective time to remember events in our lives. Under some situations, often involving large doses or combinations of memory-impairing drugs, there can be total amnesia for relevant events. Under other situations, the memory impairment may be partial with some details being recalled but not others.

5.29 This partial impairment is also seen when drugs cause misattribution errors. So a person may remember something being said but mistake who said it or when or what someone else replied. There is evidence that these types of error are increased by some benzodiazepines, anticholinergics and ketamine. For example, in one study healthy people had to respond to each of a series of words in a different way depending on whether it was spoken by a man or a woman. They were asked to say whether the 'female' word was concrete or abstract and whether the 'male' word was pleasant or unpleasant. Later they were asked to decide which of each of a series of words they had heard before, and whether it had been spoken by a man or a woman. This was fairly easy for those who were given an inactive drug (placebo) before hearing the words. However, for those given a dose of ketamine, not only was their recognition of words impaired but even for words they correctly recognized, they made significant errors in recalling whether it was spoken by a man or woman.[2] When the same task was given to people who repeatedly self-administered ketamine, they showed the same pattern of effects not only after taking the drug but also when tested in a drug-free state a few days later, suggesting long-term damage to episodic memory.[3] The possibility that drug use by a particular witness has not only impaired memory but also increased errors of misattribution should be borne in mind when evaluating their testimony.

5.30 Our memory for personally experienced events that have an *emotional* impact on us tends to be particularly durable and vivid. Most people find it easier to recall very emotional events in their lives than events of a more humdrum nature. A series of studies by Cahill, McGaugh and colleagues have shown that drugs called beta-blockers (e.g. propranolol) can sometimes reduce this effect, impairing healthy people's recall of emotionally arousing but not neutral elements of a story which involved a child in a horrendous car smash.[4] Benzodiazepines have also been shown recently to have the same effect, reducing memory globally but reducing memory for emotional information to roughly the same level as for neutral information. Surveys of university students in the US suggest that total blackouts can happen for naturally occurring emotional events—such as sexual intercourse or being involved in a fight—when large amounts of alcohol were consumed in the period before the event.

5.31 Although we have concentrated on the most researched memory-impairing drugs, there is also evidence that many other drugs can have detrimental effects on episodic memory and these include opiates (e.g. morphine, methadone), cannabis (marijuana) and 'ecstasy' (i.e. methylenedioxymethamphetamine or MDMA). A mention of memory 'enhancing' drugs is also warranted. Although the evidence is limited to date, some drugs (e.g. bromocriptine, methylphenidate) can produce transient mild improvements in working memory, notably in people whose working memory is not functioning optimally. There are also drugs prescribed for Alzheimer's Disease but these at most slow down the rate of progression of the dementia and do not improve the person's memory *per se*.

---

[2] Morgan, C.J.A., Mofeez, A., Brandner, B., Bromley, L. and Curran, H.V., 'Acute effects of ketamine on memory systems and psychotic symptoms in healthy volunteers' (2004) 29 *Neuropsychopharmacology*, 208–218.

[3] Morgan, C.J.A., Riccelli, M., Maitland, C.H. and Curran, H.V., 'Long-term effects of ketamine abuse: evidence of persisting impairment of source memory in recreational users' (2004) 75 *Drug and Alcohol Dependence*, 301–308.

[4] Cahill, L. and McGaugh, J., 'Mechanisms of emotional arousal and lasting declarative memory' (1998) 21 *Trends in Neuroscience*, 294–299.

G. Drugs do not only Affect Memory

5.32 As we noted at the start of this chapter, memory does not occur in a vacuum and psychoactive drugs do not only affect memory. Psychopharmacological research has also examined other functions that may be affected by drugs, particularly those functions which influence memory.

5.33 A wide range of drugs affects arousal levels, having either sedative or stimulant effects. A witness who was sedated around the time that relevant events occurred may have registered those events poorly, or if they had fallen asleep, not perceived them at all. Often, doses of alcohol which lead to a memory blackout end with the person falling asleep.

5.34 Drugs can also affect concentration, reducing attentional resources. For example, alcohol can induce a 'myopia' such that central features may be attended to at the expense of peripheral details. A witness who was intoxicated at the time an event occurred may thus admit having poor memory for what a person was wearing or the type of car parked nearby whilst feeling very confident in his memory for who threw the first punch. That said, a person's confidence in their memory is not necessarily predictive of accurate recall, especially so when psychoactive drugs have been taken.

5.35 Some drugs can alter perception and so memories for events occurring whilst under the influence will inevitably be distorted. Thus drugs like LSD can produce disorientation and hallucinations.

5.36 Certain drugs may make the person more impulsive and less likely to consider the consequences of their actions or to consider alternative courses of action. Several drugs, including alcohol and benzodiazepines, can induce a *disinhibition*. Thus, under the influence of such drugs, a person's decision-making ability may be severely compromised. This, for example, will impinge on their ability to give informed consent to sexual intercourse or to make rational financial decisions.

5.37 In certain people, disinhibition can lead to increased aggression. Alcohol is widely recognized for such effects, but benzodiazepines can produce a paradoxical aggression in some individuals. Steroids (e.g. 'roid rage'), crack cocaine and many other drugs have been associated with increased aggression. However, there is marked individual variation. Most people are aware of this when they think how one or two of their acquaintances may become aggressive after several drinks whereas most do not. It is often the case that a witness may blame drug X for their bad behaviour when many other people who have used the same drug X do not become aggressive or commit crimes.

5.38 Many drugs affect mood and most psychiatric drugs are prescribed for their mood-altering effects. Many drugs are self-administered for their mood-enhancing effects although often such euphoric effects are followed some time later by the opposite effect (dysphoria). Drugs may also be self-administered to relieve negative mood states, pain or withdrawal symptoms. The mood effects of drugs also depend on other factors such as the social environment in which they are taken and whether the individual is experienced in the effects of the drug. When someone has been given a drug covertly as with drug-assisted rape or robbery, the effects can be very confusing and often frightening.

People who are in drug withdrawal show mood disturbances as well as craving for their preferred drug. Increased suggestibility from leading or misleading questions has been reported in studies of people who were in withdrawal states from opiates and from alcohol.[5]

H. Assessing Evidence on Drug Use and Memory

Much of what we know scientifically about drug effects derives from controlled studies where a drug is given, often a single dose but sometimes a series of doses, and then different types of memory tests are given at specified time points afterwards. The precise dose of the drug is known, as is the exact nature of the information the person aims to remember, and the time between the drug and recall. The information they are asked to remember varies enormously but is typically lists of words, photographs of faces or short news-type stories. Some of these tests, such as news stories, are more predictive of real-life memory abilities than others. John Yuille and his colleagues in Vancouver[6] wanted to determine whether a single dose of alcohol influenced memory for a specially staged crime scene using actors, one of whom carried out a theft. Participants who had been given either alcohol (BAC 0.10%) or placebo watched the scene and were then given an interview requiring them to supply details of everything they could remember (free recall). The main conclusion from this study, that memory of someone under the influence of alcohol is reduced but is most accurate when tested as soon as possible after an event, generally accords with what would have been predicted from controlled studies where the information to be remembered is more artificial. **5.39**

In real life, it is impossible to know the actual content, dose or purity of any street drugs that a witness may have taken. Even if medical records show a person's prescribed drug regimen, it is possible that more or less of the allotted dose was taken at a certain time or that a combination of drugs was used. Forensic tests can provide very valuable information from a person's urine and/or blood which might confirm that a drug was present in the body at a time before the sample was taken. Many drugs can be detected for a day or two in blood and longer in urine. Some drugs can be detected a few weeks after use, but some are very quickly metabolized and excreted and so cannot be detected several hours after use. Hair can be analysed to detect previous drug use for longer periods and can specify the types of drug but not the amounts taken. When several drugs have been taken together, it is often difficult if not impossible to gauge their conjoint effect. **5.40**

It is impossible to determine exactly how a particular witness was affected by drug(s) around the time that the relevant events occurred. However, one can assess the evidence to try to determine whether the person's testimony and behaviour was broadly consistent **5.41**

---

[5] Murakami, A., Edelmann, R.J. and Davis, P.E., 'Interrogative suggestibility in opiate users' (1996) 91 *Addiction*, 1365–1373; Gudjonsson, G.H., Hannesdottir, K., Agustsson, T.Þ., Sigurdsson, J.F., Gudmundsdottir, A., Þordardottir, Þ., Tyrfingsson, Þ. and Petursson, H., 'The relationship of alcohol withdrawal symptoms to suggestibility and compliance' (2004) 10 *Psychology, Crime and Law* 169–177.

[6] Yuille, J.C. and Tollestrup, P., 'Some effects of alcohol on eyewitness testimony' (1990) 75 *Journal of Applied Psychology*, 268–273.

with the known effects of the drug(s). Witness statements and any other relevant evidence may be used to construct an approximate time-line of events including those concerning drug ingestion. This can be compared with what is known about the time course of the various effects of the drug(s), including physical as well as psychological effects. If a witness reports experiencing memory loss, the type of memory loss (e.g. working, episodic, semantic) can be compared with what is known about the effects of the particular drug on these different memory systems. The relation between the onset of memory impairment and the time of drug ingestion is also important given the time for absorption into the brain and the fact that drugs act to interfere with the ability to form new episodic memories. A witness's memory may be influenced by many factors besides drugs (see Chapter 1 above) and, as yet, there is insufficient research on how drugs interact with most of these factors.

Further Reading

Curran, H.V. and Weingartner, H., 'Psychopharmacology of Memory' in Baddeley, A, Wilson, B. and Kopelman, M. (eds), *The Handbook of Memory Disorders*, New York: Wiley, 2002, 123–141.

Ghoneim, M.M., 'Drugs and Human Memory (Part 2): Clinical, Theoretical, and Methodologic Issues' (2004) 100 *Anesthesiology*, 1277–1297.

Helmstaedter, C. and Kurthen, M., 'Memory and epilepsy: characteristics, course, and influence of drugs and surgery' (2001) 14 *Current Opinion in Neurology*, 211–216.

White, A.A., 'What happened? Alcohol, memory blackouts and the brain' (2003) 27 *Alcohol Research & Health*, 186–196.

H. Valerie Curran is Professor of Psychopharmacology and Director of the Clinical Psychopharmacology Unit at University College London (UCL). She is also Research Lead and Consultant Clinical Psychologist to the Substance Abuse Services in Camden and Islington Social Care and Mental Health Trust. She acts as an expert witness and advises in cases involving the affects of psychoactive drugs.

Psychopharmacology is the scientific study of the psychological effects of drugs that act on the brain. Since 1985 Professor Curran has researched the effects of a wide range of legal and illegal drugs on memory and related functions and has published widely in medical and scientific journals. Her research involves healthy volunteers, patients taking prescribed medications, recreational drug users and drug-dependent individuals.

Editors' Note

Subject to the effective performance of the prosecution's disclosure obligations, it ought to be easy enough to discover whether a witness is under the influence of prescribed drugs during the investigative or evidential processes. This may be more problematic if the individual has ingested unlawful or over-the-counter drugs and reliable scientific testing is impossible due either to the absence of samples (body fluids, hair) or the passing of time. Either way participants in the forensic process need to be alert to the risk of an unreliable account owing to the influence of drugs on the witness's memory and cognitive processes—particularly recall, reasoning and reporting. It is essential to consider what may be the potential effects of a drug—or drugs—upon the mental performance and behaviour of a contentious witness at any relevant stage. Complaints alleging sexual assault well illustrate this, where the ingestion of alcohol upon a witness's behaviour may vary from: (1) remaining able to engage in conscious decision making but nonetheless acting in a disinhibited and aberrant manner, (2) the ability to engage in conscious, albeit disinhibited, decisions but experiencing a 'memory blackout' for relevant events, to (3) unconsciousness rendering the witness incapable of making free choice concerning his or her behaviour. The employment of a medical toxicologist and/or psychopharmacologist may be necessary where it is considered that a witness's recall ability may have been affected by the ingestion of drugs.

6

RECOVERED MEMORY AND FALSE MEMORY

Chris R. Brewin

A. Introduction

Since the 1990s there has been a revival of interest in the accuracy of adults' memory for **6.01** childhood events, in particular traumatic events, and the relationship of such memories to psychopathology. Although memory is at times unreliable, the integrity of memory over long periods can sometimes be impressive, provided its limitations are not exceeded. In general, memory for the gist of childhood events is often well retained, so long as such events were reasonably significant or were repeated sufficiently often. Memory for detail, for example of conversations that may have occurred years before, or memory that involves qualitative judgements, is less reliable. There is little evidence that the presence of psychiatric disorder in the person remembering their past will in itself significantly bias or distort what is recalled.[1]

Another important limitation of memory in early life is the phenomenon known as **6.02** childhood or infantile amnesia. When adults are asked to recall their childhood there is a marked drop-off in the availability of memories from the first five to seven years of life, although this is subject to considerable individual variation. Specific requests to recall a person's very earliest memory tend to elicit events that occurred around age 3.5. Questioning about specific, highly significant events such as the birth of a sibling has resulted in memories from age 2 to 2.5 being reported. Summarizing this research, memories

---

[1] Brewin, C. R., Andrews, B. and Gotlib, I. H., 'Psychopathology and early experience: A reappraisal of retrospective reports' (1993) 113 *Psychological Bulletin*, 82–98.

from the first two years of life are extremely rare, and memories from the first five years are few and likely to involve significant personal events. Very early memories are likely to be fragmented and involve images or other sensations that are not embedded within a coherent narrative. If very early memories are reported that go beyond sensations and involve details such as conversations or sequences of events, they may reflect imaginative elaborations that have occurred when the memories were rehearsed later in life. It must be emphasized, however, that childhood memory does not develop in a completely consistent way across individuals, nor does it develop in an all-or-none fashion.

6.03 The recovered memory/false memory controversy is concerned with a specific subset of these memories. The central question is whether it is plausible, or even possible, that people can forget traumatic events that occurred in childhood and then remember them later, sometimes after a passage of many years. In the scientific literature this debate has mainly been the province of cognitive psychologists who study memory, and various mental health professionals such as clinical psychologists, psychiatrists, and psycho-therapists. In a legal context the question arises particularly in relation to allegations of sexual abuse that are made by adults in respect of experiences that happened during their childhood, but it is applicable in principle to any traumatic event. Before proceeding further, it will be useful to define and discuss some of the terms that are most commonly employed in this area.

6.04 A 'recovered memory' generally refers to the experience of remembering an actual event after a period of time in which it was forgotten. It is assumed that the individual did not just fail to think about the event, while retaining the knowledge that the event happened, but completely forgot that it ever occurred. A 'false memory' refers to the experience of remembering an event that did not in fact occur. In many cases, of course, there is no conclusive evidence to distinguish between whether any particular experience involves a recovered memory or a false memory. To make things more complicated, it is quite con-ceivable that a particular experience of remembering might involve a mixture of true and false elements. 'False memory syndrome' is a term put forward by proponents of the idea that recovered memories are often in reality false memories. It is not a term that has any scientific status. They have also coined the term 'recovered memory therapy' to refer to the practice of therapists who attempt to recover what are assumed to be forgotten trauma memories, typically of sexual abuse. Again, the term is not formally defined or recognized by mental health professionals.

6.05 It is easy to form the impression that the recovered/false memory controversy revolves around the problematic concept of repression. There are in fact two quite separate issues that are often conflated by writers on the subject. The first issue is whether or not it is possible to forget that a traumatic event ever happened and then later recall it to mind. The second issue is, assuming the recovery of trauma memories is possible, by what mechanism is it achieved? Repression refers to one particular controversial mechanism that has been proposed as an explanation for forgetting. The validity of the concept of repression is logically distinct from the question of whether or not forgetting happens. To make things even more complicated, repression has two quite separate meanings, which again are often not distinguished. In one sense (sometimes also referred to as 'suppression') it refers to a deliberate strategy on the part of a person to exclude unwanted material from consciousness. This is a relatively uncontroversial process that has been well established in the laboratory. In its second sense it refers to a completely unconscious process in which traumatic events are excluded from consciousness automatically. Although no empirical evidence has been found for such an unconscious process, it is not unreasonable to hypothesize that the repeated exercise of repression in its first usage, for example by someone who was exposed to repeated trauma over an extended period, might lead to the development of repression in its second sense. It is this second sense, however, that is particularly controversial and often rejected by sceptics.

Having outlined the scope of the controversy and defined some of the key terms, it is **6.06** important to place it within its scientific and societal context. The debate is notable for having spilled out into the popular media and having been the subject of numerous newspaper articles, TV programmes, popular books, and novels. Unfortunately the highly visible, and at times ostensibly political, nature of the controversy has not contributed to a balanced appraisal and presentation of the evidence.

B. Origins of a Scientific Controversy

The gradual revelation during the 1980s of the widespread sexual and physical abuse of **6.07** children, and the realization that for years this abuse had been ignored or simply overlooked, led to an unprecedented development in clinical services for abuse survivors, offered both by clinics and hospitals and by private psychotherapists. As these therapists started working with survivors of prolonged trauma, they began to encounter clinical phenomena for which they had received little, if any, training and with which they were often poorly equipped to deal. For example, therapists came across patients who described recalling episodes of abuse that they had completely forgotten. These apparent recovered memories were often vivid and detailed and were initially recalled with high levels of surprise and emotion.

It was commonly assumed that these early traumatic experiences were the cause of the **6.08** person's later psychological problems, that therapists needed to understand the links between the past and the present, and that the person's experience eventually had to be accepted and validated instead of being dismissed and ignored as had so often happened in the past. These assumptions were readily generalized by some to cases in which the trauma apparently had been partially or wholly forgotten, or in which the memory seemed to be vested in a subpersonality. In line with Freud's original seduction theory, the thinking was that trauma memories had been repressed and if patients were to recover, their experiences had to be brought fully into consciousness.

As trauma therapy spread, so the links of reasoning that supported its use gradually **6.09** became stretched. Initially, therapists felt reasonably confident when they could trace low self-esteem, eating problems, and other difficulties to feelings patients could consciously associate with the abuse they had always remembered. Noting that abuse was sometimes forgotten and appeared to be remembered only later, some therapists began to argue that the very existence of certain symptoms and difficulties indicated that abuse had probably occurred, even if the patient had not recalled it. The (even less) logical extension of this argument was that patients should be helped to recover these memories, and that if they had suspicions, vague feelings, or images relating to abuse, then it was very likely to have occurred. There was little questioning at first of whether vivid experiences that appeared to be memories were actually always true and whether the uncovering of abuse memories was necessarily in the patient's best interests.

6.10 Other influential trauma therapists, some of whom did have a higher level of professional training, also appeared to fall into the trap of assuming that memory was invariably a reliable guide to what had actually happened and that attempts to recover memories, for example, using hypnotic age regression, were likely to uncover the truth. It is important to emphasize that this constellation of attitudes and techniques, which as noted above has sometimes been dubbed 'recovered memory therapy', never achieved the status of an 'official' therapy or became part of standard training for therapists. Rather, they inhabited a hinterland of therapy for childhood sexual abuse and were used on an ad-hoc basis by certain therapists and counsellors when they seemed to be appropriate within the overall context of treatment. It is unclear how many practitioners could legitimately be called 'recovered memory therapists' in the sense that they operated largely or exclusively according to these principles, in the same way as hypnotherapists would routinely use hypnosis as part of their treatment.

6.11 Another consequence of the increasing focus on violence and abuse, and on the assumption that the victim should always be believed, was the mobilization of campaigners who were willing to defend some adults accused of abuse and to question the credibility of some of the accusations, whether they were made by children or by adults describing their childhoods. In 1992 the False Memory Syndrome Foundation (FMSF), an organization dedicated to supporting parents whose adult children had made what were regarded as false accusations of abuse against them, was founded by Pamela and Peter Freyd. From its outset, the FMSF was extremely successful at attracting (usually quite favourable) publicity, and over the next few years both the FMSF and other false memory societies claimed that there were many thousands of cases known to them in which previously happy families were disrupted by false accusations of childhood abuse triggered when an adult entered therapy. In addition to encouraging accused parents to call them and tell them of their experiences, one of the first actions of the FMSF was to form a scientific advisory board, mainly consisting of academic psychologists and psychiatrists. Although some of these individuals acted in a purely advisory capacity, others enthusiastically championed the notion of a 'false memory syndrome' in the media and in professional journals. One of them, John Kihlstrom, then at Yale University, put forward a definition of the syndrome that has achieved wide currency:

> A condition in which a person's identity and interpersonal relationships are centered around a memory of traumatic experience which is objectively false but in which the person strongly believes. Note that the syndrome is not characterised by false memories as such. We all have memories that are inaccurate. Rather, the syndrome may be diagnosed when the memory is so deeply ingrained that it orientates the individual's entire personality and lifestyle, in turn disrupting all sorts of other adaptive behaviors. . . . False Memory

Syndrome is especially destructive because the person assiduously avoids confrontation with any evidence that might challenge the memory.[2]

The eminence of the scientific advisors was surprising because at this stage no evidence **6.12** for the syndrome had been put forward other than the personal experience of a few individuals. In the vast majority of cases there was only the parents' testimony that the memory was objectively false, that there had been any personality or lifestyle changes, or that the sufferer was impervious to contrary facts and alternative theories.

One advisory board member who did have good reason to doubt the reliability of **6.13** memory was Elizabeth Loftus, the foremost American expert in the study of eyewitness testimony. Her article published in 1993 in *American Psychologist* was a landmark event, establishing the arguments for the false memory position in a high-profile professional journal.[3] Loftus suggested that at least some of the memories of childhood sexual abuse recovered in therapy might not be veridical but might be false memories 'implanted' by therapists who had prematurely decided that the patient was an abuse victim and who used inappropriate therapeutic techniques to persuade the patient to recover corresponding 'memories'. Among her most telling claims questioning the plausibility of recovered memories of abuse were the following:

- these memories were sometimes highly unusual, for example, of satanic rituals with human sacrifices;
- the age at which the events were supposed to have occurred sometimes was so low that it preceded the development of conscious event memory;
- there was typically no independent corroboration of the events;
- therapists sometimes seemed to have fixed ideas about the ubiquitous influence of child abuse, and
- therapists might hold mistaken beliefs about the accuracy of memory and might employ procedures such as hypnosis or guided fantasy that increased the risk of imaginary scenes and images being interpreted as actual events.

Other cognitive psychologists also reviewed relevant psychological studies on auto- **6.14** biographical memory, eyewitness testimony, suggestibility, and the fallibility of memory, concluding that the creation of false memories within therapy was a possibility that must be taken seriously.[4]

C. The Evidence Base

There are two main sources of relevant evidence: experimental evidence obtained from **6.15** the laboratory and naturalistic evidence from surveys of false memory societies, the general population, therapists, or patients in therapy. The experimental evidence is easier

---

[2] Cited in Pope, K. S., 'Memory, abuse, and science—Questioning claims about the false memory syndrome epidemic,' (1996) 51 *American Psychologist*, 957–974.

[3] Loftus, E. F., 'The reality of repressed memories,' (1993) 48 *American Psychologist*, 518–537.

[4] See e.g. Lindsay, D. S. and Read, J. D., 'Psychotherapy and memories of childhood sexual abuse: A cognitive perspective' (1994) 8 *Applied Cognitive Psychology*, 281–338.

to interpret, but is farther removed from the phenomena it purports to model. In contrast, the naturalistic evidence is more clearly relevant to the matter at hand but is plagued by problems of validity.

(1) Experimental evidence

6.16   Hyman and Loftus reviewed experimental evidence to demonstrate that a proportion of people asked to vividly imagine made-up scenes from their childhoods will later come to mistake those scenes for actual events.[5] In one example, Hyman and colleagues conducted three interviews with participants in which they were asked to recall events from their childhoods supplied by their parents. Mixed in with true events were several false events, one of which involved the six-year-old participant knocking over a punchbowl at a wedding and spilling the contents over the bride's parents. The participants generally recalled the true events and remembered more about them over the three interviews. Although none remembered the punchbowl incident at the first interview, by the third interview a quarter of the sample claimed to have a memory for it.

6.17   Participants who agree to these false memories tend to be of a more generally suggestible disposition. Just as in these experiments, it has been proposed that patients might also be willing to accept suggestions about childhood abuse made by their therapists. Lindsay and Read noted that the likelihood of suggestive influences leading to memory errors is increased by the perceived authority and trustworthiness of the source of suggestions, by repetition of suggestions, by their plausibility and imageability, and by the adoption of an uncritical attitude towards establishing the truth or falsity of apparent memories.[6] They proposed that such features might characterize a type of therapy that they called *long-term, multifaceted, suggestive memory work*, involving repeatedly encouraging a patient to imagine or fantasize about what might have happened coupled with an absence of warnings about the unreliability of memory. Pezdek *et al* demonstrated, however, that there are probably limits to people's willingness to accept such made-up experiences as their own, and that it is difficult to implant false memories about unlikely and unpleasant events.[7]

6.18   There have been some interesting studies comparing the suggestibility of women who think they have been abused but have no memory of it (the 'repressed memory' group), women who report recovering memories of abuse (the 'recovered memory' group), women who report having always known they were abused (the 'continuous memory' group), and women who say they were never abused (the 'control' group). In one study,[8] women were asked to rate their confidence that certain non-traumatic events from childhood had happened to them, such as finding a ten-dollar bill in a parking lot. On a later occasion they were required to vividly imagine a subset of these events and rerate their confidence

---

[5] Hyman, I.E. and Loftus, E.F., 'Errors in autobiographical memory' (1998) 18 *Clinical Psychology Review*, 933–947.

[6] Cited above at n.4.

[7] Pezdek, K., Finger, K. and Hedge, D., 'Planting false childhood memories: The role of event plausibility' (1997) 8 *Psychological Science*, 437–441.

[8] Clancy, S.A., McNally, R.J. and Schacter, D.L., 'Effects of guided imagery on memory distortion in women reporting recovered memories of childhood sexual abuse' (1999) 12 *Journal of Traumatic Stress*, 559–569.

that they had actually occurred. Although this procedure led to a slight increase in the belief that the imagined events had happened, this effect was larger for the control group than for the recovered memory group.

Another study[9] involved showing participants a list of related words (such as 'candy',   **6.19** 'bitter', 'sour', 'sugar') and testing whether they would later falsely remember having seen another word (such as 'sweet') that was highly associated with all of them but was never actually shown. In this experiment the recovered memory group was more prone than the other groups to agree that they had seen the non-presented word, but the repressed memory group did not differ from the control group. It is hazardous, however, to draw parallels between this kind of word experiment with its compelling associative cues and the situation of people with recovered memories of incidents of abuse. Studies are not consistent in showing that people claiming repressed or recovered memories are more suggestible than non-abused people.

In contrast, the idea that people are able to deliberately forget unwanted or irrelevant   **6.20** mental contents has come back into fashion. Interestingly, an event does not have to be traumatic to be forgotten. Rather, these are everyday processes designed to make our thinking more efficient. Without a way of screening out unwanted thoughts, memories, and associations, we would all become overwhelmed by the sheer volume of information available to us. In 'directed forgetting' experiments participants are instructed either to remember or to forget arbitrary lists of unrelated words.[10] In the list method, participants are presented with a list of words one at a time, and then midway through are instructed to forget the first half of the list and remember the second half of the list. In a surprise test in which participants have to recall all the items from both halves of the list without any retrieval cues, they remember fewer words from the to-be-forgotten set than from the to-be-remembered set. Similar processes may be involved in post-hypnotic amnesia, when participants are instructed to forget something while in a hypnotized state. After hypnosis has been lifted, they are unable to retrieve the forgotten item until their amnesia is reversed by a prearranged signal or cue.

In an even more direct demonstration of deliberate forgetting, Anderson and Green had   **6.21** their participants learn a series of word pairs such as 'ordeal-roach' so that they could remember the right-hand word when shown the left-hand word.[11] They were then presented with the first word of a pair and were instructed either to retrieve and say aloud the second word of the pair ('think' condition) or to try to prevent the word from entering their consciousness at all ('no-think' condition). Other word pairs were not presented at this time to provide a comparison. At the end of the experiment participants were once again given the left-hand word of each pair and asked to recall the right-hand word. Anderson and Green found that, compared with the comparison pairs, recall was

---

[9] Clancy, S.A., Schacter, D.L., McNally, R.J. and Pitman, R.K. 'False recognition in women reporting recovered memories of sexual abuse' (2000) 11 *Psychological Science*, 26–31.

[10] Bjork, E.L. and Bjork, R.A., 'Continuing influences of to-be-forgotten information' (1996) 5 *Consciousness and Cognition*, 176–196.

[11] Anderson, M.C. and Green, C., 'Suppressing unwanted memories by executive control' (2001) 410 *Nature*, 366–369.

significantly better when participants were in the 'think' condition and significantly worse when they were in the 'no-think' condition. Moreover, the more often their participants practiced not thinking about a word, the harder it was for them to remember it later when asked to do so. The researchers concluded that they had identified a control mechanism that was effective in keeping unwanted material out of consciousness, similar to that proposed by Freud.

6.22 Evidently, these experiments do not have too much to say about claims of false or recovered memories of traumatic events. They are useful, however, in establishing that it is not too difficult in principle, at any rate with a subgroup of individuals, to implant memories for events that never happened and, conversely, to deliberately forget unwanted mental material.

(2) Naturalistic evidence

6.23 The most compelling naturalistic evidence for the existence of false memories is the existence of individuals who are convinced they have at some time been abducted by aliens. 'Memories' of alien abductions behave similarly to real trauma memories in that they are often extremely vivid and compelling. Moreover, these 'memories' produce high levels of emotion and responses on objective physiological measures.[12]

6.24 Other relevant evidence comes from various types of survey data and has been reviewed in detail.[13] At least three studies have provided confirmation that some therapists hold beliefs that run contrary to what we know about memory. One survey compared U.S. and U.K. psychologists' practices and experiences as well as more general beliefs concerning memory recovery of sexual abuse during childhood. The British respondents (who were all chartered clinical psychologists) were less likely than their U.S. counterparts to use memory recovery techniques such as hypnosis and age regression, although both groups had similarly high rates of respondents reporting memory recovery in at least some clients. One of the problems with asking whether certain therapeutic techniques have been employed is that they may have been used for purposes other than memory recovery. For example, hypnosis is often used simply to relax people, without giving any age regression or memory recovery instructions. In one survey, use of techniques to aid recall before the first memory recovery was not associated with faster memory recovery, and these cases were just as likely to be accompanied by reports of corroborative evidence as cases in which no techniques were employed.

6.25 How robust is the claim that the false memory societies have identified thousands of people who all have had the same experience and who all tell the same story? A survey of

---

[12] McNally, R. J., Lasko, N. B., Clancy, S. A., Macklin, M. L., Pitman, R. K. and Orr, S. P., 'Psycho-physiological responding during script-driven imagery in people reporting abduction by space aliens' (2004) 15 *Psychological Science*, 493–497.

[13] See Brewin, C. R. and Andrews, B. 'Recovered memories of trauma: Phenomenology and cognitive mechanisms' (1998) 18 *Clinical Psychology Review*, 949–970, and Brewin, C. R., *Posttraumatic stress disorder: Malady or myth?* New Haven, Conn.: Yale University Press, 2003 (Chapters 7 and 8 dissecting the controversies over recovered/false memory and repression). These sources support the conclusions drawn in paragraphs 6.24 to 6.29.

around 400 British False Memory Society (BFMS) members obtained a 70 per cent response rate, with approximately 70 per cent of responders agreeing that recovered memories were involved in the accusations, 20 per cent not being sure or not answering the question, and 10 per cent denying that recovered memories were involved. Thus, clear indications of the possible involvement of recovered memories were obtained from only about half the membership of the BFMS. No comparable analysis of people contacting the American FMSF has been published. These data obviously are uncorroborated, in that we do not know whether the accusers would agree that the memories were indeed recovered from previous amnesia.

Second, how robust is the claim that memories of sexual abuse can be forgotten and later **6.26** recovered? More than twenty longitudinal and retrospective studies have now found that a substantial proportion of people reporting childhood sexual abuse (somewhere between 20 and 60 per cent) say they have had periods in their lives (often lasting for several years) when they had less memory of the abuse or could not remember that it had occurred. It is of course difficult to evaluate the performance of one's own memory accurately, and it is clear that some people's claims of forgetting are mistaken. Nevertheless, the evidence that people *believe* they have completely forgotten the events is quite substantial.

One of the major objections to these studies raised by McNally, is that when people **6.27** agree they had periods when they could not remember the trauma they may not have forgotten the events but simply not thought about them.[14] He argues that for their statement to make sense they must have tried to think about the trauma but failed. An alternative view is that when people make such a statement they are referring to a failure of memory for the fact that the trauma happened, and are expressing the view that the trauma represents such an important aspect of their life that they would expect always to be aware of it, even if they did not actively think about it. Several studies based on detailed questioning or knowledge of the individual have clarified that most people claiming recovered memories do not mean that they always knew about the trauma, and this is supported by the shock and surprise that are often described as accompanying traumatic memory retrieval.

It has been claimed that the content of recovered memories tends to be bizarre and **6.28** implausible. According to records kept by the UK and US false memory societies, between 8 and 18 per cent of callers to their organizations mentioned reports of satanic or ritual abuse. According to a sample of chartered psychologists in the United Kingdom answering questions about clients with recovered memories, 5 per cent of memories involved ritual cult abuse, and one memory involved an alien abduction. More than a quarter of the respondents reported having clients with non-abuse-related recovered memories in the past year. The most frequent categories involved other child maltreatment, traumatic medical procedures, and witnessing violence or death. Other studies have similarly reported the existence of recovered memories of events that have nothing to do with sexual abuse. Studies have also examined how many memories appear to fall totally within the period of childhood amnesia, when event memories are known to be

---

[14] McNally, R. J., *Remembering trauma*, Cambridge, Mass.: Harvard University Press, 2003.

very rare. Surveys consistently report that no more than 7 per cent of recovered memories relate exclusively to this very early period of life.

6.29 There is also quite a lot of corroborative evidence for recovered memories, some based on detailed case studies in which other explanations for apparent memory recovery were systematically considered.[15] In some of these cases the events were protracted in time, which contradicts the argument that while single events can be forgotten, people are unable to forget repeated or protracted events. Other corroborated cases have been documented by Ross Cheit's Recovered Memory Project. This Internet-based resource[16] details upward of eighty corroborated recovered memory accounts drawn from legal, academic, and other sources. Some of these, like that of Ross Cheit himself, who remembered being abused between the ages of ten and thirteen by a camp administrator, or Frank Fitzpatrick, who remembered being abused at age twelve by a priest, also involved repeated instances of victimization. In addition to these case studies, surveys have also reported the existence of corroborative evidence such as an abuser acknowledging some or all of the remembered abuse, someone who knew about the abuse telling the respondent, or someone else reporting abuse by the same perpetrator. A final issue is whether recall occurs exclusively during therapy sessions, or after the onset of therapy, as opposed to before therapy. Survey data indicate that between a third and a half of memories were recovered in other contexts.

6.30 One doesn't need to be a scientist to see the problems with all the data presented above. The information provided by members of the false memory societies is mainly uncorroborated, in that we do not know whether the accusers would agree that the memories were indeed recovered from past amnesia. Breakdown in family communications is also going to limit the accuracy of what families are able to say about the basis for the accusations. Nor in most cases does anyone other than those involved know with any certainty whether the events complained of did in fact occur. Equally, the data from surveys of patients themselves and their therapists are open to the objection that the respondents might be mistaken in thinking these were genuine memories. As we have seen, some corroborative evidence has been provided for some individuals, but while this is supportive it does not prove that even their memories are accurate.

(3) Summary

6.31 The scientific evidence is consistent neither with the idea that traumatic memories need to be exhumed and deactivated if clients are to be cured of their problems, nor with the existence of a well-defined false memory syndrome of epidemic proportions. In my view the clinical and survey data reviewed indicate that at least some recovered memories may not correspond to actual events. A minority of memories contain unusual content or refer to events that occurred at an age preceding the development of verbal memories. Some memories occur within therapy after the use of a specific technique to aid recall

---

[15] See e.g. Schooler, J. W., Bendiksen, M. and Ambadar, Z., 'Taking the middle line: can we accommodate both fabricated and recovered memories of sexual abuse?' in Conway, M.A. (ed.), *Recovered memories and false memories*, Oxford: Oxford University Press, 1997, 251–292.

[16] http://www.brown.edu/Departments/Taubman_Center/Recovmem/index.html.

and cannot be corroborated, and some practitioners appear to have important mis-conceptions about the nature of memory and adopt risky practices. Thus, false memories are a very real possibility that professionals in the field must guard against at all times. At the same time the data from these surveys suggest that many recovered memories are not amenable to this kind of explanation. Memory recovery appears to be a remarkably robust phenomenon, occurring both within and outside therapy and involving a wide variety of different types of event. Many well-trained practitioners have encountered the phenomenon, often without using techniques to aid recall. Laboratory studies of hypnotic amnesia show that memories can be routinely lost and then recovered by ordinary hypnotized subjects when the appropriate instructions are given.

To complicate matters further, memory theory and experimental research make the **6.32** strong prediction that the recall of events that have not actually happened is more likely when there are similar events that have actually happened. That is, some false memories may have a basis in reality, even though details of events, people, and places may have become confused. Interestingly, trauma therapists have arrived at exactly the same conclusion on the basis of their experiences. One leading therapist has commented:

> Traumatised patients may be (a) very suggestible and (b) very compliant (in certain respects). Both qualities make the traumatised patient more likely to generate material that fits the therapist's expectations, theoretical assumptions, emotional prejudices, etc. This means that, paradoxically, traumatised and abused patients may be more likely to produce false memory narratives of trauma and abuse.[17]

Most independent commentators now appear to accept that traumatic events can be **6.33** forgotten and then remembered. For example, two leading cognitive psychologists concluded:

> In our reading, scientific evidence has clear implications . . . : memories recovered via suggestive memory work by people who initially denied any such history should be viewed with scepticism, but there are few grounds to doubt spontaneously recovered memories of common forms of child sexual abuse or recovered memories of details of never-forgotten abuse. Between these extremes lies a gray area within which the implications of existing scientific evidence are less clear and experts are likely to disagree.[18]

Similarly, the consensus view among independent commentators, repeated in the 1995 report of the BPS Working Party on Recovered Memories and the 1994 interim state-ment of the American Psychological Association's Working Group on Investigation of Memories of Childhood Abuse, is that memories may be recovered from total amnesia and they may sometimes be essentially accurate.[19] Equally, such 'memories' may some-times be inaccurate in whole or in part. It must however be noted that some sceptical

---

[17] Mollon, P., *Remembering trauma: A psychotherapist's guide to memory and illusion*, Chichester: John Wiley and Sons, 1998, 175.

[18] Lindsay, D.S. and Read, J.D., ' "Memory work" and recovered memories of childhood sexual abuse: Scientific evidence and public, professional, and personal issues' (1995) 1 *Psychology Public Policy and Law*, 846–908, at 894.

[19] Morton, J., Andrews, B., Bekerian, D., Brewin, C.R., Davies, G.M. and Mollon, P., *Recovered memories*, Leicester: British Psychological Society, 1995; American Psychological Association (1994), *Interim report of the APA working group on investigation of memories of childhood abuse*, Washington, D.C., 1994

voices still insist it has not yet been proven that individuals are able to completely forget traumatic events and then later recover the memories, particularly when those events are repeated.[20]

6.34 In practical terms, the debate has had major effects on how psychotherapy is conducted, leading to greater safeguards for patients. The initial polarization between memory researchers and clinicians has now dissolved, so that both can largely endorse the same conclusions and recommendations. Proponents of the idea that therapists should routinely try to recover abuse memories are now almost impossible to find within the ranks of leading psychiatrists and psychologists. Despite the lack of direct empirical support, there is widespread agreement that situations in which there is sustained suggestive influence, such as therapy, do have the potential to induce false memories of traumatic events. Active attempts to recover suspected forgotten memories may sometimes be appropriate in unusual or extreme cases, but both patient and therapist must be aware of the risk of false memories. Techniques such as hypnosis and guided imagery should not be used without safeguards against potential suggestive influence. Furthermore, good practice now requires therapist and patient to adopt a critical attitude toward any apparent memory that is recovered after a period of amnesia, whether or not this is within a therapeutic context, and not to assume that it necessarily corresponds to a true event. Even highly vivid traumatic memories (flashbacks) may be misleading or inaccurate in some cases. Clinical guidelines are now available to help the practitioner avoid the twin perils of uncritically accepting false memories as true or summarily dismissing genuine recovered memories.

D. Practical Considerations in Legal Settings

(1) Relevance of the scientific controversy

6.35 Perhaps the first question to ask is whether an allegation actually involves issues of recovered memory. Defence lawyers not infrequently raise the issue when any historical allegation is involved, even in the absence of evidence that the complainant does report having completely lost the memory for some period of time. Continuous memories of traumatic events that have never been forgotten, provided they originate from after the period of childhood amnesia, have not been subjected to the same criticism as recovered memories, although they may also be inaccurate. Witness statements rarely provide the level of detail about memory needed to specify this unambiguously.

(2) When should concerns be raised about recovered memories?

6.36 As proponents on both sides of the debate acknowledge, it is common for memories of all kinds to be forgotten and then recovered. Ironically, in view of the criticisms of recovered memory, there is no scientific evidence that a recovered memory is likely to be less accurate than a continuous memory. For theoretical reasons, however, commentators have concerns about a number of situations in which recovered memories may arise. A very

---

[20] McNally, R. J., cited above at n.14 (the most detailed case yet made for the sceptical point of view).

important question concerns the presence of 'sustained, suggestive influences'. Pressure on an individual to remember events for which they initially had no memory, for example using techniques such as hypnotic age regression or guided fantasy, would in most experts' view increase the probability of false memory creation. This would be exacerbated by encouragement to take literally any image that came to mind and to assume that it corresponded to an actual event. Such encouragement could come from a therapist, but could equally come from a friend, religious advisor, or family member. Similarly, indications that the individual reporting the recovered memory was suggestible, or tended to suspend their critical faculties rather than question the nature of their mental experiences, would be of concern. For example, evidence of extensive previous fantasizing, adoption of bizarre beliefs, or claims to remember events from the first 18 months of life, would be relevant here. In contrast, it would be reassuring if there was no evidence of external persuasion and if the individual appeared to retain a questioning attitude to their mental experiences.

The kind of questions that may be helpful is to ask the individual who expresses confidence in their recovered memory experience whether they have considered the possibility that the memory might not be accurate, and how they have arrived at the conclusion that it is accurate. The interviewer would be seeking indications of initial uncertainty and that the individual made attempts to test the evidence. An interesting issue is that memory vividness and detail are two criteria which in an everyday context usually help to distinguish between a memory for an actual and an imagined event. Trauma memories, particularly involuntary ones, tend to be vivid, to contain sensory detail, and to be associated with intense emotion. Thus, complainants may assume that because their memories are vivid they must be accurate. However, there are several case reports and studies indicating that this is not necessarily the case. People may have very vivid and emotion-laden intrusions of events that never actually happened, or that represent distortions of actual events. This does not appear to be particularly common, but it is certainly possible. Thus, vividness and intensity of emotion are not reliable guides to the authenticity of a recovered memory experience. **6.37**

(3) Characteristics of a good expert report

It should be evident that strong conclusions are not warranted on the basis of the existing scientific evidence. Reports should therefore strive to be even-handed and avoid giving the impression that there is a consensus either in favour of or against the existence of recovered and false memories. They should draw attention to the different points of view and cite proponents sceptical of and supportive of the idea that some recovered memories of trauma may well be accurate. Some academic commentators as well as authors of more popular books on this issue have adopted a consistently sceptical focus (e.g. Sidney Brandon, Frederick Crews, John Kihlstrom, Elizabeth Loftus, Richard McNally, Harold Merskey, Richard Ofshe, Mark Pendergrast, and Harrison Pope), whereas others have been more favourable to the idea that recovered memories are likely to exist in reasonable numbers (e.g. Douglas Bremner, Chris Brewin, John Briere, Laura Brown, Jennifer Freyd, Steven Lindsay, Phil Mollon, Kenneth Pope, Don Read, and Jonathan Schooler). A balanced report is likely to cite a good selection of these authors. **6.38**

6.39 Expert reports should also be accurate in any attempts to summarize scientific knowledge about memory, and cite authoritative sources for any general statements they make. For example, it is sometimes (wrongly) claimed that memory in general, and highly emotional forms of memory such as flashbacks or flashbulb memories in particular, are inherently unreliable. Other erroneous claims are that memory consists solely of attempts to reconstruct the past from general beliefs, and that the longer the gap between the event and the attempt at recall, the more unreliable memory is likely to be. Researchers are largely agreed that there is a basic integrity to human memory, although errors and false beliefs are not uncommon. Memory for the gist of concrete or repeated facts that were important to the individual is likely to be well retained over many years, although memory for detail (including timing), memory that involves evaluations and judgements, and memory for unimportant events are likely to be much more fallible. There is good evidence that memory for highly emotional events remains relatively vivid even after many years, but it is not possible to distinguish scientifically between a true and a false memory.

6.40 It is generally difficult to tell from witness reports whether a complainant has completely forgotten for a period of time that the alleged events occurred, and is therefore basing such allegations on a recovered memory. Statements implying memory recovery, such as 'I suddenly remembered what he had done to me as a child', do not categorically distinguish between a continuous memory that had not been thought about and a memory that had been completely forgotten. Similarly, although counselling and clinical records are sometimes useful and should be routinely requested, it is not always possible to tell whether there has been any prolonged suggestive influence. Apparent inconsistencies in witness statements are common, and it is often not possible to tell without careful questioning whether they reflect inaccurate third party reporting, an infelicitous use of language, or an actual inconsistency.

6.41 For these reasons it is almost always necessary to interview the complainant concerning the status of their memories, whether continuous or recovered, the triggers to memory recovery, the immediate reaction to memory recovery, including any disbelief and attempts to test the veracity of the memories, the consistency of their accounts, and the presence of suggestive influences whether within or external to any therapy or counselling that has been received. At interview the complainant can also be administered structured clinical interviews to ascertain whether they at any time met criteria for a psychiatric disorder, and exhibited symptoms warning of an impaired ability to test reality.

6.42 The issue of psychiatric disorder in a complainant must be treated with great caution. General references in medical or general practitioner notes concerning episodes of anxiety and depression are very common, and often insufficiently precise to permit a judgement about whether there has been a significant episode of illness. Attempts to diagnose other conditions such as personality disorders from medical or counselling records are likewise very hazardous and should be resisted. Experts will need to consider whether the disorder arose before or after the alleged assaults, whether there is any evidence that they impaired reality testing, and whether the disorder could legitimately be seen as a possible consequence of the alleged assaults.

Expert reports should avoid focusing on theoretical issues such as the existence of repres-   **6.43**
sion, or the relationship between dissociation and forgetting. Although of clinical interest,
and possibly relevant to the motivation of therapists to adopt particular approaches to
their patients, these issues are beset by definitional problems that impede clear communication. As I have indicated above, there is little in the way of unambiguous scientific
evidence either to support or refute them, and they are largely irrelevant to the question
of whether or not a memory has been forgotten and later recovered. Finally, attempts to
rule on the reliability or unreliability of the complainant's memories should be avoided,
except in the very limited way set out in the next section.

(4) What can the expert legitimately conclude?

The veracity of any allegations is obviously a matter for the court to decide, not the expert   **6.44**
witness, and indeed scientific knowledge offers little basis for offering an opinion. It
should be evident from the above review that there is some general evidence of relevance
but little in the way of specific studies that speak directly to the kind of issues that are
likely to concern the court. There is general support, for example, for the proposition that
memory is likely to be less reliable when there are prolonged suggestive influences, when
the individual has exhibited previous beliefs that were obviously delusional, or when they
showed evidence of an unquestioning acceptance of mental experiences without any
attempt to consider or test their veracity. Some individuals have indeed been encouraged
to attempt memory recovery using guided fantasy, hypnosis, prayer, or other altered
mental states, and have been instructed that any experiences they have are likely to
correspond to actual historical events. This would be a matter of concern.

The courts are extremely well equipped to test the nature of the evidence supporting any   **6.45**
allegations, and those involving memory recovery are no exception. Experts are entitled
to point to factors that from a scientific viewpoint are likely to increase or decrease the
probability that a memory report is accurate. They should be able to identify the specific
reason for their concern and cite empirical evidence supporting their position, even if it
is based on laboratory rather than real-world evidence. The nature of this evidence and
its limitations should be commented upon. They may also be able to identify the kind of
additional evidence that would increase or allay their concern. If there is no evidence that
factors thought to compromise the validity of memory reports are present in a particular
case, they should say so.

Because in relation to sexual offences in England and Wales corroborative evidence of   **6.46**
allegations is not required, experts are also entitled to discuss the reasons why individuals
may be convinced that their recovered memories correspond to actual events, for example
the presence of high levels of vividness, sensory detail, and emotion. They should be
aware of the evidence that these factors are generally relied upon to help distinguish
between reality and imagination, but that they are not infallible guides. They should also
determine whether there are related episodes that could have become confused with
those featuring in the allegations, and possibly produced intrusive 'memories' of an event
that did not happen. Finally, experts should correct misleading statements concerning
recovered memories that may be made by others in the case, and emphasize the very
limited nature of the current evidence base.

Further Reading

Brewin, C.R., *Posttraumatic stress disorder: Malady or myth?* New Haven, Conn.: Yale University Press, 2003. (Chapters 7 and 8 dissect the controversies over recovered/false memory and repression)

Davies, G.M. and Dalgleish, T. (eds.), *'Recovered memories: Seeking the middle ground,* Chichester: John Wiley and Sons, 2001 (collection of chapters covering socio-historical, legal, scientific, and therapeutic issues)

Gleaves, D.H., Smith, S.M., Butler, L.D., *et al* 'False and recovered memories in the laboratory and clinic: A review of experimental and clinical evidence' (2004) 11 *Clinical Psychology: Science and practice*, 3–28 (detailed review of the experimental and naturalistic evidence).

McNally, R.J., *Remembering trauma*, Cambridge, Mass.: Harvard University Press, 2003 (the most detailed case yet made for the sceptical point of view).

Chris R. Brewin is professor of clinical psychology at University College London and consultant clinical psychologist with the Camden and Islington Mental Health and Social Care Trust. For the past fifteen years he has been treating patients traumatized in childhood and adulthood. He is widely known internationally for his research on traumatic memory and post-traumatic stress disorder and has published two books and over forty peer-reviewed journal articles on this topic. He was a member of the British Psychological Society's working party on Recovered Memories and has been an expert witness in numerous UK trials involving recovered memories.

Editors' Note

There seems little doubt from orthodox and prudent scientific research that a person, perhaps due to their age or the traumatic affects of victimization suffered, may undergo a 'loss' of memory of historic events but that their memory is susceptible to later retrieval. Equally, inappropriate counselling or other forms of interview technique may cause a subject to come to believe in the reality of events which, in fact, never occurred. Unless fact finders, and those who address or direct them, either through expert evidence or the communication of 'common knowledge' with which fact finders may not be familiar, are adequately informed concerning the relevant mechanics of memory, decisions in cases where 'recovered memory' is a factor will be susceptible to ill-informed error.

The question of the admissibility of expert evidence relating to childhood amnesia has been the subject of judgments of the Court of Appeal in *R v JH; R v TG (deceased)* [2005] EWCA 1828 and *R v Snell; R v Wilson* [2006] EWCA Crim 1404.

7

CRIME-RELATED AMNESIA

Sven Å. Christianson, Harald Merckelbach and Michael Kopelman

A. Introduction

Crime-related amnesia refers to a claim raised by offenders that they cannot remember **7.01** essential details of the crime they have committed. There are two obvious legal reasons why it is important to explore crime-related amnesia.[1] To begin with, amnesia raises the issue of automatism, which refers to criminal behaviour that is executed unconsciously and without intent. Second, amnesia bears relevance to the issue of competence to stand trial. An accused who has no memory of the crime cannot plead on his own behalf, simply because he is unable to inform his counsel. Thus, in some jurisdictions, such a person may be incompetent to stand trial.

For the Anglo-Saxon situation, it has been noted[2] that 'no court has found a defendant **7.02** incompetent to stand trial solely because of amnesia'. Indeed, in Anglo-Saxon countries amnesia does not figure in the list of disorders that typically contribute to 'not guilty by

---

[1] Schacter, D.L., 'Amnesia and crime: How much do we really know?' (1986) 41 *American Psychologist*, 286–295.

[2] Parwatikar, S.D., Holcomb, W.R. and Menninger, K.A., 'The detection of malingered amnesia in accused murderers' (1985) 13 *Bulletin of the American Academy of Psychiatry and Law*, 97–103.

reason of insanity' verdicts. Most of the times, such outcomes involve schizophrenia and mood disorders, especially in combination with alcohol or drug use.[3]

7.03 Still, according to some leading Anglo-Saxon authors,[4] claims of amnesia may have far-reaching legal implications. In the legal context, it is not amnesia *per se* that is considered to be informative, but what amnesia reveals about the state of the defendant at the moment he/she committed the crime. In the literature, examples of 'automatic' crimes committed during sleepwalking, epileptic seizures, or hypoglycaemic states abound. Kopelman[5] noted that offenders who commit an 'automatic' crime would always become amnesic.

7.04 In countries like the UK, Canada, and Australia, automatism has been divided into 'sane' and 'insane' types. For both categories of automatism, it is assumed that the *mens rea* (i.e. 'wicked mind') aspect of the crime is at stake.[6] 'Sane' automatism refers to a crime committed by someone who is essentially healthy, but who is in a temporary state of madness due to some external agent (e.g. insulin). Such a scenario may lead to acquittal. 'Insane' automatism refers to a crime originating from brain dysfunction. The proto-typical example is the man who killed his neighbour during an epileptic seizure.[7] Such a scenario can lead to a 'not guilty by reason of insanity' verdict.

7.05 The distinction between 'sane' and 'insane' automatism is a legal notion without clear psychological or medical rationale. The assumption is that if an automatism results from an external agent (such as insulin), the behaviour will not recur, whereas if there is underlying brain disease (such as epilepsy) recurrence is likely. Both components of this assumption are tendentious. Referring to several case examples, others[8] showed that the distinction is highly dependent on arbitrary judgements made by expert witnesses and especially their opinion as to what counts as a structural brain dysfunction. McSherry's article describes two similar cases of domestic murder. Due to expert witness testimonies, one case was classified as 'sane' automatism leading to full acquittal, whereas the other case was classified as an example of 'insane' automatism, leading to a 'not criminally responsible' verdict and admission to a psychiatric hospital. With these interpretational problems in mind, Yeo argues that it is better to conceptualize automatic states in terms of uncontrollable behaviour.[9]

7.06 The difficulties in an alleged defence of automatism and a defendant's claim of amnesia is exemplified in the following case. NN, a 40-year-old man, was at a nightclub in Malmö,

---

[3] Lymburner, J.A. and Roersch, R., 'The insanity defense: Five years of research (1993–1997)' (1999) 22 *International Journal of Law and Psychiatry*, 213–240.

[4] E.g. Bradford, J.W. and Smith, S.M., 'Amnesia and homicide: The Padola case and a study of thirty cases', (1979) 7 *Bulletin of the American Academy of Psychiatry and Law*, 219–231.

[5] Kopelman, M.D., 'Psychogenic Amnesia', in Baddeley, A.D., Kopelman M.D., and Wilson, B.A. (eds.), *Handbook of Memory Disorders* 2nd edn, Chichester, UK: John Wiley and Sons, 2002, 451–472.

[6] Hermann, D.H.J., 'Criminal defenses and pleas in mitigation based on amnesia', (1986) 4 *Behavioural Sciences and the Law*, 5–26.

[7] Fenwick, P., 'Brain, mind, and behaviour: Some medico-legal aspects' (1993) 163 *British Journal of Psychiatry*, 565–573.

[8] McSherry, B., 'Getting away with murder: Dissociative states and criminal responsibility' (1998) 21 *International Journal of Law and Psychiatry*, 163–176.

[9] Yeo, S., 'Clarifying automatism' (2002) 25 *International Journal of Law and Psychiatry*, 445–458.

Sweden, together with a female friend. They had both consumed some alcoholic beverages during the evening, and NN was tipsy. Another man and his friend had approached NN a few times during the course of the evening. They were provocative, and the third time they came to NN's table they attacked him. He received several blows to the head and tried to defend himself, but was struck on the forehead with an object and collapsed to the floor. NN was under threat from a criminal gang and feared for his life. Because of these threats, he was carrying a loaded pistol. After being struck to the ground, he immediately got up and pulled his gun. The man who had struck him fled, and NN followed him, shooting at him at every opportunity, until the weapon was empty. The man died as a result of his bullet wounds, and NN, who was picked up by the police minutes after the shooting, was charged with murder. He did not try to escape and he was completely unaware of what had happened or what he had done. His memory function improved when he was at the police station, but at that time, he had no real recollection of what happened immediately before, during, and after the shooting. Later, NN remembered brief fragments from outside the nightclub and when he was arrested.

At several times in his life, NN had suffered head trauma, with resultant effects on **7.07** memory and symptoms of epilepsy. There was reason to suspect, therefore, that the amnesia and behaviour displayed by NN in connection with the criminal event might have a neuropsychiatric basis. Additional factors that might have aggravated effects on NN's memory are that he, besides receiving a blow to the head and possibly experiencing epileptic activity, was also under the influence of alcohol, benzodiazepines, and anabolic steroids. These substances in combination have significant deleterious effects on memorial ability.

The defence argued for a state of insane (epileptic) automatism, and that his amnesia was **7.08** relevant in showing that the defendant did not know what he was doing as a result of neurological disease. The appellate court claimed that NN was conscious of his actions, that he acted highly rationally and on the basis of definite goals, e.g. '. . . in that he carried a loaded pistol, followed and shot his antagonist . . . in that almost all shots fired hit the antagonist'. NN was convicted of murder and sentenced to 10 years in prison.

Did the defendant NN have the mental state required for criminal conviction? This **7.09** chapter will offer some background information for a reasonable answer.

B. Types of Crime-related Amnesia

(1) Prevalence

Offenders who claim amnesia for their crime are by no means rare. As a rule of thumb, **7.10** one can say that 20 to 30 per cent of those who commit violent crimes claim amnesia. For example, one group of researchers[10] interviewed 34 murderers and found that 9 of

---

[10] Taylor, P.J. and Kopelman, M.D., 'Amnesia for criminal offences' (1984) 14 *Psychological Medicine*, 581–588.

them (26 per cent) claimed amnesia. Another research group[11] interviewed a further 177 murderers of whom 31 per cent reported amnesia. In another study[12] on 64 convicted criminals, 21 (32 per cent) of them claimed amnesia for their crime. While these claims are often raised in the context of murder or manslaughter cases, there are other crime categories in which claims of amnesia occur. For example, claims of amnesia regularly occur in sexual crime cases,[13] domestic violence cases,[14] and some fraud cases.[15]

(2) Dissociative amnesia

7.11 Several taxonomies have been proposed to distinguish between different types of amnesia.[16] Most of them agree that at least three forms of amnesia should be considered: dissociative amnesia (formerly termed psychogenic or functional amnesia), organic amnesia, and feigned (or simulated or malingered) amnesia. Dissociative amnesia for criminal behaviour is thought to originate from extreme emotions. Several authors[17] have argued that dissociative amnesia is typical for crimes that are unplanned, involve a significant other, and are committed in a state of strong agitation. The idea behind this is that extreme levels of arousal during the crime may hamper memory at a later point in time. Thus, a failure in retrieval processes would underlie dissociative amnesia: the offender, who eventually has come to his senses, finds it impossible to access memories stored during a moment of turbulence. A term often used in the Anglo-Saxon literature to describe amnesia as a consequence of strong emotions (e.g. rage) is 'red-out'. In the words of Swihart *et al*[18]: 'Apparently, an individual can get so angry with his/her intimate partner that s/he can severely beat or kill that partner and then not remember doing so: that is, they can experience a red-out resulting in circumscribed amnesia.'

7.12 A number of authors have emphasized that excessive alcohol use may contribute to dissociative amnesia for crime.[19] Often, the so-called 'state-dependent memory theory' is invoked to account for the combination of dissociative amnesia and alcohol.[20] In short, this theory states that when memories are stored in an exceptional context (e.g. strong

---

[11] Pyszora, N.M., Barker, A.F. and Kopelman, M.D., 'Amnesia for criminal offences: A study of life sentence prisoners' (2003) 14 *Journal of Forensic Psychiatry and Psychology*, 475–490.

[12] Gudjonsson, G.H., Petursson, H., Skulason, S. and Sigurdardottir, H., 'Psychiatric evidence: A study of psychological issues' (1989) 80 *Acta Psychiatrica Scandinavica*, 165–169.

[13] Bourget, D. and Bradford, J.M.W., 'Sex offenders who claim amnesia for their alleged offense', (1995) 23 *Bulletin of the American Academy of Psychiatry and Law*, 299–307.

[14] Swihart, G., Yuille, J. and Porter, S., 'The role of state-dependent memory in red-outs' (1999) 22 *International Journal of Law and Psychiatry*, 199–212.

[15] Kopelman, M.D., Green, R.E.A., Guinan, E.M., Lewis, P.D.R. and Stanhope, N., 'The case of the amnesic intelligence officer' (1994) 24 *Psychological Medicine*, 1037–1045.

[16] E.g. Schacter, (1986), cited above at n.1; Kopelman, M.D., 'Crime and amnesia: a review' (1987) 5 *Behavioural Science and the Law*, 323–342; Kopelman, (2002), cited above at n.5, 451–472; Kihlstrom, J.F. and Schacter, D.L., 'Functional disorders of autobiographical memory' in Baddeley, A.D., Wilson, B.A. and Watts, F.N. (eds.), *Handbook of Memory Disorders*, New York: Wiley, 1995, 337–364; Christianson, S.A. and Merckelbach, H., 'Crime-related amnesia as a form of deception', in Granhag, P.A. and Strömwall, L.A. (eds.), *The detection of deception in forensic contexts*, Cambridge: Cambridge University Press, 2004, 195–225.

[17] E.g. see Kopelman, (1987), cited above at n.16.   [18] Cited above at n.14, 200.

[19] See Kopelman, (1987), cited above at n.16 and Swihart *et al*, (1999) cited above at n.14.

[20] Swihart *et al*, ibid.

emotions and under the influence of alcohol), subsequent retrieval of these memories is facilitated when a similar context is created. However, in a different context (e.g. when the person is relaxed and sober), the pertinent memories would be inaccessible and so dissociative amnesia would occur.

(3) Organic amnesia

Organic amnesia is always caused by a neurological defect. This defect may be structural (e.g. epilepsy, brain trauma), but it may also be transient (e.g. alcohol or drug intoxication). Kopelman[21] assumes that memory loss in organic amnesia has to do with storage problems rather than retrieval problems: due to epileptic seizure, brain damage or intoxication, offenders would not be able to store their memories in the first place, which would eventually lead to a total 'blackout' for their crime.

7.13

(4) Feigned amnesia

Offenders may simulate amnesia for a crime in an attempt to obstruct police investigation and/or to avoid responsibility for their acts. In an older study,[22] it was found that 20 per cent of the offenders who claimed amnesia were malingerers. However, there are good reasons to believe that the rate of malingering is much higher (see below). The literature provides clear examples of defendants who feigned amnesia in order to gain tactical advantage in legal procedures. A recent example of how malingering might surface during legal proceedings is provided by the 'three strikes and you're out' law that has been adopted by some American states. Under this law, the third crime that a defendant commits will lead to a severe sentence. Thus, even if one's third offence consists of stealing a slice of pizza, one may face a sentence of 25 years in prison. Several psychiatrists have noted that defendants who are charged under this law often simulate amnesia in combination with bizarre symptoms. Jaffe and Sharma[23] report, for example, that in some Californian prisons there is a true epidemic of amnesia claims along with Lilliputian hallucinations (i.e. hallucinations of little green men). Offenders may report such bizarre symptoms in an attempt to be held incompetent to stand trial.

7.14

C. Instrumental versus Reactive Homicide

(1) The instrumental versus reactive dichotomy

An important distinction is that between instrumental/proactive and reactive/expressive homicide offenders.[24] In reactive homicide, the violence leading to death of another person can be construed as an impulsive response. The attack is spontaneous, immediate,

7.15

---

[21] Kopelman, (1987), cited above at n.16.

[22] Hopwood, J.S. and Snell, H.K., 'Amnesia in relation to crime' (1933) 79 *Journal of Mental Science*, 27–41.

[23] Jaffe, M.E. and Sharma, K.K., 'Malingering uncommon psychiatric symptoms among defendants charged under California's "three strikes and you're out" law' (1998) 43 *Journal of Forensic Sciences*, 549–555.

[24] Pollock, P.H., 'When the killer suffers: Post-traumatic stress reactions following homicide' (1999) 4 *Legal and Criminological Psychology*, 185–202.

and emotion-driven. Victim provocation is evident, but there is no apparent external goal other than to harm the victim following provocation or a conflict. A purely reactive homicide is an immediate, rapid, and powerful affective response (e.g. manslaughter). However, in some cases, the crime may contain some degree of planning. For example, the offender may leave to get a weapon and return for revenge, but without a 'cooling off' period between provocation and attack. Victims are typically a spouse or someone well known to the offender. The offender experiences a high level of angry arousal at the time of the violent event.

7.16 In instrumental homicide, the violence leading to death is planned and proactive. A homicide is purely instrumental when the murder is clearly goal-directed (e.g. to fulfil sexual or material needs or to obtain a thrill), with no evidence of an immediate emotional or situational provocation, and when the victim has little personal significance to the offender. Self-reported lack of arousal and anger during the offence are common in this group of offenders.

7.17 The distinction between reactive and instrumental crimes may over-simplify highly complex behaviours with multiple motivations and manifestations. For example, a bank robbery might originally have been a planned event (i.e. an instrumental crime), but during its execution an unexpected complication (e.g. victim resistance) might have created a reactive situation. Thus, some components of an event might be reactive and others instrumental. This might result in differential memory for different parts of an event. The analysis of a memory (e.g. its detail, affect, etc.) must accordingly be coordinated with the instrumental/reactive aspect of each part of the event.

(2) Associated features

7.18 The reactive versus instrumental dichotomy appears to be useful for predicting recidivism and treatment prognosis and it is associated with specific psychological characteristics of offenders. In one sample of 125 Canadian offenders, researchers[25] found that 27 per cent of the offenders could be classified as psychopaths. Over 90 per cent of the psychopaths were instrumental offenders. Because psychopaths would be expected to exhibit a general lack of affective interference and absence of empathy and remorse, and because of the pre-homicide fantasies among psychopaths, genuine dissociative memory reactions (amnesia) are unlikely to occur in this group. Genuine dissociative memory reactions and post-traumatic stress disorder (PTSD) symptoms are more likely to be found among those who committed a reactive homicide.[26] However, since the presence of re-experienced symptoms, including intrusive memories, is implied by the diagnosis of PTSD, it is likely that offenders who develop PTSD have vivid memories from their offences.

7.19 Furthermore, because there is a high degree of premeditation and preparation in instrumental homicides, one may expect that such offences are easier for the offender to

---

[25] Woodworth, M. and Porter, S., 'Historical and current conceptualizations of criminal profiling in violent crime investigations' (manuscript submitted for publication).
[26] Pollock, (1999), cited above at n.24.

remember. In cases of sexual murder—especially in offenders who plan to commit subsequent homicides—the act of killing (own actions, sexual components, victim's actions and reactions) is often compared to a script fantasy that precedes the murder. Premeditated fantasies and the act of murder are replayed over and over in the offender's mind, and the more the offender goes over the event in his/her mind,[27] the more firmly will the event be stored. Furthermore, instrumental offenders are expected to experience a lower level of intra-crime arousal rather than a state of extreme arousal (cf. red-outs), which thus will facilitate remembering the offence. However, in reporting about their offences, psychopaths are more likely than other offenders to 're-frame' the level of instrumentality that had been involved (i.e. exaggerate the reactivity). In comparing official reports and offenders' self-reported descriptions, some authors[28] found that psychopaths were more likely to commit instrumental (premeditated, goal-driven) homicides. Interestingly, the instrumentality difference disappeared when the offenders' narratives were examined: psychopaths exaggerated the reactivity of their violence, in terms of minimizing the degree of planning/premeditation and exaggerating the victim's role in, and the spontaneity of, the offence.

To test whether rates of amnesia are lower among instrumental than among reactive **7.20** homicide offenders, Christianson and von Vogelsang[29] collected data from 88 homicide cases. Of these, 54 were coded as reactive and 34 were coded as instrumental. Rage and relational themes were the two most common crime motives among reactive offenders, whereas sexual and thrill themes were the most common motives among instrumental offenders. All reactive offenders reported negative emotions at the time of the crime and 91 per cent reported such emotions for the period after the crime. In the instrumental group, 59 per cent experienced negative emotional arousal during and 44 per cent after the crime. This pattern is in line with previous research[30] revealing that 58 per cent of those who had committed reactive homicide showed PTSD symptoms compared to 36 per cent among the instrumental murderers.

In comparing offenders' memory before, during, and after the crime, Christianson and **7.21** von Vogelsang[31] found that it was more common to completely lose memory of what happened during the crime than information immediately before and after the crime. This pattern was evident for both groups, but was most pronounced in the reactive group. Note that this pattern is opposite to what is normally found when studying memory for emotional events.[32] That is, subjects typically remember the emotion-inducing event quite well, but show impaired memory for information preceding and/or succeeding the highly arousing event.

---

[27] I.e. elaborative rehearsal; Craik, F.I.M., and Lockhart, R.S., 'Levels of processing: A framework for memory research' (1972) 11 *Journal of Verbal Learning and Verbal Behavior,* 671–684.
[28] Porter, S., and Woodworth, M., 'Patterns of violent behaviour in the criminal psychopath' in Patrick, C. (ed.), *Handbook of psychopathy,* New York: Guildford, 2006, 481–494.
[29] Christianson, S-Å. and von Vogelsang, E., *Homicide offenders who claim amnesia for their crime,* Unpublished manuscript, 2003.
[30] See Pollock, (1999), cited above at n.24.   [31] Cited above at n.29.
[32] Christianson, S.-Å., 'Emotional stress and eyewitness memory: A critical review' (1992) 112 *Psychological Bulletin,* 284–309.

7.22 26 per cent of the reactive offenders (14 offenders) against 12 per cent of the instrumental offenders (4 offenders) consistently claimed to be amnesic for the act of killing throughout the investigation. Averaged across the two groups, this percentage is 21 per cent, which is highly similar to percentages reported by other studies on amnesia for homicide.[33]

D. How Offenders Describe their Amnesia

7.23 In evaluating the 21 per cent claiming amnesia in the Christianson and von Vogelsang study,[34] certain characteristics were found to be common in this group. To begin with, the offenders in this group were dogmatic about their amnesia (e.g. 'it doesn't matter if you ask me five, ten or even more times, I will never remember anything about what happened that evening'). A second feature was that they claimed to have total memory loss: 'my memory is like a black hole, everything is gone'. Further, offenders' claims of sharp limits for the beginning and end of the amnesia were quite common (e.g. 'from the moment I stepped out of the restaurant door, until I sat in the police car, everything is lost'). Finally, references to intoxication were also quite common. However, a closer look at the total sample revealed that 65 per cent of the offenders who were intoxicated by alcohol remembered the murder quite well, whereas only 19 per cent of them claimed amnesia.

7.24 The way in which offenders describe their memory loss might be helpful in distinguishing true from feigned amnesia for criminal acts. It is a well established fact that in bona fide patients with mental disorders, periods of amnesia are usually gradual and blurred in onset and termination. Moreover, in true amnesia, patients usually have 'islands of memory'. In contrast, many amnesic offenders say that they recall events immediately preceding and following the crime, with a circumscribed memory loss for the act of killing itself. Porter and Yuille[35] argued that this is an unusual pattern in clinical cases of both organic and dissociative amnesia, where more blurred demarcations between remembering and forgetting are found.

7.25 Schacter[36] argued that false claims of amnesia are characterized by a sudden onset and low ratings on feeling-of-knowing judgements. If, for example, a murder suspect is asked about the possibility of recurrence of memories after being provided with cues, recognition alternatives, more time to think about the event, additional interrogation, visits to the crime scene, and so forth, the malingerer is usually dogmatically negative.

7.26 Porter and Yuille[37] pointed out that malingerers are also more likely to relate symptoms of extreme specificity (e.g. 'I cannot recall anything from noon until midnight') and to

---

[33] E.g. see Taylor and Kopelman, (1984), cited above at n.10 and Pyszora *et al*, (2003), cited above at n.11; Cima, M., Nijman, H., Merckelbach, H., Kremer, K. and Hollnack, S., 'Claims of crime-related amnesia in forensic patients' (2004) 27 *International Journal of Law and Psychiatry*, 215–221.

[34] Cited above at n.29.

[35] Porter, S. and Yuille, J.C., 'Credibility assessment of criminal suspects through statement analysis' (1995) 1 *Psychology, Crime, and Law*, 319–331.

[36] Cited above at n.1.   [37] Cited above at n.35.

recount symptoms of extreme severity. Doubt should also arise when suspects with a diagnosis of psychopathy claim amnesia. Psychopaths do not experience the extreme emotions that may undermine encoding of information, but they do have a tendency to pathological lying and malingering. In keeping with this, Cima *et al*[38] found in their sample of psychiatric prison inmates that those who claimed amnesia displayed more antisocial characteristics, but also scored higher on an instrument tapping malingering tendencies.

Suspects often blame their amnesia on intoxication. Yet, as pointed out by Parwatikar **7.27** and co-workers,[39] amnesia for crime is unlikely to depend purely on an intoxicated state. In a study on drivers arrested during large traffic-control actions by the Dutch police, researchers[40] found that claims of alcohol amnesia (blackout) were predominantly raised by those involved in an accident. More specifically, 85 per cent of the drivers who claimed amnesia were involved in a serious motor vehicle accident against 35 per cent of those not claiming amnesia. Interestingly, during the time of the arrest, blood-alcohol concentrations ('BACs') in those who claimed amnesia were not higher than BACs of arrested drivers without amnesia. This illustrates that the combination of amnesia and intoxication claims may serve face-saving purposes.

On the other hand, some features may indicate that a claim of crime-related amnesia is **7.28** bona fide. To begin with, amnesic offenders may give themselves up or, at least, make no effort to avoid capture.[41] Secondly, there is a consistency in how they describe their amnesia, and many of their descriptions *do* in fact resemble those given by other people with psychological forms of amnesia—the memories being locked away in the back of the mind and impossible to retrieve, and sometimes there being islands or fragments of preserved memory within the amnesic gap, rather as in the amnesia which follows head injury. Thirdly, it should be noted that victims of offences sometimes describe very similar amnesic gaps, for example rape victims,[42] and eyewitnesses often make errors in recall; in neither case are their motives impugned. Fourthly, alcoholic blackouts are very common in heavy drinkers, and many offenders have a long alcohol history, including previous blackouts, and very high BACs at the time of their alleged offence. Finally, it should be noted that amnesia on its own does not have any bearing on criminal responsibility or accountability in most nation-states. The only exceptions are the very rare instances where automatism is an issue, in which amnesia is a necessary but not sufficient condition to raise an automatism defence. In practice, amnesia can be damaging to

---

[38] Cima, M., Merckelbach, H., Hollnack, S. and Knauer, E., 'Characteristics of psychiatric prison inmates who claim amnesia' (2003) 35 *Personality and Individual Differences*, 373–380.

[39] Cited above at n. 2.

[40] van Oorsouw, K., Merckelbach, H., Ravelli, D., Nijman, H. and Mekking-Pompen, I., 'Alcohol black out for criminally relevant behavior' (2004) 32 *Journal of the American Academy of Psychiatry and the Law*, 364–370.

[41] See Taylor and Kopelman, (1984), cited above at n. 10; see Kopelman, (1987), cited above at n. 16; Gudjonsson, G.H. and MacKeith, J.A., 'Retracted confessions: legal, psychological and psychiatric aspects' (1988) 28 *Medicine, Science and the Law*, 187–94.

[42] Mechanic, M.B., Resick, P.A. and Griffin, M.G., 'A comparison of normal forgetting, psychopathology, and information-processing models of reported amnesia for recent sexual trauma' (1998) 66 *Journal of Consulting and Clinical Psychology*, 948–957.

mounting a defence, and can hinder a defendant's instructions to his lawyers. A defendant claiming amnesia can guarantee that the prosecution will challenge his or her claim of amnesia very robustly.

7.29 For the expert witness, it is difficult to distinguish between dissociative, organic or feigned amnesia. This has to do with the fact that simulators can give a compelling imitation of someone with a dissociative or organic amnesia. It is only with the help of structured interviews focusing on certain memory characteristics and tests that an expert will be able to identify simulators. Ultimately, it is a matter for the jury to decide whether they believe a defendant's account, including any claim of amnesia. The expert is there only to advise on the circumstances in which amnesia may or may not arise, and the decision in any particular case is a matter for the jury. Relevant factors are discussed below.

E. Dissociative versus Feigned Amnesia

(1) Do strong emotions produce amnesia?

7.30 Dissociative amnesia is defined as 'an inability to recall important personal information, usually of a traumatic or stressful nature, that is too extensive to be explained by ordinary forgetfulness'.[43] As with many definitions in the *Diagnostic and Statistical Manual of Mental Disorders*, this definition is quite confusing.[44] It not only suggests that the cause of the memory loss is a dissociation between consciousness and memory, it also assumes that memory loss for emotional trauma does exist. Although lay people believe that it is perfectly possible that an emotionally provocative event like murder can lead to complete memory loss, specialists have more reservations about this. Some authors have argued that amnesia for offences does exist, and dissociation might be one possible mechanism, because defendants who claim amnesia often inform the police about their crime, or fail to take any measures to avoid capture.[45] However, Sadoff[46] has argued that a defendant who knows that there is extensive forensic evidence against him may speculate that he will make a more sympathetic impression on triers of fact when he simulates amnesia than when he provides them with a lucid description of crime details. Sadoff concluded that most cases of crime-related amnesia are actually feigned. Evidence in favour of this position comes from older studies reporting that criminals who raise such claims can be distinguished from other criminals by their relatively low intelligence and their hysterical traits.[47] In this context, hysterical traits refer to manipulative behaviour, including the

---

[43] *Diagnostic and Statistical Manual of Mental Disorders*, (4th ed.), Washington DC: American Psychiatric Association, 1994, 477.

[44] Pope, H.G., Hudson, J.L., Bodkin, J.A. and Oliva, P., 'Questionable validity of dissociative amnesia in trauma victims' (1998) 172 *British Journal of Psychiatry*, 210–215.

[45] See Kopelman, (2002), cited above at n.5; Porter, S., Birt, A.R., Yuille, J.C. and Herve, H.F., 'Memory for murder: A psychological perspective on dissociative amnesia in legal contexts' (2001) 24 *International Journal of Law and Psychiatry*, 23–42.

[46] Sadoff, R.L., 'Evaluations of amnesia in criminal–legal situations' (1974) 19 *Journal of Forensic Sciences*, 98–101.

[47] O'Connell, B.A., 'Amnesia and homicide' (1960) 10 *British Journal of Delinquency*, 262–276; Parwatikar et al, (1985), cited above n.2.

tendency to feign symptoms.[48] While the concept of hysteria has largely disappeared from psychiatric vocabulary, more recent studies point in the same direction. For example, Porter and co-workers[49] reported that claims of amnesia are often raised by defendants with an antisocial personality disorder. A hallmark feature of this disorder is, of course, manipulative behaviour. Similarly, Cima *et al*[50] found that criminals who report amnesia have low intelligence and display antisocial personality features. If true, the picture which would emerge from such studies is that defendants who claim dissociative amnesia often rely on a simple form of denial in an attempt to minimize their responsibility. However, the relationship between amnesia claims and low intelligence has not been replicated in all samples.[51]

A second reason to adopt a sceptical attitude towards claims of dissociative amnesia is **7.31** that the whole idea of amnesia for crime is based on the dubious assumption that 'the majority of crimes which are followed by amnesia are those accompanied by strong emotional reactions'.[52] By this view, strong emotions lead to repression or, to use a more recent notion, to dissociation and this would produce retrieval problems. If this line of reasoning is correct, one expects that, for example, concentration camp survivors would also display amnesia for the horrifying events they have experienced. However, there is controversy over this issue.[53] On a related note, eyewitnesses to extreme violence rarely report that they are amnesic for the events they have witnessed,[54] although they commonly show recall errors, and amnesic gaps have been reported in victims of rape.[55] In short, the notion that people may develop complete amnesia for highly emotional events remains controversial.[56] In this context, it is important to remember that dissociative amnesia is, in general, a rare phenomenon, and always requires an attitude of respectful scepticism.[57]

A third reason to be sceptical about claims of dissociative amnesia is that recent psychi- **7.32** atric literature shows that a non-trivial minority of people tend to feign a variety of symptoms and tend to confabulate stories if this serves their interests. For example, it is estimated that as many as 20 per cent of closed-head-injury patients pursuing financial compensation exaggerate their symptoms.[58] Likewise, in the United States there are now many well-documented cases of Vietnam veterans who have never served in Vietnam and

---

[48] O'Connell, ibid.   [49] Porter *et al*, (2001), cited above at n. 45.   [50] Cited above at n. 38.
[51] Pyszora, N., 'Amnesia for criminal offences in a cohort of life sentence prisoners', Ph.D. Thesis, University of London, 2005.
[52] Hopwood and Snell, (1933), 32, cited above at n.22.
[53] E.g. Merckelbach, H., Dekkers, T., Wessel, I. and Roefs, A., 'Dissociative symptoms and amnesia in Dutch concentration camp survivors' (2003) 44 *Comprehensive Psychiatry*, 65–69.
[54] Porter *et al*, (2001), cited above at n. 45.   [55] Mechanic *et al*, (1998), cited above at n. 42.
[56] Pope *et al*, (1998), cited above at n. 44.
[57] Christianson, S.-Å., and Nilsson, L.-G., 'Hysterical amnesia: A case of aversively motivated isolation of memory', in Archer, T. and Nilsson, L.-G. (eds.), *Aversion, avoidance, and anxiety: Perspectives on aversively motivated behavior*, Hillsdale, NJ: Lawrence Erlbaum Associates, 1989, 289–310.
[58] Binder, L.M. and Rohling, M.L., 'Money matters: A meta-analytic review of the effects of financial incentives on recovery after closed-head injury' (1996) 153 *American Journal of Psychiatry*, 7–10.

who fake their PTSD symptoms.[59] When motor vehicle accident victims feign neuro-logical complaints and when military personnel invent a complete autobiography to qualify for disability payments, why should the criminal who simulates amnesia be a rarity? Lay persons often have a notion of amnesia derived from television and films, completely at variance with the facts of either neurological or psychogenic amnesia, although they often remain healthily sceptical about its occurrence in everyday life. However, it should be noted that, when normal subjects are instructed to play the role of the murderer, confronted with abundant evidence during interrogation, the most frequently chosen strategy is to claim amnesia for the criminal act and to attribute it to an internal force that they cannot control.[60]

(2) The role of alcohol

7.33 Excessive alcohol or drug use is often said to precede criminal acts for which dissociative amnesia is claimed. At least, that is what criminals who claim such memory loss tell expert witnesses. As said before, the 'state-dependent memory' hypothesis is often invoked to explain the apparent link between alcohol and amnesia.[61] Yet, a closer look at the literature shows that this hypothesis is not based on solid evidence. For example, in a study by Wolf,[62] a substantial amount of alcohol was given to criminals who had committed murder under the influence of alcohol and who claimed to be amnesic. The 'state-dependent memory' hypothesis would lead one to predict that alcohol results in recovery from the amnesia. This is not what Wolf found. Although his subjects became emotional, they maintained that they could not remember the crime details.

7.34 Of course, the phenomenon of 'alcohol blackout' exists. However, it is best viewed as an organic form of amnesia resulting from an excessive amount of alcohol consumed within a very short time span (e.g. 5 glasses of whisky or 20 glasses of beer within 4 hours).[63] Not all alcoholics will develop an alcoholic blackout; it occurs more commonly in those who start drinking early in life, and who may have experienced multiple head injuries. Although normal people consuming this level of alcohol are not capable of the fine motor operations that are needed to carry out a criminal act[64] alcoholics who develop tolerance will be able to do so. It is always useful to try to establish the BAC following an offence. Meanwhile, defendants' reference to their alcohol or drug use may serve a specific function. That is, for those who have seriously violated the law, an appeal to alcohol or drug intoxication may give an explanation for the crime that has been com-mitted as well as for the memory loss that is claimed. The example of the Canadian

[59] E.g. Gold, P.B. and Frueh, B.C., 'Compensation-seeking and extreme exaggeration of psycho-pathology among combat veterans evaluated for Posttraumatic Stress Disorder' (1998) 187 *Journal of Nervous and Mental Disease*, 680–684.

[60] E.g. Merckelbach, H., Devilly, G.J. and Rassin, E., 'Alters in dissociative identity disorder: Metaphors or genuine entities?' (2001) 22 *Clinical Psychology Review*, 1–17.

[61] Swihart *et al*, (1999), cited above at n.14.

[62] Wolf, A.S., 'Homicide and blackout in Alaskan natives' (1980) 41 *Journal of Studies on Alcohol*, 456–462.

[63] Goodwin, D.W., 'Alcohol amnesia' (1995) 90 *Addiction*, 315–317.

[64] Kalant, H., 'Intoxicated automatism: Legal concept vs. scientific evidence' (1996) 23 *Contemporary Drug Problems*, 631–648.

Supreme Court shows that courts may be vulnerable to such an 'intoxication defence'. In the case of a rapist, who claimed not to remember the crime because he was in a state of alcohol intoxication, the Court ruled that the crime had been committed in a state of 'drunken automatism'.[65]

(3) The role of expectations

Experiments show that the effects of alcohol are to some extent guided by expectations **7.35** that people have about these effects. A straightforward procedure to demonstrate this is the 'balanced placebo design'. The rationale behind this design is that some subjects are given a non-alcoholic drink that they believe to contain alcohol, while others consume an alcoholic drink that they believe is a non-alcoholic refreshment. Under these circumstances, extrovert behaviour, tension reduction, and other positive as well as negative effects that people associate with alcohol do not depend on actual alcohol intake, but on the belief that one has consumed alcohol.[66] In a recent study, Assefi and Garry demonstrated that the mere suggestion to subjects that they have consumed alcohol makes these subjects more susceptible to misleading information.[67] These findings underline that people have strong ideas about the effects of alcohol, ideas that in turn may guide their behaviour.

Is it possible that some defendants really believe that they are amnesic because they **7.36** assume that this is a probable outcome given the traumatic character of the event and/or their large consumption of alcohol? A study by Gudjonsson, Kopelman, and MacKeith[68] demonstrates that there is such a thing as imaginary amnesia. In this case, a defendant was convicted for the murder of a little girl. During police interrogations, the defendant was encouraged to distrust his own memory, which made him more susceptible to what police officers told him about his involvement in the crime. The fact that he had no memories of the crime was interpreted as a manifestation of dissociative amnesia, an interpretation in which the defendant himself came partly to believe. Subsequently, it became clear that he was innocent.

Germane to the issue of expectations is also an experiment by Christianson and Bylin.[69] **7.37** These authors gave their subjects a case vignette of a murder. Subjects were instructed to identify themselves with the offender. Next, one group of subjects was told to play the role of an amnesic offender during a task that consisted of a series of questions about the case. The control group was encouraged to perform as well as they could on this task. After a week, subjects returned to the lab and, again, answered questions about the case.

---

[65] Ibid.

[66] Critchlow, B., 'The powers of John Barleycorn: Beliefs about the effects of alcohol on social behavior' (1986) 41 *American Psychologist*, 751–764.

[67] Assefi, S.L. and Garry, M., 'Absolute memory distortions: Alcohol placebos influence the misinformation effect' (2003) 14 *Psychological Science*, 77–80.

[68] Gudjonsson, G.H., Kopelman, M.D. and MacKeith, J.A.C., 'Unreliable admissions to homicide: A case of misdiagnosis of amnesia and misuse of abreaction technique' (1999) 174 *British Journal of Psychiatry*, 455–459.

[69] Christianson, S.-Å. and Bylin, S., 'Does simulating amnesia mediate genuine forgetting for a crime event?', (1999) 13 *Applied Cognitive Psychology*, 495–511.

This time, all subjects were instructed to perform as well as they could. During the first session, subjects who played an amnesic role gave fewer correct answers than control subjects, which is not remarkable. It only shows that the 'amnesic' subjects took their role seriously. However, at the one-week follow-up test, ex-simulators were still performing under the level of control subjects. This is remarkable, because it shows that simulating amnesia has memory-undermining effects.

7.38 The memory-undermining effect of simulating amnesia is a robust phenomenon.[70] There are several explanations for this phenomenon. One assumes that expectancies are the driving force behind the memory-undermining effect of simulating amnesia. People who initially played the role of an amnesic person may have a strong expectation that they will perform poorly on subsequent memory tasks. This, in turn, may give rise to a 'self-fulfilling prophecy' when the person is given such a memory task. This phenomenon is also known from studies on placebo effects. Subjects who receive a placebo in combination with the story that it is a memory-undermining substance, later on perform less well on memory tasks than do control subjects.[71]

7.39 The memory-undermining effects of simulating suggest that a simulated amnesia may sometimes develop into a real memory problem. Referring to such mixtures of simulated and real memory problems, Kopelman[72] argued that the various forms of amnesia 'form end-points along a continuum rather than discrete categories'.

F. Organic versus Feigned Amnesia

(1) Head injury and post-traumatic amnesia

7.40 On the face of it, organic amnesia is an unproblematic phenomenon. In many cases, organic amnesia will be a persistent symptom due to brain damage as a result of chronic alcohol abuse, epilepsy, tumours, encephalitis, or traumatic injury. Note that in this context, the word trauma has a circumscribed meaning. Whereas in psychiatric literature, it refers to emotional shock (e.g. witnessing a shooting), here it refers to an external agent that caused brain dysfunction (e.g. closed-head injury from an accident or fight). Even in cases of mild traumatic brain injury, acute loss of consciousness and subsequent Post-Traumatic Amnesia (PTA) may occur. PTA refers to a disoriented state and a serious memory problem immediately after the incident that caused the brain injury. When loss of consciousness exceeds 30 minutes and PTA duration is longer than 24 hours, traumatic brain injury is said to be severe.[73]

---

[70] van Oorsouw, K. and Merckelbach, H., 'Feigning amnesia undermines memory for a mock crime' (2004) 18 *Applied Cognitive Psychology*, 505–518.

[71] Kvavilashvili, L. and Ellis, J.A., 'The effects of positive and negative placebos on human memory performance' (1999) 7 *Memory*, 421–437.

[72] Kopelman, M.D., 'Focal retrograde amnesia and the attribution of causality: An exceptionally critical review', (2000) 17 *Cognitive Neuropsychology*, 585–621 (at 608).

[73] Faust, D., 'Assessment of brain injuries in legal cases: Neuropsychological and neuropsychiatric considerations', in Fogel, B.S., Scheffen, R.B. and Rao, S.M. (eds.), *Neuropsychiatry*, Pennsylvania: Williams and Wilkins, 1996, 973–990.

Regardless of whether brain injury is mild or severe, in the period after the PTA, the **7.41**
patient usually reports all kinds of complaints that vary from concentration difficulties to
depressive feelings. These complaints are sometimes referred to as the 'post-concussion'
syndrome, but this impressive term suggests more clarity than the neurological literature
really offers. For example, Lees-Haley, Fox, and Courtney[74] noted that most symptoms
associated with this syndrome are surprisingly non-specific and are also highly prevalent
among people who never sustained a brain injury. However, an inability to recall important details surrounding the trauma (e.g. an accident or a fight)—organic amnesia—is a
rather specific symptom of the post-concussion syndrome. Organic amnesia follows a
fixed course that was first described by the 19th century French psychologist Theodule
Ribot[75] and is therefore known as Ribot's law. This law refers to the phenomenon that
organic amnesia pertains to the traumatic incident itself and events that immediately
preceded and/or followed it, rather than events that took place long before the trauma. If
such older memories have nevertheless become inaccessible, they will return sooner in
the weeks following the trauma than more recent memories that have become inaccessible.[76] Eventually, the amnesia will largely disappear, and will be limited to the traumatic
event itself and the few seconds that preceded it.

There are reasons to believe that the vague, non-specific symptoms of the post- **7.42**
concussion syndrome are sensitive to simulation. This is mostly the case in civil law suits,
in which, for example, vehicle accident victims require financial compensation. In such
cases, it is relatively easy to feign atypical symptoms.[77] Meanwhile, organic amnesia is
considerably more difficult to simulate—at least for naïve malingerers—because of its
typical course. That is, organic amnesia requires the specific sequence of trauma, loss of
consciousness, PTA, memory loss pertaining to recent rather than old memories, and
memory recovery in such a way that old memories come back more readily than recent
ones. When complaints about organic amnesia do not follow this pattern, there is every
reason to be sceptical and to consider the possibility of malingering.

(2) Neurological conditions

As reviewed above, the various neurological conditions which can give rise to a transient **7.43**
amnesia, during which an offence is committed, are rare but legally important. However,
definitions of an automatism are unsatisfactory. One of us has suggested that an
automatism is: 'an abrupt change in behaviour in the absence of conscious awareness or
memory formation, associated with certain, specific clinical disorders, such as epilepsy,

---

[74] Lees-Haley, P.R., Fox, D.D. and Courtney, J.C., 'A comparison of complaints by mild brain injury
claimants and other claimants describing subjective experiences immediately following their injury' (2001)
16 *Archives of Clinical Neuropsychology*, 689–695.
[75] Haber, L. and Haber, R.N., 'Criteria for the admissibility of eyewitness testimony of long past events',
(1998) 4 *Psychology, Public Policy, and Law*, 1135–1159.
[76] E.g. Christianson, S.-Å., Nilsson, L.-G. and Silfvenius, H., 'Initial memory deficits and subsequent
recovery in two cases of head trauma' (1987) 28 *Scandinavian Journal of Psychology*, 267–280.
[77] Youngjohn, J.R., Burrows, L. and Erdal, K., 'Brain damage or compensation neurosis? The controversial post-concussion syndrome' (1995) 9 *The Clinical Neuropsychologist*, 112–123.

parasomnias, or hypoglycaemia'.[78] Whilst aware of the limitations of this definition, we would argue that it is more specific than (for example) that given by Fenwick.[79]

7.44 Epileptic automatisms or post-ictal confusional states occasionally result in crime. When this occurs, ElectroEncephaloGraphic (EEG) tracings subsequently reveal that the seizure activity involved the hippocampal and parahippocampal structures bilaterally as well as the mesial diencephalon.[80] As these structures are crucial for memory formation, amnesia for the period of automatic behaviour is always present and is usually complete.[81] There is no automatism without amnesia although, of course, there is very frequently amnesia without automatism. Consequently, assessment requires a convincing history of both epilepsy and amnesia. Since the *R v Sullivan* case (reported by Fenwick[82]), courts in England and Wales have regarded epileptic automatisms as a form of 'insane automatism', resulting from 'intrinsic' brain disease, liable to recur and therefore requiring compulsory psychiatric treatment, often in a secure hospital. Of course, there is no reason to suppose that such an episode will necessarily recur.

7.45 Regarding the case of NN above, he had suffered head trauma at several times in his life, with resultant effects on memory and symptoms of epilepsy. Thus, there were reasons to suspect that the amnesia and behaviour displayed by NN in connection with the criminal event might have a neuropsychiatric basis. In connection with a single-vehicle accident in 1987, NN became disoriented and amnesic (memory loss). There were suspicions of intracranial bleeding/skull injury and epilepsy, but adequate assessment and treatment did not occur because NN left the hospital. Ten years later, in 1997, NN sought medical care for muscle spasms and in 1999, an epileptic seizure was triggered in connection with playing a home-video game; this resulted in memory loss. An EEG test was conducted in 2001, after NN's repeated attempts to receive help with memory disturbances and headaches. Note that repeated episodes of memory loss or 'blackouts' are one of the primary clinical symptoms of brain injury. The neuropsychological assessment conducted on NN also showed certain symptoms of neuropsychological dysfunction, thus indicating possible problems associated with brain injury. Thus, it is fully conceivable that a blow to the head or extreme stress could have triggered epileptogenic activity in NN, at the same time as he performed appropriate motoric actions, but in the absence of conscious control of these actions, so that the attack on him was followed by marked anterograde amnesia. In clinical contexts, this type of epileptic attack has been established in patients using deep electrodes from the amygdala and hippocampus and has also been observed in association with fits of rage and violence.

---

[78] Pyszora, N., Jaldow, E. and Kopelman, M.D., 'Memory disorders in the civil and criminal courts' in Young, S., Gudjonsson, G. and Kopelman, M.D. (eds.), *Forensic Neuropsychology*, Oxford: Oxford University Press, 2006 (in press).

[79] Fenwick, P., 'Automatism, medicine and the law' [Review] (1990) 17 *Psychological Medicine Monograph Supplement*, 1–27.

[80] Fenton, G.W., 'Epilepsy and automatism' (1972) 7 *British Journal of Hospital Medicine*, 57–64; Fenwick, (1990), cited above at n.79.

[81] Knox, S.J., 'Epileptic automatism and violence' (1968) 8 *Medicine, Science and the Law*, 96–104.

[82] Cited above at n.79.

Hypoglycaemia can result from insulin-treated diabetes, alcohol intoxication, insulinoma, insulin abuse, or the 'dumping' syndrome. Insulin abuse has been implicated in a number of serious offences, including violent crimes against children.[83] Where hypoglycaemia has resulted from the administration of an 'extrinsic' agent such as insulin, the case for a 'sane' automatism can be argued, potentially resulting in acquittal (in England and Wales and many other jurisdictions) on the basis of the fact that the situation is unlikely to recur. As discussed elsewhere in this chapter, such an assumption is not necessarily very logical. The third author managed to argue successfully for an acquittal in the case of a young diabetic man who delayed taking a meal after self-administering his insulin because he had become interested in a television programme; subsequently, he killed a friend without any apparent motivation, and he was clearly hypoglycaemic when the police arrived.

Sleepwalking or somnambulism has also been used for grounds for automatism. It occurs **7.46** most commonly in childhood and adolescence, and occasionally in adult life when precipitated by fatigue, mental stress, sleep deprivation, drugs or alcohol, or a change in the sleeping environment.[84] It most commonly occurs within two hours of falling asleep, and episodes last only a few minutes. There are a substantial number of case reports in the medical and legal literature of violent attacks during sleepwalking, often involving strangulation, attempted strangulation, or the use of available implements as weapons with a sleeping partner as the victim.[85] Most commonly in these case reports, there has not been any hostility between the offender and the victim, and the behaviour is entirely out of character. Typically, episodes of violence accompanying sleepwalking terminate in the subject appearing confused on awakening, recalling relatively little of any accompanying dream, but being aware of a sense of acute dread or terror in such a dream (so-called 'night terrors'). This arises because sleepwalking and night terrors commonly occur in stage 4 of slow-wave sleep, shortly before the transition to rapid-eye movement (REM) sleep. It used to be thought that violent offences could not occur in association with REM sleep because the subject was paralysed and could not sleepwalk. However, since the identification of REM sleep behaviour disorder,[86] episodes of lashing out or more organized violence against a sleeping partner have indeed been reported. A great problem in sleep-related automatisms is the extent to which complex or prolonged abnormal behaviour can be accepted as an 'automatism', and this has given rise to extensive recent medico-legal controversies in Canada and the United States.

In the case of NN, the degree and character of his memory loss suggest organic amnesia. NN displays limited retrograde amnesia, but pronounced anterograde amnesia, which can be observed in cases of cranial trauma and epileptic attacks. The fact that NN

---

[83] Scarlett, J.A., Mako, M.E., Rubenstein, A.H. *et al*, 'Factitious hypoglycaemia' (1977) 297 *New England Journal of Medicine*, 1029–1032; 'Editorial: Factitious hypoglycaemia' (1978) I *Lancet*, 1293.

[84] Kales, A., Soldatos, C.R., Caldwell, A.B. *et al*, 'Somnambulism' (1980) 37 *Archives of General Psychiatry*, 1406–1410; Howard, C. and d'Orbán, P.T., 'Violence in sleep: medico-legal issues and two case reports', (1987) 17 *Psychological Medicine*, 915–25; Fenwick, (1990), cited above at n.79.

[85] Fenwick, ibid.

[86] Schenck, C.H., Bundlie, S.R., Ettinger, M.G., and Mahowald, M.W., 'Chronic behavioural disorders of human REM sleep: a new category of parasomnia' (1986) 9 *Sleep*, 293–308.

shows islands/fragments of memory, some—though limited—recovery of detail information, and that he has a history of memory loss suggests that his amnesia is genuine, that is, not simulated. Moreover, the fact that, in the aftermath of the violence perpetrated by him, NN did not try to hide his crime or flee from the scene of the crime, and that he is not conscious of his violent actions, but instead directs attention to his own injuries, is in good accordance with a state of disorientation following an epileptic seizure. In court, the first author therefore argued for the possibility that NN had a genuine amnesia and committed his crime in a state of automatism caused by a subclinical seizure.

G. Testing

7.47 When a defendant claims crime-related amnesia, how should an expert witness determine what type of amnesia the defendant suffers from? One possibility is that the defendant sustained brain injury and consequently developed an organic amnesia. The expert may explore this by examining if and how the defendant's amnesia disappears over time. If the defendant's amnesia follows Ribot's law, that information might be crucial for the defendant's counsel. Consider a defendant charged with murder. If the defendant has an organic amnesia and it can be shown that this amnesia originates from the victim hitting the defendant on his head before he was murdered, then a self-defence interpretation of the murder case might be considered (*cf.* the case of NN).

7.48 Another possibility is that a defendant honestly believes that he suffers from amnesia. As far as we know, there is no valid test to explore this possibility. However, with the findings of Kvavilashvili and Ellis[87] in mind, the expert might consider giving the defendant a placebo along with the instruction that it is a memory-enhancing drug. In a way, such a manipulation is deceptive. On the other hand, it is highly similar to forensic hypnosis, because that technique also capitalizes on expectancies.[88]

7.49 A third possibility is that a defendant feigns his amnesia. Again, this possibility warrants serious attention and can be explored in several ways, for example, by using Symptom Validity Testing, self-report scales or other techniques.

(1) Symptom Validity Testing

7.50 Symptom Validity Test ('SVT') has been found to be useful in identifying defendants who simulate amnesia.[89] Basically, SVT procedures consist of a forced-choice recognition test, where the defendant is asked a series of true-false questions about the crime and the circumstances under which it took place. The defendant is instructed to guess in case he does not know the right answers because of his amnesia. Typically, 15 to 100 items are presented, each followed by a forced-choice recognition task. With any number of items,

---

[87] Cited above at n.71.
[88] Kebbell, M.R. and Wagstaff, G.F., 'Hypnotic interviewing: The best way to interview the eyewitness?' (1998) 16 *Behavioural Sciences and the Law*, 115–129.
[89] Frederick, R.I., Carter, M. and Powel, J., 'Adapting symptom validity testing to evaluate suspicious complaints of amnesia in medico-legal evaluations' (1995) 23 *Bulletin of the American Academy of Psychiatry and the Law*, 227–233.

chance performance (guessing) can be determined fairly precisely. This has to do with the fact that purely random responding will result in about half of the answers being correctly answered. Individuals who perform significantly below chance strategically avoid correct alternatives.[90] This means that they must possess knowledge about the correct answers and this implies that they feign memory impairment. SVT is based on binomial statistics, which has the clear advantage that one can quantify memory performance. Thus, one can determine the exact probability that someone with genuine memory loss gives only three right answers to 15 true-false questions. On the basis of chance alone, such person should have six, seven or eight correct answers. The probability that someone with genuine memory loss produces only three correct answers is smaller than 5 per cent.

SVT does not require technical facilities. All one needs is a pencil, a paper, and basic **7.51** knowledge of statistics. It is essential, though, that the correct and incorrect alternatives are first evaluated by a panel of naïve subjects. When this panel judges the incorrect alternatives as more plausible than the correct alternatives, it is possible that someone with a genuine amnesia performs below chance level. Moreover, the test can be difficult to administer where an amnesic gap is very brief. With these restrictions in mind, we would like to recommend the SVT to experts who have to examine cases in which defendants claim amnesia.[91]

(2) Self-report scales

Another way to examine claims of amnesia is provided by self-report questionnaires that **7.52** capitalize on the tendency of malingerers to exaggerate their memory complaints. A promising questionnaire is the Structured Inventory of Malingered Symptomatology (SIMS).[92] The SIMS consists of 75 true–false items that can be grouped into 5 subscales, each subscale containing 15 items. Subscales correspond to symptom domains that are sensitive to malingering and include low intelligence (LI), affective disorder (AF), neurological impairment (N), psychosis (P), and amnesic disorder (AM). Items of the subscales refer to bizarre experiences (e.g. 'at times I've been unable to remember the names or faces of close relatives so that they seem like complete strangers') or to unrealistic symptoms (e.g. 'When I can't remember something, hints do not help'). Other items explicitly allude to a certain syndrome (e.g. amnesia) in such a way that specialists recognize that highly atypical symptoms are listed (e.g. 'my past and important events became a blur to me almost overnight'). The idea is that malingerers will tend to exaggerate and in doing so, will endorse bizarre, unrealistic, and atypical symptoms.

---

[90] For a review see Bianchini, K.J., Mathias, C.W. and Greve, K.W., 'Symptom Validity Testing: A critical review' (2001) 15 *The Clinical Neuropsychologist*, 19–45.

[91] See also Jelicic, M., Merckelbach, H. and van Bergen, S., 'Symptom validity testing of feigned amnesia for a mock crime' (2004) 19 *Archives of Clinical Neuropsychology*, 525–531.

[92] Smith, G.P. and Burger, G.K., 'Detection of malingering: Validation of the Structured Inventory of Malingered Symptomatology (SIMS)' (1997) 25 *Journal of the Academy of Psychiatry and the Law*, 183–180.

7.53   So far, a number of studies have looked at the accuracy with which the SIMS detects malingered symptomatology. Although these studies came up with promising results, most of them relied on laboratory set-ups. In this type of study, undergraduate students are instructed to feign certain psychiatric symptoms in a convincing way (e.g. amnesia). Performance of these instructed malingering groups on the SIMS is then compared to the SIMS scores of control (i.e. uninstructed) groups responding honestly. It is evident that this approach is subject to a number of limitations, not the least of which is that for undergraduates instructed to feign symptoms there are hardly any risks or incentives. Nevertheless, the results of these studies are encouraging in that the SIMS appears able to identify subjects instructed to feign, say, amnesia with a high degree of precision. For example, Merckelbach and Smith[93] reported that more than 90 per cent of the subjects instructed to malinger amnesia are identified by the SIMS (sensitivity) and more than 90 per cent of the control subjects are classified by the SIMS as honest respondents (specificity).

(3) Other techniques

7.54   Traditional tests (e.g. IQ tests, memory tests, MMPI, polygraph methods) may provide useful background information in evaluating amnesia claims.[94] For example, one could rely on well-validated tests to examine whether there are indications for clear irregularities in the suspect's memory (e.g. autobiographical memories, childhood memories, new learning capacity). One could also look for a history of memory loss due to stress, alcohol, skull injury, epilepsy, or sleepwalking. Along with psychological tests, critical information can be gathered from social authorities, medical history, journal notes, legal documents, interrogation reports, and interviews with relatives, friends, and workmates. These may give important evidence about the consistency of the amnesia claim and when it was first reported. Assessment of personality traits (psychopathy, dissociative tendencies, proneness to fantasy, and suggestibility) might also provide useful information. Hypnosis is controversial and should never be employed for trial because of the risks of contaminating a person's memory.[95] Another potentially very controversial technique is that of 'symptom suggestion'.[96] Here, the suspect is provided with false characteristics of amnesia and his behaviour is then monitored for possible incorporation of the symptoms, which would be indicative of malingered amnesia.

---

[93] Merckelbach, H. and Smith, G.P., 'Diagnostic accuracy of the Structured Inventory of Malingered Symptomatology (SIMS) in detecting instructed malingering' (2003) 18 *Archives of Clinical Neuropsychology*, 145–152.

[94] For reviews see Kopelman, M.D., 'Crime and amnesia: a review' (1987) 5 *Behavioural Sciences and the Law*, 323–342; Rogers, R., *Clinical Assessment of Malingering and Deception*, New York: Guildford, 1997; Hall, H.V. and Poirier, J.G., *Detecting Malingering and Deception: Forensic Distortion Analysis*, London: CRC Press, 2000; Allen, J.J.B. and Iacono, W.G., 'Assessing the validity of amnesia in dissociative identity disorder' (2001) 7 *Psychology, Public Policy, and Law*, 311–344.

[95] Cima *et al,* (2003), cited above at n.38.   [96] Porter and Yuille, (1995), cited above at n.35.

H. Concluding Remarks

It is not uncommon that defendants claim amnesia for the crime of which they are **7.55** accused, particularly in cases of homicide where 25–45 per cent of offenders claim amnesia. In this chapter, we have presented arguments for and against the existence of such amnesias. Against the authenticity of amnesia, empirical data from interviews with homicide offenders indicate that they often have a strong motivation for feigning amnesia, and that their memory loss may possess typical features of malingered amnesia. Simulated or imagined amnesia may be at least as common as dissociative amnesia. However, unstructured clinical interviews are not a reliable way of differentiating between these types of amnesias.

On the other hand, it can pointed out that many offenders claiming amnesia report their **7.56** own offence, or fail to take measures to avoid capture. There are consistencies across their reports which are striking, and their descriptions do indeed bear some resemblances to other patients' accounts of psychological forms of amnesia in clinical circumstances. Furthermore, victims sometimes report similar amnesias, and memory errors are common in eyewitnesses; nobody disputes the motives of these parties. Also, amnesia itself only rarely has legal implications, and may be damaging to the conduct of a person's defence; it will certainly be challenged vigorously by the prosecution. Another point is that alcoholic blackouts are common in heavy drinking populations, and there is a high rate of offending and violent crime in such groups; it is not surprising that some individuals who have consumed large quantities of alcohol report amnesia for their offence. Finally, even the sceptic will not usually query the presence of amnesia in certain neurological conditions, such as epilepsy, hypoglycaemia, and somnambulism, although these can be at least as difficult to assess as the psychological forms of memory loss.

Further Reading

Baddeley, A.D., *Your Memory: A User's Guide*, London: Penguin Books, 1993.

Baddeley, A.D., Kopelman, M.D., and Wilson, B.A. (eds.), *Handbook of Memory Disorders*, 2nd Edn., Chichester: John Wiley and Sons, Ltd, 2002.

Christianson, S.-Å. and Merckelbach, H., 'Crime-related amnesia as a form of deception', in Granhag, P.A. and Strömwall, L.A. (eds.), *The detection of deception in forensic contexts*, Cambridge: Cambridge University Press, 2004, 195–225.

Kopelman, M.D., 'Crime and amnesia: a review', (1987) 5 *Behavioural Sciences and the Law*, 323–342.

Kopelman, M.D., 'Disorders of memory', (2002) 125 *Brain*, 2151–2190.

Squire, L.R. and Schacter, D.L. (eds.), *Neuropsychology of Memory*, 3rd Edn., New York: The Guildford Press, 2002.

Tysse, J.E., 'Note: The right to an imperfect trial—amnesia, malingering, and competency to stand trial', (2005) 32 *William Mitchell Law Review*, 353–387.

Sven Å. Christianson is a Professor of Psychology, Ph.D., Licenced Psychologist, and chief of the Research Unit for Forensic Psychology, at the Department of Psychology, Stockholm University, Sweden. He has authored or co-authored over one hundred papers published in peer-reviewed psychological and medical journals, and has written or edited six books regarding crime, trauma, and memory: e.g. *Handbook of emotion and memory* (1992), *Traumatic memories* (1994), *Crime and memory* (1996), *Advanced interrogation and interviewing technique* (1998). The objectives of his current research programme are to gain an understanding of the relationship between emotion and memory, while a current research focuses on victims', bystander witnesses' and offenders' memories of violent and sexual crimes. Dr Christianson is a sought-after speaker and psychological expert witness in various criminal cases.

Harald Merckelbach has a degree in Psychology. He is a full professor of Experimental Psychology at the Faculty of Psychology, Maastricht University, but also holds an honorary Psychology and Law chair at the Law School of Maastricht University. He is a dean of the Faculty of Psychology. He frequently acts as an expert witness in court cases that require expert opinions on malingering, confessions, PTSD, schizophrenia, memory loss, and/or recovered memories. Together with professors Peter van Koppen, Dick Hessing and Hans Crombag, he edited a 1200-page Dutch handbook on psychology and law. His research articles in psychology journals mainly concern memory aberrations and how they bear relevance to the domains of psychopathology (e.g. PTSS) and law (e.g. offenders who claim amnesia).

Michael Kopelman is Professor of Neuropsychiatry in the University of London (King's College London, Institute of Psychiatry), working in the South London and Maudsley NHS Trust and based at St Thomas's Hospital. He holds qualifications in neuropsychiatry and neuropsychology and, as well as being a Consultant Neuropsychiatrist, he is also a Chartered Psychologist. He is a Fellow of the Royal College of Psychiatrists and of the British Psychological Society, President of the British Neuropsychological Society, a founder member of the Memory Disorders Research Society and a member of the Society of Expert Witnesses. He has a particular interest in memory disorders, and he has published widely in the scientific and clinical literature on various forms of amnesia. His papers include reviews of crime and amnesia, and also disorders of memory. He was co-editor with Professors A D Baddeley and B A Wilson of the 2nd Edition of the *Handbook of Memory Disorders*, published in October 2002. He has appeared in criminal trials and the Court of Appeal on many occasions, and also undertakes civil cases.

Editors' Note

In a field related to that explored by Brewin in Chapter 6, claims that witnesses—often defendants—have forgotten essential detail of relevant events are common. Whilst examination of these is frequently effected most sensibly by relevance to their previous statements and other evidence in the case, this is not always possible and the evidential gaps created by such claims can present real difficulty for the purposes of the discovery of what happened or a defendant's mental state at the time of relevant events. The contents of this chapter should help investigators and lawyers to decide whether to obtain an expert report on this issue and should assist advocates and judges in steering fact finders towards informed and just decisions where a witness's or defendant's amnesia has been raised as a relevant factor.

SECTION 2

INVESTIGATIVE PERSPECTIVES

Summary

Chapter 8. 'Have you told Management about this?': Bringing Witness Interviewing into the Twenty-first Century.
Eric Shepherd and Rebecca Milne

Many interviews of vulnerable and intimidated witnesses, and key witnesses in major investigations, are, now, video- or audio-recorded and conducted by specially trained police officers. But most evidential interviews with witnesses still are not tape-recorded and in pursuit of a desired outcome too many officers interview directively, contrary to the patterned/non-directive approach of PEACE and its subsequent developments. Hence, resultant statements hinder effective investigation, expose witnesses to unjustifiable attacks on their reliability and mislead courts. Universal electronic recording is the only foolproof way to encourage and to ensure that interviewing is patterned and non-directive, thus productive of full and faithful representations of witness accounts.

Chapter 9. Investigative Interviewing with Children: Progress and Pitfalls.
Graham Davies and Helen Westcott

Techniques used by investigators for interviewing children have been significantly improved in recent years, notably through the guidance embodied in *Achieving Best Evidence*. Nonetheless, pitfalls remain if training courses offered to investigators are not taken or adequately acted upon. Talking to children in a way which produces a reliable account requires special skills and the analysis of a child's evidence needs to take account of factors which may not be applicable to an adult's. Legal advocates, judges and fact finders need to be informed about these factors and others concerning the reliability of children's evidence generally when a child is questioned during a case and decisions are made concerning the accuracy and reliability of the child's evidence.

Chapter 10. Obtaining, Recording and Admissibility of Out-of-Court Witness Statements.
Anthony Heaton-Armstrong, David Wolchover and Annabel Maxwell-Scott

The 'hearsay' provisions of the Criminal Justice Act 2003 have revolutionized the law relating to the admissibility and status of pre-testimonial statements of those who give oral evidence in court in a way which has the potential to cause fact finders to make better sense of this material. Now, all statements by witnesses, whether written or originally oral, have the potential for being used in evidence to supplement or, even when inconsistent, act as a substitute for statements made from the witness box as part of the witness's overall account of what happened. The details and implications of the new law are discussed. The importance of discovery of the circumstances in which the previous statement is said to have been made is emphasized. Failing comprehensive disclosure of these, the dangers involved in fact finders relying on previous statements are clear.

Chapter 11. Oral Confessions to Non-Investigator Witnesses.
David Wolchover and Anthony Heaton-Armstrong

In spite of the wealth of regulation concerning the obtaining of what may turn out to be incriminating statements, or confessions, by suspects to police investigators, over the centuries the courts have been increasingly ready to accept in evidence alleged confessions made to third parties. It is not, now, uncommon for a compliant prisoner to be located in close proximity to a defendant on remand in custody in the hope of obtaining a confession in what may be an otherwise weak case. In such circumstances, the safeguards afforded to a suspect, in stark contrast to those enjoyed when in police detention, are virtually non-existent. This dichotomy is explored by reference to historical development, the conflicting law and with a focus on the proceedings in *R v Michael Stone*.

Chapter 12. Interpreters and Translators in the Criminal Legal Process.
Ann Corsellis and Amanda Clement

The incidence in the use of foreign language and other interpreters and translators in legal proceedings in United Kingdom jurisdictions has risen in line with both the increase of non-English-speaking people resident here and the obtaining of testimony from people with mental or physical disorders who might previously have been considered to be incompetent. The experience of judges, practitioners, witnesses and defendants is that the quality of interpretation and translation services offered at both the investigative and the forensic stages differs very widely and is often poor. The implications (for the interests of justice) of unreliable or inaccurate interpretation or translation, especially bearing in mind the inevitable loss in value of evidence of demeanour (such as it is) when an interpreter is used, are abundantly apparent. This chapter sets out the circumstances in which interpreters or translators are required, describes and expands upon the need for best practice and the detection of and response to poor quality and makes recommendations for the necessary improvement in procedures.

Chapter 13. Witnesses who use British Sign Language.
Jim Kyle

Those who are Deaf provide a particular example of witnesses who, owing to their physical incapacity, require an interpreter. The problems associated with Deaf people who are involved in the justice system, whether as victims or witnesses, are examined and discussed through consideration of relevant history and the author's expertise. There is a significant risk of misunderstanding, especially if the quality of interpretation services offered is poor or where judges, advocates and fact finders are ill-informed concerning Deaf people and communication issues arising from the use of British Sign Language.

Chapter 14. Investigative and Evidential Applications of Forensic Speech Science.
Peter French and Philip Harrison

This chapter comprises an introduction to the principal investigative and evidential applications of forensic speech science (otherwise known as speaker profiling), forensic speaker identification and questioned utterance analysis, the core material being audio-recorded statements or conversations, typically obtained through telephone transmission or the use of covertly placed recording devices. The science of speaker profiling, by reference to e.g. age, accent and educational or social background, is defined. Also discussed are techniques used to compare a suspect's voice with that of the speaker on an audio record in order to discover whether they are the same individual and the role of the expert.

Chapter 15. Identifying the Origins of Evidential Texts.
Tim Grant

Expert linguistic evidence may be provided as to the authorship or wider origins of evidential texts. This may be particularly useful when the need arises to analyse the authenticity of what purports to be a witness's written account, said to be free from the influence of the police officer scribe who obtained and wrote it, or where an interpreter has been used in the investigative setting and the foreign-language-speaking witness's written statement in their own tongue is subsequently translated into English. It may be necessary to subject other types of text, e.g. a ransom demand or threatening letter, to linguistic analysis by an expert. The science is in its comparative infancy and the power of the linguistic expert to reach definitive conclusions is necessarily limited.

8

'HAVE YOU TOLD MANAGEMENT ABOUT THIS?': BRINGING WITNESS INTERVIEWING INTO THE TWENTY-FIRST CENTURY

Eric Shepherd and Rebecca Milne

A. Introduction

The witness[1] statement, the police officer's[2] edited representation of the witness's disclosures when interviewed, occupies a focal position in our criminal justice system. Investigating officers rely upon statements obtained by other officers, or themselves, to **8.01**

---

[1] The term 'witness' includes victim.
[2] The term 'police officer' refers to police and civilian colleagues engaged in the investigative interviewing process.

inform and to progress the investigation. For the Crown Prosecution Service (CPS)—prior to and following charging decisions—and for the defence, statements critically determine the management of the case. Similarly the judiciary rely heavily upon statements to enable them to obtain a detailed grasp of the case. Statements are very convenient. Unlike the electronic recordings of interviews (of vulnerable and intimidated witnesses required by the Youth Justice and Criminal Evidence Act 1999 and of significant witnesses in major investigations recommended by the Association of Police Officers (ACPO)),[3] the written statements of the generality of witnesses do not demand playback equipment and at any time and any where they can be read, navigated, and annotated.[4] However, since there is no recording of the actual interviewing process that gave rise to these all important statements, we all have to trust that in each case the interviewing officer did not improperly influence the witness's disclosures and that the statement as drafted by the officer gives a full and faithful representation of what the witness actually said.

8.02 From 1993 onwards most officers have attended a basic course introducing them to PEACE, the national model of investigative interviewing. (The acronym PEACE represents the stages of the interviewing process: P—Preparation and Planning; E—Engage and Explain; A—Account; C—Closure; E—Evaluate.) PEACE guides officers to engage in 'best practice' implementing a *patterned/non-directive* style of interviewing in order to maximize disclosure by a witness or a suspect. The core aim of PEACE was to replace the traditional *directive* interviewing style adopted by officers when interviewing any person.[5] Officers' prior case knowledge, preconceptions, and the outcomes desired from the interview—a confession from the suspect or a 'good' statement from a witness—meant that traditionally they did not approach the interview with an open mind. Rather they applied a *relevance filter* to disclosed detail, selectively attending to that which fitted—or better still confirmed—what was known or desired.

8.03 On the original PEACE courses officers were guided to follow a 'cognitive approach' when interviewing a witness.[6] This involved facilitating fuller disclosure by: (1) giving the witness control of the process and the content of his or her disclosures, (2) not interrupting the witness to ask questions, and (3) using specific yet simplified cognitive interviewing techniques. Regrettably those who developed PEACE did not acknowledge the cognitive interviewing origins of the 'cognitive approach'[7] and presented cognitive interviewing in an overly formalistic and inflexible manner:[8] get interviewee in context (mentally relive; edit nothing), free recall, second recall (change order of recall), third free

---

[3] ACPO (2000) *Murder Investigation Manual.*

[4] We acknowledge that often following an electronically recorded interview a written s 9/102 statement is prepared comprising the witness's factual assertions.

[5] Shepherd, E. and Milne, R., 'Full and faithful: ensuring quality practice and integrity of outcome in witness interviews', in Heaton-Armstrong A., Shepherd E. and Wolchover D. (eds.), *Analysing Witness Testimony.* Oxford: Oxford University Press, 1999.

[6] CPTU *A guide to interviewing.* Harrogate: CPTU, 1992.

[7] Fisher, R. and Geiselman, R., *Memory enhancing techniques for investigative interviewing: the Cognitive Interview,* Springfield, Ill.: Charles C. Thomas 1992.

[8] Clifford, B. and Memon, A., 'Obtaining detailed testimony: the cognitive interview', in Heaton-Armstrong A., Shepherd E. and Wolchover D. (eds.), *Analysing Witness Testimony,* Oxford: Oxford University Press 1999.

recall (change perspective), probe, review, and produce written statement. The 'cognitive approach' as originally advocated in PEACE was eventually dropped from the PEACE course curriculum.

- *Problems putting the 'cognitive approach' into practice.* PEACE was taught in a 'cascading' manner by officers who were neither sufficiently versed nor skilled in cognitive interviewing. The cognitive interview is a demanding technique requiring specialist psychological knowledge. Furthermore the constraint of course duration meant that many officers did not have an opportunity to practise the 'approach'. In the workplace many officers found the 'approach' useful, though certain elements were difficult to apply, but the issue of time taken hindered its widespread implementation.[9] The problem of time presented a paradox: clearly witnesses were disclosing in detail and at length, hence confronting the officer with practicalities of control. In the view of one observer lengthy interviews frustratingly very often produced problems: detail that did not square with that known to the officer or detail that could not be included in a 'good' statement.[10]

- *Greater training emphasis on suspect interviews.* The requirements of the CJPOA 1994 and for greater attention to pre-interview disclosure led to a reduction in time devoted to training to interview witnesses.

8.04 Research in 1998[11] indicated that officers were disappointed with witnesses because they did not disclose as much as officers believed they could. This, it was suggested, was a failure on behalf of witnesses as opposed to the interviewers themselves. It was no surprise therefore that when Clarke and Milne[12] examined tape-recordings of witness interviews they found that officers were interviewing directively. The greater part of the interview time was devoted not to finding out new information but to drafting the statement for signature by the witness.

8.05 Selected officers now attend 'specialist' *Achieving Best Evidence* (ABE) training to prepare them to interview vulnerable and intimidated witnesses.[13] A minority of officers attend Enhanced Cognitive Interview (ECI) training[14] to prepare them to interview key witnesses or to work in specialist units (e.g. child protection, sexual offence investigation). Both ABE and ECI involve extending control to the witness. Students on these courses struggle.[15] In this they join their colleagues on advanced suspect interviewing courses.

---

[9] Kebbell, M., Milne, R. and Wagstaff, G., 'The cognitive interview: a survey of its forensic effectiveness', (1997) 5 *Psychology, Crime and Law*, 101–16.

[10] Croft, S., 'Helping witnesses to remember', (1995) November, *Police*, 13–14.

[11] Kebbell, M. and Milne, R., 'Police officers' perceptions of eyewitness factors in forensic investigations', (1998) 138 *Journal of Social Psychology*, 323–30.

[12] Clarke, C. and Milne, R., *National Evaluation of the PEACE Investigative Interviewing Course* (2001) Police Research Award Scheme. Report No: PRAS/149.

[13] Home Office *Achieving Best Evidence in Criminal Proceedings: Guidance for Vulnerable or Intimidated Witnesses, including Children.* London: Home Office 2001.

[14] Milne, R., *The Enhanced Cognitive Interview: A Step-by-Step Guide.* Unpublished Training Document 2004.

[15] Griffiths, A. and Milne, R., 'Will it all end in tiers: Police interviews with suspects in Britain', in T. Williamson. (ed.), *Investigative interviewing: Rights, research, regulation*, Cullompton: Willan Publishing 2005.

Time has to be spent engaging in remedial work because the entirety of their experience has been interviewing witnesses directively to achieve the officer's ends, in particular a written report. We have to take them back to conversational basics, using exercises to develop intent listening skills, working memory and basic questioning (i.e. asking open-ended questions).[16] However training can only raise awareness and point the way. The absence of personal and professional commitment to develop these skills in the workplace necessarily gives rise to the behaviours described by Davies and Westcott in Chapter 9.

8.06 Between us we have some forty years of experience working with the police service as operational and training consultants. Increasingly officers with whom we work ask whether we have told management about the matters that we bring to their attention concerning quality interviewing and quality outcomes. In this chapter we seek to speak to police and CPS as well as the judiciary. First we explain why witnesses disclose much less than they could when questioned, and how police officers' directive interviewing actually makes the problem worse, paradoxically helping deceivers to achieve their aim. We then summarize how appropriate interviewing overcomes these problems, securing fuller disclosure and a comprehensive grasp of fine-grain detail. We turn to why officers would not see it as sensible to interview in this way, preferring to engage in directive interviewing. We argue yet again that recording of all witness interviewing is the only way to stop dysfunctional behaviour and describe readily available inexpensive equipment options. We conclude with a summary and a request.

B. The Disposition not to Disclose Too Much

(1) 'Pitch', powerful people and the 'less is best' strategy

8.07 When conversing with another person we make decisions about how we will 'pitch' what we say—about the information we will disclose and how we will say it. We devote some thought to conversing in a way that increases the likelihood of the person arriving at a positive view of us and of letting us know that we have met that person's expectations. If the person arrives at a neutral view of us—neither positive nor negative—we might not be happy but we are usually able to cope. If we disclose details that are unwanted by the person and converse in a way that the person considers to be inappropriate, we will have 'pitched' things incorrectly. The person is highly likely to derive a negative view of us.[17]

8.08 From early childhood onward we learn that there are particular individuals whose views of us—and of how we 'pitch' things in conversation—matter much more. These are *powerful people*: parents, doctors, teachers, and the like. Their judgement and feedback really matter. They are usually very busy, do not have much time to devote to conversing

---

[16] For similar problems in Australia, see Wright, R. and Powell, M.B., 'Investigative interviewers' perceptions of their difficulty in adhering to open-ended questions with child witnesses', *International Journal of Police Science and Management* (in press).

[17] Shepherd, E., *Investigative Interviewing: the Conversation Management Approach*, Oxford: Oxford University Press (forthcoming).

with us, and want to find out specific information. They behave in a predictable way that communicates and confirms their power. They exercise significant, all too frequently excessive, control over the conversation to achieve their purpose, determining the topics and the progression of topics across the conversation. They do most of the talking: dominating the talking turn and the talking time. The way they converse indicates they are either too busy to pay, or are not interested in paying, full attention to what we say. To varying degrees they are *non-attenders*, engaged in relevance filtering of what we say. They skim our disclosures, selecting detail that they think is relevant, compressing some of this, and ignoring the greater part of what we say that does not 'fit'.[18]

Powerful people are by disposition *assumers*. They believe in great measure that they **8.09** already know, or assume they know, all that is necessary for them to find out from us and all that we are able to contribute. Because they already know the answers their questions are predominantly suggestive—leading, confirmatory, option, open-closed combin- ation—pointing us to the desired answer or restricting the scope of our reply to a confirmation of what is inside their heads. Through their control of topics, domination of the talking turn, and their suggestive questions they drive the conversation, determin- ing what gets talked about, when, for how long, and in what level of detail. Some powerful people allow their assumptions to run riot. They believe they know what we are in the process of saying or are about to say. They take the talking turn away from us finishing our utterances or, even more bizarrely, answering their own questions or speaking for us saying something like '*I know what you . . .*'.[19]

Early on in life we learn a safe '*less is best*' strategy for 'pitching' our conversations with **8.10** powerful people in order to gain their approval. If we do not disclose too much detail this occupies much less of that person's time than if we disclosed more, if not all that we could. If initially we say much less than we could say—giving a 'thin' account or descrip- tion—this allows the powerful person to come in much sooner to select topics that suit his or her notions of 'relevance' and to achieve his or her 'agenda', to use suggestive questions to determine the content of responses and to dictate what topics will be covered, for how long, and in what depth and to what outcome. 'Less is best' continues to succeed as a strategy for gaining approval if we are submissive and compliant, restrict- ing what we say spontaneously, do not seek to take the talking turn, and give responses that are not too full, accepting and endorsing the content of the powerful person's questions. At the conclusion of the conversation it is 'mission accomplished' by both parties. The powerful person is happy or at least satisfied because he or she has achieved all, or an acceptable number of, his or her objectives and has been proved right. We feel happy or at least satisfied because the powerful person's reactions and responses evince that he or she feels positively—or at least not negatively—about what we have said and about us.

Even before we enter the education system the 'less is best' strategy is well established **8.11** within us. As we progress through school, adolescence and into adulthood we generalize

---

[18] Ibid.   [19] Ibid.

it to any encounter with someone who has the power to reward or punish us socially, or to give or withhold something that we want.

(2) When 'less is best' and excessively controlling behaviour meet in the witness interview

8.12 Police officers are, of course, powerful people. When witnesses implement the 'less is best' strategy, and then go along with a police officer's controlling behaviour in order to gain his or her approval they are actually being to a lesser or greater degree compliant and suggestible in the manner described by Gudjonsson in Chapter 4. A witness being interviewed by a police officer exercising excessive control is an excellent example of the disadvantages for both when one individual follows the 'less is best' strategy and the other exercises excessive control over the conversation.

(i) What the witness wanted, or was willing, to disclose remains undisclosed

8.13 The witness might have wanted—or would have been willing—to say much more. However the 'less is best' strategy is extremely pervasive. It is risky to abandon the strategy. Fear of negative feedback from the police officer inhibits fuller disclosure. A police officer who is excessively controlling will therefore never find out very much—if anything—'new' beyond what he or she already knew, or assumed he or she knew or believed to be the case, before the interview ever took place. The witness is left feeling frustrated and alienated. Some officers might feel pleased that they have obtained sufficient information to draft a 'good' statement. The findings of Kebbell and Milne[20] suggest that officers do sense that the witness could have said much more but they believe that they nonetheless have enough detail to generate a 'good enough' statement.[21]

(ii) Excessively controlling behaviour assists the deceiver

8.14 People seek to deceive for all manner of reasons. Witnesses are no exception. There is a common misconception in the population that deception is an active process that involves disclosing a narrative, explanation or description woven from untruthful detail: real lies—'porkies' (from the rhyming slang 'porky pies'). This is extremely odd because *active lying* is the least common way in which people lie. This is because it takes mental effort to put together and to remember the false detail.[22]

8.15 The most common form of deception is *passive lying*: simply not mentioning something at all either spontaneously or in reply to a question. Evasion—avoiding not saying—is very common because it involves no effort. People also seek to deceive by saying things non-specifically—vaguely or ambiguously. This takes some mental effort, but not a lot.

8.16 Like all powerful people, police officers in pursuit of their agendas actually help the deceiver. If they feel they are under time pressure their assistance is even greater. Because they tightly control the topics, skim what the deceptive witness is saying, relevance filter and delete a very great deal—or even most—of the detail that does not 'fit' their

---

[20] Cited above at n.11.   [21] Shepherd and Milne, cited above at n.5.

[22] Ekman, P., *Telling lies: Clues to deceit in the marketplace, politics and marriage*, New York: Norton (1985/2001).

preconceptions they fail to detect passive deception: what the witness deliberately did not say at all!

Similarly preconceptions (especially when combined with perceived time pressure) set **8.17** police officers up to respond inappropriately to non-specific disclosure. Common sense argues that they should probe a witness's vagueness or ambiguity, asking for expansion or explanation. Yet police officers act counter to common sense. They do not stop to think. They make assumptions, unconsciously translating the non-specific into a specific that 'fits' their prior knowledge, preconceptions, and the 'agenda' that they have to fulfil.

Hence witnesses who seek to deceive by giving thin, under-detailed, non-specific narra- **8.18** tives, explanations, and descriptions into which they weave very little actual untruth, are not only indistinguishable from truthful witnesses who are following the 'less is best' strategy but are assisted in their deception by the police officer's behaviour.

C. Maximizing Spontaneous Disclosure and Comprehensively Capturing Detail

(1) The issue of control

An interview is a conversation with a purpose. The interviewer—the powerful person— **8.19** initiates the encounter in order to achieve one or more explicit or implicit purpose(s). Because interviewers converse as a 'job of work' there is a tendency to forget that the interviewee has a perspective on the exchange. The interviewee may not necessarily be there through choice, and may be conversing to some purpose intended prior to the meeting or in response to the interviewer's conduct, the course, and the content of the exchange. The interviewer's *conversation management*—how he or she best exercises control over the interviewee's participation and disclosure of detail to achieve the interviewer's purpose(s)—is a vital, but wholly misunderstood, issue. The origins of conversation management stem from the first author's work in the clinical psychotherapy context working with traumatized and resistant individuals. However the approach was advanced as a framework for managing *any* interview in any context.[23,24] The similarity noted by Wilson and Powell of the protocols for the *Memorandum of Good Practice* (the forerunner to the Phased Interview of ABE), the Stepwise Interview and the Cognitive Interview/ Enhanced Cognitive Interview reflect the fact that they contain the same conversation management ingredients.[25]

Directive interviewing enables the officer to retain tight control of the interview but at **8.20** some cost. The officer may well have kept the duration within time constraints and secured the necessary detail for a 'good enough' if not 'good' statement. But the whole exercise constitutes an inherently self-defeating exercise if detail that the witness could have disclosed, had they been interviewed appropriately, remains unsaid. The witness,

---

[23] Shepherd, E., 'The conversational core of policing', (1986) *Policing*, vol. 2, 294–303.
[24] Shepherd, *Investigative Interviewing*, cited above at n.17.
[25] Wilson, C. and Powell, M., *A guide to interviewing children*, Crows Nest NSW: Allen and Unwin 2001.

the police officer, colleagues involved in the investigation, everyone in the criminal justice system—all lose. Only the deceptive witness wins because his or her evasion, non-specificity and thin 'real' lies go undetected.

8.21 Given the shortcomings of directive interviewing the introductory PEACE course for new officers now guides them to conduct a Free Recall Interview of the witness.[26] An essential precondition to adopting this approach is an acceptable level of basic conversational skill, and a clear understanding that skilled conversationalists actually create openings for the other person to talk. They consciously relinquish or forgo the 'talking turn' so that the other person has maximum opportunity and time to talk on matters. Conversation management takes matters forward to a higher level of performance. The officer uses a range of techniques to manage the conversation as an event and as a process. From the outset and continuously thereafter the officer works at creating a *working relationship* with the witness that facilitates maximum spontaneous disclosure from the witness and facilitates maximum capture and comprehension of fine-grain detail by the officer. Comprehensive grasp of fine-grain detail enables rapid identification of anomalies (oddities) and areas that require timely probing or investigation beyond the confines of the interview.

(2) Creating a working relationship

8.22 Skilful conversation management is founded upon reflective practice: thinking about one's conduct and its effects on the interviewee before, during, and after the interview.[27] Fundamental is the officer signalling respect by the 'way' he or she talks to the witness: talking 'across' as equals rather than 'down'. The reality of this respect is reinforced, and empathy communicated, by being open about the joint task that faces the officer and the witness. If the officer shares with the witness an understanding of goals and respective responsibilities to achieve these, this mapping out of the working relationship is real evidence of the officer's empathy and respect for the witness. This is true rapport.

8.23 Key to creating and sustaining rapport is the content of the *explanation* in the Engage and Explain phase. This needs to overcome the 'guessing game': anxiety and apprehension experienced when a witness does not know, and is trying to work out, what it is 'all about', what is to come, what the officer wants and expects of the witness, and what the witness can expect of the officer.

- *The reason for the interview*: The 'why'.
- *The route map*: the 'what': giving the witness a 'map' of the interview stages.
- *The routines*: the 'how': the way in which the officer will capture and refer to information.
- *The expectations*: this is vital information on the 'how' of the interview in terms of straightforward *ground rules* for working together to ensure maximum disclosure and maximum grasp of detail:

---

[26] *Practical Guide to Investigative Interviewing. Tier 1.* (August 2003). Centrex (Central Police Training and Development Authority).

[27] Schon, D., *The Reflective Practitioner.* New York: Norton 1983.

- *The 'cannot be too much detail' ground rule*: this ground rule common to all interview protocols lets the witness know that: this is a conversation where the 'less is best' strategy does not apply; the officer really has an open mind; the officer is interested in learning as much as possible about what the witness has to say; and the witness should not assume the officer knows anything. For example:

  It's about detail . . . There can't be too much detail . . . Don't think I already know something . . . for instance what you have said to others before now . . . When you describe something, it will help you if you get a picture in your mind's eye of what it is that you're describing . . . People often find that it helps to close our eyes when trying to get a picture in their mind's eye . . .

- *The 'taking time' ground rule*: this ground rule, again common to all interview protocols, greatly increases the witness's potential to retrieve and to image detail within working memory, and to report detail without being pressured by immediate questions. For example:

  There's no rush . . . it's not a race . . . Take your time . . . This will give you plenty of time to remember and to think about the little bits of detail we need . . . When you've stopped talking . . . I won't rush in to ask you questions . . . Think about things before you talk . . . and after you've stopped talking . . .

These ground rules must be checked back with the witness, to establish comprehension **8.24** and 'buy in'. If the witness gives a 'thin' account this could be entirely due to innocent failure to grasp that the 'less is best' strategy does not apply in this conversation. Alternatively it could be a would-be deceiver evading and being non-specific. Taking the witness through the ground rules again, checking grasp and getting 'buy in' before requesting a second attempt assists the genuine and makes life very difficult for the deceiver.

(3) Information processing techniques integral to interviewing

A witness who 'buys in' to disclosing in detail poses the officer with a substantial infor- **8.25** mation processing task. A number of techniques enable the officer to capture, retain and respond to the fine-grain detail disclosed by the witness.

- *Imaging.* In everyday conversation most people just hear words. They do not create mental images of the descriptions, events, and episodes from the verbal information given to them. Creating an image from the incoming detail means devoting just that much more conscious attention than one would normally, thus increasing the potential for its retention in working memory and subsequent consolidation when revisited across the interview.

  We were all imagers as young children. As people acquire language many lose the facility to create images. Fortunately practice in consciously attending to the task of imaging helps most people to recapture this lost ability. A few have to work hard. Imaging in a conversation requires us to be in the listening turn and paying attention. Individuals who would rather talk than listen, who are overly concerned with their 'agenda', have to work hard overcoming these motivational blocks!

- *'Mental echoing'*. Some descriptive detail is difficult to image, e.g. names, locations, ages. The simple act of silently saying the detail to oneself—'mentally echoing'—devotes a fraction more conscious attention, increasing the potential for consolidation of this detail in memory. In effect, the officer creates a sound image in his (or her) 'mind's ear':

Witness: '*We left Northolt around 10-ish . . .*' Officer silently says (mentally echoes) '*Northolt*'.

- *Guggling.* When talking people use vocal stress to put to foreground and to direct the listener's attention to the key 'ideas' in what they are saying. 'Guggles' are movements of the head and sounds (e.g. '*uh-huh*') made to indicate that we are following what is being said: we have identified the key idea. As with imaging, the fraction of extra attention used in consciously spotting the key 'idea' and physically marking this with a guggle, assists holding this detail in working memory.

- *SE3R.* This method[28] incorporates those described above together with a format and notation technique that enables a secure memory of material without conscious effort, the rapid comprehensive capture of fine-grain detail, and the rapid identification of anomaly—oddities—and areas that require probing, i.e. a request for expansion and explanation.[29]

(4) Developing conversation management in the police service

(i) Taking PEACE forward

8.26 Awareness of the essential ingredients of interviewing and the information processing techniques has developed with:

- the introduction of a five-tier developmental approach to investigative interviewing within the PEACE model: Tier 1—new police officers; Tier 2—officers investigating volume crime and crime of intermediate level seriousness; Tier 3—advanced/specialist investigative interviewers (including officers trained in ECI and those conducting more demanding ABE interviews); Tier 4—interview supervision; Tier 5—interview adviser to an SIO in a major investigation;[30]
- training selected officers to conduct ABE interviews, and
- training selected officers in ECI.

(ii) Techniques for communicating experience non-verbally

8.27 Some experience is particularly difficult, if not impossible, for a witness to describe verbally either due to lack of vocabulary, or because words temporarily fail the witness at the time of wanting to disclose. Some individuals have markedly limited verbal ability due to educational problems, immaturity or intellectual disadvantage. Finally there is the barrier of the officer and witness having different languages, and interpreters whose ability to interpret is restricted.

---

[28] Shepherd, E., *SE3R: A resource book*, East Hendred: Forensic Solutions 2004.
[29] Shepherd, E. and Mortimer, A., 'Identifying anomaly in evidential text', in Heaton-Armstrong A., Shepherd E. and Wolchover D. (eds.), *Analysing Witness Testimony*, Oxford: Oxford University Press 1999.
[30] Griffiths and Milne, cited above at n.15.

Three techniques enable a witness to describe his or her experience non-verbally. All have **8.28** the potential, while the witness is engaged in them, to trigger further spontaneous verbal disclosure.

Illustrator representation   Illustrators are movements of a finger/fingers, hand or hands **8.29** that an individual can use to 'draw' or to indicate in space—to illustrate—shape, direction, size, route, trajectory, layout, and the like. We illustrate in this manner in our everyday lives and find no difficulty representing our visual experience. Using simple instructions, where necessary expanded by a demonstration, an officer can obtain illustrator representations from a witness. The officer can commit the image to memory or make a quick sketch.

Of course if the officer knows the object or location then an initial illustration of the **8.30** witness's non-verbal experience is instantly validated. If the officer does not have this knowledge the 'validity' of the non-verbal description can be established by a second request for illustration later in the interview.

Enactment   The officer requests the witness to demonstrate detail physically, using **8.31** himself or herself, the interviewing officer or anyone else available (e.g. another officer, relative, or another third party). Enactment enables the witness to show relative positioning, a hold, a movement, an action or reaction and the like. Of course this technique must only be used within common sense and ethical constraints, i.e. it would be bizarre to invite a victim to enact an act of gross indecency.

Enhanced drawing   Drawings are of enormous investigative and evidential value. They **8.32** are, in effect, a variation on context reinstatement and therefore assist greatly the enhancement of memory. When witnesses draw they commonly talk aloud: the act of drawing triggers them to describe detail and experience that they could never include in the drawing, not least because it might be another sensory modality (e.g. smell) or impossible to draw given the constraints of the drawing (e.g. *'it was rough at the corner . . . zigzag pattern . . . lots of holes in it'*). In addition people typically engage in what is called *commentary*, making asides (e.g. *'I was panicking and trying to keep my eyes shut at this point . . .'*) or observations about the process of describing (e.g. *'I'm not too clear about this . . .'*) and the focus of attention (e.g. *'this was in bright light, I could see everything about this bit . . .'*).

However there are potential problems. The request to draw often provokes anxiety or a **8.33** sense of inadequacy: *'oh, I'm not very good at drawing'*. The witness may start a drawing that is very small, making it difficult for the witness to insert critical detail or for anyone examining the drawing to make sense of tiny or indistinct detail. It is also no use asking some witnesses to label or to annotate their drawing, for example very young witnesses, those with learning difficulties, those who are illiterate, or who are extremely embarrassed about inability to spell. Furthermore because conventional drawing is done using one colour those examining the drawing later have no means of knowing which detail was drawn initially upon request and which was added subsequently in response to probing.

Enhanced drawing involves particular elements to overcome these problems. **8.34**

- *Simple explanation of expectations.* Consistent with the interview protocols referred to earlier the officer works to overcome the individual's performance anxiety, explaining that it is a tool to assist memory. The explanation guides the individual to use all of the paper, and to talk out loud while drawing (*'as you draw just say what comes into your mind ... Tell me what you are thinking about ... Talk me through what you are drawing'*).

- *In parallel the officer creates an annotated duplicate drawing ('manual photocopy') of what the witness is drawing.* The officer notes whatever the witness says (e.g. experience reported in a different modality, detail that it is impossible to draw, commentary), to annotate points for subsequent probing, and to label detail that the witness for whatever reason does not.

- *Parallel use of pens of different colours to signify the stage at which detail was drawn.* Both the witness and the officer simultaneously use pens whose ink colours follow the standard SE3R colour sequence:[31] *black*—original spontaneous detail; *blue*—requested further detail; *red*—additional detail requested later in the interview.

D. Why Directive Interviewing of Witnesses Remains the 'Norm'

8.35 Throughout the criminal justice process great reliance is placed upon the content of witness statements. Common sense argues that officers should interview every witness in a manner that maximizes spontaneous disclosure, makes life difficult for the would-be deceiver, and enables the officer to secure a comprehensive grasp of detail essential to the creation of a full statement, faithful to the witness's account.

8.36 Why would officers feel that it is common sense to interview directively and to generate statements of lesser, even questionable, content? Why would they feel it foolish to act otherwise? The explanation lies in the fact that the police service is a 'closed' institution. Hyman[32] observed that in such institutions people do indeed act in a manner which to external observers is clearly stupid but which is 'right' because it delivers benefits to the individual and those who manage workflow and the workforce.

(1) Directive interviewing reduces anxiety

8.37 Conversation is an inherently anxiety-inducing activity because of the potential to lose control of what gets said by the other person when we relinquish the talking turn. Posing an *open-ended* question or raising a topic then pausing exercises minimal control over the content and duration of the other person's response. In contrast *direct* or *specific* probing questions—*who, what, where*, and *when*—reduce the stress because they determine the focus of the person's response. Responses to these questions imply lesser mental demand on the officer than those to open questions. *Closed confirmatory*—yes/no—questions and

---

[31] Shepherd, cited above at n. 28.
[32] Hyman, R., 'Why and when are smart people stupid?', in R. Sternberg (ed.), *Why smart people can be so stupid*, New Haven, Conn: Yale University Press, 2002.

suggestive questions (leading and option) are extremely directive, generating responses that make no mental demand.[33]

In the unmonitored world of witness interviewing, officers engage in 'question-answer' exchanges, using directive questions to keep their anxiety to a minimum.[34] Echo probing, minimal prompts—'*and*...', '*then*...', '*so*...', verbal guggles (e.g. '*uh-huh*') and non-verbal guggles (a nod of the head)—and a questioning 'look' are all rare because they exercise no control. Officers are not convinced of the 'power of the pause' brought to their attention on the PEACE course as a means of expending no effort to induce the other person to say something. The anxious officer construes remaining silent as giving control to the witness and losing control of what gets said. Better to have no pauses: when a silence appears the wise thing to do is to 'fill the pause', i.e. to talk immediately. Paradoxically 'filling the pause' puts conversational pressure on the officer: to think of something to say next. Officers frequently fill the pause with another question, creating a confusing sequence of multiple questions. The witness who really wanted to say something is alienated. 'Filling the pause' helps the officer get the information wanted in the first place[35] but also helps the deceptive, who really want to say as little as possible spontaneously. **8.38**

(2) The assumption that observance of procedure constitutes competent practice

Across the rank, role and seniority spectrum, managers and the managed in the police service hold and act upon an entrenched assumption: being told 'how' to do something in the training context translates immediately into competent practice in the workplace. Of course this is a convenient but nonsensical assumption. Viewed simplistically PEACE is a series of explicit stages. In the case of unmonitored witness interviewing, so long as the stage has been gone through, neither officers nor their managers need to concern themselves about actual performance. **8.39**

(3) The disinclination to improve quality through reflection

The police service is a pragmatic profession. The culture—how people think, talk about, value, and engage in work—is action-orientated. It is not reflective. Hence the invitation to 'think quality'—in respect of interviewing performance, the construction and content of statements, and the witness's experience of contributing to the criminal justice process—is entirely alien. Thinking about what you have done and how you have done it makes no sense because 'what's done is done'. Looking over things that cannot be changed takes up valuable time that could more usefully be used doing something else more productive. **8.40**

Once officers have passed through the early stages of being a probationer/recruit they **8.41**

---

[33] Powell, M. and Snow, P., 'A guide to questioning children during the free-narrative phase of an interview about abuse'. *Australian Psychologist* (in press).

[34] Shepherd, E., 'Resistance in interviews: the contribution of police perceptions and behaviour', in E. Shepherd (ed.), *Aspects of police interviewing. Issues in Criminological and Legal Psychology, No 18.* Leicester: British Psychological Society, 1993.

[35] Clarke and Milne, cited above at n.12.

operate without formal scrutiny. For the rest of their careers the service leaves it up to the officer to be, in effect, the sole arbiter of the appropriateness of his or her performance. The 'informal code' of policing requires officers not to criticize the performance of others: nor must they tell management of another officer's shortcomings.[36] Officers who are poor or inappropriate performers typically know that this is the case. They become well known to colleagues, supervisors, and managers. It is just that nothing is done by anybody to change matters.

8.42 PEACE has attempted to change thinking. During the Evaluate stage it guides officers to reflect on their performance after the interview.[37] In the case of a suspect interview, or a 'specialist' witness interview (e.g. ABE or ECI) there is often an electronic record that can be examined. Indeed reflecting on the recording makes absolute sense particularly where the interview is a potential cause for concern. Recording is typically checked for observance of 'legal requirements' and for key evidential content, e.g. to prepare a s 9/102 statement, if required. Relatively few officers examine the recording with a view to developing their interviewing practice however, e.g. to identify points where their conduct appeared to influence the interviewee's disclosures and behaviour, and then to consider other ways things could have been done.

(4) The disinclination to supervise performance

8.43 There is a universal axiom that applies to the world of work whatever the context: if a job is not worth supervising it does not matter how that job is done. If management does not consider it worth checking performance why should the individual bother to think twice about what he or she did or the quality of the outcome? Supervision is essential to ensuring consistent, quality performance through monitoring—quality control and quality assurance—and mentoring the individual. Common sense argues that to perform these functions a supervisor must be motivated to do so, and have the requisite knowledge and be a competent performer of the observed behaviours.

8.44 Stockdale warned that there was no appetite to supervise interviewing practice.[38] The original PEACE package designed for supervisors never lifted off.[39] Arguably it was unrealistic to expect supervisors to mentor and to give feedback on officers' performances based on a compressed introduction to PEACE and a checklist of what to look for. Tellingly it was never resolved what supervisors should do if, when they reviewed a suspect interview, it emerged that the officer had breached PACE or had otherwise behaved inappropriately.

8.45 Tier 4 (supervisor) courses have yet to be developed and fully delivered across the country. Supervision is taking place, but unevenly and very infrequently. For selected officers (e.g. those following a professional development programme) a supervisor can 'dip

---

[36] Roberg, R. and Kuykendall, J., *Police organisation and management behaviour: theory and processes*, Pacific Grove, Cal: Brooks-Cole, 1990.

[37] Centrex, *Practical Guide to Investigative Interviewing*, cited above at n. 26.

[38] Stockdale, J., *Management and supervision of police interviews*, Police Research Series:Paper No. 5. London: Home Office, 1993.

[39] CPTU, *Developing interview skills*, Harrogate: CPTU, 1994.

sample' PACE interviews of suspects for review and discussion. Similar supervision of witness interviews does not happen. There are often no recordings and there is insufficient supervisory resource to accompany officers when they interview. Indeed there is, astonishingly, no standard assessment tool. Primarily assessment still remains a matter of opinion, emerging as a matter of interviewee ability to disclose rather than interviewer's ability to facilitate disclosure.

A recording would confirm what is already known by supervisors and by everyone else— **8.46** police managers, officers, and the CPS—and what the research of Clarke and Milne[40] confirmed. Officers are apt to interview witnesses in ways that are wholly improper and ineffective.

(5) The value attached to consistent and seamless accounts

There is a widespread belief that if a witness discloses detail that does not accord with **8.47** other information known to the police, this risks undermining the status and worth of the information as well as the witness's reliability. This is a reflection of the stereotypical thinking of lay people that if two or more people say the same thing it must be true and confers greater credibility on each individual.[41] A moment's thought will reveal that this is a nonsensical stereotype, but one which assists two or more liars giving the same account to be deemed to be telling the truth. The implications of the stereotype in the police context are great. In a run of witness interviews giving latitude to the second and subsequently interviewed witnesses to disclose as much detail as possible risks the emergence of detail that is inconsistent—does not fit or marry up—with the 'facts' disclosed by the first witness. It makes pragmatic sense to police officers to interview directively to enable the creation of statements whose content converges with that within the first witness's statement and is consistent with the officer's case theory and hypotheses.

Deliberately influencing and shaping the responses of a second and any subsequent **8.48** witness to confirm those of the first witness is dysfunctional. The officer is denying the emergence of evidence that could be of vital importance or contaminating witnesses' evidence to achieve consensus. However police officers seem to have compartmentalized thinking concerning contamination. The first officer attending a crime scene knows to instruct witnesses not to discuss matters with each other while waiting to give an account to a police officer. Outside this context officers know the 'system' works differently. Where two or more police officers are witnesses *R v Bass*[42] gives them licence to engage in collaborative recall to create a seamless script which they use to draft separate statements saying the same thing. So it should come as no surprise that officers have no qualms about shaping witnesses to say the same thing.

This common sense view however is at odds with what psychologists know about how human memory works. Due to the fact that the brain has a limited processing capacity

---

[40] Clarke and Milne, cited above at n.12.
[41] Wagenaar, W., van Koppen, P., and Crombag, H., *Anchored narratives: the psychology of criminal evidence*, Hemel Hempstead: Harvester Wheatsheaf, 1993.
[42] *R v Bass* [1953] 1 QB, 680–7.

and there is too much information in our environment to process at any one time, our perceptual processes subconsciously use selective attention to filter out what they deem as irrelevant in the environment. Thus, if there are five different witnesses to an event it should be no surprise that the five different versions of the event will emerge due to individual differences.

(6) No time, no ownership

8.49 Over the last decade the process of investigating has been divided into functional steps. Those who respond to a reported incident do the initial 'finding out', take first accounts from witnesses, arrest and place the suspect before the custody officer to be detained, interview witnesses to create statements, complete a crime report, and prepare a handover note. The entirety constitutes a 'package' that is picked up by the next link in the investigative chain: the investigating officer.

8.50 It is understandable that those attending incidents perceive that what matters is rapidity of response—being a firefighter—and rapid turn-around of work, creating a 'package' as quickly as possible. They soon work out that it is quantity—amount of work done—rather than quality of work done that matters. It does not matter how well or poorly they do their job because they have no subsequent involvement in the progress of the investigation. If they had 'ownership' of the case, i.e. they were responsible for subsequent investigative action including interviewing of the suspect, they might worry more about the way they interviewed witnesses, what they did and how they did it.

8.51 Investigating officers who inherit 'packages' bemoan the fact that statements are poor and lack content, and there are no drawings of key locations made either by officers attending or requested from witnesses. Supervisors also comment on the decline of quality in statements, as do officers in Administration of Justice Units who prepare files for court. Everyone knows that poor witness interviewing and poor statement generation hinders and even sabotages effective investigation, destines a case to fail at court, produces victims and witnesses who lose faith in the police service, and results in miscarriages of justice.[43] However, given the way the investigation process is divided up, and that there is no audit trail—no recording of what goes on when witnesses are interviewed—and given the 'informal code', no-one knows how management could be prevailed upon to change matters. This is the 'reality' of front-line policing.

8.52 These attitudes have a corrosive effect upon all involved in the investigative process. When we contribute to Tier 2 (basic detective) courses, and work to develop quality investigation and investigative interviewing we are invited to 'get real' and to recognize that students' lives are about 'quantity not quality'. Certainly they would like to do a good job interviewing witnesses but the 'job' (the police service) won't let them. If their supervising officer does let them own the case and there is no 'comeback' whether they

---

[43] Savage, S. and Milne, R. (forthcoming), 'Miscarriages of justice—the role of the investigative process' in Newburn, T. Williamson T. and Wright A. (eds.), *Handbook of criminal investigation*, Cullompton: Willan Publishing.

do a poor or a good job, why should they bother doing anything other than a rushed, 'near enough' job?

(7) Inappropriate messages from the judiciary and the CPS

All too often judges complain about statements that contain too much detail! Clearly **8.53** they want things to be within their 'comfort zone'. Their views necessarily can impact upon the local CPS. Hence we know of instances where the CPS tries to pre-empt matters by calling upon officers not to include too much detail in witness statements. Understandably these messages dishearten officers who still want—and are trying—to do a good job. They can be forgiven for their reaction: 'If the judges and the CPS don't want us to give a full and faithful account of the witness's disclosures why should we bother to do anything other than give them statements with the minimum detail?'

E. Setting Officers Free to Conduct Quality Witness Interviews

It is no coincidence that a significant trigger to the emergence of PEACE was the **8.54** widespread introduction of tape recording in the late-1980s and courts listening to tape-recordings. Technology forced the police service to face up to the realities of poor, inappropriate and improper suspect interviewing.

In *Analysing Witness Testimony* we pointed out that PEACE recommended that witness **8.55** interviews be recorded where this was considered appropriate. We indicated that this invitation had been steadfastly ignored and urged the service to move to recording all witness interviews. In due course recording will be introduced for witnesses within the ambit of ABE and the ACPO policy on significant witnesses. Interviewing of the generality of witnesses has continued to be a closed, unrecorded, unmonitored, unsupervised world where the officer is left to be sole arbiter of the worth of what he or she is doing and the statements they produce.

Recording is so obviously the key. Without an official requirement to record their inter- **8.56** views officers will continue to interview witnesses in ways that would render a suspect interview inadmissible. So long as there is no record of their behaviour officers cannot engage in reflective practice to develop their professional skills: reviewing their behaviour, its effects, and alternative ways of doing things. Nor can supervisors work with them to foster and sustain skilled practice. Nor can the CPS, the defence, the judiciary and triers of fact assess the impact of the officer's behaviour upon the witness's disclosures, or draw conclusions about the witness's behaviour in terms of acquiescence, compliance and suggestibility.

Recording of vulnerable and intimidated witnesses and key witnesses in major enquiries **8.57** has begun to liberate the interviewing officer. Things are not perfect but with recordings officers, supervisors, and training and operational consultants such as ourselves can do something to improve practice. Without these recordings nothing could be done to develop the skills of creating a working agreement, using techniques to maximize spontaneous disclosure, and techniques to capture maximum detail.

Very few of the generality of witnesses attend the police station. Interview rooms with **8.58** dual tape machines are at a premium, these being taken up with interviewing suspects. Within any force there are bulky, portable PACE dual tape machines, similar to those used in interview rooms. Few officers know of the existence of these machines, where they can be obtained, or want to stand out as taking the initiative by asking to take a machine for use on a home visit. However the world has moved on from these bulky, unused machines. A range of equipment options is available for police managers to consider.

(1) Hand-held tape recorders

8.59 These can be bought in the high street for less than £5. Bulk purchase would bring the unit price down dramatically. There are plenty of tapes in police stations since these are used for suspect interviews.

8.60 There would be no problem of tape security. Every tape has an embossed batch number and the witness could be invited to sign the paper inset panel on both sides of the cassette. (As an aside, in reality it is virtually impossible to tamper with an audio recording without sophisticated equipment and spectroscopic analysis by a forensic linguist, such as our colleagues French and Harrison in this volume, would readily reveal tampering.)

8.61 The recording could proceed as the officer contemporaneously used SE3R, obtained illustrator representations, invited enactments, and obtained enhanced drawings. At different stages in the interview (e.g. start of the first account, start of probing, start of checking back) and at key points within these stages (e.g. a significant disclosure, the creation of an illustrator representation) the officer can make a note of the time-elapsed or trip meter reading. This detail enables rapid navigation of the recording after the interview, assisting checking of the accuracy of detail captured using the comprehensive capture techniques described below.

8.62 Some might argue that hand-held recorders are bulky and tapes similarly so. However, officers could do the same as we do: put them in an easily carried small bag (about the size of a small toilet bag).

(2) Digital recorders

8.63 These are much smaller than hand-held tape recorders, some very small indeed. There are no tapes. Several hours of recording can be made on a standard memory card. Digital recorders are more expensive but again prices are falling dramatically, and bulk purchase would bring the unit price down substantially.

8.64 Digital recording has a very significant advantage over tape recording. The recording can be uploaded onto a computer as a .WAV file, making it very easy indeed to replay and to navigate from one section to another. Also .WAV files can be transmitted immediately via e-mail as an attachment, or other media (on a CD or DVD).

(3) PC tablets

8.65 We see these ultimately becoming the way ahead for the service as a professional investigative institution. PC tablets are increasingly being used by investigative professionals in both the public and private sectors who have to interview to do their jobs, and need to capture and to work with different forms of media. They are already in use in a number of forces. Tablets look like small, thin laptop computers, are lighter, cheaper and easier to carry, and like all technology are falling dramatically in price. The construction of certain models enables them to withstand heavy-duty handling.

Tablets have built-in recorders, the recording going straight to the hard disk. Their **8.66** unique property is that there is no typing involved. They have an A4-sized screen—the 'tablet'—on which the individual is able to write and to draw (in the case of an illustrator representation or enhanced drawing) using a stylus (which is in fact a mouse shaped like a biro). The information is stored immediately on the hard disk and is immediately retrievable.

The interviewer can capture on the tablet all the techniques we have described: SE3Rs **8.67** using different colours for each stage of the disclosure process, 'flat pack' diagrams of key locations, used after sketch plans drawn by the interviewee, illustrator representations being 'drawn' in the air by the witness's fingers or hands, and the annotated duplicate version of the interviewer's enhanced drawing—using the different colours to show the spontaneous drawing stage and the added detail of the probing stage.

Because a tablet functions just like a computer, before going to interview the witness the **8.68** officer can load useful material from an external database, e.g. stored still and recorded images, mapping, documents, and the like. The officer is then able to show the witness material to trigger further disclosure and to assist probing. The SE3R and any illustrator or drawing can be transmitted electronically to any addressee, e.g. a major incident room.

(4) Mobile phones

Even very inexpensive mobile phones can be used to record an exchange. A phone is a **8.69** perfect means for capturing a permanent record of a witness's very earliest disclosures, e.g. at the scene of an incident or crime. The recording can be transmitted immediately, accessed later to create an SE3R or loaded onto a PC tablet.

F. A Summary and a Request

We have delivered on our colleagues' request to tell management about things. They and **8.70** we want police and CPS managers, together with the judiciary, to know that poor and inappropriate witness interviewing is now prejudicing the service's ability to investigate crime effectively and to put reliable written evidence before the courts. But it does not stop at written evidence, given the forthcoming implementation of s17 of the Youth Justice and Criminal Evidence Act 1999 and s137 of the Criminal Justice Act 2003, both opening the door to the widespread visual recording of interviews. The service is in crisis and time is not on its side.

Speaking on behalf of a service that we jointly have worked with for four decades, we **8.71** respectfully request that management—police service and CPS managers and the judiciary—acknowledge the crisis facing the service in respect of interviewing the generality of witnesses, and prevail upon government to require the recording of all witnesses.

8.72   The Chinese ideogram for crisis is a combination of those for threat and opportunity. We should not delude ourselves. Recording of their witness interviews—required by PACE, or some other legal instrument—will constitute a threat to officers, supervisors and managers. Thus far their performances have been unmonitored, taken for granted, and they have 'got away with it' because it has not mattered to management. Management needs to say that it does matter, and that despite the painful transition recording will bring witness interviewing into the twenty-first century. If management does nothing the message will be 'carry on as normal': officers will continue to interview witnesses inappropriately and improperly. The result will be incalculable: increasing harm to the service's reputation and further decline as an investigative institution.

Further Reading

Fisher, R. and Geiselman, R., *Memory-enhancing techniques for investigative interviewing: the Cognitive Interview*, Springfield, Ill.: Charles C. Thomas, 1992.

Gudjonsson, G., *The psychology of interrogations and confessions*, Chichester: John Wiley and Sons, 2003.

Milne, R. and Bull, R., *Investigative interviewing: psychology and practice*, Chichester: John Wiley and Sons, 1999.

Shepherd, E., *SE3R: A resource book*, East Hendred: Forensic Solutions, 2004.

Shepherd, E., *Investigative Interviewing: the Conversation Management Approach*, Oxford: Oxford University Press (forthcoming).

Williamson, T., *Investigative interviewing: rights, research, regulation*, Cullompton: Willan Publishing, 2005.

Becky Milne is a Principal Lecturer at the Institute of Criminal Justice Studies, University of Portsmouth. She has performed consultancy work in the UK and abroad, and has trained a wide range of professions including police officers in witness interviewing issues. Becky is a member of the ACPO Investigative Interviewing Strategic Steering Group, as the Academic lead and is chair of the associated research sub-committee. Recently Becky was part of a writing team who wrote a national training package to support the *Achieving Best Evidence* document (Home Office, 2002) and she is currently part of the team writing the ABE part 2 document. She is a chartered Forensic Psychologist and an Associate Fellow of the British Psychological Society and an Associate Editor of the *International Journal of Police Science and Management*.

Editors' Note

If testimonial archaeology is to be a realistic and productive process the first priority is to discover critical artefacts in the generation and subsequent representation of a witness's disclosure, in the form of the statement drafted by the interviewing officer. The Code of Practice to the Criminal Procedure and Investigation Act 1996 requires the preservation of material bearing upon the statement's content. Common sense argues that an officer's notes which are exclusive of questions put to the witness are wholly inadequate to this task. In the case of interviews of suspects and special categories of witness electronic recording has proved the ideal form of preservation, enabling subsequent scrutiny by police officers, lawyers, the judiciary, and triers of fact. Recording has not only deterred inappropriate or improper interviewing but, importantly, has enabled officers to develop skill and the application of techniques to maximize disclosure and to capture detail comprehensively. This chapter starkly challenges managers—particularly the police but also the CPS and the judiciary—to face up to a sober reality: the unrecorded interviews of the majority of witnesses allow police officers to behave in ways that would never be allowed in a PACE interview. Their unacceptable directive interviewing is dysfunctional: they retain tight control but the resultant statements actually hinder investigation and undermine the prospect of a conviction. Recording technology, particularly the PC tablet which captures all forms of detail, is now accessible and inexpensive. Managers must unite in declaring to government that unmonitored witness interviewing is counter-productive, the price paid for not recording **all** witness interviewing which involved potentially contentious accounts is too high, preventing the development of the police service in enabling every witness to give the fullest possible testimony.

9

INVESTIGATIVE INTERVIEWING WITH CHILDREN: PROGRESS AND PITFALLS

Graham Davies and Helen Westcott

A. Children and the Law

A generation ago, a chapter in a legal text on interviewing children would have been **9.01** based largely on anecdote, laced with a fair measure of opinion and prejudice. This, in part, reflected the infrequent appearance of minors in the witness box and the lack of rigorous research and practical experience of forensic interviewing of children. That situation has rapidly changed in the last 30 years. Due to changes in the criminal law in relation to the admissibility of children's evidence and the availability of video technology in the courtroom[1] children's evidence is now heard more frequently in court, most notably in cases of alleged sexual or physical abuse, but also domestic violence or road

---

[1] Davies, G., Wilson, C., Mitchell, R. and Milsom, J., *Videotaping Children's Evidence: An Evaluation*, London: Home Office, 1995.

traffic offences.[2] The more widespread appearance of children in the courtroom has led to *progress*—an overdue increase in the numbers of prosecutions for assaults on children[3]— but also *pitfalls*—allegations of miscarriages of justice, based on an over-reliance on the word of a child.[4] In both instances, effective interviewing practices lie at the centre of the debate.

9.02 It has long been recognized that talking to children requires special skills and an awareness of how the world of the child differs from that of an adult. In general, children have less knowledge and experience of the world than adults, their vocabulary and comprehension is more limited and their emotional and social development makes talking to strangers difficult, especially about sensitive topics.[5] Until recent times, knowledge about interviewing children was scattered and mostly dwelled on clinical or therapeutic interventions.[6] However, the explosion of interest during the 1980s in child protection issues, especially child sexual abuse, coupled with the growth in support for children's rights, highlighted particular difficulties for children in investigative contexts. Large numbers of experiments were conducted by psychologists to explore both the strengths[7] and the vulnerabilities[8] of children's memory for events in their own lives. From such studies, evidence-based guidelines have emerged which are designed to form the basis for both training and practice for those charged with interviewing juveniles.

9.03 In this chapter we first consider the research on the reliability of children as witnesses, stressing the changes that occur with increasing age in such areas as memory, suggestibility and deceptive behaviour. We then go on to consider the progress that has been made in developing effective interviewing strategies with children of different ages. Next, we illustrate the pitfalls of interviewing: examples of bad practice which have led in some instances to unfounded allegations being levelled against adults. We then review some of the guidelines used in child witness interviewing and consider whether such recommendations are followed in practice. Finally, we consider how interviewing quality could be improved further and also maintained over time to the lasting benefit of both child witnesses and adult suspects alike.

---

[2] Wilson, C. and Powell, M., *A Guide to Interviewing Children: Essential Skills for Counsellors, Police, Lawyers and Social Workers*, Crows Nest, NSW: Allen and Unwin, 2001.

[3] See n.1.

[4] Garven S., Wood J.M., Malpass R.S. and Shaw, J.S., 'More than suggestion: The effect of interviewing techniques from the McMartin case' (1998) 83 *Journal of Applied Psychology*, 347–359.

[5] Aldridge, M. and Wood, J., *Interviewing Children: A Guide for Child Care and Forensic Practitioners*, Chichester: John Wiley and Sons, 1998.

[6] For example, see Boggs, S.R. and Eyberg, S., 'Interview techniques and establishing rapport' in A.M. La Greca (ed.), *Through the Eyes of the Child: Obtaining Self Reports from Children and Adolescents*, Boston: Allyn and Bacon, 1990, 85–108; and White, S., 'The investigatory interview with suspected victims of child sexual abuse' in La Greca, *Through the Eyes of the Child*, cited above, 368–84.

[7] Westcott, H.L. and Jones, D.P.H., 'Are children reliable witnesses to their experiences?' in P. Reder, S. Duncan and C. Lucey (eds.), *Studies in the Assessment of Parenting*, Hove: Brunner-Routledge, 2003, 105–23.

[8] Ceci, S.J., Crossman, A.M., Scullin, M.H., Gilstrap, L. and Huffman, M.L., 'Children's suggestibility research: Implications for the courtroom and the forensic interview' in H.L. Westcott, G.M. Davies and R.H.C. Bull (eds.), *Children's Testimony: A Handbook of Psychological Research and Forensic Practice*, Chichester: John Wiley and Sons, 2002, 117–130.

B. The Reliability of Children as Witnesses

Historically, lawyers and indeed, psychologists have viewed children as rather unreliable **9.04** witnesses. For example, they have been presented as prone to fantasy and the making of false allegations, and inherently suggestible.[9] Of course, adult witnesses (and defendants) can be equally unreliable and prone to error, but children have come to be seen as particularly problematic. In order to assess children's 'reliability' we need to clarify what we mean by the term: it can comprise accuracy, suggestibility, consistency and honesty, for example.[10] In this section, we explore some of these issues and consider them in the context of investigative interviewing.

(1) Children's memory accuracy

Even very young children can provide accurate testimony about events they have experi- **9.05** enced.[11] Although age-differences in children's memory are well established, with pre-schoolers facing particular challenges, age alone does not determine whether a child's memory is correct, incorrect or partially correct.[12] In a famous case in the US, a three-year-old girl who was the victim of a brutal assault, was able to describe her assailant with sufficient accuracy to enable detectives to detain him. His later confession corroborated the child's account.[13] In experimental studies, children can offer information that is 80 or 90 per cent accurate about events they have participated in, or witnessed, provided that interviewers use appropriate questioning techniques (see Section D below).

Interviewers need to be aware that memory is not akin to a photograph or video recording. **9.06** There are three stages to memory—encoding, storage and retrieval—and failure can occur at any of these stages, with implications for the conduct of investigative interviews.[14] For example, a child may not attend to all aspects of a novel experience (such as witnessing a crime), and so relevant information may not enter her memory in the first place. A child may also lack relevant knowledge and experience of a particular type of event, which affects storage of related information in his/her memory. Finally, children may be susceptible to social pressures (such as answering questions from an adult authority figure) that can influence the retrieval of information from memory. All of these effects will be modulated by the child's developmental age.[15]

Lawyers frequently invoke the effect of stress on children's testimony, to argue sometimes **9.07** that it improves memory and at other times that it impairs it.[16] The answer from psychological research is far from complete, though some research has demonstrated

---

[9] For a review, see Ceci, S.J. and Bruck, M., *Jeopardy in the Courtroom: A Scientific Analysis of Children's Testimony*, Washington DC: American Psychological Association, 1995.

[10] Ibid.

[11] Fivush, R., 'The development of autobiographical memory' in Westcott, Davies and Bull, *Children's Testimony*, cited above at n.8, 2002, 55–68.

[12] Baker-Ward, L. and Ornstein, P. A., 'Cognitive underpinnings of children's testimony' in ibid. 21–36.

[13] Jones, D.P.H. and Krugman, R.D., 'Can a three-year-old child bear witness to her sexual assault and attempted murder?' (1986) 10 *Child Abuse and Neglect*, 253–8.

[14] See Chapter 1.   [15] See Chapter 1.

[16] Christianson, S., 'Emotional stress and eyewitness memory: A critical review' (1992) 112 *Psychological Bulletin*, 284–309.

negative effects, for stress experienced both at encoding and at retrieval. That is, if the child is being interviewed about an event that was stressful at the time, then her memory for it may be adversely affected. Also, if a child is experiencing stress at the time of recall (i.e. interview or testimony) then this too can impair memory.

9.08 Lawyers also often highlight discrepancies in children's accounts, especially concerning peripheral details but, from a psychological perspective, this practice can be misleading: it is a natural phenomenon of memory that individuals remember different details at different times; inconsistency does not necessarily indicate unreliability.[17] Providing children have been asked open and non-leading questions, some inconsistency across successive retellings is to be expected, and the newly reported details are likely to be accurate. Inconsistency within interviews, or in response to extensive specific or misleading questions, is more problematic, and the information elicited may be inaccurate. For example, if a child changes their answer to a question that is repeated within an interview, this may reflect the child's response to social factors: the child may surmise that their first answer was somehow 'wrong' and so change their answer the second time.[18] It is worth emphasizing that memory accuracy is unrelated to completeness or credibility: testimony from a child who says virtually nothing about an event may be very accurate, but also very incomplete and lacking in credibility, for example.

(2) Suggestibility

9.09 All witnesses can be suggestible; that is, their answer to a question may be influenced by the person questioning them, or by persons who have interacted with them previously.[19] Suggestibility can be increased when the original memory is poor, for instance because of a long delay or the fleeting nature of the event. Social factors too, can influence suggestibility: child witnesses may feel intimidated by the interviewer. Suggestibility can be reduced or increased by the manner of the person questioning the child, or by the formality of the surroundings in which a child is interviewed. Hence suggestibility is not so much a 'trait' as a product of circumstance: children are not inevitably or uniformly suggestible. Reviewing their research on suggestibility amongst pre-schoolers, Ceci and colleagues[20] conclude that young children may be suggestible when the interviewer repeatedly makes false suggestions through misleading questions, and creates negative stereotypes about a person; when they are asked about personal events that happened a long time ago and their memory has not been 'refreshed' since; when they are questioned by a biased interviewer who pursues one line of questioning single-mindedly; when they are asked repeatedly to visualize fictitious events; and when they are asked in a suggestive or leading manner to demonstrate an event using anatomical dolls.

9.10 One reason why children may be suggestible, or may be inaccurate in their description of events, is because they have particular difficulties in monitoring the sources of their

---

[17] Janes and Krugman, (1986), cited above at n. 13.

[18] Moston, S., 'How children interpret and respond to questions: Situational sources of suggestibility in eyewitness interviews' (1990) 5 *Social Behaviour*, 155–167.

[19] See Chapter 1.   [20] Cited above at n. 8.

memories.[21] For example, they may sometimes find it difficult to identify whether they performed a particular action, or imagined themselves performing it. Recent studies have shown that children who are more able to identify the sources of their memories are better able to provide accurate accounts.[22] Interviewers should try always to explore the source of information (did the child really hear/see someone say or do something) in order to establish the reliability of an allegation.

(3) Deception

Psychological research suggests that children are capable of deceptive behaviour from as **9.11** young as three years old. However, deception at this age is likely to be simple verbal or non-verbal behaviour: for example, a child shaking his head to deny wrongdoing, or offering one-word answers like 'yes' or 'no' in response to questioning.[23] Children require more advanced cognitive understanding and language skills in order to maintain elaborate, deliberate verbal deception; for example, an appreciation of what another person is thinking in order to mislead them.[24] This level of understanding is not apparent until children are older. The relationship between deception, its detection, and witness credibility is complex. Contrary to beliefs about the value of 'face-to-face confrontation' with witnesses, available research shows that children's lies are easier to detect when listening to their voices rather than looking at them, and through verbal rather than non-verbal means. Further, introverted and socially anxious children are less likely to be believed, irrespective of whether they are telling the truth or lies. Implications for interviewing include the use of open questions as far as possible, to promote reliance on the child's original memory, and deter one-word answers (which make it easier to maintain any dishonesty).

(4) The reliability of children as witnesses

What are the implications of the various developmental issues that have been discussed in **9.12** this section?

- Children can provide highly accurate information about an event, provided they are questioned appropriately;
- children's developmental immaturity may affect all aspects of their memories, and may make them particularly susceptible to social influences (such as the adult interviewer);
- interviewers can increase or decrease suggestive influences through their behaviour or the environment in which the interview takes place;
- children may be deceptive from a young age; however, elaborate lies require a higher level of cognitive understanding and are difficult for young children to maintain;

---

[21] Lindsay, D.S., 'Children's source monitoring' in Westcott, Davies and Bull, *Children's Testimony*, cited above at n.8, 83–98.

[22] Thierry, K.L., Lamb, M.E. and Orbach, Y., 'Awareness of the origin of knowledge predicts child witnesses' recall of alleged sexual and physical abuse' (2003) 17 *Applied Cognitive Psychology*, 953–967.

[23] Vrij, A., 'Deception in children: A literature review and implications for children's testimony', in Westcott, Davies and Bull, cited above at n.8, 175–94.

[24] Called a 'theory of mind' *per* Perner, J., 'Children's competency in understanding the role of a witness: Truth, lies and moral ties' (1997) 11 *Applied Cognitive Psychology*, S21–S35.

- interviewers need to support children's memories through the use of appropriate questioning strategies, which guide the child through their account in a structured manner, and
- open questions are valuable for maintaining the child's accuracy, consistency, and honesty, and for reducing suggestibility.

C. Progress in Effective Interviewing Techniques

9.13 Much progress has been made in recent years regarding the most effective preparation for an investigation and identifying the skills necessary for a successful interview.

(1) The importance of planning

9.14 Planning needs to take place on two levels: first, for the investigation of which the interview is just one part, and second, for the interview itself. An analysis of investigative interviews in England and Wales[25] highlighted the potential difficulties that can arise when planning on either of these levels is ineffective, and the additional pressures on interviewers that can result. *Achieving Best Evidence in Criminal Proceedings*[26] gives extensive advice on how to plan the interview in the broader context of a criminal investigation, child protection enquiry and possible court proceedings, and includes a wide range of factors—such as ethnicity, gender, level of cognitive development and communication skills—that may need to be considered at the planning stage. If the child is suspected or known to have been previously abused, then planning must also take account of this and the reactions of the child and family.

9.15 Importantly, planning should also include whether an assessment of the child prior to interview could be beneficial. Such an assessment could include: the child's ability and willingness to talk in a formal interview situation, an explanation of the reason for the interview and the ground rules for the interview (see below). Some estimate can also be made of the child's cognitive, social and emotional development. The opportunity can also be taken to answer any questions the child may have about the nature of the interview process and thus secure informed consent. It can also inform the choice of lead interviewer, and clarify working arrangements if an interpreter or intermediary is required. It is important that such assessments are properly documented, so as to assuage concerns at trial over possible coaching or undue influence.

(2) Setting ground rules

9.16 An investigative interview with a child is very different indeed from almost all other interactions children experience. The adults they are talking to do not already know the answers, nor do they want the child to guess at answers: thus interviews are immediately different from school lessons. No assumptions can be made about shared knowledge or

---

[25] Davis, G., Hoyano, L., Keenan, C., Maitland, L. and Morgan, R., *An Assessment of the Admissibility and Sufficiency of Evidence in Child Abuse Prosecutions,* London: Home Office, 1999.

[26] Home Office, *Achieving Best Evidence in Criminal Proceedings: Guidance for Vulnerable or Intimidated Witnesses, including Children,* London: Home Office Communication Directorate, 2002.

shared language. For these reasons, interviewers need to set ground rules early on in the interview, which will help the child to understand what is expected of them, and to clarify how an investigative interview departs from the normal rules of conversation. One important rule is to ensure that the child understands the importance of telling the truth.[27] This will normally involve some exploration of the nature of truth and lies, but the child is not required to take an oath. Other ground rules underline the importance of precise and accurate recall: the interviewer was not present at the event, and thus is relying on the child's account; that the child should say if s/he does not understand a question; that the child can say 'I don't know' to any question, and should correct any mistakes made by the interviewer in subsequent questions; that the child can use any language ('rude' or not) in the interview, and that they should try to remember as much detail as possible.[28]

9.17 How an interviewer conveys ground rules matters—merely reciting the list in front of a passive child is unsatisfactory. It is good practice for an interviewer to ask a child a question that the child cannot answer and see how the child responds—congratulating the child if they say, correctly 'I don't know' or explaining why it was wrong to guess if they have responded incorrectly. Such a task can form part of a 'practice interview' in the rapport phase of the main interview. A practice interview involves the child being asked to recall some unrelated but salient event from their life, such as a birthday party or other family celebration. Interviewers can then use the child's account to explain the level of detail required in the main interview, for instance in their descriptions of actions or people. Practice interviews are recommended in many interviewing protocols, and had a positive impact on interview quality in a recent project with police and social work interviewers in England.[29]

9.18 Interviewers often omit some or all of the ground rules during actual interviews. For example, Westcott *et al*[30] found that ground rules were omitted in nearly 40 per cent of the interviews they examined, particularly those conducted with children under seven years old. However, experimental research has shown that, if successfully conducted, ground rules can lead to better recall from children.[31]

(3) Asking the right questions

9.19 There is now a consensus among psychologists and lawyers that the 'right' questions to be asked during an investigative interview are those that are non-leading, and that are as

---

[27] In England and Wales, judges have rejected the view that expert evidence is necessary to assess the competency of children under the 1988 and 1997 Criminal Justice Acts: the decision should be left to the judge hearing the case—see *G v DPP* [1996] QB, 919.

[28] For example, see Poole, D.A. and Lamb, M.E., *Investigative Interviews of Children: A Guide for Helping Professionals*, Washington, DC: American Psychological Association, 1998; Wilson and Powell, *A Guide to Interviewing Children*, cited above at n. 2; Home Office, *Achieving Best Evidence*, cited above at n.26.

[29] Westcott, H.L., Kynan, S. and Few, C., 'Improving the quality of investigative interviews for suspected child abuse: A case study' 2006, 12 *Psychology, Crime and Law*, 77–86.

[30] See n.29.

[31] Mulder, M.R. and Vrij, A., 'Explaining conversation rules to children: An intervention study to facilitate children's accurate responses' (1996) 20 *Child Abuse and Neglect*, 623–631.

open as possible.[32] An interviewer may have a good idea what has happened to the child from other sources, or from an assessment of the child prior to interview, but should refrain from imparting any sense of this by asking open questions such as 'what happened?', 'tell me more about that', and so on. Even specific information should be sought using the most open question format possible, such as 'what colour was the car?' Open questions require the child to rely more on their own memory and less on information contained in the question.

(4) The need for proper recording

9.20 Investigative interviews should always be video-recorded: it enables the child's responses and equally important, the interviewer's questions, to be preserved and accessible to other interested parties without the need for further interviews. Problems can arise if children make disclosures 'off camera' or make further allegations after the initial interview, either against the accused or another person. The courts will expect a written contemporaneous record of such disclosures, supplemented where necessary, with a further video interview.

(5) Taking the child's perspective into account

9.21 We know from a number of studies that children do find it very difficult to talk about abuse-related activities.[33] Even if children pre-empt the investigative interview with a verbal disclosure, they may find the speed of the subsequent investigation surprising, or the need to discuss abusive events in great detail embarrassing. Research has demonstrated that children are frequently distressed about possible outcomes for themselves, their families and the alleged perpetrators, and that this can affect how they behave and what they chose to disclose in interviews. During the interview, interviewers need to be willing to use the child's own terms for body parts and sexual activities, but they should check the precise meaning of the child's terms. Certain concepts are abstract and especially difficult for children to use competently, such as those relating to estimates of time and frequency. Interviewers need to be aware that children use language differently to adults, and that many terms used in sexual abuse investigative interviews, such as 'on top of', 'behind', 'underneath', 'once' and 'often' may be poorly understood, even by children as old as seven or eight years old.[34]

(6) Progress in effective interviewing techniques

9.22 A number of implications for practice have emerged from this section:

- planning is essential, both in any assessment prior to the interview and in preparing the child for the interview itself;

---

[32] See *Achieving Best Evidence* cited above at n.26; Poole and Lamb, *Investigative Interviews of Children*, cited above at n.28; Wilson and Powell (2001) cited above at n.2.

[33] For example, see Wade, A. and Westcott, H.L., 'No easy answers: Children's perspectives on investigative interviews' in H.L. Westcott and J. Jones (eds.), *Perspectives on the Memorandum: Policy, Practice and Research in Investigative Interviewing*, Aldershot: Arena, 1997, 51–66.

[34] Walker, A.G., 'Questioning young children in court: A linguistic study' 17 *Law and Human Behavior*, 59–81.

- ground rules need to be included which help the child to understand what is expected of them in the interview: these can be explained through a practice interview during rapport;
- open questions should be used as much as possible throughout the interview;
- interviews and any pre-interview contact with the child needs to be properly recorded and documented, and
- the child's perspective should be taken into account when organizing the interview, and in the language used by the interviewer.

D. Pitfalls, or when Interviews go Wrong

Our review of children's memory has demonstrated that children are capable of providing accurate information from memory, but that care is needed to avoid suggestion and other sources of error. The preceding section described some of the procedures that need to be followed with children to ensure that the police and the courts deal with accurate and reliable testimony. Set against this are a number of instances where misleading allegations have led to actual or potential miscarriages of justice. The problems in these cases generally lay not with the children, but with the inappropriate interviewing practices employed. A number of classic cases involved testimony from groups of pre-school children, whose more limited powers of verbal recall and increased suggestibility made them particularly vulnerable to inappropriate interviewing techniques.   **9.23**

(1) Two famous cases

Two high-profile US cases have been extensively studied by psychologists for the lessons they provide for interviewing practice: *People v Buckey*[35] and *State of New Jersey v Michaels*.[36] In the Buckey case, seven teachers at the McMartin Preschool were accused of sexually abusing children in their care over a ten-year period. Charges were eventually dropped against all the accused, but not before the proceedings had become the longest and most costly in Californian history. In the Michaels case, Kelly Michaels, a preschool teacher, was accused of a range of bizarre sexual acts with the children in her care. She was tried, convicted and sentenced to 47 years' imprisonment, before being freed on appeal, in which an *amicus* brief highlighting the suggestive nature of many of the interviewing techniques played an important role.[37]   **9.24**

(2) Failing to keep an open mind

It is important that the interviewer adopts a sympathetic, but dispassionate stance towards child witnesses. Mistakes can arise where the interviewer forms a premature hypothesis about what is likely to have occurred and focuses only on statements that are consistent with the hypothesis, ignoring incompatible information. Such ruthless over-focusing is illustrated in one interview in the Michaels case: **9.25**

---

[35] Garven *et al.*, (1998), cited above at n.4.
[36] Bruck, M. and Ceci, S.J., 'Amicus brief for the case of *State of New Jersey v. Margaret Kelly Michaels* presented by committee of concerned social scientists' (1995) 1 *Psychology, Public Policy and Law*, 246–271.
[37] Ibid.

Q: Did you ever see Kelly have blood in her vagina?
A: This is blood.
Q: Kelly had blood in her vagina.
A: Yeah.
Q: She did? Did you ever get blood on your penis?
A: No, green blood.
Q: Did you ever see any of your friends get blood on their penis from her vagina?
A: Not green blood, but red blood.[38]

9.26 In one experiment, children between three and six years old played with an accomplice before being interviewed one and two months later. Trained interviewers were supplied either with an accurate or an inaccurate synopsis of the incident. The inaccurate account included some bizarre details (e.g. licking the experimenter's elbow) reminiscent of the information supplied to investigators in the Michaels case. Interviewers who had the inaccurate synopsis typically put the false allegations directly to the child leading to around a third of the younger children agreeing to at least one. Many of these children went on to elaborate on their assent in the second interview.[39]

9.27 Interviewers in child witness cases will inevitably know something of the reasons why an interview has been requested. Indeed, such prior information is probably essential if the interviewer is to focus on relevant issues within the time available (see Section C), but it is important always to preserve an open mind and to consider alternative and possibly innocent explanations for the allegation.

(3) Inappropriate assumptions and paraphrasing

9.28 The rationale of the investigative interview is that, as far as possible, children tell their own stories with the minimum of cueing from the interviewer. Errors can occur when interviewers make inappropriate assumptions about how an incident developed and unwittingly guide children into supporting their view of events. Opportunities for error can arise both through direct questioning and from inaccurate paraphrase of what the child has said. In North America, Roberts and Lamb[40] found a total of 140 interviewer-produced errors in 68 transcripts. Children spontaneously corrected around a third of such errors, but the remainder went uncorrected, including an instance where the child said the accused 'touched me in private' which the interviewer paraphrased as 'touched you in your privates more than one time'. In 10 instances, such errors led to the child incorporating the interviewer's version of events into their own accounts.[41] Davies[42] provides an example of a paraphrase error made in an interview with a child at age nine,

---

[38] Ibid., 276.

[39] White, T.L., Leichtman, M.D. and Ceci, S.J., 'The good, the bad, and the ugly: accuracy, inaccuracy, and elaboration in preschoolers' reports about a past event' (1997) 11 *Applied Cognitive Psychology*, S37–S54.

[40] Roberts, K.P. and Lamb, M.E., 'Children's responses when interviewers distort details during investigative interviews' (1999) 4 *Legal and Criminological Psychology*, 23–31.

[41] See also Westcott, Kynan and Few, cited above at n.29.

[42] Davies, G.M., 'Coping with suggestion and deception in children's accounts' in P.A. Granhag and L. A. Strömwall (eds.), *The Detection of Deception in Forensic Contexts*, Cambridge: Cambridge University Press, 2004, 148–71.

which she then incorporated into her account when she was re-interviewed five years later.

The use of paraphrase is a useful device in interviewing: it not only allows child and interviewer to take stock, but also aids the finder of fact to comprehend and follow the substance of an allegation.[43] The rigorous use of ground rules, which encourage the child to correct any mistakes the interviewer might make in understanding the child's account, can do much to minimize the risk of inappropriate assumptions and erroneous paraphrase.

9.29

(4) Use of repeated questions

Where interviewers fail to receive the answer they expect, the temptation is simply to ask the question again. Under these circumstances, a witness will sometimes give the required answer—but this may reflect the child's perception of interviewer expectations, rather than the truth (see Section B). Examples of repeated questions occur in the McMartin interviews:

9.30

Q: Can you remember the naked pictures?
A: (shakes head 'no')
Q: Can't remember that part?
A: (shakes head 'no')
Q: Why don't you think about it for a while, okay? Your memory might come back.[44]

Again, experimental studies demonstrate the damaging effect of the repetition of closed questions with young children. Poole and White[45] asked children and adults to recall a staged incident either immediately or after a week's delay. The interview included both closed and open-ended questions that were repeated three times. Repetition had no effect for the open-ended questions, but the youngest children were more likely to change their response when asked closed questions. More damaging effects are observed when questions are repeated across interviews with additional instructions to 'think about it' as in the McMartin case. Ceci *et al*[46] repeatedly asked preschool children about a series of real and non-existent events from their past over a ten-week period and encouraged visualization as a cue to recall. By the end, some 58 per cent of the children claimed to have 'remembered' at least one of the non-existent events. Repeated questions figure frequently in investigative interviews, at least in the United States: Warren *et al*[47] examined 42 transcripts from

9.31

---

[43] Westcott, H.L. and Kynan, S., 'The application of a "story-telling" framework to investigative interviews for suspected child sexual abuse' (2004) 9 *Legal and Criminological Psychology*, 37–56.

[44] Garven *et al*, (1998) cited above at n.4.

[45] Poole D.A. and White, L.T., 'Effects of question repetition on the eyewitness testimony of children and adults' (1991) 27 *Developmental Psychology*, 976–986; Poole, D.A., and White, L.T., 'Two years later: Effects of question repetition and retention interval on the eyewitness testimony of children and adults' (1993) 29 *Developmental Psychology*, 844–853.

[46] Ceci, S.J., Huffman, M.L.C., Smith, E. and Loftus, E.F., 'Repeatedly thinking about a non-event: Source misattributions among preschoolers' (1994) 3 *Consciousness and Cognition*, 388–407.

[47] Warren, A.R., Garven, S., Walker, N.E. and Woodall, C.E., 'Setting the record straight: How problematic are "typical" child sexual abuse interviews?' (2000) Paper presented at the biennial meeting of the American Psychology-Law Society (March).

investigative interviews and reported that 95 per cent contained repeated questions, even when the child had given an unequivocal answer on the first occasion.

9.32   Clearly, repeated closed questions are not good interviewing practice, especially with very young children: they can lead at best to equivocal responding and at worst to a misleading accusation. If issues need to be revisited, interviewers should rephrase questions as open-ended probes, referring back if necessary, to the child's earlier answer. Lyon[48] has urged caution before making sweeping assertions about the impact of repeated questions on the overall veracity of interviews. He notes the generally modest effects observed in many experimental studies and their disproportionate impact on very young children.

(5) Inappropriate use of authority

9.33   As was noted in Section B, suggestibility is increased by differences in perceived status between child and interviewer. Interviewers need to take account of this dynamic in the way that questions are framed and comments made. In the Michaels case, interviewers sometimes emphasized their role in law enforcement ('I'm a policeman. If you were a bad girl, I would punish you wouldn't I?').[49] In one experiment, children interviewed by an actor produced less accurate testimony when (s)he dressed as a police officer than when (s)he wore civilian clothing.[50] Authority figures are also in a more powerful position to invoke stereotypes, which are known to be a powerful source of distortion in younger children's accounts. In their classic experiment, Leichtman and Ceci[51] demonstrated that young children could be induced to provide strikingly inaccurate accounts of the actions of a stranger at their nursery school, when his behaviour was characterized repeatedly as clumsy prior to his visit. In the Michaels investigation, interviewers consistently referred to her as a 'bad girl' who had done 'bad things'.[52] Such talk should always be avoided, even when initiated by the child.

(6) Pitfalls, or when interviews go wrong

9.34   The implications for interviewers are:

- interviewers need to preserve an open mind when interviewing children and be alert to other possible interpretations of actions or statements;
- interviewers need to be aware that leading and other inappropriate styles of questioning may have an adverse impact on the overall accuracy of a child's statement;
- interviewers should be careful when paraphrasing children's statements not to introduce new material or misrepresent what the child has said;
- interviewers should avoid putting the same question to a child, if the child has already given an unequivocal answer on the first occasion;

---

[48] Lyon, T.D., 'Applying suggestibility research to the real world: The case of repeated questions' (2002) 65 *Law and Contemporary Problems*, 97–126.

[49] Bruck & Ceci, (1995), cited above at n.36, 286.

[50] Tobey, A. and Goodman, G.S., 'Children's eyewitness memory: effects of participation and forensic context' (1992) 16 *Child Abuse and Neglect*, 807–821.

[51] Leichtman, M.D. and Ceci, S.J., 'The effects of stereotypes and suggestions on preschoolers' reports' (1995) 31 *Developmental Psychology*, 568–578.

[52] Bruck and Ceci, (1995), cited above at n.36.

- interviewers should be aware of their status as authority figures and of the potentially negative impact on testimonial accuracy of suggestive comments or stereotypical remarks about an accused, and
- these precautions apply particularly to the interviewing of very young children and/or for events where poor memory may be expected by reason of duration or delay.

E. Interview Guidelines

Both the cases discussed in the preceding section took place over a decade ago when **9.35** knowledge of investigative interviewing of children was still at an early stage. Such cases highlight the need for informed guidelines for the conduct of investigative interviews, which maximize accurate information, while minimizing suggestive or erroneous responding. In recent years, numerous sets of guidelines have been produced in the United States for child witness interviewers,[53] but none has achieved national recognition, either among interviewers or by the courts. In England and Wales, *The Memorandum of Good Practice on Video Recorded Interviews with Child Witnesses for Criminal Proceedings*[54] based on the work of a psychologist (Professor Ray Bull) and a lawyer (Professor Diane Birch) has had a much more powerful impact.

(1) The Memorandum of Good Practice

The *Memorandum* enjoyed two significant advantages over its North American counter- **9.36** parts. First, the guidance was intended to apply to all interviews conducted by police officers and social workers with children throughout England and Wales. Second, the 1991 Criminal Justice Act ensured that all such interviews were to be video-recorded, thus making it possible for all parties to assess whether interviewers had followed the *Memorandum* recommendations.

The *Memorandum* followed North American practice in calling for a phased approach: **9.37** each interview should contain four distinct phases and each phase should have a separate and identifiable function.[55] The initial *rapport phase* is designed to build social bridges between the interviewer and the child through discussion of age-appropriate topics, such as sport, school or popular culture. This phase is also used to impart to the child the *ground rules* for the interview, in particular the need to be accurate and tell the truth (see Section C). The reason for the interview will also be broached during rapport, though there should be no mention from the interviewer of the nature of the allegation: all information needs to come from the child. The *free narrative phase* is designed to capture the child's account of the event(s) in question in his or her own words. The guidelines

---

[53] For example, APSAC, *Practice Guidelines: Use of Anatomical Dolls in Child Sexual abuse assessment*, Chicago: APSAC, 1995; Berliner, L., *Guidelines for Psychosocial Evaluation of Suspected Sexual Abuse in Young Children*, Chicago: APSAC, 1990.

[54] Home Office, *The Memorandum of Good Practice on Video Recorded Interviews with Child Witnesses for Criminal Proceedings*, London: Home Office, 1992.

[55] Yuille, S.C., 'Training Programmes and Procedures for interviewing and assessing sexually abused children', in Bagley, C and Thomlinson, K., (eds), *Child Sexual Abuse: Critical Perspectives on Prevention, Intervention and Treatment*, Toronto: Wall and Emerson, 1991, 121–134.

emphasize the importance of not interrupting the child, tolerating pauses and adopting a form of 'active listening' involving verbal ('uh huh') or non-verbal (nod of the head) indications of attention. The information in free narrative normally represents the most accurate information a witness can provide.[56] However, free narrative accounts are invariably incomplete, so it is usually necessary to explore and amplify them in the *questioning phase*.

9.38 The *Memorandum* recommends starting with *open* questions, because of their value in eliciting extended answers from the child (see Section C). Follow-up questions may be *specific, yet non-leading* ('what colour was his t-shirt?') and if this too fails to elicit any response, *closed* questions can be employed ('was his t-shirt red, white or some other colour?'). Interviewers are counselled against resorting to the use of *leading* questions ('his t-shirt was red wasn't it?'), unless all other tactics have failed to engage the child in talk about the topic of the interview. Experimental research confirms that open questions invariably elicit more accurate information from children than specific or closed questions.[57] When the interviewer is satisfied that the child has nothing further to say— controversially the *Memorandum* set a limit of one hour on any interview—the final *closure phase* can begin, when the interviewer summarizes what the child has said in his/her own language, answers any queries (s)he may have before reverting to rapport topics in an effort to ensure that the child leaves the interview in as positive a frame of mind as possible.

(2) But do interviewers follow the guidance?

9.39 One of the advantages of videotaping interviews is that, with the permission of those involved, it is possible to establish how effectively the guidance is carried out in practice. Sternberg *et al*[58] examined the content of some 119 interviews conducted by 13 different police forces in investigations of alleged sexual abuse. They found an average of only 6 per cent of questions were open; some 47 per cent were specific yet non-leading and a further 29 per cent were closed. Interviewers asked leading questions only 5 per cent of the time and a later study by Westcott *et al*[59] reported an even lower figure. While the low numbers of leading questions reflects well on training, the very small number of open questions—an average of just 4 per interview—remains a major concern.

9.40 Lamb, Sternberg and colleagues have argued that the only way of ensuring that interviewers ask consistently open-ended questions is to structure the interview even more intensively. The NICHD Investigative Protocol seeks to orient both the interviewer and child toward open questioning and extended responding. Interviewers are taught to use the practice interview (see Section C) to encourage free narrative and extended answers to questions. The interviewers are taught specific scripted prompts for use at different stages of the interview and, more generally, how to rephrase closed questions in an open form:

---

[56] Westcott, H. and Jones, N. (eds), *Perspectives on the Memorandum*, Aldershot, Harts: Arena, 1993.
[57] Poole and Lamb, *Investigative Interviews of Children*, cited above at n.28.
[58] Sternberg, K.J., Lamb, M.E., Davies, G.M. and Westcott, H.L., 'The Memorandum of Good Practice: Theory versus application' (2001) 25 *Child Abuse and Neglect*, 669–681.
[59] Cited above at n.29.

specific questions are used only when all open-ended prompts have been exhausted.[60] Research in Israel and the United States suggests that the Protocol had a dramatic effect on the amount of useful information elicited in an interview. After training in the Protocol, 49 per cent of useful information was derived from the free narrative phase compared to only 16 per cent before training and the proportion of open questions rose from 10 to 35 per cent.[61]

(3) Achieving Best Evidence in Criminal Proceedings

The need for a greater emphasis on free narrative and open questioning is reflected in the new guidance *Achieving Best Evidence in Criminal Proceedings*[62] which has now replaced the *Memorandum* in England and Wales. *Achieving Best Evidence* again adheres to the four-fold interview structure of the original *Memorandum*, but there is much greater emphasis on the importance of pre-interview planning and assessment. Like the NICHD Protocol, there is great emphasis on the use of open questions and the need to revert to an open-ended approach after specific or closed questions have been posed. Similarly, scripted passages ('verbal formulae') are included, to cover raising issues of concern and exploring a child's understanding of truth and lies. There is also an acknowledgement that interviewing techniques need to be tempered to the needs of the individual child—symbolized by the disappearance of the 'one hour rule'—with special sections devoted to interviewing learning-disabled, pre-school and ethnic minority children. **9.41**

F. Conclusion

In this chapter, we have reviewed the pitfalls as well as the progress in the development of child witness interviewing. As emphasized in Section C, investigative interviewing as a technique is not a natural form of discourse. It is perhaps inevitable that errors will occur in such interviews: the interviewer may ask a leading question or the child may muddle the sequence of events. However, such errors need not be fatal to the value of the interview: a muddle here may be balanced by a revealing statement from the child elsewhere, prompted by the effective and sensitive use of open questions by the interviewer.[63] Moreover, as has been already emphasized, the interview is only part of the totality of evidence in any case. Just like any evidence, the statement of a child needs to be weighed by the judge or jury against the statements of the other parties involved, together with any forensic evidence that may be available. Free narrative provides the **9.42**

---

[60] Lamb, M.E., Orbach, Y., Sternberg, K.J., Esplin, P.W. and Hershkowitz, I., 'The effects of forensic interviews on the quality of information provided by alleged victims of child abuse' in Westcott, Davies and Bull, *Children's Testimony*, cited above at n.8, 131–46.

[61] Ibid.   [62] Cited above at n.26.

[63] The issue of breaches in procedure in the conduct of investigative interviews under *Achieving Best Evidence* has been the subject of a number of appeals. In *R v Hanton* [2005] EWCA Crim 2009, The Court of Appeal has laid down a test for the admissibility of such interviews, namely whether a reasonable jury, properly directed, could be sure that the witness had given a credible and accurate account in the interview, notwithstanding any breaches.

opportunity for the child to put his or her point of view to the jury in a way in which examination at court (and in particular, cross-examination) rarely permits.[64]

9.43 The latest guidance embodied in *Achieving Best Evidence* and the NICHD Protocol reflects much of what has been learned from research on interviewing children. Both should lead to improvements in the overall quality of interviews. However, success of both is critically dependent upon interviewers learning to use appropriate techniques and continuing to use them in their practice. Lamb *et al*[65] note that the success of their Protocol is dependent upon prolonged and systematic training and frequent review and refresher sessions. A comprehensive training package has also been developed for *Achieving Best Evidence* including explanatory notes and video clips illustrating good and poor practice in interviewing,[66] but there are no plans to move away from the intensive one-week courses typical of police interviewer training today. The advent of longer and sustained nationally-accredited courses[67] could lead to a major step-change in interview quality and better justice for all.

Further Reading

Aldridge, M. and Wood, J., *Interviewing Children: A Guide for Child Care and Forensic Practitioners*, Chichester: John Wiley and Sons, 1998.

Ceci, S.J. and Bruck, M., *Jeopardy in the Courtroom: A Scientific Analysis of Children's Testimony*, Washington DC: American Psychological Association, 1995.

Walker, A.G. and Warren, A.R., 'The language of the child abuse interview: Asking the questions, understanding the answers' in T. Ney (ed.), *True and False Allegations of Child Sexual Abuse: Assessment and Management*, New York: Brunner/Mazel, 1995, 153–62.

Westcott, H.L., Davies G.M. and Bull, R.H.C. (eds), *Children's Testimony: A Handbook of Psychological Research and Forensic Practice*, Chichester: John Wiley and Sons, 2002.

Westcott, H.L., Davies, G.M. and Spencer, J.R., 'Children, hearsay and the courts' (1999) 5 *Psychology, Public Policy and Law*, 1–22.

Westcott, H.L. and Kynan, S., 'The application of a "story-telling" framework to investigative interviews for suspected child sexual abuse' (2004) 9 *Legal and Criminological Psychology*, 37–56.

Wood, J.M. and Garven, S., 'How sexual abuse interviews go astray: Implications for prosecutors, police and child protection services' (2000) 5 *Child Maltreatment*, 109–118.

Yuille, J.C., 'The systematic assessment of children's testimony' (1988) 29 *Canadian Psychologist*, 247–262.

Graham Davies is a Professor of Psychology at the University of Leicester. His main research interests lie in the eyewitness testimony of children and adults on which he has published some five books and over 100 articles in scientific journals. He is the founder

---

[64] Henderson, E., 'Persuading and controlling: The theory of cross-examination in relation to children' in Westcott, Davies and Bull, *Children's Testimony*, cited above at n.8, 279–94.

[65] Cited above at n.60.

[66] Welsh Assembly, *Training package to accompany 'Achieving Best Evidence'*, Cardiff: Welsh Assembly Government, 2004.

[67] Davies, G.M., Marshall, E. and Robertson, N., *Child Abuse: Training Investigative Officers* (Police Research Series Paper No. 94), London: Home Office, 1998.

and editor of *Applied Cognitive Psychology* and of the *Wiley Series on the Psychology of Crime, Policing and the Law*. He is the current President of the European Association for Psychology and Law and led the writing team responsible for *Achieving Best Evidence in Criminal Proceedings* (Home Office, 2002).

Dr Helen Westcott is a Senior Lecturer at The Open University in Milton Keynes. She has a longstanding interest in issues concerning child sexual abuse and interviewing children, along with cross-examination practice, and the abuse of children who are disabled. Helen is a Chartered Forensic Psychologist, and she publishes and presents widely on topics related to children's evidence (e.g. *Children's Testimony*, Wiley, 2002, with Professors Graham Davies and Ray Bull). She was a member of the writing team that produced the 2002 Home Office guidance *Achieving Best Evidence in Criminal Proceedings*, and she works closely with practitioners and policy makers.

Editors' Note

Many investigators, judges and advocates clearly still have a long way to go in the attainment of a proper and comprehensive understanding of the best methods to be used when they communicate with children. Unless they take this road, fact finders will continue to be misled concerning the evidence of children and just verdicts will, thus, be put at risk. Inappropriately interviewed or questioned in court, a child may be presented as having provided ostensibly unreliable evidence, the essential factual features of which may, nonetheless, be true. Armed, however, with an intelligent grasp of what this chapter has to offer, those who are responsible for collating, examining and presenting the evidence of children to fact finders will be better informed for the purposes of the attainment of more reliable and just verdicts.

10

OBTAINING, RECORDING AND ADMISSIBILITY OF OUT-OF-COURT WITNESS STATEMENTS

Anthony Heaton-Armstrong, David Wolchover and Annabel Maxwell-Scott

A. Introduction

In chapter 15 of *Analysing Witness Testimony* ('Recording witness statements') two of the **10.01** present chapter's authors examined the absence of any general procedural requirement for recording (a) the interviewing of witnesses by investigators and (b) the process of writing up witness statements. We demonstrated how, with no such monitoring, the corruption of evidence gathering through the questioning of witnesses was liable to infect the conduct and fairness of criminal trials virtually unchecked. This is because, from beginning to end, witness statements play a vital role in the whole of the criminal process. For the prosecution they inform the charging decision and the nature of the way the case is put. For the defence, they provide the basic structure on which to prepare the attack on the prosecution case and to build the defendant's account. In the trial itself, pre-recorded witness statements provide the blueprint for both examination-in-chief and cross-examination, and highlighting their inconsistency with the witness's live evidence is always a crucial component of the defence strategy. The Criminal Justice Act 2003 has momentously removed the former absolute rule rendering inadmissible any statement other than one made by a person while giving oral evidence in the proceedings as evidence of any fact or opinion stated—the rule against hearsay.[1] At the same time, it has actually curtailed slightly the statutory criteria for reading at trial *contentious* whole statements in substitution for the live evidence of unavailable deponents. (In effect, such use may be regarded as a vestigial application of the old 'best evidence' rule—the principle of allowing in the best evidence the nature of the case will admit.[2]) However, previous statements introduced in order to assist or qualify the evidence of live witnesses have, under the Act, been invested with the status of evidence of the facts they purport to assert, a development which has aggravated fundamental concerns about all those deficiencies in the process of taking and recording witness statements, which have long plagued the process of evaluating eyewitness evidence.

B. Before the Criminal Justice Act 2003

(1) Emergence of the rule against hearsay

10.02 In modern times the bedrock of trials under common law has been proof by oral narrative evidence of witnesses who are present in court and who can be cross-examined by the opposing party. It was not always so. In centuries gone by verdicts were based on the jury's own knowledge; not until the sixteenth century did oral evidence in open court become commonplace, a fact recognised by the statute 5 Eliz I, c9 (1562–63) which provided a compulsory process for witnesses.[3] However, there was still little structure in the management of trials with few rules, if any, for screening out inherently unreliable assertions. Practically anything was allowed. With the transition to trial by evidence given in open court attention inevitably began to be paid to the nature of such evidence and the first objections against hearsay were voiced.[4] Nevertheless, adoption by criminal courts of the incipient principle, traced by Thayer to the thirteenth century 'and bearing marks of antiquity then,' which required witnesses in a certain kind of action for the recovery of land to state what they had seen and heard '*de visu et auditu*'[5] was still in the future. The memory of that rule, combined with the influence of Lord Coke's recently published denial of the 'strange conceit' that one might be an accuser by hearsay,[6] were

---

[1] The hearsay provisions in the CJA 2003 were to some extent inspired by the Law Commission, Report No. 245, *Evidence in Criminal Proceedings: Hearsay and Related Topics*, Cm 3670; London: HMSO, 1997, as considered in the White Paper, *Justice for All*, Cm 5563, London: HMSO, 2002. Earlier the Criminal Law Revision Committee had made important proposals for reform in their milestone 11th report, *Evidence (General)*, Cmnd 4991, London: HMSO, 1972, paras 224–265, and draft Bill, cll. 30–41. For Parliamentary consideration of what became the Act's hearsay provisions see HC Standing Committee B, 15th and 16th Sittings, 28 January, 2003.

[2] That it may be the best *available* evidence was the view of the Law Commission, cited above at n. 1, paras 3.2, and see also paras 3.3 and 3.4.

[3] See e.g. Holdsworth, Sir William, *A History of English Law* (16 vols) London: Methuen, 1903–1966, vol ix, 215.

[4] See e.g. *R v Throckmorton* (1554) 1 State Trials 875–876.

[5] Thayer, J.B., *A Preliminary Treatise on Evidence at the Common Law*, Boston: Little, Brown, 1898, 498.

[6] *Third Institute*, 1641, 25–26.

important elements in the establishment of the hearsay rule in the immediate post-Restoration period.[7] Wigmore was inclined to suppose that it was 'between 1675 and 1690 that the fixing of the doctrine takes place'[8] but if any moment can be identified as marking the judicial crystallizing of the rule, it is a resolution of the judges in *Tonge* that an out-of-court confession before a JP or Privy Counsellor 'is only evidence against the party himself who made the confession, but cannot be made use of as evidence against any others whom on his examination he confessed to be in the treason . . .'[9] Thus was the genesis of a truism heard recited every day in the Crown Court.

The affirmation of the primacy of the hearsay rule had important consequences for the use to which the pre-trial depositions of witnesses could be put at trial. Before that time, a prosecution case might rest entirely or very largely on hearsay and, moreover, of a kind at once ostensibly compelling and peculiarly untrustworthy, the written confession of an accomplice implicating the accused.[10] Instead of calling a witness the Crown might, if it wished, read to the jury any deposition taken from the witness in private. This was an option where it was feared that an awkward witness might inconveniently retract on being confronted with the defendant and there was no question but that such statements were treated as evidence of the truth of the factual assertions they contained. The trial of Sir Walter Raleigh in 1603 is often quoted as a particularly graphic example of the Crown blatantly keeping its own witness—Lord Cobham—out of the way (he was in the Tower) and reading his confession before the Privy Council instead.[11] Chief Justice Popham met Raleigh's call for Cobham's production with the somewhat ingenuous riposte that the hearsay was admissible if it merely corroborated an allegation well-proved by other means. In fact, the only evidence was the record of Cobham's confession and a codicil he wrote going back on a letter he had sent Raleigh retracting the confession. Raleigh professed his willingness to admit the legality of reading Cobham's deposition if he could 'not be had conveniently'[12] but he could safely afford to go through the motions of conceding this, given Cobham's obvious availability if the authorities had only deemed it in their interests to produce such an equivocating witness. **10.03**

In spite of the willingness of the courts to use a deposition it is indicative of the fact that the sixteenth century represented a phase of transition into trials based on live narrative that, as Professor Langbein has persuasively demonstrated, the purpose of the Committal Statue 2 & 3 Philip and Mary c.10 of 1555 was never to give evidentiary force to the **10.04**

---

[7] See e.g. Holdsworth cited above at n.3, vol ix, 214–218.

[8] Wigmore, J.H., *A Treatise on the Anglo-American System of Evidence in Trials at Common Law* (6 vols) Boston: Little, Brown, 1923, para 819, notes 29–32, recording occasional lapses. *Cf* Langbein's close scrutiny of the Old Bailey sessions papers revealing wholesale disregard of the hearsay rule until the 1740s, when defendants came to be allowed counsel to examine and cross-examine witnesses on their behalf: Langbein, J.H., 'The Criminal Trial Before the Lawyers,' (1978) 45 *Univ. Chicago Law Rev*, 263, at 307–311.

[9] (1662) Kelyng's Rep 18; 6 St Tr 226,

[10] See Wigmore, cited above at n.8, para 819, note, for a collection of cases.

[11] (1603) 2 State Trials 1.

[12] Ibid, p.19. See Holdsworth, cited above at n.3, ix, 217, n.2, for comment on the judge's strained reasoning.

written record of the preliminary examination of the witnesses.[13] Rather its chief purpose was to systematize and organize the prosecution of indictable crime and, indeed, the possibility that the examination record of a witness, provided it was taken under oath, might be read if he should die before trial is not mentioned until 1581.[14]

(2) Traditional rationale behind the rule against hearsay

10.05 A variety of reasons for objecting to hearsay have been put forward at various times.[15] Three of them are relevant to the present topic. First, before the era of modern electronic audio-visual recording it would have been impossible for the triers of fact to judge from the written record of the statement or an orally conveyed account of it, whether or not it had been faithfully taken down or was accurately recalled. Even the most experienced and skilful amanuensis keeping what purports to be a verbatim note simultaneously may have misheard, misunderstood (and so erroneously put down) or omitted what was uttered. Where a note was written up at some stage afterwards the risk of inaccuracy would have been magnified as the interval increased. In the words of the Law Commission, '[t]his risk is all the greater if the reporter had a preconceived idea of what the other person was going to say'.[16]

Second, even assuming the written record or the memory of the oral reporter was broadly accurate as to the words used—an optimistic assumption at best—the triers would have had no opportunity to observe the way in which the statement was originally delivered, to see and hear the questions which may have elicited it, the context of the answers in the light of those questions, the influence which such questions may have brought to bear on the maker, whether leading, suggestive, or 'cognitively' neutral, and finally the ostensible maker's intonation and inflexion, degree of confidence or hesitancy, and not least the myriad of his nuances of demeanour when speaking. Hence they would have had no means of judging whether any of these factors reflected, modified or belied the ostensible meaning of the recorded or reported words.[17]

Third, the triers of fact will have enjoyed no opportunity to observe cross-examination of the unavailable maker of the assertion of fact, and so be unable to evaluate its truth from the reaction of the maker when tested adversarially.[18] Not only would the triers be unable

---

[13] Langbein, J.H., *Prosecuting Crime in the Renaissance*, Cambridge, Mass: Harvard University Press, 1974, ch. 2.

[14] By William Lambarde in his *Eirenarcha: or Of the Office of the Justice of the Peace*, London: Companie of Stationers, 1581, 210, cited in ibid, p.9. See further below, para 10.06.

[15] See the Law Commission report, cited above at n.1, Part III.

[16] Ibid, at para 3.6.

[17] See Law Commission Report, cited above at n.1, paras. 3.10 and 3.11 for authoritative opinions doubting the value of demeanour as an indicator of reliability, and see chapter 18 of the present work. The Commission's view was that the significance of demeanour was not such as to justify the exclusion of hearsay, but that it did merit a judicial warning: para. 3.12.

[18] Wigmore famously extolled cross-examination as 'the greatest legal engine ever invented for discovering of truth' which, rather than jury trial, was 'the great and permanent contribution of the Anglo-American system of law to improved methods of trial procedure': cited above at n.8, para. 1367, note. The Law Commission, however, cited opinion doubting the value of cross-examination: see above at n.1, para. 3.17.

to observe the statement maker's overt demeanour but the lack of any opportunity to cross-examine would have meant no opportunity to probe the maker's mental or physical health (including, in appropriate cases, the quality of such of the maker's faculties of perception as eyesight and hearing, for example), or inner emotional state or mood at the time of the events described and at the time of narration. All in all, as Wigmore put it, the 'elusive and incommunicable evidence of a witness's deportment while testifying' and the consequent 'subjective moral effect' produced on him would have been entirely missing.[19]

(3) Witness statements exceptionally admissible in the absence of their maker

With the introduction of the new hearsay rule into law three important exceptions were **10.06** conceded by resolution of all the judges in a caucus meeting before the trial of Lord Morley for treason in 1666: a deposition might be read if the witness were proved on oath to be dead, too ill to travel or detained by means of procurement of the prisoner.[20] The first two were cited by Hale (who was one of the judges)[21] which probably explains why only they were codified in section 17 of the Indictable Offences Act 1848. Re-codification in section 13 of the Criminal Justice Act 1925 added the third *Morley* exception and a fourth, proof of the witness's insanity (which originated from a late eighteenth century case.[22]) The Criminal Justice Act 1988 controversially dropped the explicit need for proof of the defendant's involvement in procuring the absence of the witness. Instead, section 23(3)(b) enacted that any statement made to a police officer or other official investigator might be read if the maker 'does not give evidence through fear or because he is kept out of the way'. The two conditions were disjunctive so that, without any provable action on the part of the accused, statements could qualify to be read if the maker were in a state of incapacitating fear of the accused because of the nature of the offence, or too fearful of the experience of going into the witness box, to give evidence in court.[23] The distinction has been noted between fear and *distress*, fear

---

[19] Cited above at n.8, para 1365. 'The light which his demeanour would throw on his testimony is lost': *Teper v R* [1952] 2 AC 480, at 486, HL, *per* Lord Normand, cited by Law Commission, see above at n.1, para. 3.9.

[20] (1666) 6 State Trials 770. See also Kelyng Rep, 55. Other well-known 'exceptions' were also subsequently allowed.

[21] Hale, Sir Matthew, *A History of the Pleas of the Crown*, London: Sollom Emlyn, 1736 (first printing, 60 years after the author's death) ii, 24.

[22] For a detailed history of proof by missing witness in the hearsay era and an account of developments in relation to the absent-through-fear provision during the Parliamentary process leading to enactment of the 1988 Act, see a series of articles by David Wolchover in the *New Law Journal:* (1983) 133 *NLJ* 1117 (23 December); (1987) 137 *NLJ* 525 (5 June), 805 (28 August), 833 (4 September); (1988) *NLJ* 202 (25 March), 242 (8 April), 261 (15 April); 461 (1 July).

[23] Law Commission Report, cited above at n.1, para 4.42. See also ibid, paras 8.48–8.70. In *R v Acton JJ, ex p McMullen; R v Tower Bridge Magistrates' Court, ex p Lawlor* (1996) 92 Cr App R 98, the Divisional Court held that it was 'sufficient' to prove that the witness was in fear as a consequence of the commission of the material offence or of something said or done subsequently in relation that offence and the possibility of the witness testifying to it. It has been observed that this does not technically foreclose the argument that any fear of testifying, for whatever reason, may suffice: Birch, D., 'The Criminal Justice Act 1988 (2) Documentary Evidence' [1989] Crim LR 15, at 23. However, as has also been noted, a 'court bent on purposive interpretation of the section may well not be hospitable to that argument': Griew, E. and Ormerod, D, 'Criminal Justice Act 1988, ss23 and 24: the absence conditions and the cases' [1999] 12 *Archbold News* 6 (February 28).

being 'a qualitatively different state and one less easily established than mere distress, which would encompass the feelings of most [*sic*] witnesses'.[24] However, there will be cases where statement makers are palpably in fear, as might be evident from their behaviour, demeanour or words or a combination, and not merely distressed. One problem with the reform was that the witness might well be visibly but nevertheless incoherently (and therefore inexplicably) terrified—but (albeit privately) as to the consequences of committing perjury.[25] The Law Commission decided that it was unnecessary to make an express provision excluding cases in which the witness feared a prosecution for perjury 'since no court would think it "in the interests of justice" to allow a witness statement to be read on this basis'.[26] It has been noted that the fear of the consequences of perjury is not confined to that of prosecution but may include the risk of retaliation from those implicated by the evidence.[27] The 1988 Act also incorporated provision for the reception of 'business' documents and the written statements of witnesses who were abroad or were untraceable.

10.07   On the face of it taking matters much further, the Criminal Procedure and Investigations Act 1996 (s 68 and Sch 2) removed practically all legal restraints on the reading at trial of a contentious deposition or witness statement which had been processed through committal proceedings in accordance with ss 9 of the Criminal Justice Act 1967 and 102 of the Magistrates' Courts Act 1980.[28] However, stubbornly refusing to concede any amendment to the wording the Government purported in a somewhat confused declaration in the House of Lords to give assurances that the intention behind the measure was that trial courts would simply refer to the 1988 criteria in exercising their discretion whether or not to allow statements to be read,[29] a proposition which plainly nullified the essential purpose of the measure. The new provision co-existed with section 23 of the 1988 Act and in the event little or no use appears to have been made of it. Coming in from another approach were those special measures which allow—indeed require—video-recorded statements to be played as evidence-in-chief where the witness was vulnerable. However, this was not an exception to the hearsay rule because the witness would be present at court when the recording was played and available for cross-examination via a video link with the courtroom.

10.08   Contentious *depositions* under the 1925 Act had to be taken at committal proceedings in which the defendant did at least enjoy the opportunity of cross-examining the maker at that stage. The enactment of the prosecution's right, under the various conditions of the CJA 1988, to lead statements in documents in lieu of the testimony from the maker

---

[24] Ormerod, Prof D., 'Hearsay Provisions in the Criminal Justice Act 2003,' paper presented at a Criminal Bar Association conference, 21 January 2006, para 6.7.

[25] This point was originally made by David Wolchover in (1988) 138 *NLJ*, 461, at 462.

[26] Cited above at n.1, para 8.66.

[27] See Ormerod, cited above at n.24, at para 6.8. The sanction of the oath may deter some people.

[28] We lay stress on *contentious* statements. Provision for agreed section 9 statements to be read in lieu of the attendance of the deponent was of course made in the 1967 Act.

[29] See *Archbold Criminal Pleading, Evidence and Practice*, London: Sweet and Maxwell, editions prior to 2004, para 10–41. The 1996 measure was closely examined in Munday, R., 'The drafting smokescreen,' (1997) 147 *NLJ* 792 (30 May), 860 (6 June).

(with the proviso under the 'fear' head that the statement was one made to the police effectively under section 9 of the CJA 1967), and the abolition of live committal proceedings in the 1990s, meant that even that partial consolation was ended.

(4) Previous statements of witnesses who appear to give evidence

The reception in evidence of contentious statements made by persons who, for the **10.09** reasons referred to above, are not in attendance at court, is permitted by way of an exception to the hearsay rule. In contrast, previous statements made by witnesses who do come to give evidence are not really hearsay, since the maker is present in court. At common law when such statements were disclosed to the court under one of the relevant rules they were not admissible as evidence of the truth of the assertions of fact they contained. That has now changed under the CJA 2003. The use of previous statements to displace or complement a witness's evidence in court is considered in more detail in Section C below dealing with the provisions of the Act.

C. The Criminal Justice Act 2003

The 1996 provision appears to have been almost completely sidelined, with reliance **10.10** continuing to be placed directly on s3 of the CJA 1988 directly (and not by analogy, as the Government had intended). Section 23 of the 1988 Act has now been replaced by s116 of the CJA 2003, which to some extent relaxes the old rules in favour of admitting hearsay but in one respect imposes a slightly enhanced restriction on the potential excesses of the 'fear' limb. Further, as part of the out-of-court statements package of its measures the CJA 2003 changes the status of out-of-court statements of a witness introduced into evidence (a) for the purpose of impeaching consistency, (b) in order to demonstrate consistency, or (c) as an *aide mémoire*. Such statements are now admissible as evidence of the assertions of fact they contain. In the opinion of one authoritative commentator this is a radical change and may in the long term impact on witness intimidation as defendants realise there is little point in making threats if a witness's earlier statement can be admitted.[30]

(1) Proving statements by unavailable or incapacitated witnesses

With two important changes s116 broadly re-enacts the provisions of s23 of the CJA **10.11** 1988 laying down the circumstances in which a contentious statement previously made by an unavailable, incapacitated, or, as the case may be, mute, person may be led as evidence of any matter stated in it.[31] In criminal proceedings a statement not made in oral evidence in the proceedings is admissible as evidence of any matter stated if the maker of the statement is identified,[32] if oral evidence given in the proceedings by the

---

[30] Ormerod, cited above at n.24, para 3.1.
[31] For a review of the impact of the European Convention on Human Rights on the working of the provisions see Ormerod, cited at ibid, paras 6.10 to 6.24.
[32] *Quaere* whether the term 'matter,' as distinct from 'fact' in s23, would embrace opinion: see Ormerod, ibid, para 6.4. The requirement for identification is important if there is an issue as to the maker's testimonial competence: see ibid.

maker of the statement would be admissible as evidence of that matter, and if the maker (a) is dead, (b) is unfit to be a witness because of his bodily or mental condition,[33] (c) is outside the United Kingdom (the securing of his attendance not being reasonably practicable), (d) is untraceable despite reasonable steps having been taken to find him, or (e) through fear does not give evidence or continue to give evidence, either at all or in connection with the subject matter of the statement.[34] In contrast with s23, the statement need no longer be in the form of a document, although it may be envisaged that in practice it will usually be contained in either a statement taken in accordance with s9 of the CJA 1967, or an electronic record. In any event, subject to the conditions of s116 being met, witness A can now repeat in court the first-hand hearsay of absent person B. A second relaxation of the rule is that it is no longer necessary that a statement which it is proposed to adduce under the 'fear' head was made to a police officer or other official investigator. This will facilitate defence reliance on the provision. The term 'fear' is to be widely construed and (for example) includes fear of the death or injury of another person or of financial loss.[35]

10.12 With the exception of the fear limb s116 admissibility is automatic if the statutory conditions are met. The problem with purported fear is that a prospective witness can appear at court claiming to be in fear and can then rely on the very existence of the alleged fear to withstand questions about the cause. Again, a witness can be said to have disappeared, reportedly telling a police officer, for example, that fear is the reason. The claim is easily made but difficult to refute.

An important innovation designed to offset the risk of duplicity in this respect is a special leave requirement for the reading of statements under the 'fear' limb. A statement may only be read under the fear condition if the court considers that it ought to be admitted in the interests of justice, having regard—(a) to the statement's contents, (b) to any risk that its admission or exclusion will result in unfairness to any part to the proceedings (and in particular to how difficult it will be to challenge the statement if the relevant person does not give oral evidence, (c) to the fact that a special measures direction for the giving of evidence by fearful and other vulnerable witnesses could be made under s19 of the Youth Justice and Criminal Evidence Act 1999, and (d) to any other relevant circumstances.[36] These guidelines merely make explicit what would be implicit in the exercise of the PACE Act 1984, s78. More importantly, there is one feature of s116 which represents a pronounced improvement over the former position and to some extent meets the criticism which was articulated in relation to the untraceable and fear limbs during the Parliamentary process which led to the 1988 Act.[37] This concerned the removal of the old requirement under the *Morley* principle (as re-enacted in s13 of the CJA 1925) to prove that the potential witness's reluctance was attributable to some action taken by the defendant directly or 'on his behalf'. It was argued that this

---

[33] The 'unfitness' concerns the giving of evidence, not merely attendance, as under the predecessor rule.

[34] It is therefore made explicit that the fear condition is satisfied where a witness is called to give oral evidence but through fear fails to mention the relevant matter in the statement, as in *R v Ashford Justices ex p Hilden* [1993] QB 555: see Ormerod, cited above at n.24, para 6.7.

[35] S116(3), reflecting the thrust of decisions under s23 of the CJA 1988: see ibid.

[36] S116(4).   [37] See the articles by Wolchover referred to above at n.22.

created the very real risk that an ill-intentioned police officer, or other person with an interest in the conviction of the accused, might be tempted to cause an equivocating witness who he judged would be likely to fail to come up to proof, to disappear. The intent would be that the awkward witness's sterile written statement could then be read unsullied by any risk of being recanted or of successful impeachment under cross-examination. If the officer gave evidence that he had witnessed the person exhibiting all the outward physical signs of being in fear, coupled with supporting utterances, this would be admissible as indicative of the person's state of mind and the utterances would not have been hearsay. Moreover, it was argued, as a fundamental principle it would place defendants in the invidious position of having to face an inherently unsatisfactory form of evidence where it was unclear if the witness's reluctance was attributable to any action by or on behalf of the defendant.

To a very limited extent the CJA 2003 restores the 1925 position. Section 116(5) **10.13** provides that even if one of the sets of circumstances listed in the section for the witness not giving evidence is established the person's statement may not be given in evidence—

> if it is *known* that the circumstances . . . are caused—(a) by the person in support of whose case it is sought to give the statement in evidence, or (b) by a person acting on his behalf, in order to prevent the relevant person giving oral evidence in the proceedings (whether at all or in connection with the subject matter of the statement) (emphasis added).

For the purposes of the prosecution seeking to read the statement of a witness the Act does not identify who is meant by 'the person in support of whose case it is sought to give the statement in evidence'. Does it mean a civilian complainant, or more generally the 'Crown', or the officer in the case, acting as an agent of the Crown? On the assumption that it would include the latter, proof (i.e. knowledge) that the witness's absence or disabling state or condition was caused by or on behalf of that officer will preclude the reading of the statement. However, in contrast to the 1925 rule, which placed on the prosecution the onus of establishing that the disappearance of the witness was caused by the defendant as a condition precedent for invoking the subsection to prevent the missing witness's statement from being read, it is now incumbent on the defence to establish that the disappearance was caused by someone on the prosecution side. Overcoming this hurdle is hardly helped by the fact that evidence from the ill-intentioned officer that the missing witness had told him he was in fear of giving evidence would now be admissible under the section as direct evidence of the fact that the witness was indeed in fear.

(2) Witnesses in court

(i) Previous inconsistent statements

Apart from the hearsay exceptions depositions and witness statements had always been **10.14** permitted to be introduced into the trial for the essential purpose of demonstrating inconsistency with the maker's evidence in the witness box. In the words of the Court of Appeal 'other statements are one of the classic examples of material tending to undermine the credibility of a witness.'[38] At common law previous statements put to a witness

---

[38] *R v Rashid* {1994} unreported, transcript no. 89/4043/W3, judgment 17 April 1994.

to demonstrate inconsistency with their evidence given in court were not treated as proof of the truth of the assertions they contained unless the witness expressly resiled from his or her evidence in court and adopted the inconsistent statement as the truth. They merely went to the issue of the witness's credibility. Section 119 of the 2003 Act has radically altered this. Such statements are now admissible as evidence of any matter stated in them of which oral evidence by the maker would be admissible, irrespective of whether the statement is adopted in preference to the evidence given in court under oath or affirmation, and with which the statement put in is apparently inconsistent. Where an inconsistent statement is proved, either by virtue of the witness admitting to having made it, or by proof otherwise of its making,[39] it is now therefore a matter for the jury as to which version is the truth. This is an exercise which instinct would suggest juries have probably always conducted, irrespective of a direction of the kind which Sir Rupert Cross famously dismissed as 'gibberish',[40] and at last brings the law into line with reality. The new rule will advance the prosecution's case where a prosecution witness has been declared hostile as a result of giving evidence contrary to his statement implicating the accused and on being cross-examined by the Crown on his previous statement he agrees he made the previous statement but stands by the evidence given in court.[41] It will be to the advantage of the defence where his statement contains assertions favourable to the defendant but he has given evidence to the converse of those assertions.

(ii) Previous consistent statements

10.15 At common law previous statements were permitted to be adduced in a number of specified instances for the specific purpose of demonstrating consistency with the evidence given by a witness in court. Thus, they might be led—as evidence of recent complaint in a sexual allegation; to demonstrate a previous identification; as part of the *res gestae*; or to rebut an allegation of recent fabrication. When admitted in evidence in these circumstances they went only to the issue of consistency, that is to support the witness's credibility as to the evidence given in court, and were not evidence of the truth of the earlier statement. It has been observed that this was confusing for tribunals of fact and for those directing them[42] and that any change in favour of making the earlier statement evidence of the truth of the contents can only be a good thing since early recollections are invariably better than those in the witness box.[43] Conversely, however, it may be argued that the old qualification would generally have been of little or no significance since the account was before the court as evidence in any event.

10.16 Section 120 makes provision for previous consistent statements to stand as evidence of the truth of that which they assert where they are relied on:

---

[39] Under the Criminal Procedure Act 1865, ss3, 4 or 5.

[40] Cross, R., 'The Evidence Report: Sense or nonsense (a very wicked animal defends the Eleventh Report at the Criminal Law Revision Committee)', [1973] Crim LR 329, at 333.

[41] See *Joyce and Joyce* [2005] EWCA Crim 1785 (appellants unsuccessfully argued that judge should have stopped the trial under s125 on the basis that an earlier identification by witnesses who had been ruled hostile to the prosecution was unconvincing hearsay).

[42] Ormerod, cited above at n.24, at para 3.7, citing *R v Kiffin* [2005] All ER (D) 361.

[43] Ibid, para 3.7.

- to rebut allegations of recent fabrication (s120(2));
- to confirm the previous identification of a person, object or a place (s120(5)) or
- as evidence of recent complaint of the offence to which the proceedings relate—not merely a sexual offence—that is, a complaint made as soon as could reasonably be expected after the alleged misconduct (s120(7)).

(iii) Statement introduced to refresh memory

Where a document containing the narration of an event or description of a certain state **10.17** of affairs is made at a time when the witness's memory of the episode is still 'fresh' it has long been permissible for the witness to use the document to prompt the memory when giving evidence.[44] However, statements in the memory-refreshing document themselves were not evidence of their truth, although, as with previous consistent statements, this was arguably of little consequence where witnesses professed that their memories were revived by sight of the document. If the witness was cross-examined on the document, as a result of which the whole of its contents were read out to the court, or it was actually exhibited, any assertions revealed in it which the witness had not initially mentioned would only become evidence if they were adopted by the witness. This might be important if the witness resiled from assertions on which the cross-examiner relied. Section 120(3) would make such statements evidence:

A statement made by the witness in a document—
(a) which is used by him to refresh his memory while giving evidence,
(b) on which he is cross-examined, and
(c) which as a consequence is received in evidence in the proceedings,
is admissible as evidence of any matter stated of which oral evidence by him would be admissible.

The qualifiers refer to the document (not the statement) and hence any statement in the document, whether used to revive memory, adopted, repudiated or not recalled by the witness would become evidence of its truth on the qualifying conditions being met. A repudiated statement would of course also be admissible as truth under the rule for inconsistent statements. Statements which witnesses do not repudiate but which they profess not to recall may be helpful to the cross-examining party and the law reform is very welcome here.

Memory-refreshing documents are no longer restricted to cases where the earlier state- **10.18** ment was 'contemporaneous'. The CJA 2003 now permits witnesses to rely on statements made when their recollections were likely to have been 'significantly better' when they made or verified the document (or made a sound recording, if a transcript of such a recording is to be used): s139.

---

[44] The rule may have originated from around 1680: the written examination of a witness taken before justices of the peace might be read 'if the Evidence for the King falter in his Testimony to refresh his memory': Anonymous, *The Office of the Clerk of Assize . . . Together with the Office of the Clerk of the Peace*, London: Henry Twyford, 1681–2, 48. It was not mentioned in the earlier 1660 and 1676 editions: see Langbein, cited above at n.13, 29.

(iv) Contemporaneous record which does not refresh memory

10.19   A previous statement by a witness is admissible as evidence of any matter stated of which oral evidence by the witness would be admissible (a) if while giving evidence the witness indicates that to the best of his belief he made the statement and that to the best of his belief it states the truth, and (b) that it was made when the matters stated were fresh in his memory but he does not remember them, and cannot reasonably be expected to remember them well enough to give oral evidence of them in the proceedings: s120(7). At common law witnesses were allowed to refresh their memories on the basis of '*past recollection recorded*' where they had no independent recollection of the facts recorded but attested to the accuracy of the record.[45] The old rule was not particularly well known and the new rule, by upgrading the evidential status of a record relied upon under the old principle and enhancing awareness of that principle, might have secured the benefit that police officers will no longer feel any need to pretend that their notebook descriptions of a routine and eminently forgettable episode from perhaps months before have revived their memory, a reform which can only conduce to honest testimony.

(v) Statements previously video-recorded

10.20   In proceedings for offences triable on indictment or prescribed either-way offences the Act increases the scope for courts to use the previously video-recorded account by a witness of 'conduct constituting the offence or closely connected events' where the witness's memory of the offence or those events at the time the account was recorded is 'significantly better' than it is at the time of the proceedings in question and it is in the interests of justice to admit it as evidence: s137.

(3) Factors to be considered in determining whether to allow hearsay and previous out-of-court statements by a witness

10.21   The CJA 2003 provides in s114(1) that—

> (a) a statement not made in oral evidence in the proceedings is admissible as evidence of any matter stated if, but only if . . . (d) the court is satisfied that it is in the interests of justice for it to be admissible.

Paragraph (d) has been called the 'safety valve' exception. Of importance for present purposes is the provision of s114(2) that, in deciding whether a statement not made in oral evidence should be admitted under s114(1)(d) as evidence of any matter stated in it, the court must have regard to the following factors, *inter alia*:

- the circumstances in which the statement was made: (d);
- how reliable the maker of the statement appears to be: (e);
- how reliable the evidence of the making of the statement appears to be: (f);
- the amount of difficulty involved in challenging the statement: (h), and
- the extent to which that difficulty would be likely to prejudice the party facing it: (i).

It may be the objective of the defence to demonstrate inherent weakness in the process by which the out-of-court statement was elicited or was recorded. This will have a

---

[45] Terminology coined by Wigmore, cited above at n.8, para. 754A.

two-stepped impact. First it might prove invaluable in persuading the trial judge to exclude the statement on the basis that to allow it to be given would prejudice the fairness of the trial. If however the statement is received in evidence the next step will be to persuade the jury to discount its value in the light of doubts as to its veracity or the reliability of the evidence of its terms and tone.

D. Weaknesses in the Process of Obtaining and Recording Out-of-Court Statement

In this section it is proposed to discuss the question of the poverty of the means of **10.22** transmitting the totality of statements made out of court to the triers of fact. We shall conclude this discussion by focusing on the extent to which those weaknesses will cause the defence difficulty in challenging the truth of such out-of-court assertions and hence furnish grounds for seeking their exclusion from the evidence, or submitting to the jury that they should be disregarded.

(1) When was the statement made?

Sometimes a witness statement is taken almost immediately. This should be a good **10.23** starting point although it is always worth considering the impact of recent trauma and the confusion that can reign in the aftermath of a crime scene. However, most statements are taken some time after the event they describe. What may have happened between the event and the taking of the statement is of paramount importance. There are cases in which the statements are taken long after the event, not merely days or weeks but even years. The criminal courts are well used to dealing with arguments surrounding the issue of delay and it is not proposed to rehearse them here.

(2) Witness training or coaching

However, the influence and potential contamination of evidence by other people who **10.24** also witnessed the events has been a matter of recent review by the Court of Appeal. In *R v Momodou and Limani*,[46] which concerned a violent disorder in an immigration detention centre, the court focused on the dangers inherent in witness training. Immediately after the incident the staff at the centre, who were witnesses, were given counselling by the Independent Counselling and Advisory Service (ICAS) arranged by their employer, Group 4. They were seen in group sessions where they discussed feelings and reactions about what had occurred but no record was kept of the sessions and discussions. The staff in question were then warned by civil solicitors of the dangers of giving evidence to the police and the precautions which they ought to take, including not handing over their pocket notebooks. It was also suggested that they discuss their notes and statements with their managers and company solicitor. Group 4 then arranged for witness training for the staff, including the discussion of case studies and scenarios comparable to those they had witnessed. No record of the training was kept. The case

---

[46] [2005] EWCA Crim 177.

offers an extreme example of how witness evidence can be influenced and contaminated even before a statement is taken. The defence argued that the activities of these third parties were such as to render a fair trial impossible and argued abuse of process. The Court of Appeal rejected the submission but the judgment provides a valuable insight into the court's approach on contamination:

> There is a dramatic distinction between witness training or coaching and witness familiarisation. Training or coaching for witnesses (whether prosecution or defence) is not permitted. This is the logical consequence of a well known principle that discussions between witnesses should not take place, and that the statements and proofs of one witness should not be disclosed to any other witness. . . . The rule reduces, indeed hopefully avoids, any possibility that one witness may tailor his evidence in the light of what anyone else said, and equally, avoids any unfounded perception that he may have done so. . . . An honest witness may alter the emphasis of his evidence to accommodate what he thinks may be a different, more accurate, or simply better remembered perception of events . . . where . . . the witness is jointly trained with other witnesses to the same events the dangers dramatically increase. Recollections change, memories are contaminated. Witnesses may bring their respective accounts into what they believe to be better alignment with others. They may be encouraged to do so, consciously or unconsciously. They may collude deliberately; they may be inadvertently contaminated. Whether deliberately or inadvertently the evidence may no longer be their own.[47]

It is to be hoped that such an extreme example of the contamination of witness accounts narrative will rarely be seen in British courts. The judgment provides some general points of interest which it is worth extrapolating. Both prosecution and defence should, where possible, ascertain whether the witness has had contact with other witnesses prior to their accounts being recorded. The most obvious example of this is the collaboration between police officers on the writing up of their notes. The practice has long been viewed as acceptable for reasons of practicality (*R v Bass* [1953] 1 QB 680) but for the reasons set out above it is far from ideal and must be subject to rigorous cross-examination.

10.25 In December 2004 the Attorney-General announced his approval of a scheme which would, in certain instances, allow prosecution lawyers to interview witnesses who had already provided a statement to the police. This would enable prosecutors, principally, to assess the reliability of the witness by questioning them about their statement and hence to decide whether to call the witness or even to continue with the case. The scheme also anticipates that if, during the interview, the prosecutor elicits information from the witness which has not been included in or is in conflict with their earlier statement, the prosecutor might cause the investigator to take a further statement from the witness to reflect this. The process of conducting assessment interviews is regulated by a Code of Practice and other guidance, and pilot schemes were begun in four Crown Prosecution Service areas on 23 January 2006.[48] The Code includes a minimum requirement for the interview to be audio-recorded. Together with the various other code requirements this

---

[47] Para 61. See generally further Wydich, Prof R., 'The Ethics of Witness Coaching,' (1995) 17 *Cardoza Law Review*, No 1 (Yeshiva University of New York).

[48] Cumbria, Greater Manchester, Lancashire and Merseyside.

will expose the nuances of interviews to ease of scrutiny in court, a facility which is likely to go some considerable way towards overcoming the 'difficulty involved in challenging the statement' mentioned in s114(2)(h) and (i) of the Act of 2003 as a factor to be taken into account by the court in determining whether or not to allow the statement to be read. With the stringent requirement that it be audio-recorded, the assessment interview may be compared with very limited opportunities for revelation when a witness's statement is recorded by a police officer in the 'old fashioned' way, with no audio-recording.

Notwithstanding the establishment of transparency it may be hard to see how both as a **10.26** matter of principle and in practice prosecutors conducting assessment interviews will manage to avoid offending against the strictures in *Momodou and Limani* about coaching whether through overtly improper or merely suggestive questions.

Whether a witness has had external contact and discussions is something that can be **10.27** explored with the witness, but may also be established through disclosure.

(3) Evidence of complaint

Evidence of recent complaint is admissible on the basis that it is less likely that an **10.28** individual will make an account up so soon after an alleged event and is useful to show consistency and inconsistency. It is worth also considering the relationship to the complainant of the individual to whom such an account has been made.

(i) Family members

Many complainants—most obviously children—will turn to their family first. Some **10.29** children are more willing than others to talk about difficult and potentially embarrassing matters such as sexual activities. There is a possibility of the child overplaying or underplaying their account depending on their relationship with the family. Knowledge of that relationship may come through instructions from the defendant but may need more substantial investigation through social service files.

(ii) Friends

Mutatatis mutandis similar considerations apply when the complaint is made to friends **10.30** or close associates. Is the child likely to be exaggerating in order to show off or is the child reluctant to say what really happened? Again, investigation may be required.

(iii) Therapists

In an historic sexual abuse case purported complaints to therapists before a complaint is **10.31** made to the police may occasion obvious dangers of suggestion and contamination but, as *Momodou* highlighted, they may also arise in less obvious cases.

(4) Where and how accounts are given

Witnesses give statements in a variety of locations and by means of a number of methods: **10.32** from the police station, to the hospital, the home, school, the office and so on. They may give a question and answer style account at a police station or they may give a basic monologue account of events that is then built on. Following the *Achieving Best Evidence*

(ABE) guidance[49] video-recorded evidence is being increasingly utilized for witnesses at large, and not merely in the case of certain classes of vulnerable witnesses.

10.33 The vast majority of witness statements taken in the criminal investigative process are elicited and recorded by police officers although official investigators from other specialist agencies also play a significant role in witness interviewing. Little is disclosed to the outside world about what sort of training they receive to carry out this task. If civilian witnesses are asked whether it is their account or a construct of mere affirmative answers to questions put by a police officer, the latter response is not uncommon. Practitioners are of course not unaware of this difficulty. How, then, can it be known what sort of questioning techniques the police officer was using? Was the officer putting leading questions? Was he ignoring or not exploring certain assertions or both? These are the sort of questions that need answering in order to establish whether or not the statement is actually the witness's true recollection. By the time the case gets to trial it may be too late as the witness may be recollecting their account to the police (especially as they will have just read it in the witness room at court) rather than their actual memory. The distinction is too blurred by this stage. What safeguards against this are in place?

(i) Training of investigators

10.34 Proper training of police and other investigators is essential. Nowadays, police training follows a standardized national programme based on investigative, or 'ethical' interviewing, using the method of the 'cognitive interview',[50] and tuition in, and encouragement to follow, the ABE guidance referred to above. Other investigating authorities, less constrained by uniformity of method, employ techniques which tend to be shrouded in mystery unless the effort is made to scrutinize them as and when a case demands it.

(ii) Electronic recording: the decision-making process

10.35 The use of electronic recording to monitor and thereby inhibit the processes of contamination referred to above formed the subject matter of chapter 15 of *Analysing Witness Testimony* and it is superfluous to repeat or even summarize the conclusions reached there. It is however pertinent to examine such advances as have been made since publication in 1999. Although ABE guidance has regulated video interviewing of children and vulnerable witnesses for many years, there is now specific guidance also on the interviewing of 'significant witnesses'. The guidelines provide safeguards in relation to

---

[49] *Achieving Best Evidence in Criminal Proceedings: Guidance for Vulnerable or Intimidated Witnesses, including Children*, Home Office 2002 (consultation paper, 2000), available on *http://www.homeoffice.gov.uk/documents/achieving-best-evidence*.

[50] Heralded by the Home Office circular *Principles of Investigative Interviewing*, HO 22/1992, issued 20 February 1992, and introduced by a supplementary circular HO 7/1993, issued 7 January 1993. The training programme involves pre-course study of three booklets, *A Guide to Interviewing, The Interviewer's Rule Book* and *The Interview Workbook*, Home Office Central Planning Unit, 1992. There is an immense literature on investigative interviewing, too extensive to cite here. However, a good starting point, with a comprehensive bibliography, is Clifford, B.R., and Memon, A., 'Obtaining detailed testimony: the cognitive interview,' in Heaton-Armstrong, A., Shepherd, E. and Wolchover, D. (eds), *Analysing Witness Testimony*, London: Blackstone Press, 1999, ch. 10. For a recent dedicated work see Williamson, T. (ed.), *Investigative Interviewing: Rights, research, regulation*, Cullompton: Willan Publishing, 2006. See also Chapter 8 in this volume.

the investigation, preservation and integrity of the evidence. One of the principal safe-guards is the requirement to decide on the designation of significant witnesses and on the means of recording their statements. As to this there are three elements:

Identifying the significant witnesses At an early stage in an investigation the Senior **10.36** Investigating Officer must determine who the significant witnesses are and must record their decisions and reasoning as to the management of such witnesses.

Choosing between audio only and audio/visual recording The SIO must decide **10.37** whether an audio recording alone will suffice or whether audio-visual recording is desir-able and will be chosen. The decision and the reasons must be recorded.

Factors to be considered in choosing the recording method When determining which **10.38** method of recording to use the SIO must take account of the following factors:

(1) The competing benefits of audio and audio-visual recording, including:
   • an increase in the volume of recorded information from the witness;
   • safeguarding the integrity of the interviewer and the interview process, and
   • increased opportunities for planning, officer training and remote monitoring.
(2) It may not always be desirable or practicable to make an audio or audio-visual recording immediately or at all. Reasons for this would include:
   • at an early stage of an investigation the need to preserve life, preserve scenes, secure evidence, and identify suspects (but accurate records of the reasons must be kept);
   • potential delay between the making of the original complaint or the initial non-electronically recorded interview, during which the allegation emerged, and the full audio- or audio-visual memorandum interview, compromising the exped-itious progress of the investigation and an early decision to prosecute;[51]
   • witnesses may become unavailable or subsequently withdraw their cooperation while a statement is being drawn up;
   • the need to take into account identifiable risks in relation to disclosure of witness identification and security, and
   • the wishes of the witness.

Practitioners must ensure that full disclosure is received in relation to the notes and logs an officer makes throughout the decision-making process.

(5) Assessing the 'difficulty' in challenging the statement of an absent witness

Built in to the CJA 2003 is a frank acknowledgement of the risk that hearsay state- **10.39** ments—now admissible in general under the Act as a matter of law—and previous statements made by a person who is a witness in the proceedings, introduced to supple-ment, qualify or change statements made in the witness box, will nevertheless pose an obstacle to the defence in seeking to challenge or investigate the substance of the content.

---

[51] As much as anything this is a resource issue, with deficiencies in liaison between the police and the CPS, and casework overload on the part of both services, leading to delay in the monitoring and review by the CPS of material obtained in the initial stage of an inquiry.

We have seen that in determining whether to allow an out-of-court statement to be adduced as evidence of the truth of the assertions of fact contained within it, the court must have regard to the 'circumstances in which the statement was made', 'how reliable the evidence of the statement appears to be,' and, crucially, 'the amount of difficulty involved in challenging the statement'.

10.40 When considering whether to adduce a hearsay statement, or permitting a witness's out-of-court statement to stand as evidence of any matter asserted in it, this will necessitate determining if possible the extent to which the fact finders might be hampered in assessing the reliability and accuracy of such a statement, with no *entrée* to 'the circumstances in which the statement was made'. In any case where a person has not been treated as a 'significant witness', and consequently no audio-visual electronic recording was made of the interview in which the person's 'section 9' or 'section 102' written statement was taken down, recourse must be had to the bare text of the written statement itself. Inevitably the fact finders will be deprived of the opportunity to see the interview, 'warts and all'—the gamut of those factors which were referred to earlier. Having committed themselves to authenticating a written statement signatories may well be prone in the witness box to stick closely to the earlier script out of fear generated by the section 9 declaration concerning the risks of making a false statement. Again, official statement takers will be disinclined to concede any departure from the requirement to act neutrally in eliciting facts from the maker, whether out of concern to avoid disciplinary censure or purely out of professional *amour propre*. Cross-examination of both statement taker and maker is no guarantee that they will budge from insisting that all was as it should have been in the interview. In some cases the terms of the statement viewed in the context of other evidence may throw a revealing light on the reality of what was actually said in the interview, but in most cases the bare text will afford little help. Such difficulties may be exacerbated where the statement was made by a child to its mother, a pupil to another student or a teacher, a patient to a doctor or psychiatrist, or a 'client' to a counsellor. Discovery of the sort of 'circumstances in which the statement was made' for the purposes of considering whether it should be adduced as evidence of assertions of any matter, or, if so adduced, of the weight to be attached to it, may be enormously 'difficult' if these or the statement is 'challenged' and may be well nigh impossible when there is little or no prospect of finding out what the important 'circumstances' were. Nowhere is this more problematic than when a witness has made a statement to a parent or counsellor, often long after the relevant 'event'. Counsellors' records are apt to lack the sort of information which fact finders need to know when deciding whether what was said by the counsellor to the statement maker may have influenced their memory. They rarely comprise any sort of contemporaneous record of what their patient or client said, still less the manner in which it was said, and never (in the experience at least of the authors) do they include the detail of what the counsellor might have said to the patient.

E. Concluding Remarks

Subject to various criteria, the Criminal Justice Act 2003 makes provision for any state- **10.41**
ment, or factual assertion, to be adduced in evidence as part of the maker's historic account
of events, by way of complementing or replacing oral evidence given by the maker live in
the witness box or via a video link. The core basis of the orality tradition of trials under
common law has thus been significantly further qualified but this is not necessarily
unwelcome. The extent to which the Act allows complementary material to stand alone as
evidence has arguably made the law in action more comprehensible to triers of fact and
therefore more coherent as a working model for criminal justice. Again, the rules on
allowing in the hearsay evidence of unavailable or incapacitated witnesses can be said to
have been improved without necessarily being radically reformed. Arguably they have been
made more consonant with doing justice all round without necessarily prejudicing or
endangering the interests of the accused. Where it is proposed to give a statement in
evidence in the absence of an unavailable or incapacitated witness the interests of justice
proviso in s114(1)(d) requires a court of trial, in determining whether to permit the hearsay
evidence to be given, to have regard, *inter alia*, to the circumstances in which the statement
was made, to the amount of difficulty liable to be faced by the party in challenging the
statement and the extent to which that difficulty would be likely to cause that party
prejudice. These essential 'safety valve' requirements will afford the defence considerable
scope for challenging the admissibility of statements proffered in lieu of live testimony.

Further Reading

Achieving Best Evidence in Criminal Proceedings: Guidance for Vulnerable or Intimidated Witnesses,
    including Children, Home Office 2002 (consultation paper, 2000), available on *http://*
    www.homeoffice.gov.uk/documents/achieving-best-evidence.
Law Commission, Report, No 245, *Evidence in Criminal Proceedings: Hearsay and Related*
    Topics, Cm 3670, London: HMSO, 1997.
Ormerod, D., 'Hearsay Provisions in the Criminal Justice Act 2003,' paper presented at a
    Criminal Bar Association conference, 21 January 2006, para 6.7 (available in hard copy from
    the CBA).
R v Momodou and Limani [2005] EWCA Crim 177.

Annabel Maxwell-Scott graduated from Bristol University in 1994 with an Honours
degree in psychology. Her course emphasized cognition and memory research and her
thesis dealt with eyewitness testimony, focusing on the role of recollective experience in
misleading post-event suggestions. Since 1996 she has practised as a barrister in criminal
law, both prosecuting and defending, a field which provides ample opportunity for
putting psychological theory to practical use.

Editors' Note

As never before—owing to the 'hearsay' provisions of the Criminal Justice Act 2003—
previous, out-of-court, statements by witnesses have a potential status which equates
with oral evidence given 'live' from the witness box (or room). In order to inform fact

finders as to such statements' reliability and potential to add to the genuinely useful evidential picture, investigators and legal practitioners need to be wise to the risks to accuracy which the methods used to obtain and record such statements can present and the need, therefore, to reveal the circumstances and contexts in which previous statements were made.

11

ORAL CONFESSIONS TO NON-INVESTIGATOR WITNESSES

David Wolchover and Anthony Heaton-Armstrong

A. PACE: The Golden Age of Protective Investigation

Two decades have passed since the Police and Criminal Evidence Act 1984 (PACE) **11.01** momentously introduced what was little short of a revolution in the whole process by which the police and other official investigators obtain evidence from the prospective accused by questioning. With suspects protected for so many years now in a cocoon of binding safeguards it is sometimes difficult for those of us of the older generation to recall exactly how impoverished the system used to be even a quarter of a century ago. The impact of PACE in mitigating the adverse effects of the 'inherently coercive nature of

191

custodial interrogation' (to quote the celebrated 1966 American decision in *Miranda v Arizona*[1]) and guaranteeing precision in the recording of what suspects allegedly say to the police, has virtually removed disputes over confession evidence altogether from the agenda of the vast majority of criminal trials in England and Wales. This has amounted to such a radical change that younger practitioners may not always appreciate how confession issues not only used to make an appearance in practically every criminal trial but without doubt consumed more running time than any other single topic.

11.02   The many formalities by which PACE—both the Act and its associated Code of Practice on questioning suspects[2]—secures the authenticity of evidence of utterances by suspects when questioned by, or in the hands of, the police, contrasts with the necessary absence of procedures for authenticating incriminating utterances allegedly made by the accused to lay persons. An analogous contrast was reflected centuries ago in the fledgling attitude of the courts towards admissibility, considered first below.

B. The Approach of the Common Law to Confession Evidence Authenticity

(1) Confessions to officials and to private witnesses eventually equated[3]

11.03   The examinations of suspected offenders by investigating officials have been used at trial from time immemorial. As such they constituted what we would understand as hearsay, that is they were adduced as the factual narrative of a person who was not, and could not be, a witness: the accused. With the inception of the rule against hearsay in the seventeenth century some legal device had to be found for circumventing the rule in order to ensure the continued admissibility of such a valuable species of evidence. So, apparently adapted from an old Germanic rule avowing the incontrovertibility of records taken under royal seal, confession on examination quickly came to be justified by the rationale that officials such as justices of the peace, who customarily conducted the examination, were 'judges of record'.[4] The assumption was that the evidence of authentication enjoyed an extraordinary reliability. However, this limitation was challenged in the next century, when it was asserted that the accused's confession 'made in discourse with private persons hath always been allowed to be given in evidence against the party confessing'[5] and it was swiftly affirmed judicially that a confession made to a private person was not only

---

[1] 384 US 436.

[2] *Code of Practice for the Detention, Treatment and Questioning of Persons by Police Officers*, the current edition of which was issued under s66 of the PACE Act 1984 and s77 of the Criminal Justice and Police Act 2001 and was brought into force on 1 April 2003 by the Police and Criminal Evidence Act 1984 (Codes of Practice)(Codes B to E)(No. 2) Order 2003 (SI 2003 No. 703).

[3] See generally Wolchover, D., and Heaton-Armstrong, A., *Confession Evidence*, London: Sweet and Maxwell Criminal Law Library, 1996, paras 1–002 to 1–006.

[4] Hale, Sir Matthew, *The History of the Pleas of the Crown* (2 vols, London: Sollom Emlyn, 1736) ii, 284 (originally ordered by Parliament to be published four years after Hale's death in 1676). In the broader context, admissibility was rationalized as a matter of principle on the basis that, although it constituted hearsay, a confession 'well-proved' enjoyed a particular cogency which justified its admissibility because few would make a statement 'against interest' unless it were true.

[5] Hawkins, *Pleas of the Crown* (1st ed. 1716) c.46, §.31.

admissible but also sufficient to convict of the summary offence of deer-stealing.[6] By the last decade of the century there was no longer any doubt: in *R v Lambe* all twelve judges memorably agreed that no less admissible than a confession before a JP was one

> made in the adjoining room previous to his having been carried into the presence of the Justice, or after he had left him, or in the same room before the Magistrate comes, or after he quits it.[7]

With the development of the rule that the admissibility of a confession would be vitiated by threats or promises held out by a 'person in authority', many of the reported confession cases in the nineteenth century did in fact concern confessions made 'unofficially' to employers, usually about theft in the course of work, although sometimes the offences were of a sexually related nature (such as abortion) into which employers of domestic servants supposed it was their business to inquire. Confessions made to interested persons, such as family members of the victim, also featured in a number of the cases reported. However, the issue in all these cases concerned the voluntary nature of the confession, not its authenticity.[8] Once it had been settled in the eighteenth century that there were no special requirements for authentication of a confession (beyond the testimonial assertion that one had been made), there seemed little further reason for the courts to consider, as a matter of generality, any of the potential problems which might arise in assessing the weight to be attached to evidence given by different categories of lay persons who might be claiming to have witnessed a confession. There might be any number of reasons why some lay witnesses might have a 'personal agenda' to serve in alleging that the accused had confessed to them privately. For example, the father of a young woman who has been raped but is refusing to disclose the identity of her assailant strongly suspects a particular individual and concocts a confession in order either to make the case certain or to provoke his daughter into exonerating the man if by some slender chance (so he thinks) the man be innocent. Again, without any element of conscious deceit a witness's hearing, comprehension, memory or retrieval may be imperfect when it comes to assimilating and recalling an incriminating statement or remark. However, while juries could always be asked to bear these factors in mind on a case-by-case basis, these were not problems about which the courts were ever asked to decree any specific directions which judges were required to give juries, or even to express any authoritative opinions or guidance for judges in assisting juries. There was no juridical requirement, in other words, for juries to be given any special warnings about the dangers inherent in accepting evidence of oral confessions. This was surprising, in a way, bearing in mind the scepticism which has been expressed on the highest authority

---

[6] *R v Dore* (1738) Andrew's Rep. 301. The precedent was later overlooked by commentators, who attributed the provenance of the rule of sufficiency for a conviction of a confession in any form to *R v John Wheeling*, a case at first instance cited in a footnote on *R v Jacobs* (1790) 1 Leach CC 311, but the reference has been shown to lack any authenticity: see Wolchover and Heaton-Armstrong, cited above at n.3, para 1–026.

[7] (1791) 2 Leach CC 552, at 559.

[8] It is of note that there were no reported cases concerning confessions made to fellow prison inmates—a topic which forms an important aspect of the present chapter—for the simple reason that co-inmates were plainly not persons in authority over the accused and would be in no position to secure an end to the prosecution, or mitigation of the penalty, on condition that the defendant confessed.

towards evidence of oral confessions allegedly made to official investigators and lay persons alike.

(2) Juridical suspicion of evidence alleging an oral confession

11.04 Well before the judges of the late eighteenth century were extolling the virtues of a voluntary confession as 'deserving of the highest credit',[9] and '[w]hen well proved . . . the best evidence of guilt',[10] Sir Michael Foster in his treatise of 1732 was wont to offer a rather more sceptical take on the question:

> . . . hasty confessions, made to persons having no authority to examine, are the weakest and most suspicious of all evidence. Proof may be too easily procured, words are often misreported, whether through ignorance, inattention, or malice, it mattereth not to the defendant, he is equally affected in either case; and they are extremely liable to misconstruction and withal, this evidence is not, in the ordinary course of things, to be disproved by that sort of negative evidence, by which the proof of plain facts may be and often is confronted.[11]

Much later, Wigmore, too, although prone to idealize the value of confession evidence[12] acknowledged that the experience of the courts was not always encouraging:

> Paid informers, treacherous associates, angry victims, and overzealous officers of the law—these are the persons through whom an alleged confession is oftenest presented; and it is at this stage that our suspicions are aroused and our caution stimulated.[13]

In *R v Thompson*[14] Cave J noted with some irony a familiar pattern in which prisoners often seemed the more penitent as the case against them was weaker:

> I always suspect these confessions, which are supposed to be the offspring of penitence and remorse, and which nevertheless are repudiated by the prisoner at trial. It is remarkable that it is of very rare occurrence for evidence of a confession to be given when the proof of the prisoner's guilt is otherwise clear and satisfactory; but, when it is not clear and satisfactory, the prisoner is not unfrequently alleged to have been seized with the desire born of penitence and remorse to supplement it with a confession;—desire which vanishes as soon as he appears in a court of justice.

Modern empirical research has validated this scepticism[15] and, only a decade before PACE, Cave J's remarks were cited with wry approval by the Court of Appeal in *R v Pattinson*.[16] It is true that Cave J was thinking more of confession to police officers than to lay witnesses but the principle is surely applicable to oral confessions generally.

---

[9] *R v Warickshall* (1783) 1 Leach CC 263. [10] *R v Lambe*, cited above at n.7.

[11] *Crown Law*, 243.

[12] Wigmore, Prof J.H., *A Treatise on the Anglo-American System of Evidence in Trials at Common Law* (10 vols), 3rd ed, Cambridge, Mass: Little, Brown, 1940, para 1686. For a more down-to-earth analysis of confession utility see the judgment of Lord Lane CJ in *R v Rennie* [1982] 1 All ER 385, at 388.

[13] Wigmore, ibid, para 866. [14] [1893] 1 QB 12, at 18.

[15] See Moston, S., Stephenson, G.M. and Williamson T., 'The Extent of Silence in Police Interviews,' in Greer, S. and Morgan, D. (eds.), *The Right of Silence Debate*: Bristol, 1990, cited in Wolchover and Heaton-Armstrong, *Confession Evidence*, cited above at n.3, para1–017.

[16] (1973) 58 Cr App R 417, *per* Lawton LJ.

(3) Cases of confession to psychiatrists and probation officers

Reference was made earlier to admissions allegedly made to such lay witnesses as employ- **11.05**
ers and family members of victims. However, it is far from unknown for the prosecution
to rely on confessions or self-incriminatory utterances allegedly made to those who
perform a professional role in dealing with offenders in a confiding capacity outside the
context of a police investigative function.

In recent years the Court of Appeal has considered cases in which reliance was placed **11.06**
upon confessions made to professional counsellors in whom the maker must have
assumed confidentiality was assured. In *R v McDonald*[17] the appellant had written to his
victim's parents explaining that he had killed the victim after being told by him that he
(the victim) had had sex with his (the appellant's) wife in the appellant's mother's bed. At
his trial for murder he raised provocation and the prosecution called a psychiatrist, who
had seen him in order to determine fitness to plead, the issue of diminished responsibility
and mental state in general, and who gave evidence that the appellant had told him that
he had to make up some reason for his behaviour. It was contended that the evidence
ought to have been excluded on the grounds of unfairness as it related to a non-medical
issue. However, it was held that the Crown need not have adduced the letter as it was self-
serving although having done so it would have been misleading not to have adduced the
appellant's comments to the psychiatrist. It is not known if the psychiatrist had covertly
tape-recorded the consultation but it may certainly be assumed that he did not give the
appellant any opportunity to authenticate a note of the exchanges.

The decision should be contrasted with the similarly unsuccessful appeal in *R v Cavill*,[18]
another murder indictment. In that case the appellant was seen by a psychiatrist
instructed by the Crown Prosecution Service in the absence of a solicitor and was told by
the doctor that his report would be going to the CPS. In the course of the consultation the
psychiatrist asked him about his movements on the fatal night and he gave an account
which was inconsistent with the evidence he gave at trial. Accordingly the psychiatrist's
evidence of the consultation was adduced in evidence. The defence contended that it was
wholly inappropriate to conduct an interview which involved asking the appellant to
account for his movements, as there was no history of psychiatric illness or mental illness
of any sort. Dismissing the appeal the court noted that the defence disputed neither the
accuracy of the report nor the warning about the intended disclosure.

Reliance on confessions confided to a professional counsellor has not been confined to **11.07**
the medical profession. In *R v Brown*[19] the appellant made no admissions during a formal
taped police interview attended by his solicitor and a social worker acting as appropriate
adult. Afterwards the appellant was told by the social worker in private that she thought
she knew what had happened and that he had had something to do with the assault in
question, whereupon he admitted the assault to her. She did not tell the solicitor what
had been said but after consulting her superiors made a statement to the police. The trial

---

[17] [1991] Crim LR 122.   [18] (1995) unreported, 93/4506/Z3, 11 April, CA.
[19] (1999) unreported, 9807320/Y2, 21 May, CA.

judge accepted that the social worker had initiated the exchange and had not warned the appellant that anything he said might be used in evidence, and that he had in all innocence been misled therefore into thinking that he was speaking in an atmosphere wholly different from that which prevailed in the course of the formal interview. Nevertheless, he found that there was no bad faith and no unfairness in allowing the evidence to be given and it was held that there was no reason to go behind the ruling.

In *R v Elleray*[20] the appellant pleaded guilty to indecent assault but in the course of being interviewed by probation officers with a view to the preparation of a pre-sentence report admitted raping the complainant on a number of occasions when drunk. He was charged with four offences of rape and, giving evidence for the prosecution of the admissions, the probation officers admitted that they had not transcribed what the appellant had said. Dismissing the appeal and rejecting the appellant's submission that the admissions should have been excluded the court drew an analogy with an interview by a doctor and referred to the case of *R v McDonald*. Although a probation officer was under a duty to conduct a risk assessment and could not simply ignore relevant comments by a defendant the prosecution should always consider carefully whether it was right to rely on such evidence. However, in the instant case the prosecution did not act unfairly in prosecuting for the rapes.

(4) Cautioning juries

11.08 As already observed, judicial and academic scepticism towards evidence alleging oral confessions has not been translated into any *general* requirement for juries to be given warnings about such evidence. However, there will usually be a need for caution in approaching evidence of oral confessions attested to by persons who might have a personal interest in the case. The defence will certainly stress this in their closing speech and, in summing up, most competent and fair-minded judges will gladly remind the jury of the defence submission, even without any obligation to do so from 'on high'. In the discussions between Bench and Bar which are nowadays so often conducted prior to speeches or the summing-up in order to reach common ground on the issues and therefore avoid error the defence should certainly invite the judge to endorse the need for care in such cases. Again, even where seemingly disinterested witnesses are concerned it would not be amiss to instruct juries that, when dealing with the account of a disputed oral confession, they should be careful to bear in mind that utterances can be misheard, misremembered through being misunderstood and misrecorded, even when committed to writing soon after being pronounced.

11.09 Although, then, there is no formal duty in general to warn the jury of the potential weaknesses inherent in evidence of oral confessions, very significantly it has quite recently been held that, in relation to one particular category of evidence of an oral confession attested to by a private witness, special warnings are now obligatory subject to the meeting of certain conditions. This is in the case of confessions allegedly made to, or at least professedly witnessed by, a fellow inmate of the accused, in prison. Confessions

---

[20] [2003] EWCA Crim 553.

made and witnessed in these circumstances are by far the most commonly encountered example of confessions made to private witnesses. They have featured in a number of well-publicised trials in recent decades[21] and no doubt in countless others which have failed to attract media attention. It takes little imagination to appreciate that evidence purporting to attest to such confessions is inherently suspect. Quite apart from the fact that testifying co-inmates may have a bad record of dishonesty and general disregard for the law and may be persons therefore of very limited credibility, their evidence may well be tarnished by such factors as the hope of reward from the state in the form of early release or the dropping of charges or some other beneficence (even if there is no evidence of their being habitual police informants), or payment by a newspaper for their story, or even the attraction of kudos from other prisoners. It is well known that certain classes of prison inmate are unpopular with other prisoners, for example alleged or proven sex offenders, and such persons are usually at risk of unofficial (but officious) violent retribution at the hands of other prisoners. The same factor might be instrumental in inducing some prisoners to come forward 'selflessly' with allegations of confession in order to strengthen the case against an accused charged with an offence on the proscribed list—an example of 'noble cause corruption' or 'pious perjury,' as it used to be called.

Confessions witnessed by prison co-inmates represent the example *par excellence* of sus- **11.10** pect evidence of oral confessions made to lay witnesses and have been the subject matter of very intense public interest in recent years, mainly as a result of the case of Michael John Stone, whose case is discussed later. Accordingly, it is proposed to devote the rest of this chapter to concentrating on the law relating to such confessions. However, before moving on to that discussion mention should be made of a possible scenario in which it might be envisaged that a suspect who is in police detention is occupying the same holding cell as a lay informant who will allege that the detainee made incriminating remarks to him. If there be any suggestion that the witness was deliberately planted in the cell in order to 'obtain' a confession in circumstances in which the police were plainly circumventing restrictions on conducting a PACE interview at that stage (for example, because there was by now enough evidence to charge) the evidence would probably be excluded. To the knowledge of the authors there are no cases on the point recorded although there are a number of reported cases in which incriminating admissions

---

[21] E.g. James Hanratty for the 'A6' murder in 1961 (see Foot, P., *Who Killed Hanratty? An Investigation Into the Notorious A6 Murder*, London: Penguin, 1988, p151); Terry Marsh in 1990 (see *The Times* between 23.10.90 and 8.11.90 for daily reports on the progress of the trial); Reginald Dudley and Robert Maynard for the 'Torso Murder' in 1976 (see *The Times*, 17.2.02 and *The Guardian*, 19.7.02 reporting their successful appeal against conviction; for a detailed contemporary account of the case see Campbell, D., 'The Case of the Missing Evidence,' *Time Out*, No. 379, 1–7 July 1977, pp11–13); Michael Hickey, Vincent Hickey, Pat Molloy and James Robinson, tried in 1978 for the murder of the newsboy Carl Bridgewater (see Foot, P., *Murder at the Farm—Who Killed Carl Bridgewater?* London: 1982); John Bindon (cited in Morton, J., 'Prison Informers: Unreliable Evidence', (2005) 69 JCL, 89–91); David Armani (described by Dein, J., 'Non Tape Recorded Cell Confession Evidence—On Trial,' [2002] CrimLR 630, at 633; unsuccessful appeal reported at [2001] EWCA Crim. 1613); the Damilola Taylor murder trial (see *The Daily Telegraph*, 7.3.02). Summaries of the salient points in these cases are set out in Wolchover, D., 'The Vexed Issue of Gaol Cell Confessions,' published on-line at *http://www.DavidWolchover.co.uk* (with link from *http://www.7BellYard.co.uk*), 2005.

triggered by third parties in the police station have been overtly tape-recorded. But that situation is outside the scope of this chapter.

C. Oral Confessions Alleged by Fellow Prisoners Contrasted with those Adduced by the Police

11.11 It is instructive to compare the willingness of the courts to allow uncorroborated and unsubstantiated prison cell confessions to sustain a conviction, with the attitude of our lawmakers towards oral confessions witnessed by the police.

(1) Provisions under PACE for validating confessions made to police officers based on mistrust of the police

11.12 The PACE Act makes provision for the audio tape-recording of interviews with suspects at the police station.[22] Code E requires the tape-recording of all such interviews in respect of any indictable offence or offence triable either way.[23] Code C provides that following a decision to arrest a suspect the police must not interview the suspect about the relevant offence other than at a police station, unless certain conditions of urgency apply.[24] However, not all confessions are made within the context of a formal interview. Sometimes it is alleged that the accused made a spontaneous confession or other self-incriminating remark to the police, that is one not prompted by police questioning. Obviously police officers would not be expected to have their pens and notebooks permanently poised in order to record such utterances as might happen to fall from the lips of the accused. However, short of requiring all officers to carry with them at all relevant times voice-activated pocket cassette tape recorders, of the type which have long been available at low cost, PACE goes as far as it may be thought possible to go in placing obstacles in the way of concoction. Thus, inserted in the 1991 revision of PACE Code of Practice C following strictures by the Court of Appeal in *R v Matthews*[25] was the provision requiring that a written record was to be made of any comments by a suspected person, including unsolicited comments, which are outside the context of an interview but which might be relevant to the offence.[26] The Code does not require *ex post facto* notes of unsolicited comments to be offered for verification as soon as practicable but a very important counterpart of the requirement to make a note of such utterances is the

---

[22] s60. [23] *Code of Practice on Tape-Recording Interviews with Suspects*, E3.1.
[24] Code of Practice for the Detention, Treatment and Questioning of Persons by Police Officers, C11.1.
[25] (1989) 91 CrAppR. 43.
[26] C11.13. The record must be timed and signed by the maker and, where practicable the person must be given an opportunity to read the record and to sign it as correct or to indicate the respects in which it is considered inaccurate. Any refusal to sign should be recorded: C11.14. Following representations made by the present authors in 1990 and 1994 the 1995 revision of Code C contained a new Note for Guidance (11D, now 11E) which advised that when suspects agree to read records of interview and other comments and to sign them as correct, they should be asked to endorse the record with words such as 'I agree that this is a correct record of what was said' and to add their signature. Where a suspect does not agree with the record, the officer should record the details of any disagreement and then ask the suspect to read the details and then sign them to the effect that they accurately reflect the disagreement. Any refusal to sign when asked to do so should be recorded.

provision requiring that at the outset of any subsequent tape-recorded interview under caution, the suspect must be asked to verify earlier utterances not recorded on tape.[27] This is a measure clearly designed to prevent concoction after a taped interview has produced no admissions. Failure to ask for such verification will cast doubt on evidence of the making of the remark and will probably render it inadmissible. Again, if the accused is confronted with the *ex post facto* record of a spontaneous admission soon after its utterance, an indignant denial that it was ever made will lend support to the denial. People who unload their consciences to the police rarely if ever feel an instantaneous regret at having done so sufficient to mobilize defensive acting skills. Where second thoughts occur that will be much later. The reality of human experience is that people who are sorry for their actions do not recover from their remorse as soon as they express it.[28]

The whole PACE scheme for authenticating admissions was aimed at quelling disquet **11.13** over police malpractice. There was undoubtedly cause for concern in this area, yet PACE clearly embodies a fundamental mistrust of police officers as a whole. In spite of the fact that they must obviously be of impeccable character to get into the police in the first place, officers are not trusted to give reliable evidence unless it is validated by means which are unassailable.

(2) Contrasting trust reposed in habitual criminals

By the irony of a remarkable contrast, where evidence is adduced of a confession made in **11.14** private, in prison, to an individual with a proven record of serious crime and necessarily unauthenticated by any of the safeguards which are required when a spontaneous, unsolicited, oral confession has allegedly been made to a police officer, the accused may be convicted on the strength of that confession alone entirely unsupported by any other independent evidence.

In a fourteenth century case of note a fellow prison inmate was called by the Crown to **11.15** rebut a claim by the accused that he had made a confession only in order to escape the cruelties to which he had been subjected in gaol.[29] However, reliance on co-inmate witnesses in matters of confession is largely a modern phenomenon. This is because for a considerable period before the nineteenth century it had been the rule that a criminal conviction resulted in loss of testimonial competence. The rule seems to have had its origins in Germanic law, possibly with links also to the Old Testament entreaty 'Put not thine hand with the wicked to be an unrighteous witness'.[30] It is traced back as early as a fourteenth century case when it was declared that a conviction for conspiracy at the suit of the Crown would result in loss of competence.[31] Hale cited a contemporary case to show that convicted felons were similarly disqualified but pronounced the view that the king's pardon for any offence rendering the accused incompetent had the effect of

---

[27] C11.4 and E4.6.
[28] See Wolchover, D., 'The Myth of the Unsigned Confession', (1986) 136 *NLJ* 1007.
[29] *R v Robert de Skelebroke le Botiler* (1302) Y.B. 30, 31 Ed. 1 (Alfred J Horwood, ed), London 1863, 543.
[30] Exodus 23:1. [31] Y.B. 24 Edw. III, Mich. Pl., *per* Shardelowe J.

removing that incompetence.[32] Nearly two centuries later the rule of incompetence was still being justified on the basis that, as Starkie argued, the object of the oath being to bind the conscience of the witness it followed that the testimony of a person who had shown a disregard for laws human and divine ought not to be received since it could not reasonably be expected that such a person would respect the obligation of the oath.[33] The reiteration of that simplistic and inflexible view of human behaviour was swiftly gainsaid by Bentham's demonstration of the fallacy of regarding moral turpitude as an objection to competence rather than to the weight of the evidence,[34] the utilitarian appeal of which led in 1843 to the abolition of incompetence by statute.[35] Given that few remand prisoners were of good character, and that any prisoner offering himself as a witness to an alleged confession would be most unlikely to have a clean record, the old rule would have served to preclude the admissibility of most confessions attested to by co-inmates.

D. Protecting the Accused against False Attestation by Co-inmates as to Confession

11.16 The question of the admissibility of an oral confession attested to by co-inmates with a bad record could not now seriously be challenged on any basis of principle. However, what remains very much a live issue is the question whether such a confession should be permitted to sustain a conviction in the absence of other evidence. Nevertheless, it is proposed to review briefly here certain arguments which have been advanced in favour of, and against, the use of prison cell confessions as a matter of practice. Thereafter, in this section, reference will be made to possible procedural safeguards which might be deployed when such evidence is used.

(1) Should resort be made to prison cell confessions as a matter of practice?[36]

(i) In favour

11.17 It has been argued that the prosecution of serious crime is too important to tolerate a rule indiscriminately and inflexibly shutting out the evidence of a given category of witness as inherently unreliable without regard to the particular circumstances. In an age of some sophistication, it might be contended, the members of a modern jury, assisted by skilled counsel employing cross-examination techniques which have been honed to razor-sharp perfection over centuries of practice, are well able to separate the wheat from the chaff. A key safeguard against perjury is the duty of the CPS to evaluate the reliability of potential witnesses, and hence to make a judgement on whether to call them, using criteria set out

---

[32] *Pleas of the Crown*, Sollom Emlyn, London: 1736, ii, 277–278, citing *Lord Castlemain's Case* (1680) 7 St.Tr. 1067 (evidence allowed because the witness had received a pardon). On the effect of a pardon he expressly dissented from the view of Lord Coke CJ in *Brown v Crashaw* (1614) 2 Bulstrode 154.

[33] *Evidence*, London 1824, 83.

[34] Bentham, J., *Rational of Judicial Evidence*, (5 vols), London 1827, eds J.S. Mill *et al*) Bk.ix, Pt iii, c.iii, cited in Wigmore, cited above at n.12, para 579, and Holdsworth, Sir William, *A History of English Law* (16 vols), London: Methuen, 1903–66, vol. ix, 193.

[35] 6 & 7 Vict., c85.

[36] See generally Toczek, L., 'Cell confessions,' (2002) 152 *NLJ*, 805, and Dein, article cited above at n.21, at 632–634.

in the Code for Crown Prosecutors.[37] The prosecution are also bound by rules requiring the disclosure of any material which may weaken their case,[38] including the previous convictions of witnesses and any previous utterances, oral or written, which may be at odds with their evidence in court. The trial judge enjoys an overriding discretion to exclude evidence if its probative value is outweighed by its likely prejudicial effect and in any event is obligated to warn the jury that prosecution witnesses may have a purpose of their own to serve.[39] Lastly, a most important safeguard is afforded by the rule in *R v Galbraith*[40] that the judge ought to stop the trial where the case against the defendant is tenuous, a characterization which is arguably warranted when the only evidence is an alleged oral confession made to a fellow prison inmate with a bad criminal record. Where, in 'borderline' cases, there is some doubt as to whether the state of the evidence is such as would bring it into the category of 'tenuous' the judge has a discretion to stop the trial.[41]

(ii) Against

The use in evidence of a prison confession is likely to involve the inherent prejudice **11.18** which will follow from the jury learning that the defendant has been held on remand, rather than having been on bail. With the jury hearing evidence of the defendant's

> activities and associations when in custody, and all the unsavoury things that discussion about life in prison brings . . . cell confession carries with it a flavour and complexion, which, in itself, always puts the accused at unfair advantage.[42]

Although the prosecution bear the duty of disclosure, this only extends to material which they actually have in their possession.[43] More often than not such potentially crucial material as prison, medical, psychiatric, psychological and social services reports and records will be in the hands of third parties who will consider themselves bound by confidentiality if the witness refuses to authorize disclosure. The CPS might have second thoughts about relying on a witness who adopted such an attitude but if it were decided to use a witness who was unwilling to cooperate with the defence this would be a matter for comment but no more than that. There is no right to the disclosure of material which is required only for use in cross-examination, but which is not *prima facie* admissible.[44] The inmate witness attesting to a confession in prison will often have a background of complex emotional and behavioural instability. Unless they are privy to it the jury can hardly be expected to make a reasoned assessment of whether the account of the confession is reliable or fictitious. The potential instability and susceptibility to inducement of many prison inmates may be a key factor in exposing their vulnerability when offered blandishments to furnish confession evidence against a fellow prisoner. Such influences may emanate directly or indirectly from the police who may feel frustrated by the

---

[37] The prosecution must research fully the character and antecedents of a prisoner before deciding to call him to give evidence against a fellow prisoner: see *R v Molloy and Hickey*, unreported CA, 20.7.97, and *R v Causley* [2003] EWCA Crim1840, both cited in *Stone* [2005] EWCA Crim 105, para 29.
[38] Criminal Procedure and Investigations Act 1996, ss3, 7 and 9.
[39] See e.g. *R v Beck* (1982) 74 CrAppR 221.   [40] [1981] 1 WLR 1039.   [41] Ibid.
[42] Dein, cited above at n.21, at 634.   [43] Ibid, at 636, for a review of the arguments on disclosure.
[44] *R v Cheltenham JJ, ex p Secretary of State for Trade* [1977] 1 WLR 95.

prospect of not being able to adduce enough evidence against an accused in custody, particularly where the allegation is of a high profile crime. The evidence is at once easy to manufacture, potentially compelling and difficult to disprove. Yet the defence may have little means of discovering if there is a secret confiding relationship between the informer/witness and the police if the police choose to conceal its existence. If, however, rumours circulate and in order to pre-empt an attempt to discredit their witness in court the prosecution successfully seek a Public Interest Immunity certificate in relation to the prior existing informer status of a prison confession witness, the defence will be stymied in their attempts to establish a questionable background to the evidence of confession.

(2) Possible formal safeguards where resort is made to prison cell confessions

11.19   A confession may be suspect for one of two possible reasons. First, while the confession may undeniably have been uttered it may be unreliable as a testament of guilt in consequence of the circumstances in which it was uttered, in particular the state of mind of the accused at the time. Second, the evidence as to its making may be unreliable. In either case there are three possible legal mechanisms which might be chosen to guard against the possibility of a conviction being sustained only by a confession which is suspect. The introduction of a strict rule might be envisaged which prohibits any conviction based on a confession unsupported by other evidence. Second, without introducing a strict prohibition it might suffice simply to apply the rule requiring the trial judge to stop the trial where the evidence of guilt, though technically sufficient, is tenuous.[45] This would allow some confessions to sustain a conviction, although unsupported by other evidence, by reason of the particular cogency of the evidence proving that it was made and demonstrating the reliability of the accused in attesting to his own guilt. Third, rules might be laid down for a formulation of warning to the jury against convicting on confessions unsupported by evidence of another kind.

11.20   The issues involved in the debate as to whether confession evidence unsupported by evidence of another kind should be permitted to sustain a conviction are complex, lengthy and theoretical and are beyond the scope of the present chapter.[46] On the other hand, the question whether judges should be required to give juries a special warning about the dangers implicit in accepting evidence from a co-inmate as to a cell confession and the nature of any such warning is a narrower and more practical topic. Most people would regard the use of such evidence as fraught with risk at the best of times. However, the recent approach of the Court of Appeal in determining, in the case of Michael John Stone, when a warning as to the risks should be given to the jury, is unlikely to reduce the danger of miscarriage.[47]

---

[45] *R v Galbraith*, cited above at n.40.
[46] They are set out exhaustively in *Confession Evidence*, cited above at n.3, paras 1–023 to 1–044.
[47] *R v Michael John Stone* [2005] EWCA Crim 105.

E. Formal Directions to be given to the Jury in Cases of Confessions to Prison Co-inmates: the Case of Michael John Stone

In 1997 Michael Stone was convicted of the so-called Chillenden murders. His convic- **11.21**
tions were subsequently overturned and he was granted a retrial. In 2001 he was again
convicted and once again appealed against his conviction. He pursued a number of
complaints that the summing up was deficient and argued, on the basis of authorities
reported subsequent to the trial, that certain formal warnings specific to prison cell
confessions should have been given. All his grounds were dismissed and while the Court
acknowledged that those warnings would be necessary in appropriate cases, on the facts
of the case they were held to be not relevant. On all but one of the points there might be
little basis for taking issue with the court's analysis, although a broader, more imaginative
approach would have been welcome. However, on one central plank of the appellant's
case it is submitted that the court's reasoning was fundamentally flawed.

(1) The salient facts [48]

In July 1996 Dr Lin Russell and her young daughters Megan and Josie were brutally **11.22**
attacked on their way home from a swimming gala. Lin and Megan were killed but Josie
survived and was eventually able to give an account of the attack and a description of the
assailant. Other witnesses gave diverse descriptions of possible suspects seen in the vicinity, some elements of the totality of which corresponded to Michael Stone. One witness
in particular, Nicola Burchell, cooperated in the preparation of e-fit likenesses which
were televised a year after the attack and which led to Michael Stone's arrest. In interview
he denied he was the murderer but, it has been maintained, told a number of lies. No
witness made a positive identification of Stone and although Nicola Burchell said he
looked 'very familiar' she conceded in evidence that this could be because he reminded
her of an old acquaintance.

Significantly, there was not a shred of scientific evidence linking Stone to the murder **11.23**
scene. Not far from the bodies was found a metre-long black bootlace tightly knotted in
three places and bearing blood from both girls. Stone was a heroin addict who was
known to keep in his car syringes and a two- to three-feet length of boot lace with a
knotted loop at one end and knots in three places and he had been seen five or six times
to use it as a tourniquet around his bicep to raise a vein for the purposes of injecting
heroin while gripping it in his teeth. Although saliva residues were detected on the
bootlace found at the scene, tests over 64 areas along its length revealed insufficient
quantities from which to raise a DNA profile. Microscopic examination of a car known
to have been in his possession on two dates closely straddling the attack proved entirely

---

[48] A comprehensive account of the detailed facts, compiled from press reports and the 2005 appeal
judgment, is given in Wolchover, 'The Vexed Issue of Gaol Cell Confessions,' cited above at n.21. For other
commentary on the case see Wells, C. and Stevenson, M., 'Cell confessions—no stone left unturned'
(2005) 155 *NLJ* 550; Morton J., 'Prison Informers: Unreliable Evidence,' (2005) *JCL* 89; Mahmutaj, K,
'Confessions: A few considerations on the case of *R v Michael Stone*' (2005) 2 *CBA News* 11. Criticism in
the text appeared originally in Wolchover, D., and Heaton-Armstrong, A., 'Confessors of the (prison)
cloth,' [2005] 5 *Archbold News* 8.

negative in establishing any link with the crime. A single smeared bloodstained finger-print found on the girls' lunchbox could not have been Stone's and was very unlikely to have been made by Lin Russell. Hairs found on Josie's shoes, red fibres found in and around Lin Russell's body, and more red fibres found on a pair of tights used to tie one of the girls did not come from Stone or anyone in his family or from the Russells. Allegations by two associates of Stone that on the day of the murders he had been seen with bloodstains on his clothing were substantially discredited in cross-examination.

(2) Stone's alleged cell confession

11.24 In September 1997 Damien Daley was on remand in the Canterbury prison segregation unit when Stone was brought into the next cell. He claimed that the other prisoners were shouting at Stone and that he told them to be quiet. Stone thanked him and then mentioned 'something about' an identity parade and he said 'if it wasn't for that bitch, if she hadn't picked me out, I'd have been all right'.[49] He began 'rambling on about smashing eggs and the inside being mush or something'. Stone then went on to describe tying up the victims with wet towels and a shoe lace or short lace although he said he didn't need to because they were out of the game anyway. Daley thought Stone called them paupers and that they 'didn't have what he wanted'. Stone said something about one of them being disobedient in trying to run away but not getting very far and he referred to 'whores and bitches'. He said the dog made more noise than they did. He talked about making someone watch, but they closed their eyes and he hit them. He talked about a swimming costume, which he had sniffed and had been aroused to an orgasm, or nearly orgasm. Daley said it was like being told a horror story. The conversation allegedly lasted about ten minutes.

11.25 Several items in the confession tallied precisely with an article in the *Daily Mirror* which Daley had with him in his cell and the Court of Appeal acknowledged that with the exception of the opening remark there was nothing in what Daley attributed to Stone which was not already either in the public domain or capable of being inferred from material in the public domain. The defence described this as the classic hallmark of the fabricated confession.

11.26 As the Court of Appeal pointed out, the comment Stone allegedly made about being picked out at the identification parade (which presumably related to Nicola Burchell) could not have been based on information in the public domain, since the result of the parade had been withheld.[50] On the assumption, then, that Daley could not have known what Nicola Burchell had said (there being no suggestion that he had been primed by the police) the evidence of Stone's utterance indicates that he probably did make the remark to Daley and that there was some conversation between them. On the other hand, the important distinction between that remark and everything else which he allegedly

---

[49] See national press reports of first trial, cited in Wolchover, 'The Vexed Issue of Gaol Cell Confessions', cited above at n. 21. Alternatively, he was quoted as saying 'I'd been okay if that slag hadn't picked me out': see 2005 judgment, para 10.

[50] 2005 judgment, para 10.

uttered to Daley, is that it does not in any way express or imply guilt. Rude resentment at being suspected is hardly evidence.

(3) The oddity of confessing immediately after going on segregation to avoid false allegations of confession

Very importantly, it was not disputed that Stone had been moved to segregation expressly **11.27** at his own request because he wished to avoid other prisoners attributing false confessions to him.[51] Stone may have been rash to go against his own ordinance in talking to Daley about the case but, as counsel so aptly told the jury: 'having been put in isolation and segregation, you are being asked to believe that the first thing he does when he gets in his cell is start making a full confession to the man next door'.

(4) Desirability of warning the jury that cell confessions are easy to concoct but difficult to disprove

At his 2005 appeal it was submitted on behalf of Stone that the judge should have given **11.28** the jury a special caution that cell confessions are easy to concoct but difficult to disprove. Applying recent Privy Council authority it was acknowledged by the Court of Appeal that in what counsel for the Crown had described as the case of a 'standard two line cell confession' there would generally be a need for the judge to give this direction.[52] However, with seemingly irrefutable logic, Rose LJ, giving the judgment of the court, observed:

> If an alleged confession, for whatever reason, would not have been easy to invent it would be absurd to require the judge to tell the jury that confessions are often easy to concoct.[53]

Was the confession easy or difficult to invent? In the court's view there was little doubt about it:

> [T]he confession contained many points of detail which it would not have been easy to invent. Some were in the public domain, and others were capable of being deduced from material in the public domain. But the jury heard evidence both as to how much access Daley had to what was in the public domain and enabling them to assess how easy or difficult relevant deductions would have been for him, in the time scale available to him. In the circumstances, a direction that cell confessions are easy to concoct would have served no useful purpose and we reject the submission that it should have been given.[54]

This passage betrays a glaring inconsistency. As it reads, the court was clearly acknowledging the fundamental principle that its own view of the question (easy or hard to concoct?) was ultimately subordinate to that of the jury. It ought to have followed from this that the court could properly make no assumption about the jury's thinking which could have had any bearing on the appeal outcome. However, that is precisely what the court did purport to do, imposing its view of the issue, so as to make a judgement on

---

[51] 2005 judgment, para 13.

[52] 2005 judgment, para 83, citing *Pringle* [2003] UKPC 9 and *Bendetto v The Queen* and *Labrador v The Queen* [2003] UKPC 27, [2003] 1 WLR 1545.

[53] Para 84.   [54] Para 85.

what the jury did or did not need to be told. That the court fell into fundamental error is shown by the simple axiom that the absurdity or appropriateness of giving a particular direction as to how the jury should approach certain evidence can hardly depend on making an assumption as to what view the jury exercising its sovereign function will reach on that evidence. To argue otherwise is pure *petitio principii*. The real point of the direction, surely, is not to educate the jury on the state of the obvious but to underscore the risks involved in accepting evidence of a cell confession: that it is oral, made without authentication and in private and attested to by a person who is likely to be of dubious credibility with a possible agenda of secret ulterior motives unconnected with the imparting of truth. In the context of such a confession it reminds them of the defendant's unenviable predicament in having to prove the negative of what may be an only too easily alleged positive.

11.29 Even if the court were entitled to impose their view as to the ease or difficulty of invention on the question whether a warning was appropriate or absurd, it is far from certain that details of the confession were as hard to manufacture as the court were prepared to assume. The series of disjointed utterances attributed by Daley to Stone were obviously more elaborate than the 'standard two-line cell confession'. Clearly their concoction would have required a little thought, if not very much imagination; indeed, as defending counsel suggested to Daley 'he must have boned up on what was in the public domain'.[55] On the other hand, this was hardly rocket science. It surely would not have taken literary genius for a determined liar to weave out of the *Daily Mirror* report what he imagined sounded like a convincing impression of the lunatic ramblings of a psychotic killer. The Court of Appeal appear to have made rather too much of the banalities of what went into the confession and rather too little of the potential of someone like Daley to indulge himself in a bit of saloon bar hamming. Moreover, he had plenty of time to prepare his script: from the early evening of 23rd September to some time on the 26th, when he made his statement to the police. Although the court acknowledged the delay factor they sought to minimize its impact by pointing to Daley's wish to get his uncle's blessing before making a statement.[56] Such a consultation would surely not have precluded continued improvement and memorizing of the final script until the actual moment of the making of the statement.

11.30 In declaring that a warning to the jury about the ease of concoction would have been absurd (because the detail in the confession would not have been easy to invent) it was quite fanciful of the court to suppose that any more than a very basic inventive skill was required to compile what Daley purported to relate. In short, the court greatly exaggerated the supposed complexity of the confession and seemed almost to be in thrall to the supposed simplicity of the witness.

(5) Other appropriate warnings

11.31 In *Stone* the Court of Appeal accepted that it would often be necessary to give the jury certain other formal warnings about the co-inmate witness, although in the event it was

---

[55] 2005 judgment, para 72.   [56] Para 73.

held that on the facts of the particular case no such warnings were necessary. For example, it might be appropriate to give the jury a specific warning about possible motives for lying, for example the hope of reward from the authorities in terms of the dropping of charges, mitigation of sentence, the gaining of kudos from other prisoners or payment by a newspaper for a story. However, for tactical reasons resulting from Daley's performance in the witness box at the first trial, the defence preferred in cross-examination in the second trial to advance no suggestion of any such motive. However, it was submitted on appeal that, although it was only in counsel's closing speech in the second trial that the suggestion had been made that Daley may have lied in order to gain advantage from the police or kudos from other prisoners, the judge's duty to give a special warning as to the 'inherent unreliability' of a co-prisoner's evidence and the possibility of such motives did not cease simply because it had not been put to Daley in cross-examination. It was submitted that the general direction which the judge did give the jury about the need to exercise care in assessing Daley's evidence was not adequate to the need for a special warning as to the potential unreliability of the particular type of evidence in question.[57]

Rejecting the submission the court stated: **11.32**

> [I]n a case where the defence has deliberately not cross-examined the informant as to motive of hope of advantage, the law does not require the judge to tell the jury that, merely because the informant was a prisoner, there may have been such a motive. . . . We reject [the] submission that intrinsic concerns about a potential motive to gain advantage with the authorities are so great as to require a direction, even though defence counsel has not alleged any in cross-examination.[58]

Very much in keeping with the thinking behind this passage the court also commented that 'in a case where the defence has, for good reason, deliberately not asked about motive, it is difficult to know what the judge is supposed to say'.[59]

On the other hand, the court do not appear to have been suggesting that the duty to give   **11.33**
an appropriate warning arose merely because the witness had been cross-examined as to motive. The implication from what the court went on to say was that cross-examination had to produce a reply or response leaving open the possibility of motive. Referring to a passage in *R v Beck* expressing the desirability of an appropriate warning the court noted that this passage referred specifically to cases 'where there is material to suggest that a witness's evidence may be tainted by an improper motive'.[60] Again, the court referred to the fact that in *R v Pringle*,[61] and again in *Benedetto*[62] (which involved a cell confession attested to by a co-prisoner with a bad character), the Privy Council said that:

> indications that the evidence may be tainted by an improper motive, must be found in the evidence.

Cross-examination in the first trial had elicited a scornful riposte from Daley. Presumably had he been challenged to the same effect in the second trial the Court of Appeal would

---

[57] See paras 53 and 55.   [58] See paras 84, and 88.   [59] Para 79.
[60] Para 89, citing [1982] 1 WLR 461, at 469A, *per* Ackner LJ.   [61] [2003] UKPC 9, para 31.
[62] [2003] 1 WLR 1545, PC, at para 34, *per* Lord Hope.

no doubt have held that his response left 'no indication that his evidence was tainted by improper motive'. On the other hand, merely denying an ulterior motive would not necessarily remove an indication of its taint; the ebb and flow of cross-examination might reveal facts or leave unanswered questions from which the possibility of motive might reasonably be inferred. However, there would need to be some material basis for such an inference. In the first trial Daley's assertion that it had never occurred to him that the charges he was facing had been dropped because of his evidence was never gainsaid and so no taint was indicated. Had the authorities admitted that charges had been dropped because of his evidence this would clearly have featured as an important plank of the whole defence. It may be that hidden influences connected with the *Stone* case were brought to bear in the disposal of those charges, but no evidence to that effect was uncovered (if ever even pursued).

(6) A bleak conjecture

11.34 The jury in Stone's second trial were told in clear terms that they could only convict Stone if they accepted the truth of Daley's evidence. The formal assumption of course must be that they did accept his evidence and acted according to the duty imposed by their oath. On the other hand, it may be assumed that they were not a naive or gullible jury and it is difficult to believe that they would not have been at the very least highly sceptical of the idea that Stone would have felt impelled to open his heart to another prisoner immediately after arriving in the very part of the prison where it was accepted he had sought refuge from the risk of the false attribution of a confession. It would be intriguing to conjecture whether the jury, while suspecting Stone to be guilty, nevertheless believed that Daley was lying about the confession and took his pious protestations of altruism with a pinch of salt. It may be wondered whether the suspicions against Stone did not lead them to the conclusion that the public would be safer with him behind bars until such time as evidence might emerge which exonerated him. The Court of Appeal plainly enthused in itemizing a number of points of suspicion, mainly of a peripheral nature.[63] Yet those elements will not compensate for the wholly inexplicable absence of any scientific evidence linking Stone to the murder (which the court apparently felt it unnecessary even to mention).

F. Concluding Observations

11.35 The contrast between official scepticism of police evidence of oral confessions, expressed in the PACE 'verballing' provisions, and the insouciance about relying on gaol cell confessions is truly Alice Through the Looking Glass. In 1999 the Government announced plans for the indefinite detention without trial of dangerous persons with severe and untreatable personality disorders. Most press reports of the announcement[64] referred prominently to Michael Stone, who prior to the Chillenden murders could not be incarcerated under the Mental Health Act 1983. In September 2004 a Mental Health Bill embodying the original plans for detaining untreatable unconvicted psychopaths was

---

[63] Para 94.   [64] See national press, 16 February 1999.

published in draft.[65] Michael Stone's case certainly demonstrates the need for a change in the law. But the change it calls for is not the introduction of draconian measures for detention. Rather, the reform it points to is a law of evidence prohibiting convictions based on uncorroborated and unauthenticated oral confessions. Otherwise the courts will go on trying cases based on wishful thinking instead of evidence and defence counsel will find themselves having to echo the ringing words of William Clegg QC when he told the jury in the first trial:

> In an unconscious way you may think that everyone desperately wants Michael Stone to be guilty. If he's guilty the police guessed right and if he's guilty then the killer's caught and if he's guilty then all of us can sleep a little sounder in our beds tonight.

Further Reading

R v Michael John Stone [2005] EWCA Crim 105, decision 19.1.05.

Wells, C. and Stevenson, M., 'Cell confessions—no stone left unturned,' (2005) 155 *New Law Journal* 550 (8 April 2005).

Morton J., 'Prison Informers: Unreliable Evidence', (2005) 69 *JCL*, 89–91.

Mahmutaj, K, 'Confessions: a few considerations on the case of *R v Michael Stone*' (2005) 2 *CBA News* 11.

Wolchover, D. and Heaton-Armstrong, A., *Confession Evidence*, London: Sweet and Maxwell Criminal Law Library, 1996.

Wolchover, D., 'The Vexed Issue of Gaol Cell Confessions,' published on-line at *http://www.DavidWolchover.co.uk* (with link from *http://www.7BellYard.co.uk*), 2005.

Editors' Note

Evidence of gaol cell confessions or statements against interest, as notoriously exemplified in the Michael Stone case, may attain fundamental importance to the success of a prosecution case where other incriminating evidence is lacking. Discovery of the detailed circumstances in which such statements are said to have been made and the background and motivation of their recipients, or those who solicit them, is essential. Bearing in mind the lack of safeguards surrounding the obtaining, collation and recording of such statements, especially when compared to those which concern the treatment of suspects by investigators when in their custody (and to the forensic consequences of regulatory breach), it is debatable whether such cautionary directions concerning them which judges are currently required to give to fact finders are adequate to protect against unsoundly based decisions, particularly when, without the statement, there would be no *prima facie* case against the defendant.

---

[65] See *The Guardian*, 8 September 2004.

12

INTERPRETERS AND TRANSLATORS IN THE CRIMINAL LEGAL PROCESS

Ann Corsellis and Amanda Clement

The current scale of globalization is a recent phenomenon. We all now live in multi-**12.01**
lingual countries and most have regular contact with colleagues in other countries. The
principles of equality before the law, irrespective of language and culture, have long been
enshrined in domestic and EU law. Over the last twenty years, informed individuals and
groups have done what they could to develop the necessary skills and structures to
implement those principles in respect of other-language speakers. Governments have
only begun to institutionalize their implementation relatively recently. This is work in
progress. This chapter therefore looks at the broad spectrum of social imperatives,
national and international policy and practical approaches to best practice.

A. Why Interpreters and Translators are Needed

(1) The increasingly multilingual nature of societies

12.02 Given the increasing movement of people between countries, it is probable that any legal practitioner will come into contact with a non-English speaking client during their career. Indeed, it is likely that, for many, such clients will be numerous.

12.03 Between 1991 and 2001, the total number of people resident in the British Isles, who were born abroad, rose by 36.4 per cent, against an overall population increase of just 4.03 per cent.[1] There were 7,015 asylum applications in the first quarter of 2005.[2] The government policy on the dispersal of immigrants throughout the UK means that rural police forces and legal firms are now as likely to be required to conduct their business across language and culture, as their city counterparts. The recent enlargement of the EU produced, from the 10 accession countries, 176,000 applicants to the Worker Registration Scheme. Between 1 May 2004 and 31 March 2005, this levelled out at some 13–14,000 applications per month.[3] It should be noted that there are citizens of other Member States whose first language may originate outside Europe. Thus, the increasingly multi-lingual and multicultural demography of all countries will, inevitably, entail the need for reliable communication in the following three main areas: cases arising within nation-states involving other-language speakers; matters crossing national frontiers, and where judicial cooperation between countries is required, such as for the prevention of terrorism and the trafficking of drugs and people.

(2) The existence of EU and domestic law and good practice requirements

12.04 EU and domestic legislation requires that everyone is treated equally before the law, irrespective of language and culture. Such rights have been set out in the European Convention on Human Rights[4] (ECHR), more recently incorporated into UK domestic legislation by the Human Rights Act 1998. The ECHR comprises articles specific to the administration of justice in relation to anyone arrested or charged with a criminal offence (Article 5) and also to ensure a fair trial (Article 6). These articles make clear reference to the individual's right to free interpreting and translation. Furthermore, *Kamasinski v Austria*[4a] places the obligation on the authority concerned not only to ensure that an interpreter is provided but also to ensure that the interpreting is adequate to satisfy the individual and cumulative requirements of Article 6.[5] Moreover, the Proposed Council Framework Decision (PCFD) on certain procedural rights in criminal proceedings

---

[1] *http://www.bbc.co.uk/bornabroad.*

[2] Home Office Report: *Asylum Statistics: 1st Quarter 2005—United Kingdom*, 2nd edition, *http://www.homeoffice.gov.uk/rds/index.htm.*

[3] Accession Monitoring Report—May 2004 to March 2005—a joint on-line report by the Home Office, the Department for Work and Pensions, HM Revenue & Customs and the Office of the Deputy Prime Minister.

[4] Convention for the Protection of Human Rights and Fundamental Freedoms (Rome, 4 November 1950; TS 71 (1953); Cmd 8969)

[4a] (1991) 13 EHRR 66.

[5] See Corsellis, A., *Non-English Speakers and the English Legal System*, Institute of Criminology, University of Cambridge, 1995.

throughout the European Union makes further recommendations as to the implementation of the ECHR articles in respect of linguistic provision. At the time of writing, this document is being negotiated by the European Parliament.[6]

Within the UK, the rights of the non-English speaking detainee in police stations are **12.05** described in the Codes of Practice of the Police and Criminal Evidence Act 1984 (PACE), which place the responsibility on the chief officer to provide a competent interpreter in given circumstances (Code C, paragraph 13). Whilst there is currently no UK legislation which specifically guarantees the same quality of interpreting to a victim or witness, the same standard of linguist should be engaged as that set down in law for the detainee.

The majority of principal agencies of the criminal justice system in England and Wales **12.06** are signatories to the *Agreement on the Arrangements for the Attendance of Interpreters in Investigations and Proceedings in the Criminal Justice System*.[7] This document clarifies the standards to be applied and the procedures to be followed in engaging an interpreter.

(3) Risks of not engaging professional interpreters and translators

Anyone can call themselves an interpreter or translator because there is, as yet, no **12.07** protection of title. The qualities of a competent and professional legal interpreter or translator are explored further on in this chapter. Reliable communication is put at risk by the absence of any of these qualities, potentially resulting in unsafe convictions or acquittals, unnecessary cost to the public purse, and undermining public confidence in the legal system, in particular on the part of the other-language speaking communities. For example, if an interpreter is engaged at a police station to take a statement from a non-English speaker, not only would the quality of the written evidence be undermined by an incompetent interpretation, but it could also affect the credibility of that witness in a court hearing, when the oral evidence appears not to match the original statement. Inaccurate information can also mislead the course of an investigation, and undermine court proceedings. Employment of inadequate interpreters has given rise to past examples of miscarriages of justice, notably *R v Iqbal Begum*.[8] There have also been judgments made against the UK by the European Court of Human Rights (*Cuscani v UK*).[9]

Family and friends are often proposed as preferred sources of linguistic support. This **12.08** approach, if applied in an evidential or procedural context, could undermine the legal process. Family and friends will not usually be competent interpreters, or be impartial.

Legal service practitioners with second language skills will be familiar with the legal **12.09** domain in which they work, but should still have objective assessment of their language

---

[6] Further reading on ECHR and case law arising from it can be found in the reports of three EU-funded projects, supported by the EU Commission's Freedom, Security and Justice Directorate. The findings of these projects have informed the framing of the PCFD and the publications arising from them are listed under Further Reading at the end of this chapter.

[7] 1998, currently being revised under the auspices of the Office for Criminal Justice Reform—*http://www.io.org.uk*.

[8] (1991) 93 Cr App R 96.   [9] (2003) 36 EHRR 2.

skills prior to delivering their services across language and culture and may not be considered sufficiently impartial in some circumstances.[10]

12.10 Safeguards are only partially in place at the moment, which puts a greater onus upon those involved to ensure the accuracy of communication. Interviews with detained persons in police stations are tape-recorded, in accordance with PACE, although there is no obligation to video-record deaf suspects. However, interviews with witnesses are not routinely tape-recorded. Where there is no tape-recording of court proceedings, a written record is made only of what is said in English. Thus, where there is no record of what the other language speaker and the interpreter said, there is no means, in the event of a dispute, to assess definitively the accuracy of the interpretation, either during or after the proceedings, particularly in the event of an appeal.

B. When Interpreters and Translators should be Engaged

(1) The degrees of second language fluency needed to be able to communicate accurately in speech or writing

12.11 Those working in the legal system are used to identifying and accommodating the linguistic and cognitive strengths and limitations of clients with whom they share a language and culture, for example where the client has a limited education or under-standing of the legal system. Facts can be elicited and tested, nuances appreciated and contextual matters mutually understood.

12.12 This is not the case where there are only degrees of shared language and culture. Careful assessments have to be made at the outset as to how to bring the situation to one where communication is reliable. The decision is easy where a client obviously has a limited or no command of the English language and it is clear that an interpreter is needed. The decision is more problematic where the client has a degree of superficial fluency in their second language, which may mask a limited competence in such essential aspects as:

- *use of tenses*: taking instructions and evidence, for example, often involves descriptions of a sequence of events where clarity is needed over the past, present and future;
- *understanding of terminology and associated concepts*: for example, the formal terms denoting the concepts of the different types of bail and caution, the Crown Prosecution and the National Offender Management Services may not be understood, especially where there is no equivalent in the other language; the informal terms used in pubs and on the streets, by the young and in the drug culture may be equally incomprehensible, and
- *literacy skills*: reading and signing statements, which have not been fully understood, is an obvious pitfall.

12.13 Predicting the level of language difficulty can be misleading. There is often little correlation between the perceived importance of an event and the complexity of language

---

[10] CILT, the National Centre for Languages, has developed valuable frameworks for assessment in this area—*http://www.cilt.org.uk*.

used. For example, the language used in a straightforward guilty plea or adjournment hearing in a crown court may be linguistically and conceptually less complex than the hearing of a contested motoring offence in a lower court or taking instructions in domestic disputes. Furthermore the initially simple can turn into the complex. Stressful situations and state of mind affect second-language competence. Being bewildered, angry, frightened or injured can diminish anyone's language abilities, as can being under the influence of drugs or alcohol. The conclusion must therefore be that, when in any doubt, a professional interpreter or translator should be engaged. The decision should involve the non-English speaker (see PACE, Code of Practice C, paragraph 13.2), even though they may be reluctant to lose face over their language abilities or to prolong matters.

Where there can be a presumption of a valuable degree of second-language competence **12.14** on the part of the non-English speaker, but not sufficient certainty to ensure accuracy of communication, an interpreter can give language support. In such circumstances the interpreter monitors communication and can step in to provide words or phrases the non-English speaker may need help over.[10a] An interpreter can also supply such language support, in appropriate situations, where the legal practitioner is in a position to communicate in the first language of the non-English speaker.

(2) Which texts are to be translated

There is not yet comprehensive legislation or precedent as to which texts should be **12.15** translated at any stage of the legal process. Some precedent already exists, notably the judgment in the case of *Kamasinski v Austria*,[10b] under ECHR Article 6. This refers to texts to be translated that allow the defendant to understand what is being said against him and to instruct his defence. The Codes of Practice accompanying PACE set out the requirements for the translation of detainee statements in section C, paragraph 13.4.

Where there is no specific legislation, it is perhaps sufficient to be governed by the **12.16** ECHR principles which require that every individual should be treated equally, irrespective of language and culture, and for decisions to be made, on that basis, as to which texts would need to be translated in order to return the other-language speaker to the same position as a native speaker, and also to promote efficiency and best practice.

There is a range of texts involved in a legal process, which can include: **12.17**

- letters, e.g. between client and lawyer;
- forms and notifications, e.g. bail notices, arrangements for fines;
- information giving e.g. letter of rights, crime prevention leaflets, witness support, prison regulations;
- reports, e.g. medical, psychiatric and court welfare;
- documents forming part of an investigation;
- statements, e.g. police and witness;

[10a] See *R (on the application of Riaz) v Special Adjudicator* [2001] ER (D) 324 (Oct).
[10b] Cited above at n.4a.

- relevant advance disclosure documents, and
- transcripts of covert surveillance recordings.

This does not necessarily mean that every text should be translated.[11]

12.18 A national legal translation resource, in these days of secure IT systems, would be welcome. Meanwhile, it is useful to bear in mind the following:

(a) Most qualified legal interpreters in the UK, where there is an oral adversarial tradition, are equipped to translate and sight-translate short, straightforward texts into either language. If they do not possess the necessary additional qualifications, they should recommend that longer and more complex texts be referred to a professional legal translator.

(b) Translation requirements should be planned in advance to give time to commission qualified translators and to brief them adequately.

(c) Literacy levels of the readers should be taken into account in respect of any language. Individuals, whatever their intelligence, may not have had access to education as a result of war, economic conditions or lack of opportunity.

(d) Sight translation is where an interpreter orally transfers the meaning of a written text into the other language. It is a technique that can usually only be used reliably when short, straightforward texts are involved, such as a letter.

(e) The pre-lingually deaf, that is those who were either born deaf or lost their hearing before they had learnt to speak, may not be able to read or write, or not to the standard required. For sign language users, video-letters in British Sign Language are increasingly used and can be organized through national or local sign-language interpreting agencies. Some individual British Sign Language/English interpreters may also offer this service. See also Chapter 13 which explores this and related topics.

(3) Preserving the integrity of communication throughout the legal process

12.19 The legal system often involves a series of processes in a single matter. A criminal case may, for example, start with a police investigation leading to a court hearing, perhaps with participation by medical and social experts, and conclude with the implementation of one of a variety of sentencing disposals. The communication chain is as strong as its weakest link. Therefore equal standards and attention have to be applied to communication at each stage.

12.20 Forward planning and coordinated management of communication is essential and includes appropriate record keeping and links between the agencies responsible for each stage. Many legal agencies now have a form that can be attached to a file and/or passed on to other agencies. In order to preserve the desirable separation of investigative and judicial processes in an individual case, the same interpreter should not normally be engaged for both stages.

---

[11] See *Hayward v Sweden*, Application No: 14106/88—Commission Decision.

C. Which Interpreters and Translators should be Engaged

The demand for legal interpreters and translators was foreseen some twenty years ago. **12.21** During that time the basic necessary structures have been developed and piloted. There is still much to be done, however, to increase capacity and quality in order to provide the number of qualified interpreters and translators in all the languages and locations required. Therefore, those seeking to engage legal interpreters and translators should be clear as to the skills and structures needed, so that any shortcomings can be recognized and resolved responsibly.

The following five factors should be part of the training and assessment of legal **12.22** interpreters.

(i)   a background knowledge and understanding of the legal systems in question, their structure, procedures, processes and the roles of the people who work in them; interpreters in the public services must be in a position to practice competently without having much time to prepare for an assignment;

(ii)   knowledge of the formal and informal terminology commonly used in the legal context in both languages and, by definition, the cultures underpinning both languages;

(iii) the skills to transfer meaning accurately into both of their languages. This includes the ability to:
  • interpret consecutively (after someone speaks);
  • interpret simultaneously (while someone is speaking): unless headphone systems are in place, for spoken languages this involves the interpreter whispering the interpretation of what is being said to one listener;
  • translate short straightforward written texts, and
  • sight-translate short written texts into speech;

(iv)   understand their code of conduct and relevant guides to good practice and undertake to comply with them, and

(v)   adopt the strategies, common to all professions, to take care of their own continuous professional and personal development.

In the UK, the independent National Occupational Standards for interpreters and trans- **12.23** lators set out the minimum standards required.[12] The standards approximate to an honours degree in level if not always in breadth. In the UK, for spoken languages, there is as yet only one relevant specialized and nationally recognized interpreters' examination mapped against these standards and accredited by the Qualifications and Curriculum Authority (QCA). This is the Institute of Linguists' Educational Trust's Diploma in Public Service Interpreting (DPSI) which offers specialist options in English law and Scottish law, as well as in health and local government-related services. This examination is at an initial professional level and it is envisaged that higher levels and a formal structure for continuous professional development will be implemented.[13] CACDP, the Council for the Advancement of Communication with Deaf People, is the national

---

[12] See *http://www.cilt.org.uk*.   [13] See *http://www.iol.org.uk/qualifications*.

examinations body for sign language interpreters.[14] Its examinations test interpreting skill at the same level as that for spoken languages but do not yet include assessment of knowledge of the legal context. CACDP also offers assessments for lip-speakers[15] and speech-to-text reporters.

12.24 Interpreters and translators who are members of a recognized professional language body or register will be required by that body to observe a code of conduct. This should include requirements to:

(a) interpret or translate truly and faithfully to the best of their ability, without adding or omitting anything;

(b) observe confidentiality (except anonymously within recognized structures of professional support and training);

(c) act, and be seen to act, impartially;

(d) only undertake assignments within the individual's competence or, if difficulties present themselves during an assignment, to remedy them or withdraw;

(e) refrain from acting where there is a potential conflict of interest, unless there is informed consent from all parties;

(f) not delegate assignments;

(g) decline any reward, other than the agreed fees and expenses, for work in the public services;

(h) seek to increase their professional knowledge and expertise, and

(i) safeguard professional standards and offer assistance to other interpreters and translators wherever reasonable, practical and appropriate.

12.25 Guides to good practice are set out to promote the practical implementation of the code of conduct in particular contexts. A good example is the Metropolitan Police Service guide to interpreters, with its parallel guide for police officers working with interpreters. Whereas the core code is timeless and immutable, the guides to good practice are regularly revised to accommodate change and it is recognized that practical circumstances may hinder the following of a guide in all its detail.[16]

12.26 Face-to-face interpreting is normally considered to produce the most accurate outcomes in a process where, even at best, shades of meaning can be lost. Time, resources and practicalities inevitably result in other means being considered, although the interpreter has no access to non-verbal signals over the telephone and limited access to them via the two-dimensional image of a video camera. Bearing these caveats in mind:

- Telephone interpreting is useful:
  - in an emergency, e.g. to give to a police officer the description of a lost child;
  - for exchanges of simple information, e.g. to make an appointment;
  - to hold a situation until an interpreter can arrive for a face-to-face assignment, and
  - to text suitable messages to deaf people.

---

[14] See *http://www.cacdp.org.uk.*

[15] 'A lipspeaker conveys a speaker's message to lip readers accurately using unvoiced speech'. (The Council for The Advancement of Communication with Deaf People. *http://www.cacdp.org.uk*).

[16] See *Imam Bozkurt v Thames Magistrates' Court* (2002) RTR 15 and *R v Milahy Ungvari* (2003) *LTL* 18/7/2003 *Extempore* (unreported elsewhere).

- Video interpreting is useful:
  - for sign language interpreters where the telephone would have been used as above, and
  - where distance and time are pressing considerations.

The CJS Agreement on the arrangements for the engagement of interpreters[17] requires **12.27** that the CJS agencies should aim to engage members of the NRPSI or CACDP registers— who are subject to specific selection criteria and codes of conduct with accompanying disciplinary procedures—or the equivalent. It is therefore necessary to know about these registers in order to be in a position to determine, if necessary, what might be the equivalent.

The NRPSI has published selection criteria, a code of conduct and associated disciplin- **12.28** ary procedures. It is a non-profit-making subsidiary of the Chartered Institute of Linguists. The selection criteria include strategies to deal with short-term demands and shortcomings, while promoting long-term goals, and include:

(a) recognition of suitable language qualifications in addition to the DPSI;
(b) evidence of proven relevant experience;
(c) levels of registration that promote improvement towards full membership within a prescribed time limit: therefore, for example, interim membership may be awarded to those who have just passed their examinations and so far lack experience; the rare languages category includes those who satisfy other criteria but for whom there is not yet a formal assessment available in their particular language; the limited assessment category includes those who have passed a non-nationally-recognized assessment in a particular narrow domain such as for the immigration or the Metropolitan Police test;
(d) re-registration on a regular basis;
(e) evidence as to the absence of a criminal record and a requirement to inform the register should the registrant be convicted of an offence: in certain circumstances, the authorities concerned may wish to carry out higher security clearance and vetting procedures;
(f) a signed statement undertaking to observe the code of conduct and the disciplinary procedures where any breach of the code is alleged, and
(g) satisfactory references as to character and professional standing.

The CACDP has similar criteria.

Nationally consistent systems for contacting legal interpreters and translators are the final **12.29** component of the professional structures to be put in place. Various structures are being explored and currently include:

(a) for legal interpreters:
  - direct access on subscription to the NRPSI (National Register for Public Service Interpreters) secure website *http://www.nrpsi.co.uk*.

---

[17] See paragraph 12.06 above.

- direct access on subscription to the CACDP (Council for the Advancement of Communication with Deaf people) with registry through their website *http:// www.cacdp.org.uk* and for lip-speakers and other aids to communication.

- access through commercial or not-for-profit interpreter agencies who hold these registers: this approach can be attractive to legal personnel who prefer to outsource the associated administration; some of these agencies are good but some are still of variable quality and a national quality standard is therefore being proposed.

- some criminal justice agencies, such as the Metropolitan Police Service, have units dedicated to the provision of legal linguistic services.

(b) for legal translators, who can work in any part of the country via secure IT systems:
   - professional language bodies, which require members to meet specific standards and to observe a code of conduct. The main ones in the UK are the Institute of Translation and Interpreting (*http://www.ITI.org.uk*) and Chartered Institute of Linguists (*http://www.iol.org.uk/linguist/*).

   - specialist units, notably those set up by the Metropolitan Police Service.

   - translation agencies. There is no national system of accreditation of such agencies. A number are very good and engage only properly qualified, experienced individuals and will also undertake the necessary proof-reading and checking.

(c) for interpreters and translators in other countries. Increasingly, criminal and civil legal matters may cross national borders. This can present problems because few countries have nationally recognized professional structures in place. Some countries have 'sworn' interpreters and translators but the criteria vary. Therefore it is probably sensible, if appropriate, to make enquiries of the legal authorities in the countries concerned as to where reliable, independent legal interpreters or translators can be found and what their qualifications and professional standing are.

D. How Interpreters and Translators should be Engaged

(1) Contracts/letters of agreement

12.30 Most interpreters and translators work in a freelance capacity, which helps to reinforce the actuality and the perception of independence and impartiality vital to the performance of their role. It also means, of course, that the interpreter is able to work for a number of different agencies or companies, so ensuring efficient use of scarce and expensive professional resources.

12.31 The CJS Interpreters Working Group recommends discussion and agreement of the terms of engagement before either party agrees to a booking and, if time permits, to issue a letter of agreement outlining these. Common terms which should be included in such a document are:

- date, time and location of assignment;
- estimated duration;
- description of assignment, e.g. bail application, guilty plea in case of 15-year-old victim of rape;

- language (and dialect, if applicable): it may sometimes help to know where the non-English speaker comes from, as some spoken languages will be mutually intelligible between countries, but written differently;
- any special features of the assignment (e.g. child abuse, sexual offence, mentally disordered defendant, specialist vocabulary etc);
- fees payable—see below;
- practical mechanism for claiming fees, and timescales for payment;
- arrangements for tax and National Insurance;
- interpreters' professional affiliation, code of conduct and confidentiality, and
- any requirement for the interpreter to be covered by Professional Indemnity Insurance.

Fee agreements should cover minimum fees, fees relevant to interpreting time and, if applicable, waiting time, travelling time and subsistence, as well as arrangements for reimbursement of travelling expenses (e.g. on receipt) and fees payable on cancellation of an assignment (with prior notice/late notice, outright cancellation/curtailment). Current fee scales and responsibilities for payment can be established by reference to the relevant legal agency. Note that interpreters are usually paid by the hour, day or half-day, and translators, *pro rata*, per thousand words of translated text. There are not yet any nationally agreed fees for interpreters or translators working in the criminal justice system, although agencies signatory to the CJS Agreement have committed to work towards parity in interpreter fees.

Where it is not possible to issue a written record of the terms agreed prior to the commencement of the assignment, they should at least be agreed verbally when the interpreter is booked, and in the case of an ongoing assignment, a written record issued as soon as possible.

(2) Briefing interpreters and translators

The Auld review recognized the importance of briefing the interpreter, at recommendation 283.[18] In addition to the date, time and location of the assignment, further details should be given to allow the interpreter(s) the best opportunity to assess their own suitability for the job and to carry it out to the highest possible standard: **12.32**

- The name of the defendant, if known, as well as the name of the non-English speaker for whom the interpreter is required. This could alert the interpreter to a conflict of interest, which may require their withdrawal from the case, e.g. because the non-English speaker is known to the interpreter, other than in a professional capacity, or because they have interpreted for other parties in the same case and are, therefore, a potential witness. Wherever possible, the interpreter should be given the opportunity to talk to the non-English speaker over the telephone, before being booked to ensure a language and dialect match.
- Appropriate details of the nature of the case should be offered, to allow the interpreter to prepare relevant key vocabulary, assess their experience of similar cases or withdraw

---

[18] *A Review of the Criminal Courts of England and Wales*, The Right Honourable Lord Justice Auld, London: HMSO, (2001).

from the assignment where the domain is outside their area of competence, or personal experiences would indicate that another interpreter might be more suitable. Gender might be relevant in such matters as sexual abuse.

- An estimate should be given of the potential duration of the assignment, so that interpreters can organize their diaries appropriately.

- Interpreters should be advised of any specific techniques which will be used, e.g. for interviewing children, as these could impact upon the interpreting. The interpreter's task is to match as fully as possible the level of formality and type of language used by both parties, as well as the content of the message. They will need to know where it is vital, for instance, to use a non-leading question in particular circumstances: for example, there is no generic sign in BSL for 'weapon' and choices would have to be made between 'gun', 'knife' and so on.

12.33 When briefing a translator, an indication of the following should be given:

- The kind of translation required, i.e. the likely target audience and whether the translation will be used, for instance, for information (requiring immediate and accurate access to the content, which need not be stylistically perfect) or for publication, requiring a polished text.

- The urgency with which translation is required. Allow a realistic time frame—extra time will usually be required for proof-reading translated text. More than one translator could be commissioned to complete a lengthy text within tight deadlines, but this will take coordination to ensure consistency of format, layout and vocabulary.

- Any special formatting or layout considerations should be clarified at the outset. For instance, a translation may be formatted independently of its original, or it may be provided as a mirror image, page-by-page copy of its source text (where languages permit), despite the fact that this may result in translated pages being longer or shorter than the corresponding page in the original. Formatting and layout will take extra time. Such decisions should be taken as whether terms with no equivalent should be explained in footnotes or within the text.

- Delivery dates, times and methods should be agreed with translators.

- Legal practitioners should make themselves available to the translator in case problems arise such as the need to clarify ambiguities in the source text. Most professional translators will only translate into their best language, with the source language being their second language.

(3) Complaints and challenges

12.34 An essential component of any profession is its disciplinary procedures, designed to enforce its code of conduct. From the point of view of those engaging legal interpreters and translators, this means that they should enquire whether an interpreter or translator belongs to a professional language body at the time of booking and, where they suspect that an interpreter or translator has acted in contravention of a body's code, the legal practitioner should:

- report the matter to the relevant professional language body as soon as possible;

- complete any complaints form provided and append evidence supporting the allegation;
- be prepared to deal with subsequent correspondence and to attend any disciplinary hearing if the situation cannot be otherwise resolved, and
- employ a suitable substitute interpreter and make any other arrangements necessary to preserve the integrity of the proceedings in hand until the matter is resolved.

If it is found (by the disciplinary panel of the professional language body) that the code has been breached, there is a range of sanctions that might be activated depending on the severity of the breach. These include warnings, in-service training requirements, suspension or expulsion from the professional body. There might also be sanctions imposed by the courts. **12.35**

The following factors should, however, be taken into consideration: **12.36**

- Some participants in, or witnesses to, an interpreted exchange may have some level of skill in the relevant language but may not be sufficiently qualified to challenge an interpretation, although they may not be aware of this.

- Many complaints made about interpreters are, in fact, the result of a lack of awareness on the part of the legal practitioner of the boundaries of the interpreter's role. The roles of the legal interpreter and translator are clearly defined. In summary, the legal agencies are responsible for what is taking place, such as the management and content of a legal consultation, a police investigation or a court hearing. Interpreters and translators are responsible for communication between languages and their own code of conduct requires them to restrict themselves to that. This sounds self-evident but in practice many legal practitioners are tempted to pressure interpreters into doing more, such as taking witness statements on their own. Also interpreters are rarely qualified to be a source of accurate knowledge on the beliefs, perceptions, attitudes and demeanour of the individuals with whom they share a language. It is better by far, where that information is needed, to ask the individual client, through the interpreter. Suitably qualified interpreters and translators might, however, be called as expert witnesses on linguistic fact, including any underpinning cultural aspects such as any significance of honorifics, e.g. denoting family and social relationships.

- In circumstances where the interpreted exchange has been recorded and doubts are raised as to the standard of the interpretation, it is a relatively simple matter to request an independent assessment by an appropriately qualified third party or to call an expert witness. This can even be done mid-assignment, if the disputed interpretation is relatively concise. Otherwise, it may be quicker, cheaper and easier to instruct another interpreter to substitute for the first, in order to continue with proceedings until such time as the issue has been resolved, and to avoid the cost or concern of a retrial or a mistrial. The first interpreter should have no objection to this course of action, so long as they recognize the professional integrity of the second interpreter or expert witness. **12.37**

(4) Stressors

Legal practitioners should be aware of, and therefore reduce, if possible, factors that can have a negative impact upon the accuracy of interpretation. Interpreters, like lawyers, are able to draw on extremely high levels of mental energy, elasticity and stamina. They also **12.38** work long and often anti-social hours, are required to think on their feet and have unpredictable workloads. Interpreters have the right, as do lawyers, to decline assignments in the interests of justice when over-weary.

12.39 In addition, interpreters working in the legal domain often labour under other stressful conditions which include:

- travelling long distances to unfamiliar locations, often at unsociable times;
- interpreting harrowing evidence for suspects and victims of serious crimes, sometimes within the cells or at scenes of mass disaster, where theoretical training cannot adequately prepare the individual for the reality, and
- working in isolation—interpreters seldom benefit from the mutual support enjoyed by many other professions; where necessary they should have access to the same trauma support lines as do, for instance, police officers, to unload their stress in confidence.

E. Interdisciplinary Good Practice—How to Work with Interpreters and Translators and Across Cultures

(1) Mechanics of the interpreting process

12.40 In very basic terms, the stages of communication within a shared language comprise:

- thinking of the message to be given;
- assessing the person to be addressed in terms of such factors as age, background, education, perceptions, attitudes and the context of the relationship;
- encoding or composing the message by the speaker through selecting—on the basis of an understanding of the listener—the words, gestures, tone of voice and structures deemed most appropriate for the task and context;
- sending the message;
- the listener decoding the message, and
- the speaker and the listener checking and correcting comprehension.

12.41 During a conversation, the process is then reversed and so on. As the newly acquainted learn more about each other, they are better able to fine-tune the ways in which they compose what they say to meet the listener's situation and to check comprehension. Turn taking, the level of formality and so on vary according to different situations, contexts and relationships. Those working effectively in the legal system communicate well. They intuitively adapt their terminology, grammar, sentence constructions and registers according to who they are talking to. A police officer or a lawyer can be heard giving exactly the same piece of information differently to ten different people to ensure comprehension. Equally, they can listen to, and understand, those ten different people expressing themselves in their own way.

12.42 Where the assistance of an interpreter is required, there is more to it than the interpreter simply transposing the individual words spoken into equivalent individual words in the other language. That would result in a nonsense. One of the well-known examples of early machine translation illustrates the point. The phrase 'the spirit is willing but the flesh is weak' was turned into the equivalent of 'the whisky is fine but the meat has gone off'. Interpreters transfer the *meaning* of the message by decoding the concept expressed by the speaker and accurately re-encoding it into the other language.

Working across language and culture can add tensions to already problematic situations. **12.43** Those who are used to working effectively with qualified interpreters soon cease to see this as a 'problem'. The quality of the outcome can be greatly facilitated if legal practitioners observe the following:

(a) Brief the interpreter adequately in advance (see above).

(b) Set aside enough time because matters will take longer.

(c) Organize the venue so that there is sufficient space and appropriate acoustics. Comfortable seating should be organized where interpreters can see and hear and be seen and heard. Note that sign language interpreters will need to be positioned differently from spoken language interpreters.

(d) At the beginning of the interview, or event, allow the interpreter to recheck the language match with the other-language speaker. If mutual comprehension is at risk, perhaps because of a strong regional accent in either language, the interpreter should be allowed to withdraw and another found. Note that sign language also has regional variations.

(e) Make clear introductions, ensuring the correct spelling and pronunciation of names. Be aware of different naming systems for the purpose of precise and consistent record keeping. Allow the interpreters to explain their role in both languages, stating that they will:
 • interpret everything that is said (which pre-empts, for example, a defendant saying 'I'm guilty but don't tell them');
 • be impartial, and
 • observe confidentiality.

(f) Clarify the purpose of the interview or event where it fits into a legal process, the procedures to be followed and the role and function of all the parties present. Individuals from other backgrounds may have little understanding of what is happening and be too anxious to ask. An English magistrate is not the same as a French *magistrat*. The adversarial and inquisitorial systems require different approaches. Information needs to be layered, repeated and consolidated and time allowed for questions.

(g) Use clear and unambiguous language to enable the interpreters to be absolutely clear as to the meaning of what is said before they interpret. For example, the request 'to indicate a plea' confuses even native English speakers; the elements of such charges as ABH, GBH and common assault should be spelt out because the difference can be significant; it is as well to be specific, even if distasteful, and not use euphemisms in sexual matters; and to avoid the woolly clichés of the 'thank you for sharing that with me' variety. Latin terms, such as '*sine qua non*' and culture-bound phrases such as 'you must have thought it was Christmas, sunshine' can be a challenge to the most skilled interpreter.

(h) Use direct speech, i.e. 'where were you on Friday evening?' and not 'ask him where he was on Friday evening'.

(i) Address the other person, not the interpreter. This also helps to avoid transferring to the interpreter the assessments, engagement and relationship that should be directed at the other party. The interpreters will not feel excluded but prefer to concentrate on their job.

(j) Pause at appropriate moments for consecutive interpretation. In an interview, for example, interpreting is more likely to take place after each person has spoken, that is consecutively. It is better to allow this to happen after three or four sentences, or each complete unit of information, and never in the middle of a sentence—especially in languages where the verb is at the end of the sentence. This approach allows the rhythm of a dialogue to emerge between the principal parties and makes it easier for the interpreter to recall all the details of what has been said. The spoken-language interpreter may take notes as an *aide mémoire*, especially where numbers, times and proper names are involved. This consecutive technique is obviously necessary where the spoken exchange is being tape-recorded.

(k) Monitor pace of speech on the occasions where interpreters use the whispered simultaneous technique, such as during a judge's summing up. That is, interpreters will whisper the meaning of what is being said to one listener. This can also be a useful approach in a lawyer's office when a non-English speaker suddenly produces a torrent of emotion or information that flows better without interruption for consecutive interpreting. Most BSL–English interpreting will be simultaneous i.e. the interpreter will sign as the speaker speaks, and speak as the deaf person signs. More sophisticated and secure technology, and modern court-houses, are leading to the provision of portable equipment whereby interpreting can be carried out simultaneously through headphones. This will be particularly useful where there are multiple other-language speaking defendants and witnesses, perhaps speaking different languages, and in situations such as case conferences, where a number of people are present. It does, however, require additional skills and training for legal interpreters.

(l) Accommodate interpreters' interventions. These are designed to preserve the integrity of the communication and are made for four reasons:
- to clarify the exact meaning of what has been said in order for it to be interpreted accurately;
- to request those present to take account of the interpreting process, e.g. if someone is speaking too quickly or quietly or for too long; where people are trying to talk at the same time the interpreter will request and monitor turn taking but it is the legal professional's responsibility to retain control where, for example, emotions run high;
- to alert those present that, while the interpreting was correct, the listener may not have understood what was said, and
- to alert those present of a possible missed cultural inference: that is, where it may have been erroneously assumed that a party has knowledge or understanding of the other's traditions, customs.

Interpreters will interpret any necessary explanations and not seek to give their own advice or opinions. Nor should interpreters have a conversation in one language, the content of which is not known to the other parties present.

(m) Listen, and be seen to listen, carefully. Test each unit of fact with care and, if necessary, courage. This is something of an art where there is a shared language and culture when one also has to make notes, but all the more important where there is an increase in the significance of non-verbal signals denoting mutual comprehension and relationship. Be aware as always, however, that the meaning of non-verbal signals and body language differs between cultures and individuals (e.g. in the sign-language context, nodding indicates understanding of what is being signed, not agreement with it, and a lack of eye contact in some cultures indicates a respect for authority, and should not be construed as shiftiness). If in doubt of their meaning, and it is appropriate, simply ask the other party through the interpreter. Starting points may need to be explored, in terms of perceptions and attitudes towards, for example, definitions of natural justice or family structures. Cultural starting points may also affect not only the order in which information is given but also degrees of importance attached to particular factors or events when, for example, recounting events as a witness.

(n) Allow questions to be asked to ensure mutual understanding. It can take time, for example, for people from other countries to work out that, just because Englishmen would not customarily express emotion in a professional situation, this does not mean that they do not feel any. In today's multicultural societies, it would not be unusual, for example, for an Asian lawyer practicing in the UK to have an African client who had graduated from university in Moscow in engineering.

(o) Be prepared to negotiate communication strategies if necessary. It is usually acceptable, if things are not going too well, simply to say (through the interpreter) that working through an interpreter can be challenging and that mutual help over cultural and communication factors would be welcomed.

(p) Different situations give rise to different communication strategies, with or without an interpreter. For example, investigative interviews and cross-examinations in court have different conventions for turn taking, approaches, use of formal and informal language—all honed to a fine art through habitual use yet potentially fragile when exposed to having to cross languages and cultures. It is possible to accommodate these additional factors without losing the strategies for a quality of communication that have evolved over time. Training is becoming available for those working in the legal system to allow them to explore and practice, in advance and away from the workplace, the adaptations they will need to make when working with an interpreter. Legal professionals are often invited to participate in the training of legal interpreters, where they participate in training role-plays; ACPO investigative interviewing courses can be extended to cover this aspect; moot courts for law students can involve other-language speaking participants.

(q) Unless there is a team of interpreters to take over from one another, allow the interpreter a break of fifteen minutes in every hour wherever practicable. Conference interpreters work in twenty-minute shifts because it is difficult to retain that high level of concentration for longer without the quality falling.

Able linguists are an essential prerequisite where there is insufficient shared language but **12.44** it is what is said through that communication channel that is the important factor. It is time well spent to get to know something of the non-English speaker at the outset, where appropriate. Cultural stereotypes were never useful because every individual has their own unique culture arising from his or her unique life experience. Today they are even less useful as people move between countries, acquiring education, social and work experiences in each. A broad understanding of the individual's starting points and perceptions enables the right questions to be asked to elicit the necessary information and also to appreciate the significance of the answers.

F. Conclusion

12.45 Globalization cannot be reversed. Its effects will increase. It is a fact that only becomes a problem if not dealt with adequately. There is no alternative to doing so. That will demand endless vigilance against those who would seek, for example, to provide the criminal justice system with interpreters and translators with school-leaving standards of language skill for the sake of administrative expediency, cosmetic quick results and cost cutting. Legal practitioners have a duty to defend the integrity of the criminal justice system, as well as individual other-language speaking witnesses who have the right to understand fully what is happening around them and be understood, if they are to discharge their responsibilities properly.

Further Reading

Aequitas—*access to justice across language and culture in the EU*, Lessius Hogeschool, (ed. Erik Hertog) Antwerp, 2001.

Aequalitas—*access to justice across language and culture in the EU*, Lessius Hogeschool, (ed. Erik Hertog) Antwerp, 2003.

Aequilibrium—*instruments for lifting language barriers in intercultural legal proceedings*, (eds. Heleen Keijzer-Lambooy and Willem Jan Giselle) Utrecht ITV Hogeschool voor Tolken en Vertalen, 2005 (with associated teaching materials).

The Cambridge Encyclopaedia of Language, David Crystal. Cambridge, Cambridge University Press, 1999.

Equality before the law—Deaf people's access to justice, by Brennan, M. and Brown, R. The Deaf Studies Research Unit, University of Durham, 1997.

Working with the Metropolitan Police Service—Guidelines for Interpreters, 1998, MPS Linguistic and Forensic Medical Services.

Working with Interpreters—Guidelines for MPS Personnel, 2000, MPS Linguistic and Forensic Medical Services.

Ann Corsellis is Vice-Chairman of the Council of the Chartered Institute of Linguists and of the Board of the National Register of Public Service Interpreters. She coordinated the ten-year UK development of training, assessment and good practice for legal interpreters in the UK and the first EU two-year international project to establish equivalent standards for legal interpreters and translations in all member states. She led the UK team for the subsequent two EU projects. She represents the Magistrates Association on the National CJS Interpreter Working Group. Publications include *Non-English speakers and the English Legal System* published by the Institute of Criminology, University of Cambridge.

Amanda Clement holds a BA(Hons) in European Studies (French) from the University of London, an MA in Translation from the University of Surrey and an LLB (Bachelor of Law) from the University of East London. She is Deputy Head, Linguistic and Forensic Medical Services Branch, Metropolitan Police Service, London; a Member of the National CJS Interpreter Working Group and of the Interdepartmental Committee on Linguistic Services. She was also a member of the UK team for the last two EU international projects to establish equivalent standards for legal interpreters and translators in Member States.

Editors' Note

(See, also, our note for Chapter 13.) The risk to dependable and sound decisions and just verdicts posed by poor interpretation and translation services should, obviously, not be underestimated. Whereas these authors explain what safeguards against this are or ought to be in place, there continue to be frequent anecdotal accounts which justify the suggestion that the safeguards, or such machinery as exists to ensure that they are observed, are inadequate to ensure safe practice. Thus the question arises what needs to be done to ensure that both methodically and in individual cases—criminal or civil—the work of interpreters and translators in the justice system does not create a risk of unreliable decisions as to facts or the merits of a case. Perhaps some research is called for. This would, necessarily, involve the use of 'parallel' interpreters or translators employed by the researchers in both the investigative and forensic contexts.

13

WITNESSES WHO USE BRITISH SIGN LANGUAGE

Jim Kyle

A. Introduction

Social order is generally governed by assumptions about shared intentions, motives and **13.01** interpersonal communication. When those assumptions are disturbed, person perception changes—one person may be deemed ignorant, unreasonable, stupid or badly behaved. Lack of communication in interaction is usually considered to be a deviation from the norm. Since this applies to people in everyday interactions, it also applies to all those working within the legal process. Yet just because one person does not speak or does not speak well, it does not mean that the person has nothing to contribute or is lacking the capacity to contribute. The question becomes one of how the process is able to adjust to the needs of that person and how well intermediary services function to bridge the gap in communication. In this chapter we will examine a distinct challenge to the legal system: people who are Deaf and use British Sign Language.

B. Deaf People

(1) Issues for Deaf people

At present, there are major problems in applying the law to Deaf people since few **13.02** members of the legal profession, the police or the various plaintiffs have knowledge of the experience of deafness or of Deaf people's own views and beliefs. Procedures may be incorrectly applied or are inherently inappropriate, the level of training for professionals is poor or non-existent and costs incurred are relatively high.

13.03 There are no extended training facilities for sign language interpreters for the legal process (in the UK) and the outcome is that Deaf people's testimony is often inadequately relayed.[1] As things stand, it is questionable whether Deaf people can be dealt with effectively in the legal process. This puts both Deaf people and society as a whole at risk.

(2) Some definitions and clarifications

13.04 There are several understandings of 'deafness'. Deafness has been defined often in medical terms as a lack of hearing and this simplicity lies at the root of many of the problems in our dealings with Deaf people.

13.05 *Deafness, Deafhood, Deaf Community*—are terms acquiring new meaning as the description of the experience of a severe/profound hearing loss at an early age. Deaf with a capital D refers specifically to those people who are within this group. Typically, people who are 'Deaf' identify themselves as part of a community and nowadays, as part of a language minority group. They are likely to associate with other Deaf people at meetings, Deaf clubs, at social occasions and are likely (in 90 per cent of cases) to marry or cohabit with other Deaf people. Most such people (over 90 per cent) have no relatives who are Deaf—i.e. they have hearing parents and siblings and when married they have hearing children. In this family structure, only the partner is Deaf and naturally uses the same language. The community can be said to be one-generational—which raises significant issues when values and culture are to be handed on or when role models are needed. The size of the community is often over-stated but based on an examination of the numbers who have attended Deaf schools from our research, the core community is likely to be around 25,000 in the UK with around the same number in the periphery and using sign language to some extent. In this chapter we are dealing mainly with this group of people. Terms which are still apparent in legal circles—*deaf and dumb* and *deaf-mute*—are considered inappropriate nowadays. They should not be used.

13.06 *Deafened* has been applied to those who acquire a hearing loss at a later age—after early childhood (and certainly after they have learned to speak). Typically, deafened applies to those who have profound hearing impairments—Lord Jack Ashley is a prominent deafened person. Usually, such people continue to associate with hearing people—they remain 'culturally hearing'. They will also continue to use speech, have auditory memory and their problems of communication can be attributed to other people's inability to adapt to the reduction in the auditory channel. They can read subtitles, newspapers, books just as hearing people do. Despite a general myth about lip-reading capabilities, it is almost impossible to read lips because a significant proportion of English simply does not appear on the lips. People who appear to follow conversation by watching the lips are combining their existing knowledge of spoken language and of body language with expectations of what might be said in a given context.

---

[1] Brennan, M. and Brown, R., *Equality before the Law: Deaf People's Access to Justice*, Coleford: Douglas Maclean Publishing, 2004.

Hard of hearing people are those who form the vast majority of people who have a medical **13.07** hearing loss. Possibly, there are as many as 7 million in the UK. The vast majority are of retirement age and their hearing loss increases over time. Hard-of-hearingness is typically associated with elderly relatives and possibly 50 per cent of those over 70 are likely to have a significant hearing loss. Sadly, such hearing loss is often considered to be consciously adjustable ('he can hear when he wants'—which is not the case) or to be associated with lack of intelligence (dumbness—also incorrect) and to be a feature of declining faculties (which is possible, since lack of mobility and physical capacity is typical of this later period of life). People who lose their hearing later in life are very unlikely to use sign language and are likely to remain culturally hearing. There are also *young hard of hearing people* who may associate with each other or *young deaf people* who are not members of the Deaf community. Both groups tend to create problems for classification and also have to be analysed and assessed separately. Members of the first group tend to adopt some 'Deaf views of the world' while the second may lack the positive supporting effect of the Deaf community and are often easily led and manipulated by hearing people, including by their families. This may put this group at higher risk of becoming known to the police and the legal process.

A significant defining feature of the classification, *Deaf,* is the use of British Sign **13.08** Language. Deaf people use BSL—the other groups use English. The capitalization is therefore significant—*D*eaf people are users of *B*ritish *S*ign *L*anguage just as *French* people speak *French.*

British Sign Language is not new—language records of it exist at least as early as the **13.09** seventeenth century—although its description and rise to prominence has been relatively recent. It is a non-spoken language with a structure quite different to that of English. It is a language of vision and space and is articulated not only with the hands but also with the face and head, shoulders and body. In a signed conversation, it is mandatory that the viewer looks at the face (not the hands). Sign language is rich and more extensive than English in its expression of location and movement (all visual aspects) but does not mark verbs for tense and may be less rigorous about the order of elements in the sentence. In a formal setting it is likely to move towards English ordering but it is more commonly set out with a topic-comment structure. This leads to structures like SCHOOL; BOY WENT (for 'the boy went to school').[2] Signed languages (each country has its own) have evolved to meet the needs of the users and are extensive in expression. However, since Deaf people have rarely had an opportunity to practise law, there has been no real opportunity for legal use of BSL to have evolved (although there is now a website for Deaf and hard-of-hearing students of the law, where there is some introductory BSL video).[3] Single sign-for-word translations may not exist and concepts expressed in BSL or in English may need to be fully interpreted rather than simply transliterated. Some of the implications of this are explored below.

---

[2] Capital letters are used conventionally to denote a sign in British Sign Language. For more detail on BSL see Sutton-Spence, R. and Woll, B., *The Linguistics of British Sign Language*, Cambridge: Cambridge University Press, 1998, and visit the signstation website at *http://www.signstation.org.*

[3] *http://www.deaflawyers.org.uk.*

(3) Deaf people in the legal process

13.10 The legal system in the UK has developed to meet the needs of the majority of society—it is well established. It is complex and extensive, requiring professional training and extended practice. The situation of Deaf people is less well understood than that of the others who have difficulty with the legal process. For example, minority language users, those with limited cognitive abilities, speech problems or disabled people in general, may produce appropriate empathy among professionals. These groups are likely to have experienced similar processes of socialization (to the rest of the population) and, at some level, can be governed by legal assumptions. Deaf people grow up in a world of vision and as a result their experience of events and interaction and thereby, of the legal process in which they sometimes find themselves, can be different. Only recently has this begun to be realized.

13.11 By the nature of the Deaf experience (i.e. surrounded by non-communicating hearing people), the socialization of young Deaf people is often atypical and the perceptions of morality among young Deaf people may be affected.[4] Social immaturity among Deaf children in hearing families has been reported.[5] The implication is that Deaf adults may have had less access to the interaction necessary for the development of moral reasoning in the way that hearing people take for granted. This makes it all the more important that the legal process takes into account their difference in perspective and experience.

13.12 It has been suggested that there has been an increase in the number of forensic referrals since the 1980s.[6] Although this is consistent social difference, there are also circumstantial factors which could have contributed, i.e. the increase in provision of mental health services in the UK.

13.13 Despite these concerns it is inappropriate to assume that moral judgement will be limited in all Deaf people. However, we need to be sensitive to the way in which Deaf people interpret questions and the nature of their response may reflect the differences in early socialization as well as in expression. Such issues may or may not be explained within expert reports. These issues are more obvious when the Deaf person acts as a witness. In dealing with this topic, I will consider three aspects: the use of interpreters, Deaf people giving statements and Deaf people in cross-examination.

---

[4] Denmark, J.C., *Deafness and Mental Health*, London: Jessica Kingsley, 1994.

[5] Marschark, M., *Psychological Development of Deaf Children*, Oxford: Oxford University Press, 1993; Rodda, M., 'Social Adjustment of Deaf Adolescents' in *Proceedings of a symposium on the psychological study of deafness and hearing impairment*, London: British Deaf Association, 1966; and Gregory, S., *The Deaf Child and his Family*, London: George Allen & Unwin, 1976.

[6] Young, A., Howarth, P., Ridgeway, S. and Monteiro, B., 'Forensic referrals to the three specialist psychiatric units for deaf people in the UK' (2001) 12 *Journal of Forensic Psychiatry*, 19–35; Young, A., Monteiro, B. and Ridgeway, S., 'Deaf people with mental health needs in the criminal justice system: a review of UK literature (2000) 11 *Journal of Forensic Psychiatry*, 556–70.

C. Use of Interpreters

The use of interpreters in court is covered by *The Trials Issues Group Agreement: Arrangements For The Attendance Of Interpreters In Investigations And Proceedings Within The Criminal Justice System.*[7] **13.14**

It seems relatively clear that nowadays there should be an interpreter to support a Deaf person as there would be for anyone who used a language other than English. Unfortunately mistakes have been made. In one notable instance interpreters were called and although they complained that they could not communicate with the defendant, the case was allowed to proceed without interpretation.[8] **13.15**

The use of sign language interpreters however, has a very long history: **13.16**

> THOMAS JONES, (8th December, 1773) was indicted for stealing five guineas . . . When this prisoner was put to the bar to be arraigned, he appeared to be deaf and dumb; the Court directed the sheriff to impannel a Jury, to try whether he stood dumb through obstinacy, or by the visitation of God; a Jury were accordingly returned by the sheriff, who after hearing the evidence of Fanny Lazarus, who had known the prisoner several years, brought in their verdict, 'That he was dumb by the visitation of God'. Fanny Lazarus was sworn interpreter: she interpreted to the prisoner by signs.[9]

There are regular occurrences of this sort in the archives of the Old Bailey. These provisions for interpreting predate the existence of schools for the deaf and of course, the training of interpreters. This led to a situation where many inappropriate people—relatives and friends and even parents—were sworn in as interpreters. Interestingly, in one of the earliest cases, that of George Armstrong accused of theft in 1725,[10] his workmate John Hewitt rightly pointed out: **13.17**

> . . . though they understood one another well enough in Rope-making, he could not pretend to be certain of his Meaning in such a Case as this.

With reference to the Police and Criminal Evidence Act 1984 and the Human Rights Act 1998, guaranteeing a fair trial, the expectations in regard to interpreters have been described as follows: **13.18**

> The Deaf suspect is entitled to have an interpreter present at the police station and at court. The interpreter must be provided free of charge, be independent and competent for the task assigned. Relay interpreting is permitted.[11]

The duty of finding the competent interpreter is helped by the existence of a register and this is provided to all the criminal justice agencies. The competence of the interpreter **13.19**

---

[7] Casework Bulletin No 10 of 2002, issued 8 April, 2002, posted on the Crown Prosecution Service website at *http://www.cps.gov.uk/legal/section16/chapter_c.html*. See Annex A for the Agreement.

[8] Denmark, (1994), cited above at n.4, 113.

[9] *Proceedings of the Old Bailey, http://www.oldbaileyonline.org/*, case reference: t17731208–23.

[10] Ibid, case reference: t17250407–70.

[11] Tilbury, N., (2005) 'Specific attention for vulnerable groups—in particular those with hearing impairments and sign language users—legislation, practical issues and training' in Keijzer-Lambooy, H. and Gasille, J. (eds) Aequilibrium: *Instruments for Lifting Language Barriers in Intercultural Legal Proceedings*, Utrecht: ITV Hogeschool voor Tolken en Vertalen, 2005, p.62.

remains an issue however, and listing on a register is not a guarantee of the appropriate level of sign competence in that particular case. The transcripts (in theory) are a means to check the accuracy of interpretation and this is mentioned below, but the competence of the interpreter is usually only monitored by participants in the case or by other interpreters.

13.20 In certain situations, one might consider that the requirement to provide an interpreter is taken too far. In the following Scottish case, the complainer was 'a Deaf-mute' and the participants had been called to court:

> The complainer, a deaf-mute who required an interpreter, was charged on summary complaint. At the intermediate diet, at which the complainer appeared and was represented, there was no interpreter present and the complainer's solicitor objected to a motion by the Crown to adjourn the diet so that an interpreter could be obtained. The magistrate adjourned the diet for three weeks and the complainer appealed to the High Court on the ground that no proceedings could competently take place in the absence of an interpreter.[12]

This objection was then submitted as a Bill of Suspension to the High Court. The ruling however, was that the magistrate had acted appropriately but it illustrates the complexity of the situation which might arise when no interpreter is available (and they are in short supply).

13.21 Until 15 years ago there were no extended training programmes for interpreters. Even now, with several colleges and universities in the UK offering more extended degree programmes of three or four years, the supply of qualified interpreters does not even keep up with the turnover of interpreters in the field, nor will it ever (at current rates) meet the huge demand. Significantly, none of the courses fully prepares interpreters to work in courts of law or with the police. However, interestingly, around a quarter of registered qualified interpreters and a third of registered trainee interpreters responding to a survey claim to have attended some recent short courses training in legal areas. Surprisingly, 45 per cent had taken assignments in court and 55 per cent had accepted work in a police station. It has been pointed out, however, that of those who may be considered to be qualified to work in legal settings, a third refused to take work in court.[13] Some evidence has also been reported of non-qualified interpreters working in courts and police stations.[14] One of the reasons for this occurring is that a Deaf person may request a friend or member of the family to act as interpreter. This is generally considered unwise (professionally) but in one case study a solicitor was reported as indicating that, despite the pitfalls of using a family member, it was still true that they would not 'make decisions for the Deaf client'.[15]

13.22 In a very large number of the testimonies which I have examined both in court and in

---

[12] *Brown v Vannett (Procurator Fiscal, Glasgow)* (1999) SCCR 458, High Court of Justiciary.

[13] Brien, D., *The Organisation and Provision of British Sign Language/English Interpreters in England, Scotland and Wales*, In-House Report, London: Department of Work & Pensions, 2002.

[14] Ibid, and by Brennan and Brown, (2004), cited above at n.1, 95.

[15] Brien, (2002), cited above at n.13, 117.

statements, there are problems which may be attributed to the lack of training of the interpreters. Brennan and Brown have given examples of the extent of the problems from the Deaf person's point of view:

> We tried to communicate but I couldn't adequately sign to her because she didn't understand me. I thought 'she's hopeless'. She then tried to use her voice with me. She asked me to try and talk. The lady interpreter told the police, 'I can't understand his signing but he can use his voice'. Then when I used my voice, she didn't know what I was saying . . .'[16]

This interpreter did not have the correct level of competence—i.e. an interpreting level above Stage III in the national system of awards.[17]

13.23 This makes it particularly worrying that there are still perceptions of adequacy being reported which are inappropriate:

> *CPS officer to sign for deaf in court.*
> *Deaf witnesses* will now have an interpreter when appearing at courts in Derbyshire. Crown Prosecution Service caseworker [XX] has passed her Stage 2 British Sign Language (BSL) examination. She will interpret at Derby Crown Court and the county's five magistrates' courts. She will help deaf and hearing-impaired victims and other witnesses when they give evidence in trials. . . . [XX] said: 'I've already provided assistance during one trial in which the complainant and most of the witnesses were deaf'.[18]

13.24 There are strong grounds for improving the training of sign language interpreters to create a group of specialist courtroom and legal interpreters. In their case, knowledge of the law and legal practice would be a requirement as well as the development of appropriate behaviour and the appropriate register of sign language. Proper interpreter training is costly and time consuming—cheap interpreter training tends to cost the legal system in the long run—with retrials and rejected statements.

D. Making a Statement

(1) Deaf views

13.25 Deaf people are often reluctant to deal with the police or with solicitors. In a study in Scotland, Deaf people were interviewed about access through sign language.[19] There were a small number of positive experiences, usually involving policemen who could sign.

13.26 In the majority of cases, there was a sense of frustration at the lack of information available and the lack of understanding from the justice system. In some cases, the police were seen to try to obtain information from the children (who were hearing):

> I wanted to make complaint about the children outside making noises and ignoring me when I told them to stop. The police came but were reluctant to write things down

---

[16] Cited above at n.1, 93.   [17] *http://www.cacdp.org.uk/Qual_Training/PDFs/Qualifications.pdf.*
[18] *Derby Evening Telegraph*, 15 October, 2004 (name removed by author to avoid embarrassment).
[19] Kyle, J.G., Reilly, A.M., Allsop, L., Clark, M. and Dury, A., *Investigation of access to public services in Scotland using British Sign Language*, Edinburgh: Scottish Executive, 2004.

and tried to talk to my daughter. I moved her away and said they should write things down.[20]

13.27 Obviously, trying to obtain information from the child is a major issue—since the child may have little understanding of the concepts involved and may be placed in an impossible situation. One can also sympathize with the position of the police in having to build a picture of an incident as quickly as possible. The problems were seen to be worse among Deaf people if they were Deaf and Asian, for example, where there was little cultural understanding of the ethnic group in addition to the Deafness problem. Deaf people's solution was simple—all police should be taught how to communicate in sign language.

(2) Understanding the statement

13.28 It has been noted that there are situations in the police station where the PACE Code of Practice Annex C (1984) allows for direct questioning without an interpreter—where the suspect is vulnerable or because of the urgency of the situation.[21] This action has to be sanctioned by a senior officer and is not allowed to continue once 'sufficient information to avert the risk' is obtained. Of course, such a circumstance can lead to increased stress on the Deaf person if the questioning is largely inaccessible. There are additional circumstances which arise when a Deaf person has some hearing and has a capacity to speak. In this case, he/she may be asked if it is alright to continue to answer questions in speech. This has led to circumstances (in my experience) where the audio tape of the interview showed that the Deaf man had not fully understood the written statement which was presented. Despite the capacity to make himself understood through speech, the Deaf man was unable to read effectively. Inaccurate responses because the Deaf man was only able to lip-read/hear part of the question, could not be detected when the statement was presented to him. As a result of the examination of the audio tape—not the transcript—it was possible to determine that what was written down was invalid and this statement was not used in the subsequent trial.

13.29 Such circumstances are difficult to determine for a police officer or even a solicitor, as typically when at school, Deaf people are praised for their speaking and lip-reading skills, which simply do not work in the stressful situations in real life. A Deaf person may believe that he/she can understand more than is really the case. In the pressure of the police station, a Deaf person may be unable/unprepared to resist the need of others to progress the case, even without full understanding. Deaf people have been shown to be unaware of their rights in these circumstances.[22]

(3) Effects of restraint during custody

13.30 One topic of great concern to Deaf people in custody, is the issue of restraining methods used. Typically and understandably, police must have recourse to techniques to restrain a violent suspect. Normally this involves restraining the arms or handcuffing but . . .

> the BSL user is to all intents and purposes 'gagged'; s/he is completely incapacitated

---

[20] Ibid, 32, E75.   [21] Brennan and Brown, (2004), cited above at n.1.   [22] Ibid.

linguistically. Almost inevitably, the desire to communicate will be so intense that the Deaf person may make strong physical movements in an attempt to move her/his arms.[23]

That is, the net result is that the suspect may become more violent and require more pressure to stop the movement. As a result the charges against that person tend to include 'resisting arrest'. **13.31**

(4) Involving the solicitor

When a solicitor has to be instructed, the circumstances may change, as long as the Deaf person understands the role of the solicitor who is expected to help. It has been stressed that the solicitor should do everything possible to avoid misunderstandings: 'the responsibility for this lies with the solicitor and not with the interpreter'.[24] **13.32**

There is a need for the questioner to continue to look at the Deaf person when the person is answering the question.[25] This is an interesting point. When a solicitor or police officer asks a question of the Deaf person, the Deaf person has to watch the interpreter (who should be positioned ideally next to the solicitor); the solicitor while asking the question should be looking at the Deaf person (not at the interpreter). When the Deaf person answers the question, he/she will now look at the solicitor (not the interpreter). This means that the solicitor cannot write down at the same time as listening to the interpreter. If the solicitor tries to look away, a BSL user will stop the conversation as this is a signal of disinterest. In a Deaf conversation, the viewer never looks away, unless he/she wishes to be rude or when the participants are in an argument. A Deaf person answering a question, therefore, needs eye contact with the person who asked the question. Without this the answer will be problematic. **13.33**

(5) The nature of the statement

In the matter of the statement itself, much has been made of the circumstance of the translation from sign language to speech and then to written English. The discrepancies and errors which are apparent have led to questions in the House of Lords about whether the accuracy of sign language interpretation can be checked at a later date.[26] To which the answer was that there is a contemporaneous written note of the interview but that there was no requirement to tape-record interviews. **13.34**

More recently, the situation has been clarified judicially: **13.35**

> The true record of the original statement of a witness or defendant who uses sign language is a *video* recording, not the interpreter's written or oral version of what they say the defendant or witness conveyed.[27]

In this way, the statement of the Deaf person should be preserved as a video record and **13.36**

---

[23] Ibid, 96.

[24] Colin, J. and Morris, R., *Interpreters and the Legal Process*, Winchester: Waterside Press, 1996, 34.

[25] Ibid.   [26] 612 HL Deb., WA col 116, 19 April 2000, Lord Bach.

[27] *R v Raynor* (2000) *The Times*, 19 September, CA, and see *R v Governor of Brixton Prison and Another, ex p Safi* (2001) *The Times*, 24 January. See also European Court of Human Rights, *Manual of Guidance*, Chapter 16.8C, accessible as of 2005 via the CPS web page, *http://www.cps.gov.uk/legal/section16/chapter_c.html.*

this can be inspected by the Deaf person, expert witnesses and interpreters. Wherever the police are able to determine the Deaf person's need for sign language, then this procedure is expected to be in place.[28]

13.37 It should now be obvious that in all transactions with a Deaf witness or in a case of Deaf testimony, there should be a video record of the Deaf person's signing—not just the translation to speech or to text.

E. Witness Testimony in Court

(1) Signing the testimony

13.38 Although we are concerned with approaches to Deaf people in the legal process, today, there is much to be gained from understanding the position of Deaf people in the historical records. Sometimes the issues are the same as today. There are references to Deaf people (as deaf and dumb, deaf-mute) in old law reports as far back as the thirteenth century.[29]

13.39 The particular circumstance of Deaf people was also recognised in the fourteenth century as they were allowed to give testimony by signs.[30] In 1753, in the Court of Common Pleas at Westminster, Lady Mary O'Bryen was allowed to use an interpreter who signed to her.[31]

(2) Establishing Deafness

13.40 However, there was a major problem—which continued at least until the nineteenth century—of determining whether the person who was giving testimony was actually Deaf. This was expressed in terms of whether the person stood mute through 'malice' or 'obstinacy' or whether by 'the visitation of God'.[32]

13.41 There was some pressure on Deaf people as the consequences of being found mute by malice were severe, since they would be subject to the ordeal of *peine forte et dure*, in which they were forced to lie down and have weights placed on them until they either relented or died.

13.42 One may ask why anyone would remain silent in the face of this threat. The answer seems to be that being tried and found guilty might mean that one's family would be implicated, whereas by remaining silent one might limit the punishment to oneself. It has been suggested that the practice was discontinued by the 1720s.[33] However, it was usually

---

[28] See PACE Code of Practice Amendments, Code F: *Code of Practice on Visual Recording with Sound of Interviews with Suspects*, London: Home Office, 2005—available at *http://police.homeoffice.gov.uk/operational-policing/powers-pace-codes/pace-codes.html*.

[29] E.g. William the Deaf, tanner, on 14 September, 1233: London Eyre of 1244, 16 Henry III–18 Henry III, nos 77–96, Anno sextodecimo.

[30] 1339.057rs (1339) Edward III, Common Pleas: Plea of land; Folio RS 177.

[31] Notes of Cases, 1790, 168.

[32] See, e.g. the case of Nathan Soloman in 1772: *Proceedings of the Old Bailey, http://www.oldbaileyonline.org/*, case reference: t17720429–52.

[33] Till, W.J. 'Replies: Punishment—*peine fort et dure*', *Notes and Queries*, 16 April 1864, 3rd S.V, 324–5.

deemed necessary to have evidence on the person's extent of Deafness (and sign use) before proceeding.

In 1787, in the celebrated case of Betty Steel[34] the judge was clear that he would continue **13.43** even if she chose not to speak:

> 826. ELIZABETH STEEL was indicted for stealing, on the 22d day of January last, one watch inside and outside case, made of silver, value 30s. the property of George Childs.
> *Owen to prisoner.* Are you guilty, or not Guilty.
> *Prisoner.* You know I cannot hear.
> *Court to prisoner.* Your case has been considered by all the Judges, and they are of opinion that even if you cannot hear, you ought to be tried; therefore it is my duty to tell you (on a supposition that you can hear) that it will be in vain for you to pretend to be deaf, because you will only lose the opportunity of asking proper questions, but it will not prevent your trial coming on, for I shall certainly try you, whether you can hear or no.

Even so, and even bearing in mind the long history of Deaf people participating in court **13.44** proceedings, there were still occasions when counsel chose to object to Deaf testimony. In the case of William Bartlett, in 1786,[35] the jury had determined that the Deaf witness (the main witness for the prosecution) was 'Deaf by the visitation of God' and had sworn the sister as his 'interpretess' but the defendant's counsel, Mr Garrow, took a series of objections which rehearse many of the arguments that have persisted in Deaf education (and law) over the last 200 years and have led to the banning of sign language use in schools. The transcript of the dialogue between judge and counsel runs to some 14 pages and is of great interest for its intensity and the arguments put forward. Counsel objected to the Deaf witness on the basis that if he used signs he could not use/understand verbal concepts and that the nature of signs was insufficient in sophistication to understand the proceedings of the trial and to express the moral judgements necessary to press his case:

> *Mr Garrow.* I confess my Lord I begin to fancy my self almost an Ideot if not a dumb man my Objection is that there is no way in which you can possibly communicate with a deaf and dumb man.
> *Court.* You assume that.
> *Mr Garrow.* I assume it on the authority of my Lord Hale who lays it down that a man who is Sudus et Mutus &c. is in presumption & Ideot.[36]

In these cases and also in the Laws of Scotland[37] the state of being deaf and dumb was **13.45** seen as an obstacle to the use of reason and thereby disqualified the person from giving testimony.

---

[34] *Proceedings of the Old Bailey*, case ref: t17871024–15. See also Branson, J. and Miller, D., *The Story of Betty Steel: Deaf convict and pioneer*, Petersham, NSW: Deafness Resources Australia, 1995.

[35] *Proceedings of the Old Bailey*, case ref: o17860111–1

[36] The reference is to Hale, Sir Matthew, *History of the Pleas of the Crown*, London: Sollom Emlyn, 1736, vol i, 34: 'A man that is *surdus et mutus a nativitate*, is in presumption of law an idiot'. See also Blackstone, Sir William, *Commentaries on the Laws of England*, Oxford: Clarendon Press, 1765–1769, i, c.8, 293 ('Of the King's Revenue'): 'A man is not an idiot^p, if he hath any glimmering of reason, so that he can tell his parents, his age, or the like common matters. But a man who is born deaf, dumb, and blind, is looked upon by the law as in the same state with an idiot^q; he being supposed incapable of understanding, as wanting those senses which furnish the human mind with ideas.'

[37] Wallace, G., *A system of the principles of the law of Scotland*, Edinburgh, 1760, vol. i.

13.46   The exchange became rather heated and the Judge threatened to commit Mr Garrow. The Court then established that the oath could be conveyed and that the witness was able to judge the idea of right and wrong. Mr Garrow then tried to clarify for himself by asking the interpreter to confirm that he could understand a range of concepts but still concluded:

> *Mr Garrow.* Now my Lord I take the liberty of troubling your Lordship with my objection—I do admit this young woman having conversed with him, if we may so call it, from the time of his Nativity does believe that there is a certain degree of rationality about him, therefore he does understand some simple Ideas; but the evidence does not prove that he has any Idea of Complex Ideas.

13.47   At this point Mr Garrow launched a sustained attack on the thinking of sign language-using Deaf people. He argued that it is impossible to take in the necessary information for moral judgement just through sight. He then went on to argue that if the Deaf witness perjured himself, then it would have been impossible to try him for perjury and as a result the defendant would have had no recourse. He summed up with an extravagant plea to the jury:

> My Lord I wish I could also address that Jury on this trial I should be glad to ask them whether they would chuse to convict a man of felony upon the testimony of a man with whom they could not hold a conversation who has not more rationality than an Automaton, who does not appear more competent (if I may be allowed to make such a Simily) than that learned Pig which is now exhibited to the publick.

13.48   The Judge then refused the plea and maintained the Deaf man's validity and capacity to determine right and wrong. The hearing defendant was then found guilty on the testimony of the Deaf person.

(3) Significance of the case

13.49   While this lengthy example would seem to be an argument of the long-distant past, it touches on themes of suspicion and ethnocentrism which are still very much prevalent today. The notion that sign language and visual experience is insufficient for learning has been at the centre of the oral–manual controversy in the education of Deaf people since the late eighteenth century. The argument that we live in a hearing world (with a speaking/hearing legal system) implies the exclusion of those without that capacity and this position empowers those decision makers to use an oral-only approach in schools. When such a system does not work—and a consensus is that it has failed a significant group of Deaf people for over 200 years—then it also denies that person the socializing impact of sign language. In effect, Deaf people *could* end up in the situation which Mr Garrow implied if they have been denied access to their own language until later in life. Some Deaf people brought up without contact with other Deaf people and without being able to develop a language (since the speech around them is inaccessible) will have difficulty with concepts and in expressing themselves.

13.50   In these circumstances, Mr Garrow could be right but for the wrong reason—it would be the deprivation of language which would lead to an inability to make judgements and to determine the rationality of behaviour. It would be the provision of sign language which would be the medium upon which Deaf people construct the reality of the world around them. It is then only through this medium that they can adequately express their contribution to the legal process.

Circumstances of linguistic deprivation in early life may mean that certain Deaf persons **13.51** have not developed effective sign language nor effective English. In this case, it will be advisable to use a Deaf interpreter (as well as a hearing sign language interpreter). This Deaf interpreter will be better able to judge the conceptual competence of the Deaf witness. The Deaf interpreter will also be able to set an appropriate register for communication and then to relay the responses in sign language, to a hearing interpreter. Although this seems like a complex arrangement which will slow down proceedings and which appears to indicate incompetence in the witness, we know from cognitive testing that Deaf people do have normal distributions of intelligence and so the lack of spoken language and potential limitations in sign language use are not to be taken as meaning the Deaf person is unable to think or to recall events.

(4) Legal terms in BSL

Having set out this case, we do also need to consider the specific issue of legal argument **13.52** and the particular, legal terminology which might be used by a barrister in court. Not only are there potential conceptual problems for an interpreter, the unique sense of apparently simple sentences creates a problem for translation. Although a detailed description of these problems has been published,[38] it may be instructive to consider a number of questions which can be asked and to understand how these might be rendered in British Sign Language. These examples are taken from a transcript of the interaction of barrister and witness.

'Is it not right that . . .?' This phrase is often used to push the witness to agree to **13.53** implicate himself in some way by suggesting that the weight of opinion/fact is towards whatever follows in the sentence, e.g. 'that you needed the money' or 'that you were upset and angry with X'. However, a literal translation to BSL of the phrase would be entirely misleading: first, BSL has no verb to be; second, 'not right' (the part which could be rendered, consisting of negation and the sign CORRECT) gives the meaning 'incorrect'; third, the phrase which follows would then be negated, '(it is) not right that you needed the money?' to which the answer might be 'yes—I did not need the money'. More accurate would be the translation—'AGREE YOU' meaning 'you agree . . .'

Similar problems arise with the phrase 'I would suggest to you that . . .' and its represen- **13.54** tation in BSL.

Another potential problem is the question 'can you confirm that this is your statement?' **13.55** which may be a typical opening question. The difficulty here would be the use of CAN and CONFIRM. The first verb carries the meaning 'possible' and the second is commonly used in the sense of 'approve' or 'finalize'. The appropriate translation of the meaning would lead to a new sentence construction—STATEMENT POINT/ INDICATE, YOURS, RIGHT? (or AGREE)?—this statement on paper is yours?

---

[38] By Brennan and Brown, (2004), cited above at n.1.

Correct (or true)? Having set out specific circumstances around an incident, and wishing to question the witness's judgement or actions, in one transcript, the barrister said 'so we cannot assess how effective it was to XXYY . . .' This was meant to be a question of logic, that given a set of circumstances or lack of certain detail in the past, it was not possible to conclude XX or to act in such a way. However, if signed directly, the question becomes an issue of the present time, since BSL does not have a past tense. The question becomes a question of *our* opinion now and not about the circumstance of the past event. A second problem is the phrase 'how effective' which has no direct translation since it implies a causal effect and this has to be explained or exemplified. The literal translation is just confusing. To render the meaning, the set of events XXYY have to be first specified, then in a different signing space (i.e. in order to detach the viewer in order to make an objective judgement), JUDGE CANNOT, GOOD, BAD (or SUCCESS, FAIL or RIGHT, WRONG).

13.56 The problem is not so much that the meaning cannot be conveyed (because it can). The difficulty is that the barrister is no longer completely in control of the sense of the questioning and the thrust of the line of questioning. The responses are then made to the interpreter's form of question and not necessarily to the barrister's. This may cause special difficulties in certain circumstances.

13.57 The following example may also fit in the Statement section (above) but the implications are relevant here. In a video scenario of police questioning with an interpreter present (which I have analysed), the officer began by saying to the interviewee:

> Before we begin I just need to understand that you understand the difference between truth and a lie . . . to which the interpreter signed only 'DIFFERENT TRUE AND LIE'. The Deaf person replied 'TRUE AND LIE WHAT?' The police officer repeated 'do you know the difference between the truth and a lie?' while the Deaf person repeated 'WHAT? TRUE AND LIE?' Then the interpreter signed 'YOU THINK DIFFERENT?' The Deaf person replied 'NO, WHAT DIFFERENT?'

13.58 The dialogue continued with the police officer and the Deaf person becoming increasingly confused and with the Deaf person more and more anxious. In the view of the Deaf person, the question was nonsensical. The sign TRUE was an adjective and so needed a referent—hence the question WHAT TRUE?

13.59 Such examples illustrate the difficulties which are created by the use of these two languages and incomplete awareness of the structure of the translation. In certain circumstances, a barrister may need to be advised by a second interpreter who is monitoring the work of the first interpreter. The main point is that the interpreter working in a court room needs to be of the highest level of competence and the legal professionals would benefit greatly from some understanding of the nature of sign language. It also means that the video record of the interview is essential, in order that this sort of analysis can be carried out.

(5) Fitness to plead

13.60 The area of 'fitness to plead' borders on the issues of Deaf testimony and while it is not the intention here to go into this in detail, as it would require much more space than is available, it is interesting to note that it has been tackled recently in *R v M.*[39] In that decision, as often in the past, the court invoked the '*Pritchard* test'—the direction to the jury in the nineteenth century case of *R v Pritchard*[40]—which underlines the point that it is not the hearing loss nor the use of sign language (as Mr Garrow earlier had implied) but rather the general test of comprehension which indicates the validity of the person's testimony:

> There are three points to be inquired into—first, whether the prisoner is mute of malice or not; secondly, whether he can plead to the indictment or not; thirdly, whether he is of sufficient intellect to comprehend the course of proceedings on the trial, so as to make a proper defence—to know that he might challenge any of you to whom he may object—and to comprehend the details of the evidence, which in a case of this nature must constitute a minute investigation. Upon this issue, therefore, if you think that there is no certain mode of communicating the details of the trial to the prisoner, so that he can clearly understand them, and be able properly to make his defence to the charge; you ought to find that he is not of sane mind. It is not enough, that he may have a general capacity of communicating on ordinary matters.

Deaf people can and do take part effectively in the legal process and provided the communication channels are appropriate, then they are valid participants. **13.61**

F. Final Points

Dealing with Deaf witnesses turns out to be rather more complex than it might have seemed at first. While the giving of evidence in sign language has been known and permitted for hundreds of years, there has remained a suspicion that the language is somehow less than English and that the users of the language are somewhat lesser human beings. Paradoxically, based on our research, we now consider that it is those who are denied access to the sign language early in life, who may have the greatest difficulty in establishing their conceptual knowledge and who will then have the greater difficulty within the legal process. Deaf people in general are able to provide witness testimony actively and effectively in British Sign Language. **13.62**

Advances in knowledge about sign language have led to expectations that independent interpreters will be provided free in court and for the taking of Statements. However, there remain pitfalls—the use of unqualified or insufficiently experienced interpreters, the difficulties of a three-part interaction in regard to eye contact and note taking, and the challenges of the translation of highly developed legal jargon and questioning methods into a form appropriate to the users of sign language. From the research perspective, from the Deaf community's perspective and from the interpreter's perspective, there is no doubt that all these apparent problems can be overcome. At the same time, legal practitioners need to be aware that not all Deaf people are similar in early experience, that they may vary in sign language competence and that there are times when a Deaf relay interpreter is required (and possibly also, a language adviser). **13.63**

---

[39] [2003] EWCA Crim 3452, CA, judgment 14 November 2003.   [40] (1836) 7 C & P 303.

13.64 When attention is paid to these issues and with the awareness of the legal professionals, then the process is valid and appropriate.

Further Reading

Kyle, J.G., Reilly, A.M., Allsop, L., Clark, M. and Dury, A., *Investigation of access to public services in Scotland using British Sign Language*, Edinburgh: Scottish Executive, 2004.

Sutton-Spence, R. and Woll, B., *The Linguistics of British Sign Language*, Cambridge: Cambridge University Press, 1998.

Website with Deaf awareness and sign awareness materials, on-line course and dictionary: *http://www.signstation.org.*

Jim Kyle is Harry Crook Professor of Deaf Studies at the Centre for Deaf Studies, University of Bristol. For over 30 years he has researched and published studies of Deaf children and adults, deriving from data collected on infants, children, young people and adults. These studies (in all parts of the UK and throughout Europe) range from the acquisition of sign language, performance in school, employment experiences, and patterns of community activity through to old age. As an extension of this work, he is engaged in the application of video technologies, the Internet and e-learning as a means to include Deaf people in all aspects of society. As a Fellow of the British Psychological Society and Chartered Psychologist, he has been called frequently to provide assessment, analysis and to act as an expert witness for the police and the legal services.

Editors' Note

(See, also, our notes for Chapters 12 and 14.) Where poor interpretation practices are discovered in cases involving people who are Deaf or, with reasonable cause, suspected, the rectification of errors is likely to be burdensome and costly. A second sign-language interpreter may need to be employed to assist the investigator in re-interviewing the Deaf witness; where a trial has started and the discovery of poor trial interpretation is discovered at this stage, a case may need to be abandoned; in this event, where a retrial is ordered, a transcript of the interpreted evidence at the first trial may be necessary. The importance of sign-language interpreters (or others) being adequately trained and competence-tested cannot be over-stressed.

14

INVESTIGATIVE AND EVIDENTIAL APPLICATIONS OF FORENSIC SPEECH SCIENCE[1]

Peter French and Philip Harrison

A. Introduction

(1) General aim of the chapter

The purpose of this chapter is to introduce the reader to the main investigative and evidential applications of forensic speech science, namely speaker profiling, forensic speaker identification and questioned utterance analysis. **14.01**

In presenting these areas, we shall attempt to address the concerns of the—mainly legal and law-enforcement—readership of this book; namely, their strengths and limitations from both scientific and legal viewpoints. **14.02**

(2) Investigative vs evidential applications of forensic speech science

The services of forensic speech scientists are normally commissioned in criminal cases where there is audio-recorded evidence relating to an offence. The kinds of recording the **14.03**

---

[1] The term 'speech science' is used here as a cover term to encompass phonetics and elements of other sub-disciplines of linguistics and acoustics that are drawn on in conducting forensic analyses.

expert is asked to examine form a wide and varied array. They range from telephone calls to the emergency services, threats or ransom demands left on telephone answering facilities, fraudulent calls to banks and other financial institutions, recordings made by undercover 'test purchase' police officers entering into arrangements with drugs dealers and the products of probe microphones planted by the police or security service in the cars, domestic and commercial premises of those they believe to be involved in, for example, major drugs importation, 'people smuggling' or terrorism.

14.04 The distinction between investigative and evidential applications is essentially linked to the state of development of the criminal inquiry. The need for an investigative application arises at an early point in the inquiry, before any suspect for the crime has been found. The requirement for an evidential application arises at a much later point, after a suspect has been found and evidence is being gathered for a forthcoming trial.

B. Investigative Application—Speaker Profiling

14.05 Speaker profiling involves analysing a recording of an unknown, criminal speaker in order to derive as much information about him or her as possible.[2] Typical examples of inquiries in which this exercise is carried out would include those where there are recordings of masked robberies picked up on CCTV systems, where the faces of the robbers are not seen but their voices are heard, and telephone calls to the police and other organizations from people confessing anonymously to major crimes. The purpose of speaker profiling is to assist the investigating agency, by identifying the relevant sub-section of the wider population to which the speaker belongs. The types of information that might be gleaned about a speaker are considered below.

(1) Regional background

14.06 The accent is assessed by examination of the consonant and vowel pronunciations, aspects of speech rhythm and intonation (pitch movement). In some cases determination of regional influences is assisted by making reference to the many published studies of regional variation in English[3] and to accent atlases.[4] The 'shelf life' of the information provided in published sources, and in traditional dialect studies in particular, is, however, very short. Regional accents are in a constant state of flux and are sometimes subject to marked changes, both in terms of their distinguishing phonetic features and their geographical bounds, over quite short periods of time. In view of this, the analyst will often use published material only in order to gain a first approximation of regional influence. This has then to be confirmed, amended or refined from more up-to-date material. This may involve arranging to receive and record telephone calls from police officers native to different parts of the general, provisionally-identified target area for use as reference data.

---

[2] Foulkes, P. and French, J.P., 'Forensic Phonetics and Sociolinguistics' in Mesthrie, R. (ed.), *Concise Encyclopaedia of Sociolinguistics*, Amsterdam: Elsevier Press, 2001, 329–332.

[3] *Cf* papers in Foulkes, P. and Docherty, G.J. (eds.), *Urban Voices: Accent Studies in the British Isles*, London: Arnold, 1999.

[4] Orton, H., Sanderson, S. and Widdowson, J. (eds.), *The Linguistic Atlas of England*, London: Croom Helm, 1978.

Also, there is a quite narrowly circumscribed 'division of labour' among academic linguists and phoneticians specialising in regional variation, one linguist devoting most of his or her career to, say, the study of Newcastle English, another to Glaswegian, another to East Anglian, and so on. Whilst most such academics have no primary interest in the forensic application of their subject knowledge, they are sometimes the best sources of help. In several cases of speaker profiling, the authors have called on the assistance of region specialists, thereby relegating themselves to the role of GPs. In the interests of progressing an inquiry, this step is sometimes a professional necessity.   **14.07**

(2) Social and educational background

This is again assessed mainly by examination of consonants, vowels and prosodic features. In some white-collar fraud cases, for example, the authors have had to ask whether the sample reflects an entirely received pronunciation accent of the sort normally associated with an independent education, or if minor regional features are present too. The latter may suggest an attempt, conscious or otherwise, at modifying the accent and reflect upward social aspirations or mobility.   **14.08**

If the accent is essentially a regional one, one may ask whether it is the basilect—i.e. most non-standard form associated with the lowest social class—or a less regionally-marked lower middle or middle class variety.   **14.09**

(3) Foreign language influence or ethnic minority characteristics

Speakers for whom English is not their first language (L1) often display first language interference in their speech patterns. This may manifest itself in any or all phonetic parameters, including consonant and vowel pronunciations, rhythm, intonation and voice quality (timbre). It may also occur in respect of the speaker's grammar and vocabulary.   **14.10**

The extent of any interference is likely to be determined by two main factors: (i) the degree of disparity between the phonological system of the speaker's L1 and English, (ii) the level of the speaker's competence in English.   **14.11**

As in cases where regional accent is an issue, the general forensic speech scientist may find himself calling on the services of particular language specialists after initial determinations of L1 have been performed. For instance, it is often relatively easy to detect the source of L1 interference as Arabic. However, the number of L1 Arabic speakers is estimated at around 200 million, there being 22 countries for which it is the official language. Progressing the profile of the speaker beyond simply 'L1—Arabic' will inevitably involve enlisting an Arabist with detailed knowledge of dialectal variation.   **14.12**

It is possible for features that began as L1 interference to persist, often in modified form, across generations of speakers within ethnic minority communities, even where the current generation of speakers has English as its L1. This is clearly the case in relation to the English spoken by many younger members of Indian and Pakistani communities; the forms of pronunciation used operate as markers of ethnic and cultural identity. In the case of Black English as spoken by younger members of the Afro-Caribbean community, this is again very much the case. For them, it *is* their L1. Further, there are indications emerging that one cannot safely assume that all users of this variety of English are in fact   **14.13** black. Indeed, proficiency in it may be viewed as cultural capital for young white speakers too.[5] Thus, for the forensic speech scientist involved in profiling the voice of a criminal, the interpretation of any Black English features present should be approached with some caution.

14.14 Where speech patterns are examined for L1 influence not for the purposes of progressing a police investigation but to assist immigration authorities with determining the nationality of asylum seekers special considerations apply. Indeed, the involvement of speech scientists and linguists in that exercise has generated much controversy, culminating in the publication of a collection of papers and a collective position statement by senior academics internationally.[6]

(4) Age

14.15 Many studies have documented the affects of ageing on the voice, focusing on such features as fundamental frequency and phonatory irregularities. 'Fundamental frequency' refers to the average rate of vocal cord vibration, normally estimated by computer program. It is the physical correlate of perceived voice pitch; speakers who have a high rate of vibration are heard as having high-pitched voices and those with a low rate of vibration are heard as being low-pitched. For male speakers, it is generally accepted that the 'breaking' of the voice will be complete at around fifteen years old and that the fundamental frequency will thereafter decrease only gradually until around the age of forty. Generally speaking, it will then remain relatively stable until it begins to increase into old age at sometime between sixty and eighty years old.

14.16 Studies suggest that the adult fundamental frequency for female speakers is related to the onset of menstruation. The picture to emerge from research studies for the years between menarche and menopause is highly complex. However, it is again broadly agreed that there is a gradual decrease in female pitch after menopause.[7]

14.17 A number of studies have shown that the progression from midlife to old age may bring with it an increase in 'harshness' or 'roughness' in voice quality. This may be measured in terms of the degree of irregularity in cycle-to-cycle movements of the vocal cords (jitter and shimmer).[8]

14.18 The difficulty with applying the findings of such research studies to the profiling of a speaker lies in the inevitable absence of any longitudinal data for the person concerned. In other words, because the studies relate to changes in the voice, one would need to have samples of the speaker concerned at a younger age in order to estimate their age at the

---

[5] Hirson, A., Holmes, F. and Coulthrust, B., 'Street Talk,' paper presented at the International Association for Forensic Phonetics and Acoustics Annual Conference, Vienna, Austria, 29 June–2 July 2003.

[6] Lawyers and others concerned with these issues are directed to the special section devoted to this topic in (2004) 11(2) *The International Journal of Speech, Language and the Law.*

[7] For an overview of research in this area see Braun, A., 'Fundamental Frequency—How speaker-specific is it?' in Braun, A. and Köster, J.-P. (eds.) *Studies in Forensic Phonetics*, Trier: Wissenschaftlicher Verlag, 1995, 9–23.

[8] Wilcox, K.A. and Horii, Y., 'Age and changes in vocal jitter' (1980) 35 *Journal of Gerontology*, 194–198.

time when the criminal sample was produced. Even then, any estimate would be a very rough one, as the studies document general trends to which any given individual might or might not conform. Contrary to popular belief, the age of a speaker is extremely difficult to determine from a recording of his[9] voice, even in quite broad terms.

(5) Speech impediment and voice pathology

These terms encompass a wide variety of phenomena, some being physical in cause (e.g. **14.19** hypernasality resulting from cleft palate) and others being neuro-motor (e.g. stammering). The importance of such features in the profiling exercise is that anyone whose speech displays them may well have come to clinical attention and be represented in medical records.

(6) Reading vs speaking spontaneously

This question is often asked in relation to recordings of confessions to crimes made **14.20** by telephone callers to the police, ransom demands recorded in kidnap cases, food contamination threats and so on. The preparation of a text to read from may be taken by investigating officers as a measure of the degree of planning or serious intent of the perpetrator.

Phonetically, the clues to reading, as opposed to spontaneous speech, may lie in a number **14.21** of features. Many people unused to reading aloud may exhibit a relatively low degree of pitch variation, sounding monotonous. They may avoid the contractions that litter normal spontaneous speech (I will → I'll; will not → won't; she is → she's; etc). Rhythmically, the normal 'stress timing' associated with most accents of English, where unstressed syllables may be spoken very rapidly with reduced vowel forms, may be replaced by a rather 'wooden'-sounding rhythmical pattern redolent of a language teacher pronouncing words in citation form for foreign learners.

(7) Other

In addition to the above, there is a variety of further questions sometimes asked of the **14.22** speech scientist. Those that might reasonably be addressed include whether there are any signs of intoxication in the speech patterns, whether a voice changer device has been used and whether the speaker is attempting to disguise his voice. Certain practitioners and laboratories may also be able to derive important non-linguistic information from a recording. This would include analysis of the background sounds for clues to the location of the speaker; for example whether the speaker was indoors or outdoors or in a moving vehicle.

Questions that cannot justifiably be addressed include requests to derive physical or **14.23** psychological information about the speaker from analysis of the recording. Research studies have repeatedly shown that there is no correlation between speech features and, for example, height, weight or build. Despite the proliferation of 'voice stress level

---

[9] For economy of expression, masculine pronouns are used throughout without prejudice to the gender of the people referred to.

detector' devices and their sale to naïve individuals and organizations as a means of determining whether telephone callers and interviewees are being truthful, there is no empirical support for the claim that stress—or its absence—can be read from a speech signal. Neither is there any support for the view that speech scientists themselves perform any better than machines or computer software in this respect. The efforts of the consummate actor may defy their efforts at detection just as they may those of the layman. Indeed, the International Association for Forensic Phonetics and Acoustics (IAFPA) has a clause in its Code of Practice stating that 'members should not attempt to do psychological profiles or assessments of the sincerity of speakers'.

14.24   In summary, from the viewpoint of an investigating police officer, the main information that a speech scientist can reasonably be expected to derive from a criminal recording includes:

- regional background;
- social/educational background;
- foreign language influence or ethnic minority characteristics;
- age (although see caveats above);
- speech impediment or voice pathology, and
- reading vs speaking spontaneously.

14.25   In certain cases he may also be able to provide information concerning the location of the speaker, effects of intoxicants and whether a voice changer or attempted disguise has been used.

14.26   Information which a speech scientist cannot derive includes:

- height, weight or build of speaker, or
- truthfulness, sincerity or psychological state of speaker.

(8) Further practical advice

14.27   When instructing a speech scientist to undertake speaker profiling it may be useful to consider:

- Does he belong to IAFPA? Whilst membership of this organization is not a requirement for practitioners, it nevertheless provides the instructing party with an assurance that the expert's work is governed by a code of practice drawn up by an international professional organization.
- Is he prepared to consult other experts in more specialized areas such as speech pathology, specific regional accents and foreign languages, if the exigencies of the case demand it?

(9) Example case

14.28   One of the most well known high-profile cases of speaker profiling arose during the criminal investigation known as the 'Yorkshire Ripper Inquiry'. This concerned a series of 13 murders of women in the Leeds and Bradford areas of Yorkshire between October 1975 and November 1980. In June 1979, after the tenth murder, the police received an audio cassette tape containing a taunting message from a man purporting to be the murderer.

The recording was submitted to Stanley Ellis for speaker profiling. Ellis was able to associate the accent with a suburb of the north-eastern seaboard town of Sunderland.[10]

14.29 The murderer, Peter Sutcliffe, was convicted in 1981 and in fact came from Bradford, in West Yorkshire. It was only in 2005 that the hoaxer who sent the message was identified within the national DNA database from saliva residue on the seal of the envelope which had enclosed the tape. Impressively, it transpired that he had gone to school in the very area identified by Ellis and was still living only two miles away.

C. Evidential Applications

(1) Forensic speaker identification

14.30 Forensic speaker identification is an exercise normally carried out by speech scientists at a later stage in an inquiry, after the police have located a suspect. The task involves comparing the voice and speech patterns found in the criminal recording(s) with those of the suspect. Since the implementation of the Police and Criminal Evidence Act (PACE) 1984 all police interviews with suspects in the UK have been tape-recorded. It is this recording from which the known sample of the suspect's voice is usually taken.

14.31 Expert evidence arising from voice comparison has been accepted into the courts of England and Wales since 1965[11] and nowadays figures in a great number of criminal trials throughout the UK. Our aim in this section is to provide some basic information about what the comparative testing involves, to evaluate the probative status of the evidence and to provide some practical assistance for lawyers attempting to assess whether forensic speaker identification reports conform to the standards set out in the IAFPA code of practice and have been formulated in accordance with appellate court *dicta.*

(i) Comparative testing

14.32 Forensic speaker identification testing normally involves two complementary types of analysis: auditory-phonetic analysis and acoustic analysis.[12]

14.33 **Auditory-phonetic analysis** This entails listening to the known and questioned recordings analytically, and draws heavily upon the ear training provided in university courses in phonetics. The recordings are analysed on two levels: a) the segmental level, and b) the prosodic, or suprasegmental, level.

14.34 At the segmental level, the expert examines the pronunciation of the consonant and vowel sounds, i.e. the so called 'segments' that make up the speech chain. This task is

---

[10] For a detailed account of his investigation see Ellis, S., 'The Yorkshire Ripper enquiry: Part I' (1994) 1(2) *Forensic Linguistics: The International Journal of Speech, Language and the Law*, 197–206.

[11] Ellis, S., ' "It's rather serious . . ." Early speaker identification' in H. Kniffka (ed.) *Texte zu Thoerie und Praxis forensischer Linguistik*, Tübingen: Max Niemeyer Verlag, 1990, 515–521.

[12] See Baldwin, J. and French, J.P., *Forensic Phonetics*. London: Pinter, 1990; French, J.P., 'An overview of forensic phonetics with particular reference to speaker identification' (1994) 1(2) *Forensic Linguistics: The International Journal of Speech, Language and the Law*, 197–206; Hollien, H., *The Acoustics of Crime: The new science of forensic phonetics*, New York/London: Plenum Press, 1990; Rose, P., *Forensic Speaker Identification*, New York/London: Taylor & Francis, 2002.

normally assisted by the use of an extended system of symbols developed by the International Phonetic Association (IPA) for capturing the fine-grained detail of pronunciation. To give an indication of its complexity, the symbol system contains over 80 symbols for representing consonant sounds alone and these may be modified by the addition of diacritical marks (totalling 31), which alter their basic values in specified ways.

14.35   At the suprasegmental level the expert attends to features of speech that are more extensive than the segments themselves. Suprasegmental investigations focus on intonation, rhythm, voice quality and average rate of articulation. Again, there are conventional notation systems and labels for recording the patterns found in the samples.

14.36   **Acoustic analysis**   Acoustic analysis involves undertaking computer-based examinations of various physical parameters of the speech signal. As part of this testing, one would normally calculate the average fundamental frequency of the speech. (See 14.15 above).

14.37   Use is also made of sound spectrograms. Spectrograms are visual representations of the speech signal depicting sound energy across frequency over time. An advantage of spectrograms is that they allow one to make precise measurements of energy-frequency features and durational features. So, for example, there is considerable variation across individuals in terms of the frequency at which the main body of sound energy occurs when they pronounce consonants such as 's' and 'z'. By examining spectrograms one can build up a profile of the frequencies at which the energy associated with these sounds occurs. Examination of spectrograms also allows one to assemble a profile of the characteristic durations (in milliseconds) of such sounds within the samples.

14.38   An important element of the acoustic testing involves using spectrograms and other methods to analyse the trajectories and values of constituent vowel resonances or 'formants'. Each of the vowel sounds is characterized by a particular configuration of such resonances which gives it its own distinctive sound quality. In other words, it is because the vowels in the words 'seat', 'sit', 'set' and 'sat' have different resonance, or formant, structures that one hears them as different vowels. However, the formant configuration associated with empirical instances of vowel sounds produced by an individual speaker will also be affected by the anatomy of his vocal tract and by his speech habits. It is this fact that provides the rationale for measuring formant values and comparing them across the known and questioned speech samples.

14.39   More generally, one's impressions of intonation patterns, which might be gained as part of the auditory-phonetic examinations, can—if considered important to one's conclusions—be corroborated by examining visual representations of the pitch contours on the computer screen or printouts.

14.40   The features of speech and the tests mentioned here should be understood as indicative rather than exhaustive. Further, the weighting one might attach to any given feature will vary from case to case. What the speech scientist looks for in the comparison process are idiosyncratic or personally-distinguishing features of pronunciation and voice—features that serve potentially to mark the particular speaker out from others in the speech community. Such features are, by definition, departures from the norm for the regional, social or ethnic accent or dialect in question. The recognition of departures or deviations, of course, presupposes one's familiarity with the norms for the particular variety. In view of this, information about social and regional variation in the language takes a place alongside phonetics and acoustics as part of the forensic speech scientist's prerequisite knowledge.

Evaluating results   In comparing the features across samples one can never expect to **14.41** find a simple match in respect of any of the features examined, even where the same speaker is involved. The 'instrument' used for producing speech—the vocal tract—is highly plastic.[13] Its configuration and use, and consequently its output, are influenced by myriad physical, psychological and social-situational factors. These include smoking, drugs including alcohol, tiredness, emotional state, communication channel (e.g. telephone, face to face) and identity of interlocutor—leaving aside deliberate attempts at disguise. There is a growing research literature on the way in which these factors affect the various voice parameters.[14] This information can form a valuable resource for the analyst in interpreting the inevitable disparities between samples. It is this interpretive element in the evaluation of results that places forensic speaker identification evidence in the category of expert opinion rather than absolute scientific fact.

This view undoubtedly runs counter to the public misconception, often shared by legal **14.42** and law enforcement personnel, i.e. that somewhere within the speech signal of an individual there exists his 'voiceprint', something which is as individual and indelible as a fingerprint. The basis of this belief is undoubtedly the coining of the word 'voiceprint' by certain phoneticians and engineers acting in the forensic domain in the USA during the 1960s and 1970s. In fact, all that 'voiceprints' consisted of were paired spectrograms, i.e. spectrographic comparisons of words and utterances from a questioned recording with the same words and utterances spoken by the suspect. For the reasons outlined above, different instances of the same word or utterance will always yield different spectrographic patterns and there are no principled criteria for deciding whether the differences found in any particular case are diagnostic of the same or different speakers. Despite an overwhelming body of research evidence and negative scientific opinion internationally,[15] and a negative judicial review, this crude form of holistic picture matching persists today within the FBI, although—perhaps in recognition of its shortcomings—it is used for intelligence purposes only and is not presented in court as prosecution evidence. Unfortunately, even in the face of the stringent criteria for the acceptance of expert

---

[13] Nolan, F., *The Phonetic Bases of Speaker Recognition*, Cambridge: Cambridge University Press, 1983.

[14] Braun, 1995, cited above at n.7; Braun, A. and Künzel, H., 'The Effect of Alcohol on Speech Prosody', *Proceedings of the 15th International Congress of Phonetic Sciences*, 2645–2648. Barcelona, 3–9 August, 2003; Chin, S.B. and Pisoni, D.B., *Alcohol and Speech*, San Diego: Academic Press, 1997; Hirson, A., French, J.P. and Howard, D., 'Forensic aspects of telephone speech' in Windsor Lewis, J. (ed.), *Studies in General and English Phonetics: Essays in Honour of Professor J. D. O'Connor*, London: Routledge and Kegan Paul, 1994.

[15] Bolt, R.H., Cooper, F.S., David, E.C., Denes, B.D. and Stevens, K.N., 'Speaker identification by speech spectrograms' (1970) 47 *Journal of the Acoustical Society of America*, 597–613; same authors, 'Speaker identification by speech spectrograms: some further observations,' (1973) 54 *Journal of the Acoustical Society of America*, 531–534; French, (1994), cited above at n. 12; Hollien, (1990), cited above at n. 12.

evidence set down for the US courts,[16] certain US private experts, with varying degrees of success, continue to attempt to persuade courts to accept it as defence evidence. The combined auditory-phonetic *cum* acoustic approach described above is used in both the independent sector and in government laboratories and accepted by courts throughout most of the rest of the world.[17]

(ii) Legal considerations

14.43 For lawyers and others involved in cases where forensic speaker identification evidence is to be relied upon, there are a number of factors to be considered.

14.44 **Relative lack of certainty** First, it will be apparent from much of the foregoing discussion that, in the present state of the science, it is not possible for a speaker to be identified with the degree of certainty associated with, for example, an identification based upon fingerprints. The IAFPA Code of Practice states that 'members should make clear, both in their reports and in giving evidence in court, the limitations of forensic phonetic and acoustic analysis'. Where the case involves speaker identification this is usually interpreted as meaning that the extent of the probative value of the analysis should be made explicit. The consensus of scientific opinion internationally is that a criminal trial should not be brought on this type of evidence alone, for, in itself, it cannot generally meet the criminal standard of proof: beyond all reasonable doubt.

14.45 The first question that arises in a case involving this kind of evidence is, then, whether there is other evidence to accompany it. The lack of such evidence may be seen as grounds for a defence submission of no case to answer.

14.46 **Appropriate methodology** A second consideration is whether the work has been carried out appropriately, using recognised methodology. In particular, the question might be asked whether proper acoustic testing has been undertaken. Most UK phoneticians relied on auditory analysis alone until the mid- or late-1980s. This method was subject to an unsuccessful challenge in the Court of Appeal, Criminal Division for England and Wales in 1991.[18] More recently, however, the challenge was remounted in the Northern Ireland Court of Appeal in *R v O'Doherty*.[19] At the original trial the Crown had relied on expert evidence of speaker identification based on auditory analysis only. The appeal against conviction was based on the grounds that the technique was unreliable unless supported by acoustic analysis, and was this time successful. The judgment went further than the individual case in requiring 'that in the present state of scientific knowledge no prosecution should be brought in Northern Ireland in which one of the planks is voice identification given by an expert which is solely confined to auditory analysis. There should also be

---

[16] See Rule 702 of Federal Rules of Evidence revised in light of *Daubert v Merrell Dow Pharmaceuticals, Inc*, 509 US 579 (1993), and *Kuhmo Tyre Co v Carmichael* 119 S. Ct. 1167 (1999).

[17] A misleading account of the joint auditory-phonetic *cum* acoustic method was given by Ormerod, who seemed to believe that it comprises auditory examinations coupled with 'voiceprints': Ormerod, D., 'Sounding out expert voice identification' [2002] Crim LR 771–790.

[18] *R v Robb* (1993) 93 Cr App R 161.

[19] [2002] NI 263; [2003] 1 Cr App R 5, judgment 19 April 2002.

expert evidence of acoustic analysis . . . which includes formant analysis.'[20] Only three exceptions are made: (i) where the voices within 'a known group' are at issue and it is simply a matter of 'which voice has spoken which words'; (ii) where the voice in question has 'rare characteristics'; (iii) where the expert is simply attempting to identify the accent or dialect being used rather than the individual speaker. Here 'acoustic analysis is not necessary'.

Whilst this appeal ruling, emanating from Northern Ireland, is not strictly binding on   **14.47**
the lower courts of the separate jurisdictions of England and Wales or Scotland, it is nevertheless very likely that such courts would view it as persuasive.

An important aspect of the ruling that might easily be overlooked is that it does not just   **14.48**
state that acoustic analysis should be undertaken but requires specifically that it should include 'formant analysis'. We take the word 'analysis' not just to mean informal observation of formant patterns and trajectories on spectrograms, but a more systematic exercise whereby their values are logged, averaged and compared. Lawyers who are engaged in evaluating, or instructing experts to evaluate, the methodological adequacy of the work of opposing experts would be advised to bear this point in mind. Where the examinations have not included acoustic investigations generally, and formant analysis in particular, there may be grounds for a defence argument that the evidence is inadmissible or, at the least, that it should be excluded on the 'fairness' criterion written into s78 of PACE.

Formulation of the expert's conclusions   A third major legal consideration concerns   **14.49**
the formulation of conclusions in the expert's report. Until quite recently the use of impressionistic likelihood scales which presented speaker identification conclusions in such terms as 'probably' the same speaker, 'very likely' to be the same speaker, etc were almost in universal use among experts. Recently, however, a number of experts have moved away from expressing conclusions in this way, the reason being that one cannot assume that the combination of features found in a disputed recording and shared by the suspect will be associated with him alone. Such a presumption has been described as 'completely irresponsible'.[21] Once one concedes the possibility that a particular combination may be shared by others, then it becomes logically indefensible to state that the suspect is 'likely' to be the criminal speaker or is 'probably' the speaker. For the sake of argument, and somewhat arbitrarily, let us say that there were nine more speakers in the wider population who shared the cluster of features in question. If this were so, then, based on the voice comparison evidence alone, the criminal speaker would be no more likely to be the suspect than any one of the other nine.

Conclusions stating that the suspect is likely to be the criminal speaker give a false   **14.50**
weighting to the evidence. They present it within a framework which has become known

---

[20] For scientific arguments which lend support to the ruling see French, J.P., 'Analytic procedures for the determination of disputed utterances' in Kniffka, (1990), cited above at n.11, 201–213; Nolan, F., 'The Limitations of Auditory-Phonetic Speaker Identification' in Kniffka, ibid 457–479; French, (1994), cited above at n.12; Nolan, F. and Grigoras, C., 'A case for formant analysis in forensic speaker identification' (2005) 12/2 *The International Journal of Speech, Language and the Law*, 143–173.

[21] Ladefoged, P., *A Course in Phonetics*, 2nd ed, New York: Harcourt Brace Jovanovich, 1982, 194.

as the 'Prosecutor's Fallacy'.[22] Evidence of identity presented in this way was ruled inadmissible by the Court of Appeal in the DNA case of *R v Doheny and Adams*.[23]

14.51 An alternative, non-flawed way of expressing conclusions currently being adopted by a growing number of other speech scientists is one that avoids individual probability statements altogether and instead presents the findings in terms of consistency across samples coupled with a statement concerning the distinctiveness of the combination of common features and/or an estimation of its rarity or otherwise within the population.[24] An example might read as follows:

> Phonetically and acoustically, the voice and speech patterns of the man identified as 'John' in the questioned recording are consistent with those of Mr Smith in all significant respects. The combination of features common to the interview and questioned recording is quite distinctive. Whilst, in the present state of knowledge, one cannot exclude the possibility of there being others in the population who would share these features, if there are such speakers I would consider their number to be small.

14.52 The estimation of numbers of speakers sharing the features found are, perforce, vague and impressionistic. Statistical data concerning the distribution of speech features within populations are limited. Whilst certain phenomena such as stammering, average fundamental frequency and average rate of articulation have been subject to distributional analysis,[25] the vast majority have not, and attempts to remedy this situation are fraught with methodological problems arising from the nature of speech itself. Thus, the desirable step of moving away from impressionistic estimations of population sizes to statistical statements is presently impossible. The random occurrence ratio for nearly all combinations of features on which conclusions are based is just not known.[26]

14.53 Where speaker identification conclusions are framed in terms of likelihoods or probabilities, they may be argued as inadmissible by reference to the *Doheny and Adams* ruling.

14.54 **Nature of the recordings compared** Finally, legal concerns may also arise from the nature of the recordings compared. It is impossible to lay down fixed criteria in terms of the minimum duration of material required for a reliable result, as this will depend to an extent on the technical quality of the recordings and on the distinctiveness of the voice(s). In certain cases, the authors have found it impossible to reach a conclusion

---

[22] Balding, D.J. and Donnelly P., 'The Prosecutor's Fallacy and DNA Evidence' [1994] Crim LR, 711.

[23] [1997] 1 Cr App R 369.

[24] French, J.P., 'Forensic speaker identification evidence and the "Prosecutor's fallacy",' paper presented at the *International Association for Forensic Phonetics and Acoustics* Annual Conference, Marrakech, Morocco, 3–6 August 2005.

[25] Enderby, P. and Phillips, R., 'Speech and Language Handicap: towards knowing the size of the problem' (1986) 21 *British Journal of Disorders of Communication*, 151–165; Eisler, F.G., *Psycholinguistics: Experiments in spontaneous speech*, London: Academic Press, 1968; Künzel, H., *Sprecherkennung: Grundzüge Forensischer Sprachverarbeitung*, Heidelberg: Kriminalistik Verlag, 1987.

[26] A further alternative for expressing conclusions, and one that would be most desirable from a scientific viewpoint, involves the use of likelihood ratios. For a detailed exposition of this approach see Rose, (2002), cited at n.12 above. We take the view, however, that without statistics deriving from properly defined reference populations, the adoption of this approach at this point in time would be misleading. Further, it was ruled out in passing in the *Doheny and Adams* judgment, cited above at n.23.

where there were several minutes of reasonably high quality speech to work with in a questioned recording. In another, however, where the sample amounted to only 2.7 seconds and the quality was quite poor, a very strong conclusion was reached based on the occurrence of an unusual variety of stammer, a distinctively high pitch, an unusual voice quality and a relatively uncommon vowel formant feature, all of which also featured in the suspect's police interview recording.

Recordings in languages in which the expert does not have native, or at least near **14.55** native, speaker competence pose particular problems because, unless the expert is thoroughly familiar with the associated norms, he may easily misinterpret group features as individually-distinguishing ones. Cases where the known recording is in one language and the questioned recording is in another are problematic in the extreme, in that different languages have divergent phonological systems, including consonant and vowel repertoires. The IAFPA Code of Practice urges 'particular caution' in respect of both these situations. The way this is normally construed is that, if the known and questioned samples are both in the same language, but the expert is not a native speaker of that language, he may proceed if assisted by a native speaker. It is extremely desirable for this person to be also a phonetician or speech scientist. Cases where the putative comparison is across different languages are almost invariably rejected as incapable of yielding a reliable result.

Lawyers involved in cases where forensic speaker identification evidence is to be called **14.56** are advised to consult the IAFPA Code of Practice as an aid to assessing the degree to which the analysis and report conform to the international standards set down therein (*http://www.iafpa.net*).

(2) Questioned utterance analysis

The second major evidential application of speech science involves the determination of **14.57** content of recordings. Although some practitioners may become involved in the preparation of transcripts generally, the cases where the greatest expertise is required normally centre around queries or disputes over very localized sections of speech, perhaps a brief utterance or even a single word. This application is normally referred to as 'disputed' or 'questioned utterance analysis'.[27]

The call for questioned utterance analysis is much less frequent than for forensic speaker **14.58** identification. It arises in cases where the recordings are noisy or unclear, or where a speaker has unfamiliar, non-standard or impedimental speech patterns.

The approach to resolving what was said normally involves the comparison of features **14.59** of the questioned utterance with reference material drawn either from another, clear recording, or from clear, non-disputed areas of the same recording. To give a concrete illustration, a case arose recently where a man died in his flat in the presence of his (male) lover. The lover was questioned by police and his series of interviews was recorded. There was some evidence from a pathologist's report to suggest asphyxiation, but this was not

---

[27] French, (1990), cited above at n.20.

conclusive. Investigating officers suspected that the death might have occurred in the course of sexual activities, something which the suspect repeatedly denied. At one point in one of the later interviews, however, when the lover was asked to explain again what had happened, he said, according to the police transcript, that at the relevant time the deceased was 'just sleeping away on the bed after wank off'. This was taken as a possible inadvertent slip of his guard and independent corroboration of the content of the utterance was sought through expert analysis. The interviewee spoke with a hybrid Tyneside and Urdu-English accent, and an examination of the questioned utterance suggested an alternative interpretation: 'one cough'. In order to determine which of the two was correct, comparative material was drawn from unambiguous sections of the interviews. From this it was established that the speaker had a systematic difference in the pronunciation of syllable-final /k/—as in 'wan*k*'—and syllable-initial ones—as in '*c*ough'. The former were mainly unaspirated, whilst the latter were subject to heavy aspiration. The /k/ in the questioned utterance, having aspiration with a duration of 113 milliseconds, clearly fell into the syllable-initial category. Further, the formant structure of the vowel in the first syllable was also compared with clear examples of the speaker's 'a' vowels from words such as 'b*a*ck' and 'h*a*nging' and with the vowel he used in the word '*o*ne'. It aligned with the latter rather than the former. It was on the basis of these and other comparative analyses that it was possible to conclude quite firmly that the utterance was, in fact, 'one cough' rather than 'wank off'.

14.60 The case is intended merely to be illustrative of the general method, the value of which lies in its being a principled way of resolving questions or disputes over content. In its absence one is left with no more than people asserting their individual perceptions and preferences without being able to explain them. Indeed, it is not uncommon to find sound engineers proffering expert opinion on issues of content without having undertaken any comparative analysis of speech features, the claim to expert status for their evidence being simply that this is how their experience leads them to hear the words. Insofar as the expert evidence rules stipulate that the role of the expert is not simply to provide an opinion but to be able to explain its basis, then the expert status of such evidence might be subject to challenge.

14.61 A further example case involving a doctor recorded in the act of prescribing controlled drugs in return for payment to an actor posing as a drug addict is reported by French.[28] An issue that arose in the General Medical Council disciplinary hearing was whether the doctor, who spoke English with a marked Greek accent, had said 'can' or 'can't' when advising the actor how to use the tablets he prescribed him: 'you can/can't inject those things'. The article provides a description of the methods of analysis used to decide between the two interpretations and sets out the findings in some detail.

(3) Further evidential applications

14.62 Finally, in addition to speaker identification and questioned utterance analysis, speech scientists along with psychologists are occasionally called on to provide expert advice and

---

[28] Ibid, cited above at n.20.

evidence on the construction and evaluation of voice line-ups and the evaluation of lay-witness evidence of speaker recognition.[29]

D. Summary

In this chapter we have attempted to provide an overview of the main investigative and **14.63** evidential applications of forensic speech science: speaker profiling, forensic speaker identification and questioned utterance analysis. Throughout, we have attempted to provide a balanced view of the strengths and weaknesses of work in these areas and have, where appropriate, made suggestions concerning how evidence might be tested and challenged where either the methods of analysis or the formulation of conclusions departs from accepted standards or does not conform to appeal court rulings.

More comprehensive treatments of scientific and linguistic aspects of the work can be **14.64** found in the recommended further reading below.

Recommended Reading

Baldwin, J. and French, J.P., *Forensic Phonetics*, London: Pinter, 1990.
Although somewhat dated, this provides an easy and accessible introduction to forensic speaker identification.
Rose, P., *Forensic Speaker Identification*, New York/London: Taylor & Francis, 2002.
This contains a detailed and comprehensive description of forensic speaker identification—undoubtedly, the most thorough full-length text ever written on the subject.
Hollien, H., *The Acoustics of Crime: The new science of forensic phonetics*. New York/ London: Plenum Press, 1990.
This is a much more wide-ranging work than either of the above. In addition to speaker identification, it explains and discusses related areas including authentication of recordings, voice stress detectors and analysis of recorded gunshots.

Professor Peter French is an independent forensic consultant specializing in the analysis of magnetic and digital recordings, speech and language samples. He has been five times elected Chairman of the International Association for Forensic Phonetics and Acoustics, has published extensively on his specialist areas, is co-editor of *The International Journal of Speech, Language and the Law* and has acted in thousands of cases from countries across the world.

Philip Harrison is a forensic consultant with J P French Associates and has worked on over 800 cases in the areas of speaker identification, disputed utterance analysis,

---

[29] Readers with specific interest in voice line-ups are directed to Broeders, A.P.A. and Rietveld, A.C.M., (1995) 'Speaker identification by earwitnesses' in Braun, A. and Köster, J.-P. (eds.), *Studies in Forensic Phonetics*, Trier: Wissenschaftlicher Verlag, 1995, 24–40. For an overview and discussion of earwitness evidence see Bull, R. and Clifford, B., 'Earwitness testimony' in Heaton-Armstrong, A., Shepherd, E. and Wolchover D. (eds.), *Analysing Witness Testimony: A guide for legal practitioners & other professionals*, London: Blackstone Press, 1999, 194–206. An example case involving the construction of a voice line-up is reported in Nolan, F., 'A recent voice parade' (2003) 10(2) *The International Journal of Speech, Language and the Law*, 277–291.

transcription, authentication, and enhancement as well as many miscellaneous cases. He has an undergraduate degree in Acoustic Engineering from the Institute of Sound and Vibration Research (ISVR) at the University of Southampton and a postgraduate degree in Phonetics and Phonology from the Department of Language and Linguistic Science at the University of York. He is currently conducting doctoral research on the measurement and analysis of formants and frequently lectures on forensic speech science to universities and organizations in the UK and abroad.

Editors' Notes

There is an interesting conflict (albeit less so in recent years) between the regulatory and legal framework surrounding the obtaining and forensic treatment of evidence of facial identification or recognition and that concerning verbal speech. The emergence of this contrast and its reduction has been characterized by an acceptance by the Court of Appeal that the desirability of a science-based approach to the two categories of evidence is equally apparent whether identification or recognition of a face or a voice is involved. This chapter's companion in *Analysing Witness Testimony* having been cited in relevant academic text and in a number of court proceedings (most notably by being added to a skeleton argument in support of an application to dismiss in an attempted murder case where the only evidence against the defendant was provided by the surviving victim who claimed that he recognized the voice of the person who had shot at him when he had said, immediately before pulling the trigger, 'Take that, you motherfucker' in Urdu) significantly informed the debate and this is usefully and further advanced here.

In this context, albeit involving speech identification of a different kind, it is, perhaps, worth drawing attention to part of the recent history of evidence of lip-reading. In *R v Luttrell, Dawson and Hamberger, The Times*, 9 June 2004, the Court of Appeal approved as a category of admissible expert evidence that from a lip-reader who is deaf (one of whose claims has been to be able to lip-read languages with which she was not, herself, familiar, owing to her ability to reduce accurately into writing, albeit in phonetic form, sounds which she visually perceived the speaker as having uttered). Within months of the publication of the Court of Appeal's judgment, the same expert lip-reader's academic credentials were discredited in a first instance case as a result of which the prosecution abandoned her evidence and an inquiry was ordered by the Crown Prosecution Service into all cases in which she had previously given evidence.

15

IDENTIFYING THE ORIGINS
OF EVIDENTIAL TEXTS

Tim Grant

The most frequent general criticism I receive is, I think, upon the style,—'if I *would* but change my style'! But *that* is an objection (isn't it?) to the writer bodily? Buffon says, and every sincere writer must feel, that 'Le style c'est l'homme'; a fact, however, scarcely calculated to lessen the objection with certain critics.

From the first letter of Elizabeth Barrett to Robert Browning,
11 January, 1845.

'Style est l'homme même'

From *Discours sur le style*, Comte George-Louis de Buffon,
25 August, 1753.

A. Introduction

Shepherd and Mortimer provided a series of methods for examining evidential texts **15.01** through which they identify anomalies which might be useful in understanding or criticising witness testimony.[1] This chapter returns to the examination of evidential texts

---

[1] Shepherd, E. and Mortimer, A., 'Identifying anomaly in evidential text', in Heaton-Armstrong, A., Shepherd, E. and Wolchover, D. (eds.), *Analysing Witness Testimony: Psychological, Investigative and Evidential Perspectives. A Guide for Legal Practitioners and Other Professionals* London: Blackstone Press, 1999, 267–87.

from a linguistic perspective and demonstrates how such an approach can deepen our understanding of witness statements and on occasion provide forensic linguistic evidence for the origins of texts brought before the courts. In 1968 Jan Svartik carried out a ground-breaking analysis of the witness statements produced for the trial of Timothy Evans.[2] Evans had been wrongly convicted and in 1953 was hanged for the murder of his wife and child. Svartik's linguistic analysis contrasts portions of the statements which Timothy Evans was clearly capable of producing, with incriminating sections which Svartik convincingly argues are written in police language. The subtitle to Svartik's monograph is '*A case for forensic linguistics*'. Svartik's analysis was an academic exercise and was never used in court, but since his call forensic linguistics has developed, in fits and starts, into a potentially useful tool for the analysis of textual evidence in forensic contexts.

B. Some Recent History

15.02 Forensic linguistic analysis can no longer claim to be in its infancy. Varieties of linguistic advice and evidence have been presented for use in hundreds of UK cases and possibly thousands of cases worldwide, and yet methodologically it is still caught in the divide between two cultures. Linguists, experts in the nature and use of language, are largely trained in the culture of the arts, and develop skills which may be methodologically rigorous, but still tend to be interpretive. Linguists rarely claim to be scientists. In contrast, forensic scientists' training and intuitions are experimental, inductive and statistical. To aim at a forensic science of linguistics can therefore lead to confusion and misunderstanding. Analysts from other sciences can be seen as linguistically naïve, and linguists can easily fall into methodological errors, particularly in attempting analyses using statistical approaches and arriving at statistical conclusions. Into this clash of cultures can be added the additional confusion between, on the one hand, the linguistic expert, providing insight and knowledge in the description and explanation of linguistic phenomena; and on the other hand, lawyers and judges who may reasonably claim expertise in linguistic performance and the interpretation of legal texts. Forensic linguistics appears to be a recipe for disaster.

15.03 Something like a disaster for the field of forensic linguistics occurred in the early 1990s. A biblical authorship scholar, the Reverend Andrew Morton, borrowed a statistical technique, known as 'cusum analysis', from chemical processing and applied it to the flow of words which make up language.[3] Morton claimed that using his analysis, he could determine whether two texts originate from one author, and whether a purported single-author text had had insertions made into it by a second author. Morton's system was accepted by the courts in a series of cases involving Morton,[4] and also Farringdon[5] and

---

[2] Svartvik, J., 'The Evans statements: a case for forensic linguistics', *Gothenburg Studies in English*, 20 (1968).

[3] Morton, A.Q., *Proper Words in Proper Places*, Glasgow: Department of Computer Science, University of Glasgow, 1991.

[4] E.g. *R v Beck, Jaynes and Lincoln* (1992) unreported, Leicester Crown Court; *R v McCrossen* (1991), unreported, Court of Appeal (Criminal Division).

[5] E.g. *R v Nelson-Wilson* (1992) unreported, Central Criminal Court, London.

Baker[6] but subsequently the method was easily shown to be flawed. It was attacked by a number of studies[7] culminating in a report by Canter commissioned by the CPS.[8] Robertson and others track the history of cusum analysis through the courts and are critical of the systems and judgments which allowed it to be admitted as evidence in the first place.[9] They concluded that 'stylometric evidence appears only to have succeeded in obtaining acquittals [and in cases] where the prosecution was unprepared to deal with it.[10] In every case where the prosecution was given the time to challenge the analysis, it was defeated in court. 'Stylometry' is a now more widely used term applied to any technique used to measure and quantify linguistic style but Robertson *et al*'s conflation of all stylometric approaches to be equivalent to cusum analysis was an attitude which was reflected in subsequent CPS advice. This advice suggested that 'text analysis . . . is an example of a technique which is not considered to be sufficiently reliable to be used by the prosecution in criminal proceedings'.[11] Only recently was an addendum to this provided which indicates that text analysis includes a wide variety of techniques of which cusum is but one.

Following cusum, there was a fall in the use of linguistic evidence in the courts but more recently forensic linguistic analysis is again being accepted. A CPS practice seems to be developing whereby reports from two independent experts are obtained to analyse textual evidence and throughout the discipline there is a movement away from *ad hominem* linguistic expertise back towards more quantitative methods. This move towards quantification is perhaps driven in part by American federal rules of admissibility which operate under the *Daubert-Kuhmo* standard of scientific evidence.[12] It brings with it the dangers of the misapplication of statistics, exemplified by cusum analysis, but also opportunities for developing more rigorous methods. Most importantly, however, and in contrast to the approach of the cusum analysts, it is becoming generally accepted that there is no single method which can be applied to all cases and that there are no invariant 'linguistic fingerprints' which can be measured in any text an individual produces. **15.04**

The role of forensic linguistics in the courtroom is however not restricted to providing evidence for the courts, whether concerning witness statements or other texts. Linguists can also throw light on the nature of undisputed witness testimony and other textual evidence. The law is a linguistic process, yet a linguist's expertise in language differs from **15.05**

---

[6] E.g. *R v McGee* (1993), unreported, Central Criminal Court, Belfast.

[7] E.g. Hardcastle, R.A., 'Forensic Linguistics: an assessment of the Cusum method for the determination of authorship' (1993) 33/2 *Journal of the Forensic Science Society*, 95–106; Sandford, A.J., Aked, J.P., Moxley, L.M. and Mullin, J., 'A Critical examination of assumptions underlying the Cusum technique of forensic linguistics' (1994) 1/2 *Forensic Linguistics: The International Journal of Speech Language and the Law*, 151–167; Canter, D., 'An Evaluation of the CUSUM stylistic analysis of confessions' (1992) 1/2 *Expert Evidence*, 93–99.

[8] Unpublished report available from CPS area HQ libraries.

[9] Robertson, B., Vignaux, G.A. and Egerton, I., 'Stylometric Evidence,' [1994] Crim LR 645.

[10] *Ibid*, p.648.

[11] Crown Prosecution Service, *Legal Guidance Manual*, http://www.cps.gov.uk/legal/section13/chapter_f.html#_Toc7839900, accessed 23 February 2006, section on expert evidence.

[12] *Daubert v Merrell Dow Pharmaceuticals, Inc*, 509 US 593 (1993); *Kuhmo Tire Co. v Carmicheal*, 526 US 137 (1999).

that of a lawyer's, and so can contribute to a wider understanding of the nature and origins of a variety of evidential texts.

C. Identifying the Origins of Witness Statements

(1) The nature of witness statements

15.06 In an illuminating case study, Rock tracked the creation of a witness statement.[13] Taking advantage of the then new provision for the tape recording of significant witnesses, Rock examined the taped interview of a witness to a suspicious death, and then compared this to the final written statement produced on behalf of the witness. Within the tape-recorded interview Rock identified four separate 'tellings' or iterative attempts at creating the narrative. The first version, characterized by Rock as 'the witness's offering', is largely uninterrupted by the interviewer. In this first telling, the interviewer has five minimal conversational turns and the substance of the testimony is disorganized and contains few explicit time markers with the sequencing of movements between locations being submerged in the narrative. The second telling, in contrast, is led by the interviewer, who has 257 conversational turns. The witness's role this time around is largely restricted to providing answers, and many of these answers refer to time, location and sequencing details. Rock refers to this telling as 'co-construction' and during this telling the interviewer makes extensive notes which begin to form a draft for the final witness statement. The third telling of the narrative is labelled 'note checking'. As well as confirming the details already provided, more detail is sought and added to the draft statement. Finally the 'text construction' telling involves the interviewer using the notes to compose the final statement out loud, sentence by sentence, seeking the witness's consent before actually putting pen to paper.

15.07 In her discussion of this process Rock demonstrates that the view that witnesses should solely determine the content of their statements is naïve. Whilst recognizing the issues of potential contamination of a witness's statement, it can be argued that police interviewers have relevant expertise which should contribute to both the form and content of the final statement. They, for example, have a better appreciation than the witness of the use to which the statement will be put. The investigation requires certain details of time and place for comparison with evidence from other sources (either forensic evidence or further witness statements) and in the future lawyers for either prosecution or defence may seek to test the statement by searching for anomalies within the statement and between statements by different witnesses.[14] The increased use of tape recording for significant witnesses is likely to increase the discovery of co-construction of witness statements. It should be recognized, however, that some degree of co-construction is legitimate and necessary for the operation of the courts. Concerns for efficiency may require courts to persist in the use of written statements over tapes or transcripts, but the

---

[13] Rock, F., 'The genesis of a witness statement', (2002) 8/2 *Forensic Linguistics: The International Journal of Speech Language and the Law*, 44–72.
[14] See Shepherd and Mortimer, (1999), cited above at n.1.

existence of tape recordings will mean that it will no longer be tenable for the courts to persist in the 'fiction'[15] that a witness statement is simply the dictated narrative of a witness. The courts need to accept the fact that witness statements may be collaborative texts, but they must also accept that some collaboration is necessary to produce narratives, which not only represent the experiences of witnesses, but do so in a manner appropriate for the judicial purpose. Given this perspective, the questions which arise as to the validity of statements are not whether interviewer influence and language can be found in the statement, but rather whether the interviewer's role in co-constructing the narrative distorts the testimony of the witness.

(2) Identifying interviewer interference in witness statements

The identification of interviewer language, so called 'police-speak'[16] in witness statements can be fairly straightforward. Coulthard's analysis of the disputed confession of Derek Bentley suggests that several features of typical police language of the 1950s predominate in the statement.[17] His most reported example is the observation of the use of 'I then' 7 times in the 582 word 'confession' which contrasts with the use of 'then I' in general population language. 'I then', for example, can be shown to occur at a rate of 1 in 165,000 words in the millions of words in the COBUILD language database, whereas the pre-positional pronoun is shown to be typical of police language, occurring in a comparison police statement 9 times in 980 words. Rock's analysis[18] suggests that 'police-speak' may be found in many 'good' statements but that this identification of police language in witness statements only becomes important when, as in the Bentley case, it is claimed in court that the statement represents the verbatim statement of the witness. The measure of the validity of any statement has to be made against the claims which are made for it. Thus, a further claim made for the Bentley confession, that it is the record of a dictated monologue, can also be undermined using linguistic evidence. The closing paragraph of the Bentley statement can clearly be read as a series of answers to questions:

15.08

> I knew we were going to break into the place, I did not know what we were going to get—just anything that was going. I did not have a gun and I did not know Chris had one until he shot. I now know that the policeman in uniform is dead. I should have mentioned that after the plain-clothes policeman got up the drainpipe and arrested me, another policeman in uniform followed and I heard someone call him 'Mac'. He was with us when the other policeman was killed.

Linguistic clues to the fact that this is the record of one side of a dialogue include the provision of negative information: that Bentley *did not see . . . did not know . . . and did not have . . .* etc. as well as the staccato clausal structure.

---

[15] Heaton-Armstrong, A., 'Recording and disclosing statements by witnesses—law and practice' (1995) 35/2 *Medicine, Science and the Law* 136, at 138.

[16] Fox, G., 'A comparison of "policespeak" and "normalspeak": a preliminary study,' in Sinclair, J.M., Hoey, M. and Fox, G. (eds.), *Techniques of Description*, London: Routledge, 1993, 183–195.

[17] Coulthard, M., 'On the use of corpora in the analysis of forensic texts,' (1994) 1/1 *Forensic Linguistics: The International Journal of Speech Language and the Law*, 25–43.

[18] Cited above at n.13.

15.09 The fiction that witness statements represent the pure dictated narratives of the observer needs to be undermined across the legal system and across jurisdictions. Tyrwhitt-Drake demonstrates the co-authoring of statements by parties' lawyers in the Hong Kong civil process, which requires pre-trial exchange of statements.[19] He notes that as well as similarities in formal layout, the statements of witnesses share verbatim strings. The lawyers involved may view similarity between statements as positive indicators of the reliability of accounts between witnesses, but linguistically, verbatim agreement between statements is a clear marker of collusion, collaboration or plagiarism. As Elizabeth Barrett's slight misquotation of Buffon illustrates, it is very difficult to reproduce language verbatim without actually copying the text. Extensive verbatim strings will not occur in statements which have been produced independently. Paterson and Kemp further illustrate the fiction of the sole authorship and independent nature of witness statements.[20] They report that 86 per cent of Australian co-witnesses discussed their experience of a serious event with 63 per cent doing so immediately, perhaps before being interviewed by police. Again such influences may be detectable by linguistic analysis but the significant issue is not linguistic, but rather the legal understanding of the nature of witness statements. As 'the witness offering' in Rock's first telling indicates, witness statements solely authored by the witness may be unusable for investigative or judicial purposes. In contrast, the co-constructed statement can be an accurate reflection of a witness's experience which is also fit for purpose.

D. Interpreter Effects in Evidential Texts

(1) Interpreters in interviews

15.10 Just as the co-authoring of statements from monolingual settings is unacknowledged by the courts, so too is the co-authoring required by interpreters in forensic and judicial settings. The issues of interpretation and translation in the forensic context reveal a further set of fictions maintained by the legal approach to witnesses. The most obvious fiction which courts are likely to maintain is that an interpreter in an interview or courtroom situation can operate mechanistically as a neutral linguistic 'conduit',[21] or 'a mere cipher'[22] providing word-for-word exchanges of meaning. This view is reinforced by courtroom practice, although full transcripts of interviews can be provided, or indeed tapes played for the court; it is more common practice to provide a monolingual transcript, omitting the second language and the role of the interpreter altogether. Russell provides a detailed analysis of the opening of an interpreted interview where a police officer is, via an interpreter, cautioning a French-speaking detained person.[23] Russell

---

[19] Tyrwhitt-Drake, H., 'Massaging the evidence: the "over-working" of witness statements in civil cases', (2003) 10/2 *Forensic Linguistics: The International Journal of Speech Language and the Law*, 227–254.

[20] Paterson, H. and Kemp, R., 'Co-witnesses talk: A survey of eyewitness discussion,' (2006) 12/2 *Psychology, Crime and Law*, 181–191.

[21] *State v Chyo Chiagk* 92 Mo 395, 4 SW 704 (1887).   [22] *R v Attard* (1958) 43 Cr App R 90.

[23] Russell, S., ' "Let me put it simply": the case for a standard translation of the police caution and its explanation', (2000) 7/1 *Forensic Linguistics: The International Journal of Speech Language and the Law*, 26–48.

demonstrates the importance of understanding the distinction between form-based or word-for-word interpretation and broader meaning-based interpretation in the statement and explanation of the caution. Both types of interpretation are represented in Russell's data.

Translation of: **15.11**

'as I've explained the interview is being tape-recorded'

into:

'j'ai expliqué cet interview est en train d'être enregistré',[24]

is largely form-based, whereas the officer's request that,

'what I would ask you is if you could reply in French so that we can keep the interview completely and utterly in French not to confuse the issue'

is translated as

'pour des raisons de clarté il faut répondre en français' [for reasons of clarity you must answer in French][25]

which might be considered a reasonable, but not entirely accurate, meaning-based translation.

Russell's data shows that for the legally prescribed text of the caution, the word-for-word   **15.12**
interpretation is sometimes achieved only at the cost of reduced comprehensibility in French. In her paper the first attempt at the most complex middle section of the caution (that 'it may harm your defence if you do not mention when questioned something which you later rely on in court') is word-for-word. This, however, is followed by substantial explanation provided by a more meaning-based interpretation strategy. This tension between meaning-based interpretation and form-based interpretation is at the centre of the difficulties which legal interpreters face, particularly when it is considered that the meanings of utterances are not conveyed only in the words of an utterance but also in the grammatical structure, the manner of the speaker and any number of pragmatic variables. Accuracy of interpretation does not reduce to form-based interpretation.

(2) Interpreters in court

Gibbons suggests that the effect of interpretation both in interviews and courtroom   **15.13**
is that the second-language speaker loses many of the nuances of linguistic legal exchanges.[26] Gibbons lists some of the effects, such as the loss of the courtroom context, as in 'can you tell the court what happened?' being translated into the Spanish, '¿y luego qué pasó?' [and then what happened?][27]

Gibbons suggests that the loss of 'the court' along with the omission of 'can you tell . . .'   **15.14**

---

[24] Ibid, 34.   [25] Ibid, 32.
[26] Gibbons, J., *Forensic linguistics: An introduction to language in the justice system*, Melbourne, Australia: Blackwell Publishers, 2003.
[27] Ibid, 250.

removes from the witness the appreciation that the court will treat their testimony as one of possibly several versions of events. Whereas such losses in interpretation may seem to disadvantage a witness, this is not always the case. Sometimes the process of interpretation may act as a shield to the witness under legal questioning or cross-examination. Interpretation is likely to change factors such as the politeness or tenor of questions, impede the pacing of questions and leave out minor discourse markers such as 'well' and 'oh' which might indicate the scepticism of the questioner.[28] All these factors contribute to a dislocation of the witness from the process which is rarely acknowledged by the court.

15.15 A further form of dislocation can occur where substantial cultural differences arise. Russell[29] mentions that the French detained person may be culturally disadvantaged because the process of being cautioned does not exist within the French legal system; and Eades, amongst others, has long documented the cultural difficulties which Aboriginals experience in Australia's adversarial court system.[30] In the Australian case the perceived need for courtroom interpreters may be reduced as, although there are many points for potential misunderstanding, Aboriginal English and Australian English are largely mutually intelligible.[31] Walsh[32] and Eades[33] convincingly argue, however, that the cultural differences consistently place the Aboriginal witness at a disadvantage. Eades, for example, suggests that private or secret knowledge has a special and deep-rooted value in Aboriginal culture, and this impacts on the cultural practice of asking and answering questions. Direct questions to Aboriginal witnesses, such as those asked by police or lawyers in the courts, are often met with silence. Over time this likely response has been recognized and exploited by prosecutors who interpret for the court the witnesses' silence, as the witnesses' consent to the propositions of the prosecution. Eades suggests that a more reasonable interpretation of the Aboriginal silence might be a rejection of the questioning process such as 'this is not an appropriate way for me to provide information of this nature'.[34] This Australian example may seem distant to the UK experience but multiculturalism brings with it not only difference of language and general cultural expectation but also difference in legal expectations, perhaps shaped by experiences of Roman or Shari'ah law, and such expectations must be recognized and accounted for if they are not to disadvantage individuals caught up in the legal system.

---

[28] Ibid, citing: Berk-Seligson, S., *The bilingual courtroom: Court interpreters in the judicial process*, Chicago, Ill: University of Chicago Press, 1990; Cooke, M., 'Aboriginal evidence in the cross-cultural courtroom,' in Eades, D. (ed.), *Language in evidence: Issues confronting Aboriginal and multicultural Australia*, Sydney, NSW: University of New South Wales Press, 1995, 55–96; Hale, S. and Gibbons, J., 'Varying Realities: Patterned Changes in the Interpreter's Representation of Courtroom and External Realities,' (1999) 20/2 *Applied Linguistics*, 203–220.

[29] Cited above at n.23.

[30] Eades, D., 'A case of communicative clash. Aboriginal English and the legal system,' in Gibbons, J. (ed.), *Language and the Law*, London: Longman, 1994.

[31] See Walsh, M., 'Interpreting for the transcript: problems in recording Aboriginal land claim proceedings in northern Australia', (1990) 6/1 *Forensic Linguistics: The International Journal of Speech Language and the Law*, 161–195.

[32] Ibid.   [33] Cited above at n.30.   [34] Ibid, 242.

E. Identifying National Origins of Interviewees

One legal area where linguistic and cultural differences are increasingly important is that **15.16** of asylum and immigration interviews. Since 2003 the UK government has joined a number of other governments in using language tests to help determine the nationality of immigrants claiming asylum from political persecution. Interviews are carried out in the native language of the applicant with a view to analysing the language to determine their geographical origin and so political status. This process has created a storm of controversy amongst professional linguists. Not only are there potential problems in the processes and qualification of the interviewers (who can be language users rather than trained linguists) but there are also theoretical linguistic problems. The most obvious problem for such analyses is that there is no direct link between a person's language use and their nationality. Naturally there is a connection between a person's language variety and their geographical origins but languages and their varieties and dialects cross borders freely, irrespective of bureaucratic political divides, and in areas of conflict where forced migration of refugees may have occurred natural linguistic complexity will be exaggerated. In the interview situation there will be further linguistic issues; for example, polylingual speakers are likely to try to accommodate their language to the form spoken by an interviewee and it may be perceived to be better to speak a high status, standard variety of a language rather than the form which is commonly spoken within a family. An example of the frailty of this form of linguistic analysis is provided by Eades *et al*, who examined a set of 58 cases where language analysis had been used.[35] In 48 of the cases the conclusion of the linguistic analysis was contrary to the claim of the applicant, and yet 35 of the 48 cases were reversed on appeal. The conclusion of this report is that the language analysis performed clearly did not determine the nationality of the applicant. The issues and difficulties in this area have been addressed in a Code of Best Practice[36] on language testing for determining nationality and this has been adopted by a number of international linguistics organizations including the International Association of Forensic Linguists.

F. Identifying the Provenance of Other Evidential Texts

Forensic linguistics can be useful to the courts in demonstrating linguistic misunder-**15.17** standings and undermining legal fictions concerning witness statements produced by interview, but also linguists can provide direct testimony about language used in the course of potentially illegal activities. For example, forensic linguists have been used in cases involving language crimes such as bribery and making threats and also in trademark

---

[35] Eades, D., Fraser, H., Siegel, J., McNamara, T. and Baker, B., 'Linguistic identification in the determination of nationality: A preliminary report,' *http://www-personal.une.edu.au/~hfraser/forensic/LingID.pdf*, 2003.

[36] Language and National Origin Group, *Guidelines for the Use of Language Analysis in Relation to Questions of National Origin in Refugee Cases*, (2004) *http://privatewww.essex.ac.uk/~patrickp/language-origin-refugees.pdf*.

disputes.[37] However, in this section we turn to the evidence of linguists in determining the origins of texts other than witness statements.

15.18   Elizabeth Barrett's suggestion that she cannot change her style at will is, to a degree, ingenuous. There is large body of research exploring sociolinguistic factors which contribute to an individual's linguistic variation. Explanations of variation between any texts must account for many factors. Elizabeth Barrett's style will vary according to the mode of production, for example; even with her conversational style Barrett's written text will be denser than her spoken language. There will be variation according to the relationship she has with her interlocutor; her style will change as she becomes more intimate with Browning, and further differences will be apparent when she writes, for example, professional letters to her publisher. And there will be genre differences; not only the substantial differences in style expected between her poetry and prose but also differences between prose genres, such as letters and diary entries. There will however also be continuities across her style; her authorial voice will be subject to constraints; reasons why aspects of her language may remain constant. Linguists debate the existence of an idiolect (an individual's unique language style) and there is some empirical support for the construct. Coulthard (2004), for example, suggests that vocabulary differences between writers can be measured[38] and van Halteren *et al* detect the existence of a human stylome.[39] Additionally there is psychological evidence that an individual will fall into habits of use, both in terms of vocabulary selection and grammatical construction. The difficulty in identifying *l'homme* or *la femme* from *le style* is that of isolating the linguistic sources of variation and constancy between disputed texts and texts of known authorship.

15.19   One myth of forensic authorship identification is that texts will be short and material will be sparse. Whilst this clearly can be the case—there has been recent linguistic evidence, for example, based on the analysis of mobile telephone text messages[40]—it is not always so; other cases have involved substantial amounts of text, for example, in the analysis of substantial plans associated with terrorist conspiracy. Typically a successful analysis requires not only the disputed texts but also a good collection of comparison texts. Ideally the comparison corpus should include texts known to have been written by the suspected author(s) but an additional criterion is that these texts should be as linguistically similar as possible to the disputed text. Thus if a threatening letter is at issue, what would be needed for comparison are other letters from the suspected writer and their linguistic community, and further to this, these letters should be interpersonal or with strong emotional content. Problems in analysis are as likely to be caused by an inadequate comparison corpus as by the amount of disputed text.

---

[37] E.g. Shuy, R.W., *Language crimes. The use and abuse of language evidence in the courtroom*, Oxford: Blackwell Publishers, 1993; Shuy, R.W., *Linguistic battles in trademark disputes*, New York: Palgrave Macmillan, 2002.

[38] Coulthard, M., 'Author identification, idiolect and linguistic uniqueness' (2004) 25/4. *Applied Linguistics*, 431–447.

[39] van Halteren, H., Baayen, R.H., Tweedie, F., Haverkort, M. and Neijt, A., 'New machine learning methods demonstrate the existence of a human stylome' (2005) 12/1 *Journal of Quantitative Linguistics*, 65–77.

[40] *R v Campbell* (2002) Chelmsford Crown Court.

Just as there is no typical length of forensic text, any type of text may acquire forensic **15.20** interest. Threatening and abusive letters, or sexual communications between a 40-year-old man and a 12-year-old girl, may have inherent evidential value, but in other cases the use to which a text is put makes it forensically interesting. In the mobile phone text message analysis cited above[41] the issue was that of alibi. The timing of a text message from a victim's phone indicated a time of death, which provided an alibi for the accused; the linguistic evidence, however, suggested that the crucial text message had in fact been sent from the victim's phone by the accused.

Forensic linguistic analysis for the identification of an author is at a disadvantage in **15.21** comparison with other forensic sciences, such as forensic phonetics (see Chapter 14, above). In most forensic sciences there is some population knowledge of the distribution of variables and features. In phonetics, for example, the distribution of formant frequencies (the essential pitch of the voice) is known to vary systematically according to gender (amongst other factors). Because of this it is possible not only to establish the gender of a speaker, but also where a sample of a male voice is high-pitched it may be possible to estimate the proportion of a population with such a voice.

In contrast, such general information on base rates is difficult to obtain for most linguistic variables. This is because there are so many sociolinguistic and pragmatic reasons for language variation. Authorship analysis requires the identification of 'interesting' or salient features in an individual's written style and then comparing these features in the disputed text and/or comparison texts of candidate authors. To some degree the recognition of salient linguistic features in a text relies upon the skills and intuitions acquired during linguistic training and this is the essence of the expertise provided. However, base rate knowledge can and should be sought for the reinforcement of linguistic intuitions and the presentation of linguistic evidence to the courts. This can be achieved either through corpus searches, such as that carried out by Coulthard[42] in relation to the Bentley case, or through the collection of primary data from a relevant linguistic community. Both methods have advantages and disadvantages; corpus searches are quick and cheap and will involve many millions of words of data, but it may be difficult to argue that the data is relevant to the problem at hand; primary data collection is slow and expensive and will result in only a small amount of data but the linguistic relevance of the text is better controlled. There will always be variables and cases where base rates of salient features cannot be satisfactorily established and in these cases the analysis will continue to rest upon the expert intuitions of the hired linguist.

Authorship identification may be difficult and in some cases may prove impossible. Even **15.22** where a certain identification cannot be reached a more broadly focused authorship analysis may be useful. It can be possible to indicate, for example, the level of linguistic competence of a writer and perhaps some information about their social background and this can provide collaborative evidence or information which may have a wider value in an investigation.

---

[41] Ibid.   [42] Cited above at n.17.

G. Some Limits of Forensic Linguistic Analysis

15.23 Forensic text analysis can be used imaginatively to answer issues other than the authorship origins of texts. Shuy analysed tape transcripts of covert conversations between John de Lorean, the sports car manufacturer, and operatives of the US Drug Enforcement Agency.[43] The prosecution argued that de Lorean had agreed to an illegal drug deal, but Shuy's analysis demonstrated that this was not the case. De Lorean and the agent in the sting operation were talking at cross-purposes and conversational analysis was able to show that de Lorean neither accepted nor acquiesced in the deal. Another example from evidence which did not reach a court would be an analysis which was able to throw light on diaries and letters written by a man accused of his wife's murder. An analysis of the content and use of tense in the texts was able to demonstrate when and how the accused started to refer to the victim in the past tense. The power of linguistic analysis in answering forensic questions is still developing, however; just as there is potential for forensic linguistic analysis to be used imaginatively, so there is potential for such analysis to overstep its limits.

15.24 Perhaps the most tempting line which linguists may cross is the line between linguistics and psychology. Generally speaking, linguists in their analyses should not extend their conclusions into the area of a writer's intentions. A linguist may for example be invited to analyse a letter which is thought to contain a threat. In such a case the linguist might legitimately determine what constitutes the threat in the letter and separately may undertake analysis to help identify the writer, but they have no role in commenting on how likely the threat is to be carried through. Research into threat analysis demonstrates clearly that it is not possible to predict by linguistic means alone the outcome of a threatening communication.[44] Further to this area, current research into deception generally suggests that it is not possible using linguistic evidence alone to come to a conclusion that a communication is deceptive.[45] A final role which ought to be retained by suitably qualified psychologists or psychiatrists is that of offender profiling; determining a person's psychology or future actions from linguistic analysis is not yet possible.

H. Conclusion

15.25 Forensic linguistics continues to provide useful analysis of the linguistic processes of the law. It is not restricted to the production of linguistic evidence but where such evidence has been produced and accepted by the courts this has mostly been in areas where there

---

[43] See his 1993 work, cited above at n.37.

[44] Meloy, J.R., James D.V., Farnham, F.R., Mullen P.E., Pathe, M., Darnley, B. and Preston, L., 'A research review of public figure threats, approaches, attacks, and assassinations in the United States' (2004) 5 *Journal of Forensic Science*, 1–8; Scalora M.J., Baumgartner, J.V., Zimmerman, W., Callaway, D., Maillette, M., Covell, C., Palarea, R., Krebs, J. and Washington, D.O., 'An epidemiological assessment of problematic contacts to members of Congress' (2002) 47 *Journal of Forensic Science*, 1360–1364.

[45] Shuy, R., *The language of confession, interrogation and deception*, London: Sage Publications, 1998; Vrij, A. and Mann, S., 'Detecting deception: The benefit of looking at a combination of behavioral, auditory and speech content related cues in a systematic manner,' (2004) 13 *Group Decision and Negotiation*, 61–79.

have been either disputes over the level of linguistic competence of a witness or defendant, or disputes over the origins of spoken or written communications. At its best forensic linguistic evidence draws upon the base of the research literature and demonstrates the rigorous application of academic linguistic methods to draw conclusions about forensically interesting texts.

Witness statements constitute a peculiar genre of personal narrative. Many of the narrative **15.26** peculiarities, such as the density of time and place information, are not naturally produced in other narrative forms. Because of this, the narrative of the witness must be shaped by the expertise of the interviewer. Largely due to the fear of contamination of witness memory and testimony, there has recently and properly been considerable concentration on the removal of interviewer artefacts from witness narratives. Linguistic analysis, however, suggests that the interviewer's role is, and must continue to be, more than that of a mnemonic amanuensis. The stories of witnesses, such as those they relate to co-witnesses before being interviewed, would not be adequate for judicial purposes. The legal process requires co-construction of witness narratives and should recognize the legitimacy of its occurrence. Just as the interviewer inevitably co-constructs witness testimony so too does the interpreter. With the increased use of tape recording of significant witnesses, interviewer and interpreter influence on witness narratives will become increasingly apparent to the courts. The interests of justice require that these effects of co-construction on testimony should not be ignored or condemned but understood and managed.

Linguistic evidence can also be provided as to the authorship or wider origins of eviden- **15.27** tial texts. In these cases the issues of individual linguistic variation need to be accounted for, and features which are identified as being typical of an individual's style tested through the acquisition of base rate information. Whilst there will be many cases where useful linguistic evidence can be provided it has to be recognized that there will also be cases where the analysis fails to reach a useful conclusion. This is not necessarily a failure of the linguist, or of the methods they are applying, but rather the result of linguistic complexity and individuals' exploitation of the possibilities of linguistic creativity.

Perhaps the greatest difficulty facing a lawyer requiring input from a forensic linguist is **15.28** that of choosing the expert. The field is still relatively immature; there is no accreditation or regulation process and there are few external markers of expertise. The primary organization is the International Association of Forensic Linguists but this is still largely an academic association and does not maintain a list of recognized experts. Because of this lack of regulation anyone may call themselves a forensic linguist and offer their services. When hiring an expert linguist for court work it may be advisable therefore to request good references involving casework and also references from other linguists. *Caveat emptor.*

Further Reading

For detailed and varied coverage of all areas of forensic linguistics there is *The International Journal of Speech Language and the Law*, Equinox Press.
Berk-Seligson, Susan, *The bilingual courtroom. Court interpreters in the judicial process*, Chicago, Ill: University of Chicago Press, 1990.

Gibbons, John, *Forensic linguistics: An introduction to language in the justice system*, Melbourne, Australia: Blackwell Publishers, 2003.

Shuy, Roger W., *Language crimes: The use and abuse of language evidence in the courtroom*, Oxford: Blackwell Publishers, 1993.

Shuy, Roger W., *The language of confession, interrogation and deception*, London: Sage Publications, 1998.

Tiersma, Peter. M., *Legal Language*, Chicago, Ill: University of Chicago Press, 1999.

Tim Grant is a lecturer in Forensic Psychology at the University of Leicester. His BA was in Philosophy, followed by an MSc in Cognitive Science (Psychology Department) and a PhD in forensic authorship analysis (English Department), all from the University of Birmingham. He has worked in forensic linguistic analysis for more than 10 years in criminal and civil cases. In the criminal field he has provided expert evidence in cases involving terrorist conspiracy, murder and stalking, working for both prosecution and defence. He has also assisted in cases of literary and student plagiarism and intellectual property theft.

Editors' Note

More than any other, this chapter underlines the inherent superiority of sound-only or audio-visual recording of interviews and oral exchanges, as a vital tool of testimonial archaeology. By contrast written records created by the interviewer characteristically omit assertion-loaded questions and are apt to 'tidy up' what the witness said in a way which might well reflect the interviewer's perception of what he supposed the witness was likely to have seen or heard, as opposed to what the witness said he remembered. Nonetheless, whilst the science of forensic linguistics remains in its comparative infancy, it may be useful to instruct a forensic linguist to use such analytical skills as have been developed to report on the authenticity of a suspect text, whether as to its accuracy as a record of what the speaker is claimed to have said or as to the identity of its originator. Where no such expert is engaged, there is in this chapter much of value to assist those needing to cross-examine the makers of written texts or their scribes and to address or direct fact finders tasked to assess their authenticity and to compare their detail with oral testimony.

SECTION 3

EVIDENTIAL PERSPECTIVES

Summary

Chapter 16. Forensic Facial Identification.
Tim Valentine

Bitter experience has shown that ostensibly convincing evidence of identification, even when obtained through the use of the most stringent safeguards, can be wrong, and technology brings with it an increased risk of mistakes. This is a comprehensive summary, from a broadly psychological angle, of the uses to which identification can be put in the investigative context, the techniques used in methods of identification, the relationship between witness confidence and identification accuracy and identification through comparison between images of suspects on film and the appearance of defendants. Recommendations for improvements in procedures are made.

Chapter 17. Improving Visual Identification Procedures under PACE Code D.
David Wolchover and Anthony Heaton-Armstrong

Continuing on the themes of Chapter 16, this explores the same subject from the viewpoint of practising lawyers and in a more legal context. The risks inherent in current procedures are explained and suggestions made for the implementation of further refinements to these, which would serve to improve the quality of identification evidence and to reduce the risk of wrong identification and, thus, future miscarriages of justice.

Chapter 18. Assessing Contentious Eyewitness Evidence: A Judicial View.
Tom Bingham

Judicial experience has shown that a structured approach to the assessment of contentious eyewitness testimony is more likely to lead to reliable conclusions as to truth or falsehood and guilt or innocence than those which are based on 'hunch'-type reactions to witnesses and their evidence. The demeanour of a witness is likely to be of much less value than other clues, available from other sources, which point towards or away from truthfulness and accuracy. Honest witnesses whose evidence may be perfectly plausible might, nonetheless, be utterly mistaken. Relying on his own and his colleagues' experience as judges, the author points the way towards a more intelligent treatment of witnesses and their testimony.

Chapter 19. Judging Eyewitnesses, Confessions, Informants and Alibis. What is Wrong with Juries and Can they do Better?
Saul Kassin

Building on Bingham's conclusions, this chapter emphasizes the need for fact finders to be informed concerning psychological knowledge relating to the behaviour of eye-witnesses in a way which helps to avoid conclusions concerning disputed factual issues being reached on a series of false premises. The need for testimonial archaeology, through explorations as to how witnesses reached their conclusions and what may have contributed to this, is essential if fact finders are to avoid making decisions based on superficial appearances. Those who address and direct fact finders, whether advocates or judges, need to be aware of the potential inadequacies of evidence in the four categories. The use of electronic recordings is recommended to capture stages of the process during which prospective evidence is provided and collated.

Chapter 20. Oral Testimony from the Witness's Perspective—Psychological and Forensic Considerations.
Peter Dunn and Eric Shepherd

Recent legislative and other initiatives designed to improve the quality of witness testimony and the provision of facilities for witnesses' comfort and welfare reflect a recognition of past failure to take account of witnesses' needs and priorities. The relevant statutory provisions, notably those comprised within the Youth Justice and Criminal Evidence Act 1999, are detailed and discussed. Witnesses' perceptions as to what is important and helpful to them are considered. Witnesses' experience of the investigative and forensic processes have been apt to exacerbate the effects of their original victimization. Unless their needs are actually and realistically catered for, the prospect of the experience of being a witness will deter people from consenting to become willingly involved in the criminal justice system.

Chapter 21. Disclosure of Unused Material by Prosecution Authorities and Third Parties.
Anthony Heaton-Armstrong, David Corker and David Wolchover

'Testimonial archaeology' of the kind that many of the other chapters have shown is essential, in order to enable fact finders' conclusions to be sound and just, can only be possible if the route to the origins of testimony is cleared and discoveries made during the process both by investigators and others are shared, where relevant, with those representing the interests of accused people. Beginning with a telling summary of the history of the development of disclosure law, this chapter explains the disclosure process as it affects the remaining contents of the book, concentrating on issues concerning previous statements by witnesses and physical and mental health factors relating to witnesses which might have a bearing on the accuracy and reliability of their evidence.

Chapter 22. The Admissibility of Expert Evidence.
David Ormerod and Andrew Roberts

The desirability is recognized of preventing expert evidence which constitutes no more than what is commonly available knowledge, or is of poor quality or insufficiently impartial, from being placed before fact finders. The higher courts' approach to the admission of expert evidence concerning the issues raised in this book has become more liberal, although the definition of what constitutes 'common knowledge' gives rise to continuing debate and controversy. The currently applicable law is described, the difficulties involved in using expert evidence are identified and some suggestions offered as to likely or desirable developments in this field.

Chapter 23. Judicial Training.
William Young and Sam Katkhuda

Those who direct fact finders as to their task need to be adequately informed concerning the desirable mechanics of testimonial archaeology to enable them to reach just conclusions concerning contentious evidence and guilt or innocence. Experience in previous forensic practice may be inadequate for this purpose. Judges, also, need to be alert to the perceptions of juries as to how to perform their role and as to what considerations need to be applied in doing so. Jury research is, for this reason, informative. The importance of directing juries concerning a structured approach to decisions concerning contentious evidence and, thus, to verdict is emphasized. Comprehensive training which includes consideration of the issues raised in this book is essential.

16

FORENSIC FACIAL IDENTIFICATION

Tim Valentine

A. The Role of Mistaken Identification in Wrongful Conviction

16.01   All criminal prosecutions rely on identifying the culprit. In some cases, it may be possible to establish identification through fingerprints, DNA or other forensic evidence. In other cases identification may not be disputed. Nevertheless, in many criminal cases identification by eyewitnesses is the only means of establishing a disputed identification. Concerns about the role of mistaken identification in wrongful convictions in England and Wales led eventually to the report of the departmental committee chaired by Lord Devlin.[1]

---

[1] *Report to the Secretary of State for the Home Department on the Departmental Committee on Evidence of Identification in Criminal Cases*, HC 338, London: HMSO, 1976.

Within a very short time the Devlin Report inspired a milestone judgment of the Court of Appeal which laid down an obligatory set of standard warnings to the jury on the dangers of eyewitness identification.[2]

16.02 Analysis of cases of known wrongful conviction has highlighted the role of mistaken identification in both the USA and the UK.[3] The most dramatic evidence comes from the work of the Innocence Project in the USA. At the time of writing 180 people who were wrongly convicted have been exonerated by DNA evidence that was not available at their trial.[4] Analysis of these cases has shown that mistaken eyewitness identification was the leading cause of wrongful conviction. Mistaken identification was a factor in the conviction of 61 of the first 70 exoneration cases (87 per cent).[5] Inspired by the American project, innocence projects have been established in Australia and the UK.[6]

B. Introduction to Identification Procedures and Technologies

16.03 Identification procedures have been relatively unregulated in the USA, where practice differs from one area to another. Identification from arrays of photographs is commonplace, with no minimum number of innocent foils in the array specified. Many photograph arrays comprise only 2 or 3 foils and a suspect.[7] Expert evidence from psychologists on eyewitness identification is admissible in American courts. This practice has encouraged a significant body of empirical research on American identification procedures.[8] As a result of the evidence from the Innocence Project the US Department of Justice has recently produced guidance on best practice.[9]

16.04 In contrast to the USA, the approach taken in England and Wales has been to regulate identification procedures, but not to permit expert evidence on eyewitness identification in court.[10] The assumption of the courts is that eyewitness identification is within the ordinary experience of the jury. Procedures are set down in Code D of a code of practice

---

[2] *R v Turnbull* (1977) 98 CrAppR 313.

[3] See *e.g.* Brandon, R. and Davies C., *Wrongful imprisonment. Mistaken convictions and their consequences*, London: Allen & Unwin, 1973; Huff, C.R., Ratner, A. and Sagarin, E., 'Guilty until proven innocent: wrongful conviction and public policy' (1986) 32 *Crime & Delinquency*, 518–544.

[4] Scheck, B., Neufield, P. and Dywer, J., *Actual innocence*, New York: Doubleday, 2000; *http://www.innocenceproject.org*, downloaded 8 September 2005.

[5] *http://www.innocenceproject.org/causes/index.php*, downloaded 8 December 2005.

[6] For the Australian Innocence network see *http://www.gu.edu.au/school/law/innocence/network/network.html*. For the UK Innocence network see *http://www.innocencenetwork.org.uk/*.

[7] Wells, G.L., 'Police lineups: data, theory and policy' (2001) 7 *Psychology, Public Policy and Law*, 791–801.

[8] For a recent view see Wells, G.L., Small, M., Penrod, S., Malpass, R.S., Fulero, S.M. and Brinacombe, C.A.E., 'Eyewitness identification procedures: recommendations for lineups and photospreads' (1998) 22 *Law and Human Behavior*, 603–647.

[9] Technical Working Group on Eyewitness Evidence, *Eyewitness Evidence: A Guide to Law Enforcement*, Washington DC: US Department of Justice, 1999 (downloaded 20 January 2005 from *http://www.ncjrs.org/nij/eyewitness/tech_working_group.html*).

[10] It should be noted that, although expert testimony on *eyewitness* identification is not usually admissible, expert testimony on identification of faces from CCTV is often allowed.

required by the Police and Criminal Evidence Act (1984)[11] (PACE). Traditionally, identification evidence has been based on a live line-up or 'identity parade'. Minimum standards for the line-up are set out in the code of practice. For example, the code requires that there must be at least eight foils, who resemble the suspect in 'age, height, general appearance and position in life' and the witness must be cautioned that the person they saw may or may not be present. The most recent version of Code D has changed the traditional reliance on live line-ups in favour of requiring the line-up to be presented on video unless there is a reason why a live parade would be more appropriate. As a result of concern about the reliability of eyewitness identification, and development in the technology available, there is unprecedented interest and change in identification procedures in both the USA and the UK.

The difficulties inherent in eyewitness identification may suggest that whenever possible **16.05** it is better to rely on CCTV images for identification. Development of CCTV technology has had a particularly marked impact in the UK. CCTV has proved so popular with politicians and the public, that with an estimate of more than 4 million cameras, the UK is believed to have the highest density of CCTV cameras in the world.[12] The prevalence of CCTV means that images of either the perpetrators or the victims of crime are often available to police investigations. Recent psychological research has demonstrated, however, that the human ability to match the identity of unfamiliar individuals across video and photographic images can be highly error-prone even under ideal conditions and with high-quality images available (see paragraph 16.56 below).

A further technological step is to attempt to remove human judgement from the system **16.06** entirely and either use computers to recognize faces from video images or employ expert analysis of facial images (often referred to as facial mapping) to establish identification. Technological development has contributed to advancement in this area but an effective and efficient technical solution to the problem of facial recognition in the real world has continued to ellude us (see paragraph 16.72 below).

C. Investigative Use of Eyewitness Identification

(1) Investigative and evidential use of eyewitness identification distinguished

Investigative use of eyewitness identification can be distinguished from *evidential* use. The **16.07** police might take steps to collect identification evidence, either to obtain an identification of a possible suspect (e.g. by releasing CCTV images to the media), or to obtain evidence that their suspect is indeed the culprit (e.g. by asking a witness to attend a video identification). In either case the witness identification might form part of the evidence against the defendant in court. This would constitute *evidential* use of facial identification.

---

[11] Police and Criminal Evidence Act (1984) codes of practice, edition of 2005 (which came into force on 1 January 2006), downloaded 3 May 2006 from: *http://police.homeoffice.gov.uk/operational-policing/powers-pace-codes/pace-codes.html.*

[12] McCahill, M. and Norris, C., 'Estimating the extent, sophistication and legality of CCTV in London', in.Gill, M. (ed.), *CCTV*, Leicester: Perpetuity Press, 2003, 51–66.

(2) Investigative use generating a suspect

16.08 Another possibility is that the identification generates a suspect whom the police then investigate. As a result of the police investigation other evidence might be obtained, which forms the case in court. For example an identification of a suspect from CCTV might provide a reason to arrest a suspect and search their premises. A recent example of *investigative* use of identification from CCTV is provided by the wide publicity given to CCTV images of people suspected of carrying out the London bombing on 7 July and the attempted bombing on 21 July 2005. Information obtained through the publicity may have led the police to find incriminating material at an address linked to a possible identification. These investigations demonstrate an important investigative role for CCTV cameras. It remains to be seen whether any identification evidence from CCTV will be put to evidential use in these cases.

(3) When the identity of a suspect is unknown

16.09 The most common investigative use of witness identification is in cases in which the police have not identified a possible suspect. There are a number of procedures that can be used, depending on the circumstances of the case. The police may show a witness photographs of people who have previous convictions for similar crimes and whose appearance is broadly consistent with the witness's description. The procedure for showing photographs in this manner in specified in PACE Code D.

(i) CCTV

16.10 If CCTV images are available a still image might be made available in the police station in the expectation that an officer might recognize the person depicted as somebody previously arrested. Recognition by police officers from CCTV is currently outside the scope of PACE Code D. CCTV images might also be made available through the media in the hope that a member of the public would recognize the culprit. The degree of familiarity of the person recognized is a critical factor that determines the reliability of facial recognition from CCTV. This issue is discussed further in paragraph 16.56 below.

(ii) Street identifications (UK), confrontations (UK) and showups (USA)

16.11 PACE Code D distinguishes between a 'street identification', which may be conducted in the immediate aftermath of a crime being reported when there is insufficient evidence to make an arrest, and a 'confrontation' when a single suspect, who has been arrested, is shown to a witness for the purpose of identification. Different procedures are set out in PACE Code D for street identifications and confrontations. This distinction is not made in the USA—the showing of a single suspect is referred to as a 'showup'. Showups are most commonly used when there is insufficient evidence to arrest a suspect without identification evidence.

16.12 A typical street identification or showup may proceed as follows. Having taken a description of a street robber, the police might drive the victim around the area to see if they can identify the perpetrator. If the victim sees somebody who is recognized as the robber, they will be pointed out to the police. Alternatively, a description might be circulated by radio and other police officers driving into the area might stop somebody who matches the description. The police might set up a situation whereby the witness is able to see the suspect to establish whether an identification can be made. In essence a street identification or showup involves allowing a witness to see a single suspect and make a decision as to whether or not he or she is the perpetrator of a crime.

A street identification could be put to investigative or evidential use. The procedure is **16.13** similar to a confrontation when a witness is allowed to see a suspect, who might already have been arrested, perhaps in a police station. In principle, a confrontation (or showup) could be conducted by showing a photograph (which can be used in the USA) or on video. PACE Code D does allow a 'live' confrontation, although it is considered very much a last resort, only to be used if all other identification procedures are impracticable. Showing a single person in a photograph or on video, in a manner analogous to a live confrontation, is not included in PACE Code D. A street identification can serve an important investigative role. For example, a suspect may be subsequently identified by forensic evidence. The most controversial aspect of street identification is its use as formal identification evidence. Therefore, street identifications are discussed further in paragraph 16.45 below.

(iii) Construction of facial likeness

A further method that can be used to find a suspect is to ask a witness to construct a facial **16.14** composite from memory (for example by use of E-fit or similar systems). The first method employed was to use an artist to construct a likeness. In the 1970s paper-based systems were used to construct composite faces by slotting together individual facial features chosen from a selection of many different eyes, eyebrows, noses, mouths etc. Photo-fit, based on photographed facial features, was widely used in the UK. Identi-Kit, based on drawn facial features, was widely used in the USA. Subsequently computerized systems were developed that gave more control of the placement of features, and allowed the global configuration of the face to be manipulated. Computerized systems include E-fit, Pro-fit, Mac-a-Mug Pro and FACES. Evaluation of all of these systems has consistently shown that they perform poorly. Witnesses find the task of selecting individual features difficult. Often composites constructed with a photograph present throughout the construction are no better than composites constructed from memory. This finding suggests that people have difficulty constructing good look-alike composite faces with these systems even when there is no need to rely on memory. The computerized systems are not reliably better than the systems they replaced. Both mechanical and computerized systems are less effective than a good police artist.[13]

A new generation of facial composite systems is currently under development which **16.15** makes use of a statistical model of facial appearance and a genetic algorithm to converge on the desired facial appearance under the guidance of the witness. Initially a set of random photographic-quality synthetic faces are generated by the software and displayed on the screen. The witness is asked to select the face that most resembles the culprit. The software then generates a new 'generation' of faces that use the witness's selection to

---

[13] For a recent review of this research see Davies, G.M. and Valentine, T., 'Facial composites: forensic utility and psychological research,' in Lindsay, R.C.L., Ross, D.F., Read, J.D. and Toglia, M.P., *Handbook of eyewitness psychology* (2 vols.), Mahwah: LEA (in press), vol. 2, 'Memory for people.'

guide the search through the range of facial appearance (or 'face space'). The software also introduces random variation to generate the new set of faces. This process continues repeatedly in an iterative manner. At first the faces are dissimilar and none may look similar to the culprit. Gradually the facial appearance of the culprit is selected for. With each successive generation the facial appearances converge on the desired appearance. Systems under development include Eigen-Fit and Evo-FIT.[14] The great advantage of these systems is that the witness only ever has to look at whole faces and does not have to select individual facial features. This is important because experimental evidence shows that face recognition is an holistic process and people find it very difficult to analyse a face into its constituent parts or features.

16.16 In early evaluations the new generation of facial composite systems do not outperform current systems. However, the technology is still at a relatively early stage of development, and does show considerable promise. The new technology allows a number of innovations which are currently under development. A 3D facial model would allow the witness to rotate the head to see a three-quarter or profile view. Hand-held devices could be used permitting rapid deployment to allow a witness to construct a facial likeness at the crime scene within minutes of reporting the crime. The facial appearance generated under guidance by the witness could be used to search a database of known offenders while the police are still at the crime scene.

D. Factors Involved in the Selection and Design of Formal Methods of Identification

16.17 A range of formal procedures has been or is currently in use for testing the ability of witnesses to make an identification: live identity parades; photospreads (in the USA and Canada); video identification; and 'group' identification (England and Wales), the last of which remains nominally available but is seldom used and will not be discussed here. The first three methods involve the placing of the suspect, either in person (live parade) or in image form (still photograph or moving image) among volunteer 'foils' in order to test whether the witness is able to pick out the suspect. The choice, design and reliability of these methods must be considered in the context of three topics: the distinction between estimator variables and system variables; whether to present the array simultaneously or sequentially; and whether to select the foils according to a culprit-description strategy or a suspect-resemblance strategy.

---

[14] Frowd, C., Hancock, P. J. B. and Carson, D., 'EvoFIT: A holistic evolutionary facial imaging technique for creating composites' (2004) 1 *ACM Transactions on Applied Psychology*, 1–21; Frowd, C., Carson, D., Ness, H., McQuiston-Surrett, D., Richardson, J., Baldwin, H. and Hancock, P., 'Contemporary composite techniques: The impact of a forensically-relevant target delay' (2005) 10 *Legal and Criminological Psychology*, 63–91; Gibson, S., Pallares Bejarano, A. and Solomon, C., 'Synthesis of photographic quality facial composites using evolutionary algorithms' in Harvey, R. and Bangham, J. A., (eds.), *Proceedings of the British Machine Vision Conference 2003*, London: British Machine Vision Association, 2003, 221–230.

(1) Estimator and system variables

The outcome of an identification procedure can be affected by *estimator* variables and **16.18** *system* variables.[15] Estimator variables are the factors associated with an individual witness and their view of the crime. For example, estimator variables include the distance of the witness from the perpetrator, how much attention they paid, how long they viewed the suspect, the witness's age and eyesight, and whether the culprit was from a different ethnic origin to the witness. Estimator variables are generally not under the control of the criminal justice system. In contrast, system variables are under the control of the criminal justice system. System variables include the identification method selected (e.g. photospread, live identity parade, video identification, street identification), the method used to select foils, the similarity and number of foils, and the instructions given to the witness.

Any procedure needs to be both *sensitive* and *fair*. If the culprit is present, the procedure **16.19** must be sensitive enough to allow a reliable witness to be able to make an identification. The procedure should also be fair enough to keep the possibility of a witness making a mistaken identification to an acceptably low level. The skill in designing identification procedures is to manipulate system variables that increase sensitivity while simultaneously maintaining or increasing fairness. It is relatively easy to increase sensitivity but decrease fairness (e.g. using foils who do not fit the description of the witness and are not similar to the suspect) or to increase fairness at a cost of sensitivity (e.g. a lineup of clones).[16]

(2) Sequential and simultaneous presentation compared

In relation to photospreads it has been proposed that the array should be presented one at **16.20** a time, in a sequential presentation, rather than simultaneously.[17] Traditionally photospreads have been presented as an array of photographs set out in a single sheet; thus all faces were presented simultaneously. Under sequential presentation instructions, the witness is shown one face at a time. They are not told how many faces will be presented, but must decide whether each face is or is not the culprit before the next face is presented. The line-up administrator should be blind to the identity of the suspect to avoid any possibility of providing non-verbal cues.[18] The rationale is that when all faces are seen simultaneously, there is a tendency for the witness to identify the person who *most* resembles the culprit (i.e. to make a *relative* judgement). The use of relative judgements is believed to be a factor that makes identification evidence less reliable.[19] Sequential

[15] Wells, G.L., 'What do we know about eyewitness identification?' (1993) 48 *American Psychologist*, 553–571.

[16] Concern with the issues of fairness and sensitivity of identification procedures is central in *R v Marcus* [2004] All ER (D) 351; [2005] CrimLR 384.

[17] Lindsay, R.C.L. and Wells, G.L., 'Improving eyewitness identification from lineups: Simultaneous versus sequential lineup presentation' (1985) 70 *Journal of Applied Psychology*, 556–564.

[18] Ibid.

[19] Gronlund, S.D., 'Sequential lineups: shift in criterion or decision strategy?' (2004) 89 *Journal of Applied Psychology*, 362–368; Kneller, W., Memon, A. and Stevenage, S., 'Simultaneous and sequential lineups: decision processes of accurate and inaccurate witnesses' (2001) 15 *Applied Cognitive Psychology*, 659–671.

presentation prevents the witness from making a relative judgement, but instead requires an absolute judgement of whether each face is that of the culprit.

16.21 The accuracy rates from sequential and simultaneous presentations of photograph line-ups based on data from 9 published and 14 unpublished papers have recently been systematically compared.[20] With the culprit present in the line-up more witnesses identified the culprit from simultaneous than from sequential lineups (50 per cent vs 35 per cent respectively). Incorrect rejections of the line-up (i.e. no identification of any line-up member) were less frequent from simultaneous line-ups than from sequential line-ups (26 per cent vs 46 per cent). When the culprit was not in the line-up, there were substantially fewer correct rejections from simultaneous line-ups than from sequential line-ups (49 per cent vs 79 per cent), and fewer incorrect identifications of a foil from sequential line-ups (51 per cent vs 28 per cent). In summary, sequential presentation reduces the rate of choosing from both culprit-present and culprit-absent line-ups. The effect of sequential presentation is to provide some protection against mistaken identification from culprit-absent line-ups (i.e. to make line-ups fairer), but it does so at a cost to the sensitivity of the identification procedure when the culprit is in the line-up.

16.22 The analysis by Steblay *et al*[20a] provides a systematic assessment of the literature, but nevertheless some shortcomings in the literature should be noted. There are still only a few published studies that have tested the sequential presentation procedure. A large proportion of the studies analysed were unpublished and almost 70 per cent of studies were carried out at a single research laboratory. Studies published since the analysis was carried out have provided further evidence that the reduced rate of correct identifications from sequential culprit-present line-ups is a robust phenomenon.[21] Although sequential presentation was developed in the context of photospreads, it can be applied, in principle, to video identifications (see paragraph 16.39).

(3) Selecting foils by match to culprit description or by suspect resemblance

16.23 PACE Code D specifies that the foils for line-ups must 'resemble the suspect . . .'. Therefore, the strategy used to construct line-ups in the UK has been a suspect-resemblance strategy. It has been argued that a better strategy is to select foils who match the witness' description of the culprit.[22] Use of a culprit-description strategy has some practical implications. Foils must be selected separately for each witness if their descriptions differ. Special consideration must be made if the witness's description does not match the appearance of the suspect in any way. First, use of a culprit-description strategy

---

[20] Steblay, N., Dysart, J., Fulero, S. and Lindsay, R.C.L., 'Eyewitness accuracy rates in sequential and simultaneous lineup presentations: A meta-analytic comparison' (2001) 25 *Law and Human Behavior*, 459–473.

[20a] Ibid.

[21] Memon, A. and Gabbert, F., 'Unravelling the effects of a sequential lineup' (2003) 6 *Applied Cognitive Psychology*, 703–714; Memon, A. and Gabbert, F., 'Improving the identification accuracy of senior witnesses: Do pre-lineup questions and sequential testing help?' (2003) 88 *Journal of Applied Psychology*, 341–347; Memon, A. and Bartlett, J.C., 'The effects of verbalisation on face recognition' (2002) 16 *Applied Cognitive Psychology*, 635–650.

[22] This line of argument was first made by Luus, C.A.E. and Wells, G.L., 'Eyewitness identification and the selection of distracters for lineups' (1991) 15 *Law and Human Behavior*, 43–57.

will be considered in the situation where the witness has given a description that fits the appearance of the suspect in all attributes mentioned in the description.

(i) When the description of the culprit matches the suspect

16.24 At an identification parade the witness is asked whether any of the people in the line-up is the same person as the culprit. It is reasonable to assume that the witness can remember the description that he or she gave to the police. A witness might expect to identify somebody who matches the description they gave previously. Therefore, they might be inclined to disregard any foils that do not match their description, or conversely pay special attention to anybody who is a better match to their description than the rest. To be fair, all line-up members should match the witness's description of the culprit. Therefore, the witness's description should play a special role in selecting line-up members.

16.25 It does not introduce a bias against the suspect if line-up members differ on some feature that was not mentioned in the original description. For example, imagine a witness who described the culprit as 'white, male, mid-forties, with long, dark hair'. The suspect fits this description and has a pale complexion and prominent dark eyebrows. A culprit-description strategy would require that all lineup foils would be white males, say between 43 and 47 years old with long, dark hair. No attempt would be made to match the prominent eyebrows or the pale complexion. Indeed there should be a range of variability around these and other features not mentioned in the description (e.g. build, face-shape etc.). Heterogeneity of features not mentioned in the description will help a witness with a reliable memory to distinguish the culprit from the foils. If the police suspect is the culprit, the witness might able to identify the suspect, because on seeing the line-up, she recognizes the man with the pale complexion and prominent eyebrows. A line-up that consists of a number of people chosen because they closely resemble the suspect in all aspects of their appearance, will make it difficult even for a reliable witness to identify the culprit, if present. However, if the suspect was not the culprit, the pale complexion and prominent eyebrows are no more likely to trigger a mistaken identification than some other features on a foil (maybe thin eyebrows and an olive skin tone) because *the witness has not seen the suspect before*. A strategy of suspect resemblance, which attempts to match all features including the pale complexion and the prominent eyebrows, will produce a procedure that is less sensitive than a line-up constructed of foils chosen to match the witness's description of the culprit. As the culprit description strategy does not introduce any systematic bias against the suspect both procedures should be equally fair.

16.26 When constructing a culprit description line-up it may be necessary to take account of default values in descriptions. Sometimes people may not describe the sex or race of the person. This may occur because the witness assumes a default value, rather than implying that the witness did not notice the sex or ethnicity of the offender. It is not recommended that people of different sex or ethnic background are put on the same line-up simply because sex or ethnicity was not mentioned in a description. Similarly people may neglect to say that somebody did not have a beard or was not wearing glasses.[23] If a

---

[23] Lindsay, R.C.L., Martin, R. and Webber, L., 'Default values in eyewitness descriptions: A problem for the match-to-description lineup foil selection strategy' (1994) 18 *Law and Human Behavior*, 527–541.

description is taken carefully by the first police officer who interviews a witness the problem of missing descriptors can be minimised.

An experimental study reported by Wells, Rydell and Seelau supports the argument that foils selected to match the witness's description of the culprit produce more reliable identification evidence.[24] Students witnessed a live staged theft and were asked to identify the perpetrator from an array of photographs in an immediate test. There were more correct identifications from culprit-description line-ups (67 per cent), than from suspect-resemblance line-ups (22 per cent). When the culprit was not present in the line-up, there were fewer mistaken identifications of foils from culprit-descriptions line-ups (32 per cent) than from suspect-resemblance line-ups (47 per cent), but this difference was not statistically significant. Two further studies failed to find any statistically significant difference in the rate of correct or mistaken identification between culprit-description and suspect-resemblance line-ups.[25] At present there is surprisingly little empirical evidence on which to base a recommendation that a match-to-description strategy is a superior method for constructing a line-up than a suspect-resemblance strategy.[26]

(ii) When the description of the culprit does not match the suspect

16.27 A culprit description strategy is more problematic if the suspect does not match the witness's description in respect of some attributes. Taking the example given above, what should a line-up administrator do if the suspect is a white male with long, dark hair but is 30 years old, rather than in his mid-forties? Perhaps the witness simply made a mistake estimating his age, or perhaps the suspect is innocent. In cases such as this it is recommended that a suspect resemblance strategy should be used for the features that do not match the description. In the current example, the foils should match the age of the suspect rather than the age in the description. The aim in constructing all line-ups should be to ensure that the suspect does not stand out in any way that would draw extra attention from the witness.

E. Methods of Formal Identification by Witness Selection

(1) Identity parades (live line-ups)

16.28 A sound understanding of the sensitivity and fairness of identification procedures requires evidence from real witnesses of crime. A problem with interpreting such data is that there is no standard by which to ascertain which police line-ups contained the culprit. However, analysing large data sets and testing to determine whether effects established in laboratory studies are replicated in field studies can add confidence to the interpretation of the data. Three studies of live line-ups conducted in England and Wales

---

[24] Wells, G.L., Rydell, S.M. and Seelau, E., 'The selection of distractors for eyewitness lineups' (1993) 78 *Journal of Applied Psychology*, 835–844.
[25] Lindsay, Martin and Webber, (1994), cited above at n.23; Tunnicliff, J.L. and Clark, S.E., 'Selecting foils for identification lineups: Matching suspects or descriptions?' (2000) 24 *Law and Human Behavior*, 231–258.
[26] Wells *et al*, (1998), cited above at n.8, 632.

under PACE Code D show remarkable consistency.[27] Approximately 40 per cent of witnesses identified the suspect, approximately 40 per cent of witnesses did not make any identification, either because they were not sure or because they judged the culprit not to be in the line-up, and 20 per cent of witnesses made a mistaken identification of an innocent foil. The known mistaken identifications were made despite the witness having been cautioned that the person they saw 'may or may not' be present in the line-up. Archival data collected by the police from 1,776 identity parades showed that the suspect was identified in 48 per cent of cases, but did not distinguish non-identifications from identification of a foil.[28] An archival analysis of 58 live line-ups conducted in US criminal cases found that the suspect was identified in 50 per cent of cases, a foil was identified in 24 per cent of cases and the witness was unable to make an identification or rejected the lineup in 26 per cent of cases.[29]

Valentine *et al* examined the effect of a range of estimator variables on the outcome of **16.29** identification attempts made by approximately 600 witnesses who viewed over 300 live line-ups organized by the Metropolitan Police during the investigation of criminal cases.[30] The suspect was more likely to be identified if the witness was younger than 30, the suspect was a white European (rather than African–Caribbean), the witness gave a detailed description, and (s)he viewed the culprit for over a minute and made a fast decision at the line-up. There were no independent, statistically reliable effects of the use of a weapon during the incident, cross-race identification or of the delay before the identification attempt. However, the data did suggest that the proportion of witnesses who identified the suspect was higher for identifications made after a very short delay (less than one week after the offence). 65 per cent of witnesses identified the suspect from line-ups held within 0–7 days, while only 38 per cent of witnesses identified the suspect in line-ups held 8 days or more after the incident. Pike *et al* (2002) also reported an effect of witness age, no effect of the use of a weapon during a crime, and no effect of cross-race identification on the outcome of live line-ups.[31]

(2) Photospreads

Most research on eyewitness identification has focused on the use of photographs to **16.30** obtain formal identification evidence, because this procedure is widely used in the USA and Canada. The typical format is to present the witness with six photographs simultaneously arranged in two rows of three images in a single array. Behrman and Davey's

---

[27] Slater, A., *Identification parades: A scientific evaluation*, London: Police Research Group (Police Research Award Scheme), Home Office, 1994; Valentine, T., Pickering, A. and Darling, S., 'Characteristics of eyewitness identification that predict the outcome of real lineups' (2003) 17 *Applied Cognitive Psychology*, 969–993; Wright, D. B. and McDaid, A. T., 'Comparing system and estimator variables using data from real lineups' (1996) 10 *Applied Cognitive Psychology*, 75–84.

[28] See Table 1 in Pike, G., Brace, N. and Kyman, S., *The visual identification of suspects: procedures and practice*, Briefing note 2/02, Policing and Reducing Crime Unit, Home Office Research Development and Statistics Directorate, 2002 (*http://www.homeoffice.gov.uk/rds/prgbriefpubs1.html*).

[29] Behrman, B. W. and Davey, S. L. 'Eyewitness identification in actual criminal cases: An archival analysis' (2001) 25 *Law and Human Behavior*, 475–491.

[30] Valentine, Pickering and Darling (2003), cited above at n.27.

[31] Pike, Brace and Kyman (2002), cited above at n.28.

archival analysis of eyewitness identification in American criminal cases included an analysis of the outcome of 289 photographic line-ups.[32] They found that 48 per cent of witnesses identified the suspect. In common with the British studies cited above, there was no effect of the presence of a weapon in the crime on the likelihood of the suspect being identified. There was an effect of delay prior to the identification. Line-ups held within 7 days of the incident produced a higher rate of identifications of the suspect (64 per cent) than line-ups held after 8 days or more (33 per cent). Although Valentine *et al*[32a] reported a non-significant effect of delay in the whole sample of live line-ups in London, the delays involved were much longer. Most live line-ups were held between one and three months after the event. As noted above, a comparison similar to that made by Behrman and Davey showed a similar effect of delay. However, in contrast to the British data, Behrman and Davey did find an effect of cross-race identification in their sample of US photograph line-ups. 60 per cent of witnesses of the same ethnicity as the suspect identified the suspect, compared to 45 per cent of witnesses of different ethnicity.

16.31 There is an extensive experimental literature of laboratory studies of identification from photospreads, which includes several comprehensive reviews.[33] The importance of using non-biased instructions has been demonstrated.[34] An example of good practice would be to include the warning to the witness, specified in PACE Code D, that 'the person you saw may or may not be present'. It has been recommended that the photospread should be administered blind. That is to say the administrator should not know who is the suspect in the lineup.[35] Not only is it good scientific practice to keep the administrator blind to the suspect's identity, but it removes all possible suspicion of police malpractice. In addition to these two principles of best practice, two significant methods to enhance the reliability of identification from photospreads have emerged from this literature. Reference has already been made to the proposal that the photographs should be presented one at a time, in a *sequential presentation*, rather than simultaneously.[36] The argument that foils in a line-up should be chosen to match the witness's description of the culprit rather than selected to match the appearance of the suspect (i.e. a *culprit-description* strategy rather than a *suspect-resemblance* strategy) has also been outlined above.[37]

(3) Video identification

(i) VIPER and PROMAT

16.32 Video identification has become the primary method for obtaining formal identification evidence in the UK since the introduction of a new code of practice (see paragraph 16.04 above). Two different IT systems are in widespread use in British police forces. VIPER™ (Video Identification Procedure Electronic Recording) was developed by West Yorkshire

---

[32] Behrman and Davey (2001), cited above at n.29.   [32a] Cited above at n.27.
[33] Wells (1993), cited above at n.15; Wells *et al* (1998), cited above at n.8.
[34] Steblay, N., 'Social influence in eyewitness recall: A meta-analytic review of lineup instruction effects' (1997) 21 *Law and Human Behavior*, 283–298.
[35] Wells *et al* (1998), cited above at n.8.   [36] Lindsay and Wells (1985), cited above at n.17.
[37] Luus and Wells (1991), cited above at n.22; Wells, Rydell and Seelau (1993), cited above at n.24.

Police and is used by approximately half of the police forces in England and Wales and by all forces in Scotland.[38] PROMAT™ (Profile Matching) is used by approximately half of the police forces in England and Wales. Both systems produce similar formats of video line-up but use different databases of foils. In both systems line-ups consist of 15-second clips of each line-up member shown sequentially. The sequence starts with a head-and-shoulders shot of the person looking directly at the camera, who slowly turns their head to present a full right profile to the camera. The person then slowly rotates their head to present a full left profile to the camera. Finally the person returns to looking directly into the camera in a full-face pose.

16.33 Each person is shown one at a time in a line-up with a minimum of eight foils. The witness must view the entire line-up twice before making any identification. As is the case for a live line-up, the foils should resemble the suspect, the witness must be cautioned that the person they saw 'may or may not' be present and be told that if they cannot make a positive identification they should say so.

16.34 VIPER and PROMAT differ most in the nature of their databases. VIPER is run from a national centre. Images are collated and quality-checked to ensure that they meet stringent requirements of standardization. Currently there are approximately 12,000 images in the database, which are available to all users to select for inclusion in their line-ups. The police forces that use PROMAT collect and share their own database of foils. Conditions for recording video images is standardized but the specifications are less stringent than for VIPER.

(ii) Research on VIPER

16.35 VIPER has been the subject of research which showed that VIPER video line-ups from real criminal cases were fairer to the suspects than conventional 'live' line-ups,[39] and that VIPER video line-ups were equally fair to white European and African–Caribbean suspects.[40] In these studies, participants (known as 'mock witnesses') were shown a set of videos of VIPER line-ups or a set of photographs of a live line-up held as part of the investigation of the case. For each line-up they were given the first description of the offender made by the original witness. The mock witnesses were required to guess, on the basis of the witness's description, which line-up member was the suspect. Therefore, a 'mock witness' simulates a witness who (a) has no memory of the culprit at the time of the identification procedure; (b) can remember the description they previously gave to the police, and (c) nevertheless, makes an identification from the line-up. If the line-up is perfectly fair, and all members fit the description, the mock witness would have no basis on which to make their selection and would merely have to guess who is the suspect. Therefore, if a large number of the mock witnesses are asked to make a selection they

---

[38] The Police and Criminal Evidence Act (1984), and therefore Code D covering identification procedures, does not apply in Scotland. Nevertheless, all Scottish police forces now have the VIPER system available in their area.

[39] Valentine, T. and Heaton, P., 'An evaluation of the fairness of police lineups and video identifications' (1999) 13 *Applied Cognitive Psychology*, S59–S72.

[40] Valentine, T., Harris, N., Colom Piera, A. and Darling, S., 'Are police video identifications fair to African–Caribbean suspects?' (2003) 17 *Applied Cognitive Psychology*, 459–476.

would select the suspect on 11 per cent of occasions (1 in 9) from each line-up, because the line-ups all contained a suspect and eight foils. Using this procedure Valentine and Heaton (1999) found that 25 per cent of mock witnesses (1 in 4) chose the suspect in the live line-ups. The mock witnesses were able to identify the suspect in the live line-ups more frequently than by chance (25 per cent vs 11 per cent), notwithstanding the fact that, by definition, they had no memory of the culprit. Therefore, the structure of the live line-ups (i.e. the selection of foils) showed some bias against the suspect. In comparison, 15 per cent of mock witnesses selected the suspect from the videos of VIPER line-ups, which also consisted of one suspect and eight foils. Statistical tests showed that the VIPER line-ups were significantly fairer than the live parades (15 per cent vs 25 per cent), and the VIPER line-ups were not significantly less fair than expected by chance (15 per cent vs 11 per cent).

16.36 Previous data from real cases suggested that live line-ups may be less fair to ethnic minorities than to white Europeans.[41] Therefore, Valentine, Harris, Colom Piera and Darling (2003) compared the fairness of VIPER line-ups of African–Caribbeans and of white Europeans using equal numbers of mock witnesses from both ethnic backgrounds. The VIPER parades were found to be equally fair to suspects of both ethnic groups, with very similar measures of fairness to Valentine and Heaton's data for VIPER line-ups.

(iii) Benefits of video identification as against live parades

16.37 Video identification has a number of important benefits compared to live line-ups. First, use of video can dramatically reduce the delay before an identification can be organized. Live line-ups have been subject to long delays to enable a selection of appropriate foils to be available to stand on a line-up (typically of 1–3 months).[42] In contrast VIPER can produce a video line-up for most suspects and transmit it via a secure network within two hours of request.

16.38 Second, approximately 50 per cent of live line-ups are cancelled, for example, due to failure of a bailed suspect to attend, failure of the witness to attend, or lack of suitable volunteers. Cancellations contribute to a further increase in delay before the witness can view a line-up. Since the introduction of video identification, the proportion of procedures cancelled has fallen to around 5 per cent.[43] Third, availability of a large database of video clips from which to select foils can make line-ups fairer to the suspect as demonstrated in the research discussed above. Fourth, use of video is less threatening to victims, who no longer have to attend an identification suite where their attacker might be physically present. A further advantage is that video equipment can be taken to a witness who is unable to attend the police station. In a recent case, Abigail Witchalls, a victim of an attack who was left paralysed, was able to view a video line-up from her hospital bed, and a suspect was eliminated from the inquiry as a result.[44]

---

[41] Wright and McDaid (1996), cited above at n.27.
[42] Valentine, Pickering and Darling (2003), cited above at n.27.
[43] Pike, G., Kemp, R., Brace, N., Allen, J. and Rowlands, G., 'The effectiveness of video identification parades' (2000) 8 *Proceedings of the British Psychological Society*, 44.
[44] *http://www.guardian.co.uk/crime/article/0,2763,1473862,00.html*, downloaded 31 August 2005.

(iv) Naturally sequential presentation

Video identification naturally yields a sequential presentation. Sequential presentation **16.39** can reduce mistaken identifications when coupled with appropriate viewing instructions (see paragraph 16.20). Under sequential viewing instructions the witness is required to make a decision after viewing each person as to whether he or she is the culprit. However, the current PACE code of practice does not allow any advantage of sequential presentation to be realized because it requires witnesses to view the entire line-up twice before making any decision. Thus, the question arises of whether video identification procedures could be improved by allowing strict sequential viewing instructions to be used.

My colleagues and I have examined this issue in a current research project.[45] When **16.40** combining the sequential viewing instructions with culprit-absent VIPER video line-ups, there was a reduction in mistaken identifications of foils, but the effect was not statistically significant. However, there was a significant reduction in the number of correct identifications from culprit-present video line-ups with sequential viewing instructions. The sequential instructions appear to reduce the rate of choosing from witnesses overall, and therefore suppress correct identifications as much as, if not more so than, incorrect identifications. In conclusion, we do not recommend combining sequential viewing instruction with video identification.[46]

(v) Moving images compared with stills

As part of the same project we have also investigated whether the moving images used in **16.41** video identification contribute to its success compared to single full-face images, as frequently used in American photospreads. Intuition suggests that witnesses might be more likely to be able to identify a culprit from a moving image that allows the face to be seen from a variety of angles. However, results from a staged-incident experiment using VIPER line-ups showed that this was not the case. The rate of correct identification from culprit-present video line-ups was the same for moving clips (as described in paragraph 16.32 above) as for static full-face images presented on a monitor. When the culprit was not in the line-up, there were fewer mistaken identifications of foils from moving clips than from still images. Thus the use of moving video clips improves the fairness of line-ups without affecting the sensitivity of the procedure.

(vi) Research comparing selection of foils by culprit description and by suspect resemblance

A final aspect of this project is to investigate whether video identifications can be **16.42** improved by using a culprit-description strategy rather than a suspect-resemblance strategy to select the foils. This work is continuing, but early results suggest that both strategies tend to result in similar line-ups being selected from the VIPER database.

---

[45] We acknowledge funding from the Nuffield Foundation for this project.
[46] Valentine, T., Darling, S. & Memon, A., 'Do sequential viewing instructions and moving images increase the reliability of police video identification procedures?' (in preparation).

F. Non-selection Modes of Identification

(1) Street identifications, showups and confrontations

16.43 In both the USA and the UK a person detained in an area where a crime has been recently reported (e.g. within a few hours) and who fits a general description given, may be shown to the witness to enable an identification to be made (see paragraph 16.11 above). This procedure is known as a showup in the USA and a street identification in the UK. A showup or street identification is used when there is insufficient evidence to arrest the suspect without a positive identification. In England and Wales, if the suspect has been arrested any identification must follow PACE Code D, and a video identification procedure would usually be carried out. Following a positive street identification, a video identification should normally be used to obtain identifications by any other witnesses. In effect, a street identification is a confrontation between the witness and a potential suspect. A confrontation, in which a witness is allowed to see a single suspect who has been arrested, is available under PACE Code D as a method of last resort. A confrontation may be used if the suspect refuses to cooperate with any other method of obtaining formal identification evidence.

(i) Street identification and PACE Code D

16.44 If there is only one witness, a positive street identification may provide the main evidence against a suspect. Therefore, a question arises over the reliability of street identifications. The procedure can be highly suggestive, as the witness may be aware that the police suspect the person they see. Furthermore a street identification provides no test of witness memory as there is no possibility of a witness making an identification that is demonstrably mistaken, as may occur if a witness picks a foil from a video identification. PACE Code D (2004) contains guidance for conducting street identifications, including the instruction that 'care should be taken not to direct the witness's attention to any individual unless, taking into account all the circumstances, this cannot be avoided' (paragraph 3.2). It is not clear how this recommendation is implemented when the police have already stopped a suspect. In *K v Director of Public Prosecutions*[47] a conviction for robbery was overturned on the grounds that a street identification was suggestive. A police officer held a suspect close to a car window for the victim of a street robbery to identify him. The court took the view that there were sufficient grounds for arrest prior to the street identification and an identity parade should have been held instead of a street identification.

(ii) Research

16.45 There is very little research on street identifications or showups, despite evidence that these procedures are often used by the police. American estimates suggest that showups account for between 30 and 77 per cent of all identification procedures.[48] I am not aware of any formal estimate of the frequency of street identifications in the UK. Field data

---

[47] [2003] EWHC Admin 351.
[48] Steblay, N., Dysart, S., Fulero, S. and Lindsay, R. C. L., 'Eyewitness accuracy rates in police showup and lineup presentations: A meta-analytic comparison' (2003) 27 *Law and Human Behavior*, 523–540.

from the USA gives a conflicting picture of the outcome of showups conducted by the police. Gonzalez, Ellsworth and Pembroke report that from a sample of 224 identification procedures recorded by a police officer, 172 were showups and 52 were photospreads. An identification was made in 22 per cent of the showups and 56 per cent of the photospreads.[49] They also found in laboratory studies that the identification rate from showups was lower than from photographic line-ups. In contrast Behrman and Davey[50] found higher identification rates from showups than from photospreads in their archival study of identification in cases in the USA. From 284 photographic line-ups, 48 per cent of witnesses made an identification. From 258 showups, 77 per cent of witnesses made an identification. Laboratory studies of showups, which with the exception of the study by Gonzalez *et al* (1993) involved presentation of a photograph in the showup, generally found lower rates of identification from showups than from photospreads (27 per cent vs 54 per cent).[51]

16.46 The comparison between showups and photospreads reveals conflicting results in the few data that are available. However, the important issue to appreciate is that all identifications in showups are forensically significant. The person identified is always the suspect, will often not have an alibi by virtue of the fact that they have been detained in the relevant area shortly after a crime has been committed, and will fit a general description provided by the witness. In contrast we know that mistaken identifications frequently occur from photospreads and live line-ups, because many are identifications of a foil which are known to be a mistake on behalf of the witness and have no consequences for the person identified. In summary, evidential use of street identifications should be treated with caution. However, the reliability of street identifications is an issue that would benefit from further research data.

(2) Dock identifications

16.47 Under Scots law an identification of the defendant in the dock made by a witness called to give evidence at the trial can constitute formal identification evidence. Identification evidence, however, requires corroboration under Scots law. The use of dock identifications was recently challenged in *James Holland v. HMA*.[52] James Holland was convicted on two charges of assault and robbery. In both cases he was first identified from photographs shown to a witness by the police. Subsequently, at the direction of the court in a preliminary hearing, an identity parade was organized. There was one principal witness in each case, both of whom were the victims of an assault. In the first offence the witness identified two foils from the line-up. The police told her that she 'had not done too well'. However, the victim's son, whose arrival home prompted the robbers to flee, identified James Holland at the identity parade. In the other offence, the witness picked a foil but was unaware that he had made a mistaken identification. At the trial both witnesses, who had failed to identify the accused at the identity parade, were invited to identify the

---

[49] Gonzalez, R., Ellsworth, P. and Pembroke, M., 'Response biases in lineups and showups' (1993) 64 *Journal of Personality and Social Psychology*, 525–537.
[50] Behrman and Davey (2001), cited above at n.29.
[51] Steblay, Dysart, Fulero and Lindsay (2003), cited above at n.48.   [52] [2005] UKPC D1.

accused in the dock. Both made positive identifications, on which the prosecution case relied.

16.48 James Holland's conviction was upheld at the first appeal. Subsequently he appealed to the Privy Council on the grounds that he had been denied a fair trial. In the judgment the principle of using dock identifications was upheld, but the appeal was allowed on the grounds that the prosecution failed to disclose exculpatory information.

G. The Relationship between Eyewitness Confidence and Accuracy

16.49 Evidence shows that the confidence of a witness is probably the most important factor that determines whether an identification will be believed by a jury.[53] In the past psychologists have argued, from the available experimental evidence, that the confidence of an eyewitness bears little or no relationship to their accuracy. Recent research has given us a more sophisticated understanding of the confidence–accuracy relationship in eyewitness identification, and enabled conditions to be identified which optimize the confidence–accuracy relationship.

16.50 Many studies have examined the confidence–accuracy relationship amongst a group of participants who all viewed the same simulated crime or event in an experiment, and therefore all experienced similar viewing conditions. More recently, it has been discovered that if the participants experience a wide range of different viewing conditions, their confidence shows a moderately strong positive relationship with the accuracy of their eyewitness identification.[54]

16.51 It has been found that the relationship between confidence and accuracy is considerably higher amongst witnesses who identify somebody from a line-up than it is amongst people who make no identification from a line-up. For non-choosers the confidence–accuracy relationship is close to zero, but choosers show a moderately strong positive relationship.[55]

16.52 The two findings described in the paragraphs above suggest that the confidence of an eyewitness in court may be more diagnostic of identification accuracy than psychologists have previously believed. However there are still some very important reasons for caution. It should be stressed that the confidence–accuracy relationship is only moderate (a correlation coefficient of approximately 0.5). Therefore, confident but mistaken eyewitnesses may be encountered fairly frequently.

16.53 In a real investigation, the police routinely ask a witness when taking an initial statement whether they would recognize the man if they saw him again. A witness who expresses doubt at this stage is unlikely to attend an identification procedure. However, confidence

---

[53] See Wells *et al* (1998), cited above at n.8, for a brief review of this evidence.

[54] Lindsay, D. S., Read, J. D. and Sharma, K., 'Accuracy and confidence in person identification: The relationship is strong when witnessing conditions vary widely' (1998) 9 *Psychological Science*, 215–218.

[55] Sporer, S., Penrod, S., Read, D. and Cutler, B. L., 'Choosing, confidence and accuracy: A meta-analysis of the confidence–accuracy relations in eyewitness identification studies' (1995) 118 *Psychological Bulletin*, 315–327.

measured before an attempted identification is not as predictive of accurate identification as confidence measured immediately after the identification attempt.[56] This is one reason why it is good practice to take a clear statement of confidence from the witness immediately after the identification attempt and before the formal procedure has ended.

A very important research finding is that witness confidence is changeable and is influenced by information that the witness acquires after the original incident. Receiving feedback that the suspect has been identified, or that somebody else made the same identification will increase the witness's confidence in their identification. Not only does confirming feedback tend to make the witness more confident in their identification, but it also tends to inflate estimates of a range of testimony including how long the culprit was seen for, how close they were, how much attention the witness paid etc.[57] Furthermore, confirming post-identification feedback tends to make eyewitnesses overconfident. That is, they express more confidence in their identification than is warranted.[58] By the time a witness gives evidence in court they will have received confirming feedback, if only by virtue of the fact that they have been called upon to give evidence. The witness is unlikely to be asked to attend court if they had identified the wrong person. The effect of confidence malleability is particularly important in the cases that rely on dock identifications. **16.54**

H. Identification by Viewing CCTV Footage

CCTV images can be used in a number of ways for investigative and evidential purposes. One use, which we are all familiar with, is the release of CCTV footage to the media, in the hope that a member of the public will recognize the person in the footage as somebody they know. The results of psychological studies show that this can be an effective use of CCTV because people are extremely good at recognizing a highly familiar person across a variety of viewing and lighting conditions. Familiar people can be recognized from poor quality CCTV images with over 90 per cent accuracy.[59] David Copeland, the London nail bomber, was caught in 1999 after being recognized by a work colleague from broadcast CCTV images.[60] **16.55**

---

[56] For a review of pre-identification confidence and accuracy see Cutler, B. L. and Penrod, S. D., 'Forensically-relevant moderators of the relationship between eyewitness identification accuracy and confidence' (1989) 74 *Journal of Applied Psychology*, 650–652. For a review of post-identification confidence and accuracy see Bothwell, R. K., Deffenbacher, K. A. and Brigham, J.C., 'Correlations of eyewitness accuracy and confidence: Optimality hypothesis revisited' (1987) 72 *Journal of Applied Psychology*, 691–695.

[57] Wells G. L. and Bradfield, A. L., ' "Good you identified the suspect": Feedback to eyewitnesses distorts their reports of the witnessing experience' (1998) 66 *Journal of Applied Psychology*, 688–696.

[58] Semmler, C., Brewer, N. and Wells, G. L., 'Effects of postidentification feedback on eyewitness identification and nonidentification confidence' (2004) 89 *Journal of Applied Psychology*, 334–346.

[59] Bruce, V., Henderson, Z., Newman, C. and Burton, A. M., 'Matching identities of familiar and unfamiliar faces caught on CCTV images' (2001) 7 *Journal of Experimental Psychology: Applied*, 207–218; Burton, A. M., Wilson, S., Cowan, M. and Bruce, V., 'Face recognition in poor quality video: evidence from security surveillance' (1999) 10 *Psychological Science*, 243–248.

[60] *http://www.guardian.co.uk/bombs/Story/0,2763,338345,00.html*, downloaded 1 September 2005.

(1) Matching identities from CCTV

16.56 A more controversial, and scientifically less sound use of CCTV, is to use a CCTV image as identification evidence of a suspect who is not well known to the witness who makes the identification. Thus CCTV images may be presented in court with the prosecution case being that it is an image of the defendant. The defence case may be that the defendant is not the person in the image. However, the defendant will not be familiar to the members of the jury, with whom a decision of whether the CCTV image depicts the defendant ultimately lies. Psychological science shows that we are surprisingly poor at matching images, taken by different cameras, of an otherwise unfamiliar person. For example, Bruce *et al* asked participants to choose from an array of ten high-quality photographs the face that they thought matched a target face.[61] The photograph of the target was taken from a studio video recording made on the same day as the still photographs in the array. The available set of faces from which the arrays were selected consisted of 120 young, male, clean-shaven Caucasian police trainees supplied by the Home Office. The arrays consisted of faces judged to resemble each other so that selections could not be based on substantial differences in hairstyle, weight or age. When the viewpoint and facial expression of the target and the correct image in the array matched (i.e. a comparison is made under ideal conditions), participants only made the correct selection in 79 per cent of the arrays. Bruce *et al* conclude 'the implication of these findings is that courts must be aware that caution should be used when the impressions of resemblance are used to establish the identity of unfamiliar people, *even when the quality of video tape is high*' (emphasis in the original).

16.57 The forensic implications of a separate study of recognition of faces from a poor-quality video, typical of that recorded by a commercial security CCTV system, was summarized as follows: '. . . identification of these types of video sequences is very unreliable, unless the viewer happens to know the target person'.[62] Referring to the performance of participants unfamiliar with target faces, Burton *et al* state: 'although there were reliable differences on the judgements between the targets that were present and those that were not present, differences were comparatively small'. Furthermore, the same study showed that police officers, with experience in forensic identification and an average of over 13 years' service, performed as poorly as other participants unfamiliar with the targets. A police officer is no more likely to correctly identify somebody from video than anybody else who has a similar level of familiarity with the target.

16.58 A study conducted in our laboratory examined people's ability to match video images of a person to somebody physically present in the room.[63] This comparison occurs when the jury watches a video sequence in a court in the presence of the defendant. Participants (n = 198) matched a previously unfamiliar actor filmed on high-quality video with a single live 'defendant'. The video, which lasted 40 seconds, displayed views of each

---

[61] Bruce, V., Henderson, Z., Greenwood, K., Hancock, P., Burton, A. M. and Miller, P., 'Verification of face identities from images captured on video' (1999) 5 *Journal of Experimental Psychology: Applied*, 339–360.

[62] Burton, Wilson, Cowan, and Bruce (1999), cited above at n.59.

[63] Davis, J. & Valentine, T., (in preparation).

actor's face and body from a number of different angles. In half of the trials the defendant was not the person in the video. The overall error rate was approximately 20 per cent (22 per cent target present; 17 per cent target absent). That is, one in five participants was mistaken under ideal conditions when there was no requirement to remember the culprit's face, and there was no time pressure. The video sequence could be played up to three times or until the participant made their decision. Error rates varied considerably across different actors. In one case 44 per cent of participants (7 out of 16) incorrectly judged an 'innocent defendant' to be the actor in the video sequence. Inspection of the photographs of the two men involved in this comparison shows that they have similar hair length, hair texture and face shape; however they do not closely resemble each other.

Other studies have found similarly high error rates in identifying previously unfamiliar **16.59** persons from CCTV. Davies and Thasen report identification accuracy between 15 and 30 per cent with false alarm rates between 60 and 65 per cent, showing that people are particularly prone to making a mistaken identification when the person they expect to identify is not present.[64]

Why is recognition of familiar faces so robust but recognition of previously unfamiliar **16.60** faces so vulnerable? It is known that familiar faces are better recognised from their internal features (eyes, nose, mouth). When looking at unfamiliar faces more reliance is placed on the external features (hair, face shape).[65] The configuration of the internal features is a more reliable cue to identity across different views and lighting conditions. When recognizing unfamiliar faces we are more likely to rely on superficial similarities that are changeable (e.g. hairstyles, hairline).

(2) Identification by police officers

Images from CCTV are often circulated amongst police officers in the expectation that **16.61** the person to be identified might previously have had some contact with the police and might be recognized. This practice has obvious investigative value in suggesting an identity for an unknown suspect. However, use of an identification obtained in this manner as evidence in court, raises the issue of how reliable it would be. The first point to be made is that in England and Wales identification by a police officer from CCTV is outside the scope of PACE Code D. A record of the formal identification is usually kept and is available to the court. However, typically there is no record of when the police officer first saw the CCTV or a still taken from it, why the officer was asked to make a formal identification in the case, whether an identity was suggested to the officer prior to the 'identification' or whether the identification had been discussed with colleagues prior to the formal identification. All these issues are highly relevant to evaluating the reliability of the identification.

---

[64] Davies, G. and Thasen, S., 'Closed-circuit television: How effective an identification aid?' (2000) 91 *British Journal of Psychology*, 411–426; Henderson, Z., Bruce, V. and Burton, A. M., 'Matching the faces of robbers captured on video' (2001) 15 *Applied Cognitive Psychology*, 445–464.

[65] Ellis, H. D., Shepherd, J. W. and Davies, G. M., 'Identification of familiar and unfamiliar faces from internal and external features: some implications of theories of face recognition' (1979) 8 *Perception*, 431–439; Young, A. W., Hay, D. C., McWeeney, K. H., Flude, B. M. and Ellis, A. W., 'Matching familiar and unfamiliar faces on internal and external features' (1985) 14 *Perception*, 737–746.

16.62 A police officer is unlikely to be highly familiar with the person he or she recognises from CCTV. Typically, the identified person might have been stopped on one or two occasions, perhaps interviewed for 30 minutes once or twice and might have been seen during a court appearance. These encounters might occur over a period of a year or more. The science tells us that matching unfamiliar facial identities from CCTV can be error-prone. On the other hand, we know that a reliable identification of a familiar person (e.g a work colleague) can be made even from poor quality CCTV. Where within this range of reliability does identification by a police officer lie in the circumstances described above?

16.63 There is little direct evidence of how familiar one has to be with a face to recognize the person reliably from CCTV. Bruce *et al* looked at matching performance for faces that had been familiarized by 30 seconds' or 1 minute's exposure of a wide range of different views of the face immediately before performing the matching task.[66] The task required matching of a target photograph to an array of 8–10 photographs. In half of the trials the target was not present in the array. There was little benefit from previous familiarization, except when two participants viewed the faces together and were encouraged to discuss the faces during familiarization. In these circumstances when matching *good quality images in the same view*, participants who had received the previous 'social' familiarization identified 98 per cent of targets and correctly rejected 68 per cent of 'target-absent' arrays. This compares to 81 per cent and 39 per cent respectively for participants who received no previous familiarization. In conclusion, previous brief social familiarization can enhance matching under ideal conditions with no memory load. However, even under these ideal conditions (good-quality video images in the same view) there is a substantial false alarm rate when the 'target' is not present in the array (32 per cent of responses). The conditions of familiarization (i.e. brief exposures immediately prior to identification) are very different from familiarization in the real world (longer exposures with very long delays). These differences make the research findings described difficult to generalize to the real world.

(3) Facial comparison by experts

16.64 In a case of disputed identification, can the identity of a person in a CCTV image be determined by an objective analysis of the facial image? The question often arises whether a facial image captured by CCTV is of the same person as a photograph of the suspect (e.g. an arrest photograph). In contrast to the situation in relation to identification by eyewitnesses, expert evidence is admissible in English courts in relation to analysis of facial images from CCTV.[67] There is no single method with an agreed procedure to compare the identity of two facial images. Facial image comparison (often referred to as 'facial mapping') refers to a number of techniques adopted by experts from a variety of different backgrounds.[68] The methods differ substantially in their approach and scientific rigour.

---

[66] Bruce, Henderson, Newman and Burton (2001), cited above at n.59.

[67] *Attorney General's Reference* (No. 2 of 2002) [2003] 1 Cr App R 321.

[68] For a brief description of methods of facial image comparison used by expert witnesses see Association of Chief Police Officers (ACPO) *National working practices in facial imaging 2003*, available from *http://www.acpo.police.uk/asp/policies/Data/garvin_facial_imaging_guidelines.doc* downloaded 30 September 2005.

No method of facial comparison can give absolute certainty that two images are of the **16.65** same person. For example, in the extreme it would be impossible to distinguish between identical twins from typical CCTV images. The major problem for anybody comparing facial images is that faces of different people can look very similar and yield very similar measures of facial proportions. The issue is made even more difficult because images of the same person can look very different under different lighting conditions and measurements are sensitive to slight differences in pose. In addition the quality of CCTV images available for comparison is often very poor. Thus, similarity cannot establish absolute identification, especially when the images to be compared are limited in the views available and in their quality. However, significant differences between facial images may provide exculpatory evidence.

There are three main approaches to facial comparison. Morphological comparison, **16.66** anthropometric comparison and video superimposition. Morphological comparison involves categorizing facial features according to their type or shape and counting the number of similar categorizations across the comparison images. For example, the face shape may be classified as elliptical, round, oval, etc. The facial profile may be jutting, forward curving, vertical etc.[69] The method is based upon subjective judgements of facial features. Anthropometric comparison involves comparing measurements of distances and angles between facial landmarks. Video superimposition involves wiping from one video image to another that has been scaled and rotated to provide the best match. Video superimposition can provide compelling graphics in court and is presented by expert witnesses in English courts. Its weakness is that it requires a human judgement of similarity with no treatment of error or of possible matches between faces of different people.

Any sound method of facial comparison should include three features. First, a formal **16.67** treatment of the error of measurement that arises due to the quality of the images, the reliability of the measurement process, differences between measurements taken by different people, error due to minor changes in pose, changes in lighting, etc. Second, comparison of the differences in measurements, or other data taken from the comparison images, with comparable data from an appropriate database of facial images. Are the differences between the two images in question less than the differences between the CCTV image and the faces in the database, who are known to be of a different person? Third, evaluation of the comparison between the images that is informed by both the error of measurement and comparison with the relevant database. Few facial comparisons presented by expert witnesses in English courts have all of these features.

Anthropometric measurement offers the best potential to meet these requirements. **16.68** Measurements can be taken from a set of images agreed to be of the same person (e.g. different frames in a CCTV clip) by more than one operator. These data can be used to estimate the error of measurement. Differences between the facial images for

---

[69] Iscan, M. Y., 'Introduction of techniques for photographic comparison: potential and problems,' in Iscan, Y. K. and Helmer, R. P. (eds), *Forensic Analysis of the skull: Craniofacial analysis reconstruction and identification*, New York: Wiley, 1993, 57–70.

comparison can be determined and their significance assessed in the light of the error estimate. Differences between the faces to be compared can be evaluated by comparing the disputed facial image (from CCTV) to a database of facial measurements, restricting the comparison to facial landmarks that could be measured in the forensically relevant comparison. If it is possible to find a match with a face from the database which is as good or better than the match between the CCTV image and the defendant, it would suggest that either the defendant is not the person in the CCTV image or the measurements that can be taken for comparison are not adequate to distinguish faces of different people.

16.69 The reliability of expert evidence on facial comparison was recently considered by the Court of Appeal in *R v Gray*.[70] A conviction for robbery was based partially on the evidence of a facial comparison expert who stated that facial characteristics of the accused provided 'strong support' for the identification of the robber from CCTV as the accused. At appeal the conviction was overturned. In the judgment, the court noted that there is no national database of facial characteristics or any accepted formula from which conclusions of the probability of occurrence of facial characteristics or their combinations can safely be drawn. In their absence estimates of probability or expressions of degree of support provided by a facial comparison expert must only be the subjective opinion of the witness. The court expressed doubt that, in the absence of a national database or agreed formula, opinions of probability or the strength of evidential support from a facial comparison should ever be expressed by an expert witness.

16.70 Subsequently, in *R v Gardner*[71] the Court of Appeal considered another case which concerned expert evidence on a facial comparison from CCTV images. Notwithstanding the judgment in *Gray* and despite quoting a long passage from it, the court held: 'there is no rule [. . .] that in cases such as the present an expert witness cannot go further than saying "there are the following similarities", leaving the ultimate decision to the jury, as opposed to the expert witness actually giving a view to the degree of probability of the images being the same'. In conclusion, the manner in which the courts treat expert evidence on facial comparison appears somewhat confused and will require further consideration.

I. Biometric use of Facial Images

16.71 The events of 11 September 2001 and subsequent terrorist attacks around the world have heightened concerns about personal identification especially for international travel. The UK government has commissioned trials of the feasibility of using facial images as a biometric in passports. The face is unique as a biometric because a facial image can be obtained remotely without the knowledge or cooperation of the person concerned. From November 2005 new biometric passports will be issued in the UK. The only biometric information they contain will be a digitized photograph.

---

[70] [2003] EWCA Crim 1001.   [71] [2004] EWCA Crim 1639; [2004] JCL 372.

Media reports can give the impression that face recognition by computer has reached a **16.72** level of development that makes it highly reliable. However, the reality is very different. The state of the art in face verification (i.e. is this the same person as in the photograph?) is about 90 per cent accurate verification with a 1 per cent false acceptance rate.[72] This means that 10 per cent of airline passengers would not have their identity confirmed. Even if a failure rate of only 1 per cent could be obtained in face verification, it would still pose severe practical difficulties in screening international airline passengers at a busy airport. Face identification (is this person one of the targets on a wanted list?) is even more problematic. With a small database (800) under favourable conditions about 85 per cent correct identification can be achieved. However, this rate falls in direct proportion to the size of the database to be searched. Changes in illumination and pose between images, and images obtained under outdoor illumination, pose particular challenges to machine face recognition.[73] Although pose and lighting might be controlled to some extent in passport photographs and at the airport check-in, an additional problem will be to verify and identify faces from images that may be several years out of date.

In practice automatic face recognition systems may be used to screen large numbers of **16.73** facial images, leaving the final decision to a human operator. The weakness of such a system is that the psychological science demonstrates that humans are prone to error in matching facial identity of unfamiliar people from images taken with different cameras. We do not yet have the technology to take the human error out of facial recognition. It is debatable whether a facial image alone will ever provide sufficient information to support reliable automatic recognition. For this reason, a current research area is to combine automatic face recognition with some other biometric such as voice or gait.

J. Conclusions and Recommendations

Mistaken identification has a long and dishonourable tradition in the criminal justice **16.74** system. In England and Wales some legal safeguards have been introduced, principally through the Police and Criminal Evidence Act 1984 and its associated and updated code of practice for identification (Code D). In the USA, where there is strong evidence of many wrongful convictions from mistaken identification, the first very tentative steps towards introducing some safeguards are only just beginning. Examples of poor practice are still commonplace in both the USA and the UK. Widespread evidential use of street identifications (or showups) is a matter for concern. Continuing judicial support for dock identifications in Scotland contradicts 35 years of intensive scientific study of eyewitness identification.

Technology for facial identification has developed rapidly in the last five years. The **16.75** adoption of video identification procedures in England, Wales and Scotland provided a good example of best practice, which was informed by research findings. Video

---

[72] Zhao, W., Chellappa, R., Phillips, P.J. and Rosenfeld, A., 'Face recognition: A literature survey' (2003) 35 *ACM Computing Surveys*, 399–458.
[73] Ibid.

identification will improve the reliability of eyewitness identification evidence because it makes available a larger database of appropriate foils, and can dramatically reduce delay prior to an identification attempt. However, technology also brings with it an increased risk of mistaken identification. Evidential use for identification of images from ubiquitous CCTV cameras in the UK creates new possibilities of mistaken identification. In England, a case of disputed identification from CCTV has already been overturned on appeal.

16.76 Development of identification procedures should be informed by relevant experimental evidence. The current code of practice should be extended to include procedures for identification from CCTV by police officers or other witnesses who may be able to make an identification because the suspect is known to them.

16.77 Wells *et al* (1998)[74] made two recommendations that could easily be accommodated within revisions to PACE Code D. First, the line-up administrator should not know the identity of the suspect. Second, a clear statement of confidence should be obtained from the witness immediately after they make their response to the line-up.

16.78 Use of live line-ups made it difficult in the past for the line-up administrator to be 'blind' to the identity of the suspect.[75] However, now that most identification procedures are conducted on video it would be easy to implement blind testing. We routinely use blind testing in our laboratory when administering VIPER line-ups. In the presence of the accused's legal representative, the witness could choose at random from a number of DVDs that have the line-up recorded with the suspect in a different position on each. This is current best practice. Therefore, nobody present will know in which position the suspect will appear. The witness watches one screen. Everybody else present watches a different screen. The two monitors should be placed back to back, so that nobody can see more than one screen. The operator's screen is covered so that only the number identifying which position in the line-up is being presented and any on-screen controls can be seen. The line-up is administered in the normal way. The legal representative can see that the line-up administrator cannot see when the suspect is on screen. Any possibility of anybody giving any non-verbal cues to the identity of the suspect is eliminated. When the witness makes an identification or rejects the line-up a clear statement of confidence is obtained and recorded in the presence of the legal representative. Only after this statement is recorded and the witness has left the room, should the cover obscuring the image on the operator's screen be removed. The legal representative can see the image and the outcome of the identification should be recorded in his/her presence. This procedure would be very cheap and easy to implement, it would demonstrate to all concerned that there is no possibility of unconscious bias in the administration of the line-up, and it would record a clear statement of witness confidence before there was any possibility of influence from post-identification feedback or other information. The case from psychological science for amending PACE Code D in this minor way is compelling.

---

[74] Cited above at n.8.

[75] Davies, G. M. and Valentine, T., 'Codes of practice for identification' (1999) 7 *Expert Evidence*, 59–65.

Further Reading

Scheck, B., Neufeld, P. and Dwyer, J., *Actual innocence: Five days to execution and other dispatches from the wrongly convicted*, New York: Doubleday, 2000.

Wells, G. L., Small, M., Penrod, S., Malpass, R. S., Fulero, S. M. and Brinacombe, C. A. E., 'Eyewitness Identification Procedures: Recommendations for line-ups and photo spreads' (1998) 22 *Law and Human Behavior*, 603–653.

Valentine, T., Pickering, A. and Darling, S., 'Characteristics of eyewitness identification that predict the outcome of real lineups' (2003) 17 *Applied Cognitive Psychology*, 969–993

Valentine, T. and Heaton, P., 'An evaluation of the fairness of police lineups and video identifications' (1999) 13 *Applied Cognitive Psychology*, S59–S72.

Bruce, V., Henderson, Z., Newman, C. and Burton, A. M., 'Matching identities of familiar and unfamiliar faces caught on CCTV images' (2001) 7 *Journal of Experimental Psychology: Applied*, 207–218.

Tim Valentine is Professor of Psychology at Goldsmiths College, University of London. He has authored or co-authored more than 50 scientific articles on the psychology of face recognition, eyewitness identification and memory for people's names. He edited *Cognitive and Computational Aspects of Face Recognition* (Routledge, 1995), co-authored *The Cognitive Psychology of Proper Names* (Routledge, 1996), and is a member of the editorial board of *Applied Cognitive Psychology*. His recent work includes research on video identification procedures, now widely used in the UK. He works as an expert witness on issues related to eyewitness identification and facial identification from CCTV.

Editors' Note

It might be thought that, following Lord Devlin's report concerning the inherent dangers of evidence of facial identification, the judgment of the five-judge Court of Appeal in *R v Turnbull* and, latterly, the use of technology for the composition and conduct of 'video' identification parades and yet another revised edition of Code D to the Police and Criminal Evidence Act 1984, the days of mistaken identification are over. Sadly, this is not the case and, together with Chapter 17, this chapter, replete as it is with references to the latest cutting edge research (much of it led by the author), amply demonstrates that the need for care and vigilance where an identification is disputed (or, even, where it is not, in view of the continuing risk of false confessions) is as great as it ever was.

17

IMPROVING VISUAL IDENTIFICATION PROCEDURES UNDER PACE CODE D

David Wolchover and Anthony Heaton-Armstrong

A. Introduction

Although the pursuit of criminal justice increasingly depends upon forensic science a **17.01** crucial instrument in the detection and prosecution of offenders remains that of establishing the identity of the culprit by visual, which is to say facial, recognition. The procedures regulating visual identification of suspects are contained in Code D, *The Code of Practice for the Identification of Persons by Police Officers*, issued under the Police and Criminal Evidence Act 1984 (PACE) originally in 1985 and subsequently re-issued through a number of editions, most recently on 1 January 2006, although the latest version introduces changes to the much reworked, 2004, edition which are only of marginal relevance. Since 2003 video identification procedure has virtually been the only method allowed by the code for testing whether a known suspect is the culprit.[1] In recent

---

[1] For a comprehensive account of video identification procedure under the Code see Wolchover, D., *Visual Identification Procedures Under PACE Code D*, accessible through a link from

years development of the code and of investigative procedures in step with it have been driven by joint interaction between the police, the academic world, the legal profession, and Home Office experts, to the point that it is now reckoned by some commentators to be the world's leading manual on the subject. However, despite just cause for satisfaction with such an excellent document there is always room for improvement. The purpose of this chapter is to offer suggestions for improving the form and application of a number of code procedures but this implies no assumption that there are not other features of the code which may require improvement.

B. Methods of Eliciting First Descriptions

17.02 A physical description of the culprit is not only a basic requirement of crime detection but will also furnish an invaluable check against retrospective self-corroboration where a witness makes a positive identification following an arrest. Surprisingly, it was only as recently as 1995 that it became obligatory under Code D to make a record of a 'first description' prior to the participation of the witness in a formal identification procedure (D3.1). The method of drawing out the description will be crucial in assessing its value. The 'cognitive interview', involving an invitation to directed free recall, is now widely regarded as much more efficient in eliciting reliable detail than value-laden questioning.[2] However, it requires the luxury of time and so hardly works best in the police operations room or when officers are setting off with a witness on the look-out for the perpetrator in the immediate aftermath of some street crime. Inappropriate questioning on the hoof can undermine the mental processes of encoding, storage and retrieval, particularly through the phenomenon of *overshadowing*, which research suggests can cause interference by a verbal description with the memory trace of the actual person observed. Suitable techniques in the training of emergency telephone operators and patrol officers alike need to be developed and applied, yet although this has been urged from time to time[3] very little has so far been done to implement such a programme. It follows that Code D contains no provisions designed to avoid the dangers implicit in poor technique.

C. Perusing the Photographic Rogues' Gallery

(1) Hard albums and electronic compilations

17.03 Where the police have no known suspect to a crime and are working blind in the hunt for the perpetrator it has been the practice for as long as the police have kept a photographic 'rogues' gallery' to show witnesses a variety of photographs of relevant known offenders in the hope that the culprit might be recognized. To a greater or lesser extent locally held

---

http://www.7BellYard.co.uk. For a recent general study of the law relating to identification generally see Bogan, P., *Identification: Investigation, trial and scientific evidence*, London: Legal Action Group, 2004.

[2] For a good general summary with comprehensive bibliography see Clifford, B.R. and Memon, A., 'Obtaining detailed testimony: the cognitive interview,' in Heaton-Armstrong, A., Shepherd, S. and Wolchover, D. (eds.), *Analysing Witness Testimony*, London: Blackstone Press, 1999, 146–161.

[3] McKenzie, I. and Dunk, P., 'Identification parades: psychological and practical realities,' in ibid, at 183–184.

albums have been maintained in categories. The use of 'hard' albums has now commonly given way to computerized presentation by means of DVD compilations made up from databases of the images of known offenders. The use of compilations has facilitated the narrowing down of possible suspects to those corresponding to the witness's description as well as to those within other relevant categories, something which was not practicable in the past when hard albums were used. The Code expressly prohibits the showing of still photographs 'if the identity of the suspect is known to the police and the suspect is available to take part in a video identification. . . .'[4] Where there is no known suspect the showing of photographs is regulated by Annex E to the Code.[5]

(2) Recording the perusal

Whether or not an identification is made, a record must be kept of the showing of **17.04** photographs on forms provided for the purpose.[6] This includes anything said by the witness about the identification or the conduct of the procedure, any reasons it was not practicable to comply with any of the provisions of Code D governing the showing of photographs and the name and rank of the supervising officer.[7] The supervising officer must inspect and sign the record as soon as practicable.[8] It is noteworthy that these provisions do not preclude audio- or video-recording of the showing of photographs, although the common practice is to maintain only a written record. A written record will not pick up nuances of vocal intonation and inflexion or the subtleties of facial expression and body language of the kind which may prove significant in the context of assessing the validity of a formal identification made later and the weight to be given to the witness's evidence in court. There is therefore a very strong argument for making it compulsory to video-record the procedure, more particularly to compensate for the necessary absence of any prospective defence legal representative.

(3) Restricting the number of photographs perused or the exposure time to each

Research has shown a negative correlation between the accuracy of identification and the **17.05** number of photographs inspected.[9] As the number of faces inspected by the witness increases the greater will be the extent to which those images interfere with the witness's memory of the culprit's face, the phenomenon of overshadowing. Similarly, viewing faces in photographs can create some confusion in memory that interferes with the ability to make a subsequent identification.[10] Annex E provides that witnesses must be told that they should not make a decision until they have viewed at least twelve photographs.[11] A

---

[4] D3.3. It has been pointed out that the showing of stills is permissible if a known suspect is unavailable, although if resort has to be made to stills they ought to be shown in video format in conformity with D3.21 when a known suspect is not available: Bogan, P., cited above at n.1, para 3.12, citing *R v Kitchen* [1994] CrimLR 684 where the suspect had escaped from custody and the equivalent provision under the 1991 edition (D2.18) was held to permit an identification by photographs.

[5] D3.3.   [6] Annex E.11.   [7] Ibid.   [8] Annex E.12.

[9] See Lindsay, R.C.L., Nosworthy, G.J., Martin, R. and Martynuck, C., 'Using mug shots to find suspects' (1994) 79 *Journal of Applied Psychology*, 121–130.

[10] Gorenstein, G.W. and Ellsworth, P., 'Effect of choosing an incorrect photograph and later identification by an eyewitness,' (1980) 65 *Journal of Applied Psychology*, 616–622.

[11] Annex E.5.

partial amelioration of the shortcomings alluded to above may be to restrict the total number of photographs selected for viewing, rather than allowing open-ended search through albums until a face is recognized. This would not necessarily mean fixing an absolute maximum but it is certainly feasible to reduce the number of photographs which are worth inspection. With Home Office funding the University of Aberdeen developed a system of coding witness descriptions to compile a relatively smaller number of photographs for inspection, leading to more accurate performance than was possible using the full albums.[12] In this way reduction in the number of photographs to be viewed may be achieved in practice without necessarily imposing any formal limit on the number. Paring down the gallery to this end would necessitate the witness being asked to provide as precise a verbal description of the facial features recalled as possible. It might be suggested that a likeness construct such as photofit or E-fit could be employed as a first stage. Then, using the construct, a trained officer could conduct a trawl through the available albums picking out only those faces which correspond to the description or which resemble the construct. However, the problem with this strategy is that verbal overshadowing or overshadowing as a result of cooperating in the preparation of a composite can also interfere with the accuracy of an identification.[13] Since research has shown that the performance of witnesses in attempting to create constructs tends to be poor[14] it may be best therefore to restrict preparation to concentrating on taking as detailed a verbal description as possible, making the selection from that and imposing a strict limit on the number of images viewed.

17.06   Any notion of restricting the number of images viewed would inevitably face official resistance. However, an alternative means of avoiding the problem of overshadowing would be at least to limit the exposure time of witnesses to each image shown, an advantage of the use of DVD. Since research shows that accurate identifications tend to be swift[15] (a phenomenon probably related to the holistic nature of facial recognition) this is a limitation which may serve to reduce the effect of overshadowing without diminishing the comprehensive ambit of the rogues' gallery trawl.

---

[12] Shepherd, J., 'An interactive computer system for retrieving faces', in Ellis, H.D., Jeeves, M.A., Newcombe, F. and Young, A., *Aspects of face processing*, Dordrecht: Martinus Nijhoff, 1986, 398–409.

[13] Subjects who had attempted an Identikit of a suspect did not perform as well as a control group at a later identification parade and in the two hours it took to create a likeness an immense amount of verbal overshadowing could have occurred to contaminate the memory of the witnesses by the time they participated in the identification test: research by Cornish, referred to without full citation by McKenzie, I. and Dunk, P., cited above at n.3, 178–193, at 184, note.

[14] This is considered in chapter 16 at paras 16.14–16, in which Professor Tim Valentine describes the development of a new generation of potentially much more effective computerized programmes for constructing composite likenesses.

[15] See e.g. Stern, L.B. and Dunning, D., 'Distinguishing accurate from inaccurate eyewitness identifications: a reality monitoring approach,' in Ross, D., Ceci, S.J., Dunning, D. and Toglia, M. (eds.), *Adult Eyewitness Testimony*, Cambridge: Cambridge University Press, 1994, 144–160; Deffenbacher, K.A., *Forensic Facial Memory: Time is of the Essence*, New York: Elsevier Science Publishers, 1989; Shepherd, J.W., Gibling, E. and Ellis, H.D. 'The effects of distinctiveness, presentation time and delay on face recognition' (1991) 3 *European Journal of Cognitive Psychology*, 137–145.

D. The Difficult Problem of 'Street' Identification

(1) The common scenarios: extrinsic factors of weakness in identifications

The criminal courts frequently have to deal with cases where the police arrive on the **17.07** scene within a very short time of an alleged offence and the complainant or an eyewitness is then taken on a tour of local streets to search for the culprit or culprits on the supposition that they may still be in the vicinity. A potential suspect is spotted, is positively identified by the witness, and is duly arrested.[16] A variation on the theme occurs where the suspect has been stopped by police nearby on the basis of a description and the complainant/witness is then brought to the location where the suspect is being detained by the police, and makes a positive identification.[17]

Another not uncommon circumstance of 'street identification', is that of the complainant **17.08** or witness who by chance sees the alleged offender in the street or elsewhere on some occasion perhaps weeks or days or even hours after the relevant incident and then calls the police.[18] Purposive, as distinct from fortuitous, street identifications after a lapse of time are occasionally arranged by the police where, for example, the culprit is thought to make the same journey regularly or to frequent the same location, in which case officers will take up a speculative observation with the witness.[19]

The imperatives of prompt search and capture necessitating these exercises are funda- **17.09** mental to law enforcement and are likely to offer the only chance of bringing offenders to book. On the other hand, the obvious weaknesses implicit in street identification require a balance to be struck between the detection of offenders and the protection of defendants. That balance is expressed in D3.2, which allows street identification where the suspect's identity is not known.[20] So long as the accumulated information, then, does not furnish reasonable grounds to suspect the person on whom attention has focused street identification is permissible.

The potential pitfalls in street identification are fairly obvious. The environmental condi- **17.10** tions in which they often take place may in themselves undermine their reliability. The

---

[16] See, e.g. *R v Brown* [1991] CrimLR 368, C.A.

[17] See, e.g. *Coulman v DPP* [1997] COD. 91 QBD. In the leading case of *R v Forbes* [2001] 1 AC, at 487, the witness spotted the assailant minutes after the offence, called the police and was then driven around by them until he pointed out the appellant as his assailant.

[18] Noted in the report of the Committee chaired by Lord Devlin, *Report to the Secretary of State for the Home Department of the Departmental Committee on Evidence of Identification in Criminal Cases*, H.C. 338, 26 April 1976, para 4.16. In *R v Wait* [1998] CrimLR 68, CA, the complainant saw two of his assailants some days after the attack and flagged down a police vehicle whereupon they were arrested.

[19] In *R v Popat* [1998] 2 CrAppR 208, CA, the victim of an attack subsequently saw her assailant in the same vicinity and then, over a number of days, kept observation there with a police officer until identifying the assailant. The surveillance need not necessarily be live. Thus, where there were no known suspects following an outbreak of violence at a public house and the police installed a video system which enabled a witness to make an identification from recordings of people subsequently using the premises, the procedure was apparently treated as analogous to a street identification or group identification: *R v Jones and others* (1994) 158 JP 293, CA.

[20] 'In cases when the suspect's identity is not known, a witness may be taken to a particular neighbourhood or place to see whether they can identify the person they saw.'

lighting at the place of identification may be poor, or no better than at the location of the crime, and the witness may be at a distance from the person to be identified when the identification is made. In any event, there will be little prospect of keeping an unassailable record of these factors. Again, the limited recording facilities available to the police may admit of uncertainty and ambiguity as to the manner in which the purported identification was expressed. If it was by pointing at individuals in a group there is obvious scope for error if the exact target was misinterpreted and not clarified in words. It is always to be hoped that the police will take the greatest pains to ensure fairness and accuracy in their recording of detail but, especially where there is a need to watch out for possible escapes, or to prevent further eruption of public disorder, the ideal is often unachievable.

17.11   The very presence in the vicinity of a person who may in broad terms resemble the culprit or one of a group of perpetrators may lead the complainant or witness to presuppose that the person is indeed the culprit, particularly where there are few members of the public in the vicinity at the time and the witness is in an excited and suggestible state. In the experience of practitioners identifications on the hoof frequently appear to be influenced by a distinctive article of attire (which may in fact be in common currency) rather than the emphasis on precise physical characteristics such as facial appearance, gait or voice and speech pattern. The importance of clothing is clearly not to be discounted, because the shorter the lapse of time the less likely that it will have occurred to the culprit to discard a distinctive item or to exchange it with a confederate in the hope of sowing confusion. On the other hand, the more distinctive and unusual the item the more likely will be the formation of reasonable grounds for suspicion and hence the requirement for a formal procedure.

17.12   Again, where a street robbery, for example, has been committed by a group the purported identification of individuals within a group observed afterwards often appears suspiciously to lay stress on group resemblance as between the perpetrators and those pointed out afterwards, in terms of number, approximate age, mode of dress and ethnic origin. It may be that in certain circumstances the sighting of no other persons in the vicinity, coupled with the short interval of time between the offence, and the stop and group resemblance, may by a process of elimination justify the inference that the group is one and the same. By the same token, however, these factors may very well form the basis of reasonable grounds for suspicion against each member of the group, necessitating formal procedures.

17.13   Apart from the weaknesses discussed above, street identification involves the problem of influence by the force of suggestion which inheres in its very mechanics. This is discussed next in the context of the measures designed to reduce its impact.

(2) Identification of potential suspects who have been stopped by the police

(i) The fundamental problem of inherent suggestion

17.14   One of the benefits of 'all cars, all points' rapid response to street crime and the pervading ownership of mobile telephones is that the police often arrive in the vicinity so quickly and in such numbers that they are able to spot and stop possible suspects on the basis of information received over the air even before there has been any opportunity to take the complainant or other eyewitness on a tour of the neighbourhood to hunt down the culprits.

The fundamental problem with identification of persons who have already been stopped **17.15** by the police when the witness is brought to the location of the stop is that the very fact that the police will manifestly already have targeted a possible culprit, and will be standing very near to the individual, in itself carries the strongest taint of suggestion that the person would not have been stopped unless the police had very good reason to suspect guilt.[21] The antidote to the problem provided by the 1995 version of Code D was supposedly set out in the well known paragraph D2.17 which perfunctorily instructed:

> Care should be taken not to direct the witness's attention to any individual.

The sentiment was pious but the advice offered little protection against the influence of suggestion which inevitably arises where police officers are necessarily having to stand at close quarters to a provisional suspect. The basic problem is always going to exist of balancing the need to keep a close eye on would-be escapers who are not yet in custody[22] with that of trying to avoid too obviously 'nudging and winking' by the mere fact of physically juxtaposing a single individual or a group of persons with police officers in uniform. A new sense of realism in acknowledging the basic conundrum was injected into the 2003 edition of the code (reissued in 2004), which makes the admonition that care should be taken not to direct the witness's attention to any individual conditional on this being unavoidable.[23]

(ii) Statutory attempt to mitigate the problem of inherent suggestion

The measure removing from the code the former absolute prohibition on drawing the **17.16** witness's attention to a particular individual where it is unavoidable is contained in a somewhat forlorn attempt to introduce features of a more formalized controlled procedure to be followed where 'a witness [is] taken to a particular neighbourhood or place to see whether they can identify the person they saw'.[24] The most controversial of the required measures is that contained in D3.2(b). While the need for police officers to stand close to a potential suspect may be unavoidable, it will rarely if ever be necessary to point directly at a particular person and to ask whether he or she is the perpetrator. To do so would clearly be regarded as a leading question, as the Court of Appeal observed in *R v Brizey*, although in that case the actual effect of the officer's words was held merely to

---

[21] See *R v Vaughan* (1997) *The Independent*, 12 May, CA (judgment 30 April). Such a preconception might have been reinforced as a result of overhearing police conversation: see Bogan, cited above at n.1, para. 5.14.

[22] Because the police are supposedly constrained by the belief they have as yet insufficient information to justify arrest but who may very soon be in custody after being identified; see *R v Malashev* [1997] CrimLR 587.

[23] See Roberts, A. and Clover, S., 'Managerialism and Myopia: The Government's Consultation Draft on PACE—Code D', [2002] CrimLR 873, at 888; Clover and Roberts, 'Short-sighted or forward-looking?' (2002) *New Law Journal* 870, at 872 (June 7).

[24] C3.2. The required measures were based on guidance provided by Mitchell J in *R v Hickin* [1996] CrimLR 584, CA.

have widened the ambit of the complainant's attention.[25] D3.2(b), which now adds an important qualification to the old rule D2.17, provides—

> [C]are must be taken not to direct the witness's attention to any individual unless, taking into account all the circumstances, this cannot be avoided. However, this does not prevent a witness being asked to look carefully at the people around at the time or to look towards a group or in a particular direction, if this appears necessary to make sure that the witness does not overlook a possible suspect simply because the witness is looking in the opposite direction *and also to enable the witness to make comparisons between any suspect and others who are in the area . . .*[26]

What was doubtless a valiant attempt to make the best of a bad job in difficult circumstances in the event achieves little more than dressing up a confrontation as a quasi-identification parade. However, in most cases in a deserted street late at night there will be few members of the public about, either walking past or stopping to watch, who may be used or invited to stand in as foils. In most cases the only people present who are not in police uniform are likely to be members of a group who have been stopped and all or most of whom may be suspects. It is plainly undesirable that they should be used as foils for each other, particularly when the group may well have been stopped on the basis of a group description. This is reminiscent of the practice of some of the states in the USA, in which it is quite permissible for the police to put together a line-up in which all of the suspects of a crime might be placed together and the witness is invited to select the culprit—a procedure which has been referred to as similar to a multiple-choice examination question with no wrong answer.[27] The sanction in the code for directing the witness's attention to any individual where this is unavoidable amounts to a sensible recognition of the fact that in general it is in practice impossible to avoid drawing a witness's attention to an individual who has been stopped at the roadside by uniformed police on mobile patrol. The measure has been criticized as being likely to be taken as a warrant for inviting the witness—expressly, it is assumed—to concentrate on a particular person or group.[28] Strictly speaking and for what it is worth, this seems to be precluded by the generalized, almost deliberately vague, terms of the language which is to be used in inviting the witness where to look. In reality, however, the coy hints sanctioned by the passage may convey a stronger message than a blunt question as to whether the person is the culprit. If a casual identification is going to be permitted where there is no option but to place a potential suspect immediately next to a uniformed officer it seems farcical to prohibit an express invitation to participate in what would amount to nothing short of a confrontation. Any officer advancing such an argument might well feel justified in expecting to receive a sympathetic hearing from a court.

---

[25] (1994) unreported, 10 March, CA. See Bogan, (2004), cited above at n.21, para 5.23.

[26] Emphasis added. Note for Guidance 3F warns that the admissibility and value of any street identification may be compromised if, before a person is identified, the witness's attention is specifically drawn to that person.

[27] See McKenzie and Dunk, (1999) cited above at n.3, 185.

[28] Roberts and Clover, [2002] CrimLR, cited above at n.23, at 888.

(iii) A general solution to the problem of inherent suggestion

Where there are multiple witnesses to a street crime the prohibition on further casual **17.17**
identification procedures as soon as one witness has made a positive identification affords
some relief from the risk of multiple error.[29] However, this does not eradicate the problem
of auto-suggestion in the case of the witness making the first identification. Moreover, in
many instances there will only be one witness to an incident—usually the complainant.
While it may be useful to hold a second, formal, procedure later, since this *might* cause an
honest witness to have second thoughts when the suspect is viewed against an array of
near-look-alikes, this hardly offers a guaranteed cure for hasty error. One solution which
has been suggested is to require officers standing with a potential suspect to be in plain
clothes, where possible, and that uniformed police and marked police vehicles should not
be in the immediate vicinity.[30] This supposed antidote ignores operational constraints
and, although in many instances plain-clothes robbery squad officers will be in attendance, the system should not have to depend on the instant availability of plain-clothes
officers, or on uniformed officers switching tunics and police headgear with anoraks or
sports jackets and back-to-front baseball caps conveniently kept in the boot as stage
props, or on the hope that witnesses will fail to notice size 12 police issue boots, or the
fact that three diminutive youths are flanked by large well-built men in their thirties
dressed self-consciously in the latest designer sports casual wear.

What is a fundamentally very serious problem should be addressed by a vastly more **17.18**
decorous solution than the frankly ridiculous measures necessitated by staging the semb
lance of a controlled test in the street. Fortunately there is a far simpler and more effective
solution made available by modern technology, although not one which may be to the
taste of everyone associated with liberal opinion.

In the classic situation, if not in the majority of cases, where the police arriving on the **17.19**
scene in answer to a call within a short time of the offence stop a possible culprit or group
of individuals on the street, it will almost invariably be on the basis of a matching of
the physical description of the culprits with the persons stopped, combined with an
assessment of the relative times, location, direction of travel of the temporary detainees,
and degree to which the vicinity is devoid of pedestrians. Although it has been held that a
person is not a 'known suspect' merely because he or she matches the description of an
offender circulated to police officers[31] a combination of the above factors may well
furnish reasonable grounds for suspicion justifying an arrest, even without a positive
identification.[32] Stops are rarely random or even based on description alone but are
usually driven by a combination of circumstances which in themselves will almost certainly
raise reasonable grounds for suspicion justifying arrest. If there are reasonable grounds for
arrest, even without a positive identification, formal procedures for visual identification are
obligatory under the code where identification is disputed (D3.12) and arrest (as distinct
from reliance on voluntary attendance at the police station) is likely to be the only
practical means of securing the suspect's cooperation in carrying out these procedures.

---

[29] D3.2(d).   [30] Ibid.   [31] *Coulman v DPP* [1997] COD 91, DC.
[32] See e.g. *R v Nunes* [2001] EWCA Crim 2283; 10 *Archbold News* 1, CA.

Where the suspect has said nothing of relevance prior to, or on arrest, D3.12 will arguably necessitate a prompt, formal interview at the police station to determine if identification is likely to be in issue. It can hardly be denied that with its attendant distress and inconvenience, an arrest would deprive an innocent, albeit suspected, person of the opportunity of being cleared forthwith. This is the understandable attraction of street identification and the police might well seek to demonstrate its efficacy by pointing to the presumably significant numbers of people whom it clears.[33]

17.20 On the other hand, arrest and formal procedure will afford a strong measure of protection against a hasty identification which may well be mistaken. A formal video identification procedure can now be arranged within a matter of hours, in under an hour in urgent cases, and the fastest one on record took a mere 15 minutes. The suspect's stay at the police station need not be protracted and might well result in his elimination from the inquiry where he might otherwise have been implicated on the basis of a woefully imperfect procedure. Although many suspects might understandably prefer in the short run to take their chances on instant elimination from the inquiry, the interests of justice surely require a more objective, if paternalistic, regard for reliability. If the grounds for suspicion are reasonable enough to justify a stop, then they will probably be enough to justify an arrest and, if so, there should be an arrest and not a street confrontation. Indeed, the police should be discouraged from declining to arrest ostensibly on the basis of insufficient grounds for suspicion and therefore for arrest, since this might furnish an improper pretext for circumventing the protection of a formal procedure in favour of holding an inherently unsatisfactory casual one. Advocates should be prepared to counter any police claim that they lacked grounds for arrest and to seek exclusion of visual identification evidence under s78 of PACE if it appears that grounds for arrest clearly existed, irrespective of the professed belief or motivation of the officers.

(iv) Stops initiated by an eyewitness on tour

17.21 The problem of auto-suggestion arises too, although less acutely, where the witness is taken on a tour of the vicinity and sees a person on foot who matches the description of the culprit and who, at least viewed from a distance, he thinks he can identify. Here again, the description, coupled with such elements as timing, distance, direction of travel, and the fact that the streets of the locality are deserted—factors which might in themselves induce the witness to believe that the person is the culprit—might give rise to reasonable grounds for suspicion without a positive identification. Questioning on prior movements might enhance the suspicion. If there are sufficient grounds for arrest the formalities of video identification become obligatory and the witness should be kept at a safe distance and not given a chance to make a close facial examination of the suspect before the latter is taken away.

---

[33] See Valentine, chapter 16 above, at paras 16.45 and 16.46, for a review of some American field and laboratory studies on the rates of identification as between 'showups' (the American term for street identifications) and photographic line-ups.

E. Video Identification Procedure

(1) Requirement for the selection of foils conforming to the suspect's 'general appearance'

Applying the long-established rule for live identification parades the rule for video iden- **17.22** tification parades was that they had to be made up of the images of the suspect and at least eight volunteers 'who, so far as possible, resemble the suspect in age, height, general appearance and position in life'.[34] Under the code revision which came into force on 1 January 2006 the rule is modified to delete the requirement for height conformity on the ground that within reason it is impossible to tell a discrepancy in height from the images displayed.[35] Psychologists have argued that the use of foils whose appearance matches a previous description given by the witness rather than the suspect will furnish a more sensitive test and for that reason is preferable, at least where the description involves no obvious or radical disparity with the suspect.[36] The code emphasis on '*general* appearance' would certainly permit the use of foils whose facial description might differ on some specific points from that of the suspect and would arguably allow for a choice to be made between match to culprit description and suspect resemblance methodology.

From an objective standpoint although there is some experimental evidence to suggest **17.23** that foils selected by culprit description might produce more reliable identification evidence than those selected by suspect resemblance, taking all relevant studies into account there is, as Valentine points out in Chapter 16, little empirical evidence on which to base a contention that a match-to-description strategy is a superior method of constructing an array than a suspect-resemblance strategy.[37]

Since the available empirical evidence on effectiveness places no particular premium on **17.24** the need to select by culprit description there remains one compelling reason for selecting by suspect-resemblance. The suspect may have a facial feature which though not idiosyncratic, such as a tattoo, is nevertheless uncommon, for example an abnormally large nose. No such feature is mentioned in the witness's written description, though that would not necessarily mean that the culprit had a normal nose. The witness might have forgotten that the culprit's nose was large or might have no immediately conscious memory of the fact and the officer taking a description might have neglected to take the witness through the appearance of particular facial features in order to stimulate his or her memory on a feature by feature basis. If foils are selected with a normal range of nose sizes, an identification of the suspect would raise suspicions that the witness had been told privately about the suspect's nose size and was therefore on the look-out for a face with such a feature.

---

[34] Annex A.2.

[35] The change was proposed by the CPS: see schedule of proposals and HO responses.

[36] Originally argued by Luus, C.A.E. and Wells, G.L., 'Eyewitness identification and the selection of distractors for lineups' (1991) 15 *Law and Human Behavior*, 43–57. See also Wells, G.L., Small, M., Penrod, S., Malpass, R.S., Fulero, S.M. and Brinacombe, C.A.E., 'Eyewitness identification procedures: Recommendations for lineups and photospreads' (1998) 22 *Law and Human Behavior*, 603–647.

[37] See para 16.27.

(2) The rule against witness reminders

17.25 The witness might previously have made an identification from a photograph, or computerized or artist's composite likeness, of a person who appears not to be the suspect. Again, the witness might have given a previous description which is significantly different from the suspect's appearance. In such a case the suspect would plainly have an interest in seeing that the witness is reminded of the photograph, likeness or description immediately before embarking on the video identification procedure. Such a reminder might well reinforce any disinclination to identify a person resembling the suspect. However, after expressing the warning against directing the witness's attention to any one individual or giving any indication of the suspect's identity, Annex A.13 continues:

> Where a witness has previously made an identification by photographs, or a computerised or artist's composite or similar likeness, the witness must not be reminded of such a photograph or composite likeness once a suspect is available for identification by other means in accordance with this Code. Nor must the witness be reminded of any description of the suspect.

Although the rule relates to the position where the suspect has become 'available for identification by other means' it is assumed that the proscription lasts until the conclusion of the witness's participation in the identification procedure, and in any event the paragraph comes under the section of the Annex captioned '(b) Conducting the video identification'.[38] It is to be noted that in the final sentence against reminding the witness of a description of the suspect the rule is not confined to a description given by the witness.

17.26 It is easy to understand the purpose of the rule where the previously viewed photograph plainly depicts the suspect or where the construct, or a previous description given by the witness, matches the suspect's appearance. A previous reminder will be equivalent to self-prompting from a previous statement, a form of leading question. However, the same cannot be said where the photograph is not of the suspect or where there is an obvious disparity between the construct or description and the appearance of the suspect. In such a case the rule might be seen to be designed almost to suppress the disinhibition to commit an error. The mandatory terms of A.13 are regrettable. It would surely be better to give identification officers some measure of latitude in conceding a defence request for a reminder to be given. There is no leeway at all in Annex A.13 as it currently stands.

(3) Statements of confidence: a plea for the status quo

17.27 Reference is made in Chapter 16 to recent research suggesting that the expressed confidence of an eyewitness in court may be more diagnostic of identification accuracy than psychologists had previously believed.[39] Reference is also made there to research suggesting that confidence measured before an attempted identification is not as predictive of accurate identification as confidence measured immediately after the identification attempt, which it is argued is one reason why it is good practice to take a clear 'statement of confidence' from the witness immediately after the identification attempt and before

---

[38] This would seem to be confirmed by reference to the contrasting provision in Annex A.14.
[39] See para 16.52.

the formal procedure has ended.[40] While Code D does not preclude the taking of a statement of confidence after the identification procedure has been concluded, the code procedure for conducting a video identification has been criticized on the basis that the question of whether a witness can make a 'positive identification' does not allow a witness to express any degree of certainty crucially during the procedure itself.[41] It is therefore suggested that although the witness might have harboured such thoughts as 'I'm fairly sure', 'it might well be number four', 'it looks like him' or 'it could be number three', the form of the instruction includes no cue for uttering them, with the result that a qualitative assessment of the identification may be precluded. If the witness is not in fact asked any qualitative question until trial, a considerable time later, slight misgivings at the time might not be recalled, or an identification might be fortified by the subsequently acquired knowledge of another identification of the same suspect. Again, the witness might simply feel under pressure to express greater certainty before the jury, especially if the prosecution is dependent on the identification.

Instead of using the formulation 'positive identification' the idea has been canvassed of **17.28** using alternative questions such as one in open form as to how sure the witness is, or a request to grade the degree of certainty in terms of whether the person was possibly, probably or certainly the same person as previously seen.[42] Again, it has been suggested that the degree of confidence could be expressed in terms of a numerical gradation scale of the kind used by scientific experts.[43] During the consultation process which preceded the code revision which came into force on 1 January 2006, the Home Office was urged to amend Annex A by introducing in effect a request for a statement of confidence. Thus, it was proposed that use of the phrase 'positive identification' should be reconsidered to allow for degrees of certainty to be expressed and that witnesses should be asked to express their degree of certainty on a scale of 1 to 10.[44] Devlin had considered the question 'does anyone on the parade closely resemble the person you saw?' but rejected it as liable to confuse some witnesses.[45] Possibly in ignorance of Devlin's authoritative view, it was also proposed to the Home Office that on failing to make an identification the witness should be asked if anyone shown on the film was similar to the person previously seen.[46] These proposals were rejected by the Home Office on the ground that 'the current wording is sufficient and the Codes deliberately only allow for a positive identification because anything less than that opens the potential to flawed identification'.

---

[40] See para 16.53.

[41] See *e.g.* Bogan, (2004) cited above at n.21, para 5.56. The topic was originally discussed in depth in the *Devlin Report*, cited above at n.18, paras 5.58 to 5.62.

[42] Bogan, ibid, para 5.56, noting that the procedure for group identification and showing photographs makes provision for a selection by a witness who is unable to confirm the identification, when the witness is then asked how sure he or she is (Annexes C.23 and E.9, respectively).

[43] Ibid, para 5.57.

[44] Proposed by West Yorkshire Police and the Crown Prosecution Service: see schedule of recommendations and responses posted on the relevant Home Office webpage. The gradation scale idea is an adaptation of the scheme employed by scientific experts and may have been inspired by Bogan's treatment.

[45] *Devlin Report*, cited above at n.18, paras. 5.58–5.62.

[46] Proposed by Karl Burn, Identification Officer.

17.29   The undoubtedly sensitive analysis in the previous paragraph of the supposed inflexibility of the existing instruction overlooks the fact that the instruction requires witnesses to be told 'that if they cannot make a positive identification, they should say so'.[47]

This is a conventional linguistic form of encouragement to people to speak their mind and not be afraid to express reservations. It is difficult to see why such an exhortation will be insufficiently effective in eliciting such commonplace phrases for expressing various degrees of reservation as those instanced above, with any specific explanatory reasons (e.g. 'the hair looks different, somehow'). In contrast with the idea of using the three degrees of confidence referred to above or the numerical scale, it is maintained nevertheless that the nuanced colloquialisms liable to be elicited by the existing form of entreaty are more apt to express a range of subtle variation, including at one extreme the negative assertion 'none of those shown', than are the relatively inflexible three options or a 10-point gradation scheme.

17.30   Criticism has also been levelled at the code scheme for its exclusive reference to positive identification rather than also to positive exoneration of the suspect, there being 'little reason not to ask whether the witness can exclude the persons viewed', though it is conceded that such a direct challenge might provoke a qualified identification.[48] While it may be argued that the existing terms of the instruction provide a reasonably effective means of prompting the witness (if so minded) to exonerate the suspect without raising any such counter-productive risk, it has been usefully suggested that the code should require witnesses to be cautioned that it is as important to clear innocent persons from suspicion as it is to identify the guilty, and that regardless of whether or not an identification is made, the police will continue to investigate the incident.[49]

(4) Preventing reinforcement feedback by informing identification witnesses that they have picked out the suspect

17.31   A significant shortcoming in the code which may need to be redressed in any future revision is that it imposes no prohibition on witnesses being told that they have either identified the suspect or have failed to do so. It has been argued that there is a danger in such confirmation that a witness who may have harboured some doubt could feel fortified in an initially tentative identification. The process of such reinforcement of confidence has been described as 'bolstering' or 'firming up'.[50] Such a contention appears to be supported by research cited in Chapter 16 of the present work, demonstrating not only that receiving feedback that the suspect has been identified, or that another witness has made the same identification, will increase the witness's confidence in their identification,

---

[47] Annex A.11.   [48] Bogan, (2004), cited above at n.1, para. 5.58.

[49] Roberts and Clover, [2002] CrimLR, cited above at n.23, at 887, citing a recommendation by the Technical Working Group for Eyewitness Evidence of the U.S. Department of Justice Office of Justice Programmes, *Eyewitness Evidence: A Guide for Law Enforcement*, National Institute of Justice, Washington D.C., 1999.

[50] Originally described by Loftus, E.F., *Eyewitness Testimony*, Cambridge, Mass: Harvard University Press, 1979, chap 1, instancing in particular the notorious Sacco and Vanzetti case in the United States in 1920.

but also that it may inflate a range of assertions tending to enhance the professed reliability of the original sighting, for example, its duration, the quality of lighting conditions, the proximity of the suspect to the witness, the witness's attentiveness, and so forth.[51] Other research demonstrates that post-identification feedback tends to make eyewitnesses over-confident, expressing more certainty in their identification than may be merited.[52]

It has also been suggested that informing witnesses of a *failure* to identify the suspect may **17.32** induce them to adjust their evidence, although how exactly is not explained.[53] It is assumed that what is meant by 'adjustment' in this prognosis is the danger that witnesses who think they may have recognized the person but say nothing out of a punctilious regard for fairness and propriety might feel less inhibited about implicating the person they think they may have recognized once they receive confirmation that the suspect was among the images depicted (whether or not they are told at which number the suspect appeared in the array).

The Court of Appeal have advised that a witness ought not to be told that the person **17.33** picked out was the suspect *until after making a statement about the parade.*[54] This will prevent a suspiciously rapid process of firming up between the identification procedure and the making of the routine statement which is usually taken immediately afterwards. However, it is difficult to see what significant protection it will offer against potentially much more insidious long-term bolstering of a tentative recognition as a result of being told subsequently to the making of a statement that the right person was picked out. Thus, it has been persuasively argued[55] that the principle of non-disclosure ought to be maintained right up to trial:

> [F]airness to the suspect surely requires that the witness be not told at any time before trial whether the person identified was the suspect, unless there is a particular reason for doing so. The reality is that any witness is going to be fortified in a belief as to the correctness of the identification by being given such information. It is no answer to say that, if the witness says in a post-parade statement, 'I think it was the person I identified, but I am not entirely sure' and at trial says 'I am in fact 100% sure', the evidence at trial may be undermined by cross-examination on the previous statement. It is notorious that honest but mistaken identification witnesses can be convincing. If the witness says that he has given it considerable thought, and has in consequence become sure, this may be extremely plausible. This may be so even if the jury are informed of the fact that the witness has been told that the suspect was the person identified.

It has been reported that in the light of pronouncements by a number of Crown Court judges the policy has been adopted in some police areas (including, notably, Kent) of not

---

[51] Wells, G.L. and Bradfield, A.L., ' "Good you identified the suspect": feedback to eyewitnesses distorts their reports of the witnessing experience' (1998) 66 *Journal of Applied Psychology*, 688–696, cited para 16.54 above.

[52] Semmler, C., Brewer, N. and Wells, G.L., 'Effects of postidentificaiton feedback on eyewitness identification and nonidentification confidence' (2004) *Journal of Applied Psychology*, 334–346, cited ibid.

[53] Bogan, cited above n.1 para 5.47.   [54] *R v Willoughby* [1999] 2 CrAppR 82.

[55] See Richardson, P.J., commentary on *Willoughby*, [1999] 25 *Criminal Law Week* 4.

confirming or denying the accuracy of any identification made by a witness.[56] This local practice ought to be incorporated in the code as a provision. As the prevention of secret approaches to a witness would be virtually impossible to enforce it might be worth considering whether to introduce a routine practice of withholding the details of the procedure and of the witness's performance from officers involved in the investigation, even from the officer in the case. The details would be confidential to the supervising identification officer and the Crown Prosecution Service.

(5) Preventing non-verbal cues during the identification process

17.34 The process of reinforcement referred to in the last section might conceivably take place during the identification procedure itself, with the supervising officer indicating or signalling to the witness that a tentative identification had indeed been correct. This might be conveyed in speech or by some other vocal cue (a cough or grunt) or by a non-vocal cue (the raising of an eyebrow or a head tilt) or by a combination. Non-verbal and non-vocal cues may also induce the witness to assert an identification in the first instance, expressed either with certainty or tentatively. Audio recording of the procedure will pick up vocal cues, but only comprehensive video monitoring of the procedure will furnish direct evidence of non-vocal ones. While identification procedure administrators can be deterred from giving conscious signals by the presence of the suspect's legal representative or by the installation of electronic monitoring such safeguards will not preclude unconscious ones or those which the administrator may contrive to give at a 'dead' point out of view of the cameras or when the suspect's representative, if present, is not looking. Total prevention can only be guaranteed by a code provision requiring that the actual administrator of the video identification procedure (the official taking the witness through the video array, not the identification officer in overall charge of the operation) must be kept in ignorance of the identity of the suspect to eliminate the possibility of the giving of cues. The legal representative also should not know in which position the suspect appears on the array, to avoid any possibility of an unconscious cue coming from that source (such as the drawing-in of breath). Such a provision could be coupled with an inexpensive and simple scheme of procedure of the sort proposed in Chapter 16 of the present work.[57] This would involve the current best practice use of random selection by the witness from multiple DVDs each with the suspect shown in a different position in the array, in combination with the use of two back-to-back monitors, one viewed by the operator and the suspect's legal representative showing only the number identifying the suspect's position in the array being presented.

(6) A flaw in the validation requirements for video identification

(i) Live parades

17.35 It is a key component of any reliable identification procedure that an unassailable record be maintained of the behaviour and reactions of the witness to the live participants of a parade or to video images as they are displayed. Written records are subjective, prone to

---

[56] See McKenzie, I., and Dunk, P., (1999), cited above at n.3, 178–193, at 190.
[57] See above para 16.78.

error and can hardly convey the full flavour of the events they describe. Still photography of the volunteers to a live parade can of course provide a record for assessing resemblance to the suspect (although the Devlin Committee thought it might be deceptive as to colour[58]) but can hardly furnish a record of the witness's behaviour. The obvious solution lies in technology but without explanation the Devlin Committee believed that a 'ciné film' would not be as valuable as a still photograph.[59] The original edition of Code D required a video or photograph of the parade where it was held without a solicitor or friend of the suspect being present but, following a recommendation of the Royal Commission on Criminal Justice,[60] the qualification was removed from the 1995 revision and it became mandatory to take a colour photograph or to video-record the parade. In the 2004 version the rule has been refined still further and now provides that a video film of a live parade must be made unless it is impracticable, in which case a colour photograph must be taken.[61]

(ii) Video identification procedure: the fundamental flaw

A serious flaw of video identification is that Annex A provides, *inter alia*: **17.36**

> The suspect's solicitor, if practicable, shall be given reasonable notification of the time and place the video identification is to be conducted so a representative may attend on behalf of the suspect. If a solicitor has not been instructed, this information shall be given to the suspect. The suspect may not be present when the images are shown to the witness(es). *In the absence of the suspect's representative, the viewing itself shall be recorded on video.* No unauthorised people may be present.[62]

The words in emphasis stand in stark contrast to the mandatory requirement for live identification parades. The qualification for video identification is the same as the pre-1995 rule for live parades. It is not apparent why it should be stuck in a time-warp. It is conceivable that the lacuna was unintentional but if so the failure by the Home Office to correct the deficiency in the 2006 revision is regrettable.[63] It has been noted that some constabularies make a video recording of the identification as a matter of routine.[64] Ideally, the record for case preparation and court presentation will consist of a split screen in which the images shown and the witness's viewing of them are recorded and displayed simultaneously.[65]

Where the viewing is not routinely recorded in all cases irrespective of the presence or **17.37** absence of a legal representative the only way for the suspect to ensure that the procedure

---

[58] *Devlin Report,* cited above at n.18, para. 5.47.   [59] Ibid.

[60] Report, Cm. 2263, July 1993, Recommendation No. 6, para. 10.   [61] Annex B.23.

[62] Annex A.9, emphasis added.

[63] The flaw presently under discussion has been highlighted since 2004 in the first co-author's on-line monograph, cited above at n.1, prominently referred to in [2003] 7 *Archbold News* 4 and [2004] 3 *Archbold News* 5, and prominently advertised in *Counsel/Bar News*, September 2005, 47. Attention was focused on Annex A.9 in consequence of an unrelated proposal from the Humberside Police Administration of Justice Unit: see Home Office on-line schedule of proposals and responses, 2006 revision consultation.

[64] Bogan, cited above at n.1, para. 5.54.   [65] Ibid.

is video-recorded is to instruct the solicitor to stay away from the procedure.[66] It is inconceivable that the rule was designed to force a choice between having a solicitor or a video-recording. A mounted camera is no guarantee against surreptitious signalling, which a vigilant defence representative in attendance might pick up.

Further Reading

Bogan, P., *Identification: Investigation, trial and scientific evidence*, London: Legal Action Group, 2004.

McKenzie, I. and Dunk, P., 'Identification parades: psychological and practical realities' in Heaton-Armstrong, A., Shepherd, S. and Wolchover, D. (eds.), *Analysing Witness Testimony*, London: Blackstone Press, 1999, at 183–184.

Police and Criminal Evidence Act 1984, Code of Practice D, *The Code of Practice for the Identification of Persons by Police Officers*, 5th ed, London: HMSO, 2004 (in force 1 August 2004).

Roberts A. and Clover, S., 'Managerialism and Myopia—The Government's Consultation Draft on PACE Code D' [2002] CrimLR 873.

Wolchover D., *Visual Identification Procedures Under PACE Code D*, frequently updated online monograph accessible through *http://www.7BellYard.co.uk*.

Editors' Note

(See, also, our notes for Chapter 16.) The authors' conclusion that the Code D requirements relating to 'foil' selection and the composition of parade line-ups are adequate is at odds with Valentine's views on this. Such healthy debate on fundamental identification procedures ought to inform future consideration of further improvements to Code D, the text of which, in the light of a constantly changing landscape of academic and practitioner views and experiences, will never be perfect.

---

[66] In *R v Elson* (1994) unreported CA94/0547/Y3, 27 May, the foils bore so little resemblance to the defendant that the solicitor's clerk took the view that a photograph was desirable and he stayed away from the parade in order to ensure that a photograph was taken in accordance with the code. In the event no camera was forthcoming.

18

ASSESSING CONTENTIOUS EYEWITNESS EVIDENCE: A JUDICIAL VIEW*

Tom Bingham
The Right Honourable Lord Bingham of Cornhill

A. The Judge's Role as a Fact Finder

(1) A lowly but onerous and crucial duty

In the hierarchy of legal skills, pride of place is given, and quite rightly, to the great **18.01** exponents of legal principle, those (whether academic or judicial) who weave disparate

---

* Originally included as part of a paper published in *Current Legal Problems*, vol. 38, London: Stevens & Sons Ltd, 1985, 1–27, and subsequently incorporated as part of Chapter 1 in Bingham, T. H., *The Business of Judging: selected essays and speeches*, Oxford: Oxford University Press, 2000. The text is virtually unchanged but the insertion of section headings and a small number of deletions and additions by the editors in the interests of consistency of chronology and house-style has been kindly approved by the author.

threads of authority into coherent doctrine or plant the flag of legal principle in hitherto untrodden factual territory. In comparison with these mandarin arts, the judicial determination of factual issues occupies a somewhat lowly place, an activity of its nature ephemeral, uncreative and particular. In short, a task appropriately left in criminal cases to the legally unqualified lay juror.

18.02 But reference to the criminal juror perhaps gives one pause for thought. His obstinate survival into modern times is, after all, at least in part, a reflection of public belief that where guilt and innocence depend on them factual decisions are too important to be left to judges. To the civil litigant also, whose case will almost always be tried by a judge sitting alone without a jury,[1] findings of fact are likely to be crucial. This is because, first, most cases turn largely, if not entirely, on the facts; as Justice Cardozo observed:

> Lawsuits are rare and catastrophic experiences for the vast majority of men, and even when the catastrophe ensues, the controversy relates most often not to the law, but to the facts.[2]

18.03 And secondly it is so because factual findings once made at first instance are very hard to dislodge on appeal,[3] for reasons to which I will return. Of the litigants who each year tramp out of the law courts muttering darkly of a bad day for British (never, curiously, English) justice, I strongly suspect that a large majority have been outraged not by a decision against them on the law but by a factual decision which they know or believe or claim to be wrong. To the judge, resolution of factual issues is (I think) frequently more difficult and more exacting than the deciding of pure points of law. In deciding the facts, the judge knows that no authority, no historical enquiry and (save on expert issues) no process of ratiocination will help him. He is dependent, for better or worse, on his own unaided judgment. And he is uneasily aware that his evaluation of the reliability and credibility of oral evidence may very well prove final. So it is, I hope, worth considering what his factual task involves, and how he sets about it.

(2) The common law judge's fact-finding role compared with other assessors

18.04 The judge's role in determining what happened at some time in the past is not of course peculiar to him. Historians, auditors, accident investigators of all kinds, loss adjusters and doctors are among those who, to a greater or lesser extent, may be called on to perform a similar function. But there are three features of the judge's role which will not all apply to these other investigations. First, he is always presented with conflicting versions of the events in question: if there is no effective dispute there is nothing for him to decide. Second, his determination necessarily takes place subject to the formality and restraints (evidential and otherwise) attendant upon proceedings in court. Third, his determination has a direct practical effect upon people's lives in terms of their pockets, activities or reputations.

---

[1] Section 6(I) of the Administration of Justice (Miscellaneous Provisions) Act 1933 is in practice little used save in libel cases.

[2] Cardozo, B. N., *The Nature of the Judicial Process*, New Haven, Conn: Yale University Press, 1921, 128–129.

[3] See, e.g. *Hontestroom (Owners) v Sagaporack (Owners)* [1927] AC 37; *Powell v. Streacham Manor Nursing Home* [1935] AC 243; *Onassis v Vergottis* [1968] 2 Lloyd's Rep. 403.

Some would draw attention to a further difference. The common law judge, it is often **18.05** said, unlike his counterpart in a civil law system and unlike the other investigators I have mentioned, is not concerned with establishing the truth of what did or did not happen on a given occasion in the past but merely with deciding, as between adversaries, whether or not the party upon whom the burden of proof lies has discharged it to the required degree of probability. The Court of Appeal has said that 'the due administration of justice does not always depend on eliciting the truth. It often depends on the burden of proof.'[4] This may be unreservedly accepted, and it is of course true that the judge's independent power to remedy deficiencies in the evidence in civil cases is extremely limited.[5] The Court of Appeal has nonetheless defined the English judge's object as being, 'above all . . . to find out the truth, and to do justice according to law', and as being, 'at the end to make up his mind where the truth lies'.[6] This, I respectfully suggest, accords with the reality of what occurs in an English civil trial of any substance where factual issues are important. The mills of civil litigation may grind slowly, yet they grind exceeding small. By the time both parties have explored every point which they think may help them or damage their adversary not much remains obscure, and it is not (I think) a common complaint of judges at the end of such a case that the material submitted has been inadequate in quantity. While the burden of proof always exists, few substantial cases turn upon it and in making his factual findings the judge is usually expressing his considered judgement as to what in truth occurred. The crucial difference between him and his civil law counterpart is not, surely, in their respective objectives but in the means which have been evolved under the two systems for achieving the objective common to both, the ascertainment of the truth. 'In practice,' as Lord Devlin observed, referring to the two systems, 'there is not, at any rate in the civil case, all that much difference.'[7]

B. Tackling the Assessment of Eyewitness Reliability

(1) The key questions

Let me then turn to the central questions. Faced with a conflict of evidence on an issue **18.06** substantially effecting the outcome of an action, often knowing that a decision this way or that will have momentous consequences on the parties' lives or fortunes, how can and should the judge set about his task of resolving it? How is he to resolve which witness is honest and which dishonest, which reliable and which unreliable?

(2) Isolating common ground

The normal first step in resolving issues of primary fact is, I feel sure, to add to what is **18.07** common ground between the parties (which the pleadings in the action should have identified, but often do not) such facts as are shown to be incontrovertible. In many

---

[4] *Air Canada v Secretary of State for Trade* [1983] 2 AC 394 at 411, *per* Lord Denning MR.
[5] *Re Enoch and Zaretsky, Rock & Cos Arbitration* [1910] 1 KB 327.
[6] *Jones v National Coal Board* [1957] 2 QB 55 at 63, 64 *per* Denning LJ, these references forming part of a passage described by Lord Devlin in Devlin, P., *The Judge*, Oxford: Oxford University Press, 1979, 56, as 'a classic account of the judge's function in the adversary system'.
[7] Ibid, at 60.

cases, letters or minutes written well before there was any breath of dispute between the parties may throw a very clear light on their knowledge and intentions at a particular time. In other cases, evidence of tyre marks, debris or where vehicles ended up may be crucial. To attach importance to matters such as these, which are independent of human recollection, is so obvious and standard a practice, and in some cases so inevitable, that no prolonged discussion is called for. It is nonetheless worth bearing in mind, when vexatious conflicts of oral testimony arise, that these fall to be judged against the background not only of what the parties agree to have happened but also of what plainly did happen, even though the parties do not agree.

(3) The judicial process of determining credibility

18.08 The most compendious statement known to me of the judicial process involved in assessing the credibility of an oral witness is to be found in the dissenting speech of Lord Pearce in the House of Lords in *Onassis v Vergottis*.[8] In this he touches on so many of the matters which I wish to mention that I may perhaps be forgiven for citing the relevant passage in full:

> 'Credibility' involves wider problems than mere 'demeanour' which is mostly concerned with whether the witness appears to be telling the truth as he now believes it to be. Credibility covers the following problems. First, is the witness a truthful or untruthful person? Secondly, is he, though a truthful person, telling something less than the truth on this issue, or, though an untruthful person, telling the truth on this issue? Thirdly, though he is a truthful person telling the truth as he sees it, did he register the intentions of the conversation correctly and, if so, has his memory correctly retained them? Also, has his recollection been subsequently altered by unconscious bias or wishful thinking or by overmuch discussion of it with others? Witnesses, especially those who are emotional, who think that they are morally in the right, tend very easily and unconsciously to conjure up a legal right that did not exist. It is a truism, often used in accident cases, that with every day that passes the memory becomes fainter and the imagination becomes more active. For that reason a witness, however honest, rarely persuades a Judge that his present recollection is preferable to that which was taken down in writing immediately after the accident occurred. Therefore, contemporary documents are always of the utmost importance. And lastly, although the honest witness believes he heard or saw this or that, is it so improbable that it is on balance more likely that he was mistaken? On this point it is essential that the balance of probability is put correctly into the scales in weighing the credibility of a witness. And motive is one aspect of probability. All these problems compendiously are entailed when a Judge assesses the credibility of a witness; they are all part of one judicial process. And in the process contemporary documents and admitted or incontrovertible facts and probabilities must play their proper part.

18.09 Every judge is familiar with cases in which the conflict between the accounts of different witnesses is so gross as to be inexplicable save on the basis that one or some of the witnesses are deliberately giving evidence which they know to be untrue. There are, no doubt, witnesses who follow the guidance of the Good Soldier Švejk that 'the main thing is always to say in court what isn't true',[9] as a matter of principle, but more often

---

[8] [1968] 2 Lloyd's Rep. 403, at 431.
[9] Hašek, J., *The Good Soldier Švejk*, Harmondsworth: Penguin, 1983, 382.

dishonest evidence is likely to be prompted by the hope of gain, the desire to avert blame or criticism, or misplaced loyalty to one or other of the parties.

(4) Five tests of credibility

The main tests needed to determine whether a witness is lying or not are, I think, the **18.10** following, although their relative importance will vary widely from case to case:[10]

(i)   the consistency of the witness's evidence with what is agreed, or clearly shown by other evidence, to have occurred;

(ii) the internal consistency of the witness's evidence;

(iii) consistency with what the witness has said or deposed on other occasions;

(iv) the credit of the witness in relation to matters not germane to the litigation;

(v)   the demeanour of the witness.

The first three of these tests may in general be regarded as giving a useful pointer to where the truth lies. If a witness's evidence conflicts with what is clearly shown to have occurred, or is internally self-contradictory, or conflicts with what the witness has previously said, it may usually be regarded as suspect. It may only be unreliable, and not dishonest, but the nature of the case may effectively rule out that possibility.

(5) Cross-examination as to credit on collateral issues

The fourth test is perhaps more arguable. Much time is spent, particularly in criminal **18.11** but also in civil cases where the honesty of witnesses is in issue, cross-examining as to credit, that is, in cross-examining witnesses on matters not germane to the action itself in order to show that they are dishonest witnesses whose evidence on matters which are germane to the action should be rejected. The underlying theory is that if a witness is willing to lie or can be shown to have acted dishonestly in one matter, he will be willing to lie or act dishonestly in another. As the Latin maxim put it, *falsus in uno, falsus in omnibus*. The practice of many advocates would suggest that the reliability of the principle is beyond doubt. And no doubt to any witness who from earliest youth, like Matilda's aunt, 'had kept a Strict Regard for Truth', the telling of any lie, large or small, on a matter relevant or irrelevant, would be unthinkable. There must nonetheless be many other witnesses who regard questions concerning their previous career or personal history or habits as an unwarranted intrusion into their privacy, in no way bearing on the substance of their testimony and undeserving of an honest answer. Or the truth may, for reasons right or wrong, be thought to be embarrassing. Let me give one very familiar example. A husband and wife both witness an event the subject of an action tried years later. Some months before the trial both give statements to the lawyers for the party wishing to call them. Both are in due course called to give evidence and are asked by cross-examining counsel whether their evidence has been the subject of discussion between them. Much more often than not, in my experience, the witness vehemently denies that there has been any discussion at all. It usually does not matter whether there

---

[10] For this, as for much of the ensuing discussion, I acknowledge my debt to the Hon. Sir Richard Eggleston QC, *Evidence, Proof and Probability*, Littleton, Colorado: Fred B. Rothman & Co, 1978, 155.

has been discussion or not, but counsel who has obtained such an answer habitually points to the extreme unlikelihood of its being true and urges that the whole of the witness's evidence should be treated as suspect. Sometimes, taken in conjunction with other grounds for suspicion, this indication may be significant. I have on occasion relied on it.[11] But I very strongly suspect that many witnesses, not being untruthful people, infer from the asking of the question that any discussion of their evidence with their spouse will be criticized as improper; so, to avoid such public criticism, they deny that such discussion occurred, contrary to the very strong probability that most unestranged husbands will discuss with their wives matters which involve and concern them both. Equally, I strongly suspect that many honest witnesses, who would do their very best to ensure that the substance of their evidence was reliable and accurate, would nonetheless be willing to prevaricate, or if necessary lie, when asked why they lost their previous job or how their first marriage came to break up. Cross-examination as to credit is often, no doubt, a valuable and revealing exercise, but the fruits of even a successful cross-examination need to be appraised with some care.

C. Assessing Reliability by Witness Demeanour

(1) Traditional emphasis on the importance of demeanour

18.12 And so to demeanour, an important subject because it is the trial judge's opportunity to observe the demeanour of the witness and from that to judge his or her credibility, which is traditionally relied on to give the judge's findings of fact their rare degree of inviolability. Lord Loreburn reflected such thinking when he said in *Kinloch v Young*:[12]

> Now, your Lordships have very frequently drawn attention to the exceptional value of the opinion of the judge of first instance, where the decision rests upon oral evidence. It is absolutely necessary no doubt not to admit finality for any decision of a judge of first instance, and it is impossible to define or even to outline the circumstances in which his opinion on such matters ought to be overruled, but there is such infinite variety of circumstances for consideration which must or may arise, and it may be that there has been misapprehension, or that there has been miscarriage at the trial. But this House and other Courts of appeal have always to remember that the judge of first instance had had the opportunity of watching the demeanour of witnesses—that he observes, as we cannot observe, the drift and conduct of the case; and also that he has impressed upon him by hearing every word the scope and nature of the evidence in a way that is denied to any Court of appeal. Even the most minute study by a Court of appeal fails to produce the same vivid appreciation of what the witnesses say or what they omit to say.

Lord Pearce, in his speech from which I have already quoted, makes the same point:

> One thing is clear, not so much as a rule of law but rather as a working rule of common sense. A trial Judge has, except on rare occasions, a very great advantage over an appellate Court; evidence of a witness heard and seen has a very great advantage over a transcript of that evidence; and a Court of Appeal should never interfere unless it is satisfied both that the judgment ought not to stand and that the divergence of view between the trial Judge

---

[11] E.g. *The Zinovia* [1984] 2 Lloyd's Rep. 264, at 278–9.   [12] [1911] S.C. (H.L.) 1, at 4.

and the Court of Appeal has not been occasioned by any demeanour of the witnesses or truer atmosphere of the trial (which may have eluded an appellate Court) or by any other of those advantages which the trial Judge possesses.[13]

What, then, is meant by the demeanour of the witness in this context? The answer is: his conduct, manner, bearing, behaviour, delivery, inflexion; in short, anything which characterizes his mode of giving evidence but does not appear in a transcript of what he actually said. In *Clarke v Edinburgh Tramways*[14] Lord Shaw put it in this way:

> witnesses without any conscious bias towards a conclusion may have in their demeanour, in their manner, in their hesitation, in the nuance of their expressions, in even the turns of the eyelid, left an impression upon the man who saw and heard them which can never be reproduced in the printed page.

Lord Justice Ormrod emphasized the importance of demeanour as a pointer to the truth. Referring to our system of oral trial, he said:

> As a method of communication, it is very complex, involving not only what is actually said, but how it is said. Inflections in both questions and answers may be highly significant, and demeanour, not only of the witness, but of others in court may be revealing.[15]

(2) Latter-day tendency to distrust demeanour as an indicator of truthfulness and accuracy

I have a hunch, which I cannot begin to justify, that in days of yore trial judges rather **18.13** prided themselves on and had considerable confidence in their ability to discern the honesty of a witness from the showing which he made in the witness box. Be that as it may, the current tendency is (I think) on the whole to distrust the demeanour of a witness as a reliable pointer to his honesty. Let me quote passages from the extra-judicial utterances of three very experienced trial judges. First, Lord Devlin:

> The great virtue of the English trial is usually said to be the opportunity it gives to the judge to tell from the demeanour of the witness whether or not he is telling the truth. I think that this is overrated. It is the tableau that constitutes the big advantage, the text with illustrations, rather than the demeanour of a particular witness.[16]

Second, Mr. Justice MacKenna, in a passage which Lord Devlin later adopted as his own:

> I question whether the respect given to our findings of fact based on the demeanour of the witness is always deserved. I doubt my own ability, and sometimes that of other judges, to discern from a witness's demeanour, or the tone of his voice, whether he is telling the truth. He speaks hesitantly. Is it the mark of a cautious man, whose statements are for that reason to be respected, or is he taking time to fabricate? Is the emphatic witness putting on an act to deceive me, or is he speaking from the fullness of his heart, knowing that he is right? Is he likely to be more truthful if he looks me straight in the face than if he casts his eyes on the ground, perhaps from shyness or a natural timidity? For my part I rely on these considerations as little as I can help.[17]

---

[13] [1968] 2 Lloyd's Rep. 403, at 431.   [14] [1919] S.C. (H.L.) 35, at 36.
[15] 'Judges and the Process of Judging' *Jubilee Lectures*, Holdsworth Club Presidential Address, 7 March, 1980.
[16] *The Judge*, cited above at n. 6, 63.
[17] MacKenna, B., 'Discretion,' (1974) IX (new series) *The Irish Jurist*, 1, at 10.

Third, Lord Justice Browne:

> So the main job of the judge of first instance is to decide the facts. How does he do it? When there is a conflict of evidence between witnesses, some judges believe that they can tell whether a witness is telling the truth by looking at him and listening to him. I seldom believed that. . . .[18]

18.14 To these powerful voices may be added two from Australia, suggesting that a loss of faith in the value of demeanour is not a purely local phenomenon. The Hon. Sir Richard Eggleston, QC wrote in 1978:

> Many judges think they can tell from the demeanour of a witness when he is lying, but in the course of my practice at the Bar there were several occasions on which witnesses, whom I firmly believed to be honest and to be telling the truth, displayed evident signs of embarrassment and discomfort in the witness-box, sufficient to make them appear to be lying. I am therefore very sceptical of such claims. A more complicated case in which demeanour was deceptive was that of a man whom I knew well, who was employed as a book-keeper on a sheep station. When called upon to tell a social lie, he was covered with blushes and showed every sign of acute embarrassment. He always spent much more than his salary and was believed to have wealthy parents, but so transparent did he appear to be that it did not occur to anyone to question his honesty until a query came from head office about the accounts, when he asked for the afternoon off, and was found dead some distance away. He had been systematically defrauding his employers for years, and almost everything he had told his associates about himself was fiction.[19]

And lastly, an advocate's view from Mr A. M. Gleeson, QC.:

> Reasons for judgment which are replete with pointed references to the great advantage which the trial judge has had in making the personal acquaintance of the witnesses seem nowadays to be treated by appellate courts with a healthy measure of scepticism. What might be called the Pinocchio theory, according to which dishonesty on the part of a witness manifests itself in a manner that does not appear on the record but is readily discernible by anyone physically present, seems to be losing popularity.[20]

(3) The limited value of demeanour, subject to three specific areas of doubt as to its utility

18.15 Seeing that we have so great a cloud of witnesses, any additional observations by me are plainly unnecessary. But I shall of course make some. There are, I feel sure, occasions on which a witness leaves a judge with a profound conviction that he is, or is not, telling the truth. This may not derive from anything he has said or failed to say but may be based ultimately on impression. As such it is probably impossible to explain or justify in rational terms. Whether his conviction was soundly based the judge is unlikely ever to know, so that he has little or no check on the accuracy of his own impressions, but if an impression is strong enough he will be unable in conscience to deliver a judgment which does not give effect to it. A firm judgment of this kind formed by one whose judgment is supposed to be his stock in trade is, I think, not lightly to be overridden. I would

---

[18] Browne, P., 'Judicial Reflections' (1982) 35 *Current Legal Problems*, 5.
[19] Cited above, at n.10, at 163.
[20] 'Judging the Judges' (1979) 53 *Australian Law Journal*, (July number), 344.

furthermore suggest that many judges, with years of forensic experience behind them, are likely to have developed some skill at recognizing certain types of rogue, particularly if the type is one they have met before. But subject to those qualifications I ally myself with the doubters. The cases which vex a judge are not those in which he is profoundly convinced of a witness's honesty or dishonesty. In those cases, whether his conclusion is right or wrong, the decision for him is easy. The anxious cases are those, which arise not infrequently, where two crucial witnesses are in direct conflict in such a way that one must be lying, but both appear equally plausible or implausible. In this situation I share the misgivings of those who question the value of demeanour—even of inflexion, or the turn of an eyelid—as a guide. To Mr Justice MacKenna's percipient remarks I would simply add three addenda:

(a) Plausibility can be the hallmark of the accomplished liar   First, the ability to tell a   **18.16**
coherent, plausible and assured story, embellished with snippets of circumstantial detail and laced with occasional shots of life-like forgetfulness, is very likely to impress any tribunal of fact. But it is also the hallmark of the confidence trickster down the ages.

(b) Intimidation of the witness box   Second, there is (I think) a tendency for professional   **18.17**
lawyers, seeing themselves as the lead players in the forensic drama, to overlook how unnerving an experience the giving of evidence is for a witness who has never testified before. The architecture of the Law Courts in the Strand, with its blend of the ecclesiastical (in the entrance hall) and the custodial (in many of the upper corridors), and the lay-out of the courts themselves, with the witness raised up and isolated like a lone climber on a peak in the Dolomites, might almost have been designed to maximize his unease. It would rarely, in my view, be safe to draw any inference from the fact that a witness seemed nervous and ill-at-ease; and if he did not it could well be because he had taken a tranquillizer to fortify himself for the ordeal, so that his apparent calmness would be equally lacking in significance.

(c) Foreign language witnesses   Third, however little insight a judge may gain from the   **18.18**
demeanour of a witness of his own nationality when giving evidence, he must gain even less when (as happens in almost every commercial action and many other actions also) the witness belongs to some other nationality and is giving evidence either in English as his second or third language, or through an interpreter. Such matters as inflexion become wholly irrelevant; delivery and hesitancy scarcely less so. Lord Justice Scrutton once observed: 'I have never yet seen a witness who was giving evidence through an interpreter as to whom I could decide whether he was telling the truth or not.'[21] If a Turk shows signs of anger when accused of lying, is that to be interpreted as the bluster of a man caught out in a deceit or the reaction of an honest man to an insult? If a Greek, similarly challenged, becomes rhetorical and voluble and offers to swear to the truth of what he has said on the lives of his children, what (if any) significance should be attached to that? If a Japanese witness, accused of forging a document, becomes sullen, resentful and hostile, does this suggest that he has done so or that he has not? I can only ask these questions.

---

[21] *Compania Naviera Martiartu v Royal Exchange Assurance Corporation* (1922) 13 Lloyds L. Rep. 45, at 97 CA, (Court of Appeal judgment in case cited at n.22).

I cannot answer them. And if the answer be given that it all depends on the impression made by the particular witness in the particular case that is in my view no answer. The enigma usually remains. To rely on demeanour is in most cases to attach importance to deviations from a norm when there is in truth no norm.

(4) Danger in relying on ambiguities of demeanour or intonation

18.19   There are of course occasions when the simple language used by a witness, reproduced on the printed page, may be ambiguous although its meaning is, to anyone who hears the answer, apparent. For example, a witness may assent to a suggestion of cross-examining counsel with a shrug of the shoulders to indicate that though theoretically possible the suggestion is in practical terms absurd, or the assent may come after a long pause and in a manner indicating full acceptance. But responsible counsel do not allow a case to proceed on the basis of a single answer without making sure that the witness's position is clearly established, and were they to do so the judge would intervene to ensure that there was no room for doubt. The occasions on which the flavour of a witness's evidence is more accurately derived from the inflexion attached to a single answer, or his demeanour when giving it, than from the gist of a series of answers must, I suggest, be few.

(5) Consequences of justifying doubts as to the significance of demeanour

18.20   If these doubts concerning the significance of demeanour are justified, certain consequences logically follow. An appellate court, reading the transcript of the evidence given, could decide the facts as well as the trial judge. There need be no bias in favour of the judge's factual conclusions. There could on an appeal be a complete re-hearing, on fact as well as law. The result would be to increase very substantially the burden on the appellate courts, to delay the *finis litium* which is held to be in the public interest, to increase uncertainty (because a litigant could never be sure on what version of the facts a point of law was to be decided) and to increase the already frightening cost of litigation. These are, without doubt, ills to be avoided if possible, and it would in my view be a respectable rule that every litigant should be entitled to a full contest on the facts at one level only and that the facts should be open to review thereafter only if some glaring and manifest error could be demonstrated. This is not, I think, very different from the substance of the present practice, but that practice might perhaps be better justified on that ground than by reference to the peculiar advantage enjoyed by the judge who has seen and heard the witnesses.

(6) Doubts: a cautionary tale

18.21   Before finally leaving the subject of demeanour—to which I have already, probably, devoted too much time—perhaps I may briefly digress to recount a somewhat remarkable cautionary tale. In *La Compania Martiartu of Bilbao v Royal Exchange Assurance Corporation*,[22] the owners of the steamship *Arnus*, which had been lost at sea off the coast of Brittany, sued the defendant insurers upon a time policy issued on the hull and

---

[22] (1922) 11 Lloyds L. Rep. 174, at 186, KBD (first instance hearing of appellate case cited at n.21).

machinery of the vessel, alleging that the loss was caused by perils of the sea. The insurers denied a loss by perils of the sea and alleged that the vessel had been wilfully cast away—scuttled—by those on board with the knowledge and consent of the owners. After a trial lasting five days (which contrasts with the four comparable cases tried since 1960, none of which lasted less than forty) the learned trial judge reserved judgment. When he gave judgment eight days later, he referred to powerful evidence in favour of scuttling but concluded on balance that the vessel had sunk as a result of striking a piece of floating wreckage.

The crucial factor in the owners' favour was the evidence of the second mate, as to which **18.22** the judge observed:

> If I do not believe the second mate it is quite clear this vessel was scuttled. I have to make up my mind whether in fact, when he says he saw this floating mass there was this mass or not. I was from the first and am still deeply impressed with the second mate's evidence. He gave his evidence in commission and repeated it here. I was impressed with his demeanour and frankness. . . . He gave his evidence quite fairly and frankly, and with great reticence. In my judgment that was a witness of truth. . . . The main reason why I decide in favour of the owners is that I accept the evidence of the second mate. . . .[23]

The learned judge had apparently formed the view that his decision, being based almost **18.23** entirely upon facts, was not open to review, and indeed spoke of it with what was later described as 'some degree of sanguineness' as practically unappealable.[24] No doubt his conclusion founded on the demeanour of the second mate fortified that belief. But he proved to be mistaken. A finding of scuttling, made by the Court of Appeal, was upheld by the House of Lords. The task of the appellate courts was made easier when it emerged that the second mate, although he had testified on commission, had never attended the trial or given evidence at all and had (as Lord Birkenhead put it) 'enjoyed therefore small opportunity of exhibiting either his demeanour or his frankness'.[25]

D. Assessing Reliability from Probability

If too much attention has over the years been paid to the demeanour of the witness in **18.24** guiding the trial judge to the truth, too little has perhaps been paid to probability. I do not use that word in any mathematical or philosophical sense, but simply as indicating in a general way that one thing may be regarded as more likely to have happened than another, with the result that the judge will reject the evidence in favour of the less likely. I think most judges give weight to this factor in reaching their factual conclusions. Mr Justice MacKenna, in the paper from which I have already quoted, has said that he habitually did:

> When I have done my best to separate the true from the false by these more or less objective tests, I say which story seems to me the more probable, the plaintiff's or the defendant's, and if I cannot say which, I decide the case, as the law requires me to do, in the defendant's favour.[26]

---

[23] Ibid, at 188–9.   [24] (1924) 19 Ll.L. Rep. 95.   [25] Ibid, at 95–6.
[26] Cited above at n.17, at 10.

18.25   Lord Justice Browne spoke to rather similar effect, also in the paper previously quoted:

> Sometimes one has to rely on probabilities and on circumstantial evidence; which I always thought was less unreliable than oral evidence. But the judge's own opinion about probabilities can be dangerous, being based on his own, perhaps limited, experience. Like all motorists, I thought I could see what the probabilities of a motor accident were, but I was quite incapable of judging the probabilities of a factory accident.[27]

In choosing between witnesses on the basis of probability, a judge must of course bear in mind that the improbable account may nonetheless be the true one. The improbable is, by definition, as I think Lord Devlin once observed, that which may happen, and obvious injustice could result if a story told in evidence were too readily rejected simply because it was bizarre, surprising or unprecedented. The most striking illustration of this which I know of, although given by Wigmore,[28] is one for which I am indebted to Sir Richard Eggleston:[29]

> A woman living in Lancaster, Massachusetts, on the hill that leads to the gaol, was considered to be suffering from hallucinations, because of her complaint that the head of her late husband (a negro) had rolled down the steps into her kitchen and had been retrieved by the devil wearing a black cloak. In fact, the devil was an eminent scientist, who had been making a study of the heads of criminals, and had, on the night in question, been carrying the head of a negro who had died at the gaol; he dropped the head in the street and it rolled down the steps of the old woman's house. As the removal of the head was not strictly lawful, be had wrapped his cloak round his face and calling out 'Where's my head? Give me my head!', gone to retrieve it, confident that he would not be recognized.

18.26   American fact is stranger than English fiction. A second note of caution must also be sounded. An English judge may have, or think that he has, a shrewd idea how a Lloyd's broker, or a Bristol wholesaler, or a Norfolk farmer, might react in some situation which is canvassed in the course of a case but he may, and I think should, feel very much more uncertain about the reactions of a Nigerian merchant, or an Indian ship's engineer, or a Yugoslav banker. Or even, to take a more homely example, a Sikh shopkeeper trading in Bradford. No judge worth his salt could possibly assume that men of different nationalities, educations, trades, experience, creeds and temperaments would act as he might think he would have done or even—which may be quite different—in accordance with his concept of what a reasonable man would have done.

18.27   Nonetheless, and despite these important disclaimers, I think that in practice judges do attach enormous importance to the sheer likelihood or unlikelihood of an event having happened as a witness testifies in deciding whether to accept his account or not. If, for example, a witness who is shown to have been a meticulous diarist, log-keeper, letter-writer or note-taker testifies to the happening of an event which he claims to have been of importance to him at the time but of which he made no record, then in the absence of some convincing explanation the court is likely to infer that the event did not occur at

---

[27] Cited above, at n.18, at 6.
[28] Wigmore, J.H., *The Science of Judicial Proof*, 3rd edn., Boston, Mass: Little, Brown, 1937, 443–445.
[29] Cited above, at n.10, at 164.

all, or that if it did occur the witness did not know of it, or that if it did and he did know of it the event did not then strike him as important. This is no more than ordinary common sense. Examples could be multiplied, but perhaps I can give one from my recent experience.[30] A seaman who was due to fly out to join a new ship went to the airport with his wife and children and there met a First Officer bound for the same ship. There being some delay before the aircraft took off, they all (according to the seaman-witness's evidence) had a meal together in a public restaurant at the airport. The witness's wife commented on the heat in India, where the ship was sailing, whereupon the First Officer told the witness and his wife not to worry about the heat, because he proposed to run the ship aground before she reached India in order to earn extra overtime. It was not suggested that the First Officer had ever met the witness's wife before, or that the witness and the First Officer (although they were acquainted) had ever discussed a crime of this character before or that the witness's children (although very young) were out of earshot. As it happened, there were other strong reasons for doubting the honesty of this witness, and in addition he did not make a favourable impression as a person, nor did his evidence accord closely with his earlier statements. But I should, dealing with a foreigner and with statements taken either through interpreters or in very different circumstances, have been unhappy to rely on these last points alone. As it was the story struck me as so highly improbable—although not, of course, impossible—that I would, if necessary, have rejected it on grounds of sheer unlikelihood alone. It is, I think, a common occurrence for a judge to find, after using his imagination to place himself in the position of the witness and in the context of the case as a whole, that an account given in evidence is one that he simply cannot swallow. While this is not a very scientific test nor is it in my view, if carefully and imaginatively applied, any the worse for that.

E. Perceptions as to the Frequency of Deliberate Untruthfulness

Different views have been expressed of the frequency with which judges encounter **18.28** deliberately untruthful witnesses. Sir Richard Eggleston took a rather gloomy view:

> In my experience, judges tend to overrate the propensity of witnesses to tell the truth. Since judges regard breach of the obligation imposed by the oath as a serious crime, as indeed it is, they tend to think that witnesses will be as overawed as those who impose the sanction of an oath think they ought to be. In fact, I do not think many people feel any sense of wrongdoing when they swear falsely, so long as they can persuade themselves that they are doing it in a good cause.[31]

One must certainly accept that of the thousands who take the oath each year it would be a tiny minority who would be constrained thereby to tell the truth for fear of spiritual penalty. But Lord Justice Browne expressed a more generous opinion—not, I feel sure, accounted for by the difference of national jurisdiction:

> I think that in civil cases (unlike criminal cases) the witnesses are seldom lying deliberately. But I am very sceptical about the reliability of oral evidence. Observation and memory are

---

[30] *The Zinovia* [1984] Lloyd's Rep. 264, at 281.   [31] Cited above at n.10, at 159.

fallible, and the human capacity for honestly believing something which bears no relation to what really happened is unlimited.[32]

18.29 I respectfully agree although, regrettably, somewhat less wholeheartedly than I should have done some years ago.

F. Honest Witnesses: the Three Sources of Unreliability

18.30 The tests used by judges to determine whether witnesses although honest are reliable or unreliable are, I think, essentially those used to determine whether they are honest or dishonest: inconsistency, self-contradiction, demeanour, probability and so on. But so long as there is any realistic chance of a witness being honestly mistaken rather than deliberately dishonest a judge will no doubt hold him to be so, not so much out of charity as out of a cautious reluctance to brand anyone a liar (and perjurer) unless he is plainly shown to be such. There are three sources of unreliability commonly referred to by judges when rejecting the evidence of honest witnesses.

(1) Omissions and errors of observation and memorization

18.31 The first source of unreliability, arising principally when the evidence relates to an accident or incident occurring over a very short space of time, is where the witness although present at the scene and in a position to see what happened does not in truth see, or in any event register mentally, exactly what did happen. Most of those who witness events of this kind are in the position of casual watchers of football on television, denied a commentary or a slow-motion replay: they see that a goal is scored; they know which side has scored it; they may (just) be able to identify the player who scored it; but they could not to save their lives give an accurate description of the moves and passes which led up to it. As witnesses so regularly say, 'it all happened so quickly, it was over in a flash'. There is of course a minority of accurate and very perceptive observers, although I doubt if there would be many even of that select band who could with any pretence of accuracy answer the sort of question habitually asked in motor accident cases: 'Had you reached the second telegraph pole on the left in photograph number 3 when you first saw the oncoming vehicle?'

18.32 Work done by psychologists on the operation of the human memory throws a very interesting sidelight on this point.[33] There is good reason to accept that with a significant number of witnesses, exposure to later misinformation gives rise to an inaccurate recollection as a result of supplementation or alteration. An account of this was given by Elizabeth Loftus, of the University of Washington, in a paper presented to the Royal Society:

> In a typical experiment, subjects see a complex event and are then asked a series of questions which exposes them to post-event information. Typically some of the questions

---

[32] Cited above at n.18, at 5.
[33] I am indebted to Gillian Butler, of The Warneford Hospital, Oxford for her expert guidance through this, to me, unknown terrain.

are designed to present misleading information, that is, to suggest the existence of an object or detail that did not in fact exist. Thus, in one study, subjects who had just watched a film of an automobile accident were asked, 'How fast was the white sports car going when it passed the barn while travelling along the country road?' Whereas no barn existed. The subjects were substantially more likely to later 'recall' having seen the non-existent barn than were the subjects who had not been asked the misleading questions.[34]

The scope for quite unintentional distortion of a witness's recollection by police or **18.33** enquiry agents or solicitors taking pre-trial statements is obvious. The same psychological testing suggested a number of other interesting conclusions, potentially significant to litigation: that once the memory is altered in this way, it is difficult to retrieve the original memory; that there is a tendency to reject misinformation if it comes from a source which the subject regards as biased or other than independent; that a warning against possible misinformation has an effect if given before the feeding of the misinformation but not after; that the longer the interval between the original event and the misinforma- tion, the greater the chance of distortion; that misinformation is less likely to be rejected the less prominently it features in the question put to the subject; and that exposure to an incident of extreme and ugly violence tends to limit a subject's recollection and also render him more vulnerable to later misinformation. I am not of course competent to discuss these conclusions, but they do perhaps go some way towards showing that the judges' habitual caution in accepting evidence of this kind reflects an approach justified by science as well as common sense.

(2) Loss of recollection

The second source of unreliability is loss of recollection. It is an unfortunate but **18.34** inescapable fact that most factual issues come to be determined, at any rate in the High Court, several years after the material events occurred. It is almost axiomatic that a witness cannot recall an event which happened several years ago as clearly and accurately as one that happened the day before. As it is often put, recollections fade with the passage of time. I do not doubt the essential truth of this proposition, although there is (I believe) a school of thought which holds that memories, once stored in the human mind, last for ever, the only problem being one of retrieval.[35] But I would add two comments:

Does memory fade uniformly with the passage of time? First, it is often assumed—or **18.35** appears to be assumed—that recollection fades in a more or less constant way, such that if loss of recollection were plotted against time the result would be a straight line. Thus judges sometimes speak as if a lapse of time, no matter how long after an event, must deprive a witness of some significant recollection of it. As Lord Pearce put it, 'with every day that passes the memory becomes fainter. . . .'[36] Taken very literally this is no doubt true, but I have often wondered whether loss of recollection, particularly of rather ordinary events not regarded as very striking or noteworthy at the time, does not occur in the main early on—say, the first six months or a year—with relatively little loss thereafter of what remains at the end of that period. I am reassured to find that the results of

---

[34] *Misfortunes of Memory,* paper presented at meeting of the Royal Society in January 1983.
[35] Ibid   [36] Cited above at n.8.

psychological investigation tend to confirm this hunch.[37] Although related to an entirely different subject matter (the retention of nonsense syllables) and a time scale altogether inappropriate to the sort of event with which litigation is likely to be concerned, these investigations appear to show a very high rate of loss immediately following the event and then no more than a minimal loss. If this pattern applied generally, it would strongly justify the attention habitually paid to the date when a witness made his first statement, that being identified as the same at which his recollection crystallized.

18.36   *Is the fading of memory selective?*   Second, I strongly suspect that recollection fades in a selective and not in a uniform way: in other words, that the circumstantial detail falls away or becomes blurred while recollection of the crucial and striking features of the event (as perceived by the witness) survive. This is suggesting no more than what is perhaps obvious, that the dominant impression lasts longest. My own experience suggests to me that the crucial features of any real emergency in which one has been personally involved remain clear for a very long time, if not indefinitely. Psychologists would not, I think, challenge that view, but tests reported by Bartlett as long ago as 1932[38] tended to show that the loss of recollection by subjects of the test asked to reproduce a narrative after a lapse of time followed a systematic pattern: as one would expect, the summary given became shorter and details were omitted, but omitted also were features which did not fit in with the subject's prior expectations, and there was a tendency to introduce material to explain incongruous features of the original narrative; certain detail might become dominant: words and names would be changed so as to become more familiar; and sometimes even the order of events would change. In a platitude, the memory plays funny tricks.

(3) Wishful thinking and self-exoneration

18.37   The third source of unreliability which I would mention is wishful thinking. I have already quoted passages in which Lord Pearce and Lord Justice Browne refer to this. Many other similar citations could be made. There can be few trial judges who have not at some time said something to this effect: 'X testified that so and so happened. I am sure that X was being entirely truthful in giving this evidence. I am also sure that so and so did not happen. In my judgment X has, over the years, erroneously but quite genuinely persuaded himself that so and so happened as he described.' This approach has philosophical support; Nietzsche observed:

> 'I did this,' says my memory, 'I cannot have done this,' says my pride, and remains inexorable. In the end memory yields.[39]

I certainly do not challenge that such wishful thinking, usually a process of unconscious self-exoneration, occurs. But I do a little question how often, in normal (unhallucinated) people, it does so. One cannot usefully make a clinical experiment upon oneself, because that which one has wishfully persuaded oneself to be true is (if the theory is sound)

---

[37] Baddeley, A.D., *The Psychology of Memory*, New York: Harper & Row, 1976.

[38] Bartlett, F.C., *Remembering*, Cambridge: Cambridge University Press, 1932.

[39] Nietzsche, F., *Also sprach Zarathustra*, Prologue.

indistinguishable to oneself from the truth. I must, however, confess a personal belief that the effect of time is often quite the opposite: acts or omissions which at the time one persuades oneself are in every way proper and justifiable become, in retrospect, embarrassingly obvious as grounds of criticism. Perhaps it all depends on the individual. The consensus appears to be that this is not an uncommon phenomenon, and if, as I have suggested, the memory is vulnerable to misinformation from without, it is perhaps to be expected that the urgings of the subconscious will be no less efficacious.

Further Reading

Cardozo, B., *The Nature of the Judicial Process*, New Haven, Conn: Yale University Press, 1921, 128–129.
Devlin, P., *The Judge*, Oxford: Oxford University Press, 1979.
Eggleston, R., *Evidence, Proof and Probability*, Littleton, Colorado: Fred B. Rothman & Co, 1978, 155.
MacKenna, B., 'Discretion' (1974) 9 *The Irish Jurist* (new series), 1.
Brown, P. (Lord Justice) 'Judicial Reflections' (1982) 35 *Current Legal Problems* 5.

Lord Bingham was a barrister in independent practice between 1959 and 1975; a Recorder of the Crown Court 1972–1975; a High Court Judge 1975–1980; a Lord Justice of Appeal 1986–1992; Master of the Rolls 1992–1996; Lord Chief Justice 1996–2000 and, since 2000, has been the Senior Lord of Appeal in Ordinary. He was Chairman of the Butler Trust 2001–2004. His numerous honours include the award of an Honorary Fellowship of The American College of Trial Lawyers in 1994. He was made a Knight of the Garter in 2005. Some of his collected essays and speeches were published as *The Business of Judging* by Oxford University Press in 2000.

Editors' Note

Occasionally, a judge may express an opinion of general application in an individual case, hence Smith, J: 'although witnesses might lie, that did not necessarily mean that the entirety of that witness's evidence should be rejected. A witness could lie in a stupid attempt to bolster a case, but the actual case could, nevertheless, remain good irrespective of the lie' (in *EPI Environmental Technologies Inc. and Another v Symphony Plastic Technologies plc and Another*, *The Times*, 14 January 2005). However, it is rare that the views of an experienced judge, let alone one whose opinions are as sought after as this author's, concerning the subject of the treatment of contentious witness testimony, are published in any wider context and the judiciary have, traditionally, been shy to expound their opinions on topics which might be the subject of consideration in cases which they might be called upon to try.

This chapter, originally written in 1985 when Lord Bingham had been sitting as a first instance judge for ten years, is, therefore, a particularly valuable contribution to the question of the best and most logical approach to the resolution of disputed issues arising from the evidence of eyewitnesses, free of the consideration of potentially misleading material such as their demeanour when giving evidence.

19

JUDGING EYEWITNESSES, CONFESSIONS, INFORMANTS AND ALIBIS: WHAT IS WRONG WITH JURIES AND CAN THEY DO BETTER?

Saul Kassin

A. Introduction

This chapter will address lay people's ability to assess the accuracy and credibility of **19.01** oral testimony at trial in the form of eyewitness identifications, confessions to police, informants, and alibis. The DNA exoneration literature reveals that there are systemic problems at two levels. First and inevitably, human-produced evidence is imperfect, often being flawed and biased. Second, however, police, prosecutors, judges, and juries too often assess that evidence at insufficient levels of accuracy. In particular, recent DNA exoneration cases reveal a glaring failure among juries that had convicted innocent defendants because they mistakenly believed mistaken but confident eyewitnesses, perjured testimony from informants and other cooperating witnesses, and vividly detailed false confessions—all while disbelieving credible denials and defence alibis. These research literatures are reviewed, after which it is argued that juries are informationally handicapped in their task, as they typically observe the final product (i.e. the witness's confident identification, the suspect's admission and detailed confession, and an informant's rehash of the defendant's statements) but not the process through which it came about (i.e. how the eyewitness made his or her identification, how the suspect was induced to confess, and how the informant was recruited to serve as a cooperating witness). To the extent that diagnostic information resides in these eliciting situations, and to the extent that juries are denied access to that information, they are structurally handicapped in their ability to make accurate judgements of accuracy and credibility. For this reason, the use of videotaping is proposed as an important means of reform.

19.02 Every tragic tale of a wrongful conviction—in which an innocent person is sent to prison while the criminal escapes detection—is a tale of two layered flaws in the criminal justice system. The first occurs when bad evidence is gathered in the street, the police station, or the crime laboratory. In recent years, forensic researchers have uncovered a host of problems both in the data collection processes and in the objectivity and accuracy of such core forms of human-produced evidence as eyewitness identifications,[1] police-induced confessions,[2] sworn testimony from jailhouse snitches and other informants[3] and an array of forensic sciences[4]—including fingerprints.[5] The second flaw occurs in the courtroom, when judges and juries fail to serve as a safety net, using the bad evidence that is presented in reaching a verdict—often while discounting credible denials and defence alibis.[6]

19.03 This chapter will address lay people's ability to assess the accuracy and credibility of oral testimony in the form of eyewitness identifications, police-induced confessions, government informants, and defence alibis.

B. Eyewitness Identifications

19.04 The annals of criminal justice reveal that wrongful convictions occur on a regular basis. In the light of recent advances in the science of DNA testing, the number of post-conviction exonerations has drawn a great deal of consternation. As these numbers accumulate, revealing the tip of an iceberg the size of which is unknown, it is clear

---

[1] Wells, G.L., Malpass, R.S., Lindsay, R.C.L., Fisher, R.P., Turtle, J.W. and Fulero, S.M., 'From the lab to the police station: a successful application of eyewitness research' (2000) 55 *American Psychologist*, 581–598.

[2] Kassin, S.M., and Gudjonsson, G.H., 'The psychology of confession evidence: A review of the literature and issues' (2004) 5 *Psychological Science in the Public Interest*, 33–67.

[3] E.g. Yaroshefsky, E., 'Symposium: The cooperating witness conundrum: Is justice attainable?' (2002) 23 *Cardozo Law Review*, issue 3.

[4] E.g. Faigman, D.L., Kaye, D.H., Saks, M.J. and Sanders, J., *Science in the law: Forensic science issues*, St. Paul, Minn: West, 2002.

[5] Cole, S.A., *Suspect identities: A history of fingerprinting and criminal identification*, Cambridge, Mass: Harvard University Press, 2001.

[6] E.g. Olson, E.A. and Wells, G.L., 'What makes a good alibi? A proposed taxonomy' (2004) 28 *Law and Human Behavior*, 157–176.

that mistaken eyewitnesses are the most common source of error. Indeed, one or more eyewitness identifications were in evidence in roughly three-quarters of these cases.[7]

(1) System and estimator variables

Beginning with Munsterberg's 1908 work *On the witness stand*,[8] psychologists have **19.05** systematically identified a number of factors that compromise an eyewitness's ability to perceive, store, and ultimately retrieve a perpetrator's face and crime from memory.[9] Following a distinction introduced by Wells,[10] some of this work has focused on *estimator variables* that enable researchers to identify possible sources of error (e.g. whether the witness is under stress; whether there was a weapon present); other work focuses on *system variables* that can be controlled, making it possible to improve eyewitness accuracy by altering identification procedures (e.g. using the unbiased instruction that the perpetrator might or might not be in the line-up; making sure that the suspect's photograph is not more salient than the others; presenting the line-up alternatives sequentially rather than in a simultaneous array). On the basis of these latter variables, researchers in the U.S. helped produce for the Justice Department a 'How to' manual, the first of its kind, entitled *Eyewitness Evidence: A Guide for Law Enforcement*.[11]

In light of all the research that has been conducted, there is a general consensus within **19.06** the scientific community as to the factors that affect the accuracy of eyewitness identifications. In a survey of 64 eyewitness experts, for example, at least 80 per cent agreed that the following 16 phenomena are reliable enough to be presented in court:

- that an eyewitness's report can be shaped by how questions are worded;
- police instructions can affect an eyewitness's willingness to make an identification;
- an eyewitness's confidence can be influenced by factors unrelated to accuracy;
- exposure to mugshots of a suspect can increase the likelihood that a witness will later select the suspect in a line-up;
- eyewitness memories are influenced by post-event information;
- young children are more suggestible than adults;
- eyewitness perceptions can be tainted by attitudes and expectations;
- hypnosis increases the impact of leading questions;
- alcoholic intoxication impairs the recollection of persons and events;
- eyewitnesses are more accurate at identifying members of their own race than of other races;
- the presence of a weapon reduces identification accuracy;
- confidence is not a good predictor of accuracy;
- eyewitness memory loss over time is patterned after the classic forgetting curve;

---

[7] Scheck, B., Neufeld, P. and Dwyer, J., *Actual innocence: Five days to execution and other dispatches form the wrongly convicted*, New York: Doubleday, 2000; *http://www.innocenceproject.org*.

[8] Munsterberg, H., *On the witness stand*, Garden City, NY: Doubleday, 1908.

[9] For a historical overview see Doyle, J. M., *True witness: Cops, courts, science, and the struggle against misidentification*, New York: Palgrave MacMillan, 2005.

[10] Wells, G. L., 'Applied eyewitness testimony research: System variables and estimator variables' (1978) 36 *Journal of Personality and Social Psychology*, 1546–1557

[11] See Wells *et al*, 2000, cited above at n.1, discussing how the guidelines were developed.

- brief exposure time reduces accuracy;
- witnesses are more likely to misidentify someone when presented with a simultaneous array than a sequential lineup, and
- eyewitnesses sometimes identify as a culprit someone they had seen in another context.[12]

(2) Impact of eyewitness identifications on juries and others

19.07   Many years ago, researchers found that juries are not proficient at evaluating the accuracy of eyewitnesses. Wells, Lindsay, and their colleagues conducted a series of experiments in which they staged a theft in the presence of participants who were later cross-examined after trying to identify the culprit from a photospread.[13] Serving as mock jurors, other participants observed the examination and judged the witnesses. The results revealed two patterns of results that were subsequently replicated. One is that the jurors over-estimated how accurate the eyewitnesses were, relative to observed accuracy rates; the second is that they could not distinguish from the examinations between witnesses whose identifications were correct and those who were incorrect.

19.08   Additional studies suggest that there are two problems. First, laypeople are not sophisti-cated as implicit cognitive psychologists, the subject of human memory being something about which they have little knowledge as a matter of common sense. Survey studies have shown that people lack awareness of many of the eyewitness phenomena described above, including those on which experts strongly agree.[14] Even in the context of a trial, mock jurors are not sufficiently responsive to the effects of line-up instructions and other cognitive factors involved in the acquisition, storage, and retrieval of the eyewitness information[15]—such as the race of the culprit.[16] This lack of knowledge among legal decision makers is not limited to trial juries. Wise and Safer surveyed 160 US judges for their beliefs about eyewitness testimony and found that although the judges were correct on some issues, they were incorrect on numerous important questions—such as whether eyewitness confidence at trial is a strong indicator of accuracy, and whether jurors can distinguish accurate from inaccurate witnesses.[17]

---

[12]   Kassin, S. M., Tubb, V. A., Hosch, H. M. and Memon, A., 'On the "general acceptance" of eyewitness testimony research: A new survey of experts' (2001) 56 *American Psychologist*, 405–416.

[13]   Lindsay, R. C. L., Wells, G. L. and Rumpel, C., 'Can people detect eyewitness identification accuracy within and between situations?' (1981) 66 *Journal of Applied Psychology*, 79–89. See also Wells, G. L., Lindsay, R. C. L. and Ferguson, T. J., 'Accuracy, confidence, and juror perceptions in eyewitness identification' (1979) 64 *Journal of Applied Psychology*, 440–448.

[14]   Brigham, J. C. and Bothwell, R. K., 'The ability of prospective jurors to estimate the accuracy of eyewitness identifications' (1983) 7 *Law and Human Behavior*, 19–30; Kassin, S. M. and Barndollar, K. A., 'The psychology of eyewitness testimony: a comparison of experts and prospective jurors' (1992) 22 *Journal of Applied Social Psychology*, 1241–1249.

[15]   Cutler, B. L., Penrod, S. D. and Dexter, H. R., 'Juror sensitivity to eyewitness identification evidence' (1990) 14 *Law and Human Behavior*, 185–191; Cutler, B. L., Penrod, S. D. and Stuve, T. E., 'Juror decision making in eyewitness identification cases' (1988) 12 *Law and Human Behavior*, 41–55.

[16]   Abshire, J. and Bernstein, B. H., 'Juror sensitivity to the cross-race effect' (2003) 27 *Law and Human Behavior*, 471–480.

[17]   Wise, R. A. and Safer, M. A., 'What U.S. judges know and believe about eyewitness testimony' (2004) 18 *Applied Cognitive Psychology*, 427–443. See also Stinson, V., Devenport, J. L., Cutler, B. L. and Kravitz, D. A., 'How effective is the motion-to-suppress safeguard? Judges' perceptions of the suggestiveness and fairness of biased lineup instructions' (1997) 82 *Journal of Applied Psychology*, 211–220.

The second problem is that typically people, including mock jurors, are highly influenced **19.09**
in their assessments of eyewitness accuracy by a host of cues that are not diagnostic of
accuracy. For example, research shows that people infer accuracy from a witness's memory for vivid and trivial details[18] from internal consistencies in the witness's testimony,[19]
and from self-reported confidence—a cue that is influenced by extraneous factors, such
as post-identification feedback, and is only modestly predictive of accuracy.[20]

(3) Mechanisms for improving jury performance

It is not clear whether jurors can be sufficiently educated about human memory to **19.10**
become more discerning and more accurate judges of eyewitness evidence, though there
is some encouraging research on this front. One possibility is to videotape all eyewitness
identifications so that juries can observe not only the witness's decision but the process
by which that decision was made. A number of mock eyewitness studies have shown that
accurate witnesses are more likely than inaccurate witnesses to make their identification
decisions quickly[21] and to describe the process as automatic and effortless rather than
involving an elimination of alternatives.[22] To the extent that jurors are permitted to
observe the identification process, they may shed their conventional reliance on confidence and base their judgements more on the speed and ease with which witnesses
made their decisions—a cue that is diagnostic.[23]

A second means of educating trial juries is through expert testimony on the psychology of **19.11**
perception, memory, and eyewitness identifications. Cutler, Penrod, and Dexter[24] identified two possible effects of such testimony: (1) that juries become more *sceptical* of
eyewitness identifications, and less likely in general to convict on the basis of such

---

[18] Bell, B.E., and Loftus, E.F., 'Trivial persuasion in the courtroom: The power of (a few) minor details'
(1989) 56 *Journal of Personality and Social Psychology*, 669–679.

[19] Berman, G.L. and Cutler, B.L., 'Effects of inconsistencies in eyewitness testimony on mock-juror
decision making' (1996) 81 *Journal of Applied Psychology*, 170–177.

[20] Bradfield, A.L., Wells, G.L. and Olson, E.A., 'The damaging effect of confirming feedback on the
relation between eyewitness certainty and identification accuracy' (2002) 87 *Journal of Applied Psychology*,
112–120; Penrod, S.D. and Cutler, B., 'Witness confidence and accuracy: Assessing their forensic relation'
(1995) 1 *Psychology, Public Policy, and Law*, 817–845; Sporer, S.L., Penrod, S.D., Read, J.D. and Cutler,
B.L., 'Choosing, confidence, and accuracy: A meta-analysis of the confidence–accuracy relation in
eyewitness identification studies' (1995) 118 *Psychological Bulletin*, 315–327; Wells, G.L. and Murray, D.,
'Eyewitness confidence' in Wells, G.L. and Loftus E.F. (eds.), *Eyewitness testimony: Psychological perspectives*,
New York: Cambridge University Press, 1984.

[21] Kassin, S.M., 'Eyewitness identification: Retrospective self awareness and the accuracy–confidence
correlation' (1993) 49 *Journal of Personality and Social Psychology*, 878–893; Sporer, S.L., 'Eyewitness
identification, accuracy, confidence, and decision times in simultaneous and sequential lineups' (1993)
78 *Journal of Applied Psychology*, 22–33; Dunning D. and Perretta, S., 'Automaticity and eyewitness
accuracy: a 10- to 12-second rule for distinguishing accurate from inaccurate positive identifications'
(2002) 87 *Journal of Applied Psychology*, 951–962; Weber, N., Brewer, N., Wells, G.L., Semmler, C. and
Keast, A., 'Eyewitness identification accuracy and response latency: The unruly 10–12 second rule' (2004)
10 *Journal of Experimental Psychology: Applied*, 139–147.

[22] Dunning, D. and Stern, L.B., 'Distinguishing accurate from inaccurate eyewitness identifications via
inquiries about decision processes' (1994) 67 *Journal of Personality and Social Psychology*, 818–835.

[23] Kassin, S.M., 'Eyewitness identification procedures: The fifth rule' (1998) 22 *Law and Human
Behavior*, 649–653.

[24] Cutler, B.L., Penrod, S.D. and Dexter, H.R., 'The eyewitness, the expert psychologist, and the jury'
(1989) 13 *Law and Human Behavior*, 311–332.

evidence; and (2) that juries become more *sensitized* to the factors that are predictive of eyewitness accuracy and error, customizing their verdicts according to the details of the eyewitnessing situation. Over the years, mock jury research has produced mixed results. Although some studies have demonstrated increased sensitization as a function of expert testimony,[25] the predominant effect has been less surgical, to generally increase juror scepticism.[26] Moreover, recent studies seem to indicate that when an expert's testimony is embedded in a full trial, and lacks prominence, it has even less effect.[27]

19.12 At least when it comes to system variables, a third possible avenue is to educate jurors via instructions from the bench that describe accepted standards of practice. In one recent study, mock jurors read one of three versions of a trial transcript that contained an eyewitness's identification. In one version, the identification was taken properly. In a second version, the police officer made two procedural errors in taking the identification (assembling a line-up in which the defendant was distinctive and failing to instruct the witness that the culprit might or might not be present). In a third version, the same errors were committed and jurors were told that it violated Justice Department guidelines. In this last condition, where the investigator's errors breached government guidelines, subjects saw him as less professional, found the identification evidence to be less credible and were less likely to vote for conviction.[28]

C. Police-Induced Confessions

19.13 Without a doubt, the most compelling and persuasive of all witness statements are the self-incriminating statements made by the suspects who later become defendants. As in the research on jurors' perceptions of eyewitness testimony, there are two problems. One is that people uncritically accept confessions, sometimes despite the circumstances under which they were taken. The second problem is that people cannot distinguish at high levels of accuracy between true confessions and false.

(1) The primary source of error: coercive police interrogations

19.14 Most wrongful convictions in which there were false confessions in evidence are the product of two sources of error. The first is that certain police interrogation tactics lead innocent people to confess. Over the years, false confessions have been documented in a number of ways—as in cases where it was revealed that the confessed crime

---

[25] Ibid; Devenport, J. L., Stinson, V., Cutler, B. L. and Kravitz, D. A., 'How effective are the cross-examination and expert testimony safeguards? Jurors' perceptions of the suggestiveness and fairness of biased lineup procedures' (2002) 87 *Journal of Applied Psychology*, 1042–1054.

[26] Leippe, M. R., 'The case for expert testimony about eyewitness memory' (1995) 1 *Psychology, Public Policy, and Law*, 909–959.

[27] Devenport, J. L. and Cutler, B. L., 'Impact of defense-only and opposing eyewitness experts on juror judgments' (2004) 28 *Law and Human Behavior*, 569–576; Leippe, M. R., Eisenstadt, D., Rauch, S. M. and Seib, H., 'Timing of eyewitness expert testimony, jurors' need for cognition, and case strength as determinants of trial verdicts' (2004) 89 *Journal of Applied Psychology*, 524–541.

[28] Lampinen, J. M., Judges, D. P., Odegard, T. N. and Hamilton, S., 'The reactions of mock jurors to the Department of Justice Guidelines for the Collection and Preservation of Eyewitness Evidence' (2005) 27 *Basic and Applied Social Psychology*, 155–162.

did not occur, where the real perpetrators were apprehended, where the confessor's involvement was found to be physically impossible, and where exculpatory evidence was discovered. Indeed, 20–25 per cent of all the recent DNA exoneration cases reported by the Innocence Project had contained evidence of confessions, apparently false.[29]

The pages of history reveal that people sometimes confess to crimes they did not **19.15** commit voluntarily, without external pressure. When Charles Lindbergh's baby was kidnapped in 1932, two hundred people stepped forward to confess. In the 1980s, Henry Lee Lucas falsely confessed to hundreds of unsolved murders, making him the most prolific serial confessor in history. More often than not, however, innocent suspects confess to crimes they did not commit as a result of coercive methods of police interrogation—methods that include isolation, confrontation, the presentation of false evidence, and minimization. In many of these cases, the suspects *complied* with the demand for a confession in order to escape an aversive situation, avoid an explicit or implied threat, or gain a promised or implied reward. In other cases, innocent but vulnerable suspects—presented with apparently incontrovertible but false evidence—capitulated not only in their behavior, but also *internalized* the belief that they committed the crime in question, sometimes confabulating false memories in the process. In short, there are three types of false confessions: voluntary, compliant, and internalized.[30]

(2) The secondary source of error: where is the safety net?

The second source of error is that trial juries are influenced by these confessions. Mock **19.16** jury studies have shown that confessions have more impact than eyewitness and character testimony, other potent forms of human evidence,[31] and that people do not fully discount confessions even when coerced and even when it is logically and legally appropriate to do so.[32] In a study that illustrates the point, Kassin and Sukel[33] presented mock jurors with one of three versions of a murder trial transcript. In a low-pressure version, the defendant was said to have confessed to police immediately upon questioning. In a high-pressure version, participants read that the suspect was in pain and interrogated aggressively by a detective who waved his gun in a menacing manner. In a control version, there was no confession in evidence. Confronted with the high-pressure confession, participants appeared to respond in the legally prescribed manner, at least as assessed by two measures: they judged the statement to be involuntary and said it did not influence their decisions. Yet when it came to the all-important measure of verdicts, this confession significantly boosted the conviction rate. This pattern appeared even in a condition in

---

[29] Scheck *et al*, 2000, cited above at n.7; *http://www.innocenceproject.org*, cited above at n.7.

[30] For reviews see Gudjonsson, G. H., *The psychology of interrogations and confessions: A handbook*, Chichester: John Wiley & Sons, 2003; Kassin, S. M., 'The psychology of confession evidence' (1997) 52 *American Psychologist*, 221–233; Kassin and Gudjonsson, 2004, cited above at n 2.

[31] Kassin, S. M. and Neumann, K., 'On the power of confession evidence: An experimental test of the "fundamental difference" hypothesis' (1997) 21 *Law and Human Behavior*, 469–484.

[32] Kassin, S. M. and Wrightsman, L. S., 'Prior confessions and mock juror verdicts' (1980) 10 *Journal of Applied Social Psychology*, 133–146.

[33] Kassin, S. M. and Sukel, H., 'Coerced confessions and the jury: An experimental test of the "harmless error" rule' (1997) 21 *Law and Human Behavior*, 27–46.

which subjects were specifically admonished by the judge to disregard confessions they found to be coerced.

19.17 Confessions tend to overwhelm alibis and other forms of exculpatory evidence, resulting in a chain of adverse legal consequences—from arrest through prosecution, conviction, incarceration, and even execution. Archival analyses of actual cases containing confessions later proved false tell a horrific tale. When the false confessors pled not guilty and proceeded to trial, the jury conviction rates ranged from 73 per cent[34] to 81 per cent.[35] These figures led Drizin and Leo to describe confessions as 'inherently prejudicial and highly damaging to a defendant, even if it is the product of coercive interrogation, even if it is supported by no other evidence, and even if it is ultimately proven false beyond any reasonable doubt'.[36]

(3) The assumption that innocent people do not confess

19.18 There are four bases for pessimism on the question of whether people can detect as false the confessions of innocent suspects. First, generalized common sense leads us to trust confessions on the assumption that 'I would never confess to a crime I did not commit'. Over the years, social psychologists have found in a wide range of contexts that people fall prey to the fundamental attribution error, or correspondence bias—that is, they tend to make dispositional attributions for a person's actions, taking behaviour at face value, while neglecting the role of situational factors.[37] Gilbert and Malone[38] offered several explanations for this bias, the most compelling of which is that people draw quick and relatively automatic dispositional inferences from behaviour and then fail to adjust or correct for the presence of situational constraints. Common sense also compels the belief that people present themselves in ways that are self-serving and that self-destructive behaviours, like false confessions, must be particularly diagnostic. Reasonably, most people believe they would never confess to a crime they did not commit and they cannot imagine the circumstances under which anyone would do so.

(4) The difficulty of distinguishing true and false confessions

19.19 A second general basis for pessimism is that people are not particularly adept at deception detection.[39] As to whether people can specifically distinguish between true and false confessions, Kassin, Meissner, and Norwick[40] conducted a two-part study in which they

---

[34] Leo, R. A. and Ofshe, R. J., 'The consequences of false confessions: Deprivations of liberty and miscarriages of justice in the age of psychological interrogation' (1998) 88 *Journal of Criminal Law and Criminology*, 429–496.

[35] Drizin, S. A. and Leo, R. A., 'The problem of false confessions in the post-DNA world' (2004) 82 *North Carolina Law Review*, 891–1007.

[36] Ibid, at 959.   [37] Jones, E. E., *Interpersonal perception*, New York: Freeman, 1990.

[38] Gilbert, D. T. and Malone, P. S., 'The correspondence bias' (1995) 117 *Psychological Bulletin*, 21–38.

[39] For reviews of this extensive literature see Vrij, A., *Detecting lies and deceit: The psychology of lying and the implications for professional practice*, Chichester: John Wiley and Sons, 2000; Strömwall, L. A., Granhag, P. A. and Jonsson, A.-C., 'Deception among pairs: "Let's say we had lunch and hope they will swallow it!" ' (2003) 9 *Psychology, Crime and Law*, 109–124.

[40] Kassin, S. M., Meissner, C. A. and Norwick, R. J., ' "I'd know a false confession if I saw one": A comparative study of college students and police investigators' (2005) 29 *Law and Human Behavior*, 211–227.

compared the performance of police investigators and lay people. First, they recruited and paid male prison inmates in a correctional facility to take part in a pair of videotaped interviews. Each inmate was instructed to give a full confession to the crime for which he is in prison, a narrative that was followed by responses to a standardized set of questions ('Tell me about what you did, the crime you committed, that brought you here'). In a second videotaped interview, each inmate was provided with a skeletal, one- or two-sentence description of the crime committed by the preceding participant and instructed to concoct a false confession ('I'd like you to lie about it and make up a confession as if you did it'). In this yoked design, the first inmate's true confession thus became the basis of the second inmate's false confession, the second's true confession became the basis of the third's false confession, and so on.

Using this procedure, we created a stimulus videotape that depicted ten different **19.20** inmates, each giving a single confession to one of the following five crimes: aggravated assault, armed robbery, burglary, breaking and entering, and automobile theft and reckless driving. With research showing that people are better judges of truth and deception when they use auditory cues than misleading visual cues,[41] we also created audiotapes of these same confessions. Two groups of subjects served as judges in this study: 61 college students and 57 federal, state, and local investigators, two-thirds of whom had received training in interviewing and interrogation. The results closely paralleled those obtained for judgements of true and false denials. From the videotapes, neither students nor the investigators performed significantly better than chance, though once again investigators were far more confident in their judgements. Consistent with research showing that people are more accurate when they attend to the voice than to facial cues, accuracy rates were higher when participants listened to audiotaped confessions than when they watched the videotapes. Importantly, the students but not the investigators exceeded chance level performance in this condition; the investigators, however, were more confident.

There are two possible explanations for why investigators were unable to distinguish true **19.21** and false confessions in this study and why they were generally less accurate than naïve college students. One possibility is that law enforcement work introduces systematic bias that reduces overall judgement accuracy. This hypothesis is consistent with the finding that police investigators as a group are generally and highly suspicious of deception.[42] It is also not terribly surprising in light of the behavioural deception cues that form part of the basis for training.[43] For example, Inbau *et al*[44] advocate the use of visual cues such as

[41] Anderson, D.E., DePaulo, B.M., Ansfield, M.E., Tickle, J.J. and Green, E., 'Beliefs about cues to deception: Mindless stereotypes or untapped wisdom?' (1999) 23 *Journal of Nonverbal Behavior*, 67–89; DePaulo, B.M., Lassiter, G.D. and Stone, J.I., 'Attentional determinants of success at detecting deception and truth' (1982) 8 *Personality and Social Psychology Bulletin*, 273–279.

[42] Masip, J., Alonso, H., Garrido, E. and Anton, C., 'Generalized communicative suspicion (GCS) among police officers: Accounting for the investigator response bias' (2005) 35 *Journal of Applied Social Psychology*, 1046–1066.

[43] Vrij, 2000, cited above at n.39.

[44] Inbau, F.E., Reid, J.E., Buckley, J.P. and Jayne, B.C., *Criminal interrogation and confessions* (4th ed.), Gaithersberg, MD: Aspen, 2001.

gaze aversion, non-frontal posture, slouching, and grooming gestures that, as an empirical matter, are not diagnostic of truth or deception.[45] Furthermore, research has shown that people are more accurate when they rely on auditory cues than on visual information.[46] The results replicated this effect: discrimination accuracy was higher in the audio condition than in the video condition without a significant influence on response bias. In short, it is conceivable that training in the use of visual cues would impair performance, not improve it.

19.22 Another possibility is that investigators' judgement accuracy was compromised by the use of a paradigm in which half of the stimulus confessions were false—a percentage that is likely far higher than the real world base rate for false confessions. To the extent that law enforcement work leads investigators to presume guilt and to presume most confessions true, then the response bias they imported from the police station to the laboratory might have proved misleading for a study in which they were told merely that some statements were true and others false. So instructed, investigators judged 65 per cent of the statements to be true, compared to only 55 per cent among students. Hence, our investigators might have performed poorly because of a gross mismatch between the expected and presented base rates for false confessions. To test the hypothesis that investigators' judgement accuracy was depressed relative to students because of differences in their base rate expectations, Kassin, Meissner and Norwick[47] conducted a second study to neutralize the response bias. In this experiment, all participants were shown the ten videotaped confessions but they were instructed prior to the task that half of the statements were true and half were false. It was predicted that this manipulation would neutralize the dispositional response bias of investigators relative to students—and perhaps increase judgement accuracy in the process. The manipulation was successful, both in reducing the overall number of 'true' judgements that had produced the response bias and in eliminating the differences between participant samples. But on the question of whether this would improve performance, the results were mixed. Compared to their counterparts in the videotape condition of the first experiment, investigators in this study had a comparable hit rate but a much lower false alarm rate. They still were not more accurate than students, however, and they still were overconfident. Although the response bias was neutralized, the investigators maintained the pattern of low accuracy and high confidence.

(5) Interrogation as a corrupting, guilt-presumptive process

19.23 A third reason for pessimism is that police-induced confessions, unlike most other types of verbal statements, are corrupted by the very process of interrogation that elicits them—designed for persuasion, even if false. By definition, interrogation is a theory-driven social interaction led by an authority figure who holds a strong *a priori* belief about the target and who measures success by his or her ability to extract an admission.

---

[45] DePaulo, B.M., Lindsay, J.J., Malone, B.E., Muhlenbruck, L., Charlton, K. and Cooper, H., 'Cues to deception' (2003) 129 *Psychological Bulletin*, 74–112.

[46] Anderson *et al*, 1999, cited above at n.41; DePaulo *et al*, 1982, cited above at n.41.

[47] Cited above at n.40.

For innocent people who are initially misjudged, one would hope that investigators would remain open-minded enough to monitor the suspect and situation and re-evaluate their own beliefs. However, research suggests that once people form a belief, they wittingly or unwittingly create behavioural support for that belief. Variously termed the self-fulfilling prophecy, interpersonal expectancy effect, and behavioural conformation bias, this phenomenon was first demonstrated by Rosenthal and Jacobson[48] in their classic study of teacher expectation effects on students' academic performance, with similar results obtained in military, business, and other organizational settings.[49] In the laboratory, researchers have found that behavioural confirmation is the outcome of a three-step chain of events by which a perceiver forms a belief about a target person, behaves towards that person in a manner that conforms to that belief, leading the target to respond in ways that often support the perceiver's initial belief.[50]

19.24 When it comes to confessions, it is reasonable to expect that the presumption of guilt leads interrogators to adopt an approach that is aggressive and confrontational, and that leads even innocent suspects to become anxious and defensive—and supportive of the presumption. Illustrating the process, Akehurst and Vrij[51] found that increased bodily movement among police officers triggered movement in interviewees, behaviour that is interpreted as suspicious. More recently, Kassin, Goldstein, and Savitsky[52] looked at whether the presumption of guilt shapes the conduct of student interrogators, the behaviour of student suspects, and ultimately the judgements made by neutral observers. This study was conducted in two phases. In Phase I, suspects stole $100 as part of a mock theft or took part in a related but innocent act, after which they were interviewed via headphones from a remote location. Other subjects, participating as investigators, were led to believe that most of the suspects in the study were truly guilty or innocent. These sessions were audiotaped for later analysis and followed by post-interrogation questionnaires. In Phase II, observers listened to the taped interviews, judged the suspect as guilty or innocent, and rated their impressions of both sets of participants.

19.25 The results indicated that student interrogators who were led to expect guilt rather than innocence asked more guilt-presumptive questions, saw the suspects as guilty, used more interrogation techniques, tried harder and exerted more pressure to get a confession, and made innocent suspects sound more defensive and guilty to observers. Consistently, the

---

[48] Rosenthal, R. and Jacobson, L., *Pygmalion in the classroom: Teacher expectation and pupils' intellectual development*, New York: Holt, Rinehart, & Winston, 1968.

[49] McNatt, D. B., 'Ancient Pygmalion joins contemporary management: A meta-analysis of the result' (2000) 85 *Journal of Applied Psychology*, 314–322.

[50] For reviews, see Darley, J. M. and Fazio, R. H., 'Expectancy confirmation processes arising in the social interaction sequence' (1980) 35 *American Psychologist*, 867–881; Nickerson, R.S., 'Confirmation bias: A ubiquitous phenomenon in many guises' (1998) 2 *Review of General Psychology*, 175–220; Snyder, M., 'Motivational foundations of behavioral confirmation' (1992) 25 *Advances in Experimental Social Psychology*, 67–114; Snyder, M. and Stukas, A., 'Interpersonal processes: The interplay of cognitive, motivational, and behavioral activities in social interaction' (1999) 50 *Annual Review of Psychology*, 273–303.

[51] Akehurst, L. and Vrij, A., 'Creating suspects in police interviews' (1999) 29 *Journal of Applied Social Psychology*, 192–210.

[52] Kassin, S. M., Goldstein, C. J. and Savitsky, K., 'Behavioral confirmation in the interrogation room: On the dangers of presuming guilt' (2003) 27 *Law and Human Behavior*, 187–203.

most pressure-filled interrogation sessions, as rated by all participants, were those that paired investigators who presumed guilt with suspects who were actually innocent. Observers who listened to the tapes later perceived the suspects in the guilty expectations condition as more defensive and as somewhat more guilty. In short, the presumption of guilt, which underlies all interrogation, may set in motion a process of behavioural confirmation, as it shapes the interrogator's behaviour, the suspect's behaviour, and ultimately the judgements of judges, juries, and other neutral observers.

(6) The presence of credibility cues in false confessions

19.26 A fourth reason for pessimism concerning juries is that real-life false confessions, when elicited through a process of interrogation, contain content cues that people naturally associate with truth-telling. In most documented false confessions, the statements ultimately presented in court are compelling, as they often contain vivid and accurate details about the crime, the scene, and the victim—details that can become known to an innocent suspect through the assistance of leading interview questions, overheard conversations, photographs, visits to the crime scene, and other secondhand sources of information invisible to the naïve observer. To obfuscate matters further, many confessions are also textured with 'elective' statements in which innocent suspects describe not just what they allegedly did, and how, but *why*—as they self-report on revenge, jealousy, desperation, capitulation to peer pressure, and other prototypical motives for crime. Sometimes they add apologies and expressions of remorse. In some cases, innocent suspects find and correct minor errors that appear in the statements that are derived from them, suggesting that they read, understood, and verified the contents. To the naïve spectator, such statements appear to be voluntary, textured with detail, and the product of personal experience. However, the taped confession is much like a Hollywood drama—scripted by the police theory, rehearsed during hours of unrecorded questioning, directed by the questioner, and enacted on camera by the suspect.[53]

19.27 The Reid technique offers advice on how to create these illusions of credibility. In *Criminal Interrogations and Confessions*, Inbau *et al*[54] recommend that interrogators insert minor errors (such as a wrong name, date, or street address) into written confessions so that the suspect will spot them, correct them, and initial the changes. The purpose is to increase the perceived credibility of the statement and make it difficult for the defendant later to distance himself or herself from it. As only guilty suspects should be in a position to spot these errors, this technique has diagnostic potential. However, Inbau *et al* advise that to play it safe, 'the investigator should keep the errors in mind and raise a question about them in the event the suspect neglects to do so'.[55] Similarly, they advise investigators to insert into written confessions irrelevant personal history items known only to the 'offender'. 'For instance, the suspect may be asked to give the name of the grade school he attended, the place or hospital in which he was born, or other similar information.'[56] Of course, for the suspect who is not the offender but an innocent person, the insertion of

---

[53] Kassin, S.M., 'False confessions and the jogger case' *New York Times*, 1 November 2002, A31.
[54] Cited above at n.44.   [55] Ibid, at 384.   [56] Ibid, at 383.

crime-irrelevant biographical details from his or her own life has no diagnostic value. Like the error correction trick, it creates a false illusion of credibility, making it more and more difficult for a jury to determine its veracity.

D. Informants, Snitches, and Other Cooperating Witnesses

'The history of the snitch is long and inglorious, dating to the common law. In old **19.28** England, snitches were ubiquitous. Their motives, then as now, were unholy.'[57]

Many recent DNA exonerations, as with other wrongful convictions discovered over the **19.29** years, contained confessions that defendants had yielded to police during the process of interrogation. Even more common in the annals of wrongful convictions, equally disturbing but seldom scrutinised, are confessions that defendants had allegedly made to fellow inmates while in jail awaiting trial. As a result of conversations and negotiations with authorities, these inmates step forward to report on these confessions—bringing into trial testimony from informants, jailhouse snitches, and other cooperating witnesses.

(1) The cooperating witness problem

History shows that the first documented wrongful conviction in the United States **19.30** involved a snitch. In Manchester, Vermont, in 1819, brothers Jesse and Stephen Boorn were accused of killing their brother-in-law. Both men denied the charge, but Jesse was placed in a jail cell with Silas Merrill, a forger, who reported that Jesse had confessed to him. In exchange for his testimony, Merrill was released. For their part, the Boorn brothers were found guilty and sentenced to death—until the brother-in-law was found alive in New Jersey. Lest one mistakenly think that jailhouse snitches reveal a problem of ancient history, it is worth nothing that in the United States, where more than 100 innocent death row inmates have been exonerated over the past 30 years, perjured testimony from snitches was present in 46 per cent of their cases.[58]

As described in several thoughtful articles contained within a special issue of the *Cardozo* **19.31** *Law Review*, the tragic errors so often discovered in cases involving cooperating witnesses are self-evident and hardly surprising.[59] Describing the process by which prosecutors garner an informant's cooperation, Cohen[60] notes that there is a correlation between the magnitude of an informant's past criminal conduct and the demanded extent of his or her cooperation. The risk of perjury in such cases is substantial for three reasons: (1) the cooperating witnesses themselves have a tainted track record for credibility, having previously engaged in criminal conduct; (2) their testimony is invariably 'incentivised' by promises of leniency, immunity, release, transfer, cash, or other benefits; and (3) prosecutors are confident in their common-sense ability to know when cooperating witnesses are

---

[57] Warden R., *The snitch system: How snitch testimony sent Randy Steidl and other innocent Americans to death row*, Northwestern University School of Law, Center of Wrongful Convictions, 2004.
[58] Ibid.   [59] Cited above at n.3.
[60] Cohen, S.M., 'What is true?': Perspectives of a former prosecutor' (2002) 23 *Cardozo Law Review*, 817–828.

telling the truth or lying.[61] Indeed, as the recent trend in the US towards increasingly severe sentencing has raised the stakes for cooperating witnesses, 'the consequences of disappointing prosecutors can be devastating'.[62] To complicate matters further for judges and juries who must assess this evidence, these witnesses—once recruited—are routinely prepared by prosecutors for their testimony, a practice that often crosses a blurry line into improper witness coaching.[63] All considered, it is no wonder that a US federal appeals judge so forcefully argued that 'the judicial process is tainted and justice is cheapened when factual testimony is purchased, whether with leniency or money'.[64]

(2) Unknowns, and prospects for reform

19.32 Recognizing the dangers inherent in the self-serving testimony of cooperating witnesses, a number of structural recommendations have been made to improve the veracity of their testimony. Among these recommendations are that all cooperating witness statements be electronically recorded, that prosecutors disclose to defence counsel the terms of all deals struck with informants, and that prosecutors take steps to ensure that the resulting statements are true and corroborated by additional evidence. In the case of jailhouse snitches, an added recommendation is that the informants be wired to record electronically their conversations with the defendants who had allegedly confessed.

19.33 The problems associated with informants have been clearly and forcefully articulated. Indeed, Gershman described the cooperating witness as the most dangerous prosecution witness of all: 'no other witness has such an extraordinary incentive to lie. Furthermore, no other witness has the capacity to manipulate, mislead, and deceive his investigative and prosecutorial handlers.'[65] Despite the known abuses, criticisms, and recommendations for reform, little has changed—at least in the United States. Ultimately, and in the context of an adversarial forum that permits cross-examination, rebuttal witnesses, and closing arguments by counsel, the credibility and impact of informants, snitches and other cooperating witnesses is a matter for the judge or jury to decide.

19.34 To this author's knowledge, there is no published research on the specific question of how jurors use evidence from cooperating witnesses. According to attribution theory, jurors should discount, or at least underweight, testimony from snitches and other cooperating witnesses who stand to benefit personally and substantially from testimony that implicates the defendant. Yet research consistently has shown that people often fail to discount motivated testimony even when it is logically appropriate to do so. In numerous studies, for example, participants have inferred a college student's true attitudes from his or her writings and speeches—even when he or she was assigned by an instructor to espouse those particular attitudinal positions.[66] In light of this

---

[61] Yaroshefsky, E., 'Cooperation with federal prosecutors: Experiences of truth telling and embellishment' (1999) 68 *Fordham Law Review*, 917–964.

[62] Glaberson, W., 'Trading in lies, some informers build cases for prosecutors,' *New York Times*, 7 April 2004, Section B, 1.

[63] Gershman, B.L., 'Witness coaching by prosecutors' (2002) 23 *Cardozo Law Review*, 829–863.

[64] *United States v Singleton*, 144 F.3d 1343 (10th Circuit, 1998).

[65] Cited above at n.63, at 847.   [66] For a review, see Jones 1990, cited above at n.37.

phenomenon, as well as the numerous wrongful convictions by juries who heard testimony from informants, it seems clear that there is reason for concern.

E. The Alibis of Innocents

Countering eyewitness identifications, confessions, and incriminating secondhand testimony from informants, juries routinely must assess the defendant's protestations of innocence—denials that offer corroboration through the use of alibis. An alibi is a story, accompanied by some means of proof, which places a suspect at the time of the crime in another place, making it impossible for him or her to have committed the crime.[67] An alibi might place the defendant in any other setting (e.g. at home, at work, or in a public place) and engaged in any other activity (e.g. sleeping, working, recreation), and the corroborating proof that is offered might consist of physical evidence (e.g. surveillance camera footage, ATM receipts) or personal evidence (e.g. sworn testimony from friends, family members, or strangers). What makes alibis important is that they often contradict the state's eyewitnesses, informants, confessions, and other incriminating evidence—forcing juries to choose between the conflicting accounts. As to how juries assess alibis and manage the contradictions, it is interesting that among innocent people who were convicted but later exonerated by DNA, alibis were often presented and prosecutors often cited 'weak alibis' as proof of guilt.[68]

19.35

(1) People are poor alibi detectors

There are two reasons why juries cannot be trusted to assess a defendant's denials with accuracy. One is the now familiar phenomenon described earlier that people are poor judges of truth and deception.

19.36

In a two-part study of forensic relevance, Kassin and Fong[69] recruited college students to commit one of four mock crimes, which they found to be moderately stressful: breaking and entering a locked office building, shoplifting in a local gift shop, vandalizing a building by chalking it with graffiti, or breaking into someone's personal computer account. Afterward, they were apprehended by a security officer and brought into the laboratory for questioning. Others innocently reported to the same crime scenes, at which point they too were apprehended and brought in for questioning. All participants were pre-instructed to deny involvement if questioned and all were issued an incentive to be judged innocent by their questioner. During the brief interviews, which were videotaped, all suspects denied their guilt, offering alibis that were true (among those who were innocent) or false (among those who committed the mock crimes). In a second part of the study, other participants watched the tapes and judged the mock suspects. Regardless of whether these participants were first 'trained' in the Reid technique, they were unable to differentiate between suspects whose alibis were true and false.

19.37

---

[67] Garner, B.A. (ed.), *Black's Law Dictionary* (7th edition). St. Paul, Minn: West, 1999.
[68] Olson and Wells, 2004, cited above at n. 6.
[69] Kassin, S. M. and Fong, C. T., ' "I'm innocent!" Effects of training on judgments of truth and deception in the interrogation room' (1999) 23 *Law and Human Behavior*, 499–516.

19.38 In a follow-up study using the same tapes, Meissner and Kassin[70] tested police samples from the United States and Canada and found that they too could not distinguish between true and false alibis. In studies conducted in Sweden, researchers separately interviewed each member of truth-telling pairs and lying pairs of suspects about their alibis for a lunch that they did or did not have together. Replicating past research, they found that lay observers could distinguish only modestly between the truthful and deceptive alibis on the basis of these interviews. Interestingly, the problem stemmed from the fact that observers most frequently cited 'consistency within pairs of suspects' as a basis for their judgements. Yet the lying pairs, forewarned that they would be interviewed, fabricated alibis that were particularly consistent in their details.[71]

(2) People are sceptical of alibis

19.39 There is a second reason for concern over the way in which juries are likely to use alibi evidence. As a general rule, most people, when they are not alone, spend most of their time with family, friends, acquaintances—precisely the kinds of defence-interested parties that may elicit scepticism in juries.[72] As noted earlier, attribution theory predicts that jurors would discount the testimony of alibi witnesses who provide friendly support for defendants with whom they have a positive relationship. At the same time, research described earlier shows that people often do not discount what others say even when it is logically appropriate to do so.[73] To test these propositions in the context of alibi evidence, Lindsay *et al*[74] presented mock jurors with a trial involving a defendant who was positively identified by an eyewitness but whose innocence was supported by an alibi provided either by a relative or by a stranger. As measured by a lowered conviction rate, they found that jurors were influenced by the stranger but not by the relative. In a second study, Culhane and Hosch[75] presented mock jurors with a witness who corroborated or failed to corroborate the defendant's account that he was at home during an armed robbery for which he was identified. As in the Lindsay *et al* (1986) study, jurors were significantly influenced by the alibi when it was the defendant's neighbour ('Yes, I saw him working in his yard from 5:00 to 7:30') but not when it was his girlfriend ('Yes, he was with me at his home from 5:00 on').

19.40 In an effort to understand what constitutes a strong and believable alibi to social perceivers, Olson and Wells[76] proposed a taxonomy consisting of two dimensions:

---

[70] Meissner, C.A. and Kassin, S.M., ' "He's guilty!": Investigator bias in judgments of truth and deception' (2002) 26 *Law and Human Behavior*, 469–480.

[71] Granhag, P.A., Strömwall, L.A. and Jonsson, A.C., 'Partners in crime: How liars in collusion betray themselves' (2003) 33 *Journal of Applied Social Psychology*, 848–868; Strömwall, Granhag, and Jonsson, 2003, cited above at n.39.

[72] Martin, G.A., 'Closing argument to the jury for the defense in criminal cases' (1967) 58 *Journal of Criminal Law, Criminology, and Police Science*, 2–17.

[73] Jones, 1990, cited above at n.37.

[74] Lindsay, R.C.L., Lim, R., Marando, L. and Cully, D., 'Mock-juror evaluations of eyewitness testimony: A test of metamemory hypotheses' (1986) 15 *Journal of Applied Social Psychology*, 447–459.

[75] Culhane, S.E. and Hosch, H.M., 'An alibi witness' influence on mock jurors' verdicts' (2004) 34 *Journal of Applied Social Psychology*, 1604–1616.

[76] Cited above at n.6.

(1) whether the proof comes in the form of physical or personal evidence, and (2) the extent to which the alibi is easy or difficult to fabricate. To test this model, they presented participants, instructed to play the role of detectives, with brief descriptions of crimes, each followed by the alibis of three suspects. In all cases, participants were asked to rate the credibility of the alibis—which varied in the nature of the physical evidence (none; easy to fabricate; difficult to fabricate) and the person evidence (none; motivated familiar other; non-motivated familiar other; non-motivated stranger).

Overall, the results supported the proposed taxonomy—though there were also two **19.41** noteworthy findings. One was that participants were generally sceptical of alibis, yielding a mean believability score of only 7.4 out of 10 even in the strongest condition containing difficult to fabricate physical evidence (e.g. the defendant's presence on a timed and dated security camera) and difficult to fabricate personal evidence (e.g. a store clerk). This result led Olson and Wells to wonder, 'what kind of proof would it take to get a believability score of 8, 9, or 10?'[77] Second, participants were more likely to believe physical evidence than personal evidence—even when the physical evidence was easy to fabricate (e.g. a cash receipt). This latter result more specifically confirms that social perceivers are inherently sceptical of human alibi providers that are familiar to a defendant—even when not motivated by familiarity, friendship, and personal interest.

F. Closing Statement

In evaluating eyewitness identifications, confessions from defendants, testimony from **19.42** informants, and alibis, juries are informationally handicapped in two ways: first, juries were not present at the crime scene and must invariably rely on the evidentiary model of the event in question that is built in the courtroom; second, juries are typically not privy to the process by which the evidence presented in court was gathered. They typically see the final product (i.e. the witness's confident identification, the suspect's detailed confession, the informant's recruitment and rehash of the defendant's statements, and the alibi's description of the defendant's whereabouts) but not the process (the 'how') through which that evidence came about. To the extent that relevant diagnostic information resides in the eliciting situation, and to the extent that judges and juries are denied access to that information, they are structurally handicapped in their ability to make accurate judgements of accuracy and credibility.

Specific to each type of testimonial evidence, numerous proposals for reform have been **19.43** suggested, all designed to increase accuracy—of eyewitness identifications, confessions, and informants and alibi witnesses. Across these same domains, the second important issue concerns how to improve the performance of fact finders, notably judges and juries. Toward this end, research offers little reason to believe that expert testimony or cautionary instructions from the bench will substantially improve the accuracy of decision making. Future research should thus be directed at the most promising means of reform: the question of whether judges and juries would become more proficient at

---

[77] Ibid, p.174.

distinguishing accurate and mistaken eyewitnesses, guilty and innocent confessors, and truthful and lying witnesses for the prosecution and defence, if provided with electronic recordings of the *processes* by which these forms of evidence were gathered.

Further Reading

Doyle, J. M., *True witness: Cops, courts, science, and the struggle against misidentification*, New York: Palgrave MacMillan, 2005.

Granhag, P.A. and Strömwall, L. (eds.), *Deception detection in forensic contexts*, Cambridge: Cambridge University Press, 2004.

Kassin, S. M., and Gudjonsson, G. H., 'The psychology of confession evidence: A review of the literature and issues' (2004) 5 *Psychological Science in the Public Interest*, 33–67.

Vrij, A., *Detecting lies and deceit: The psychology of lying and the implications for professional practice*, Chichester: John Wiley and Sons 2000.

Williamson, T. (ed.), *Investigative interviewing: Rights, research, regulation*, Devon: Willan Publishing, 2005.

Saul Kassin is the Massachusetts Professor of Psychology and founder of Legal Studies at Williams College, in Williamstown, Massachusetts. He is author of *Psychology* (4th edition) and *Social Psychology* (6th edition) as well as many scholarly books, including: *Confessions in the Courtroom, The Psychology of Evidence and Trial Procedure*, and *The American Jury on Trial: Psychological Perspectives*. In his research lab, Dr. Kassin studies interviewing, interrogation, and confessions; eyewitness identifications; and the impact of such evidence on juries. Dr. Kassin is a Fellow of the American Psychological Association and the American Psychological Society. He has testified as an expert witness; lectures frequently to judges, lawyers, psychologists, and law enforcement groups; and has appeared as a frequent media consultant on psycho-legal issues.

Editors' Note

Those responsible for the formulation of specimen Judicial Studies Board directions by judges to juries concerning the areas covered by this chapter would be assisted by its contents. Criminal court advocates would also do well to recognize that, in the resolution of disputed factual issues arising from conflicting evidence from eyewitnesses, approaches which are based on long-held presumptions concerning what an honest or dishonest witness is likely to say and how they say it, or the way in which they behave when giving evidence, may be unsound or unhelpful. The direction concerning witness demeanour still commonly given to juries in Crown Court cases—'you've seen and heard the witnesses, make of them what you will'—and adopted as a valuable reassurance in appeal courts when a first instance fact finder's analysis of disputed evidence is criticised—'he [or she] saw and heard the witnesses'—patently ignores both scientific research and judicial experience that assessing a witness's truthfulness or accuracy by reference to their physical mannerisms can be highly dangerous. (Even assuming that the witness box is positioned in a place which enables the jury to see the witness face-on when they are giving evidence which, at least in Court 2 at the Central Criminal Court, it is not).

20

ORAL TESTIMONY FROM THE WITNESS'S PERSPECTIVE—PSYCHOLOGICAL AND FORENSIC CONSIDERATIONS

Peter Dunn and Eric Shepherd

'I needed far more counselling after I had gone through the police investigation and the court case than I had after the attack itself', rape victim, *The Observer*, 1 May 2005.

'The distress of the victim is almost integral to the success of their case.' Kelly Rust, Co-ordinator of Central Criminal Court Witness Service, *The Observer*, 1 May 2005.

A. Introduction

Witnessing is a long journey. In *Speaking Up for Justice*[1] the Government recognized the **20.01** stresses involved in this journey. The Youth Justice and Criminal Evidence Act 1999 implemented provisions to extend to vulnerable or intimidated witnesses pre-existing *special measures* introduced for child witnesses. The Act also included measures to protect witnesses from cross-examination by the accused in person.

In this chapter we open with a summary of the Act's key provisions and associated

---

[1] Home Office, *Speaking Up for Justice*, London: Home Office, 1998.

guidelines before reviewing the evidence from research and practice upon their application. This enables us to draw some conclusions about the need for criminal justice system practitioners to be more mindful, be more motivated, and be given more means to change their behaviour towards witnesses.

B. Changing Witnesses' Experience of Giving Testimony

(1) Narrowing the 'justice gap'

20.02 The Government wishes to narrow the 'justice gap'. It wants the criminal justice system to convict more offenders on the basis of recognizably sound evidence. To achieve this aim even greater reliance will have to be placed on witnesses coming forward and giving testimony. It makes sense to spell out some common-sense key starting points concerning witness testimony and the experience of witnesses:

- unless we get the witness testimony right the guilty will go unpunished and, with every negative witness experience, confidence in the criminal justice system will decline;

- witnesses who have a bad experience in court won't want to give evidence again;

- the bad experience in court often begins with an over-zealous police officer who, naturally keen to make a case, sets the witness up for making a witness statement that they will have difficulty explaining if they are cross-examined on it in court;

- being treated badly in court, including being publicly called a liar or described as unreliable, will have seriously damaging effects on the health and wellbeing of some witnesses: these effects can be long-term;

- the experience of giving evidence is bad enough for most witnesses: it is likely to be even worse for victims of serious personal crime such as rape, for young people, and for people who often experience unfair discrimination such as black and ethnic minority people, lesbians and gay men, transgender and disabled people, and

- the adversarial system requires the reliability of witnesses' testimony to be undermined in the eyes of the judge and the jury to enable one side to 'win' the case. The inherent nature of the system is not likely to change, but better informed and more humane legal practice can make a difference by ameliorating the damaging effects of this process.

20.03 Given the core contribution of witness testimony, the Government has introduced a programme of reforms that 'puts victims and witnesses at the heart of the criminal justice system'.[2]

In the view of the Government:

> public confidence in the criminal justice system is low, and too few offenders are brought to justice . . . too often victims and witnesses are treated without due consideration. They are not kept properly informed, or provided with a sense of security. Too often they are expected to turn up at court for cases that are then adjourned, or are subjected to

---

[2] Home Office, *A New Deal for Victims and Witnesses*, London: Home Office, 2003, available from *http://www.crimereduction.gov.uk/victims24.htm*.

unnecessarily stressful courtroom experiences. Too often they are not even thanked. Too often those most seriously affected are not given the long term support they need.[3]

The Government is talking here about the potential experience of *all* witnesses. However the Government has thus far focused on ameliorating the experiences of those defined as *vulnerable* within the ambit of the Youth Justice and Criminal Evidence Act 1999.

(2) The Youth Justice and Criminal Evidence Act 1999

The Youth Justice and Criminal Evidence Act 1999 specifies *special measures* to assist **20.04** *vulnerable* or *intimidated* witnesses to overcome barriers to them giving 'best' evidence. It also prohibits defendants cross-examining the victim in certain types of offence.

(i) Vulnerable witnesses

These include witnesses under the age of 17 and those with a physical or mental **20.05** impairment, health problem, or learning disability.

The Act defines three categories of child witness:

1. Children giving evidence in a sexual offence case.
2. Children giving evidence in a case involving an offence of violence, abduction or neglect.
3. Children giving evidence in all other cases.

Children in categories 1 and 2 are in need of *special protection*. The court will make strong presumptions about which special measures are put in place to help them give evidence. They *will* have a video-recorded statement, if there is one, admitted as their evidence-in-chief. They *will* be cross-examined via a live TV link. However children in category 3 *are eligible* to have a video-recorded statement, if there is one, admitted as their evidence-in-chief. They *may* give further evidence, or be cross-examined, via a live TV link.

(ii) Intimidated witnesses

Research indicates that sexual offences, assaults, domestic violence, hate crimes, and **20.06** offences that feature repeat victimization—such as stalking—are likely to lead to witness intimidation. Witnesses to these offences need protection. Witnesses to other crimes might also experience fear and distress and might require similar safeguarding and support. The Act defines an *intimidated* witness as being a witness (other than the accused) in respect of whom 'the court is satisfied that the quality of evidence given by the witness is likely to be diminished by reason of fear or distress on the part of the witness in connection with testifying in the proceedings'. The police or CPS should notify the court of the necessary arrangements to protect the intimidated witness.

(iii) Special measures

The Act incorporates most of the recommendations within *Speaking up for Justice* for **20.07** special measures to assist the giving of 'best evidence':

---

[3] Ibid.

- the use of a screen in court between the witness and the defendant;
- giving evidence by live TV link;
- giving evidence in private;
- removal of wigs and gowns;
- video-recorded evidence-in-chief;
- video-recorded cross-examination (though this special measure has not been implemented);
- examination of a witness through an intermediary (a specially trained person appointed by the court to help a witness to communicate), and
- the use of aids to communication.

The Act also recognizes that pre-trial support and preparation for the court process—without discussing the evidence—help witnesses give better evidence. Either the prosecution or the defence will apply for special measures at a pre-trial review or the plea and directions hearing. When assessing the application the court must decide whether the absence of special measures might diminish the witness's evidence. It will take into consideration:

- the witness's circumstances, e.g. age, disability, communication difficulties, a history of self-harming, and ethnicity;
- the offence, which can also be a factor, e.g. a hate crime, a sexual offence, murder;
- if the defendant is the witness's carer, and
- the views of the witness.

(iv) Cross-examination by the defendant

20.08 A defendant charged with rape or certain other sexual offences, who is not legally represented, may not cross-examine the complainant. This prohibition extends to any other offence with which the defendant has been charged in the proceedings.

An unrepresented defendant also may not cross-examine a child witness in a case involving sex or violence or who was witness to kidnapping, false imprisonment or abduction. The age limit for child witnesses in this context is 17 for sexual offences and 14 for the other offences.

A court can also prevent the unrepresented defendant cross-examining witnesses in other cases if it is satisfied that the circumstances merit this and it would not be contrary to the interests of justice. In all instances the court will invite the defendant to appoint a legal representative to conduct the cross-examination. The court may appoint one for the defendant who declines.

(3) Achieving 'best evidence'

20.09 Viewed as key to the implementation of the Youth Justice and Criminal Evidence Act is *Achieving Best Evidence in Criminal Proceedings*.[4] These are excellent, comprehensive,

---

[4] Home Office, *Achieving best evidence in criminal proceedings: guidance for vulnerable or intimidated witnesses, including children*, London: Home Office, 2002.

detailed guidelines covering the planning and conduct of interviews, witness support and preparation, and treatment of witnesses at court.

It would appear that prior to the Act there was no assessment of the potential demand for **20.10** special measures, i.e. how many individuals might meet the qualifying criteria for vulnerability. There is insufficient funding, staff resources and technology to implement the Act for all those who notionally qualify.

For its part the police service has juggled limited resources to organize and train officers to interview the vulnerable appropriately, and to provide support and protection. Every force has child protection units staffed by specialist officers. Some—but certainly not all—'front-line' police officers attend Achieving Best Evidence (ABE) courses and Vulnerable and Intimidated Witness (VIW or VI) courses. Some ABE/VIW trained officers are trained in sexual offence interviewing techniques. A select few are trained to conduct Enhanced Cognitive Interviewing in which memory-enhancing techniques are used.

C. The Journey of the Witness: Research and Practice

(1) Initial and subsequent treatment by the police

According to a MORI survey for the Audit Commission[5] difficulties encountered in **20.11** reporting crime greatly affects perceptions of the eventual police response. Respondents strongly criticized common difficulties in accessing help:

- being connected by telephone to the wrong person;
- being asked to leave a message with a person or on an answering machine;
- leaving messages that remained unanswered, and
- impersonal attitudes of central switchboard or call centre staff.

Home Office research found that by 2002 conviction rates for rape had fallen to **20.12** 5.6 per cent and remain very low level despite increasing reporting to the police.[6]

Although three-quarters of the sample had reported the offence the vast majority of cases did not proceed beyond the investigative stage. The police classified about a quarter of complaints as 'no crime'.

Evidential issues accounted for over one-third of cases not surviving the investigative stage. Given the numbers who are trained in ABE, VIW and sexual offence interviewing, investigators seemed unable to cope where the complainant had learning difficulties or could not give a clear account. Necessary DNA testing did not happen. Identified offenders were not traced. The decision not to proceed was often linked with doubts about the complainant's credibility. Consultation between police and CPS rarely led to enhanced case-building.

---

[5] Audit Commission, *Victims and Witnesses: providing better support,* London: Audit Commission, 2003.
[6] Kelly, L., Lovett. J. and Regan, L., *A gap or a chasm? Attrition in reported rape cases,* Home Office Research Study 293, London: Home Office, 2005.

Disclosing to the police is a powerful deterrent. One-third of complainants withdrew at the investigation stage, not wanting further involvement in the criminal justice process. This decision was associated with age (more 16–25 year olds withdrew), being disbelieved, and fear of going to court.

20.13 Since 1991 cases of perverting the course of justice have increased six-fold; more than doubling since 1997/98. Intimidation as a crime includes threatening witnesses. The Audit Commission's MORI survey[7] uncovered a disturbing growth in this form of intimidation. The intimidation problem is large: just under 10 per cent of all reported crime and 20 per cent of unreported crime. In many more cases, victims and witnesses *feared* such intimidation.

Reporting intimidation creates an expectation of police protection: one which often goes unmet. The survey quotes a victim of serious crime: 'they [the police] were on about having protection for us but they just didn't want to listen no matter how many times I rang them'.

20.14 Personal communication from police officers indicates that the practicalities—including inability to ensure the extended contact and time of a supporting officer, especially the same designated officer—are barriers to continuity and quality of support between the initial investigation phase and court. There is a greater effort to assign the same family liaison officer (FLO) in cases of murder. For other offences, demand outstrips resource.

It is not just about the same 'dedicated' officer, or any officer, being assigned to support the witness. The quality of support matters. Victim Support research[8] into the needs of people bereaved by homicide found that FLOs failed to give many bereaved relatives accurate information about Victim Support and other support organizations. Often FLOs did not refer people for support until the officer was withdrawing. By this time many bereaved relatives did not feel they wanted to 'start again' with someone else. Officers can therefore perversely act as powerful gatekeepers to sources of support for victims: either by withholding referral to other agencies or by failing to 'sell' early on the potential benefits of support from such agencies.

20.15 The comprehensiveness and the accuracy of a witness's disclosures in a video-recorded interview, or to a police officer interviewing in order to draft a written statement, have profound implications for the witness's experience at court. It matters that the police facilitate maximum disclosure and, where this is not recorded, they generate full and faithful accounts of what the witness disclosed.[9]

Chapter 9 by Davies and Westcott in this volume highlights persistent shortcomings in the interviewing of child witnesses. In Chapter 8, Shepherd and Milne cite a number

---

[7] Cited above at n.5.

[8] Victim Support, *In the Aftermath: the support needs of people bereaved by homicide*, London: Victim Support, 2006.

[9] Shepherd, E. and Milne, R., 'Full and faithful: ensuring quality practice and integrity of outcome in witness interviews', in Heaton-Armstrong, A. Shepherd E. and Wolchover D. (eds.), *Analysing Witness Testimony: a guide for legal practitioners and other professionals*, Oxford: Oxford University Press, 1999.

of studies indicating that officers interviewing witnesses to generate written statements engage in interviewing behaviours that would be wholly unacceptable within an interview of a suspect. They explain how previous case knowledge and established practices combine all too often to create a 'relevance filter' that narrows the interviewing focus. It shapes what the witness discloses, shapes the officer's perceptions of the witness's disclosures, determines in advance what questions are posed, the officer's remembrance of responses, and the wording of the statement given to the witness for checking and signature.

Witnesses rarely assert themselves to give corrective feedback to an officer who is 'driving' the interview, which can all too easily degenerate into an exercise in inviting the witness to confirm what is inside the officer's head. Similarly witnesses rarely tell the officer that what is in the statement is not exactly—or may even not be—what the witness said. Only later at court when cross-examined will the witness pay the price for this lack of assertion and absence of corrective feedback.

(2) Experience of criminal proceedings

(i) The 2002 Witness Satisfaction Survey

A Home Office Witness Satisfaction Survey[10] found that the greatest predictors of witness dissatisfaction with the experience of giving evidence were feeling intimidated by an individual or the court process, and feeling that they were being taken for granted. **20.16**

42 per cent of adult witnesses and 60 per cent of young witnesses felt intimidated, giving rise to a range of negative experiences:

- feeling frightened or scared;
- loss of confidence;
- feeling like a liar or a bad person;
- feeling as if they were on trial, and
- feeling stressed.

According to the survey 86 per cent of victims attending court were satisfied with the CPS lawyer.[11] The same proportion of victims was satisfied with the police. More were satisfied with the judiciary (92 per cent), court staff (96 per cent) and the Witness Service (98 per cent).

However nearly a quarter of witnesses felt their contribution had been taken for granted. Having steeled themselves for an anxiety-provoking and at best unpleasant experience, their anxiety and their efforts to overcome it seemed of no interest to those operating the criminal justice system. The survey found that 'very vulnerable' witnesses are the most likely to be seriously unsettled by this. These witnesses are the most likely to need support but the least likely to ask for it. They are the most likely to be intimidated. They are the least confident. They are seriously damaged by a bad experience at court.

---

[10] Angle, H., Malam, S. and Carey, C., *Key findings from the Witness Satisfaction Survey 2002*, London: Home Office, 2003.

[11] The report does not state whether or not these are victims who are attending court to give evidence.

Because of their vulnerability they are also the most likely to be repeatedly re-victimized by the system.

(ii) The Audit Commission MORI survey

20.17 The findings of the Audit Commission MORI survey of witnesses' experience contrasted with those of the Home Office Witness Satisfaction Survey.[12] Strikingly the survey found that involvement with CPS solicitors and barristers was the element of the criminal justice system with which victims and witnesses were *least* satisfied. People were concerned about the lack of contact prior to the hearing and by lawyers being unfamiliar with the case. This led to a lack of confidence in the quality of advocacy being received. Some witnesses also felt that they were not treated with respect or were ignored altogether.

20.18 The Audit Commission survey generated a very practical typology of witnesses:

- The *very vulnerable*. These are likely to:
  - be a victim of serious crime;
  - have very specific needs;
  - be subject to intimidation;
  - know, or live in close proximity to the defendant;
  - be unconfident about their own abilities;
  - have no experience of court;
  - in need of considerable support, and
  - describe their feelings about engagement with the criminal justice process as, for example, feeling 'physically sick' and 'traumatic'.
- The *nervous*. These are likely to:
  - be a victim or witness of a crime that concerned them;
  - have received little information and not know who to ask;
  - want support but not know how to get it;
  - be very affected by delays and changes in the criminal justice process, and
  - describe their feelings about the process as being 'anxious and worried' and 'in two minds'.
- The *unconcerned*. These are likely to:
  - have been a victim or witness of minor crime;
  - have received information about the criminal justice process;
  - have a good personal support network, and
  - describe their feelings in terms of 'am not bothered' and 'I'm not worried, it's just a pain'.
- The *confident*. These are likely to:
  - have had previous experience of going to court;
  - be strong minded, self-confident;
  - have little interaction with the defendant;
  - have been kept well informed throughout, and be able to ask for information, and

---

[12] Cited above at n. 5.

- describe their feelings in terms of being 'relaxed, quite happy to go' and 'I take pleasure in seeing justice served'.

These findings have important implications.   **20.19**

1. Criminal justice practitioners who are aware of this typology of witnesses and their characteristics can look out for them and adjust their actions accordingly. Most lawyers engage in categorical—typology-based—thinking when assessing the credibility of a potential witness. The Audit Commission-generated typology assists more: it points to the witness's needs.
2. While criminal justice practitioners cannot control some of the factors that determine the category in which the witness exists, e.g. the severity of the offence, they are able to control other factors. For example police, lawyers, and Witness Care Unit staff can ensure that those they are dealing with are kept well informed throughout, and that they are referred for available support.

Indeed thoughtful and well-focused action can move the individual up the scale from, say, 'very vulnerable' to 'nervous'. Such mindfulness could make all the difference. 'Best evidence' emerges because the potential for trauma or damage arising from giving evidence is lessened if not removed.

The Audit Commission appositely commented: 'it is important that these different types of victims and witnesses are recognised so that agencies can provide a more targeted approach to the delivery of guidance, advice and support services prior to and at court. Currently, however, this targeting rarely happens, with more vulnerable and nervous victims and witnesses not always getting the level of help that they need.'[13]

(iii) Research into young witnesses' experience of criminal proceedings

The NSPCC and Victim Support research study *In their own words*[14] reports the experi-   **20.20**
ences of 50 young witnesses in criminal proceedings: the run-up to the court appearance; witness preparation; waiting at the court itself; giving evidence, being cross-examined, and after the trial is reported.

(1) *Waiting for the trial.* Witnesses waited on average 11.6 months for Crown Court trials. 35 witnesses described themselves as being very nervous or scared in the pretrial period. 6 reported having specific difficulties at school during this period and significantly, none of these had been kept informed about what was happening with the court case. Some ceased attending school because of anxiety and some were prescribed anti-depressant medication.
(2) *Special measures.* 18 said they were offered no choice about anything associated with being a witness. Most gave evidence by TV link at court. One was very nervous about giving evidence but the equipment in the TV link room was not working. Although she wanted to go into open court to 'get it over and done

---

[13] Cited above at n.5.
[14] Plotnikoff, J. and Woolfson, R., *In their own words: the experiences of 50 young witnesses in criminal proceedings*, London: NSPCC and Victim Support, 2004.

with' it was not allowed. She had to wait a further few days while the equipment was repaired.

(3) *Pre-trial preparation.* 14 had no contact with a supporter before the trial. 11 were critical of the lack of information and support before the trial.

(4) *Refreshing the witness's memory.* Of the 39 witnesses who made a videotaped statement, 14 saw it before trial. Almost all found this helpful. 9 who did not see it until the trial thought that seeing it at an earlier stage would have been helpful. Of the 10 who had made a written statement, one who asked to see it was refused.

(5) *Meeting the advocates and judiciary.* Over half had met the prosecutor, defence lawyer or judge, but several were confused about the identity of the person they had met. 13 said the meeting had helped them cope with the court process.

(6) *Answering questions.* 25 were clear that the defence lawyer had accused them of lying. 5 thought that they had been asked about things it was unrealistic to expect them to remember. 29 were very upset or angry while giving evidence, mentioning crying or feeling sick. 3 girls mentioned their embarrassment having to describe intimate details to lawyers.

Young witness supporters were interviewed as part of the research and many were concerned about the way cross-examination had been conducted, variously describing it as being confusing, complex, rushed, repetitive and bullying.

(7) *After court.* 36 witnesses recalled being thanked for giving evidence and that they appreciated this. Of these, only 6 found out the eventual outcome of the case, through media reporting of it. 16 were extremely negative about the experience of court.

20.21 The young people contributing to the NSPCC and Victim Support research had the following suggestions to make to the judiciary, to lawyers, to supporters and to other young witnesses:

- *to the judiciary:* 'intervene to make sure things are fair in court, when lawyers intimidate people and witnesses get confused';
- *to lawyers:* 'introduce yourselves'; 'stop being aggressive'; 'slow down, explain what you mean and use simple words';
- *to supporters:* 'tell the witness things may go wrong in court';
- *to other young witnesses:* 'ask to meet the judge and lawyers'; 'be prepared to be accused of lying'.

20.22 In 1997 the NSPCC produced a video *A Case for Balance: demonstrating good practice when children are witnesses.*[15] The production was aimed primarily at judges and lawyers dealing with child witnesses, and its purpose was to stimulate discussion about practice among the judiciary and the wider criminal justice community. Seven years, one Act of Parliament, and a comprehensive set of guidelines later, the NSPCC and Victim Support research indicates that there is still a long way to go before court processes can be said to not be re-victimizing, certainly where young people are concerned. Lawyers, the

---

[15] NSPCC, *A Case for Balance: Demonstrating good practice when children are witnesses,* London: NSPCC, 1997.

judiciary, court staff and witness supporters all need to ask themselves whether the types of court experiences described, including behaviour so unacceptable that it is described by professional adults as among other things 'bullying', is tolerable in a modern criminal justice system.

(iv) Other vulnerable witnesses' experience of criminal proceedings

We need research, akin to that of *In their own words*, to enable those within other **20.23** categories of witness to give voice to their experience of the court process. It is appropriate to provide an illustrative, real-life case example, from Victim Support's volunteer learning materials for supporting vulnerable and intimidated witnesses.

Ken is a male adult victim of aggravated burglary who was attending court to give **20.24** evidence against his attacker. The Witness Service manager had not been notified of Ken's attendance prior to the day of the trial nor that he had any particular difficulties. But as soon as Ken arrived at court it became very obvious to her that he had great difficulty in communicating and being understood. Ken told her that he suffered from epilepsy as a result of a previous assault.

He also said that he was concerned about giving evidence as the defendant's friends had threatened him with a gun. He had informed the police of this and they had installed a panic alarm in his home. The police had not communicated this information to anyone. No special measures had been applied for. No witness preparation had taken place.

With Ken's consent the Witness Service manager spoke with counsel who immediately made a late application for special measures. This was granted, allowing Ken to give his evidence over the TV link. The manager also contacted the Victim Support Vulnerable and Intimidated Witness worker who came to court to prepare Ken for the court attendance and to offer support through the process of giving evidence.

As a result of his epilepsy Ken became very sick during the day while waiting to give his evidence. The Witness Service manager had to call for the court first aider on several occasions. Ken was finally called to give evidence, but he was still very sick and the jury saw this. An application was made for the jury to be discharged and a new jury was to be sworn. The defence counsel then decided Ken's statement could be read rather than call Ken in person. Ken was allowed to leave, much to his relief.

Later the defence decided that, after all, that Ken should be cross-examined. He was called back to court again the following week. There were more delays due to a problem with the TV link equipment. Ken became very upset and again became ill. The Witness Service manager became very concerned for Ken's well-being. The first aider was called. Ken had several consecutive seizures, rendering him incapable of speech. An ambulance took Ken to hospital where, by now unconscious, he was placed on a ventilator in intensive care.

The judge finally made the decision not to call Ken back to court and his evidence was read out.

Cases such as that of Ken serve to underline the pervasiveness of the inappropriate **20.25** mental set of criminal justice professionals, identified in the Audit Commission survey. It is yet another recent illustration of the way in which mindless behaviour of the 'professionals' before and during the court process renders for some vulnerable witnesses going to court to give evidence—and the prospect of cross-examination—an exercise in secondary victimization.

(v) Rape and domestic violence victims' experience of criminal proceedings

20.26 The Home Office researchers into the decline in convictions for rape[16] observe that 'in no other crime is the victim subject to so much scrutiny at trial, where the most likely defence is that the victim consented to the crime. Powerful stereotypes function to limit the definition of what counts as "real rape".' The researchers also found that:

- where a full trial took place, acquittal was the likely outcome, and
- police and CPS over-estimate the scale of false allegations, feeding into a 'culture of scepticism'. Some complainants might interpret police officers' early assessments of the difficulties of investigation and prosecution as discouragement to continue.

The authors comment that 'from the perspective of complainants, the difference in perceptions between themselves and CJS personnel was too often not just a gap but a chasm. If, however, each point in the attrition process is examined in detail, what emerges is a series of smaller gaps, each of which could be bridged by targeted interventions.' They recommend that 'a shift occurs within the CJS from a focus on the discreditability of complainants to enhanced evidence gathering and case-building'. This places the onus squarely upon the police to conduct quality investigations and to do justice to the witness's testimony, taking to heart some of the advice given in Chapter 8 above.

20.27 Hartley argues that lawyers should adopt a 'therapeutic jurisprudence' approach to prosecution. She argues that by meeting with the victim early and often, by listening and understanding the context and history of the victimization, prosecutors can transform victims' experience of giving evidence from one that is re-victimizing to one that can be empowering and therapeutic. Her insights also help us understand why the victim quoted in the opening of this chapter felt as she did. Quoting several research studies, Hartley writes that 'rape victims report that it was difficult to deal with the realization that it was not their trial . . . and that they had little control over what happened during the trial. By taking away their control, this state-controlled approach to prosecution has the anti-therapeutic effect of disempowering victims participating in the process.'[17]

D. The Findings of Research and Practice: a Summary

(1) The negative experience of being a witness

20.28 There is substantial convergence on factors that all too frequently turn the witness's journey into a negative experience.

---

[16] Kelly, Lovett and Regan (2005), cited above at n.6.

[17] Hartley, C., 'Therapeutic jurisprudence approach to the trial process in domestic violence felony trials' (2003) 9/4 (April) *Violence Against Women*, 410–437.

1. The justice gap is widening with increasing rates of discontinuance and acquittal. Allegations of rape exemplify the causes for this: inadequate police investigation; poor investigative interviewing; witnesses not being believed and being encouraged to withdraw; lack of evidence-building.
2. Witnesses wait a long time to give evidence (almost a year according to the NSPCC and Victim Support research). During this period many witnesses experience anxiety so severe that they require medication or are unable to go about their normal lives.
3. Many witnesses wait for hours at court, only to be told to go away and come back another day.
4. Many witnesses are intimidated at court—by an individual or by the process—and this, combined with feeling taken for granted, is a major source of dissatisfaction with the court process. It is also a source of unwillingness to be a witness in criminal proceedings again.
5. Most young witnesses are denied any choice about what special measures are put in place for them.
6. Young witnesses in particular report being accused of lying, being intimidated by aggressive lawyers, feeling sick and tearful. Their supporters at court describe the behaviour of some lawyers as 'bullying'.
7. Many are not thanked for attending court.
8. Many witnesses are not told the outcome of the case.
9. Many victims and witnesses are not given accurate information about support, or are not referred by statutory criminal justice agencies to Victim Support and the Witness Service.[18]
10. For very many victims and witnesses, the investigation and court process is a source of secondary victimization.

(2) What helps the witness

There is also substantial consensus as to what can make things better for the witness.   **20.29**

---

[18] In April 2006 the government established the Code of Practice for Victims of Crime. Introduced under the Domestic Violence, Crime and Victims Act 2004, the Code of Practice replaces the old Victim's Charter, which was introduced in 1990 and revised in 1996. The Code of Practice sets out what services victims can expect to receive from each of the criminal justice agencies. For the first time the statutory criminal justice agencies are required by law to provide minimum standards of service to victims of crime, whereas the old Victim's Charter gave victims no legal right of redress in the event of a criminal justice agency failing to offer a satisfactory service. The Code of Practice is designed to ensure all victims receive timely, relevant information: about the progress of their case, including when someone is arrested, charged, bailed and sentenced; about provisions for vulnerable and intimidated witnesses, and about eligibility for criminal injuries compensation. It gives victims the right to be referred, with their consent, to Victim Support and to receive the services of a police family liaison officer if they have been bereaved by homicide.

The government considers it is important that victims are aware of their rights and that they challenge criminal justice agencies if they do not feel they are receiving a satisfactory service. Victims can make a complaint to the agency involved. If they are not happy with the response, they can complain to the Parliamentary Ombudsman through their MP. The government is also appointing, in 2006, a Commissioner for Victims, whose role will include coordinating government work concerning victims of crime and reviewing the Victim's Code of Practice. Further information about the Code of Practice is available from *http://www.cjsonline.gov.uk/victim/coming_forward/your_rights/index.html.*

1. The regular provision of accurate information about progress in the case helps reduce witnesses' anxiety in the run-up to giving evidence.
2. Support services such as the Witness Service, which are highly rated by those who are referred to them.
3. Witnesses and young witnesses in particular, benefit from meeting lawyers, the judiciary and court staff before giving evidence.
4. Witnesses appreciate being thanked for coming to court.
5. Relatively simple and easy measures, such as keeping witnesses informed about progress, have a tremendously beneficial effect on witnesses' overall experience of the criminal justice process.

E. A Coordinated Infrastructure for Witness Support and Care

20.30 The introduction of Witness Care Units has the potential to assist matters. Staffed by CPS and police, sometimes with secondments from Victim Support, they have the task of assessing witness needs and referring witnesses to organizations who can provide support. Given their gradual introduction during 2004 and 2005 they have yet to succeed in the basic task of reliable identification of support needs.

In 2004–5 Victim Support's Witness Service received 26,311 referrals of vulnerable and intimidated witnesses who had been identified as such by the referring criminal justice agency. The Witness Service identified a further 20,697 witnesses (a similar number were recorded in the previous year) who they assessed as vulnerable or intimidated but who were not referred as such. This was despite many of them being young witnesses, entitled to special measures simply on the basis of their age.[19]

Although the Witness Service is now located in every criminal court in England and Wales, it struggles to attract referrals. Furthermore it lacks adequate resources and the necessary influence within the criminal justice system to provide the quality of service to which it aspires.

20.31 Returning to Ken's experience (para. 20.24) if there had been a coordinated infrastructure of witness care multiple steps could have been taken to prevent him being re-victimized:

1. *During the investigation.* Ken had told the police he had been threatened after reporting the crime, and the police had installed a panic alarm in his home. We are not told whether he was referred to Victim Support but this is unlikely given that he had not been referred to Victim Support's Witness Service.
   The police could have fulfilled a number of caring responsibilities:
   • discussed options for ongoing support with Ken and referred him to Victim Support;
   • with his consent, taken steps to ensure that his doctor was aware of the offence;

---

[19] Victim Support, *Annual Review 2005*, London: Victim Support, 2005.

- informed the Witness Care Unit of Ken's vulnerability so that they would be able to make a proper assessment of his needs;
- kept him informed of progress in the case in the run up to the court hearing, and
- taken steps to provide an enhanced level of protection for Ken as the trial date approached.

2. *Waiting to go to court.* The police had not told the Witness Care Unit or the CPS about Ken's needs, no special measures had been applied for, and he had not been referred to the Witness Service.

The CPS could have fulfilled a number of caring responsibilities:

- recognized his vulnerability and applied for special measures;
- passed this information to the Witness Service so that he could be offered pre-trial witness preparation and support, and
- ensured that prosecuting counsel was properly briefed about Ken's vulnerability and his needs as a witness.

3. *At court.* Because nobody at court was aware of Ken's vulnerability there had been no special measures application, no preparation had taken place and there had been no arrangements made to receive Ken at court.

If Ken had been referred to the Witness Service, the Service could have fulfilled additional caring responsibilities:

- arranged for Ken to enter the court by a separate entrance to avoid the defendant and the defendant's associates;
- liaised with the Witness Care Unit or the police to obtain transport to court for Ken;
- undertaken witness preparation with Ken;
- liaised with Victim Support, Ken's doctor and other carers about his health needs in relation to giving evidence;
- explained any special measures that the court had granted to Ken, and
- offered Ken a pre-trial visit and, in areas where the Witness Service is resourced to offer an enhanced level of service to vulnerable and intimidated witnesses, supported Ken over a longer period of time in the run up to the trial, including visiting him at home.

Meanwhile, at court the CPS could have taken additional steps:

- ensured that prosecuting counsel met Ken at the earliest possible opportunity;
- liaised with defence counsel earlier in the proceedings;
- advocated for Ken with the court about the use of the TV link room;
- thanked Ken for coming to court to give evidence, acknowledging the great personal cost to Ken of doing this, and
- ensured that arrangements were in place to inform Ken about the outcome of the trial.

4. *After court.* In this particular example Ken, the witness, was left with unusually high support needs. The experience of giving evidence re-victimized him, creating and greatly exacerbating a range of personal problems.

All relevant agencies could have made preparations to attempt the reduction of damage experienced by Ken:

- the police: to tell him the outcome of the case;

- the police: to monitor any continued intimidation;
- the Witness Service: to refer him to Victim Support, with his consent, for further support in the aftermath of the trial, and
- adequate health care that recognized the impact of his victimization, and his secondary victimization by the criminal justice system, on his deteriorating health.

20.32 It should be a source of considerable concern to criminal justice agencies that many of the 'could have' statements above are already required standards of practice. Monitoring of these is clearly inadequate (see *The Victim's Charter*, Home Office 1996, replaced in April 2006 by a Victim's Code of Practice; and the *Statement of National Standard of Witness Care in the Criminal Justice System*, Home Office 1996).

It is a sad reflection that Witness Service managers notice how, for example, some CPS lawyers see it as fundamental to their role to find the time to meet and talk to witnesses before a trial, which witnesses find enormously helpful. In contrast other CPS lawyers are known never to have the inclination and have not therefore found the time to meet witnesses beforehand.[20]

In summer 2005, the Government announced plans to introduce 'victims' advocates' in homicide cases, to be piloted in five areas during 2006. A similar scheme for rape cases may follow later. The purpose of the scheme is to 'enable the bereaved relative, if they wish, to make a personal statement in court before sentence on how the death has affected them, either directly themselves, or through a lawyer or suitable representative' and 'achieve a step change in the ability of the relative to communicate effectively with prosecution decision makers at all stages of the criminal justice process'.[21] Bereaved

---

[20] In February 2006 the Director of Public Prosecutions announced a new standard for communication between victims and witnesses and the prosecution advocate. This builds on existing CPS guidance on the care and treatment of victims and witnesses and the Prosecutor's Pledge. Further information about these is available from the CPS web site at: *http://www.cps.gov.uk/legal/section16/chapter_a.html*. The standard builds on the CPS responsibilities specified in the Victim's Code of Practice.

The new standard is designed to ensure that 'prosecuting advocates . . . have a responsibility to ensure that victims and witnesses who are affected by the court process are accordingly treated with respect and decency'. It requires that prosecutors consult and liaise with victims and witnesses and the Witness Service, to ensure witnesses have satisfactory information and support and that their needs are taken account of when arranging the business of the court. The standard gives prosecuting advocates a range of responsibilities towards victims and witnesses. These range from introducing themselves and explaining court processes to ensuring special measures are arranged if appropriate, and taking steps to avoid undue delay and waiting. Prosecutors are also required to challenge derogatory or inaccurate statements put forward by the defence.

[21] CJS, *Hearing the Relatives of Murder and Manslaughter Victims: the government's plans to give the bereaved relatives of murder and manslaughter victims a say in criminal proceedings—consultation*, September 2005. On 24 April 2006 the government began piloting new provisions for family impact statements in five Crown Courts: the Old Bailey, Birmingham, Cardiff, Manchester and Winchester. The scheme will enable people bereaved by homicide to tell the court, after the defendant's conviction but before sentence, how they have been affected by the crime. Bereaved relatives will be able to address the court themselves, or do so via a lawyer, a victim's advocate or a 'lay friend'. The government notes that bereaved relatives sometimes feel they are completely excluded from the system, and that it is wrong that the people for whom the case matters most have to be silent in court. The scheme is designed to correct this by giving relatives the chance to speak. Further information about the scheme is available from: *http://www.cjsonline.gov.uk/the_cjs/whats_new/news-3204.html*. On 3 May 2006 Lord Justice Judge, in his capacity as President of the Queen's Bench Division of the High Court of Justice issued a Protocol setting out the procedure to be followed in the victim's advocate pilot areas. (Available from: *<www.judiciary.gov.uk>*.)

relatives of homicide victims will be able to address the court directly about how the killing has affected them, or an advocate could be appointed at public expense to do this on their behalf. This initiative is designed to give bereaved relatives a voice in court, and to enable them to refute evidence about the victim's bad character that is sometimes put forward by the defence in mitigation. Many victims' organizations welcome the initiative, stating that it is what victims have for years been asking for. However, it can also be argued that current plans for the CPS to have much more extensive and effective communication with victims or their relatives before and during a trial is a better way of achieving improved representation of victims' views in criminal proceedings, without the risk that they might be led to believe they can influence sentencing.

F. Concluding Remarks

We will always rely upon witnesses to contribute to our criminal justice system—from **20.33** initial contact with the police through to court—and to enable offenders to be justly convicted on their 'best evidence'. The Government is right to say that it is unacceptable and that it inevitably erodes confidence in the criminal justice system if the system mindlessly re-victimizes witnesses as they make their journey through the system. Thus far it has focused on the vulnerable as requiring mindful behaviour by those who operate the system. We need to remind ourselves that the law defines vulnerability narrowly—arguably too narrowly. Yet we know that many more in our society are vulnerable by virtue just of being who and what they are.

The wish is not the fulfilment. Specifying what should be the case does not make it the case. It is an exercise in delusion for the Government to believe that people are doing what they ought to be doing. Significant numbers of the police service, the CPS, the defence, the judiciary, the magistracy, the Witness Service, Victim Support, and all others with express and implicit responsibilities to witnesses will be neither ready, willing, nor able to put law and policy into effect if there are no sanctions for not doing so—and no continuing resource to permit them to do so.

Without the motivation and the means to behave differently—common-sensically—the prospects are not good. Critical numbers of those who work in the criminal justice system will continue to excuse themselves for not acting mindfully, humanely towards victims and witnesses. They will continue to damage these people—most particularly and unforgivably those who are vulnerable. People upon whom they rely for their living. People who over time will constitute nemesis for our criminal justice system. Based on first- or second-hand experience people will conclude that coming forward as a witness and going to court is 'just not worth the grief'. Increasingly victims and witnesses will not engage with the justice system. The justice gap will grow.

Further Reading

Crawford, A. and Goodey, J., *Integrating a Victim Perspective within Criminal Justice: international debates*, Ashgate: Dartmouth, 2000.

Kemshall, H. and Pritchard, J., *Good Practice in Working with Victims of Violence*, London: Jessica Kingsley, 2000.

Shute, S., Hood, R. and Seemungul, F., *A Fair Hearing? Ethnic minorities in the criminal courts*, Cullompton, Devon: Willan, 2005.

Peter Dunn worked as a probation officer from 1984 to 1999, during which time he managed a probation hostel and developed his local probation service's victim contact work. Joining the Youth Justice Board as a policy adviser in 1999, he was responsible for producing the first National Standards for Youth Justice. He is now Head of Research and Development with Victim Support and is doing doctoral research on the impact of hate crime at the London School of Economics. He has written articles about young victims, hate crime and victimology for a range of journals and was elected a Fellow of the Royal Society of Arts in 2005.

Editors' Note

For a witness the ordeal involved in participating in a police investigation or the process of giving evidence in court has, until recent years, been the subject of scant consideration by the authorities, who were not, previously, sufficiently appreciative of the fact that the circumstances in which witnesses were interviewed or gave evidence could have a bearing on the perception of their statements and testimony amongst investigators and fact finders. A witness who is appropriately treated and handled by investigators, prosecuting and defence lawyers, court staff and advocates will, whether their evidence is considered to be truthful and reliable or not, be more likely to give an account which is the product of their genuine memory and be realistically articulated in a way which is not corrupted by extraneous factors such as fear or physical discomfort. Conversely, one who, consequent upon their experience, feels that this was no better or even worse in its effects than their original victimization or involvement in the crime scene, will be less likely to do so. Whilst government and prosecution initiatives to improve the treatment of and facilities for witnesses have, undoubtedly, served to reduce the risk to reliable testimony, legal professionals at all levels need to be better informed concerning what the experience of being a witness involves. This chapter should help to achieve this.

21

DISCLOSURE OF UNUSED MATERIAL BY PROSECUTION AUTHORITIES AND THIRD PARTIES

Anthony Heaton-Armstrong, David Corker and David Wolchover

'He who knows only his side of the case knows little of that.'

John Stuart Mill, *1859*

A. Introduction

During the course of an investigation into an allegation of crime and its prosecution in **21.01** court proceedings the investigating and prosecution authorities will collect a body of material. Typically this will consist of written witness statements, transcripts of electronically recorded interviews with witnesses or defendants and documentary and other exhibits, which constitute the evidential basis on which their case is advanced—hence 'used' material. 'Unused' material comes into two broad categories: first, that which is collated by the police during the course of an investigation but which, necessarily, does not form the basis of their prospective evidential resources; and, second, that which is held by other individuals or bodies who do not form part of the prosecution team and which, at least prior to intervention by defence lawyers, may not be sought by investigators. Such unused material may or may not be relevant, subject, amongst other things, to the issues in the case. Whether material becomes 'used' or 'unused' depends on decisions made by investigators and prosecutors in their selection of such resources as will form the basis of prospective prosecution evidence. Used material is, as a matter of course, disclosed to the defence prior to trial. Whether unused material is disclosed, at least in the earlier stages of proceedings, depends, in essence, on decisions by the prosecutor as to its relevance. Material is relevant if it might reasonably be considered capable of undermining the case for the prosecution against the accused, or of assisting the case for the accused. This is the 'disclosure test.'

B. Focus of this Chapter

21.02 Comprehensive and effective disclosure of unused material which touches on the issues raised in criminal litigation is clearly an essential prerequisite of fair trial proceedings. Much of the focus of this book's contents concerns information which comes under the broad heading of 'unused material' and it is, thus, desirable that professionals engaged in the conduct of criminal cases should be adequately informed concerning the complexities and pitfalls which are commonplace in the disclosure process. This chapter will concentrate on those aspects of disclosure law and practice which bear relevance to the balance of the book's contents and to assist practitioners—the judiciary, the legal profession, prosecuting authorities and the police—in the performance of their roles in this field.

21.03 In England and Wales, as in other jurisdictions, a large proportion of those notorious miscarriages of justice which have come to public notice in recent years have involved failures by investigating and prosecution authorities, amongst others, to disclose to the defence unused material which might have assisted accused people in establishing their innocence. Alert to the problem, Parliament, the appellate courts and government institutions have responded to this through Royal Commissions and other forms of inquiry, statute, case law and written guidance. Through reaction and counter-reaction this has involved something of a pendulum effect, characterized by a more liberal approach to disclosure; in turn, this has been followed by a tightening up of statutory procedures in response to what have been perceived as the costly and wasteful consequences of an excessively 'open door' attitude. Such developments will be briefly chronicled. Those categories of unused material which have particular relevance to the themes and issues underlying the contents of this book will be listed and discussed. The existing law and guidance relating to it provide a raft of detailed mechanisms intended to ensure that proper disclosure is effected comprehensively and expediently. These are summarized. The mechanics of the effective operation of the disclosure process and the strategies available to defence lawyers to stimulate and achieve appropriate levels of disclosure in practice are detailed and considered.

C. Principles

In the England and Wales accusatorial and adversarial system of criminal justice, it is the **21.04** prosecution team—the investigating police, the prosecution authority's case workers, lawyers and their trial advocates—who are responsible for investigating and prosecuting any allegation of crime. Consequently they enjoy something of a monopoly over the creation, collection and search for much of the material which may be relevant to an allegation and any defence to it during the investigative stage. Furthermore, the prosecution are likely to enjoy much easier access than defence lawyers to unused material held by third parties, whether these are individuals or organizations. Holding, for this reason, the disclosure whip hand, prosecution agencies therefore hold a high degree of responsibility to ensure that relevant material is created, sought, stored and, if it is relevant to an issue in the case, disclosed to the defence, and to maintain, when performing these tasks, an impartial and open mind as to the guilt or innocence of the accused person.

In the words of Glidewell LJ in The *Judith Ward* case.[1]   **21.05**

> Non-disclosure is a potent source of injustice and even with the benefit of hindsight, it will often be difficult to say whether or not an undisclosed item of evidence might have shifted the balance or opened up a new line of defence.

Subsequently, the importance of the conduct of a fair and just disclosure process has, understandably, been emphasized on numerous occasions. Hence, in the *Criminal Procedure Rules* of 2005,[2] it is defined as one of the 'overriding objectives' of any criminal trial. In the case of *R v Winston Brown*[3] Steyn LJ said that '. . . an accused's right to fair disclosure is an inseparable part of his right to a fair trial'. Again, in *R v H and C*[4] Lord Bingham of Cornhill referred to 'the golden rule of full disclosure'.

D. History

Until the coming into force of the disclosure provisions of the Criminal Procedure **21.06** and Investigations Act 1996 (CPIA), the law relating to disclosure was statutorily unregulated. The first major signs of a more methodical approach to the disclosure process than hitherto came in 1981 when the Attorney-General issued a set of *Guidelines on Disclosure*.[5] In the wake of the ruling by Henry J in the *Guinness* prosecution, in 1992 the Director of Public Prosecutions circulated to Chief Officers of Police what became known as her '*Guinness* advice'.[6] Whilst intended to mitigate the effects of unjust non-disclosure, these initiatives were clearly inadequate to achieve their desired ambitions, as reflected in the judgment of the Court of Appeal in *R v Judith Ward*[7] and *R v Winston Brown*,[8] when Steyn LJ pointed out that neither the Attorney-General's guidelines of 1982 nor the Director of Public Prosecution's *Guinness* advice attracted the force of the law.

---

[1] [1993] Crim App R 1, at 22.   [2] SI 2005 No. 384.   [3] [1995] Cr App R 191, at 198F.
[4] [2003] EWCA 2847, HL.   [5] [1982] 74 Cr App R 302.
[6] Crown Prosecution Service, 14 August 1992.   [7] Cited above at n. 1.
[8] Cited above at n. 3.

21.07 On the day following the delivery of the judgment of the Court of Appeal and its quashing of the convictions in the notorious 'Birmingham Six' case,[9] the Home Secretary announced the setting up of the Runciman Royal Commission, whose recommendations on disclosure formed much of the basis of the relevant provisions of the CPIA.[10] These set out a complex and tightly defined procedure for the operation of a now statutorily defined disclosure process. This caused responsibility for the making of decisions as to whether unused material should be shown to the prosecuting authority's lawyer and for the latter's decisions whether to disclose this to the defence, to be placed clearly in the hands of the investigating police and prosecuting lawyers respectively, albeit subject to some judicial oversight where the defence were able to make an application to the court, in accordance with s8 of the Act, for an order requiring the prosecution to disclose to them material which the defence believed they possessed. Whereas, following the *Ward* judgment, many police forces and prosecuting authorities had pursued a more or less 'open house' policy on the disclosure process, the Act's provisions necessitated an abandonment of any liberal or 'let the defence see what they want' policy in favour of a 'we'll let you see what we think is relevant' alternative.

21.08 Predictably, as evidenced by limited research conducted by the then Chairman of the Bar, Heather Hallet, and followed up by the results of more wide-ranging surveys of their members by the Criminal Bar Association (in association with the British Academy of Forensic Sciences) and the Law Society, the police and, to a lesser extent, the Crown Prosecution Service (CPS) were found to be incapable, in numerous cited instances, of making sensible and sound decisions on the relevance and disclosability of unused material in accordance with the terms of the CPIA, a conclusion similarly reached by a University of Manchester School of Law survey conducted by Hannah Quirk.[11] These informal initiatives were succeeded by reports of the CPS Inspectorate,[12] and, in the light of official concern over the impartiality of the Criminal Bar Association and Law Society surveys, by that of independent researchers commissioned by the Home Office.[13] The conclusions of both these reports were, nonetheless, broadly in accordance with those of the professions' surveys.

21.09 Consequent upon concern arising from the conclusions of these surveys and the CPS Inspectorate's report, the Attorney-General issued another set of *Guidelines on Disclosure*

---

[9] *R v McIlkenny and others* [1991] 2 All ER 417.

[10] *Report of the Royal Commission on Criminal Justice* (ch. Viscount Runciman of Doxford) Cm 2263, London: HMSO, 1993, paras 33–73. For a discussion of the then-existing law, see O'Connor, P., 'Prosecution Disclosure: principle, practice and justice' [1992] Crim LR 464.

[11] Details of the CBA/BAFS/Law Society survey, carried out between February and May 1999, are contained in an unpublished report copies of which are available from Anthony Heaton-Armstrong, 9–12 Bell Yard, London WC2A 2JR. For the University of Manchester survey see Quirk, H., 'The significance of culture in criminal procedure reform: why the revised disclosure scheme cannot work' (2006) 10 *Evidence and Procedure*, 42–59.

[12] *Report on the Thematic Review of the Disclosure of Unused Material*, March 2000; 2/2000 Crown Prosecution Service.

[13] Plotnikoff, J. and Woolfson, R., 'A Fair Balance? Evaluation of the operation of disclosure law' Home Office, Research, Development and Statistics Directorate, Home Office Occasional Paper No. 76, London: Home Office, 2001 (published 6 December).

on 29 November 2000, designed to mitigate the ill effects of police and prosecuting authority perceptions of the rigours of the CPIA provisions.

The review of the criminal justice system by Lord Justice Auld—yet another attempt **21.10** to come to grips with the need for an effective solution to the disclosure quagmire— concluded:[14]

> The CPS Inspectorate, in its Thematic Review of the Disclosure of unused Material found that the [CPIA] was not working as Parliament intended and that its operation did not command the confidence of criminal practitioners . . . Our findings confirmed the conclusion of the . . . Review that poor practice in relation to disclosure was widespread. The study also revealed a mutual lack of trust between the participants in the disclosure process and fundamental differences of approach to the principles that underpin the CPIA. There is enormous scope to improve and monitor the working practices of all those involved.

Since the *Ward* judgment, disclosure practice 'at the coal face' has varied in its intensity **21.11** and efficiency both in overall tendency and in individual cases, varying between, at one extreme, defence lawyers being given 'the key to the warehouse', thus enabling them to have free access to all unused material, often at huge and unnecessary public expense and, at the other, to prosecution lawyers following, in rigid adherence, the specific requirements of the CPIA in a way which has frequently led to fruitless exchanges of often unanswered correspondence with defence solicitors and 'non-disclosure' court hearings to the frustration of all involved. The liberal approach was unpopular with the police, the restrictive with defence lawyers. The Auld recommendations led in significant degree to yet another set of disclosure measures, encapsulated in the disclosure provisions of the Criminal Justice Act 2003 (CJA 2003). In general terms, whilst preserving many of the disclosure provisions of the CPIA, these place a much greater onus on the defence than hitherto for disclosure purposes and, in essence, require that defence case statements (the notification to the prosecution and the Court of the defendant's prospective defence and the factual and legal issues in the case) should be more detailed, specific, focused and particularized—to enable the prosecution to be better informed for disclosure purposes, thus facilitating expedient and non-wasteful decisions concerning whether or not to disclose unused material. Ominously, the CJA 2003 is silent in response to Lord Justice Auld's call for the 'monitor[ing of] the working practices of all those involved', and it is the absence of any audit process which continues to give rise to concern.

E. The New Disclosure Regime

The Attorney-General has issued a revised set of *Guidelines* to accord with the disclosure **21.12** provisions of the CJA 2003—particularly in relation to defence disclosure. In introducing them he stressed, in his foreword, that the days of 'blanket' prosecution disclosure

---

[14] *Review of the Criminal Courts of England and Wales* (ch. Sir Robin Auld), London: HMSO, 2001, paras 163–164; available at *http://www.criminal-courts-review.org.uk*.

to the defence were over and that, henceforth, disclosure is to be made on a focused, case-by-case basis, strictly compliant with the CPIA and its revised Code of Practice and the CJA 2003, which meet the particular issues involved.

(1) Implementation dates of the new disclosure law

21.13 The disclosure provisions of the CJA 2003 and the revised CPIA Code of Practice came into force on 4 April 2005. The new *Attorney-General's Guidelines* were published on the same day.[15] The immensely valuable *Disclosure Manual*, the result of a collaboration between the Crown Prosecution Service and the Association of Chief Police Officers,[16] was published in June 2005 and applies to all investigations commencing on or after 4 April 2005. Amounting to nothing less than a disclosure encyclopaedia, it contains comprehensive legal and practical guidance concerning the whole disclosure process and includes the essential texts of the CPIA and CJA 2003 disclosure provisions, the revised CPIA Code of Practice and the new *Attorney-General's Guidelines*.

(2) The *Disclosure Protocol*

21.14 Following what has doubtless been continuing judicial, prosecutorial and police concern about practitioners' inattention to the requirements of statutory disclosure law and the continuation of wasteful and unnecessary 'trips to the disclosure warehouse' by defence lawyers, on 20 February 2006 the Court of Appeal issued a *Disclosure Protocol*.[17] Authored by two High Court judges, this lambasts improper, unlawful and wasteful disclosure practices and, in condemning 'a general laxity of approach' points out that all too frequent failures 'properly to apply the binding [statutory] provisions as regards disclosure have proved extremely and unnecessarily costly and has obstructed justice . . . there needs to be a sea-change in the approach of both judges and the parties to all aspects of the handling of the material which the prosecution do not intend to use in support of their case.' In spite of its strictures this, together with the *Disclosure Manual*, is another invaluable document concerning disclosure law and practice.[18]

21.15 As it therefore currently stands, disclosure law and the way in which it has been said it must be applied in practice places very substantial burdens of responsibility on police and prosecution authority personnel, albeit, in accordance with the terms of the CJA 2003, as better informed by the defence as to the issues in the case. The days when, concerned about the possibility of having 'missed' a crucial item of unused material, the prosecution—in their nervousness—allowed defence lawyers unrestricted access to the disclosure warehouse have gone. Henceforth, the disclosure process must be effected strictly in accordance with the terms of the CPIA and CJA 2003 and related secondary legislation

---

[15] Printed in *Archbold Criminal Pleading, Evidence and Practice*, Supplement, Annex A, London: Sweet and Maxwell, 2006, paras 242a and 243.

[16] Available from the CPS website at *http://www.cps.gov.uk/legal/section20/Chapter_a.html*.

[17] *Disclosure: A protocol for the Control and Management of Unused Material in the Crown Court*, Y Llys Apel/Court of Appeal, 20 February 2006, *http://www.hmcourts-service.gov.uk/cms/files/disclosure_protocol.pdf*.

[18] For useful summaries and commentaries, see [2006] 51 *Criminal Law Week*, para. 08, and Zander, M., 'Mission Impossible?' (2006) 156 *New Law Journal* 618.

relating to procedures and all the often complicated, time-consuming paperwork and court hearings that this inevitably involves. Essentially, therefore, whilst, now, intensively regulated, the success of the operation of the disclosure process continues to depend on the open-mindedness, intelligence, efficiency and conscientiousness of those at the forefront of the investigation and prosecution of any allegation of crime—the police and prosecuting lawyers—and their ability and level of determination to do what the law requires. Whereas, without doubt, the intensity and enormity of their task is emphasized by the wealth of exhortation, regulation, and guidance and improved training programmes[19] (as pronounced by Parliament, the Higher Courts, the *Disclosure Manual*, the Court of Appeal's *Disclosure Protocol, et alia*) the best cards in the disclosure pack have undoubtedly been placed back in the hands of the prosecution team. Cynics might say that the disclosure fox is back in the henhouse, with no realistic possibility of any effective audit of his activities there. Henceforth, the prosecution can go about their disclosure tasks safe in the knowledge that the gates to their disclosure store will remain firmly locked to forays by defence lawyers with no fear that any judge will order these to be opened.

In June 1991 Alison Shaughnessy was stabbed to death at her home in Battersea in **21.16** London. Just over a year later Michelle and Ann Taylor, who were both white, were convicted of Shaughnessy's murder. Unknown to their defence team at trial, the detective sergeant in charge of the investigation had information that a passer-by at the scene of the killing, who was the principal witness as to identification, had seen two females fleeing from the victim's flat, and had described one of these as being black. Neither had this information been passed to the Crown Prosecution Service. A week before the appeal, hitherto advanced on other grounds, was due to be heard the Court of Appeal delivered their judgment in *Ward*. Armed with this, junior counsel for the appellants obtained open access to all the unused material retained by the police in the case, fortunately still retained at a police station, and discovered the record of the identification witness's inconsistent description. The appeal was allowed and the convictions quashed, partly owing to non-disclosure of this by the police.[20]

Whether, in the brave new world of strictly CPIA- and CJA 2003-compliant disclosure **21.17** practice, examples of such blatant and unjust disclosure as, by complete good fortune and coincidence, occurred in the Taylor sisters' case will continue to arise remains to be seen (or concealed). Such disclosure would have been in stark disobedience to the current law, and something which, in their *Disclosure Protocol*, the Court of Appeal said 'must stop'. However, the message for those involved in 'testimonial archaeology'—which this book indicates is necessary—is clear: the performance of the disclosure process, by both prosecuting and defence lawyers, merits great conscientiousness and meticulous attention to detail, in the absence of which miscarriages of justice are likely to continue to recur.

---

[19] For some detail of training programmes available to and undertaken by the police and CPS personnel, see Monteith, C., 'Disclosure! CPIA revisited,' [2006] *Counsel*, March ed, 33.

[20] [1994] 98 Cr App R 361.

F. Categories of Unused Material Relevant to the Themes and Contents of this Book

(1) Previous statements

21.18 In *R v Rasheed* Lord Justice Steyn observed:[21]

> The classic examples of material tending to undermine the credibility of a witness, which must be disclosed, are other statements . . .

As is apparent from several other chapters,[22] it may be crucial to obtain discovery of witnesses' pre-testimonial statements and the circumstances in which they were made for the purposes of assessing the accuracy and reliability of their evidence in court. As we have pointed out in Chapter 10, this was, and continues to be, important for the purposes of comparing courtroom testimony and previous statements for consistency. The significance of out-of-court statements, as we also observe in Chapter 10, has now, with the coming into force of the hearsay and related provisions of the CJA 2003, assumed a much greater importance owing to the new potential for adducing such statements as evidence of the truth of what a witness said before giving evidence. Thus something said by a witness immediately after the alleged crime, whether to another civilian or to an investigator, can now be used to assist the prosecution to establish a defendant's guilt even when this is inconsistent with an assertion made when in the witness box.

21.19 For disclosure purposes, previous statements by a witness come into two categories— statements made to police investigators and statements made to third parties. This is because statements made to investigators, assuming these to be relevant, are required to be recorded and retained whereas statements made to third parties may only be discovered in the pursuance of 'Further Reasonable Lines of Enquiry'. This has obvious implications for the reliability and accuracy of the record of the statement. The investigator, if conscientious, should make a record of the statement as soon as possible after it was uttered when his memory of events is likely to have been fresh. A third party may not be required to make or contribute to the making of a record until long, even years, after the event.

21.20 As well as the statement itself, the circumstances in which it was made are likely to be influential. Questions which may need to be answered are: what was the physical and mental health of the witness at the time they made the statement? What were the physical circumstances in which the statement was made? How long after the event described in the statement was it made? Had the witness earlier spoken to others about the subject matter of the statement? Had the statement been made in response to what may have been influential questions by the person to whom the statement was made? What was the relationship and its dynamics between the statement maker and the person to whom it was made?[23]

---

[21] (1994) unreported, CA, 89/4043/W3, judgment 17 May.
[22] See, e.g., chapters 1, 8, 10, 18 and 19.
[23] Such factors are indicated in Chapter 1, by Loftus and others.

(2) Statements to police investigators

'Traditionally', legal practitioners and police investigators have been apt to consider **21.21** 'statements' as being a reference to written witness statements recorded in accordance with, respectively, ss 9 and 102 of the Criminal Justice Act 1967 and the Magistrates' Courts Act 1980 while oral statements made in other less formal circumstances, e.g. in the immediate aftermath of an alleged crime, have tended to be accorded less, if any, significance. However, it hardly needs to be said that a first report of crime made to a police officer fresh at the scene may acquire unforeseen significance especially if, as in the Taylor sisters' case cited above, this is inconsistent with something else said later.

Questions put to witnesses by police investigators are as likely to be influential and **21.22** potentially productive of unreliable answers if, because they are leading, they are improper, in whatever the circumstances in which they were made—whether immediately after a crime, shortly before the stage at which a written s9/102 statement is begun to be recorded or during this process. Disclosure of the questions which elicited the responses may be as important as the responses themselves. With the increase in the use of electronic recording devices by the police when witnesses are interviewed, the capture of such questions can be made unassailably. But where a witness is interviewed at a crime scene albeit briefly, or a witness statement is written out by a police officer scribe at the supposed dictation of a witness and given the witness's later unexaminable 'approval' when reading it through, it is likely to be extremely difficult, if not impossible, to discover the detail of eliciting questions.

(3) Statements made to non-police investigators

The discovery of the circumstances in which previous statements were made to non- **21.23** investigators or third parties, whilst potentially highly important, may be infinitely more problematic. Being human, witnesses are likely to speak to other witnesses about their experience. A previous statement which constitutes the witness's first report of an alleged crime may be made in a setting or to a person the details of which it is necessary to discover in order to assess its reliability and that of subsequent statements. This is, especially, the position when the witness is alleged to have made the statement to a person in authority, such as a parent or school-teacher or to a professional such as a counsellor or psychiatrist, who might perceive their role as discovering, out of concern for their well-being, whether the witness has been previously victimized.

(4) Previous statements made to mental/medical health professionals

Where a complaint of crime to the police has been preceded by one to professionals **21.24** whose role is to look after or investigate the welfare of the witness, many of the same considerations which are detailed under 'Statements to police investigators', above, will also apply. Experience has shown that some ill-trained or -motivated doctors, social workers or counsellors, for example, may question their patients or clients in a way that risks the emergence of confabulated or, occasionally, wholly untrue accounts which, because of the witness's vulnerability to suggestion, may become ingrained in their memory as real-life events. If the circumstances in which such statements are made are not susceptible to realistic forensic examination owing to the absence of any records against which their reliability can be properly tested, it may be that a fair trial is rendered impossible.[24]

G. Health and Other Issues

(1) General

21.25   Also addressed in a number of other chapters are other factors bearing on the reliability and accuracy of a witness's account (whether in a previous statement or in courtroom testimony) which might need to be the subject of detailed disclosure concerning their mental or physical health.[25] A witness may suffer from a learning disability; be pathologically compliant or suggestible; be under the influence of drugs at the time of making a previous statement or when giving evidence; be suffering from amnesia or claiming to be; be suffering from a physical defect which inhibits 'normal' communication styles; have a low intelligence quota; be psychopathologically damaged and, consequently, prone to confabulation or mendacity; suffer from disturbed sleeping patterns so that they might have difficulty in distinguishing between real and dreamed events; be suffering from the early, as yet undiagnosed, effects of senile dementia or Alzheimer's disease.

21.26   The conditions mentioned above (the list is, of course, not exhaustive) might be discoverable by reference to the witness's health records. Alternatively, whilst it may be suspected that the witness is affected by one of the conditions listed, this might not have been previously investigated and, thus, not be the subject of record.

(2) Health records

21.27   Difficulties in the discovery of relevant information relating to a witness's mental or physical health may arise in various circumstances. Assuming that the records are available and, if held in different locations (e.g. in a number of G.P.s' surgeries, at (a) hospital(s), by a school doctor, by a prison medical officer, in a residential home), collated, they may not be sufficiently clear or comprehensive to enable prosecution and defence lawyers or any expert instructed by them to reach reliable conclusions as to their relevance. The records may not address the relevant issue: for example, where the witness is under the influence of prescribed or illicit drugs at the time a statement is made or evidence given, what the effects of such drugs might be on recall and memory.

(3) Psychopathological issues

21.28   A witness may, owing to the influence of environmental and social factors, have a tendency to mendacity, exaggeration or to the making of false complaints of bad behaviour by others. Where this is not reflected in any criminal record or police files concerning

---

[24] See Brewin, chapter 6.
[25] See, e.g. Chapters 3, Murphy and Clare; 4, Gudjonsson; 5, Curran; 7, Christianson and others; 9, Davies and Westcott; and 13, Kyle.

complaints previously made and health records are silent on this issue, recourse may need to be had to Social Services or school records, an employer's disciplinary file or to individuals—friends or associates of the witness—who might be in a position to provide information concerning the witness's previous conduct.

H. Language Communication Issues

The 'typical' witness speaks English as their first language, is literate and can communi-   **21.29**
cate orally in a way which will readily be understood by English-speaking fact finders. However, in an increasingly cosmopolitan world and with the increasing use of facilities which permit evidence from witnesses who might previously have been considered incompetent owing to an inability to communicate coherently, courts are much more frequently becoming used to hearing from witnesses who communicate through an interpreter.[26] Inevitably, interpreters and interpreters/translators will have been used to facilitate communication with such witnesses earlier in the prosecution process, e.g. when their prospective evidential account is obtained by an investigator. Necessarily, participants in the criminal justice process—investigators, prosecution and defence law- yers, trial advocates, judges and fact finders—must rely on the professionalism, integrity and capability of interpreters and translators and to assume that what they say, in oral English, the witness has said or what they present in written translated English as being the witness's written statement—albeit, originally, in a foreign language or other- wise incomprehensible style—represents his or her actual account without misleading qualification.

However, it is the common experience of practitioners that standards of interpretation   **21.30**
and translation vary greatly and are prone to often significant error. Where a witness's statements are, if made in a foreign language, audio-recorded or, if made using visual aids, e.g., where the witness is deaf, video-recorded, any independent analysis of the accuracy of the original interpretation is greatly facilitated. However where only a written record is obtained, as in the 'traditional' method for recording s9/102 witness statements which does not include an electronically recorded version of the witness's utterances or use of visual aids, any later investigation as to whether the interpreter or translator 'got it right' is, effectively, rendered impossible. This may cause insuperable difficulty for a witness who claims that an interpreter did not interpret what they said to an investigator, as well as making well-nigh meaningless any attempt to assess a witness's courtroom evidence by reference to previous statements.

In these circumstances, disclosure of out-of-court statements to investigators by witnesses   **21.31**
communicating through an interpreter can only be effected usefully if they have been audio tape- or video-recorded. This is subject to the style of communication used, whether oral or through visual aids. Such records will include the questions put to the witness.

---

[26] See chapters 12, Corsellis and Clement and 13, Kyle.

I. The Prosecution's Disclosure Obligations

(1) General

21.32 The prosecution's disclosure obligations are set out in the CPIA and its Code of Practice, and their broader implications are usefully expanded upon in the *Attorney-General's Guidelines*, the *Disclosure Manual* and the Court of Appeal's *Disclosure Protocol* (all referred to earlier). Here, we highlight such aspects of these as bear relevance to the overall themes of this book. These relate, principally, to a witness's mental and physical health and statements made by them prior to giving evidence.

21.33 The extent to which members of the prosecution team perform their disclosure obligations effectively and comprehensively will depend to a great extent on the level of impartiality, open-mindedness and intelligence which they apply to their tasks. An approach which relies on slavish adherence to the niceties of the language used in the core texts might cause crucial material to be missed. It is, thus, as well for investigating and disclosure officers and prosecuting lawyers and advocates to adopt a defence mindset and to be proactive rather than to focus on strict compliance with disclosure law in the narrow sense, waiting before effecting their obligations until the defence have pointed the way. In *R v Rasheed*[27] Lord Justice Steyn made this clear:

> There is a positive duty to give fair disclosure. That duty is not contingent upon a request for disclosure, and the activation of that duty is not affected by the question whether, by due enquiries, the defence could have obtained [the document] in other ways.

(2) Recording and retaining information

(i) Previous statements to investigators

21.34 The CPIA Code of Practice sets out the police investigator's obligation to record and retain information which 'may be relevant to the investigation'. When conducting an investigation, the police investigator should, furthermore,

> . . . pursue all reasonable lines of inquiry, whether these point towards or away from the subject . . . Negative information is often relevant to an investigation . . . Where relevant information is obtained . . . it must be recorded at the time it is obtained or as soon as practicable after that time.[28]

21.35 Both the CPIA Code of Practice and the *Disclosure Manual* provide guidance concerning the type of material which might need to be recorded, retained and listed on the MG6C, the schedule of unused material, and which might relate to the mental or physical health of witnesses and their previous statements.

21.36 Whilst specifying that records of interviews with witnesses should be retained, there is little guidance as to what the record should include. Audio—or video—recorded interviews with witnesses necessarily include the whole record, warts and all, and provide a valuable resource for testimonial archaeologists concerned to know whether questions asked might have corrupted the witness's memory. Annex A of the *Disclosure Manual*

---

[27] Cited above at n. 21.   [28] Paras 3.5, 3.6 and 4.4.

lists, generically, various categories of material which might include forms of record of interviews with or statements made by witnesses and which need to be listed on the MG6C; hence: '999 voice tapes; crime reports; road traffic crash reports; family liaison logs; first descriptions of all suspects however and wherever recorded; draft statements or preparatory notes; records of information provided e.g. in conversation.'

The *Manual* adds that '[unused] material [which needs to be recorded and retained] **21.37** includes information given orally. Where relevant material is not recorded in any way, it will need to be reduced into a suitable form.'

Increasingly, police interviews with potential witnesses are being either video-recorded, **21.38** usually because the witness's video-recorded interview is eligible for use as their evidence-in-chief at trial, or audio-recorded, because the witness is treated as a 'significant' witness. Predictably, such records tend to reflect an appropriate and proper interview style which avoids 'leading' the witness or otherwise infecting their real memory. However, a large proportion of evidential interviews with witnesses, either because they are informal or because they involve the taking of s9/102 statements in the 'traditional' way described above, will continue to omit the very material—the investigator's questions and, perhaps, much of what the witness said orally—which is an essential prerequisite for those needing to know about the precise subject matter of previous statements to investigators and the circumstances in which they were made.

(ii) Previous statements to non-investigators

Whether previous statements made to those who are not part of the investigation **21.39** team are sought and consequently recorded and retained will depend on investigators' perceptions concerning their relevance and the question as to whether seeking them constitutes a 'reasonable line of enquiry'. Where a witness has spoken to another concerning the subject matter of their prospective evidence and this has the potential for being contentious there seems little doubt that, subject to any issues raised by the defendant whether in police interview or through a defence case statement, such statements or conversations will usually have the potential for relevance in case they either add to subsequent evidence and, thus, constitute material which can be used in evidence to prove the truth of their contents, or form the basis for cross-examination as to inconsistency.

Where investigators decide, nonetheless, not to seek details of previous statements to **21.40** third parties, it may be necessary to discover these through a direct approach to the third party, for example, a civilian, a social services employee, a member of school staff, a counsellor or doctor, or by using the third party witness summons procedure.[29]

(iii) Witness's mental and physical health and other issues concerning the reliability of a witness

The CPIA Code states, simply, that one of the categories of material falling within the **21.41** duty of retention by the investigator is 'any material casting doubt on the reliability of a

---

[29] See *Disclosure Manual*, chapter 4.

witness'. Chapter 4 of the *Disclosure Manual*, which concerns reasonable lines of enquiry and third parties, lists those categories of person frequently encountered as third parties who might hold relevant material under this heading. These include social services departments, forensic experts, police surgeons and GPs and hospital authorities. Otherwise, both the Code and the *Manual* offer little guidance to investigators which might inform them when decisions are made as to whether a reasonable line of enquiry might include making further investigations into a witness's mental or physical health or some other aspect of their character or past behaviour which has a bearing on their reliability as a witness.

21.42 Relevant material may be obvious to an investigator. A witness might have a record of previous cautions or convictions; have expressed an interest in a reward or compensation; have made previous ill-founded or mendacious complaints; have unsuccessfully applied for compensation in relation to a previous complaint to the Criminal Injuries Compensation Authority; or have a patent symptom of physical or mental ill-health or incapacity. In such circumstances, the investigator's obligations to retain and record relevant material and to pursue further reasonable lines of enquiry will be clearly apparent. In other situations, such tendencies or conditions will be known to or reasonably suspected by only the defence and investigators' initiatives to make appropriate enquiries will need to be stimulated through a defence case statement which is drafted specifically to address such issues. Alternatively, they might need to be discovered through the third party witness summons procedure.

(3) Scheduling unused material, revelation to the prosecutor and disclosure to the defence

21.43 Where the investigator has recorded and retained relevant unused material, whether in the form of records of previous statements or information casting doubt on the reliability of a witness, the items in question must be listed, by the disclosure officer, on a disclosure schedule, the MG6C, in a way which informs the prosecutor and the defence about the item's contents sufficiently to allow a decision to be made concerning whether it could satisfy the disclosure test.[30]

21.44 Having scheduled the material, the disclosure officer must copy to the prosecutor 'any material casting doubt on the reliability of a prosecution witness'.[31]

21.45 Having reviewed the disclosure schedule and any item copied to him by the disclosure officer, the prosecuting lawyer must cause the disclosure officer to copy to the defence any material which satisfies the criteria for disclosability. Such material ought, unarguably, to include all records of previous statements by a prosecution witness concerning the subject matter of their complaint or prospective evidence.

---

[30] *Disclosure Manual*, chapter 7, paras 3 and 4.   [31] CPIA Code paragraph 7.2.

J. Defence Disclosure and Obtaining Prosecution Disclosure

Initial disclosure by the prosecution is intended to cover material which is disclosable **21.46** regardless of any issue raised by the defence or which concerns issues which arise during the defendant's police interview before the Defence Case Statement is served. Experience has shown that it is far from safe for the defence to assume that the prosecution has comprehensively performed its initial disclosure tasks—recording, retention, scheduling, the pursuance of further reasonable lines of enquiry, revelation, disclosure to the defence. Notably, the disclosure schedule may not include relevant items or, if it does, describe these with a sufficient degree of specificity to inform the prosecutor as to disclosability— for example, if the item is a note of a pre-written statement conversation with a witness, what the witness said. In these circumstances, the only means of securing disclosure of material hitherto undisclosed is through correspondence with the prosecutor or police. This is something for which disclosure law—assuming, as it does, that the prosecution performs its initial disclosure tasks comprehensively—makes no provision. CPIA s8 applications can be made to the court for a direction as to disclosure of material previously undisclosed only after a defence case statement has been served. Written requests for unused material which is said to satisfy the test for initial disclosure can be fruitful but often are not and prosecution authorities, particularly the Crown Prosecution Service, have a reputation for poor response to any written enquiries which do not, as they perceive them, strictly comply with the CPIA's disclosure provisions.

Thus, where the prosecution have not remedied inadequate initial disclosure or are **21.47** disinclined to enter into correspondence with the defence about it, the defence can have recourse only to the defence case statement.

(1) Defence case statements

Where these are used in an attempt to flush out unused material which, arguably, ought **21.48** to have been disclosed already during initial disclosure or to assist in effecting further disclosure consequent upon the issues raised in them, their texts need to be sufficiently specific to inform the prosecutor and police disclosure officer for the purposes of their decisions as to whether to make further disclosure. As the CJA 2003 and the Court of Appeal's *Disclosure Protocol* make clear, bald assertions of the defendant's innocence are completely unhelpful. The defence case statement needs to address those issues upon which further disclosure of unused material will depend. They should, therefore, explain the extent of factual dispute with assertions made by prosecution witnesses, detail the prospective defence and raise any specific issues concerning, for example, prosecution witnesses' mental or physical ill-health which are known to or suspected on reasonable grounds by the defence. Suggestions for the pursuance by the police of further reasonable grounds of enquiry, or 'shopping lists' of previously undisclosed material of the kind which are usefully added to defence case statements, should be referable to the factual disputes detailed and issues raised. Whilst some requests for generic material are justifiable, such as records of previous statements by witnesses whose prospective evidence is contentious, those which, simply, refer to 'all police officer's notebooks' or 'social services records' without more detail, for example, will understandably meet a negative response.

A suggestion that the police should seek access to any documents within Social Services' records which constitute the basis of a suggestion that the complainant or a witness has a reputation for dishonesty or a history of confabulation ought, if such material exists, to be more productive.

(2) Applications for orders for further disclosure under section 8 of the CPIA

21.49 Once a defence case statement has been served, the defence have the option to apply to the Court for an order requiring further disclosure of any material which they have reasonable cause to believe the prosecution has in its possession which satisfies the disclosure test. The making of s8 orders is, strictly, the only opportunity afforded by the law to the court for making binding orders relating to disclosure—a factor strongly highlighted in the *Disclosure Protocol*. But the ambit of s8 orders is limited for two principal reasons: first, they do not empower the court to require the prosecution to pursue further reasonable lines of enquiry which might lead to the obtaining of material which is not yet but ought to be in their possession and, second and connected, such orders cannot relate to material which, whilst they might have easy access to it, is not in the prosecution's possession.

(3) Material held by third parties

21.50 Until the publication of the Attorney-General's *Guidelines on Disclosure* of 29 November 2000, it was thought by many that the search for material held by third parties was of no legitimate interest to the prosecution and was a matter for defence initiatives only. The 2000 *Guidelines* made it clear that this was not the case. This was replicated in paragraph 51 of the 2005 *Guidelines*:

> There may be cases where the investigator, disclosure officer or prosecutor believes that a third party (for example, a local authority, a social services department, a hospital, a doctor, a school, a provider of forensic services) has material or information which might be relevant to the prosecution case. In such cases, if the material or information might reasonably be considered capable of undermining the prosecution case or of assisting the case for the accused prosecutors should take what steps they regard as appropriate in the particular case to obtain it.

The obligation was confirmed in the judgment of Longmore LJ in *R v Alibhai and others*:

> The Crown does have obligations in respect of material in the hands of third parties and a conviction would, in any event, be unsafe if the absence of disclosure of material in the possession of a third party meant that an accused could not have a fair trial.[32]

---

[32] [2004] EWCA Crim 681, judgment 30 March, at para 31. In *R v Derek A* (2000) unreported, CA reference 1998/07511/Y5, judgment 14 March, *per* Lord Bingham CJ, a case involving allegations of sexual assault on a child, the non-disclosure at trial of material relating to the credibility of the complainant which was obtained by the police from third parties and should clearly have been disclosed to the prosecutor and thence to the defence, was held to warrant quashing of convictions obtained prior to the implementation of the CPIA. In *R v K* [2002] EWCA Crim 2879, judgment 11 December, *per* Rose LJ, similarly involving allegations of sexual assault against a child, non-disclosure of third-party material, apparently disclosed later at the behest of the Criminal Cases Review Commission, led on review by the Court of Appeal to the convictions being quashed (prosecution not criticized).

Exceptionally, the prosecution may decide to seek access to material held by a third party **21.51** independently of defence stimulation, whether through the defence case statement or otherwise. Alternatively, they may yield to defence suggestions that they should do so, particularly if these are articulated in a way which justifies such an approach. In either event, the defence should take steps—usually through an appropriately drafted defence case statement—in advance of the approach by the prosecution to the third party, to ensure that both the prosecution and the third party are fully informed concerning the issues in the case and the category and specificity of material which should be searched for and sought.

It should be borne in mind that simply because there exists material held by a third party **21.52** which 'might' have a bearing on the issues in the case, it should not be assumed that it will necessarily be relevant. As the Attorney-General's *Guidelines* indicate, the prosecution need, if they are to take the initiative to approach the third party, to be satisfied that they have a 'belief' that the third party, indeed, holds relevant material. This was emphasized in the judgment of the Court of Appeal in *R v Alibhai*:[33]

> . . . even if there is the suspicion that triggers these provisions [of the 2000 edition of the Attorney-General's *Guidelines*], the prosecutor is not under an absolute obligation to secure the disclosure of the material or information. He enjoys what might be described as a 'margin of consideration' as to what steps he regards as appropriate in the particular case. If criticism is to be made of a failure to secure third party disclosure it would have to be shown that the prosecutor did not act within the permissible limits afforded by the *Guidelines*.

It might not always be appropriate to allow or encourage the prosecution to take the **21.53** initiative in seeking third-party disclosure. Either for reasons of expedience, the need for timely preparation or because the defence feel more confident that the third party will be comprehensively informed through a defence approach, it might be more apt for the defence to make the first move.

The complex mechanics of the process of seeking third-party disclosure are fully set out **21.54** in the *Disclosure Manual*,[34] referred to usefully in the *Disclosure Protocol*[35] and, where it becomes necessary to summons the holder of the records to court to produce them, either by s2 of the Criminal Procedure (Attendance of Witnesses) Act 1965 or s97 of the Magistrates' Courts Act 1980,[36] and it is not proposed to reiterate their contents or requirements here. However, when the defence decide to approach a third party, the following need to be particularly remembered.

The third party must be fully informed concerning the issues in the case—most easily **21.55** effected by copying for them the police or prosecuting advocate's case summary and the defence case statement. Their attention must be drawn either to the category of material or specific documents which are sought and the reason for the request for their disclosure must be detailed by reference to the issues in the case. Where using the process set out in the statutory provisions for securing the attendance of the holder of the records at Court,

---

[33] Ibid, at para 63.   [34] Cited above at n.16, chapter 4 and Annex B.
[35] Cited above at n.17, paragraphs 52–62.
[36] A s2 application must comply with the Criminal Procedure Rules 2005, paras 28.3–28.6.

the material sought must be, at least potentially, material evidence, that is, evidence which would be admissible in evidence in the proceedings in relation to which disclosure is sought. Owing to the hearsay provisions of the CJA 2003, records of previous statements by witnesses concerning the subject matter of their prospective evidence would normally come into this category, as would records of statements made by others which might form the basis of a suggestion that the witness had a reputation for dishonesty or suffered from a mental or physical condition which rendered their evidence otherwise potentially unreliable or inaccurate.

K. The Use of Experts

21.56 As indicated above, mental and physical health records, assuming that disclosure of these has been obtained, might not be sufficiently informative to enable the parties to assess whether a mental or physical illness suffered by a witness might have caused previous statements by them or their evidence in Court to be inaccurate or unreliable. In such circumstances, it may be necessary for steps to be taken to cause an expert—typically a doctor, medical specialist or psychiatrist—to examine the witness and to provide a report which addresses the issue. If the witness is a prosecution witness and this initiative is taken by the defence, it will be necessary for access to be sought to the witness through the police and for the prosecution to be informed, either in correspondence or through an appropriately drafted defence case statement, as to the purpose for which the examination is required.

L. Conclusion

21.57 There is no question that problems relating to the enormously complex and difficult area of disclosure law will continue to arise, especially when so much trust is placed in the hands of state servants to ensure that the process is effected comprehensively and fairly. When it comes to the operation of the disclosure machinery it is clear that all those involved—whether members of the prosecution team or those representing the interests of defendants—should leave no stone unturned in what needs to be a highly focused, often time-consuming, expensive and methodical search for material which might have a bearing on the determination of the guilt or innocence of the accused. One could do little better than to recall the terse comment of Lord Hope in *R v Brown (Winston)* when, in referring to the practical difficulties which might be involved in implementing the duty of disclosure, he said 'if fairness demands disclosure, then a way of ensuring that disclosure will be made must be found'.[37]

Recommended Reading

The Disclosure Manual: http://www.cps.gov.uk/legal/section20/chapter_a.html.
Disclosure: A protocol for the Control and Management of Unused Material in the Crown Court, Y

---

[37] [1998] AC 367, at 390.

Llys Apel/Court of Appeal, 20 February 2006, *http://www.hmcourts-service.gov.uk/cms/files/disclosure_protocol.pdf.*

Heaton-Armstrong, A. and Wolchover, D., 'Recording witness statements' in Heaton-Armstrong, A., Shepherd, E. and Wolchover D., *Analysing Witness Testimony*, London: Blackstone Press, 1999, 222–250.

Heaton-Armstrong, A., 'Recording and Disclosing Statements by Witnesses: Law and Practice' (1994) 35 *Medicine, Science and the Law*, 136.

Bond, T. and Sandhu, A., *Therapists in Court: Providing Evidence and Supporting Witnesses*, London: Sage Publications, 2005.

Quirk, H., 'The significance of culture in criminal procedure reform: Why the revised disclosure scheme cannot work' (2006) 10 *Evidence and Procedure* 42–59.

David Corker is a criminal defence specialist solicitor at Corker Binning and since the mid-1990s he has had a particular interest in matters relating to disclosure in criminal cases. His authorship of *Disclosure in Criminal Proceedings*[38] has led to numerous invitations to address legal audiences on disclosure-related subjects and he is now working on a second edition for Oxford University Press, due in 2007. He has also published *Abuse of Process in Criminal Proceedings*, now in its second edition.[39]

Editors' Note

Without comprehensive and focused disclosure of 'unused' material which touches on issues raised in a case, a fair trial which enables fact finders to see a realistic and integral evidential picture is rendered impossible. Recent initiatives in the field of disclosure law, influenced by concerns over wasted cost and defence lawyers arguably taking unfair and improper advantage of information contained in unused material which ought not to have been disclosed, have further secured the barriers to any route to effective audit of the performance of the prosecution's disclosure role. The responsibility of state servants to ensure that defence lawyers are properly informed concerning unused material which may point away from guilt or towards innocence is, therefore, greater than ever. Those representing the interests of defendants should leave no moveable stone unturned in their quest for the discovery of material which might assist fact finders in resolving issues of truth and accuracy and guilt and innocence.

---

[38] London: Sweet and Maxwell, 1997.
[39] London: Butterworths, 2000 (1ˢᵗ ed.); 2003 (2ⁿᵈ ed).

22

THE ADMISSIBILITY OF EXPERT EVIDENCE

David Ormerod and Andrew Roberts

A. Introduction

Expert evidence is a dynamic and controversial area of the law of evidence, particularly **22.01** criminal evidence. In this chapter we aim to describe the current law, identify and examine principal difficulties in using expert evidence and, finally, to offer some suggestions as to likely developments in this area. Although expert evidence relates to a broad range of subject matter, as far as possible the emphasis of this chapter reflects the book's dominant themes. In particular, we deal with expert evidence on identity, the veracity of the testimony of non-defendant witnesses and evidence concerning the reliability of defendants' confessions and mental state when criminal acts were committed.

B. Expert Evidence in the Context of the Rules of Evidence

(1) Relevance and admissibility

22.02 Whether an item of evidence is to be received at trial is determined on the application of two issues: *relevance* and *admissibility*. A fundamental principle is that all relevant evidence is admissible. The notion of *relevance* in this context is concisely stated in Rule 401 of the US Federal Rules of Evidence, which defines relevant evidence as 'evidence having any tendency to make the existence of any fact that is of any consequence to the determination of the action more probable or less probable than it would be without the evidence'. The *admissibility* of *relevant* evidence is dependent on the absence of any exclusionary rule which might operate to prevent its reception.

(2) Opinion evidence

22.03 Generally, while witnesses may testify to relevant facts within their knowledge there is an exclusionary rule rendering inadmissible their 'opinion' on those facts. 'Opinion' has been defined as 'an inference drawn or to be drawn from observed and communicable data'.[1] The general rule excluding opinion evidence has a number of rationales.[2] The principal objections are that allowing opinion would tend to usurp the fact finder's function without assisting their determination of the issues. It is for the tribunal of fact to draw inferences from the testimony of witnesses in applying the law to the facts of the particular case. Wigmore explained the rationale of the rule excluding opinion evidence as one based on superfluity:

> It simply endeavours to save time and avoid confusing testimony by telling the witness: 'the tribunal is in possession of the same materials of information on this subject as yourself; thus, as you can add nothing to our materials for judgement, your further testimony is unnecessary, and merely cumbers the proceedings'.[3]

(3) The admissibility of the opinion of an expert

22.04 However, where a witness possesses some knowledge, experience or skill which the tribunal of fact does not, his or her opinion as to the meaning or implications of some piece of evidence might assist the tribunal of fact to discharge its function. Accordingly, *expert* opinion evidence is admissible under a long-standing exception to the general prohibition on opinion evidence.[4] Whether any particular item of expert opinion evidence is to be received at trial is dependent on its relevance and admissibility within this

---

[1] *Allstate Life Insurance Co. v ANZ Banking Group Ltd (No. 5)* (1996) 64 FCR 73, 75.

[2] See generally, Dennis, I.H., *The Law of Evidence*, 2nd ed, London: Sweet & Maxwell, 2002, 699; Australian Law Reform Commission, Report (Interim) No. 26, vol 1, *Evidence*, Canberra: ALRC: 1985, 406–407.

[3] Wigmore, J.H., *A Treatise on the Anglo-American System of Evidence in Trials at Common Law, Evidence*, 3rd ed (10 vols) Boston, Little, Brown & Co., 1940, para 1917.

[4] See e.g. the 16th century case, *Buckley v Thomas* (1554) 1 Plowden 118, 124, *per* Saunders J: 'If matters arise in our law which concern other sciences or faculties, we commonly apply for the aid of that science or faculty which it concerns which it is an honourable and commendable thing for our law. F thereby it appears that we do not despise all other sciences but our own, but we approve of them encourage them as things worthy of commendation.'

exception to the rule. The main considerations are whether the individual proffering the opinion qualifies as an expert and whether the subject matter involved is one on which the tribunal of fact needs assistance.

C. Who is an Expert?

(1) The pragmatic approach of the English courts

The English courts have adopted a pragmatic approach to determining whether a witness is qualified to proffer expert evidence. There is no prerequisite that a witness possesses formal qualification or training. An early case illustrating this flexibility is *R v Silverlock*,[5] where a solicitor was permitted to testify on handwriting analysis. He had no qualifications nor had he undertaken any formal training in the techniques that he applied. His skills had been acquired during the course of his business and in pursuit of his hobby of studying historic documents. Nonetheless his evidence was admissible as expert opinion.

22.05

(2) Traditional disciplines and other fields of expertise

The need to avoid a formalistic approach to acknowledging expertise is induced in part by the diversity of subject matter on which expert evidence might assist the fact-finder. In *R v Robb*[6] it was stated that witnesses practising in traditional academically-based sciences such as medicine, geology and metallurgy present no problem, as expertise will be established by relevant qualification, membership of a professional body, etc. Beyond the 'traditional sciences' the relevant question is 'whether the witness in question is [skilled and has an adequate knowledge] . . .'[7] In a trial by jury, the trial judge acts as a gatekeeper to ensure (i) that the witnesses who purport to hold expertise do in fact possess it, and (ii) that the evidence that they give is reliable and ought to be received (this is dealt with in the following section).

22.06

(3) The increasing need for vigilance in vetting claims to expertise

The sufficiency of a witness's expertise continues to pose problems despite the pervading judicial pragmatism. In recent years there has been an increased willingness to call expert evidence. This is owing in part to the greater reliance on forensic science at trial, but also to the wider availability of putative experts on the broader range of subjects now attracting research. More generally, this desire to call experts might reflect the greater emphasis in modern society on science and pseudo-science, and the legal profession's perception of an increased expectation from fact finders that some scientific explanation will be available for any event. With this in mind, it will become increasingly important that judicial evaluation of the sufficiency of expertise is appropriately rigorous. At the same time, as the subject matter on which experts are prepared to testify expands well beyond the

22.07

---

[5] [1894] 2 QB 766.   [6] (1991) 93 Cr App R 161, CA.
[7] Ibid, 165, *per* Bingham LJ. *Robb* also raises the problem of the 'ad hoc expert'—one who has only gained his expertise by studying materials in the case in issue. See further Munday, R., 'Videotape Evidence and the Advent of the Expert ad hoc' (1995) 159 JP 412.

boundaries of traditional sciences, it will become more difficult to establish whether the relevant degree of knowledge and learning is possessed.[8]

22.08 Arguably, the degree of scrutiny of expertise ought to vary depending on the level of organization that exists in the witness's field of practice. For example, the 'expert' might belong to a professional body, for which membership depends on attainment of some academic or vocational qualification, or successful completion of some entrance examination, and compulsory Continuing Professional Development training. In such circumstances the court might properly defer to the judgement of the witness's peers on his expertise.

(4) Requirement for expertise on the specific matters in issue

22.09 This proposition is subject to one important caveat: the witness must possess expertise in relation to the matters on which he proposes to offer an opinion. Among the principles set out by the High Court when considering the role of an expert witness in *The Ikarian Reefer* was that '[a]n expert should provide independent assistance to the court by way of objective unbiased opinion *in relation to matters within his expertise* . . .'[9] This principle has all too often been overlooked. In the recent case of *R v Barnes*[10] the evidence of an arboriculturalist called to testify that woodgrain impressions incidentally lifted in the recovery of fingerprints at a crime scene did not match the grain in the wood surface on which they were purportedly found was held to be inadmissible on the grounds that the expert had no experience in the interpretation of impressions and relevant comparisons.

22.10 Although this might appear an obvious point, it was the courts' failure to keep sight of the nexus between a witness's field of expertise and the nature of his testimony that recently led to notorious miscarriages of justice. *R v Clark*[11] involved multiple 'cot deaths' in one family. An eminent and well-respected paediatrician gave expert testimony on the possible causes of death. In evidence he suggested that the odds of two such unexplained deaths occurring in the same family were some 73,000,000 to 1. This figure was derived by multiplying the risk of a mature, non-smoking couple suffering the loss of an infant in such circumstances that was found in one study (8,543 to 1), by itself. Despite possessing no expertise in statistics, the paediatrician was permitted to testify as to the statistical probabilities of a family suffering two such deaths. The calculations were seriously flawed, failing to take account of relevant factors such as genetics, common family living conditions and the type of bedding used, and sleeping positions, all of which would have made a second death much more likely.[12]

---

[8] There will be an increased need for judicial training on evaluating expertise. See the interesting review by Odgers, S. and Richardson, J., 'Keeping Bad Science out of the Courtroom—Changes in American and Australian Expert Evidence Law' (1995) 1 *Univ. New South Wales Law Journal* 108.

[9] *National Justice Cia Naviera SA v Prudential Assurance Co Ltd (The Ikarian Reefer)* [1993] 2 Lloyd's Rep 68, 81–82. For further recent guidance on the role and duties of expert witnesses, see *R v Harris* [2005] EWCA Crime 1980; *R v Puaca* [2005] EWCA Crim 3001; *R v Bowman* [2006] EWCA Crim 417.

[10] [2005] EWCA Crim 1158.

[11] *R v Clark (Sally)* [2004] EWCA Crim 1020; [2004] 2 FCR 447. See also *R v Cannings (Angela)* [2004] EWCA Crim 1; [2004] 2 Cr App R 7; *R v Harris* cited at n. 9 above.

[12] 'Cot death numbers don't add up, says eminent statistician', *The Times*, June 25, 2005. See the helpful information on the flaws as explained by the Royal Statistical Society at *http://pass.maths.org.uk/*

(5) The problem of establishing competence in non-regulated fields

Where the expertise of a witness lies in a field which is not subject to any formal **22.11**
regulation, establishing whether he has sufficient skill or knowledge is more difficult.
Those best placed to assess competence are persons working in that field, but reliance on
their view is hazardous in the absence of a formal accreditation system and particularly
where there are few people engaged in the field of study. Despite these dangers, English
courts' acceptance of such individuals' expertise appears sometimes to be based on a
rather too uncritical and limited appraisal of a witness's credentials. In this regard *R v
Luttrell*[13] ought to sound a cautionary note. The appellant was alleged to have been
involved in a criminal conspiracy. The mainstay of the prosecution case was analysis of
CCTV footage by a lip-reading expert, R, who claimed to have been able to decipher
incriminating conversations between the appellant and others. After acknowledging that
there were only four such witnesses in the UK the Court of Appeal stated:

> As and when new witnesses appear, it will be entirely appropriate, when they first give
> evidence, for their expertise to be challenged and tested by reference, in appropriate cases,
> to disclosed material bearing on their skill or lack of it. But so far as [R] and [H—another
> expert lip-reader who gave evidence in the case]—are concerned, if they give evidence in
> future cases we would not expect a trial judge to permit extensive trawling through their
> past 'successes' and 'failures'. As we have indicated, the material before us establishes
> conclusively that [R] is one of the very best lip-readers.[14]

These comments were unfortunate since at a subsequent trial, R's qualifications were
challenged by defence counsel, which led to the Crown Prosecution Service reviewing
cases in which she had provided important evidence and declining to instruct her in
any future case.[15] Similar concerns arise with other narrow specialisms such as voice
identification[16] and facial mapping.[17]

(6) The trend towards accreditation and registration

There is a discernible and welcome trend towards expanding accreditation and registration **22.12**
schemes regulating those who might be called to give expert testimony, which would
seem to be in the interests of both experts and the criminal justice system. For example,
the Council for the Registration of Forensic Practioners maintains a register of competent
forensic practitioners[18] with the aim of maintaining public confidence. Registration
entails evaluation of an applicant's competence through examination of his casework by a

---

issue21/features/clark/. See also the Society's letter to the Lord Chancellor at *http://www.rss.org.uk* and
follow links to 'Current Hot Topics' and Statistics and the Law.

[13] [2004] EWCA Crim 1344; [2004] Crim LR 939.   [14] Ibid, [38].

[15] See 'Lip-reader's CV claims lead to case reviews', *The Times*, July 4, 2005; Jackson, S., 'Read My Lips'
(2004) 154 *NLJ* 1146.

[16] *R v O'Doherty* [2003] 1 Cr App R 5, NICA and Ormerod, D., 'Sounding Out Expert Voice Identification' [2002] Crim LR 771. See also Chapter 14 above.

[17] See especially *R v Ward* [2003] EWCA Crim 3191, and *R v Gray and Nugent* [2003] EWCA Crim
3434; *R v Mitchell* [2005] EWCA Crim 731; *R v Ciantar* [2005] EWCA Crim 3559; *R v Cakir* [2005] All
ER (D) 129 May. See also Chapters 16 and 17 above.

[18] Registration is currently limited to those working in one of 13 specified fields of forensic science,
although at the time of writing the CRFP was in the process of extending it to encompass two further areas
of practice.

Council assessor. A significant current development is a government proposal[19] to extend the statutory registration scheme[20] to anyone using the title 'forensic psychologist'. Inclusion on the register would require an applicant to meet and maintain standards of proficiency.

D. Matters on which Experts may Testify

(1) Relevance, reliability and the test of admissibility

22.13 As for the conditions for admissibility of expert evidence, the English courts have cited[21] with approval the position expounded in the leading textbook, *Cross & Tapper on Evidence*, that 'so long as a field is sufficiently well-established to pass the ordinary tests of relevance and reliability, then no enhanced test of admissibility should be applied'.[22] However, the adequacy of this as a definitive and authoritative statement of the principles of admissibility is questionable owing to its generality. What is meant by *relevance* in the context of expert evidence? How is the issue of *reliability* to be approached? The adequacy of this vague test in ensuring that the court is best served by the available expert evidence is under greater pressure as research expands into ever more esoteric areas.

(2) Relevance and the 'common knowledge' rule

22.14 To be admissible, expert evidence must be relevant. In this context, relevance is used in two senses. First, in the orthodox sense, that the testimony of the expert must be logically probative of some fact which will form part of the basis of the fact finder's adjudication. The second sense concerns the issue of superfluity. This can be demonstrated by reference to the decision of the High Court of Australia in *Smith v The Queen*,[23] where the evidence of two police officers who purported to identify the appellant, with whom they had had previous dealings, as the person in still images taken during a bank robbery was held to be inadmissible under s55 of the (Australian) Evidence Act 1995 (Cth). That section defines *relevant evidence* as 'evidence that, if it were accepted, could rationally affect (directly or indirectly) the assessment of the probability of the existence of a fact in issue in the proceedings'. The images were available to the jury and the police officers were no better placed than the jury to determine whether the appellant was the person depicted:

> The fact that someone else has reached a conclusion about the identity of the accused and the person in the picture does not provide any logical basis for affecting the jury's assessment of the probability of the existence of that fact when the conclusion is based on material that is not different in any substantial way from what is available to the jury . . .

---

[19] *Applied Psychology, Enhancing Public Protection: Proposals for the statutory regulation of applied psychologists*, (Department of Health: March 2005).

[20] Health Act 1999, s60 permits registration of persons concerned wholly or partly with the physical or mental health of individuals.

[21] See *R v Dallagher* [2002] EWCA Crim 1903; *R v Luttrell*, cited above at n.13

[22] Tapper, C., *Cross & Tapper on Evidence*, 9th ed, London: Butterworths, 1999, 523. See now 10th ed, 2004, 558 *et seq*.

[23] (2001) 206 CLR 650.

[The jury's] task is neither assisted nor hindered, by knowing that some other person has, or has not, arrived at that conclusion.[24]

In English law this notion of relevance as a condition for admissibility finds articulation in what is known as the 'common knowledge' rule. Although its provenance can be traced to much earlier decisions,[25] the most often cited statement of it is found in *R v Turner*:[26]

> An expert's opinion is admissible to furnish the court with scientific information which is likely to be outside the experience or knowledge of a judge or jury. If on the proven facts a judge or jury can form their own conclusions without help, then the opinion of an expert is unnecessary . . . The fact that an expert witness has impressive scientific qualifications does not by that fact alone make his opinion on matters of human nature more helpful than that of the jurors themselves; but there is a danger that they may think it does.

The rule is problematic because the trial judge is obliged to determine whether the subject matter on which it is proposed to adduce expert evidence is 'within the common knowledge and understanding of the jury'. Moreover, the foundation for the test—that there is a 'common understanding'—is flawed, and leads to arbitrary and inconsistent decisions.[27]

In respect of evidence regarding human behaviour, the common knowledge rule has also **22.15** been cogently criticized on the grounds that a considerable body of research indicates that lay people find many forms of 'normal behaviour' as difficult to understand as mentally disordered behaviour.[28] Moreover, psychological research produces findings that are often at odds with intuition about everyday human behaviour.[29] The common knowledge rule has proved particularly difficult to apply consistently across a range of disciplines, and we consider here some of the more controversial.

(3) The common knowledge rule in application

(i) Identification evidence

There is no authority in English law as to admissibility of the evidence of a psychologist **22.16** concerning factors that might affect the reliability of eyewitness identification evidence. The presumption must be that it would be excluded by the operation of the common knowledge rule. In Australia, s80 of the Evidence Act 1995 (Cth.) abolished the common knowledge rule although it appears to have been subsumed, in substance if not form, by the definition of relevance in s55 Evidence Act 1995 (Cth.), as applied in *Smith v The Queen* (see paragraph 22.14 above). While the impugned testimony in that case was not expert evidence, the decision indicates the basis on which expert evidence might be

---

[24] Ibid, para 11, *per* Gleeson LJ.   [25] See *e.g. Folkes v Chadd* (1782) 3 Doug KB 157.
[26] [1975] QB 834, at 841. For a detailed analysis of *R v Turner* and its implications, see Redmayne, M., *Expert Evidence and Criminal Justice*, Oxford: Oxford University Press, 2001, Chapter 6.
[27] It has been rejected in the High Court of Australia; see Heydon, J., *Cross on Evidence*, 7th Australian ed, Chatswood, NSW: Butterworths, 2004, 930.
[28] Mackay, R., Colman, A. and Thornton, P., 'The Admissibility of Expert Psychological and Psychiatric Testimony,' in Heaton-Armstrong, A., Shepherd, E. and Wolchover, D., *Analysing Witness Testimony*, London, Blackstone Press: 1999, 324.
[29] Redmayne, cited above at n. 26, 160.

excluded as irrelevant (or to use more appropriate terms redundant or superfluous) in Australia. It also provides an example of the divergence in judicial assumptions regarding human behaviour and the psychological research findings underlying the criticism directed at the common knowledge rule. The court assumed that the police officers who were familiar with the appellant prior to observing the images from the bank robbery were no better placed than the jury when it came to identifying him. This assertion appears to be confounded by psychological research which suggests that attempts at identification are likely to be far more accurate in cases where a witness and the person depicted in the images are already known to one another than where there is no such familiarity.[30]

In *R v Smith*[31] the New South Wales Court of Criminal Appeal recognized that, following the abolition of the common knowledge rule, expert evidence concerning identification might theoretically be admissible in that jurisdiction.[32] However, it then appeared to foreclose this possibility in practice by holding that the expert evidence in question would be inadmissible at a retrial as being likely to cause or result in undue waste of time.[33] This anxiety about the distraction caused by expert evidence is also seen in the Canadian case of *R v McIntosh*[34] where Finlayson JA held inadmissible expert opinion on cross-racial identification on the ground that it would be too prejudicial and would distort the fact-finding process.[35]

22.17   Since identification evidence is recognized by the courts to be so hazardous that it is not safe to be left for the jury's consideration without explicit warnings and guidance, it is surprising that the courts eschew the opportunity to offer the jury the best guidance available—that from an expert psychologist.

(ii) The defendant's state of mind

22.18   The courts have been equally resistant to the reception of expert evidence on the defendant's state of mind. Evidence concerning a defendant's *abnormal* mental condition is presumptively outside the jury's common knowledge. Expert evidence is, therefore, admissible and may in certain circumstances be necessary[36] where a defendant claims to have been suffering from some reduced mental capacity which limits or obviates any culpability in respect of an offence with which he is charged.

---

[30] See Bruce, V., *et al*, 'Matching Identities of Familiar and Unfamiliar Faces Caught on CCTV Images', (2001) 7 *Journal of Experimental Psychology: Applied* 207; Burton, M., *et al*, 'Face Recognition in Poor-Quality Video: Evidence from Security Surveillance,' (1999) 10 *Psychological Science* 243. Such testimony would be admissible in England: *Attorney-General's Reference (No.2 of 2002)* [2003] 1 Cr App R 21, CA. See also Chapters 16 and 17 above.

[31] (2000) 16 A Crim R 1.   [32] See s79 Evidence Act 1995 (Cth.).

[33] Ibid, s135(c).   [34] (1997) 117 CCC(3d) 385 (Ont CA), para 23.

[35] See more generally in Canada *R v Fengstad* [1994] BCJ No. 80 (BCCA), para 74: 'the dangers of misidentification, while they can never be completely overcome, can adequately be minimized by a proper jury charge without the assistance of expert testimony. We need only mention that the difficulties of identification could be compounded if the jury should be visited with questioned or conflicting expert opinion evidence.'

[36] E.g. with diminished responsibility *R v Dix* (1982) 74 Cr App R 306, CA. It is also admissible in cases of duress: *R v Bowen* [1996] 2 Cr App R 157, CA, *R v Hurst* [1995] 1 Cr App R 82; and in provocation: *R v Smith (Morgan)* [2001] 1 Cr App R 5, HL.

Expert evidence is, generally, inadmissible where it is relied upon in relation to a defendant **22.19** who is not suffering from some mental illness/abnormality, usually in an attempt by the defendant to support his claim that he lacked the necessary mental element of the offence alleged. In *R v Chard*[37] C appealed his conviction for murder on the grounds that the trial judge had wrongly excluded evidence from the prison doctor. The doctor had reported that on examination of C there was no evidence of mental abnormality, and opined that in light of the appellant's personality C had not formed the necessary intent or *mens rea* to commit murder as alleged. In dismissing the appeal, the court held that it was not permissible to call a witness to tell the jury how an accused's assumedly normal mind operated in relation to the issue of his intention at the time of the alleged crime. This position was been reiterated in numerous cases[38] including, for example, *R v Coles,*[39] emphasizing that unless some factor of the defendant's mental health or psychiatric state was raised, expert evidence relating to the defendant's *mens rea* was inadmissible.

While this remains authoritative as a general principle it has been significantly under- **22.20** mined in a series of decisions relating to defendants who, on being jointly tried, ran 'cut-throat' defences, i.e. each blaming the other. In *Lowery v R*[40] the Privy Council considered the admissibility of evidence from a psychiatrist as to the respective person- alities of two co-defendants, L and K. They had been accused of the sadistic murder of a 15-year-old girl. A psychologist, C, called on behalf of K had interviewed both K and L and submitted them to the same tests commonly employed by clinical psychologists in making assessments of personality. C gave evidence that K was an immature, emotionally shallow youth, who seemed likely to be led and dominated by more aggressive and dominant men and who could conceivably act out or behave aggressively to comply with the wishes or demands of another person. He further testified that L showed little evidence of capacity to relate adequately to others, that he had a strong aggressive drive with weak controls over the expression of aggressive impulses, and a basic callousness and impulsiveness. The attribute of callousness had not been found in K. Furthermore, L found sadistic pleasure in observing the suffering of other people. The accused were both convicted and L appealed, principally on the ground that evidence of the psycho- logical condition of an accused person as tending to prove his guilt ought never to be introduced either by the prosecution or by the defence of a co-accused person. The Privy Council concluded that the psychiatrist's evidence was admissible because there was 'no reason of policy or fairness which justifies or requires the exclusion of evidence relevant to prove the innocence of an accused person'.[41] Essentially K's argument was that he did not have the kind of personality that would lead him to murder, and that L was an aggressive sadist who was more likely to kill. This does not appear to be evidence merely concerning which of the defendants was the more credible, but which was more likely to have killed with the necessary intent.

This case has attracted criticism on the grounds of the lack of clarity in the reasoning **22.21**

---

[37] (1971) 56 Cr App R 268, CA. [38] See e.g. *R v Raghip, The Times,* December 9, 1991.
[39] [1995] 1 Cr App R 157, CA. [40] [1974] AC 85. [41] Ibid, 102.

which led to the conclusion.[42] However, for our purposes it is notable insofar as it appears to provide authority for the proposition that expert evidence is occasionally admissible on the issue of *mens rea*. Until recently the decision in *Lowery* might have been viewed as a circumscribed exception to the general principle regarding the admissibility of expert evidence on the issue of *mens rea*. However, recent cases raise the question of whether wider admissibility of expert evidence concerning personality and propensity relating to *mens rea* can logically be resisted. In a joint trial involving two defendants, the conceptual position is that the Crown is involved in two separate proceedings against D1 and D2 respectively. The traditional view was that evidence received in the case against D1 could not be used against D2 unless the rules of evidence permitted the prosecution to adduce that evidence in its case against D2.

22.22   In *R v Randall*,[43] a murder case in which two defendants ran cut-throat defences, the House of Lords took *Lowery* to be 'high authority' for the proposition that a defendant (D1) could in his defence adduce evidence of a co-defendant's (D2's) propensity to show that it was more likely that D2 committed the killing. However, Lord Steyn went on to state that where D1 adduced evidence of D2's propensity for violence for the purpose of exonerating himself, the jury should not be prevented from considering that evidence in the prosecution's case in determining guilt against D2.[44] If expert evidence on the issue of D2's personality in relation to his propensity to form the necessary *mens rea*, such as that adduced in *Lowery*, is relevant and may be used in this way when adduced by D1, there appears no logical reason for prohibiting the prosecution from adducing it in the case against D2. However, if the prosecutor were permitted to call such evidence to show propensity to form *mens rea*, it would be unjust, and probably a violation of D2's right to a fair trial under Article 6 of the European Convention on Human Rights,[45] to prevent him adducing expert evidence to support his denial of *mens rea*. If this analysis is correct, then *Randall* raises the possibility of a significant relaxation of the prohibition of expert evidence relating to the *mens rea* of defendants in joint trials involving cut-throat defences. Admissibility of such evidence rests on its relevance and probative value in assisting jury evaluation of whether D1 or D2 was more likely to have formed the necessary *mens rea*. On this basis it might be difficult to defend any prohibition on such evidence in trials involving a lone defendant.

22.23   If it is accepted that psychiatric evidence relating to the 'normal' range of personality traits can assist a jury in determining which one of two co-defendants might have killed with the necessary intent, why should it not assist a jury in determining the issue of *mens rea* in the trial of a single defendant? This is, we submit, an area in which it is inevitable that sole defendants will soon attempt to adduce expert evidence as to *mens rea*. It will be

---

[42] See Dennis, cited above at n.2, 703–704; Tapper, *Cross & Tapper on Evidence*, 10th ed, cited above at n.22, 372–373; *Phipson on Evidence*, 17th ed, London: Sweet & Maxwell, 2005, para 21–04.

[43] [2003] UKHL 69.   [44] Ibid, para 35.

[45] It is also important that the expert is perceived, objectively, to be independent. Cf. *Matadeen and Peebles*, unreported, January 25, 2001, Southwark CC, HH Judge Jackson (police officer from the same station as those investigating the offence lacked the appearance of fairness required of an expert). See further Fortson, R., *Misuse of Drugs and Drug Trafficking Offences*, 5th ed, London: Sweet & Maxwell, 2005, paras 11–68 to 11–87.

interesting to see how resolutely the courts resist any such attempt to usurp what might be seen as a core element of the jury task, and how they balance that against the defendant's claim that he is adducing relevant evidence. As one of the leading commentators on the area has suggested,[46] '[w]hen it comes to establishing lack of *mens rea* . . . the interpretation of *Turner* as establishing a normal/abnormal rule is unsatisfactory. Given that the prosecution bears the onus of proving *mens rea* beyond reasonable doubt, rules limiting the ability of defendants to show lack of *mens rea* raise serious criminal justice issues.'

Nonetheless, it is clear that for now the general position regarding the prohibition of **22.24** expert evidence on the issue of *mens rea* remains intact. *R v Henry*[47] provides a recent example of its restatement. The appellant having been convicted of soliciting to murder and conspiracy to murder sought to appeal to rely on expert evidence on the issue of his intention from two psychologists. His defence was that he had never intended to harm the proposed victim and that his co-conspirator was lying, manipulative and obsessive, with whom H had played along in order to pacify her. The psychologistsy' reports stated that while H was not mentally ill, he was in the borderline range of learning disability and had serious emotional problems. They suggested that H was easily imposed upon. His psychological problems would make him susceptible to fall under the influence of others as he would have difficulties in coping with the stress and demands placed upon him. The Court of Appeal held that while neither of the reports opined that the intellectual impairment of H might have negated the specific intention, as H was not suffering from mental illness or abnormality the rule in *Turner* would have rendered any such evidence inadmissible.

(iii) Reliability of confessions

In contrast to the courts' resistance to expert evidence relating to the *mens rea* of a **22.25** defendant of 'normal mental capacity' in respect of expert evidence regarding the reliability of confessions made by suspects there has been progressive liberalization of the rules on admissibility. The reliability of a confession may be challenged under ss76 and 78 of the Police and Criminal Evidence Act 1984. Section 78 provides a trial judge with a general discretion to exclude prosecution evidence.[48] Not only can a confession made by the defendant be adduced by the prosecution, but D1 may adduce a confession made by a co-accused, D2.[49] Section 76 provides that a confession must be excluded where it is suggested to the court that it was obtained in circumstances in which any confession made by the defendant was likely to have been unreliable. It is for the trial judge to determine whether or not this was the case and in doing so he is obliged to consider any medical evidence concerning any mental abnormality on the part of the confessor.[50]

---

[46] Redmayne, cited above at n. 26, 157.

[47] [2005] EWCA Crim 1681. However, for recent examples of cases which appear to undermine the general principle see *R v Flinders* [2004] EWCA Crim 3186; *R v Cash* [2004] EWCA Crim 666.

[48] Where 'in all the circumstances, including the circumstances in which it was obtained, it would have such an adverse effect on the fairness of proceedings that it ought to be excluded.'

[49] See s76A of PACE as inserted by the Criminal Justice Act 2003, s128.

[50] *R v Everett* [1988] Crim LR 826, CA.

22.26   The greater willingness to accept expert evidence on confessions can be traced through a number of cases. The narrow approach to the issue of admissibility is apparent in *R v Weightman*[51] where the Court of Appeal held that 'a psychiatrist's evidence is inadmissible where its purpose is in effect to tell a jury how a person who is not suffering from mental illness is likely to react to the stresses and strains in life'.[52] However, relatively shortly thereafter the constraints on the reception of expert evidence began to be relaxed significantly. In *R v Raghip*[53] the court stated that the approach to determining the admissibility of an impugned confession should not be governed by which side of an arbitrary line delineating the normal from the mentally abnormal the suspect's IQ fell. The relevant question was whether the mental condition of the defendant was such that the jury would be assisted by expert help in assessing it. In *R v Ward*[54] it was held that expert evidence from a psychiatrist or psychologist could be admitted in respect of a defendant who was suffering from personality disorder, which while not considered to be a mental illness, was so severe as to be categorized as mental disorder. Acknowledging the state of flux in this area of the law, the Court of Appeal in *R v Strudwick*[55] suggested that the range of mental conditions on which the jury might require expert assistance was non-exhaustive and extended to forms of 'psychological damage'. In *R v O'Brien*[56] the court moved still further away from a strict medicalized basis for determining admissibility of expert evidence relating to the reliability of confessions by stating that the existence of some recognized mental disorder or abnormality was neither a necessary nor sufficient condition of admissibility:

> . . . the test cannot, in our judgment, be whether the abnormality fits into some recognized category, such as anti-social personality disorder. That is neither necessary nor sufficient. It is not necessary, because . . . the real criterion must simply be whether [an] abnormal disorder might render the confession or evidence unreliable. It is not sufficient because an anti-social personality disorder does not necessarily mean that the defendant is a compulsive liar or fantasist or that his confession or evidence might be unreliable.

22.27   More recently, in *R v Blackburn*[57] the Court of Appeal permitted expert evidence relating to situational factors, rather than the mental attributes of the suspect, which might have a bearing on the reliability of confession evidence. The appellant, PB, had been convicted of attempting to commit buggery on and then murder a nine-year-old boy. At the time of his conviction in 1978, PB was 15 years old. During the course of the investigation three different youths had confessed to carrying out the assaults, including one of PB's brothers, but all retracted these confessions. PB was interviewed informally by the police on a number of occasions over the course of a few days before being cautioned and subjected to a formal police interview. During the series of interviews he had been asked about an incident two years earlier in which he and another boy had been convicted of

---

[51] (1991) 92 Cr App R 291, CA.   [52] 92 Cr App R 291, 297 *per* McCowan LJ.
[53] Cited above at n. 38.   [54] (1993) 96 Cr App R 1.
[55] (1993) 99 Cr App R 326, 332: 'It is not suggested here that the appellant is suffering from a mental illness, but that of itself is not conclusive against the admission of his evidence. The law is in a state of development in this area. There may well be other mental conditions (including psychological damage) about which a jury might require expert assistance in order to understand and evaluate their effect on the issue in the case.'
[56] [2000] Crim LR 676.   [57] [2005] EWCA Crim 1349; *The Times*, June 10, 2005.

causing actual bodily harm to two nine-year old boys. During the fourth of a series of interviews conducted on the same day in the absence of any legal representative but the presence of a House Warden at the institution to which PB had been sent, the interviewing officers intimated to him that there might also be the possibility of further charges relating to that previous incident. Immediately after this was said, following three hours of questioning, PB confessed to committing the buggery and murder. At his trial the confession was admitted by the trial judge who found that there had been no threat or improper pressure applied by the police.

In the appeal proceedings the appellant made an application to call the evidence of a **22.28** forensic psychologist who had extensive experience of interrogation methods and of their effects. This was resisted by the Crown on two grounds. The first was that such matters were within the range of experience of a jury. The other ground was that the psychologist who was to be called had never interviewed or examined the appellant and there was no suggestion that he was suffering from any mental disorder. The Court, however, took the view that the expert's evidence which concerned research into the extent to which 'normal people not suffering from any personality disorder or abnormal disorder could be rendered compliant by prolonged interrogation'[58] ought to be admitted. The possibility of a suspect making an unreliable *coerced compliant confession*[59] in such circumstances was considered to be outside the normal range of experience of a jury.[60]

The cases highlight how ill-suited is a test of admissibility based on 'normality'. Once **22.29** the concept is divorced from a narrow medicalized definition it loses any objective benchmark.

The courts' approach to confessions stands in stark contrast to the attitude to expert **22.30** evidence on witness identification. Both identification and confessions are renowned for their potential unreliability, both are acknowledged by the courts as requiring special caution, both are seen by jurors as critically important pieces of evidence, both are areas in which there is a wealth of academic learning from psychologists shedding light on the hazards, and yet only in relation to confessions is that expert evidence being received to assist the jury.[61]

(iv) Competence

The court must be satisfied of the 'competence' of any witness to testify. Formerly the **22.31** test was a controversial one, particularly in its application to children, requiring as it did a demonstrable comprehension of the oath and divine sanction. The test is now a secular one based on the ability of the tendered witness to understand questions put and to give an intelligible account.[62] If necessary, for example with a young child or a person with a learning disability, the court can be assisted in the determination of competence.[63]

---

[58] Ibid, at para 30.

[59] See the Report of the Royal Commission on Criminal Justice (1993); Mirfield, P., *Silence, Confessions and Improperly Obtained Evidence* Oxford: Clarendon Press, 1997.

[60] See also Chapter 8 above.

[61] See also Chapters 1 (paras 1.40–1.46), 4, 8, 11, 16, 17, 18 and 19 above.

[62] Youth Justice and Criminal Evidence Act 1999, s53(3).

[63] Section 54(5). See also Chapters 3 (paras 3.45–3.50) and 9 (paras 9.34 and 9.36–9.41) above.

(v) Credibility of witnesses

22.32 Once a witness is accepted as competent, the question arises whether expert evidence can be adduced as to the witness's likely reliability and credibility in the testimony he or she provides. The trend in the admissibility of expert evidence concerning the reliability of confessions seems to be mirrored by a similar relaxation in the approach to the reception of expert opinion on the reliability of witness testimony. This is clearly illustrated by the stark contrast in the outcome of two appeal hearings in the same case separated by some 22 years. The appeals[64] related to a series of six murders committed between 1974 and 1978. John Childs pleaded guilty to those murders and gave evidence at the trial of his co-accused who included Pinfold and MacKenney. Pinfold was convicted of one murder but acquitted of three. MacKenney was acquitted of one murder and convicted of four of the others. The prosecution's case had depended upon Child's evidence being accepted by the jury. In the first appeal the appellants sought to adduce the evidence of a psychologist who had examined the witness and was willing to testify that in his opinion Childs was a psychopath and incapable of giving reliable evidence. At the first appeal, *R v MacKenney & Pinfold (No.1)* in 1981, the Court of Appeal held that while *psychiatric* evidence was admissible to show that a witness suffers from a disease or defect or abnormality of mind that affects the reliability of his testimony, a *psychologist* with no medical qualifications could not be called to give evidence of whether a defendant was suffering from any specific disease or defect or abnormality of mind. The marked change in the courts' approach to admissibility is evident in the second appeal hearing, *R v MacKenney & Pinfold (No.2)* in 2003. Here, the Court noted that while at the time of the original appeal the psychologist's evidence was not admissible, on the contemporary approach to expert evidence, such evidence was admissible and should be taken into account.

22.33 The appellants also sought to rely on fresh medical evidence provided by a forensic psychiatrist as to Child's ability to give credible evidence and the difficulty the jury might have faced in detecting that his evidence was not reliable. The Court held that the approach set out in *R v O'Brien* (see paragraph 22.26 above) applied whether the expert evidence being considered related to a witness's testimony or a defendant's confession. However, the principle is subject to qualification in the case of expert opinion relating to the credibility of witness testimony. If the testimony of the witness, in respect of which it is proposed to call expert evidence, is of little significance to the issues at the trial the admission of expert evidence ought not to be admitted. This qualification appears unobjectionable: the value of expert evidence about the credibility of witness testimony is contingent on the value of that testimony in the context of the trial. At some point the disadvantages associated with the reception of expert evidence—additional complexity, capacity to confuse the jury and increases in the length and cost of trials—will, on policy grounds, tip the balance in favour of its exclusion.

---

[64] *R v MacKenney & Pinfold (No.1)* (1981) 76 Cr App R 271; *R v MacKenney & Pinfold (No.2)* [2003] EWCA Crim 3643; [2004] Crim LR 468. See Roberts, P., 'Towards the Principled Reception of Expert Evidence of Witness Credibility in Criminal Trials' (2004) 8 E & P 215.

22.34 A controversial question in this area is whether expert evidence should be admitted to bolster the credibility of a witness who has testified. The orthodox position is set out in *Robinson*[65] where the appellant was charged with sex offences against a 15-year-old girl with a learning disability. The trial judge declared her competent and allowed a psychologist to testify for the Crown as to the suggestibility of the complainant. The Court of Appeal quashed the conviction, accepting that evidence from a psychiatrist or psychologist was admissible to show that a witness or a confession was *un*reliable, but qualifying that by stating that a psychologist or psychiatrist could *not* be called to explain to a jury why a witness who had testified was reliable.

22.35 More recently, in *Huckerby*[66] the Court of Appeal adopted a more liberal approach when accepting that expert evidence should be admitted of whether H had willingly cooperated with and assisted robbers who seized his security van or whether his ineffective behaviour was attributable instead to his alleged mental condition (PTSD). The court stated that:

> the evidence now sought to be adduced to the effect that the appellant was in fact suffering from PTSD at the time of the robbery is, if taken at face value, evidence which is potentially admissible. It falls within the category of a recognised mental condition with which the jury would not be expected to be familiar and is relevant to an essential issue bearing upon the appellant's guilt or innocence.[67]

It remains to be seen whether the distinction between expert opinion on a witness's unreliability owing to some mental abnormality and the reliability of a witness's testimony will be maintained.[68]

22.36 The narrowing ambit of the common knowledge rule across a range of important topics raises questions as to how best the admissibility of expert evidence might be regulated. We return to this issue in section F.

E. Ensuring the Reliability of Expert Evidence

(1) The English approach

22.37 The English courts have resisted persistent calls for the admissibility of expert evidence to be subject to some formal assessment of its reliability.[69] The most recent attempt was seen off in *R v Luttrell*[70] in which the Court of Appeal considered a submission that the admissibility of expert lip-reading evidence ought to be subject to a particular test of reliability: that the methods used were sufficiently explained to be tested in cross-examination so to be verifiable or falsifiable. This was rejected on the ground that valuable evidence is often received from experts whose skill or experience could not be

---

[65] (1994) 98 Cr App R 370, CA.   [66] [2004] EWCA Crim 3251.

[67] *Per* Potter LJ, at para 104. See also *Cash* [2004] EWCA Crim 666.

[68] The Home Office has recently made proposals to allow for 'general' expert evidence on rape myths and 'imperically validated behaviours or reactions of victims and witnesses'; see *Convicting Rapists and Protecting Victims—Justice for Victims of Rape*, Home Office, 2006, p.19.

[69] See *R v Clarke* [1995] 2 Cr App R 425, CA; *R v Dallagher* [2004] 2 Cr App R 520, CA.

[70] Cited above at n. 13.

subjected to such scientific scrutiny, but was nevertheless helpful. It is unfortunate that the Court of Appeal failed to address in more detail the issue of a requirement of reliability. The court's broad brush assertion that a formal reliability test would inhibit the reception of helpful evidence surely begs the question. Evidence from an expert can only be helpful in any meaningful sense if it is reliable.

(2) The approach of the United States Supreme Court: the 'general acceptance' test supplanted

22.38 Two decisions of the United States Supreme Court have been particularly influential in the search in many jurisdictions for appropriate criteria to determine the reliability of expert evidence. In the first of these decisions, *Frye v US*,[71] the Supreme Court considered the admissibility of expert evidence on the systolic blood pressure deception test which was a crude predecessor to the polygraph machine. In finding the evidence to be inadmissible, the Court set out a 'general acceptance' test:

> Just when a scientific principle or discovery crosses the line between the experimental and demonstrable stages is difficult to define. Somewhere in this twilight zone the evidential force of the principle must be recognised, and while the courts will go a long way in admitting expert testimony deduced from a well-recognised scientific principle or discovery, the thing from which the deduction is made must be *sufficiently established to have gained general acceptance in the particular field to which it belongs.* (emphasis added)

22.39 In *Daubert v Merrell Dow Pharmaceuticals Inc*,[72] the Supreme Court considered the continuing application of the 'general acceptance' condition of admissibility in light of the adoption of the Federal Rules of Evidence. It found that the *Frye* test had been superseded by Rule 702, which provided:

> if scientific, technical or other specialized knowledge will assist the trier of fact to understand the evidence or to determine a fact in issue, a witness qualified as an expert by knowledge, skill, experience, training or education, may testify thereto in the form of an opinion or otherwise.

The Court noted that Rule 702's liberalizing thrust was intended to relax the traditionally conservative approach to the admissibility of expert opinion and that the 'general acceptance' test was out of step with this approach. Under the Rules the trial judge has the task of scrutinizing an expert's evidence to establish that it is sufficiently reliable. A number of factors which might be relevant were identified by the Court:

(i) whether the expert's technique or theory can be or has been tested, that is, whether the expert's theory can be challenged in some objective sense, or whether it is instead simply a subjective, conclusory approach that cannot reasonably be assessed for reliability;

(ii) whether the technique or theory has been subject to peer review and publication;

(iii) the known or potential rate of error of the technique or theory when applied;

(iv) the existence and maintenance of standards and controls, and

---

[71] (1923) 293 F 1013.   [72] (1993) 509 US 579.

(v) whether the technique or theory has been generally accepted in the scientific community.

It was emphasized that this was not a definitive test or checklist and that the factors were neither exhaustive nor dispositive. Although the potential extension of its reach, to non-scientific evidence, depending on the circumstances of the case at issue, was recognized in *Kumho Tire Co. v Carmichael*,[73] it has been acknowledged that not all of the *Daubert* factors are relevant to every form of expert testimony. There has followed a reflexive process in which the application of *Daubert* in subsequent decisions led, in 2000, to the revision of Rule 702:

> if scientific, technical, or other specialized knowledge will assist the trier of fact to under-stand the evidence or to determine a fact in issue, a witness qualified as an expert by knowledge, skill, experience, training or education, may testify thereto in the form of an opinion or otherwise, if (1) the testimony is based upon sufficient facts or data, (2) the testimony is the product of reliable principles and methods, and (3) the witness has applied the principles and methods reliably to the facts of the case.[74]

In essence the distinction between the approaches in *Frye* and *Daubert* lies in who, in **22.40** practice, determines the issue of admissibility. The general acceptance test in *Frye* created what in form appeared to be a rule of admissibility. It was the scientific community which determined the reliability of the methods used by the expert with the courts putatively deferring to the judgement of that community. However, the vagaries of establishing whether there is general acceptance of a method or technique does in prac-tice leave a judge with a considerable degree of discretion.[75] *Daubert* confirmed that under the Federal Rules of Evidence it is the judge who performs a gate-keeping role to ensure that unreliable expert evidence is excluded. Rule 702 confers discretion to deter-mine whether the evidence will assist the trier of fact and the Supreme Court opinion in *Daubert* provides guidance on the exercise of that discretion.

(3) Pragmatism or incoherence? The influence of US decisions in England

English law has on at least two occasions flirted with the general acceptance standard set **22.41** out in *Frye*. The first occasion amounted to an intentional but misguided encounter, and the second was arguably an unwitting one which attests to the English courts' failure to take an analytical grasp on the issue of reliability. The former occurred in *R v Gilfoyle (No.2)*.[76] The appellant had been convicted of his wife's murder after she had been found hanged in the garage of their home. At his appeal he sought to introduce fresh evidence given by a forensic psychologist who had examined the deceased's diary and interviewed some of those who knew her. The evidence of the psychologist was that the material before him demonstrated convincing support for the deceased having taken her own life. The Court of Appeal held that such evidence was inadmissible for a number of reasons. The psychologist had never previously undertaken the task which he set himself

---

[73] 119 S Ct 1167 (1999).
[74] This demonstrates, contra *Luttrell* (see paragraph 22.37 above) that helpfulness is dependent on reliability.
[75] See further Redmayne, cited above at n. 26, 102–103.   [76] [2001] 2 Cr App R 57.

in the case. His reports identified no criteria by reference to which the court could test the quality of his opinions. In particular there was no database comparing real and questionable suicides and there was no substantial body of academic writing approving his methodology. Moreover, in a draft article on psychological autopsy he had stated: 'it has taken off and been used before it has reached the maturity needed to be allowed safely out of the careful confines of its professional birthplace'. Influential in the court's determination that the profiling evidence was inadmissible was the approach of the United States Supreme Court. It considered the guiding principle in that jurisdiction to be the general acceptance test set out in *Frye*. However, as the Court of Appeal in *R v Dallagher*[77] observed subsequently, when *Gilfoyle* was decided *Daubert* had already supplanted *Frye* as the guiding principle on admissibility.[78] Under that approach general acceptance of the methods used within the scientific community or peer group may be particularly relevant in determining the admissibility of novel techniques, and doubts as to the reliability of the methods used by the psychologist would have remained.

22.42 In the context of the general approach to determining the admissibility of expert evidence on the issue of reliability *Gilfoyle* stands out as an anomalous decision. The classic position of the English courts is that set out in *R v Clarke*[79] where it was said that the policy has been to be flexible in admitting expert evidence and to 'enjoy the advantages to be gained from new techniques and new advances in science'.[80] Since *Gilfoyle*, the courts have endorsed this orthodox position, resiling from any suggestion that specific criteria are to be applied in determining admissibility. In *Dallagher* (above), the Court of Appeal stated that the approach adopted in English courts was analogous with Rule 702. This might be so, but whereas the US Supreme Court laid down reasonably detailed guidance in *Daubert* on the application of the principles set out in Rule 702, English appellate decisions have been lamentably vague.

22.43 The second flirtation with an enhanced reliability test arose in *Luttrell* (above). It was held that the admissibility of expert evidence was to be determined according to ordinary principles of relevance and reliability, although those principles were not articulated in that judgment. Moreover, the extent of the guidance offered was limited to the statement that 'while reliability can be relevant to whether the conditions of admissibility are met, in itself reliability goes to weight'. Ironically, while rejecting any enhanced test of reliability as a condition of admissibility, in elucidating the conditions of admissibility the court referred, with apparent approval, to the decision of the South Australian Supreme Court in *R v Bonython*.[81] In *Bonython*, King CJ had stated that the admissibility of expert evidence depended, *inter alia*, on 'whether the subject matter of the opinion forms part of a body of knowledge or experience which is sufficiently organized or recognized to be accepted as a reliable body of knowledge or experience'.[82] It is through reliance on *Bonython* that the English courts appear to have unwittingly endorsed the *Frye* general

---

[77] [2003] 1 Cr App R 195.

[78] Though the adoption of the *Daubert* approach would have been unlikely to produce a different outcome in *Gilfoyle*.

[79] Cited above at n. 69.   [80] *Per* Steyn LJ, 430.   [81] (1984) 38 SASR 45.

[82] Ibid, 46–47.

acceptance test. The irony of the reference to it in *Luttrell* lies in the fact that, as the Australian Law Reform Commission recently observed, in respect of the reception of evidence concerning novel science, South Australia is one of the Australian jurisdictions which has adopted the *Frye* 'general acceptance' test.[83]

(4) A reliability test for novel techniques?

There are cases which suggest that the English courts' *laissez-faire* approach to the issue of **22.44** reliability is a cause for concern. In *R v Robb*[84] expert evidence on voice identification based on auditory techniques was found to have been properly admitted, notwithstanding that the great weight of informed opinion, including world leaders in the field, was to the effect that auditory techniques unless supplemented and verified by acoustic analysis were an unreliable basis of speaker identification. Only a handful of other professionals advocated the approach adopted by the expert and he had published no material which would allow his methods to be tested or his results checked. Furthermore, he had conducted no experiments or tests on the accuracy of his own conclusions. Notably the appellate courts in Northern Ireland recently declined to follow the conclusion in *Robb*, taking the view that, exceptional cases apart, given the state of scientific knowledge at that time, no prosecution ought to proceed in Northern Ireland in which the Crown proposed to rely predominantly on auditory analysis of voice samples.[85]

In light of subsequent events, the decision in *Dallagher* provides a salutary warning of the **22.45** inadequacies of the treatment of the current approach to the issue of reliability in English courts. Dallagher's conviction for murder was based in part on ear-print evidence. The Court of Appeal accepted that the expert evidence on that subject was properly admitted at trial but quashed the conviction on other grounds. Subsequently, at Dallagher's retrial, the prosecution offered no evidence when it was discovered that DNA evidence proved conclusively that he was not the culprit. The ear-print evidence, endorsed by the Court of Appeal, was shown to be fatally flawed in the first case in which it was used in an English court. Astonishingly, the Court of Appeal has continued to accept such evidence as sufficiently reliable to be admitted.[86]

F. Reform

As the frontiers of scientific knowledge continue to expand and new technologies are **22.46** developed, the courts will increasingly be faced with difficult decisions concerning the reception of expert evidence. The English courts, recognizing the advantages that such evidence might offer, have adopted a (perhaps too) liberal approach to the reception of such evidence. However, it is an approach that has developed in unsatisfactory fashion. The courts have shown a willingness to receive expert testimony on certain subject matter

---

[83] See the Australian Law Reform Commission, *Review of the Uniform Evidence Acts*, Discussion Paper 69, 2005.
[84] Cited above at n. 6.   [85] See *R v O'Doherty*, cited above at n.16.
[86] *R v Kempster* [2003] EWCA Crim 3555. See also *State v Kunze* 988 P.2d 977 (1999); the discussion in Ormerod, cited above at n.16; and O'Brien, W., 'Court Scrutiny of Expert Evidence: Recent Decisions Highlight the Tensions' [2003] 7 *E & P* 172.

while maintaining seemingly arbitrary distinctions to prevent its reception on others. The wider admissibility of expert evidence has not been accompanied by any move towards any formal regulation as to who may testify as an expert. Moreover, the issue of reliability is subject to rather vague and inadequately articulated principles which appear to be of little assistance in guiding practical decision making. English law's inadequacies in this respect have already demonstrated that miscarriages can easily follow.[87] These failings are not just a failure of the expert witness in individual cases—that would be an easy place to lay blame—but a failure of the criminal justice system.[88]

22.47 The law of evidence has undergone dramatic legislative change in recent years with most of the major admissibility rules being overhauled. It is now time for expert evidence to be examined as part of the codification of English criminal evidence.[89] It is promising to note that codification of criminal evidence has been included in the Law Commission's Ninth Programme of Law Reform. We suggest that reforms need to focus on the following.

(1) The obligation to adopt clear and rigorous rules of admissibility for expert evidence

22.48 The House of Commons Science and Technology Committee recently recommended the development of a 'gate-keeping' test for expert evidence based on the *Daubert* approach.[90] As the Committee implies, this should not necessarily amount to a straightforward assimilation into English law of the *Daubert* criteria.[91] Specific reform proposals ought to draw upon the abundance of empirical research concerning judges' application and understanding of the criteria,[92] and on the effects that *Daubert* has had on the reception of expert testimony in the United States.[93]

---

[87] *R v Cannings* [2004] 1 All ER 725; [2005] Crim LR 126 and commentary.

[88] See House of Commons Science and Technology Committee, Seventh Report of the Session 2004–2005, *Forensic Science on Trial*, HC 96–I, at para 170; see also Munshi, L., 'Forensic Science in the Dock' (2005) 155 NLJ 1162.

[89] It would be preferable to have legislation rather than judicially created changes in this area given the difficult policy issues that arise. We note also the possibility for the Criminal Procedure Rules to play an important part in providing an optimal system for the admissibility of expert evidence, given the availability of the US and Australian systems on which to draw and the Civil Procedure Rules. See also Elsmore, K. and Langford, C., (2005) 155 NLJ 1155. See also the Civil Justice Council's *Expert Protocol* (2005).

[90] Cited above at n. 88.

[91] The Australian Law Reform Commission rejected the suggestion of enacting *Daubert*-style statutory criteria on the grounds that doing so might simply introduce new uncertainties and that such criteria could not easily be applied to fields such as psychiatry and psychology: report cited above at n. 2, paras 8.53 and 8.54. See also McEwan, J., *The Verdict of the Court: Passing Judgment in Law and Psychology*, Oxford: Hart, 2003, Ch 7, and 180–190.

[92] See also the empirical work by Odgers and Richardson on Australian judicial attitudes, cited above at n. 8.

[93] Groscup, J., *et al*, found that the *Daubert* decision did not impact on the admission rate of expert testimony and that while judges understood the importance of *Daubert* only passing attention was paid to its criteria: 'The Effects of *Daubert* on the Admissibility of Expert Testimony in State and Federal Criminal Cases' (2002) 8 *Psychology, Public Policy and Law*, 339. See also *e.g.* Schuman, D. and Scale, B., 'The Impact of *Daubert* and its Progeny on the Admissibility of Behavioral and Social Science Evidence' (1999) 5 *Psychology, Public Policy and Law*, 3 (the courts have rarely articulated how the *Daubert* criteria are to be applied to behavioural and social science evidence); Gatowski, S., *et al*, 'Asking the Gatekeepers: A national

(2) Practitioners' obligations

The practitioners' obligations to the Court also need to be the subject of scrutiny. It may **22.49**
be incumbent on the regulatory bodies and the Criminal Procedure Rules Committee
to ensure that practitioners shoulder some of the responsibility for keeping poor expert
evidence out of the court. It is worth noting that other jurisdictions have already acknowledged such an obligation. In *Lewis*,[94] it was stated that

> . . . whenever the Crown wishes to rely upon forensic evidence the prosecutor has a clear
> duty, not just to his client, the Crown, but to the trial judge and the jury to acquaint them,
> in ordinary language, through the evidence he leads with some sort of evaluation of the
> opinions he expresses. Where the evidence is of a comparatively novel kind, the duty
> resting on the Crown is even higher: it should demonstrate its scientific reliability. It is not
> an answer to considerations that dictate these things to be done to say the defence may
> draw it out in cross-examination; that is an abdication of the Crown's primary function in
> a criminal prosecution.

(3) Regulation of experts

We suggest that there should be a greater obligation on the expert practitioners to **22.50**
regulate themselves. Systems of accreditation, continuing professional development, and
protocols of good practice are all seen as positive steps not just by those working in the
criminal justice system but by the expert practitioners themselves. It has been suggested
that the problem of regulating small groups of experts working in emerging disciplines
might be overcome by reliance on overseas experts for the purposes of peer assessment
and review.[95]

(4) Judicial training

We would encourage measures to create a greater judicial awareness of the forms of **22.51**
expertise and the hazards present in relying on such evidence. Judicial training and
Judicial Studies Board materials have proved successful in many areas—e.g. to deal with
vulnerable witnesses etc—and this is an area where benefits would be obvious.[96]

(5) Empirical research

Finally, arguments either, (i) for the adoption of strict rules governing the admissibility of **22.52**
expert evidence, (ii) for *Daubert*-type statutory criteria to guide judicial discretion in
determining admissibility, or (iii) that such criteria should go to assessment of the probative value (a matter for the jury) rather than admissibility (a matter for the trial judge),[97]
are predicated on various assumptions regarding the inability of juries, and the capacity

---

survey of judges on judging expert evidence in a post-*Daubert* world,' (2001) 25 *Law and Human Behavior*,
433 (only a small proportion of State trial court judges display a clear understanding of the *Daubert*
scientific criteria of falsifiability (6 per cent) and error rate (4 per cent)); Dahir, V., *et al*, 'Judicial Application of *Daubert* to Psychological Syndrome and Profile Evidence: A research note' (2005) 11 *Psychology,
Public Policy and Law*, 62.

[94] (1987) 88 FLR 104, 123–4.
[95] House of Commons Science and Technology Committee, cited above at n. 88, para 136.
[96] See also Ch 23 below.
[97] See generally, ALRC Discussion Paper, cited above at n. 2, paras. 8.33 to 8.55.

of the judiciary, to deal appropriately with such evidence. Without sufficient empirical research into such issues a programme of law reform runs the risk of seeking to prescribe on the basis of an inadequate diagnosis of the problem. Section 8 of the Contempt of Court Act 1981 presents a substantial impediment for jury research in this jurisdiction. It has been suggested that a review of jury research carried out in other jurisdictions indicates that 'the often asserted claim . . . that juries tend to be "awestruck by the expert's mystique" is not warranted'.[98] On the other hand, there is research which suggests that, despite the courts' concerns about the jury being over-influenced by the evidence relating to 'junk science', they are in fact swayed by the physical characteristics and demeanour of the expert!'[99] Further research, relating particularly to the manner in which English juries deal with expert evidence, would be valuable and to facilitate this, the Contempt of Court Act ought to be suitably amended.

Further Reading

Redmayne, M., *Expert Evidence and Criminal Justice*, Oxford: Oxford University Press, 2001.

Hodgkinson, T., *Expert Evidence: Law and Practice*, London: Sweet and Maxwell, 1990.

House of Commons Science and Technology Committee, *Forensic Science on Trial*, Seventh Report of Session 2004–2005, HC 96–1.

Carson, D., 'Expert Evidence in the Courts' (1992) 1 *Expert Evidence*, 13.

Edmond, G. and Mercer, D., 'Recognising *Daubert*. What judges need to know about falsificationism' (1997) *Expert Evidence*, 29.

Faigman, D., 'To Have and Have Not: Assessing the Value of Social Science to the Law as Science and Policy' (1989) 38 *Emory LJ*, 1005.

Freckleton, I., *The Trial of the Expert: A Study of Expert Evidence and Forensic Experts*. Melbourne: Oxford University Press, 1987.

Gudjonsson, G., 'The Implications of Poor Psychological Evidence in Court' (1993) 2(3) *Expert Evidence*, 120.

Kenny, A., 'The Expert in Court' (1983) 99 LQR, 197.

Andrew Roberts is a lecturer in the School of Law at the University of Warwick. His research interests lie in the fields of criminal procedure, the law of evidence, and the interface between the disciplines of law and psychology. He has published widely on various aspects of criminal procedure and regularly acts as a consultant to Liberty on consultation responses to government reform proposals. He is currently co-authoring a book on eyewitness identification which will be published shortly.

David Ormerod is Professor of Criminal Law at the University of Leeds and a Door Tenant in the Chambers of David Etherington QC, 18 Red Lion Court. He is the Cases Editor for the *Criminal Law Review*; Editorial Advisor, *Blackstone's Criminal Practice*; and serves on the Editorial Board of the *International Journal of Evidence & Proof* and *Covert*

---

[98] See Sanders, J., Diamond, S. and Vidmar, N., 'Legal Perceptions of Science and Expert Knowledge', (2002) 8 *Psychology, Public Policy and Law*, 139, 153. See also McEwan, J., *The Verdict of the Court: Passing Judgment in Law and Psychology*, Oxford: Hart, (2003), 192–193.

[99] See Shuman, D., Champagne, A. and Whitaker, E., 'Juror Assessments of the Believability of Expert Witnesses: A Literature Review' (1996) 36 *Jurimetrics Journal*, 371.

Policing Review. He lectures regularly to the profession and to the judiciary. David is the author of numerous journal articles and editor of *Smith and Hogan, Criminal Law* (11th ed 2005) and *Smith and Hogan, Cases and Materials on Criminal Law* (9th ed 2005). He is also the co-author of *Bailey Harris and Jones on Civil Liberties* (5th ed. 2001), and *Modern English Legal System* (4th ed. 2002).

Editors' Note

'Common knowledge' or admissible expert evidence?

Where a court decides that the subject matter of prospective expert evidence might be outwith the common knowledge and experience of a jury it may, subject to the issues in the case, relevance and various other factors such as the question concerning whether the witness is, genuinely, an expert, admit the expert evidence, even where this concerns the reliability of eyewitness testimony. Difficulties in this arena arise for various reasons, partly connected to the distaste for expert psychological evidence still felt by many judges in the United Kingdom jurisdictions and partly owing to the continuing debate over the definition of common knowledge, linked to the question as to the mechanics for the discovery of how widespread 'knowledge' has to be before it becomes 'common'. Knowledge might become common over widely varying periods of time, dependent, for example, on the vagaries of reporting on topical issues by the popular press and government-backed publicity campaigns concerning, for example, how females are apt to behave when they are inebriated or following sexual assault. Whether knowledge is common amongst members of an individual jury may depend on its make-up by reference to racial, cultural and intellectual characteristics amongst its members.

One proposition in this problematic field has to be right, however: if learning contained within this book is attempted to form the basis of expert evidence, and is ruled inadmissible because the court decides that it forms no more than the basis of 'common knowledge', the advocate cannot be criticized for making submissions to the jury which comprise propositions advanced by this book's contributors. It may be that, assuming that what Loftus, Kassin and others have to offer becomes better known, their 'knowledge' will become more 'common', at least amongst this book's readership and, in consequence, they will be ready to share this knowledge with fact finders who may not have read this book.

23

JUDICIAL TRAINING

Justice William Young[1] and His Honour Judge Sam Katkhuda[2]

A. Introduction

The 1215 abolition, by Pope Innocent III, of the institution of trial by ordeal left a major **23.01** gap in the fact-finding methodologies available to the then-rudimentary English legal system. Over the following centuries this gap has been filled by processes that depend primarily on the evaluation of witness testimony by professional judges (including part-time judges and legally trained magistrates), lay magistrates, and juries.

There are many rules regarding the way that trial judges should direct (or not direct) **23.02** juries as to the facts. Such rules sometimes operate formalistically and often require warnings against forbidden types of reasoning or certain types of evidence. Overall these rules have a piecemeal character and their combined effect falls well short of ensuring that jurors are given comprehensive assistance as to how to determine factual issues. Nonetheless, where the applicable rules have been complied with, a factual determination by a jury is unlikely to be interfered with on appeal.

In cases that have not been tried by juries, appellate courts are becoming sceptical of **23.03** findings of fact that are either unsupported by adequate reasons or strikingly inconsistent

---

[1] President of the Court of Appeal of New Zealand. This paper to some extent draws on his article, 'Summing-up to Juries in Criminal Cases—What Research says about Current Rules and Practice' [2003] Crim LR 665.

[2] A Circuit Judge of the Crown Court (South Eastern Circuit).

with the probabilities.[3] Nonetheless appellate practice still involves substantial deference to factual findings; a deference that is justifiable not so much by the inherent reliability of first instance findings but rather by the reality that appellate courts are unlikely to do any better.

23.04 Comparatively little judicial attention has been devoted to the way that triers of fact can best evaluate witness testimony, how judges can best help jurors to do so, and thus to the development of best practice standards.

B. Professional Judges

(1) Forensic experience

23.05 Those who practise extensively in the courts necessarily pick up some expertise in general fact finding.

23.06 Judges become aware of the strengths and frailties of memory: that memory is more reliable regarding the core elements of an incident than the peripheral detail, that witnesses who cannot recall all the detail tend to reconstruct (and often do so in different ways on different occasions, thus leading to exploitable inconsistencies), and that there is a real risk of memory contamination from false cues.[4] It is a commonplace of forensic experience that witnesses may be affected, consciously or unconsciously, by what they desire to be the outcome of the case.

23.07 Likewise, forensic experience in cases involving children necessarily leads to an awareness of the limited vocabulary of young children and their suggestibility. So judges learn that it may be desirable for children to be asked open rather than closed questions (not always easy to insist on when children are being cross-examined) and to control their examination closely to ensure that the questions asked are fairly within their ability to answer.[5]

23.08 Judges are conscious of the risks inherent in identification evidence. In part, this awareness results from necessary familiarity with the *Turnbull*[6] line of cases. But in any event, the way that evidence routinely comes out in criminal trials reinforces the reality that identification evidence is often not reliable.

23.09 Those who have practised at the defence bar are likely to have developed scepticism of verbal admissions attributed to defendants by police officers and the evidence of prison informants.

23.10 A judge's evaluation of evidence is necessarily affected by his or her awareness of the dynamics and conventions of litigation. For example, a defendant in a civil case

---

[3] See for instance *Flannery v Halifax Estate Agencies* [2000] 1 All ER 373. In Australia, findings of fact that are 'glaringly improbable' or 'contrary to compelling inferences' have been set aside even though based on credibility findings: see the discussion by Gleeson CJ in *Fox v Percy* (2003) 214 CLR 118, 128.

[4] Explored in several chapters in Section 1 above: see particularly Chapters 1 and 6. See also *Campbell's Psychiatric Dictionary*, (8th edn) Oxford: Oxford University Press, 2004 under 'memory', 'primary response', 'short-and long-term memory', and 'retrieval'.

[5] See particularly *Stack v Western Australia* (2004) 29 WAR 526 which is discussed later in this chapter.

[6] [1977] QB 224.

who does not give evidence by way of denial of the plaintiff's core allegations will almost inevitably lose.

Professional judges tend to decide cases primarily by reference to how they view the **23.11** probabilities and inherent plausibility of the competing narratives. The hard incontrovertible facts, perhaps physical evidence or relevant contemporaneous written material, are very important to this process. An account of events that differs from the written record is unlikely to carry the day.

This approach does not solve all problems. An improbable account may be true. In any **23.12** event, judges are often required to resolve factual conflicts where the evidence on both sides is inherently plausible and ties in closely with the incontrovertible facts.

So what other fact-finding techniques do judges use? **23.13**

The motives of the witnesses and parties (including police officers and prison inform- **23.14** ants) will be allowed for; the tendencies of plaintiffs to exaggerate and defendants to minimize. Internal consistency (or inconsistency) in the account given by a witness and its consistency (or otherwise) with accounts given by that witness on other occasions may be a critical factor. The same is true where error or falsehood on the part of the witness has been demonstrated in any respect. A judge will often be influenced by his or her view of the characters and personalities of the key protagonists in the case. That said, demeanour-based credibility assessments are unlikely to loom large in the reasoning process. Judges are, or should be, conscious of the scientific evidence that casts doubt on the ability of anyone to determine the truth of conflicting accounts based on the demeanour of witnesses.[7]

(2) Limitations on the value of professional and life experience

Changes to the way that the judiciary is appointed mean that not all judges have served **23.15** the sort of apprenticeship in the courts which, until very recently, was a necessary prerequisite for judicial office. Further, the professional experience of judges is not the equivalent of professional experience in other occupations where the consequences of wrong decisions are likely to become rapidly apparent. The engineer who designs a bridge badly, which later fails, can be expected to learn from the mistake. The judge who makes a wrong finding of fact and then moves on to the next case may never learn of his or her error.

More importantly, there are limits as to the extent to which judicial experience (and **23.16** associated experience of life) equip judges to evaluate the probabilities of competing narratives.

Until comparatively recently the courts approached cases involving alleged sexual offend- **23.17** ing on the basis that such allegations were inherently suspect and that it was therefore dangerous to convict on the uncorroborated evidence of a complainant. By the mid-1980s

---

[7] See for instance *State Rail Authority (NSW) v Earthline Constructions Pty Ltd (in liq)* (1999) 160 ALR 588, 617–618 and *Trawl Industries of Australia Pty Ltd v Effem Foods Pty Ltd* (1992) 27 NSWLR 326, 348 *per* Samuels JA.

predominant thinking had radically altered and with this came changes in the rules of evidence and court practice. Indeed there may have been something of an overshoot, illustrated by the occasionally uncritical reception of implausible allegations of widespread sexual abuse (perhaps of a ritualistic or satanic nature) and repressed memory syndrome cases.

23.18 With the associated moral panics now having subsided, judges should know that false sexual abuse allegations are sometimes made. But they have little idea of the incidence of false complaints and thus no real idea of the likelihood of a particular complaint being false. Common sense, and perhaps experience, might suggest that false sexual abuse allegations are likely to be associated with a motive on the part of the complainant to harm the defendant or to explain away an embarrassing sexual encounter. But the existence (actual or alleged) of such motives is common in sexual cases and the professional experience of judges usually provides little assistance in deciding the significance of the actual or asserted motive. Straightforward 'she says: he says' cases are by no means uncommon. Yet there may be little in a judge's professional experience that will enable him or her to develop a genuine understanding of the inherent probabilities of the competing narratives. Perhaps fortunately for judges, juries usually determine such cases.

23.19 Judges risk debilitating controversy when they explicitly decide cases by reference to stereotypical beliefs even if based on professional or personal experience. This is illustrated by *RDS v R*.[8] An African–Canadian provincial court judge from Nova Scotia dismissed summary charges against a 15-year-old African–Canadian arising out of a fracas between him and police officers. Her reasons for dismissing the charges included her assertion that 'certainly police officers do overreact, particularly when dealing with non-white groups'. Her decision was reversed (for bias) in the superior courts of Nova Scotia but reinstated (amidst much furore and polemical debate) by the Supreme Court of Canada. Central to this furore was the racial overlay to the case, but more generally the case raises the question whether judges should make findings of fact on the basis of generalizations (even of a plausible and *bien pensant* nature) as to how particular groups of people behave.

23.20 A similar problem arose in the recent Western Australian decision *Stack v Western Australia*[9] which concerned, *inter alia*, the appropriateness of the judge directing the jury as to the way in which Aboriginal people give evidence (characterized, he thought, by avoidance of eye contact, long periods of silence, and, most significantly, by a tendency to answer leading questions in the affirmative). The judge went so far as to stop defence counsel using leading questions in his cross-examination of the principal prosecution witness (who was of Aboriginal descent but who spoke only English, lived in a Perth suburb and was studying art and photography at a tertiary educational institution). The resulting conviction was set aside and a new trial was ordered.

(3) Judicial training

23.21 In both England and Wales and New Zealand there is only limited judicial training directed towards fact finding. The limited nature of this training is associated with the

---

[8] [1997] 3 SCR 484.   [9] Cited above at n. 5.

way in which the bench is recruited (almost always from active legal practitioners) and the associated expectation that the experience of those who are appointed will equip them adequately for their roles as triers of fact.

In New Zealand, there have been seminars on particular problems associated with child **23.22** witnesses and the science behind DNA evidence. Seminars on appellate practice have extended to consideration of the infirmities of demeanour-based credibility findings. Further, in judicial orientation programmes carried out since 2003, new judges have been exposed to a reasonably sophisticated session addressed to making findings of fact. But, to date, there has been no specific focus on fact finding and witness evaluation (as a topic in itself) in the programmes offered to existing judges.

The position is broadly similar in England and Wales: there has been a good deal of **23.23** training addressing topics which are relevant to fact finding and the evaluation of evidence, but fact finding as a topic has not been the subject of discrete focus.

C. Juries

(1) General

Trial judges are understandably inclined to conduct criminal trials so as to avoid or limit **23.24** the prospect of successful appeals. In this environment, it is easy to overlook practical considerations regarding jury comprehension and functioning. In the past, this was not such a problem. The requirements of a summing-up were less onerous and complex than they are now. In any event, jurors tended to look to the judge for guidance as to the appropriate verdict—guidance that was often provided in terms more robust than would now be acceptable.

As it is not now customary for a judge to give the jury direct advice as to the appropriate **23.25** verdict, there is an enhanced need for the judge to provide the jury with practical assistance in how it should go about its task. Aspects of this are necessarily at an elementary level. The judge should bring home to the jury the issues which require determination. Particularly in a long case, the jury may require judicial help to ensure that they remember the evidence which was given. Ideally the judge should marshal the evidence around the central issues of fact which arise. These are the core respects in which a judge must provide assistance. Fundamental in all of this are organization of the relevant evidential material and effective communication techniques.

(2) Jury research

Jury research in England and Wales has necessarily been very limited given the constraints **23.26** imposed by s8 of the Contempt of Court Act 1981.[10] There is, nonetheless, a great deal

---

[10] Reference, however, should be made to a recent Home Office report prepared by Roger Matthews, Lynn Hancock and Daniel Briggs, *Jurors' Perceptions, Understanding and Confidence in the Jury System* (No.05/04, 2004) and this is available online: see *http://www.homeoffice.gov.uk/rds/pdfs2/rdsolr0504.pdf.* As well, in the aftermath of the House of Lords decision in *R v Mirza* [2004] 2 Cr App R 8, the Department of Constitutional Affairs issued a consultation paper, *Jury Research and Impropriety* (Consultation paper CP 04/05 21, 2005).

of published material based on jury research on the way in which juries function.[11] What comes out of jury research projects tends to be reasonably predictable—pretty much what might be expected by an experienced judge or advocate who turned his or her mind to the way that a jury is likely to operate. For this and other reasons, judges have been slow to take on board what has emerged from these projects.[12] On the other hand, judicial interest in jury research tends to be associated with, and certainly encourages, a jury-centred approach to criminal trial practice. The recent New Zealand jury research project[13] engaged the interest of New Zealand judges and encouraged the judiciary as a whole to think carefully about the ways in which existing criminal trial procedures could be modified to be more juror-friendly and thus efficient. In this way it has had significant effects on trial practice in New Zealand.

(3) How well do judges do?

23.27 Current judicial practice seems to be reasonably effective and is perceived in this way by jurors. For instance, the recent Home Office report, *Jurors' Perceptions, Understanding, and Confidence in the Jury System*,[14] generally found high levels of understanding of the proceedings and evidence among jurors. Most jurors were impressed with the judge's summing up which had helped them to develop a clear perception of the evidence and facts in issue.

23.28 It is sensible, nonetheless to proceed on the basis that there remains scope for improvement in judicial practice.

(4) Communication techniques

23.29 It is now trite that, when speaking to juries, judges should use short and simple sentences, the active and not the passive voice and concrete rather than abstract language. Jargon or unusual words should be avoided.[15] This means that the judges should speak to the jury by reference to the facts of the case at hand rather than in general terms. A judge who takes this approach to its logical conclusion will sum up in the way recommended by Professor Edward Griew:

> It should be the function of the judge to protect the jury from the law rather than to direct them on it. The judge does in practice typically tell the jury that the law is for him and facts are for them. This should become more profoundly true than it now is. A brief statement of the law will be unavoidable if the case is to be intelligible. But what is said should not be by way of formal instruction. When it comes to instructing the jury on their task, the job of the judge should be to filter out the law. He should simply identify for the

---

[11] See William Young J (cited above at n.1).   [12] Discussed at ibid, 669.

[13] *Juries in Criminal Trials, Part 11A Summary of the Research Findings* (New Zealand Law Commission, Preliminary paper 37, vol 2, 1999). The authors (and principal researchers) were Warren Young, Neil Cameron and Yvonne Tinsley.

[14] Matthews, Hancock and Briggs (cited above at n.10).

[15] There is a great deal of literature on this; see for instance, Charrow and Charrow, 'Making Legal Language Understandable; A Psycholingual Study of Jury Instructions' (1979) *Columbia LR* 1306; Steele and Thornburgh, 'Jury Instructions: A Persistent Failure To Communicate' (1988) 67 *North Carolina* LR 77; and Severance and Loftus, 'Improving the Ability of Jurors To Comprehend and Apply Criminal Jury Instructions' (1982) 17 *Law and Society Review* 153.

jury the facts which, if found by them, will render the defendant guilty according to the law of the offence charged and of any available defence.[16]

The results of the New Zealand jury research project when read in their entirety, suggest that this approach does indeed represent best practice.[17]

23.30 When explaining the elements of the charge to the jury, a judge should identify, with respect to the defendant and what is alleged by the prosecution, specific questions that the jury must answer in favour of the prosecution before it can convict.[18] It is clear that juries find it helpful if the issues they are required to address are identified at the start of the trial and not left for the judge's summing up.[19] Indeed, in New Zealand it is increasingly common for the judge to give to the jury, at the outset of the trial, directions as to the elements of the offence alleged against the defendant.

23.31 In England and Wales judges sometimes provide the jury with written guidance (e.g. a 'duress' direction) but this practice is far more widespread in New Zealand where it is increasingly common for judges to give their key directions in writing. However, judicial practice remains mixed. Whether judges give written directions may be influenced by their own word-processing skills and the availability of judicial support.

23.32 Judges who do not put their key directions in writing (or do so only in complex cases) underestimate the extent to which such material is appreciated by juries. In six of the 48 cases that were the subject of the New Zealand jury research project, the judge provided the jury with a written summary of the law. In two of the cases, the jurors were provided with a flow chart and a sequential list of questions to address. For these two cases, all the jurors interviewed felt that they were assisted by the flow chart. The researchers recorded that 62 per cent of the jurors who did not receive such material said that they would have found it helpful had it been provided.[20]

(5) Remembering the evidence

23.33 Although the recent Home Office report, *Jurors' Perceptions, Understanding and Confidence in the Jury System*,[21] does not suggest that recalling the evidence is a major problem for jurors, the results of the New Zealand research project suggest otherwise:

> A . . . reported consequence of the fact that testimony was in oral form was that jurors had difficulty in recalling the details of it during deliberations. Such difficulties were reported to have occurred in 21 trials, and were particularly acute where the evidence was confused or contradictory, or where the sequence of events was unclear. They were also particularly likely to arise where there was more than one complainant and a number of charges: jurors

---

[16] Griew, 'Summing Up the Law' [1989] Crim LR 768, 779.

[17] Young, Cameron and Tinsley (cited above at n. 13) paras 5.5, 6.7, 7.37 and 7.61.

[18] This is also in accordance with the recommendations made by Sir Robin Auld in his *Review of the criminal courts of England and Wales: Report*, London: HMSO (2001) 534–536.

[19] See, for instance, Matthews, Hancock and Briggs (cited above at n.10), 41.

[20] Young, Cameron and Tinsley (cited above at n.13) para 7.60. The New South Wales Law Reform Commission, *The Jury in a Criminal Trial* (1986) reported that nearly half the jurors they surveyed would have appreciated a written copy of all or part of the judge's summing-up: see 92.

[21] Cited above at n.10.

reported that they got the stories between complainants mixed up; that they mistook names, dates or times; and that they sometimes had difficulty in recollecting what evidence related to which charges. The fact that jurors had significant difficulty in recalling evidence or in agreeing about what testimony had been given was reflected in the fact that they requested that evidence be read back to them in 16 trials.[22]

23.34　The New Zealand research project of course, was not subject to the constraints imposed by the Contempt of Court Act 1981 and thus involved a more detailed and case-specific analysis of jury functioning than is possible in England and Wales. This might explain why it revealed rather more in the way of jury recall difficulties than projects that have proceeded on the basis of self-assessments of understanding on the part of former jurors. Another possible explanation is that recall difficulties are largely overcome by the way in which judges in England and Wales sum up on the evidence, which is far more detailed than in New Zealand. This is an issue that is discussed later in this chapter.

23.35　It is clear that where juries experience difficulties as to recall of the evidence, resolution of these difficulties can be time consuming, distracting, and disheartening. A jury that cannot agree on what was said by the witnesses or the judge is not well positioned to reach a rational decision.

23.36　Most of the jurors interviewed during the New Zealand research had taken some notes during the trial.[23] However, jurors are seldom given assistance as to what aspects of the trial should be recorded by them. Many, and indeed perhaps most, jurors have no experience in taking notes. The New Zealand jurors interviewed sometimes mistrusted the accuracy or completeness of notes taken by other jurors. These concerns were not necessarily misplaced because the researchers recorded that some of the notes made by jurors were inaccurate.[24]

23.37　Jurors can also seek assistance from the judge as to the detail of the evidence. If this happens, the judge might read his or her notes to the jury, which is the practice invariably employed in the English and Welsh Courts. In New Zealand (where a running written transcript of the evidence is maintained and is distributed to the judge and counsel) the practice was for the judge, after consulting counsel, to read the relevant passages of evidence back to the jury. This could be a ponderous process and in some of the cases which were the subject of the jury project, the juries, having experienced this procedure, were not prepared to make further requests to have evidence read. Instead they tried to resolve amongst themselves any further disagreements as to the detail of what had been said.[25]

23.38　Some of the jurors who were interviewed as part of the New Zealand research complained that they had not received the transcript. Where there is a transcript, it is odd

---

[22] Young, Cameron and Tinsley (cited above at n.13), para 3.5.

[23] Young, Cameron and Tinsley (ibid), para 3.6, record that 75 per cent of the jurors interviewed had taken notes. This seems a very high proportion of note takers. The New Zealand jurors knew that the cases they were hearing were the subject of research. Perhaps they were on their best behaviour.

[24] Ibid, para 3.6. The same problem occurred in the NSW trials examined by Chesterman, Chan and Hampton, *Managing Prejudicial Publicity: An Empirical Study of Criminal Jury Trials in New South Wales* (2001), paras 468 and 469.

[25] Young, Cameron and Tinsley (cited above at n.13), paras 4.19–4.21 and 4.25.

that it should be provided to the judge and counsel but not to jurors, given their decision-making role.[26]

As a result of the publication of the results of the research, a number of New Zealand **23.39** judges have given transcripts of evidence to juries. The New Zealand Court of Appeal has upheld this practice.[27] Giving the jury the transcript of the evidence raises some practical problems,[28] but providing these are addressed, it can hardly do any harm. Indeed, there are real advantages in doing so. It avoids dispute in the jury room over the detail of the evidence that is given. As well, and from a judicial perspective, it makes it easy (or comparatively easy) to sum up on the evidence.

(6) Tying the evidence to the issues that have to be determined

It is one thing for jurors to be able to remember the evidence; it is another to be able to **23.40** recognize the relevance of the evidence to the issues which fall for determination.

In Australia, England and Wales and Canada, judges refer to the evidence when sum- **23.41** ming up in what is often considerable detail. When done well, the summing-up is along the lines described by Lord Devlin in *Trial by Jury* (1966):

> All the material which gets into the ring that is kept by the rules of evidence is not of course of equal value, and the task of counsel and then of the judge is to select and arrange. In discharging this task counsel can be helpful but not disinterested and the jury must look chiefly to the judge for direction on the facts as well as the law. It is his duty to remind them of the evidence, marshal the facts and provide them, so to speak with the agenda for their discussions. By this process there emerges at the end of the case one or more broad questions—jury questions—which have to be decided in the light of common sense.[29]

The limited empirical evidence points to juries generally regarding a summing-up on the **23.42** facts as of assistance particularly in longer cases.[30]

New Zealand judges have developed the practice of summing up on the facts briefly and **23.43** sometimes do no more than paraphrase the closing addresses of counsel. Given the problems encountered by some New Zealand jurors in the cases which were studied, it seems clear that this short-form style of summing up is insufficient to bring the issues and associated evidence clearly to the attention of a jury, at least where the jury must address more than one issue:

> Jurors routinely encountered problems in assessing evidence in multiple charge trials. In particular, they found it difficult to identify what evidence related to which charges.

---

[26] Ibid, para 3.9. Juror complaints about not having a transcript are neither new nor confined to New Zealand: see New South Wales Law Reform Commission, (cited above at n. 20) 90–92 and Chesterman, Chan and Hampton (cited above at n. 24), paras 462–471.

[27] See *R v McLean (Colin)* [2001] 3 NZLR 794, 802 and *R v Haines* [2002] 3 NZLR 13, 20.

[28] For instance, ensuring that the transcript the jury receives refers only to what happened in the presence of the jury and checking it for accuracy before the jury receives it.

[29] London: Stevens and Sons Ltd, 1956 (one of The Hamlyn lectures, published under the auspices of The Hamlyn Trust). At 115–116.

[30] See Zander and Henderson, *The Crown Court Study* (Royal Commission on Criminal Justice Research Study No. 19) London: HMSO (1993) 214. Also see Matthews, Hancock and Briggs (cited above at n.10), 31, where favourable juror perceptions of judges are discussed.

This problem arose in at least 11 trials involving multiple counts. Although this may have been in part attributable to the personal limitations of individual jurors, and their inability to analyse and differentiate complex information about a range of similar events, it was at least as much a consequence of the way in which the case was conducted: too many charges were brought; insufficient effort was made to distinguish the various charges for the jury; or the presentation of the evidence did not link it explicitly enough to the charge to which it related.[31]

23.44 Although the criticisms in the passage just cited were directed at counsel, it is a judicial function to ensure that the issues in the case are before the jury and that the evidence associated with those issues is identified. Overall, the New Zealand research suggests that problems with juror understanding could have been reduced if the juries had received more judicial assistance with the facts, for instance, by the judge clearly identifying the issues the jury had to address and identifying the evidence that was relevant to each issue. Such issues may be, and often are, the same as the questions that the jury must be able to answer affirmatively in order to find the defendant guilty. But sometimes (particularly in a case that is reliant on circumstantial evidence) there will be a number of topics around which the judge should marshal the evidence.

(7) An agenda for deliberations

23.45 The New Zealand juries that were studied deliberated most efficiently (both in terms of process and result) when they adopted a systematic structure for assessing the evidence and applying the law. The adoption of such a systematic structure was facilitated when the judge's summing-up provided what was, in effect, an agenda for jury deliberations.[32]

23.46 Judges in England and Wales try to sum up along the lines recommended by Professor Griew (as to the law) and Lord Devlin (as to the facts) and such a summing-up should provide the sort of agenda which juries find most useful.

(8) Advice to juries on how to determine factual issues

23.47 Judges are well placed to give juries assistance as to general methodologies for deciding disputed factual issues. This is, after all, what judges do for a living. So they can be expected to build up relevant expertise. Further, they should be familiar with relevant research, perhaps as a result of judicial training.

23.48 In an ideal jury system, the judge would share with the jury his or her expertise and knowledge. To some extent, judges do so, but such sharing of expertise and knowledge is comparatively limited and usually at a fairly general level.

23.49 Judges frequently tell juries that they should use their common sense and to look at the probabilities of the competing accounts. There may be a discussion of the differing concepts of credibility and reliability. Where circumstantial evidence is relied on, there is usually some explanation of the underlying reasoning process sometimes using the strands of a rope analogy. But assistance that is targeted at the actual issues in the case is not particularly common.

---

[31] Young, Cameron and Tinsley (cited above at n.13), para 3.13.   [32] Ibid, para 6.7.

The hands-off approach of trial judges is open to criticism. This can be illustrated with **23.50** an uncontroversial example. It is not uncommon for both prosecution and defence counsel when addressing juries to emphasize the demeanour of key witnesses. Most judges are well aware that demeanour-based credibility assessments usually provide an unreliable basis for determining where the truth lies. Therefore one might expect judges to caution juries against that approach. Yet such cautions are rarely given, save in cases where the key witnesses come from an ethnic or cultural minority.

The limited assistance that judges give to juries is very much associated with legal **23.51** requirements as to what must (or must not) be said to juries. Appellate courts and legislatures have required certain types of direction to be given and prohibited other directions. A number of overlapping premises underpin these requirements.

Sometimes the experience of the judiciary as an institution is that there are particular **23.52** dangers associated with certain types of evidence. This is why identification warnings are required. In Australia, similar warnings (known as *Longman*[33] warnings) are required in cases involving historical sexual abuse allegations. This requirement is based on the premise that the judiciary has a special awareness (which will not be shared by individual jurors) of the risks of forensic disadvantage to a defendant in a trial which relates to events that allegedly took place years or decades before. Often enough a defendant is disadvantaged forensically by delay, but the rigidity with which the courts in Australia have insisted on such warnings in cases where there might be thought to be no real risk of forensic disadvantage seems unwise.[34] The way in which this problem is addressed in England and Wales[35] and New Zealand[36] is more flexible and focused on tailoring the direction to the facts of the case at hand.

Some rules in this area are based on the view that juries will reason unfairly from certain **23.53** types of evidence. The rules as to how judges are required to direct juries where the defendant has lied are premised on the assumption (which would appear not to be warranted from actual jury research)[37] that jurors are likely to jump to the conclusion that a defendant who has lied must be guilty.[38]

Also material are theories as to legitimate and illegitimate lines of reasoning which in turn **23.54** are sometimes connected with underlying values which are thought to be inherent in the criminal law. Considerations of this sort underpin the rules as to similar fact evidence and evidence of bad character on the part of the defendant. They are also relevant to the rules as to what comment a judge can legitimately make when the defendant has not given evidence, and the extent to which a judge should steer the jury away from a focus on the motivations of the key witnesses. In Australia and New Zealand this last point has arisen acutely in relation to the use by prosecutors in sexual abuse cases of the 'why should she

---

[33] *Longman v R* (1989) 168 CLR 79.   [34] See for instance *Doggett v R* (2001) 208 CLR 343.
[35] See for instance *R v H (Henry)* [1998] 2 Cr App R 161 and *R v M (Brian)* [2000] 1 Cr App R 49.
[36] *R v Meaclem* (CA187/95, 18 May 1995).
[37] See Young Cameron and Tinsley (cited above at n.13), paras 3.22 and 7.34.
[38] See *R v Broadhurst* [1964] AC 441, 457 and *Zoneff v R* (2000) 200 CLR 234, 257. Reference should also be made to *R v Lucas* (1981) 73 Cr App R 159.

lie' argument.[39] In Australia, judges do not permit prosecutors to run this line of argument,[40] although it is permitted to a qualified extent in New Zealand.[41] It is never legitimate for a judge to invite the jury to focus on what will usually be the reality, that the witness with the strongest motive to lie is the defendant.[42]

23.55 The result is that many of the decision-making techniques which are available to judges are either off-limits in jury trials or, alternatively, the ability to deploy them is hedged about with restrictions. Leaving aside the rules as to identification evidence, a key feature of these restrictions is the lack of empirical evidence supporting the premises that underpin them.

(9) Judicial training

23.56 In England and Wales, the Judicial Studies Board provides judges and recorders with helpful guideline specimen directions to juries. As well, judges and recorders are issued with a 'Handbook on Ethnic Minority Issues' and other useful guides regarding 'equality before the courts', 'belief systems', 'disability', 'children', 'gender inequality' and 'sexual orientation'. Judges are also required to regularly attend seminars and exercises addressing practical issues associated with contemporary criminal law and procedure.

23.57 For many years New Zealand judges have had the benefit of a bench book addressed to criminal jury trial practice, which, at least broadly, corresponds to the specimen directions provided by the Judicial Studies Board. This is updated from time to time and is currently being rewritten.

23.58 The New Zealand jury research project sparked a good deal of interest within the New Zealand judiciary as to how criminal trial practice might be improved. This produced much discussion among judges (particularly in formal sessions at judicial conferences) as to what innovations are appropriate. This has been an important facet of the process because it has involved not only trial judges but also those who hear criminal appeals. The result of these discussions has been that trial judges have been able to implement such innovations with a reasonable level of confidence as to how the appellate courts will react.

D. Drawing the Threads Together

23.59 Past professional and on-the-job experience provide judges with a measure of expertise as to the evaluation of witness testimony. But a system which operates on the basis that such experience is sufficient is necessarily haphazard. It is not safe to assume that all who are appointed to judicial office have the sort of experience which is of assistance in this

---

[39] This particular issue does not seem to have caused difficulties in England and Wales: see *R v Feltrin* (CA, 8 November 1991).

[40] *Palmer v R* (1998) 72 ALJR 254.   [41] *R v T* [1998] 2 NZLR 257.

[42] *Robinson v R* (1991) 102 ALR 493. Lord Goddard CJ was recently reprimanded posthumously for making such a comment in the celebrated case of Derek Bentley: see *R v Bentley* [2001] 1 Cr App R 307, 326.

context. As well, as the other chapters of this book illustrate, there is an existing body of knowledge which is highly relevant to witness evaluation. Much (and particularly the detail) of this lies outside the awareness of most practising lawyers.

Similar comments can be made about the way judges direct juries. Experience at the **23.60** criminal bar provides an opportunity to develop a measure of understanding of what works with juries. But not all those who are appointed to try criminal cases have such experience. As well, there is such a difference between the roles of advocate and judge that even extensive practice at the criminal bar will not necessarily assist the newly appointed judge (perhaps primarily concerned about the possibility of appeals) to take an effective and jury-centred approach when summing up to a jury.

Against that background, a methodical approach to judicial training is appropriate: one **23.61** which builds on the knowledge which newly appointed judges have developed in their professional lives but also ensures that all who are appointed to the bench have ready access to information which is fundamental to their developing the skills necessary to perform effectively as judges.

Further Reading

William Young J, 'Summing-up to Juries in Criminal Cases—What Research says about Current Rules and Practice' [2003] Crim LR 665.

Darbishire and others, 'What Can We Learn from Published Jury Research? Findings for the Criminal Courts Review 2001' [2001] Crim LR 970.

Stone, M., 'Instant Lie Detection? Demeanour and Credibility in Criminal Trials' [1991] Crim LR 821.

The Law Commission for England and Wales LC245 *Evidence in Criminal Proceedings: Hearsay and Related Topics*, 3.9.

Friedland, S. I., 'On Commonsense and the Evaluation of Witness Credibility' (1989/1990) *Case Western Law Review* 165.

Blumenthal, J. A., 'A Wipe of the Hands, A Lick of the Lips: The Validity of Demeanour Evidence in Assessing Witness Credibility' [1993] *Nebraska Law Review* 1157.

Wellborn, O. G. III, 'Demeanour' (1991) *Cornell Law Review* 1075.

William Young. After graduating from the Universities of Canterbury (NZ) and Cambridge, William Young practised law in New Zealand from 1978 until his appointment to the New Zealand High Court in 1997 (having taken silk in 1991). He had a general litigation practice including both prosecution and defence work in criminal cases. In 2004 he was appointed a Judge of the New Zealand Court of Appeal and, in 2006, its President. He is a former member of the governing board of the New Zealand Institute of Judicial Studies and is currently the senior editor of its Criminal Jury Trials Benchbook.

Sam Katkhuda was appointed to the Circuit Bench in 1995 and is now located at the Crown Court at Isleworth. From 1964 to 1973 he was employed at the Central Criminal Court on the staff of the Clerk of the Peace. He was called to the bar in 1973 and practiced at the criminal bar until appointment on the bench. Amongst other trials he was defence junior for the survivor in the Iranian Embassy siege case. Published *Forms of*

Indictment (London: Longman, 1990) and is co-author in the 2006 edition of the *Crown Court Index* (London: Sweet & Maxwell, 2006).

Editors' Note

Judges' directions to juries concerning their assessment of contentious witness testimony will depend, first, on their perceptions as to what they consider it safe to assume juries will be aware of—concepts of 'common knowledge'—second, on their own experiences in life and as legal practitioners which inform them for the purposes of guiding fact finders in their role as assessors of contentious evidence; and, third, on such training as they have been given—for example, through the use of Judicial Studies Board 'Specimen Directions'—on the way to direct juries concerning their fact-finding task. If the legitimate use of experts to give evidence on the subjects covered in this book is not to proliferate, the extension of judicial training to incorporate these skills and knowledge is undoubtedly essential. The answer to the questions as to whether such 'knowledge' is actually 'common' and whether juries apply such 'common knowledge' as they ought when reaching their decisions should, perhaps, be the subject of the sort of research which is, currently, beyond the scope of legal endeavour owing to the restrictions on jury research imposed by the provisions of s8 of the Contempt of Court Act 1981. It is, arguably, unfortunate that the United Kingdom government's initiative to consult on the possibility of an amendment to s8 which might have allowed limited jury research to take place (see n. 10, above) resulted in a decision to take the matter no further. However, now that the removal of the bar on judges and practising barristers, amongst others, has begun to take affect it may be that articles such as 'Twelve men and women without a clue', by Devis Lyons, a barrister (618 SJ 19/05/06) will achieve similar results to those to which jury research might have lead. Hence:

> As to the relevant law, in my view, the jury did not understand its meanings and ramifications . . . fundamental concepts like evidential burden and standard of proof were only vaguely apprehended. The vital difference between civil and criminal standards of proof was not really grasped . . . Better judicial guidance is needed . . . Also where credibility is the central part of the prosecution case, inferences based on potted psychology seem to be the order of the day.

EDITORS' LIST OF RECOMMENDED
FURTHER READING

Ede, R. and Shepherd, E., *Active Defence*, 2nd ed, London: Law Society Publishing, 2000.

Gudjonsson, G.H., *The Psychology of Interrogations and Confessions: A Handbook*, Chichester: John Wiley & Sons, 2003.

Gudjonsson, G.H. and Haward, L.R.C., *Forensic Psychology: A Guide to Practice*, London: Routledge, 1998.

Heaton-Armstrong, A., Shepherd, E. and Wolchover, D. (eds), *Analysing Witness Testimony*, London: Blackstone Press, 1999.

Redmayne, M., *Expert Evidence and Criminal Justice*, Oxford: Oxford University Press, 2001.

Townley, L. and Ede, R., *Forensic Practice in Criminal Cases*, London: The Law Society, 2004.

See, also, the Editors' List of Recommended Reading in *Analysing Witness Testimony* (at page xvi).

INDEX